Achieving Price, Financial and Macro-Economic Stability in South Africa

Nombulelo Gumata • Eliphas Ndou

Achieving Price, Financial and Macro-Economic Stability in South Africa

The Role of the Central Bank Balance Sheet, Macro-Prudential Tools, Financial Regulations and Analysis

palgrave
macmillan

Nombulelo Gumata
South African Reserve Bank
Pretoria, South Africa

Eliphas Ndou
South African Reserve Bank
Pretoria, South Africa

ISBN 978-3-030-66339-1 ISBN 978-3-030-66340-7 (eBook)
https://doi.org/10.1007/978-3-030-66340-7

This Palgrave Macmillan imprint is published by the registered company Springer Nature Switzerland AG.
The registered company address is: Gewerbestrasse 11, 6330 Cham, Switzerland

Preface

This is the first manuscript to explore the interactions of monetary policy, financial regulation and macro-prudential tools within the context of the role and structural changes in the central bank balance sheet to assist in the achievement of the objectives of fiscal sustainability and price, financial and macro-economic stability in South Africa. The contributions of the book come at a time when inflation and the policy rate have moved to structurally low levels and these developments have not been accompanied by robust output growth, employment growth and a meaningful decline in the unemployment rate. To the contrary, the low inflation environment post-2009 has been associated with an increase in the unemployment rate, subdued and very volatile output growth, leading to calls for the South African Reserve Bank (SARB) to expand its mandate to include maximum employment. The mandate of maximum employment will be over and above those of price stability, financial stability and macro-economic stability, and that the SARB should use all the policy tools at its disposal to achieve these mandates. Throughout the times, the main mandates of central banks have always evolved to meet changing needs of their economies and society. In the same vein, most central banks are embarking on reviews of their mandates. Significant shifts are happening, with central banks changing their mandates and creating more potent tools to assist them in achieving these set objectives. There are immense and intense discussions about how the co-ordination between monetary policy and fiscal policy with the objective of achieving fiscal sustainability, greening the financial sector to mitigate the adverse effects of climate change, reducing income inequality and poverty ought to be conducted going forward.

This book brings empirical analysis which is lacking in the current academic and policy discussions and debates in South Africa. The book presents a dispassionate collection of empirical results and policy recommendations based on using time-series data from South Africa. The book has 36 chapters, with clearly defined research and policy questions explored. Research and policy questions are clearly stated at the beginning of each chapter. Each chapter in the book derives policy implications and recommendations from the findings. The book provides a comprehensive chapter that concludes by summarising the main findings and the policy implications of these findings. We use a variety of quantitative methods and approaches to test the applicability of several theories and hypothesis on the South African data, the robustness of the results and the policy implications of the results. In some instances, we explore the joint dynamics of monetary policy variables, fiscal policy variables, financial variables and real economic aggregates over time. Thereafter, we draw case-by-case policy lessons to be learned from specific regressions results using various statistical and econometric techniques, which could be useful to policymakers, market analysts, policy researchers, academics and financial institutions around the world.

This book contributes to policy and academic research aimed at putting forward strategies, policy interventions and tools that can help achieve the set targets on a variety of economic objectives, including those set in the National Development Plan (NDP) by 2030. In addition, the NDP has earmarked small-, micro- and medium-sized enterprises (SMMEs) as one of the key sectors that will contribute meaningfully to employment creation. To reach the growth and employment targets, the NDP projects that more than 90 per cent of new employment opportunities will be generated by SMMEs. As such, it calls for urgent measures to reform the mandates and operations of development finance institutions, in line with initiatives to bring services to the SMME sector. This is a timely manuscript that provides much needed contribution in the evolving academic and policy debates of how best to move forward in pursuing the objectives of fiscal sustainability, price stability, financial stability and macro-economic stability. Prior to the Global Financial Crisis in 2007, it was widely accepted that money played a passive role in the monetary policy transmission mechanism and that financial stability was implied in the existing price stability mandates of central banks. However, post-2007, policy and academic research has focused on understanding the role of financial frictions, the transmission of financial shocks to the macro-economy, and the adjustment of balance sheets to various shocks. As a result, the financial stability mandate of the central banks has been made explicit and policy makers are exploring various tools to achieve it.

The book is divided into five parts. Part I deals with capital flow episodes, fiscal shocks, commodity price and house price boom effects on credit growth dynamics. Part II deals with the interaction of the South African Reserve Bank (SARB) balance sheet with those of the Public Investment Corporation and private banks and the effects on fiscal and monetary policy tools. Part III deals with financial regulation tools, selected macro-prudential tools, the quality of banks' loan books and the transmission of monetary policy shocks. Part IV deals with money demand, exchange rate depreciation shocks, household wealth and credit conditions. Last, Part V explores the role of the flow-of-funds approach in monetary and financial policy analysis.

In the book, we show that the repo rate alone is not a sufficient monetary policy tool to achieve the mandates of price stability (low and stable inflation below 4.5 per cent), maximum employment and macro-economic stability, especially in uncertain operating conditions such as those presented by the unforeseen effects of the COVID-19 pandemic shock. In addition, we also strongly advocate for a foreign currency reserves accumulation policy as another balance sheet policy tool to assist the SARB in achieving the mandates of price stability, financial stability, macroeconomic stability and maximum employment. At the same time, we do not equate monetary policy in South Africa to that in developed economies such as the United States, United Kingdom, euro area, Switzerland or Japan, in particular with respect to the extraordinary and unconventional monetary policy measures these countries have embarked on. Neither do we group South Africa with other Emerging Market Economies (EMEs). This is because, while it is possible, to group South Africa with other EMEs, this book did not conduct a cross country comparison study or use any form of panel data where South Africa was compared to advanced economies and even to other EMEs. However, we use all the available literature on the conduct of various forms of unconventional monetary policy tools, which currently mostly happens to be that from advanced economies. These countries have been using various forms of unconventional monetary policy tools since 2007 and have thus accumulated considerable data and empirical analysis. We are also aware that with the onset of the COVID-19 pandemic in early 2020, most EMEs, including South Africa, have conducted various forms of balance sheet tools to supplement conventional monetary policy tools. There is now data and literature on several EMEs on their conduct of balance sheet monetary policy tools, albeit that the sample is still exceedingly small. As time progresses beyond 2020, we will be able to get data and enough sample size to use to conduct a comparative analytical study to assess whether there are distinct characteristics that differentiate advanced economies to EMEs.

Pretoria, South Africa — Nombulelo Gumata
Johannesburg, South Africa — Eliphas Ndou

Acknowledgements

We would like to thank our colleagues at the South African Reserve Bank and private banks. We owe a great deal of gratitude to the anonymous reviewers.

Contents

About the Authors

Nombulelo Gumata is an economist and has authored several books in the areas of money and banking regulation, international finance and macro-economics, macro-prudential tools and financial stability, labour markets, monetary and fiscal policy.

Eliphas Ndou is an economist at the South African Reserve Bank and lectures at the University of the Witwatersrand, Johannesburg, South Africa. He has authored several books which cover areas in international finance and macro-economics, applied macro-economics and micro-economics, monetary economics, public economics, labour economics, applied time-series econometrics, banking regulation and macro-prudential policy.

List of Figures

List of Tables

CHAPTER 1

Introduction

This book explores the macro-financial effects of monetary policy, financial regulation and macro-prudential tools, and the role that the central bank balance sheet can play in achieving the objectives of price stability, financial stability and macro-economic stability in South Africa. The spill-over effects from these policy interactions have implications for the dynamics of fiscal policy variables and whether the positive effects can assist in achieving or improving fiscal sustainability. After the global financial crisis, central bank balance sheets have become complementary monetary policy tools which are used to reinforce the effects of conventional monetary policy tools. We explore the role of the central bank balance sheet in South Africa in achieving price, financial and macro-economic stability considering the arguments and recommendations put forward in Gumata and Ndou (2019) to operationalise the 2030 goals of the National Development Plan (NDP). The authors stated that policy co-ordination becomes pertinent and binding to implement economic reforms. Furthermore, the authors argued that in operationalising the goals of the NDP and to contribute to the economic recovery post the COVID-19 health pandemic, it may be necessary for the central bank to expand its mandate to include maximum employment as an objective. A pertinent question that arose in their analysis was that the repo rate (monetary policy rate) alone is an insufficient instrument to simultaneously achieve an expanded mandate and a lower inflation target. This is in tandem with the experiences of

N. Gumata, E. Ndou, *Achieving Price, Financial and Macro-Economic Stability in South Africa*,
https://doi.org/10.1007/978-3-030-66340-7_1

other central banks, which have shown that the use of the policy rate alone is not enough, especially in times of economic crisis and the recovery phase. This book offers the empirical analysis that answers this question and many other important questions relating to the co-ordination of policies in pursuit of fiscal sustainability and price, financial and macroeconomic stability. The book strengthens the arguments in policy discussions regarding the use of the central bank balance sheet in its entirety by presenting theoretical perspectives and empirical analysis.

We formulate the arguments in the book under five main themes and these are:

- Capital flow episodes, fiscal shocks, commodity price and house price boom effects on credit growth dynamics.
- The interaction of the South African Reserve Bank (SARB) balance sheet with that of the Public Investment Corporation and private banks and the spill-over effects of the interactions of monetary policy, financial regulation and macro-prudential tools on fiscal policy.
- Financial regulations, selected macro-prudential tools, the quality of banks' loan books and the transmission of monetary policy shocks.
- Money demand, exchange rate depreciation shocks, household wealth and credit conditions.
- The role of the flow-of-funds approach in monetary and financial policy analysis.

1.1 Why Did We Write This Book?

The period post-2009 was characterised by the widening of the budget balance as a ratio of nominal GDP (NGDP), which was accompanied by the increase in the debt-to-GDP ratio. The increasing debt-to-GDP ratio has been accompanied by a declining investment-to-GDP ratio. At the same time, the persistently widening budget deficit has existed alongside a persistently widening output-gap. Whereas the inflation rate has been largely contained within the 3–6 per cent inflation target range since mid-2017, the unemployment rate has increased unabatedly. These trends in the South African data contrast with those observed in, for example, the United States, where the unemployment rate has declined to pre-global financial crisis levels without triggering any inflationary pressures. The nominal GDP growth (NGDP), which is the denominator for the fiscal variables, continued to trend downwards. There are implications of the observed trends post-2009. The trends include, the persistently widening budget deficit that has coexisted alongside a persistently widening output-gap, and the increasing debt-to-GDP ratio has been accompanied by a declining investment-to-GDP ratio. The implication, is that a countercyclical, and highly accommodative fiscal policy stance post-2009 that was accompanied by accommodative monetary policy[1], performed poorly as nominal demand management policies that are aimed at increasing output growth, potential output and lower the unemployment rate. A successful countercyclical and accommodative fiscal policy stance is supposed to dampen the economic slump during recessions and quickly pull the economy out of a slump. Thus, the policy mix that has been implemented post-2009 has not been as potent as initially thought. Hence, we have written this book to assess other policy tools that can assist in the pursuit of price, financial and macro-economic stability and whether the spill-over effects from their interactions can assist in the achievement of fiscal sustainability.

Furthermore, there is lack of empirical studies which empirically assess the macro-financial effects of financial regulation, macro-prudential tools, and the central bank balance sheet as an additional monetary policy tool in South Africa. As such, to a large extent the academic and policy debates and discussions have not been backed up by a wholistic approach and empirical evidence to establish the facts. The book fills these gaps in academic and policy discussions and debates. We offer insights from an empirical perspective on several monetary policy tools that can be used by the South African Reserve Bank (SARB) to pursue the price stability, financial stability and maximum employment mandates. In addition, we show what happens to certain economic indicators when some central bank balance sheet tools are used as additional monetary policy tools.

1.2 Role of Positive Capital Inflows Shocks in the Banks' Credit Constraints, Credit Growth and Transmitting the SA–US Interest Rate Differential to Domestic GDP Growth

The book explores the role of capital inflows into South Africa from various perspectives. We explore whether positive capital inflows shocks lead to the loosening of credit conditions. In addition, we explore whether shocks to capital inflows impact the excess capital adequacy ratio (CAR),

[1]The repo rate was decreased by a cumulative 700 basis points, from 12 per cent in November 2008 to 5 per cent in December 2012.

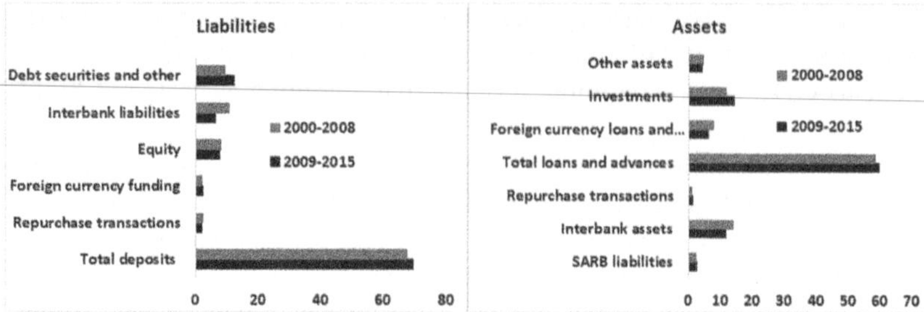

Fig. 1.1 Banks' assets and liabilities. (Source: South African Reserve Bank and authors' calculations)

excess liquid asset holdings (LAH) and the loan loss provisions of banks. We find that positive (negative) gross capital inflows shocks lead to a significant reduction (increase) in banks' excess CAR, excess LAH and loan loss provisions as shown in Fig. 1.1.

1.3 Relevance of the Credit Conditions Channel in the Transmission of Various Shocks

The analysis in the book shows how the credit conditions channel impacts the repo rate responses to positive inflationary shocks, and, also shows the importance of determining the state of credit conditions in the economy and how these interact with other variables. Credit conditions play a significant role in the transmission of inflationary shocks and the responses of the repo rate to GDP growth.

1.4 Role of Economic Thresholds in Guiding Policy Settings and Decisions

The experience from the recent financial crisis shows that economic thresholds matter, hence we show the role of credit growth thresholds on GDP growth, inflation and household consumption growth. Recent theoretical models and empirical evidence show that financial markets and institutions can be sources of shocks and conduits in transmitting shocks domestically and across borders. Furthermore, some studies establish evidence that credit conditions exert threshold and asymmetric effects on macroeconomic responses over the lending cycle. For instance, Balke (2000),

Calza and Sousa (2005) and Avdjiev and Zeng (2014) establish a nonlinear relationship between credit market conditions, monetary policy and real economic activity. They show that the impact of credit shocks on economic activity tends to be substantially larger when the economy is in a tight credit growth regime than when it is in a normal credit growth regime.[2] Sectorial credit growth above moderate credit growth may not necessarily result in a high level of GDP growth and household consumption growth. Aggregate, sectorial and mortgage credit growth above the normal credit growth thresholds tend to generate more inflationary pressures that are not accompanied by higher GDP growth and household consumption growth.

1.5 Impact of Synchronised Credit and House Price Booms on the Monetary Policy Response to Inflationary Pressures

The book offers insights into how synchronised credit and house price booms impact the monetary policy reaction to inflationary pressures. This follows vast literature post-2007 global financial crisis, which shows that synchronised credit growth and house price growth booms have an impact on the monetary policy reaction to inflationary pressures. We explore the applicability of this hypothesis on the South African data in the book.

1.6 Role Played by Contractionary Fiscal Policy Shocks in Credit Growth Dynamics

The analysis in the book determines the extent to which contractionary fiscal policy shocks impact credit growth dynamics and if these shocks are transmitted via GDP growth to dampen credit growth. The period post-2009 domestic recession was characterised by a series of sovereign debt credit rating downgrades and upward adjustments in several taxes, revised revenue deficits or short-falls and credit growth that was much lower than that observed pre-crisis. The book dedicates several chapters and explores the role of contractionary fiscal policy shocks in credit

[2] In addition, Avdjiev and Zeng (2014) extend empirical evidence of asymmetric effects of shocks over the business cycle by estimating two-thresholds or a three-regime threshold model. They argue that single-threshold models tend to be too restrictive and cannot capture all the non-linearities in the data.

growth dynamics and determines whether these shocks are transmitted via GDP growth dampen credit growth. We find that a positive tax shock has an adverse effect on credit growth.

1.7 Interaction Between Macro-prudential Policy and Monetary Policy and the Role of the Bank Risk Channel

We show the effects of the interaction between macro-prudential policy and monetary policy. This includes showing the role of the quality of the banks' balance sheets in propagating the excess LAH and tight monetary policy shock effects on credit growth. The quality of the banks' balance sheets as measured by the non-performing loans (NPLs) matters for how various shocks are transmitted from the banking sector to real economic activity. We dedicate several chapters in the book to assess the role of bank credit risk as captured by NPLs in propagating the excess LAH and tight monetary policy shock effects on credit growth.

1.8 Effectiveness of the Countercyclical Capital Buffer

We also show the effectiveness of the relaxation of the countercyclical capital buffer at a time when other residential macro-prudential tools are tight. We extended the analysis of the interaction between financial regulation tools and other macro-prudential tools in the book. This is especially important in considering the role of financial regulation tools and residential macro-prudential tools.

1.9 Role of the Central Bank Balance Sheet

The book sheds light through discussion from empirical perspective on large-scale asset purchases (LSAPs) in South Africa. The book dedicates several chapters in search of empirical evidence on how the SARB balance sheet can be strategically used as part of monetary policy tools and policy interventions. Post-2007, central banks across the globe have increasingly relied on their balance sheets to create new monetary policy tools to amplify the effects of conventional monetary policy tools to achieve the set objectives. Across the globe, central banks implemented different combinations of unconventional monetary policy tools (UMPTs) and adapted their operations to the circumstances in their jurisdictions. Central banks used a combination of negative interest rate policies, created new central bank lending operations, used various designs of large-scale asset purchase programmes, adjusted their communications strategies and relied more on forward guidance (BIS 2019). We also show the conditions under which these policies work effectively.

It is also important to show the impact of LSAPs on banks' balance sheets. Over and above a balance sheet strategy that uses LSAPs and the foreign currency reserves accumulation policy, we provide evidence showing that the lengthening of the maturities of funding available to banks at the SARB's repurchase window will help achieve some of the set objectives in the NDP. The book also identifies whether there are any amplification effects of positive shocks to SARB assets and forex reserves on long-term yields dependent on government debt regimes. Evidence in the book also shows that it may be important to use the interest rate corridor as an effective instrument to dampen the accumulation of excess reserves and lower the inter-bank rate volatility. We explore this question in the book because trends from central banks that have conducted LSAPs show that these policy interventions are also associated with an increase in excess banks' reserves with central banks.

We show the impact of LSAPs on non-resident purchases of South African assets. The analysis also explores the impact of stock and flow effects of LSAPs by looking at the effects from persistent vs transitory shocks. D'Amico and King (2013) define the stock effects of LSAPs as persistent changes in prices that result from movements along the Treasury demand curves. For instance, Altavilla et al. (2015) find that the bulk of the impact of the asset purchase programmes arises at the announcement of the key programme parameters, that is, the stock effects, whereas the flow effects generated by the actual implementation of the purchases are limited.[3]

[3] See also D'Amico and King (2013), Joyce and Tong (2012), Breedon et al. (2012) and De Santis and Holm-Hadulla (2017).

1.10 Selected Issues Regarding Large-Scale Asset Purchases by a Central Bank

In our analysis contained in the book, we present empirical evidence to show that LSAPs programmes are not a de facto monetisation of government debt that leads to high inflation. We show the results that control for the exchange rate and inflation to temporary shocks and find that the exchange rate appreciates while inflation tends to decline. Thus, the exchange rate appreciation channel tends to dampen the inflationary pressures and contributes to the price stability mandate. Furthermore, we show that the government debt growth thresholds play an important role in the effectiveness of monetary policy. We assess how the fiscal policy stance as measured by government debt growth regimes interacts with selected monetary policy balance sheet tools to amplify the effects of government debt growth regimes on the R/US$ exchange rate and inflation. Vast studies have explored the disinflationary effects of LSAPs and show that these disinflationary effects are mostly on account of the persistent effects of financial shocks. In addition, because LSAPs are expansionary financial shocks which substantially lower long-term interest rates, they tend to be disinflationary, if the supply effects dominate the demand effects.

However, we acknowledge that the direct financing of government deficits is a legitimate monetary policy tool with its own merits and trade-offs. The book did not explore the role of the direct financing of government deficits by the SARB. The direct financing of government deficits is an important monetary policy tool that has been used by other central banks and deserves careful statistical and empirical analysis.

We are aware that Venezuela, Argentina[4] and Zimbabwe have struggled with hyperinflation, which is often pointed out as an example to deter countries from embarking on excessive large-scale asset purchases and the direct financing of government deficits. We note that these countries were experiencing balance of payments problems, suffering severe foreign currency shortages, and could not meet their debt obligations, especially foreign currency dominated debt, and were using direct government deficit financing as a last stop-gap measure. At the same time, these countries were also experiencing severe supply side shocks, which on their own have

[4] In December 2015, the central bank of Argentina announced that it was moving towards the adoption of an inflation-targeting regime. The central bank launched the Inflation Targeting Regime in September 2016. The inflation targets were 12–17 per cent for 2017, 8–12 per cent for 2018 and 5 per cent from 2019 onwards.

significant and long-lasting inflationary consequences. The confluence of these events resulted in the severe negative economic factors these countries are experiencing. As such the initial economic conditions that existed in these countries are not observed in South Africa. Furthermore, none of these countries were conducting their monetary policy under the inflation targeting framework. Thus, when citing these country cases, it is important to be clear about the sequence of how the financial and economic events in these countries evolved. The SARB has not directly financed government deficits and is constrained by the inflation target.

1.11 This Book Does Not Conduct a Comparative Analysis with Other Countries

We do not conduct a comparative analysis of LSAPs effects in South Africa with other countries, such as advanced economies and emerging market economies (EMEs). This is because EMEs are not homogeneous; they are also different in many aspects. For instance, when conducting a study on LSAPs among EMEs, dimensions such as the size and liquidity of bond markets in that country matter. It is common knowledge that most of the EMEs have exceedingly small and relatively illiquid bond markets compared to South Africa. Thus, such factors must be accounted for. We are also aware that EMEs tend to be much more concerned about capital flight during crises than is the case in developed economies. During times of distress many EMEs tend to raise nominal interest rates to mitigate capital outflows at home, whereas advanced economies almost always lower policy rates.

We caution that the observation that presupposes that all the EMEs are affected by the capital flow shock episodes in the same way is extremely dangerous and highly generalised. In the South African case, the overriding objective of a policy response is the price stability mandate as measured by the inflation target band. In this regard, policy makers have always been clear that to the degree that capital flow episode impact the Rand exchange rate movements and this affects the direct and indirect channels of transmission to inflation outcomes and the outlook, they will respond. Thus, the monetary policy responses will not necessarily be directed to stem capital outflows per se, but to dampen the inflationary pressures associated with the exchange depreciation and a high exchange rate pass-through.

Furthermore, unlike most EMEs, the South African credit growth developments are not largely dominated by external developments. For instance, in the case of Turkey, the exchange rate developments are a particularly important determinant of credit growth.[5] This is not the case in South Africa.[6] Most EMEs, especially in Asia and Latin America, are highly susceptible to capital flow shocks largely because of their influence on cross-border dollar funding.[7] This is not the case for South Africa as shown in Fig. 1.1 that foreign currency funding on the liabilities of the banks' balance sheets accounts for less than 2 per cent. Thus, EMEs are not homogenous and generalising economic events and factors among this grouping of economies can be very misleading.

1.12 Interaction Between Financial Regulation, Macro-prudential Tools and Monetary Policy

The book expands the discourse on the interaction between financial regulation, macro-prudential tools and monetary policy. This includes assessing whether the impact of the unexpected positive (tightening) repo rate shock on inflation expectations is different to those due to positive excess LAH and forex reserves accumulation shocks. We assessed how the effects of the tightening in the banks' required reserves (RR), unexpected increase in excess LAH and the accumulation of forex reserves on inflation expectations differ. We also explored whether these monetary, financial regulation and macro-prudential tools complement or propagate each other's effects on inflation expectations.

1.13 Information Content of the Money Demand and Flow-of-Funds Analysis for Financial Analysis and Monetary Policy

We show that there is a need to revisit the role of monetary aggregates in policy making. The book assesses the relevance and information content of the monetary aggregates by assessing whether there is a case to redefine

[5] https://www.tcmb.gov.tr/wps/wcm/connect/a131bc0f-d754-4fc2-b775-0e7c92083e8b/OR2.pdf?MOD=AJPERES&CACHEID=ROOTWORKSPACE-a131bc0f-d754-4fc2-b775-0e7c92083e8b-krmWR0N.

[6] See Gumata and Ndou (2017) Bank Credit Extension and Real Economic Activity in South Africa: The Impact of Capital Flow Dynamics, Bank Regulation and Selected Macro-prudential Tools.

[7] See for instance https://www.bis.org/publ/qtrpdf/r_qt1903b.pdf.

and improve the money demand function to be relevant for the price and financial stability policy objectives. The monetary aggregates have largely played a passive role in policy making since the late 1980s and early 1990s. It is a well-established fact that the information content of the money supply aggregates and the income velocity of money weakened in the 1990s in part due to financial liberalisation and globalisation. We also find that the exchange rate depreciation and volatility shocks drive money demand in South Africa. In addition, we fill the gaps in financial intermediation via the flow-of-funds analysis, which may contain relevant information for policy making. To conclude the analysis contained in the book, we consider whether the flow-of-funds analysis contains valuable information for policy makers.

References

Altavilla C, Motto R, and Carboni G. 2015. Asset purchase programmes and financial markets: lessons from the euro area. ECB Working Paper Series No. 1864.

Avdjiev F, and Zeng Z. 2014. Credit Growth, Monetary Policy, and Economic Activity in a Three-Regime TVAR Model. BIS Working Papers No 449.

Balke N. S. 2000. Credit and Economic Activity: Credit Regimes and Nonlinear Propagation of Shocks. The Review of Economics and Statistics, MIT Press, 82(2), 344–349.

BIS Committee on the Global Financial System. 2019. Unconventional monetary policy tools: a cross-country analysis. Report prepared by a Working Group chaired by Simon M Potter (Federal Reserve Bank of New York) and Frank Smets (European Central Bank). CGFS Papers No 63.

Breedon F, Chadha J S, and Waters A. 2012. The financial market impact of UK quantitative easing. BIS Papers chapters in: Bank for International Settlements (ed.), Threat of fiscal dominance?, 65, pp. 277–304. Bank for International Settlements.

Calza A, and Sousa J. 2005. Output and Inflation Responses to Credit Shocks: Are There Threshold Effects in the Euro Area? Studies in Nonlinear Dynamics & Econometrics 10 (Issue 2, Article 3).

D'Amico S, and King T B. 2013. "Flow and stock effects of large-scale Treasury purchases: Evidence on the importance of local supply", *Journal of Financial Economics* 108(2): 425–448.

De Santis R A, and Holm-Hadulla F. 2017. Flow Effects of Central Bank Asset Purchases on Euro Area Sovereign Bond Yields: Evidence from a Natural Experiment. ECB Working Paper No.2052.

Gagnon J, Raskin M, Remache J, and Sack B. 2010. Large-scale asset purchases by the Federal Reserve: Did they work? Federal Reserve Bank of New York, Staff Report No. 441.

Gumata N, and Ndou E. 2017. Bank Credit Extension and Real Economic Activity in South Africa: The Impact of Capital Flow Dynamics, Bank Regulation and Selected Macroprudential Tools. Palgrave Macmillan. ISBN 978-3-319-43550-3.

Gumata N, and Ndou E. 2019. Accelerated Land Reform, Mining, Growth, Unemployment and Inequality in South Africa: A Case for Bold Supply Side Policy Interventions. Palgrave Macmillan. ISBN 978-3-030-30884-1.

Joyce M A S and Tong M. 2012. QE and the Gilt Market: a Disaggregated Analysis. The Economic Journal, Volume 122, Issue 564, November 2012, Pages F348–F384.

Joyce M, Lasaosa A, Stevens I, and Tong M. 2010. The financial market impact of quantitative easing. Bank of England Working Paper No. 393.

CHAPTER 2

A Review of the Central Bank Balance Sheet Tools That Can Be Deployed to Assist in the Achievement of Price, Financial and Macro-economic Stability

Research Questions Explored

- What are the key channels through which large-scale asset purchases are transmitted?
- Why does the size, duration and composition of asset purchases matter?
- Why should the South African Reserve Bank conduct large-scale asset purchases?
- When are the right conditions for the central bank to pursue large-scale asset purchases?

2.1 Introduction

This chapter provides a preliminary review of the chapters that conduct empirical analysis of the use of various South African Reserve Bank (SARB) balance sheet tools. With the onset of the market dislocations induced by the uncertainty that was accompanied by the COVID-19 health pandemic and the spill-overs to real economic activity, central banks across the globe embarked on new rounds of large-scale asset purchases or LSAPs (quantitative easing or QE). This book dedicates several chapters using empirical evidence to demonstrate how the SARB balance sheet can be

N. Gumata, E. Ndou, *Achieving Price, Financial and Macro-Economic Stability in South Africa*,
https://doi.org/10.1007/978-3-030-66340-7_2

strategically used as part of various monetary policy tools or policy interventions that can help achieve the set objectives and targets in the National Development Plan (NDP) by 2030. As such, the motivation for conducting LSAPs and using other central bank balance sheet tools is different to that of responding to the COVID-19 health pandemic. Post-2007, central banks across the globe have increasingly relied on their balance sheets to create new monetary policy tools to amplify (reinforce) the effects of conventional monetary policy tools to achieve the set objectives. Across the globe, central banks implemented different combinations of unconventional monetary policy tools (UMPTs) and adapted their operations to the circumstances in their jurisdictions. Central banks used a combination of negative interest rate policies, created new central bank lending operations, used various designs of LSAP programmes, adjusted their communications strategies and relied more on forward guidance (BIS 2019). Empirical evidence shows that UMPTs helped the central banks to address the immediate severe adverse circumstances presented by the crisis and the ensuing economic downturn.

2.2 What Are the Key Channels Through Which Large-Scale Asset Purchases Are Transmitted?

The key channel of transmission of QE is the portfolio balance effect and can be decomposed into:

1. The *signalling channel*, when central banks conduct QE through the purchase of long-term securities. The signalling effects of the asset purchase programmes can lower yields by influencing the two main components that shape long-term interest rates, namely expectations of future short-term rates and a term premium. Asset purchases compress the term premia by removing duration risk from the market.
2. The traditional *supply-induced portfolio balance effect*, associated with the decrease in yields due to the shortage (reduction in supply) of long-term bonds.
3. The *reserve-induced portfolio balance effect*, which occurs due to the increase in the supply of bank reserves that accompanies asset purchases.
4. The *liquidity effects*, via the bank lending channel and cost of borrowing. These effects occur as QE squeezes the liquidity premium

on various assets and the liquidity injected via QE into the economy in return for other assets increases the liquidity of the private sector balance sheets.

5. The *risk-taking channel*, which occurs as central bank asset purchases alter investor risk preferences and risk tolerance.
6. The *duration-risk channel*, which occurs when the central bank reduces the duration risk in the hands of investors by altering the yield curve as long-maturity bond yields relative to short-maturity yields adjust to central bank asset purchases. This is because a change in the relative supply of long-term versus short-term securities affects the spread between long-term and short-term securities.
7. The *confidence, risk aversion and uncertainty channels*, which are activated as QE reduces the amount of volatility in markets or uncertainty about the outlook. Under this channel of transmission, QE is expected to affect the risk premia more broadly.

All the channels discussed are transmitted into the real economy and affect wealth, spending and investment decisions, output and employment growth, inflation, the unemployment rate and income inequality.

2.3 When Are the Right Conditions for the Central Bank to Pursue Large-Scale Asset Purchases?

Literature shows that LSAPs are effective when deployed during crisis and non-crisis periods. The size of the central bank balance sheet has became a major monetary policy tool to complement the interest rates as monetary policy tools. Central banks in the United States (US), United Kingdom (UK), Europe and Japan embarked on LSAPs or QE and purchased trillions of dollars of assets in an effort to reinforce accommodative monetary policy and stimulate their economies as policy rates hit the zero-lower bound (ZLB). The effectiveness of central bank large-scale asset purchases does not depend on QE being deployed during a period of market turbulence (Bernanke 2020). Similarly, Altavilla et al. (2015) establish that in contrast to existing literature findings of a large impact of asset purchases only in periods of high financial distress, the impact of the asset purchase programme on asset prices in the euro area was sizeable even though the programme was announced at a time of low financial distress. This is because targeting assets at long-term maturity and spanning the investment-grade space supported the duration and the credit channels. At the same time, the low degree of financial stress prevailing at the announcement of the asset purchase programme, while weakening the local supply channel, facilitated the spill-overs to non-targeted assets.

Haldane et al. (2016) indicate that as monetary policy tools, central bank asset purchases can be used for a variety of price, financial and macroeconomic stability objectives. First, to provide liquidity support to the banking sector and improving the functioning of the monetary policy transmission mechanism. This was the case in the early stages of the financial crisis when the US Fed, Bank of England and the European Central Bank (ECB) expanded their balance sheets using repurchase programmes. During the 2007 global financial crisis, central banks went further along the credit risk spectrum by purchasing private sector assets through 'credit easing'. Ito (2014) states that at its core, comprehensive credit easing is aimed at purchasing assets of dysfunctional markets, whilst QE is aimed at expanding the monetary base to stimulate demand.

Similarly, Clarida (2012) distinguishes between different types of LSAPs, namely, (i) QE, which he refers to as the purchases of long-term government bonds and (ii) credit easing, which entails the purchases of privately issued debt. Gagnon et al. (2010) show that LSAPs by the US Fed worked via the risk premium on the asset being purchased and the reduction in longer-term yields come through the narrowing in risk premiums. The LSAPs removed a considerable amount of assets with high duration from the markets thus lowering the most important component of the risk premium, namely the term premium.

Second, to influence credit and duration risk in the private sector, the central bank conducts outright purchases of long-maturity government debt funded by the creation of central bank reserves. The creation of central bank reserves is essentially at zero credit risk and zero duration risk. This is because in the case of government debt purchases, the extent of credit risk transfer is minimal since most government debt is perceived as low risk.

Motto et al. (2015) find that euro-area asset purchases had a sizeable effect on asset prices although the programme was announced at a time of low financial distress. These findings contradict existing literature that find a large impact of asset purchases only in periods of high financial distress. Andrade et al. (2016) and Motto et al. (2015) find that large-scale asset purchases reinforced other channels due to the interaction between

LSAPs and the asset composition of the asset purchase programme. They find that argeting assets at long maturities supported the duration and the credit channels and that euro-area sovereign ten-year bond yields fell by 30–50 basis points. At the same time, the low degree of financial stress prevailing at time of the announcement of the asset purchase programme weakened the local supply channel and facilitated spill-overs to non-targeted assets.

2.4 Why Does the Size, Duration and Composition of Asset Purchases Matter?

Evidence on bond purchases by central banks shows that they reinforce the effectiveness of loose policy rates, they tend to be more potent and have incremental effects when conducted over time. The persistence of the effects of asset purchases is also affected by the stock and flows. In addition, it matters how a given stock of asset purchases is built up over time, as well as how this building-up interacts with the other elements of the monetary policy stance. The parameters of the purchase programme, such as its size, duration and composition, matter (Cœuré 2018). For instance, Krishnamurthy and Vissing-Jorgensen (2011) show that the effects of LSAPs on assets depend critically on which assets are purchased. Cœuré (2018) shows that there are sizeable announcement effects related to the stock of asset purchases. These effects materialise whenever investors receive new information about the parameters of the asset purchase programme, such as its size, duration and composition. To this effect, evidence shows that the persistence of the effects of asset purchases matters. Literature also shows that there are stock and flow effects involved in the conduct of LSAPs and the persistence of these effects matters. Altavilla et al. (2015) show that the stock effects of asset purchases on bond yields are transmitted via financial markets' reactions to current and expected future withdrawals of bond supply, in anticipation to the actual purchases taking place. These effects to bond yields are largely transmitted via the local supply or asset scarcity and duration channels.

Gagnon et al. (2010) show that LSAPs by the US Fed worked via the risk premium on the asset being purchased and the reduction in longer-term yields comes through the narrowing in risk premiums. The LSAPs removed a considerable amount of assets with high duration from the markets thus lowering the most important component of the risk premium, namely the term premium. Borio and Disyatat (2009) show that by providing funding at more attractive terms and larger quantities than market participants would, the central bank can boost the volume of lending and asset prices. Joyce et al. (2010) show that the presence of the central bank in the market as a significant buyer of assets may improve market functioning and reduce the risk premia for illiquidity via the liquidity premia channel effect. Andrade et al. (2016) show that the uncertainty channel also affects the 're-anchoring channel', which refers to the ability of the central bank implementing quantitative easing to reassure the private sector of its ability to anchor inflation expectations to levels consistent with price stability. Ampudia et al. (2019) find that the ECB's asset purchase programme decreased income inequality, mostly by reducing the unemployment rate for poorer households and to a lesser extent, by increasing the wages of the employed.

2.5 Is Quantitative Easing Only Effective at the Zero-Lower Bound?

Sims and Wu (2019) find that unconventional policies such as QE, forward guidance and negative interest rates are an (almost) perfect substitute for conventional monetary policy. They show that the zero-lower bound (ZLB) or effective lower bound (ELB) on policy rates is ultimately not much of a hindrance to effective stabilisation policy. Hence, QE policies can be undertaken whether conventional policy is constrained by the ZLB or not. Nonetheless, QE is more effective when short-term rates are fixed.

Contrary to the intentions of QE in advanced economies, which was to reinforce or propagate the impact of monetary policy accommodation on financial markets and real economic activity, in the book we argue that there is a case for the SARB to increase its holdings of government securities to supplement interest income and neutralise losses due to foreign investment and the foreign currency reserves accumulation programme. In this regard, our motivation is intricately linked to that of the Swiss National Bank (SNB). However, the fact that our motivation for the SARB to embark on LSAPs differs from that of the major advanced central banks does not mean that the LASPs by the SARB will not have a positive effect on inflation, output and employment growth and lower the unemployment rate. In fact, we show that as part of the monetary policy tools, even with a different motive, embarking on LSAPs operates through the same channels of transmission as those that would be active and potent in the case of dealing with financial market dislocations, depressed economic activity and subdued inflationary pressures, as was the case in most advanced economies. Furthermore, considering the effects of QE on yields and the exchange rate, we argue that it can help in anchoring inflation expectations.

2.6 Are Open-Ended Large-Scale Asset Purchases Effective?

One of the important aspects of the design of the LSAP programme is the choice between a programme with an end date for the purchases that is announced in advance and a programme that remains open ended. Burlon et al. (2019) test the effectiveness of an open-ended asset purchase programme in the euro area. The asset purchase programme is left open ended with the possibility of extending it in future conditional on inflation developments. They find that the open-ended asset purchase programme is more effective in immediately stimulating macro-economic conditions than committing ex ante to an ending date. They show that not announcing a closing date when phasing out from the asset purchase programme can be an effective policy choice. The open-ended dimension of the asset purchase programme provides a hedge against the materialisation of negative aggregate demand shocks that push inflation away from its path towards the target.

From the central bank communication perspective, the authors show the relevance of an open-ended programme from theoretical and quantitative perspectives. First, it affects the way agents form expectations about future purchases. Second, it affects the extent to which the central bank can design an asset purchase programme in an effective way. The effectiveness of open-ended asset purchases is further reinforced by a forward guidance on monetary policy rates. Similarly, Burlon et al. (2019) find that the more distant in the future the announced closing date of the asset purchase programme, the larger the (current and future) effectiveness of the programme itself.

2.7 Does Forward Guidance Reinforce the Effectiveness of Large-Scale Asset Purchases?

Literature on the effectiveness of LSAPs shows that its effects are amplified by forward guidance. Studies show that with monetary policy at the ZLB, forward guidance regarding the path of interest rates can be very effective in preserving macro-economic stability in the face of a contractionary demand shock. Theory also implies that private sector decisions depend on the entire path of the expected future short-term interest rates, not just the current level of the overnight rate or the policy rate. For instance, Swanson (2018a) shows that forward guidance and LSAPs had substantial and highly statistically significant effects that are comparable in magnitude to those of the federal funds rate before the ZLB. The author finds that forward guidance was more effective than LSAPs at moving short-term Treasury yields, whereas LSAPs were more effective than forward guidance and the federal funds rate at moving longer-term Treasury and corporate bond yields. Furthermore, the effects of LSAP announcements were very persistent compared to the effects of forward guidance. Nonetheless, he finds that the differences were not statistically significant and were probably due to the Federal Open Market Committee's (FOMC) shorter-horizon forward guidance announcements. He concludes that the Federal Reserve (Fed) is not very constrained by the lower bound on nominal interest rates and this implies that the Fed does not need to raise its inflation target.

Similarly, Levin et al. (2010) show that a combination of forward guidance and other monetary policy measures such as LSAPs is effective in responding to a 'Great Recession' style shock. The authors show that forward guidance on its own is quite effective in offsetting a natural rate shock of a moderate size and persistence. However, the macro-economic outcomes are much less satisfactory when considering a larger and more persistent shock, especially when the interest elasticity parameter value of aggregate demand is low. Filardo and Hofmann (2014) investigate the extent to which forward guidance has affected the level and volatility of interest rate expectations and the sensitivity of markets to economic news. They find that recent increased reliance on forward guidance has been helpful in clarifying policy intentions in highly unusual economic circumstances.

2.8 Why Should the SARB Conduct Large-Scale Asset Purchases?

In the book, we explore whether there is a compelling case to increase the SARB holdings of government securities to supplement interest income and neutralise losses due to foreign investments and foreign currency reserves accumulation? Evidence in this chapter establishes that there is. This question arises because the costs associated with reserves accumulation and the sterilisation of Rand liquidity created in the process have resulted in the SARB incurring persistent losses post-2009. Foreign currency reserves constitute 90 per cent of the SARB balance sheet and in the period post-2009, which was associated with exceptionally low global interest rates and yields, the returns on foreign investments have been insufficient for the SARB's operational costs. For instance, post-2009, as the policy rates in the US hit the lower bound, the Treasury Bill (TB) rates and the ten-year government bond yields declined, negatively affecting the returns. In addition, during this period the interest rate differentials widened in favour of South African assets. The widening in the interest rate differentials means that an asset allocation strategy that sought to increase the share of South African assets on the SARB's balance sheet would have greatly neutralised losses due to foreign investments. Whereas foreign investments were earning less than 2 per cent depending on the maturities of the investments, local currency investments were consistently recording returns above 5 per cent and these were not associated with the exchange rate (exchange rate valuation) risks as shown in Fig. 2.1.

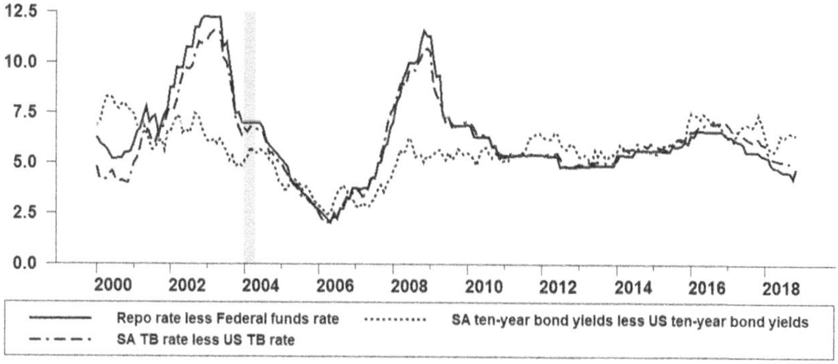

Fig. 2.1 SA and US policy rates and government yields differentials. (Source: South African Reserve Bank, Fred data and authors' calculations)

In addition, there are risks posed by large holdings of domestic assets by non-residents. The trends in Fig. 2.2 show that non-residents hold around 40 per cent of government bonds. Data shows that on a net cumulative basis, non-residents have bought more South African bonds post-2009 compared to shares. These trends can be partly explained by the increase in the budget deficit considering the conduct of the countercyclical fiscal policy and the inclusion of South African government bonds in the World Global Bond Index (WGBI) in October 2012. South African government bonds constitute 0.32 per cent of the WGBI. The GFSR (2019) refers to the trends shown in Fig. 2.2 as an unusually large share of the local currency government debt held by foreign investors.

Evidence in the book shows that LSAPs by the SARB depress the non-resident's cumulative net purchases of South African shares and bonds, especially the purchase of bonds.

The results also imply that positive shocks to SARB assets will also spillover to non-resident purchases of shares or equities. These results concur with international evidence showing that LSAPs by central banks, due to the fact that they constrain the supply of government assets (supply effects or supply-induced portfolio rebalancing) available to private investors, result in the rebalancing of assets held by investors largely due to the portfolio rebalancing channel. Thus, a balance sheet strategy by the SARB also addresses the main financial stability risks associated with changes in global

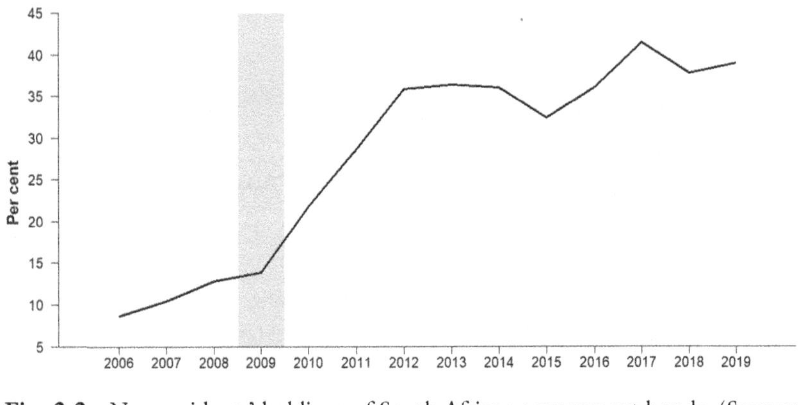

Fig. 2.2 Non-residents' holdings of South African government bonds. (Source: National Treasury)

investor risk appetite emanating from what the GFSR (2019) refers to as an unusually large share of their local currency government debt held by foreign investors.

2.8.1 Large-Scale Asset Purchases Have Not Been Inflationary in the US, euro area, the UK, Switzerland and Japan and Other Countries as Initially Thought

Post the global financial crisis in 2007 most advanced economies conducted LSAPs and even moved interest rates to negative territory, and this has not resulted in inflationary pressures. This is because all these central banks have been clear that the conduct of LSAPs is conditioned on achieving the price stability mandate.[1] Such that, once inflation rises above the inflation target, the monetary policy authorities will view that the objective of using LSAPs has been achieved and thus scale back their use of this tool. Similarly, given the price stability mandate as defined by the inflation target band, the SARB can scale back the LSAP programme if inflation breaches the preferred inflation level. We have stated that our motivation for the SARB to conduct LSAPs and other balance sheet tools is to assist the SARB to achieve the mandates of price stability (low and stable inflation below 4.5 per cent), maximum employment and macro-economic stability.

[1] 'As yet the evidence continues to indicate insufficient progress towards a *sustained adjustment in the path of inflation* towards levels below, but close to, 2 per cent over the medium term, which is a condition we have indicated for the ECB to start a gradual process of normalisation in its monetary policy stance'. https://www.bis.org/review/r170505d.htm.

'The reason central banks have been given mandates that are expressed in terms of numerical objectives for inflation is because legislatures realised that central banks' discretion had to be constrained. Their reaction functions had to be made predictable within a horizon which is realistic and, at the same time, verifiable by electorates'. https://www.bis.org/review/r150928a.htm.

'We continue to state that an inflation rate of 2 percent over the longer run is most consistent with our mandate to promote both maximum employment and price stability. In this regard, the statement now highlights that the Committee is prepared to use its full range of tools to achieve its dual-mandate objectives'. https://www.piie.com/events/fed-vice-chair-richard-h-clarida-us-monetary-policy.

2.9 Role of the Public Investment Corporation Balance Sheet

The Public Investment Corporation (PIC) is an asset management firm wholly owned by the government of the Republic of South Africa. It manages assets to the value of more than R2 trillion. The book dedicates a chapter on the role of the PIC balance sheet and how it can be used to reinforce the SARB balance sheet tools in achieving mandates of price, financial and macro-economic stability. The book explores questions related to the impact of the increased participation of the PIC in the primary and secondary government bond markets and its effects on government bond yields. We assess the impact of increasing the share of government bonds and Treasury bills in the PIC balance sheet on government bond yields. The intention is to assess the role the asset reallocation by the PIC can play in achieving the set objectives of price stability, financial stability and macro-economic stability.

The trends in Fig. 2.3 show that the share of government fixed income securities (bonds) and bills (Treasury bills) has declined over the years. Hence, the book explores whether the PIC balance sheet is another tool that can be used to achieve the set objectives of price stability, financial stability and macro-economic stability in a prudent manner. The analysis in the book assesses whether the PIC balance sheet can be used alongside

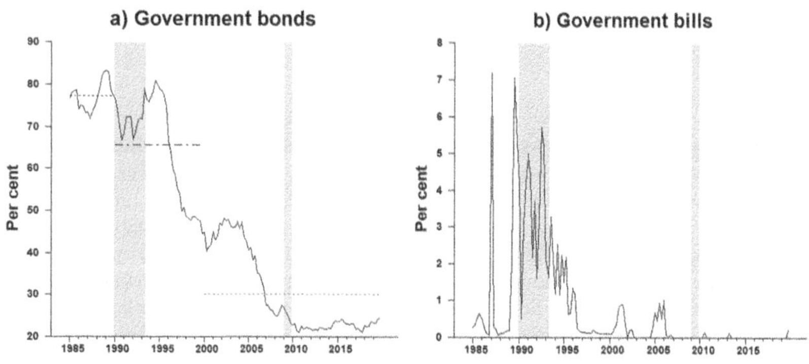

Fig. 2.3 Government bonds and bills as a share of PIC assets. (Source: South African Reserve Bank and authors' calculations. Note: The grey-shaded areas denote the periods of recessions. The dotted lines in (a) indicate the averages referred to in the text)

the SARB balance sheet to achieve these national objectives. Do bond purchases in the primary and secondary bond markets by the PIC reinforce the positive shock effects of LSAPs by the SARB?

2.10 What Are the Benefits of Increasing the Level of Foreign Currency Reserves?

The accumulation of foreign currency reserves is another SARB balance sheet tool that can be an integral part of an approach to achieve fiscal sustainability, and price, financial and macro-economic stability. The book argues for a broad approach to the reserves accumulation policy over and above the motives of holding forex reserves as a buffer against crisis, alternatively, a rainy-day fund, in case there is a balance of payments crisis. We argue for a broad approach to the reserves accumulation policy, namely (i) to maintain confidence in the monetary policy and to support the exchange rate policy, and (ii) for non-precautionary reasons such as to provide a stream of investment income to help finance part of the annual government budget, alternatively, for intergenerational savings or an endowment fund. Such a broad approach to reserves accumulation complements sound fiscal, monetary, prudential and macro-economic policy frameworks and limits a country's vulnerability to multiple shocks. Furthermore, Chang (2008) shows that within the inflation targeting framework, most importantly, the implied exchange rate stabilisation policy is derived from the objectives of stabilising inflation and the output-gap. These are the two variables in the monetary policy makers' objective function. Alternatively, there is a policy trade-off. In addition, Gumata and Ndou (2017) showed that the accumulation of foreign exchange reserves plays a role in appreciating the exchange rate, lowering permanent and overall R/US$ exchange rate volatilities, lowering inflation and lessening the burden of adjustment on the repo rate whilst supporting the price stability mandate. Thus, concluding that a reserves accumulation as a complementary policy approach can induce additional benefits of reduced welfare costs of elevated inflation, hence minimising the policy trade-off. To this effect, the trends in Fig. 2.4c show that the period post-2012, when forex reserves in US dollar terms declined, was associated with the prolonged R/US$ exchange depreciation. These trends imply that the reserves accumulation policy has an important role to play in the exchange rate policy.

Fig. 2.4 Forex reserves in US dollar terms and the R/US$ exchange rate. (Source: South African Reserve Bank and authors' calculations)

Furthermore, the broad approach to the policy of forex reserves accumulation argued for in this book also brings into sharp focus the role of the PIC as an asset manager and how the national forex reserves are managed.

2.11 Is It Important for the SARB to Lengthen the Maturities on Repurchase Agreements?

The book also considers another SARB balance sheet tool in the form of lengthening the maturities of repurchase agreements. Currently, the SARB accommodation system operates on short-dated (maturity) repurchase agreements on a weekly basis (six days) financed at the repo rate. As such, the book argues that there is a case for augmenting the current accommodation system by introducing longer-dated (maturity) accommodation window instruments. Figure 2.5 shows the long-term structure of the South African banks' assets and liabilities. It is evident that banks largely source their funding from deposits, and the interbank and debt securities.

On the asset side, banks largely extend credit to households and firms. For a shortage-based refinancing system such as in South Africa, Fig. 2.5 shows that banks only use roughly about 2 per cent of funds sourced at the repurchase agreements market to fund themselves. Banks largely fund themselves in the retail and wholesale (non-convertible debentures or NCDs), interbank and debt securities markets as opposed to the repurchase agreements market, alternatively, the discount window. This aspect of the banks' balance sheet speaks directly to the ability of banks to transmit changes in the repo rate to the economy at large.

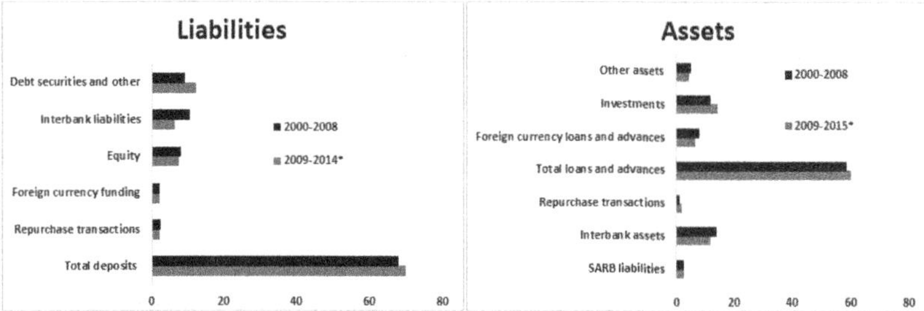

Fig. 2.5 Banks' assets and liabilities. (Source: South African Reserve Bank and authors' calculations)

Literature shows that central bank LSAPs also affect the banks' balance sheets by influencing their balance sheet developments, funding conditions and risk-bearing capacity. The ECB (2015) indicates that as an attractive source of long-term funding, the targeted longer-term refinancing operations (TLTROs) are intended to allow banks to replace more costly sources of funding and extend the maturity of their liabilities in order to better match that of the lending targeted by the measure. Furthermore, evidence shows that the funding substitution took place because of the TLTROs and resulted in a significant extension of the maturity of bank funding. The extension of maturity provides banks with funding certainty over a longer period and allows them to better match the maturity of their liabilities with that of assets such as loans to households and firms. Evidence also shows that TLTRO borrowers also reduced their recourse to wholesale funding, that is, issuance of debt securities and interbank borrowing. The book argues that lengthening of the maturities of funding options available at the accommodation can loosen the funding constraints experienced by banks and this will spill over to the funding of important markets such as the housing sector and small, micro and medium enterprises (SMMEs). In addition, from a policy and regulatory perspective, the lengthening of the maturity of the funding options for banks is especially important given the long-standing regulatory concern of the maturity mismatch risks induced by funding long-term assets such as housing using deposits which are of a short duration. At the same time, such a strategy will neutralise the impact of sterilisation and other costs associated with the forex reserves accumulation programme.

2.12 How Should the Bank Manage Excess Reserves Emanating From the LSAPs and Reserves Accumulation Policies?

It is common knowledge that in the process of conducting the LSAPs and reserves accumulation policies, central banks create bank reserves. The book addresses this matter by assessing how the SARB can deal with excess reserves that need to be sterilised to manage liquidity and the functioning of the interbank market. We assess whether the interest rate corridor is an effective instrument to dampen the accumulation of excess reserves and interbank rate volatility. Evidence from several countries that have embarked on LSAPs shows that countries adopt different approaches in dealing with excess reserves and their impact on bank liquidity and the interbank market.

Contrary to the US Fed and the ECB as shown in Fig. 2.6, excess banks' reserves in South Africa are mainly on account of the programme of reserves accumulation and the R/US$ exchange rate fluctuations. In this sense the South African case explored in the book is like the Swiss National Bank (SNB). For instance, Fig. 2.6 shows that in the US and the ECB, banks' excess reserves increased post-2009 coinciding with LSAPs. For the ECB, the amount of excess reserves stood at the beginning of 2018 above 1 trillion euros. However, in the US, as the US Fed has scaled back its LSAPs, the level of excess reserves has declined. As the US Fed

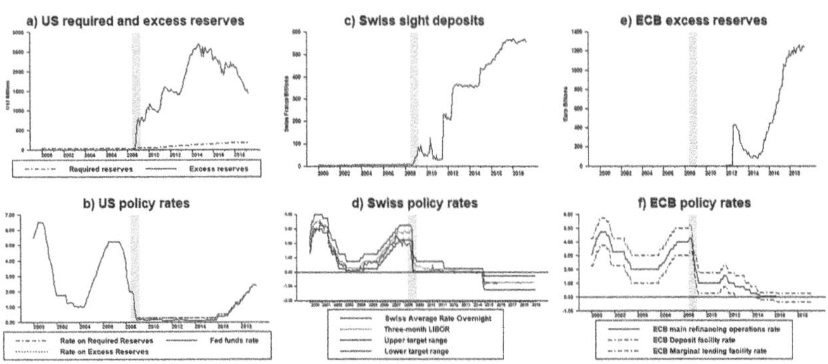

Fig. 2.6 Required reserves and policy rates in the US, Switzerland and euro area. (Source: Fred data, Swiss National Bank, ECB data warehouse and authors' calculations)

balance sheet grew to unprecedented size, the Open Market Desk at the New York Fed found it increasingly difficult to achieve the FOMC's target funds rate. In October 2008, the Federal Reserve began paying interest on required and excess reserve balances.

This interest rate was expected to establish a floor under the federal funds rate, whereas the discount rate, which since January 2003 has been set as a penalty rate above the funds rate target, was expected to limit upward pressure on the funds rate. According to Kahn (2010), with these changes the Federal Reserve's operating framework incorporated the essential elements of a 'channel' or 'corridor' system.

Contrary to the US, the ECB faced with a build-up of excess reserves opted to use a negative interest rate policy (negative deposit rate facility). In the case of the ECB, the negative rate applies also to average reserve holdings in excess of the minimum reserve requirements and all other deposits held with the Eurosystem. The negative deposit facility interest rate also applies to: (i) banks' average reserve holdings in excess of the minimum reserve requirements; (ii) government deposits held with the Eurosystem that exceed certain thresholds; (iii) Eurosystem reserve management services accounts if not currently remunerated; (iv) participants' account balances in TARGET2—Trans-European Automated Real-time Gross Settlement Express Transfer System; (v) non-Eurosystem national central bank (NCB) balances (overnight deposits) held in TARGET2; and (vi) other accounts held by third parties with Eurosystem central banks when stipulated that they are not currently remunerated or are remunerated at the deposit facility rate.

With respect to the SNB, as the central bank increased its interventions in the currency markets, so did the sight deposits of banks as shown in Fig. 2.6. At the same time, the SNB implemented its monetary policy by fixing a target range for the reference interest rate, the London Interbank Offered Rate (Libor), for three-month interbank loans in Swiss francs. Nonetheless, on 13 June 2019, the SNB introduced the Swiss Average Rate Overnight (Saron) as a new monetary policy tool replacing the Libor. As shown in Fig. 2.6d, the Saron and the Libor move in tandem. The SNB steers the Libor/Saron into the defined target range through its monetary policy operations as shown in Fig. 2.6d. As a rule, the SNB maintains the Libor/Saron in the middle of the defined range. Like the ECB, as excess reserves continued to accumulate, the SNB decided to impose an interest rate of negative rates on sight deposit account balances in December 2014.

Since January 2015, the SNB has applied negative interest rates within a target range downwards of -1.25 per cent and -0.25 per cent.

The book explores whether the interbank rate volatility is dependent on excess reserves regimes and if there is a direct relationship between the level of excess reserves and the interbank rate volatility. We use a bivariate logistic relationship between excess reserves, South African Benchmark Overnight Rate (Sabor) and the overnight forex rates in a symmetric interest rate corridor to assess the role of the level of excess reserves in determining and predicting the position of short-term rates within the interest rate corridor. The bivariate logistic function allows the position of short-term rates in the interest rate corridor to be determined and predicted depending on the level of excess reserves. Furthermore, the logistic function demonstrates how the anchoring of interbank and short-term interest rates transitions from one state to another. The intention is to assess whether the excess reserves threshold (inflection point) effects for the interbank rate occur at the same level of excess reserves when we adjust the sample size. We use the estimated threshold for excess reserves to guide the tiering of excess reserves and how they can be remunerated between the mid-point and the lower part of the interest rate corridor.

2.13 Conclusion and Policy Implications

This chapter presents a preliminary review of the central bank balance sheet tools that can be deployed to assist in the achievement of price, financial and macro-economic stability in South Africa. The chapter discusses the key channels through which LSAPS (QE) are transmitted and whether the size, duration and composition of central bank asset purchases matter. We provide vast literature review of when are the right conditions for the central bank to pursue LSAPs and whether QE is only effective at the zero-lower bound. The chapter discusses the motivation as to why the SARB must conduct QE beyond the COVID-19 period, increase the pace at which it accumulates foreign currency reserves, lengthen the repurchase agreement maturities, and adopt the excess reserves tiering approach and an interest rate corridor floor that allows the central bank to separate the monetary policy stance from the liquidity management policy. In addition, the analysis in the book assesses whether the PIC balance sheet can be used alongside the SARB balance sheet to achieve the national objectives of price, financial and macro-economic stability.

References

Altavilla C, Motto R, and Carboni G. 2015. Asset purchase programmes and financial markets: lessons from the euro area. ECB Working Paper Series No. 1864.

Ampudia M, Georgarakos D, Slacalek J, Tristani O, Vermeulen P, and Violant G L. 2019. Monetary Policy and Household Inequality. ECB Working Paper No. 2170, July 2018.

Andrade P, Breckenfelder J, De Fiore F, Karadi P, and Tristani O. 2016. "The ECB's asset purchase programme: an early assessment". ECB Working Paper 1956.

Bernanke B S. 2020. The New Tools of Monetary Policy American Economic Association Presidential Address.

BIS Committee on the Global Financial System. 2019. Unconventional monetary policy tools: a cross-country analysis. Report prepared by a Working Group chaired by Simon M Potter (Federal Reserve Bank of New York) and Frank Smets (European Central Bank). CGFS Papers No 63.

Borio C, and Disyatat P. 2009. Unconventional Monetary Policies: An Appraisal. BIS Working Papers No. 292.

Borio C, and Disyatat P. 2010. "Unconventional Monetary Policies: An Appraisal", The Manchester School, 78(s1), 53–89, September. Also available as BIS Working Papers, No. 292, November 2009.

Burlon L, Notarpietro A, and Pisani M. 2019. Macroeconomic effects of an open-ended asset purchase programme. Journal of Policy Modeling, Elsevier, 41(6), pp. 1144–1159.

Chang R. 2008. Inflation Targeting, Reserves Accumulation, and Exchange Rate Management in Latin America. Bank of Colombia Working Paper No. 487.

Clarida R H. 2012. What Has—and Has Not—Been Learned About Monetary Policy in a Low-Inflation Environment. Journal of Money Credit and Banking, 44(s1), 123–140.

Clarida R H. 2019. The Federal Reserve's Review of Its Monetary Policy Strategy, Tools, and Communication Practices. Speech given at The Bank of Finland Conference on Monetary Policy and Future of Economic and Monetary Union, Helsinki, Finland.

Cœuré B. 2018. The Persistence and Signalling Power of Central Bank Asset Purchase Programmes. Speech at the 2018 US Monetary Policy Forum, New York City, 23 February 2018.

ECB. 2015. Targeted longer-term refinancing operations (TLTROs).

Filardo A, and Hofmann B. 2014. Forward Guidance at the Zero-Lower Bound. BIS Quarterly Review, March 2014.

Gagnon J, Raskin M, Remache J, and Sack B. 2010. Large-scale asset purchases by the Federal Reserve: did they work? Federal Reserve Bank of New York, Staff Report No, 441.

Global Financial Stability Report. 2019. Vulnerabilities in a Maturing Credit Cycle. IMF.

Gumata N, and Ndou E. 2017. Bank Credit Extension and Real Economic Activity in South Africa: The Impact of Capital Flow Dynamics, Bank Regulation and Selected Macroprudential Tools. Palgrave Macmillan. ISBN 978-3-319-43550-3.

Haldane A G, Roberts-Sklar M, Wieladek T, and Young C. 2016. QE: The Story So Far. Bank of England Staff Working Paper No. 624.

Ito T. 2014. "We Are All QE-sians Now", IMES Discussion Paper Series 2014-E-5, Bank of Japan.

Joyce M, Lasaosa A, Stevens I, and Tong M. 2010. The financial market impact of quantitative easing. Bank of England Working Paper No. 393.

Kahn G A. 2010. Monetary policy under a corridor operating framework. Economic Review, Federal Reserve Bank of Kansas City, 95(Q IV), pp. 5–34.

Krishnamurthy A, and Vissing-Jorgensen A. 2011. "The Effects of Quantitative Easing on Interest Rates: Channels and Implications for Policy," Brookings Papers on Economic Activity Fall, 215–265.

Krishnamurthy A, and Vissing-Jorgensen A. 2013. "The Ins and Outs of LSAPs," in Global Dimensions of Unconventional Monetary Policy: Federal Reserve Bank of Kansas City Symposium Proceedings from Jackson Hole, Wyoming (Kansas City: Federal Reserve Bank of Kansas City) 57–111, available at http://www.kansascityfed.org/publications/research/escp

Levin A, Lopez-Salido D, Nelson E, and Yun T. 2010. "Limitations on the Effectiveness of Forward Guidance at the Zero Lower Bound", International Journal of Central Banking, 6(1).

Motto R, Altavilla C, and Carboni G. 2015. Asset purchase programmes and financial markets: lessons from the euro area. ECB Working Paper Series 1864.

Sims E, and Wu J C. 2019. Evaluating Central Banks' Tool Kit: Past, Present, and Future.NBER Working Papers 26040.

Swanson E T. 2018a. Measuring the Effects of Federal Reserve Forward Guidance and Asset Purchases on Financial Markets NBER Working Paper No. 23311.

Swanson E T. 2018b. The Federal Reserve is Not Very Constrained by the Lower Bound on Nominal Interest Rates. Working Paper.

Swanson E T, and Williams J C. 2014. "Measuring the Effect of the Zero Lower Bound on Medium and Longer-Term Interest Rates," American Economic Review, 104(10).

PART I

Capital Flow Episodes, Fiscal Shocks, Commodity Price and House Price Boom Effects on Credit Growth Dynamics

CHAPTER 3

Do Capital Inflows Relieve Banks' Credit Constraints and Boost Credit Growth? Evidence from Credit Conditions and Bank Credit Risk

Research Questions Explored

- Investigate whether various components of capital inflows relieve credit constraints by loosening credit conditions?
- What are the direct and indirect impacts of adverse credit conditions and the global and domestic recessions in the transmission of the effects of a positive capital inflow shock on credit growth?

3.1 Introduction

Igan and Tan (2015) find capital inflows loosen the credit constraints of domestic banks and boost credit growth. This is particularly the case when banks are not in good health. When credit constraints are severe, capital inflow shocks tend to have a significant effect on credit growth. Based on this view, this chapter tests the following hypothesis on the South African data:

Hypothesis 3.1 *Capital inflows relieve credit constraints by loosening (easing) credit conditions.*

N. Gumata, E. Ndou, *Achieving Price, Financial and Macro-Economic Stability in South Africa*,
https://doi.org/10.1007/978-3-030-66340-7_3

First, as a precursor to the empirical analysis, this chapter shows that non-performing loans (NPLs) as a ratio of all loans and the credit conditions index (CCI) have an inverse relationship with credit growth, as also shown in Fig. 3.1.[1] Testing Hypothesis 3.1 above means that we are determining the extent to which credit conditions and bank credit risk act as conduits of positive capital inflow shocks into credit growth. Gumata and Ndou (2019) show that the capital inflow surge shock increases credit and GDP growth in contrast to the contractionary effects induced by a sudden stop and positive net portfolio flow volatility shock. Furthermore, a capital inflow surge shock increases credit growth more than GDP growth and explains a relatively large proportion of fluctuation in credit growth. The capital inflow episode amplifies the impact of shocks on the economy as was the case prior to 2004Q1 and after 2009Q3. These findings indicate that capital inflow shocks do impact credit. However, they are silent on the role of capital inflow shocks in credit conditions and bank credit risk in credit growth.

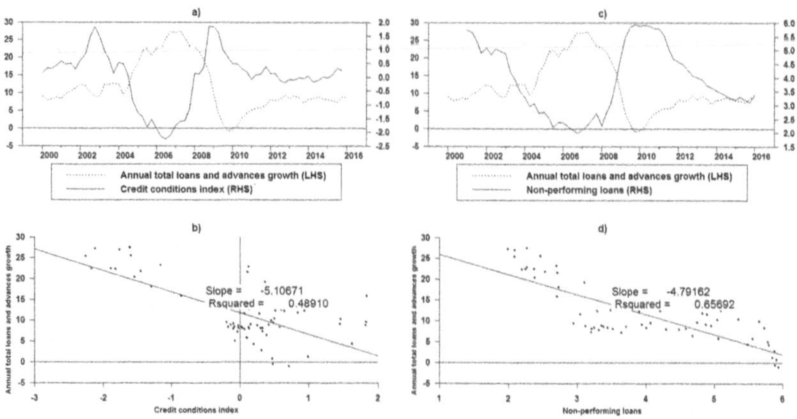

Fig. 3.1 Credit growth, credit conditions index and non-performing loans. (Source: South African Reserve Bank and authors' calculations. Note: Positive (negative) values of credit conditions index indicates tightened (loosening))

[1] See Gumata and Ndou (2017) for the detailed methodology of the construction of the credit condition index (CCI). The CCI is obtained from Gumata and Ndou (2017). The evolution of the CCI over time is presented in later chapters of the book.

This chapter contributes to literature and policy research by exploring the role of capital inflow shocks in credit conditions and bank credit risk in credit growth. We use several different statistical and econometric approaches to investigate whether various components of capital inflows relieve credit constraints by loosening credit conditions. We also establish the direct and indirect impacts of adverse credit conditions and the global and domestic recessions in the transmission of the effects of a positive capital inflow shock on credit growth.

3.2 Did Adverse Credit Conditions Since 2007Q3 Impact the Ability of Positive Capital Inflows to Influence Credit Growth Dynamics?

To examine this question, this section relies on the modified Pentecôte and Rondeau (2015) and Cerra and Saxena (2008) approaches to estimate the credit Eq. (3.1).

$$Credit_t = constant + \sum_{i=1}^{4} \beta_i credit_{t-i} + \sum_{i=0}^{4} c_i Flows_{t-i} + \sum_{i=0}^{2} d_i CCI\_D2007_{t-i} + \varepsilon_t \tag{3.1}$$

where ε_t denotes error term, *Flows* denotes the capital inflows variable and *CCI_ D2007* refers to a dummy variable for the CCI. We use two dummy variables for the CCI to capture separate effects. The first dummy variable is defined to equal the value of the CCI for the period 2007Q3 to the end of the sample and zero otherwise. The second dummy variable is defined to be equal the value of the CCI for the period 2000Q1 to 2007Q2 and zero otherwise. Credit refers to credit growth. The actual (counterfactual) responses refer to credit growth responses when the CCI channel is included (excluded) in the model. The propagating (magnifying) or restraining (stifling) ability of the CCI is determined by the gap between the actual and counterfactual responses. The analysis uses quarterly (Q) data spanning 2000Q1 to 2015Q3. We use the CCI, NPLs, GDP growth, credit growth and capital inflows. The net capital inflows are expressed as a percentage of the GDP. The data is sourced from the South African Reserve Bank database. All growth rates are at annual rate. The model is estimated using two lags and 10,000 bootstrap draws.

3.2.1 *Do Credit Conditions Impact the Transmission of Portfolio Banking Flows?*

Figure 3.2a shows that beginning in 2007Q3 the CCI led to lower actual credit growth than the counterfactual responses indicate. This evidence suggests that tight credit conditions post-2007Q3 led to a lower transmission of positive portfolio banking inflows shocks into credit growth. In contrast, the looser credit conditions index before 2007Q3 did not lead to a much higher actual impulse response than the counterfactual reactions. This evidence corroborates the findings in Gumata and Ndou (2017, 2019) indicating that capital inflows play a limited role in influencing domestic credit growth. In addition, while capital inflows into non-banks and banks result in the sectorial reallocation of credit extension between the household and corporate sectors, the sectoral credit reallocation is weak.

Furthermore, Fig. 3.2c shows that there seems to be asymmetric effects in the transmission of portfolio banking inflow shocks due to prevailing credit conditions.

3.2.2 *Evidence from Positive Shock Effects Due to Portfolio Inflow For the Period Beginning 2008Q1*

Would the effects that have been identified in the section above change when adjusting the sample size and using the values of portfolio inflows starting in 2008Q1? The period starting in 2008Q1 coincides with the beginning of the global recession and heightened global uncertainty. To answer this

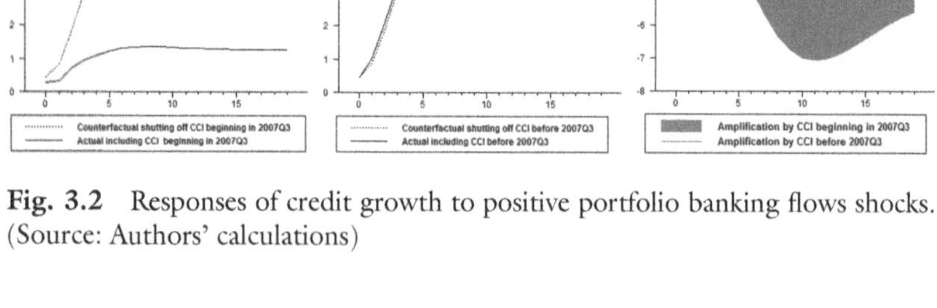

Fig. 3.2 Responses of credit growth to positive portfolio banking flows shocks. (Source: Authors' calculations)

question, we modify Eq. (3.1) to examine the dynamics of portfolio inflow effects by using the specification in Eq. (3.2), where ε_t denotes the error term and *Flows _ D2008* denotes the dummy variable which equals the value of portfolio banking inflows beginning in 2008Q1 to the end of the sample and zero otherwise. On the other hand, *CCI _ D2008* refers to the dummy variable for the CCI which equals the value of the CCI beginning in 2008Q1 to the end of the sample and zero otherwise.

$$Credit_t = constant + \sum_{i=1}^{4} \beta_i credit_{t-i} + \sum_{i=0}^{4} c_i Flows\_D2008*_{t-i} + \sum_{i=0}^{2} d_i CCI\_D2008_{t-i} + \varepsilon_t \qquad (3.2)$$

Figure 3.3a shows the responses to a positive portfolio banking inflow *Flows _ D2008* shock based on Eq. (3.2). Evidence in Fig. 3.3 indicates that the counterfactual credit growth responses are much higher than the actual impulse responses suggest. This indicates that tighter credit conditions had a larger dampening effect on credit growth. Thus, tighter credit conditions post-2008Q1 dampened credit growth more compared to the period pre-2008.

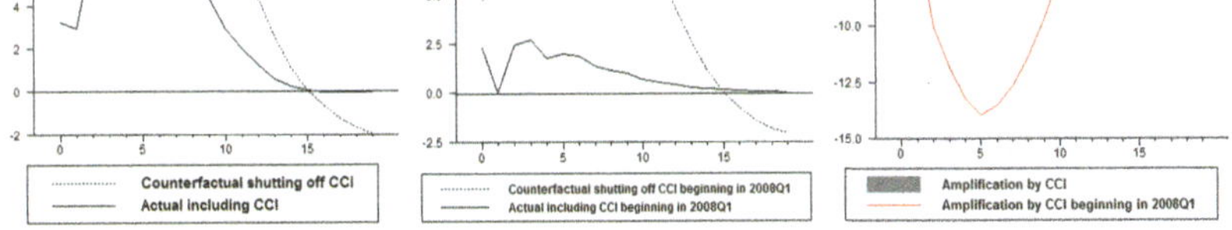

Fig. 3.3 Responses of credit growth to positive portfolio banking inflow shocks for sample starting in 2008Q1. (Source: Authors' calculations)

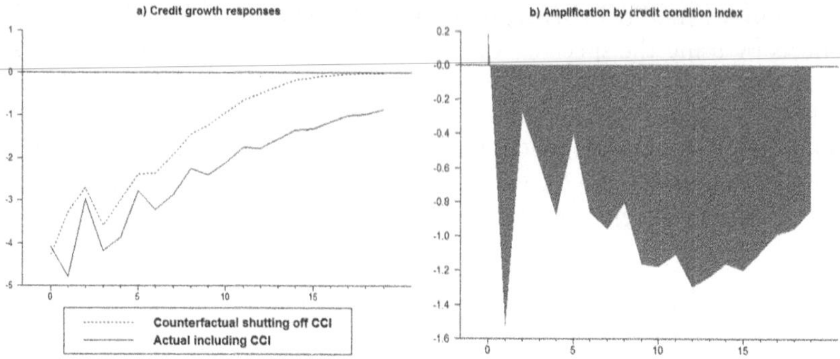

Fig. 3.4 Responses of credit growth to a recession shock and the role of the CCI. (Source: Authors' calculations)

3.2.3 *Evidence from a Recession Shock*

This section applies a similar approach to the earlier section to examine the transmission of the recession shock via its impact on credit conditions and credit growth. The recession dummy is defined to equal one in 2009Q1–Q3 and zero otherwise. Figure 3.4 reveals that the recession shock had a negative effect on credit growth. The effects are severe when the CCI is not shut-off in the model.

Therefore, evidence in this section indicates that during periods of severe global and domestic financial constraints, the ability of positive capital inflow shocks to stimulate credit growth is highly neutralised by the prevailing tight credit conditions. This was particularly the case since the onset of financial crisis in 2007Q3 and the global and domestic recessions.

3.3 Inferences from a Vector Autoregression (VAR) Model and a Counterfactual Approach

The preceding sections did not assess the influence of positive capital inflow shocks on credit constraints, but only assessed the role of prevailing credit constraints in the transmission of positive capital inflow shocks. Hence, this section examines the direct effects of positive capital inflow shocks on credit constraints. We use the counterfactual approach that shuts-off the role of the CCI channel in the model. The counterfactual impulse responses refer to the results arising when the CCI channel is shut-off in the model. Then the gap between the actual and the

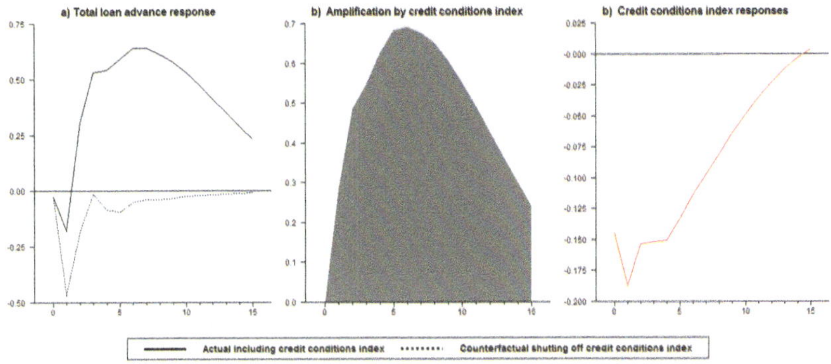

Fig. 3.5 Responses to a positive net capital inflow shock. (Source: Authors' calculations)

counterfactual impulse responses measures the amplifying effects of the credit conditions index channel. Figure 3.5 shows that positive capital inflow shocks raise the actual credit growth more than the counterfactual response. The results indicate that credit conditions play an important role in the transmission of positive capital inflow shocks to credit growth.

How is this possible? The results indicate that the shock effects are transmitted via the depressing effects of the CCI in Fig. 3.5c, which implies the loosening of credit conditions following a positive capital inflow shock. Thus, in the absence of looser credit conditions the positive capital inflow shock would not lead to a meaningful increase in credit growth.

On the other hand, Fig. 3.6 shows the effects of a positive portfolio banking inflows shock on credit growth and the role of the CCI. Evidence indicates that credit growth would be higher than the counterfactual when the credit conditions channel is included in the model. The positive capital inflow and portfolio banking inflow shocks have a direct and indirect impact on credit growth via the loosening of credit conditions. Thus, policy initiatives that loosen credit conditions tend to lead to the amplification of capital inflow shocks on credit growth.

3.3.1 Are the Results Sensitive to Changes in the Model Size?

This section concludes by estimating a vector autoregression (VAR) model with additional variables. The estimated VAR model includes the capital inflow variables as per cent of GDP, GDP growth, credit growth, inflation

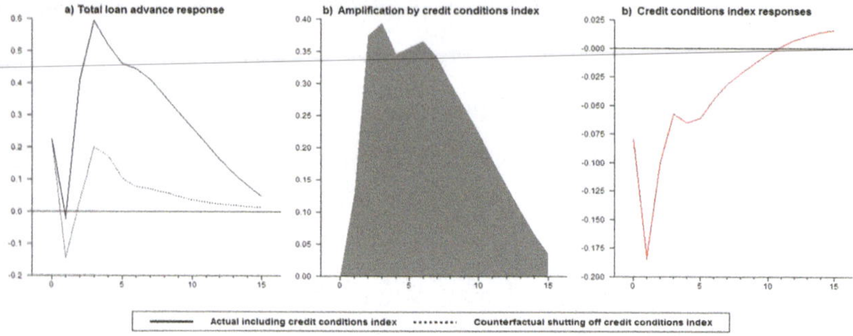

Fig. 3.6 Response to a positive portfolio banking inflow shock. (Source: Authors' calculations)

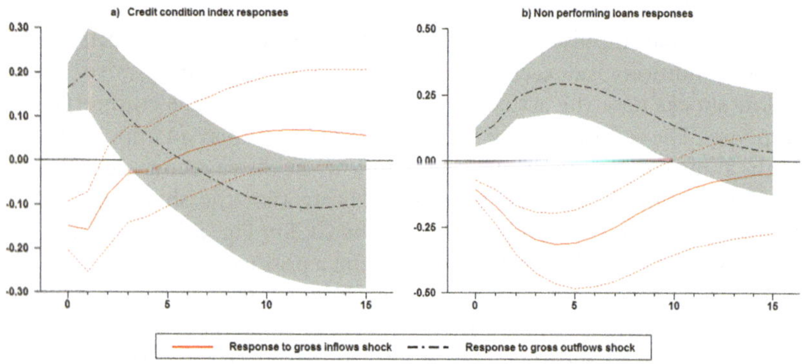

Fig. 3.7 Credit conditions index and non-performing loans responses. (Source: Authors' calculations)

and the credit constraints or risk variables captured by the NPLs and CCI. The model is estimated using two lags and 10,000 Monte Carlo draws. We differentiate between the shock effects exerted by positive gross capital inflows and outflows shocks on tight credit conditions and NPLs. Figure 3.7 shows that these shocks exert different effects on credit conditions and NPLs.

A one positive standard deviation gross capital inflow (outflow) shock leads to loosening (tightening) of credit conditions for nearly three quarters. In addition, these shocks affect credit growth via their impact on credit risk captured by NPLs. The loosening of credit condition is not only

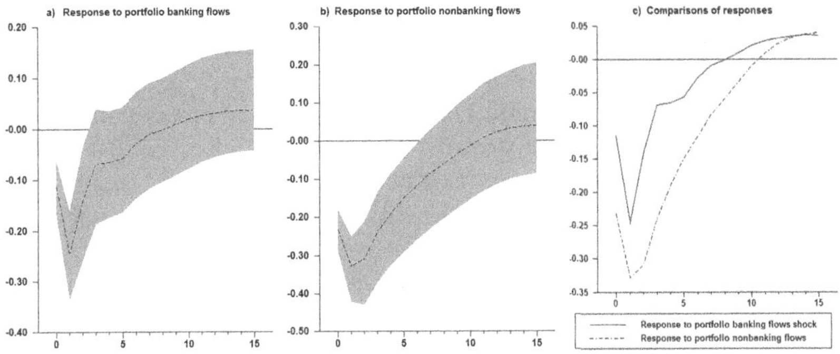

Fig. 3.8 Credit conditions index responses to portfolio banking and non-banking inflow shocks. (Source: Authors' calculations)

restricted to capital inflows shocks. Figure 3.8 shows that portfolio banking inflows and non-banking inflows lead to a significant loosening of credit conditions. A positive portfolio non-banking inflow shock leads to the loosening of credit conditions for a prolonged period compared to a positive portfolio banking inflow shock of same magnitude.

3.4 Conclusion and Policy Implications

This chapter explored whether capital inflows relieve credit constraints by loosening credit conditions. First, we establish that non-performing loans and the credit conditions index have an inverse relationship with credit growth, meaning that high (low) levels of non-performing loans and tight (loose) credit conditions result in low (high) credit growth. Second, evidence shows that beginning in 2007Q3 the CCI led to lower credit growth suggesting that tight credit conditions post-2007Q3 led to a lower transmission of positive portfolio banking inflow shocks into credit growth. Nonetheless, looser credit conditions pre-2007Q3 did not lead to much higher credit growth. Furthermore, there are asymmetric effects in the transmission of portfolio banking inflow shocks due to prevailing credit conditions.

Second, we establish that tighter credit conditions had a larger dampening effect on credit growth post-2008Q1 compared to the period pre-2008. Thus, evidence indicates that during periods of severe global and domestic financial constraints and heightened uncertainty, the direct and indirect ability of positive capital inflow shocks to stimulate credit growth is highly neutralised by the prevailing tight credit conditions. Prevailing credit conditions are conduits through which capital inflow shocks are transmitted to credit growth. In addition, credit conditions are sources of shocks to credit growth. Thus, policy initiatives that loosen (tighten) credit conditions tend to lead to the amplification (dampening) of capital inflow shocks on credit growth. Third, the data fails to reject the hypothesis that a capital inflow shock leads to the loosening of credit conditions. Capital inflow shocks affect credit growth via their impact on credit risk as captured by non-performing loans. Thus, evidence shows that capital inflow shocks affect credit growth directly and indirectly via the credit conditions and credit risk channels.

References

Cerra V, and Saxena S W. 2008. Growth Dynamics: The Myth of Economic Recovery, *American Economic Review* 98 (1), 439–457

Igan D, and Tan Z. 2015. Capital Inflows, Credit Growth, and Financial Systems. IMF Working paper WP/15/193.

Gumata N and Ndou E. 2017. Bank Credit Extension and Real Economic Activity in South Africa: The Impact of Capital Flow Dynamics, Bank Regulation and Selected Macroprudential Tools. Palgrave Macmillan. ISBN 978-3-319-43550-3.

Gumata N and Ndou E. 2019. Capital Flows, Credit Markets and Growth in South Africa: The Role of Global Economic Growth, Policy Shifts and Uncertainties. Palgrave Macmillan. ISBN 978-3-030-30887-2.

Pentecôte J S and Rondeau F. 2015. Trade Spill Overs on Output Growth during the 2008 Financial Crisis, *Journal of International Economics* 143, 36–47

CHAPTER 4

Credit Conditions and the Amplification of Macro-economic Responses to Unexpected Shocks: Implications for Monetary Policy

Research Questions Explored

- What is the impact of tighter credit conditions on how the repo rate responds to positive inflation shocks?
- What are the effects of tighter credit conditions in amplifying the responses of other macro-economic variables to several shocks?
- How are the repo rate responses to positive inflation shocks amplified or dampened by tight credit conditions and subdued GDP growth?
- Does inflation respond differently to the R/US$ exchange rate depreciation shocks in the absence of the credit conditions index?

4.1 Introduction

Earlier chapters showed that prevailing credit conditions and the bank credit risk channel as captured by the non-performing loans (NPLs) are conduits over and above being direct channels through which capital inflow shocks are transmitted to credit growth. Thus, dynamics in credit markets can lead to tighter credit conditions and heightened bank credit risk independent of changes in the monetary policy stance. In addition, we

N. Gumata, E. Ndou, *Achieving Price, Financial and Macro-Economic Stability in South Africa*,
https://doi.org/10.1007/978-3-030-66340-7_4

concluded that policy initiatives that loosen (tighten) credit conditions tend to lead to the amplification (dampening) of capital inflow shock effects on credit growth. This chapter extends the analysis of the role of credit market conditions by exploring the role of the policy rate tightening in response to inflationary pressures. This aspect has not been explored in South Africa. What are the implications of tighter credit conditions on how the repo rate responds to positive inflation shocks? Is the repo rate response to positive inflation shocks amplified or dampened by tight credit conditions and GDP growth?

Figure 4.1 shows that the credit conditions index (CCI) has been largely neutral with a tightening bias.[1] At the same time, post-2009, the output-gap has remained largely negative. Ndou and Gumata (2017) provide evidence that the negative output-gap tells us less about inflationary pressures post-2009. Hence, the suggestion that the Philips curve, alternatively, the relationship between inflation and the output-gap, has flattened.[2]

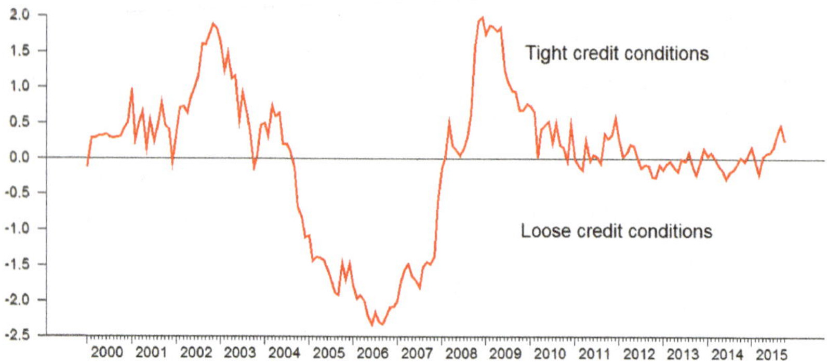

Fig. 4.1 The credit conditions index. (Source: Authors' calculations)

[1] See Gumata and Ndou (2017) for the detailed methodology of the construction of the credit condition index (CCI). The CCI is obtained from Gumata and Ndou (2017).

[2] Yellen (2017), Brainard (2017), Kashkari (2017) and IMF World Economic Outlook (2017), amongst others, raise the persistent disconnect (divergence) between the price stability and maximum (full) employment mandates in the US post financial crisis. Vast literature post-2009 documents that the insensitivity of inflation to slack is pervasive across the developed world.

This chapter fills policy and academic research gaps by establishing the impact of tighter credit conditions on how the repo rate (monetary policy stance) responds to positive inflation shocks. We also show the effects of tighter credit conditions in amplifying the responses of other macro-economic variables to several shocks. In addition, we fill research gaps by showing whether the repo rate (monetary policy stance) response to positive inflation shocks is amplified (propagated) or dampened (neutralised) by tight credit conditions and subdued GDP growth. The chapter also determines the size of the amplifications (propagation effects) induced by credit conditions on selected macro-economic variables. We further explore whether inflation would respond differently to the R/US$ exchange rate depreciation shocks in the absence of the credit conditions channel. Lastly, we establish the impact of positive inflation shocks on the repo rate response to inflationary pressures in the absence of the credit conditions channel in the model.

4.2 How Do Credit Conditions and Lending Standards Impact GDP Growth?

This section begins by showing the effects of the CCI, and the Bureau for Economic Research (BER) Ernest and Young (EY) lending standards index on GDP growth. The data spans the sample period 2000Q1 to 2015Q4. The EY lending standards index the data is only available starting 2002Q1. The data is sourced from the South African Reserve Bank and the Bureau for Economic Research databases. Figure 4.2(b and d) shows that the CCI is positively related to the EY lending standards index. This means that tight credit conditions also capture the tightening of lending criteria by banks.

On the other hand, the negative relationships between GDP growth, credit conditions index and the lending standards suggest that improved GDP growth results in the loosening of the lending standards and credit conditions. What does the tightening in credit conditions tell us about the household sector conditions? The bigger slope magnitude in Fig. 4.3(d) compared to Fig. 4.3(c) shows that households' credit growth is more sensitive to changes in the credit conditions index compared to credit to companies.

In addition, we isolate credit to the household sector by assessing the evolution of the housing sector and mortgage credit growth, which

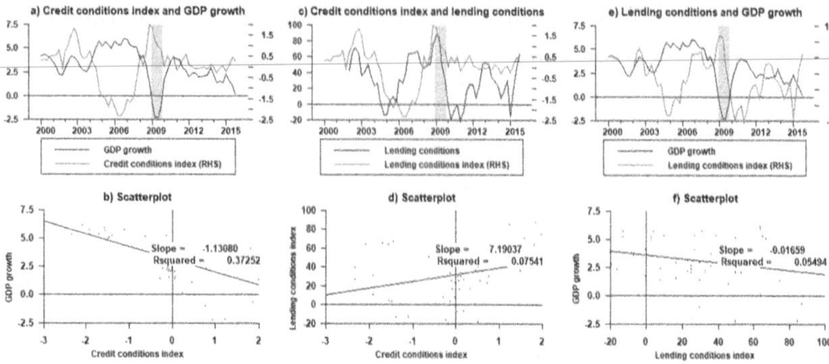

Fig. 4.2 The credit conditions index, GDP growth and lending standards. (Source: South African Reserve Bank, Bureau for Economic Research, and authors' calculations)

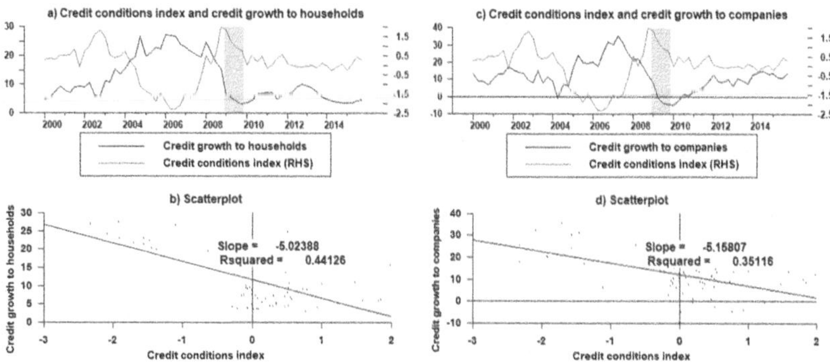

Fig. 4.3 Relationship between the credit conditions index and credit growth to companies and households. (Source: South African Reserve Bank and authors' calculations)

constitutes a larger share of household finances. Figures 4.4 and 4.5 show the relationship between the CCI, repo rate (monetary policy stance), nominal house price growth and the average mortgage repayments on an 80 per cent mortgage bond as calculated on the Absa house price index.

The relationship in Fig. 4.4 shows that tight credit conditions are positively related to mortgage repayments. However, in Fig. 4.5 the R-squares suggest that the repayments are highly responsive to changes in the repo

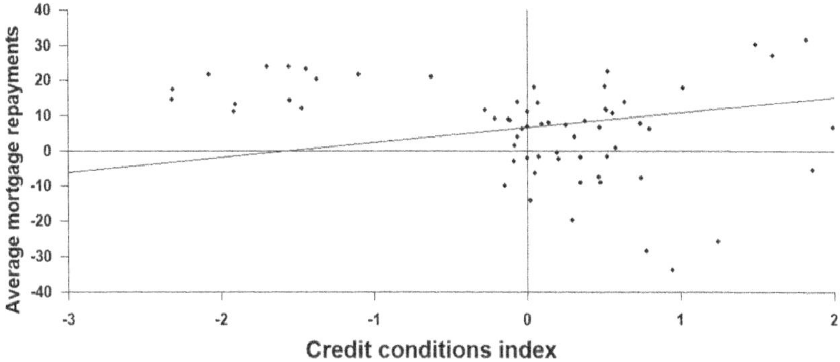

Fig. 4.4 Relationship between the credit conditions index and average mortgage repayments. (Source: Authors' calculations)

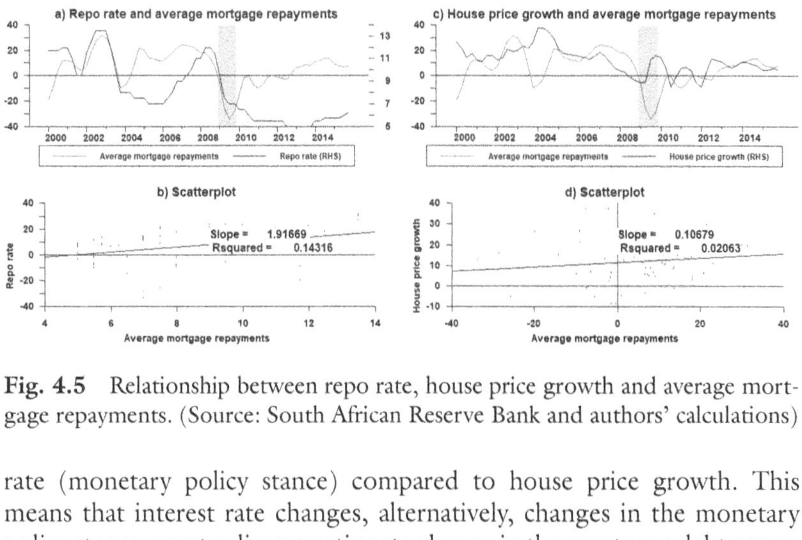

Fig. 4.5 Relationship between repo rate, house price growth and average mortgage repayments. (Source: South African Reserve Bank and authors' calculations)

rate (monetary policy stance) compared to house price growth. This means that interest rate changes, alternatively, changes in the monetary policy stance, exert a disproportionate change in the mortgage debt repayment burden compared to changes in house prices.

Last, the results in Fig. 4.6 show that house price growth matters more for household credit. The relationship is positive for the corporate sector but flat.

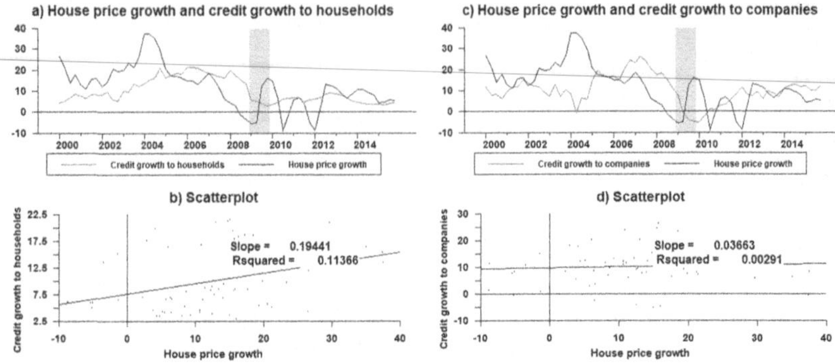

Fig. 4.6 Credit to households and companies, and nominal house price growth. (Source: South African Reserve Bank and authors' calculations)

4.3 Fluctuations and Non-linearities

This section examines two aspects, namely, (i) the fluctuations induced by the CCI shock relative to those induced by the repo rate (monetary policy stance) on inflation and GDP growth; and (ii) the non-linear (threshold) effects exerted by credit and financial conditions on inflation and GDP growth. Some literature studies indicate that credit and financial conditions exert non-linear (threshold) effects on output with implications for potential output and the output-gap trajectories. This also means that credit and financial conditions have implications for inflationary pressures and the outlook.

4.3.1 How Much Fluctuations Do Credit Conditions Induce on Other Macro-economic Variables?

To examine whether the CCI amplifies the responses of macro-economic variables to various economic shocks, this section begins by showing the fluctuations induced by the credit conditions shocks in inflation and GDP growth. We estimated a four-variable VAR model that includes headline consumer price index (CPI) inflation, GDP growth, repo rate and the credit conditions index. All growth rates are at an annual rate (12-month percentage changes). The model is estimated using two lags selected by the Akaike information criterion and 10,000 Monte Carlo draws. Figure 4.7(a) shows that credit conditions explain about 8 per cent of inflation after eight quarters and this less than 10 per cent is explained by the repo rate (monetary policy) shocks.

In contrast, credit conditions induce more fluctuations in GDP growth compared to those induced by the repo rate (monetary policy stance).

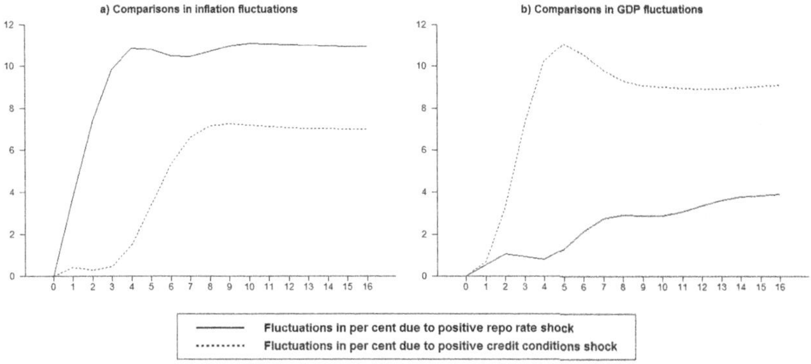

Fig. 4.7 Fluctuations induced by the credit conditions index and the repo rate. (Source: Authors' calculations)

Thus, evidence indicates the ability of credit conditions to induce large movements and possibly amplifying macro-economic responses.

4.3.2 Is There a Non-linear Effect of Credit Conditions on GDP Growth?

To determine the non-linear effects of tight credit conditions CCI_t on GDP growth, this section estimates a non-linear Eq. (4.1):

$$GDP_{\text{growth}} = \text{Constant} + \alpha_i CCI_t + \gamma_i CCI_t^2 + \partial_i D * CCI_t + \omega_i D \times CCI_t^2 + \rho_i X_t + \varepsilon_t, \quad (4.1)$$

where, CCI_t^2 is the credit conditions index squared, and X_t is the set of variables which includes the CPI inflation rate, current output growth, lagged output growth, and the crisis dummy *D*, which is equal to 1 post-2008Q4 and 0 otherwise. We further distinguish the effects before and during the global financial crisis through the interaction of the dummy variable for the global financial crisis with the credit conditions as shown in Eq. (4.2).

$$D \times CCI_t \text{ and } D \times CCI_t^2 \quad (4.2)$$

Equation (4.1) is estimated with instrumental variable techniques to deal with the possible endogeneity between credit conditions and output growth. The instruments include four to five lags of each variable. The results in Table 4.1 show a negative sign on current output growth, which indicates convergence.

Table 4.1 Results from Eq. (4.1)

Variable	*Model 1*		*Model 2*		*Model 3*		*Model 4*	
	Coefficient	*p-Value*	*Coefficient*	*p-Value*	*Coefficient*	*p-Value*	*Coefficient*	*p-Value*
Initial GDP	–	–	-0.03	(0.01)	-0.03	(0.01)	-0.06	(0.00)
CCI	-0.35	(0.01)	-0.47	(0.00)	-0.61	(0.00)	-0.69	(0.00)
D*CCI	–	–	-0.93	(0.01)	–	–	1.42	(0.17)
CCI^2	-0.12	(0.18)	–	–	-0.25	(0.01)	-0.27	(0.05)
$D*CCI^2$		–	–	–	–	–	-1.07	(0.09)

Source: Authors' calculations

We find that tighter credit conditions have adverse effects on output growth and the effects are accentuated post-2008Q4. Overall, evidence shows that credit conditions affect output growth in a non-linear way.

4.4 How Big Are the Amplifications?

This section determines the effects of the amplification or dampening abilities of credit conditions on selected macro-economic variables. We estimated a four-variable VAR model as done in the earlier section and compare the actual and counterfactual responses when the credit conditions index is shut off in the models. The counterfactual GDP response refers to the impulse response when the credit conditions index channel is shut off in the inflation equation. The gap between the impulse responses measures the amplifying ability of the credit conditions index channel. We start by asking: Do the credit conditions amplify (propagate) the responses of output growth to positive repo rate (monetary policy stance) and CPI inflation shocks? Figure 4.8(a) shows that output growth declines more in the presence of credit conditions compared to when the credit conditions are shut off (not active) in the CPI inflation equation. This suggests that tight credit conditions worsen the GDP growth decline due to positive inflation shocks. The amplification magnitudes in Fig. 4.8(b) indicate that the peak shock effects occur during the sixth quarter.

The amplification (propagation) is not only restricted to positive CPI inflation shock effects. Figure 4.9 shows that the decline in the output growth rate due to positive repo rate (monetary policy stance) shocks is

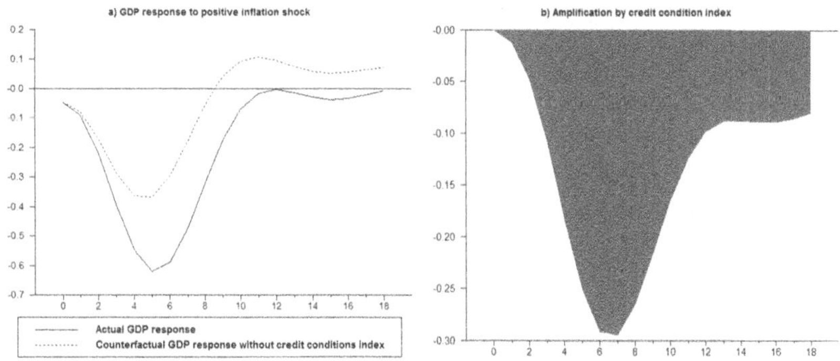

Fig. 4.8 GDP growth responses to the inflation rate shock and amplification by the credit conditions index. (Source: Authors' calculations)

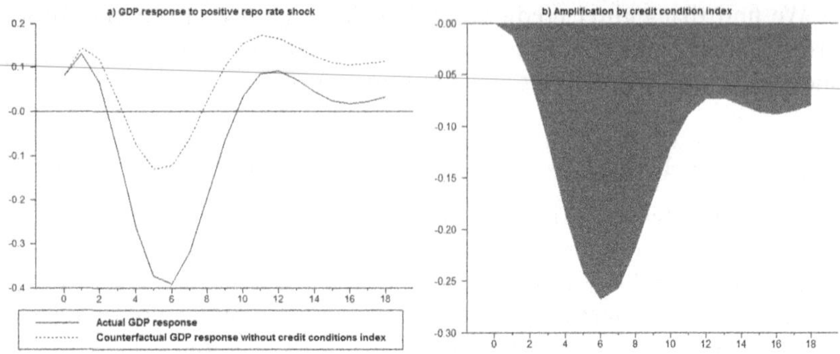

Fig. 4.9 GDP growth responses to a positive repo rate shock and amplification by the credit conditions index. (Source: Authors' calculations)

pronounced in the presence of tight credit conditions compared to when these are shut off or not active in the model.

This evidence shows that credit conditions play a significant role in output growth dynamics as a transmitter of positive CPI inflation and repo rate (monetary policy stance) shocks.

4.4.1 How Would Inflation Respond to the Exchange Rate Depreciation Shocks in the Absence of the Credit Conditions Index?

This section extends the analysis in the previous sections by including the rand per US dollar (R/US$) exchange rate depreciation effects. We are interested in the inflation responses to the R/US$ exchange rate depreciation shock in the presence and absence of credit conditions. Evidence in Fig. 4.10(a) shows that inflation would be much lower in the presence of tight credit conditions or when credit conditions are active in the model compared to when they are absent in the model due to the R/US$ exchange rate depreciation shock.

In cumulative terms, CPI inflation would increase by a peak of 5 percentage points when the credit conditions index is shut off (not active in the model) compared to 2 percentage points when credit conditions are included (active) in the model. As shown in Fig. 4.10(b), tight credit conditions dampen (neutralise) the CPI inflationary pressures associated with the R/US$ exchange rate depreciation effects.

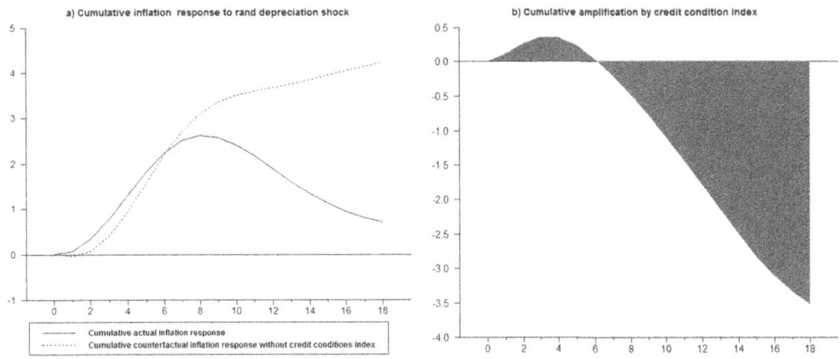

Fig. 4.10 Inflation responses to the exchange rate depreciation shock and amplification by the credit conditions index. (Source: Authors' calculations)

4.5 Implications for the Monetary Policy Conduct

The preceding sections showed that credit conditions amplify (propagate) as well as dampen (neutralise) macro-economic responses to unexpected shocks. These effects have implications for the conduct of monetary policy. This section examines the effects of credit conditions on the repo rate response to inflationary pressures. This is done by determining the actual and counterfactual repo rate responses in the presence and absence of the credit conditions in the estimated models.

4.5.1 Is the Repo Rate Reaction to Positive Inflation Shocks Amplified or Dampened by Tight Credit Conditions and Subdued GDP Growth?

The results show that the repo rate is tightened in response to a positive inflation shock, but the tightening differs in cases when credit conditions are included and shut off in the model. Figure 4.11(a) shows that the repo rate is aggressively tightened in response to positive inflation shocks when credit conditions are shut off in the model. This evidence suggests that tight credit conditions lead to less aggressive policy tightening towards inflationary pressures. Figure 4.11(b) shows the dampening effects of tight credit condition index on the repo rate (monetary policy stance) in response to CPI inflation shocks.

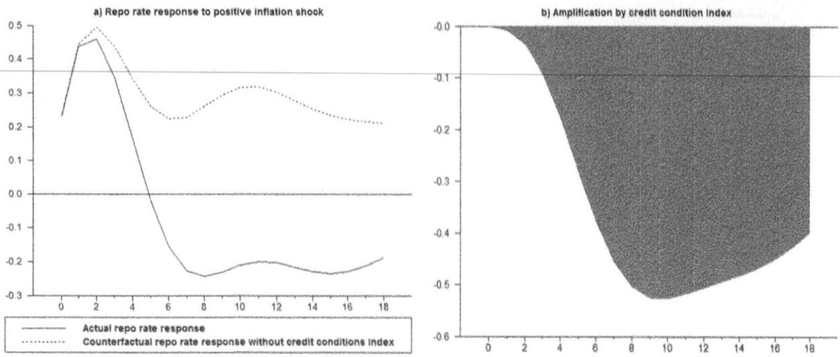

Fig. 4.11 Repo rate responses to positive inflation shocks and amplification by the credit conditions index. (Source: Authors' calculations)

What happens to the repo rate response to inflationary shocks due to the prevailing conditions of lower economic growth? To answer this question, the counterfactual VAR model is estimated to assess the repo rate responses to positive CPI inflationary shocks in the presence and absence of output growth. In Fig. 4.12, the repo rate is tightened in response to positive CPI inflationary shocks. The repo rate is tightened more due to positive CPI inflation shocks in the presence of output growth compared to when output growth is shut off. Figure 4.12(b) shows that higher output growth leads to aggressive repo rate (monetary policy stance) tightening in response to positive CPI inflation shocks.

4.5.2 *Historical Decomposition and Counterfactual Analysis*

This section applies a historical decomposition approach and decomposes the output growth, CPI inflation, and the repo rate (monetary policy stance), respectively, into their own trend, own contributions, and contributions from other variables. The counterfactual CPI inflation and repo rate (monetary policy stance) responses are calculated by purging the contributions of the credit conditions index to CPI inflation and repo rate (monetary policy stance). On the other hand, the output growth counterfactual values are calculated by purging-off the combined contributions of the repo rate (monetary policy stance) and the credit conditions index. This is to isolate the effects of financial variables on the output growth evolution.

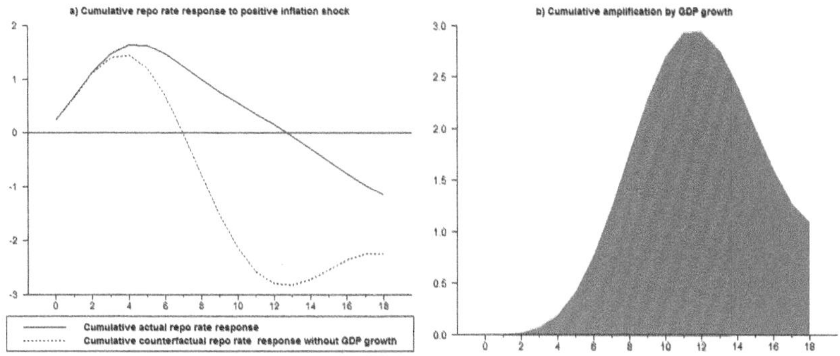

Fig. 4.12 Repo rate responses to positive inflation shocks and amplification by GDP growth. (Source: Authors' calculations)

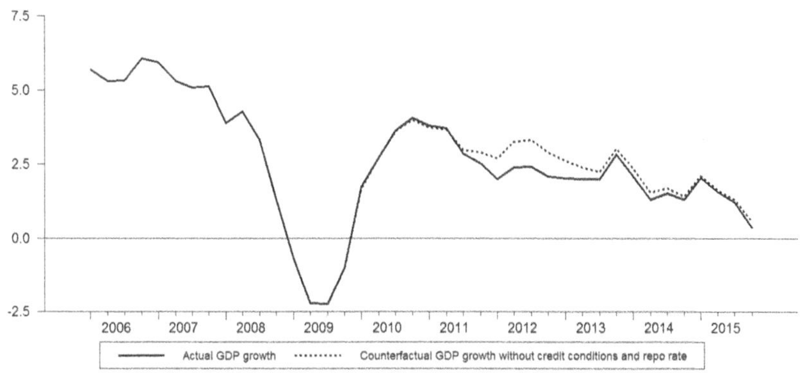

Fig. 4.13 GDP growth and the combined role of the repo rate and the credit conditions index. (Source: Authors' calculations)

Figure 4.13 shows that the actual output growth rate is lower than the counterfactual, suggesting that tight credit conditions possibly mitigated the accommodative monetary policy stance effects. However, the gap between actual and counterfactual output growth is smaller in 2015, indicating that the output growth phenomenon post-2009 recession period may be one of the factors that explain the persistently negative output-gap.

Figure 4.14 compares the actual and counterfactual inflation rate post-2009. The results indicate that between 2011Q1 and 2015Q2, actual inflation was lower than the counterfactual value. This suggests that tight credit conditions contributed to lower inflation than that would prevail in

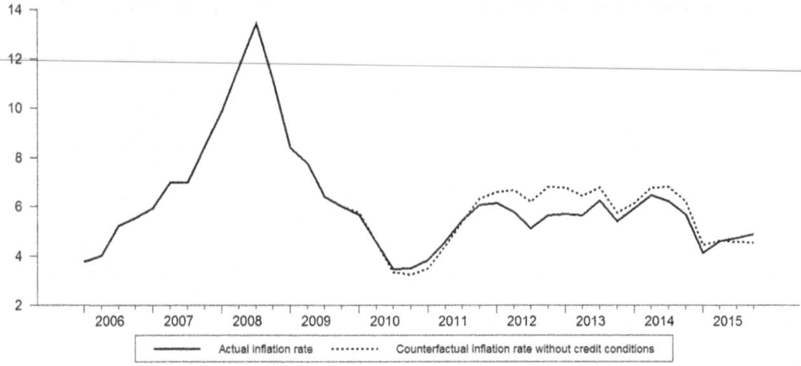

Fig. 4.14 Inflation and the role of the credit conditions index. (Source: Authors' calculations)

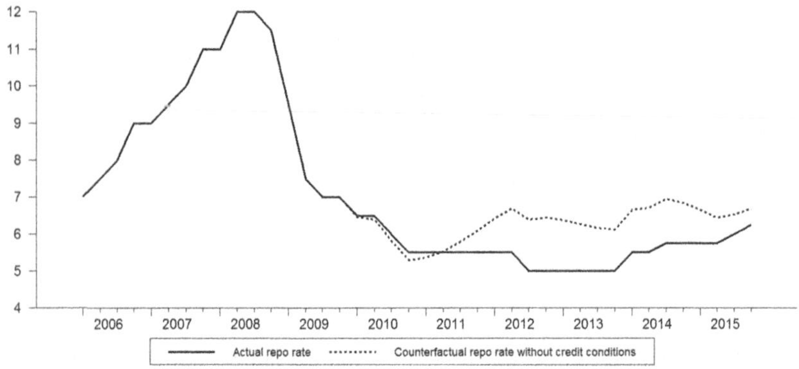

Fig. 4.15 Repo rate and the role of the credit condition index. (Source: Authors' calculations)

the absence of tight credit conditions. Thus, this could be another explanation for a low or muted exchange rate pass-through to CPI inflation post-2009. The low credit-driven demand pressures are exerting downward pressure on CPI inflation. However, actual CPI inflation exceeds the counterfactual in the last two quarters of 2015. This may be reflective of the persistent shock effects of the exchange rate depreciation as opposed to aggregate demand pressures.

We conclude the analysis by looking at the evolution of the repo rate. The results in Fig. 4.15 indicate that tight credit conditions lead to a lower repo rate level, alternatively, a looser monetary policy stance than would prevail in the absence of tight credit conditions. This evidence further corroborates earlier results of less aggressive repo rate (monetary policy stance) responses due to tight credit conditions and muted output growth.

4.6 Conclusion and Policy Implications

This chapter investigated the extent to which credit conditions amplify (propagate) macro-economic responses to unexpected shocks. First, evidence in this chapter shows that credit conditions and lending standards are positively related, meaning that tight credit conditions also capture the tightening of lending criteria by banks. On the other hand, the credit conditions and lending conditions are negatively associated with output growth. This suggests that improved output growth results in the loosening of the lending standards and credit conditions. Furthermore, tightening in credit conditions, lending standards, house price growth and the monetary policy stance have a disproportionate effect on the household sector compared to the corporate sector.

Second, evidence shows that the credit conditions index shocks induce less variation in CPI inflation compared to those due to the repo rate (monetary policy stance) shocks. But credit conditions induce more fluctuations in output compared to the repo rate. Thus, evidence shows the ability of credit conditions to induce large movements in output growth and possibly amplifying macro-economic responses. Furthermore, we find that tighter credit conditions exert threshold effects on GDP growth and the effects were accentuated post-2008Q4. Third, we examined whether credit conditions amplify the responses of output growth to positive repo rate and CPI inflation shocks. Evidence shows that output growth declines more in the presence of credit conditions compared to when the credit conditions are shut off in the inflation equation. This suggests that tight credit conditions worsen the output growth contraction due to positive inflation shocks. In addition, the amplification effects are not only restricted to positive inflation shock effects. The decline in output growth rate is pronounced in the presence of tight credit conditions compared to when these are shut off. Thus, credit conditions play a significant role in output growth dynamics as a transmitter of positive inflation and repo rate shocks.

Fourth, we establish that tight credit conditions neutralise the effects of the R/US$ exchange rate depreciation shock on inflationary pressures.

Thus, tight credit conditions dampen the inflationary pressures associated with the R/US$ exchange rate depreciation effects. This has implications for the repo rate response to inflationary pressures. Evidence shows that tight credit conditions and muted output growth lead to less aggressive repo rate responses to inflationary pressures. In the absence of credit-driven demand pressures on inflation, tight credit conditions and muted output growth have a significant impact on the pace and magnitude of repo rate responses to CPI inflation.

References

Brainard L. 2017. Navigating the different signals from inflation and unemployment. Speech at the New York Association for Business Economics, New York City.

Gumata N, and Ndou E. 2017. Bank Credit Extension and Real Economic Activity in South Africa: The Impact of Capital Flow Dynamics, Bank Regulation and Selected Macroprudential Tools. Palgrave Macmillan. ISBN 978-3-319-43550-3.

IMF World Economic Outlook. 2017. Seeking Sustainable Growth: Short-Term Recovery, Long-Term Challenges. October 2017.

Kashkari N. 2017. Why I Dissented a Third Time. Blog post. https://medium.com/@neelkashkari/why-i-dissented-a-third-time-fccbdf0f16.

Ndou E, and Gumata N. 2017. Inflation Dynamics in South Africa: The Role of Thresholds, Exchange Rate Pass-through and Inflation Expectations on Policy Trade-offs. Palgrave Macmillan. ISBN 978-3-319-46701-6.

Yellen J. 2017. Inflation, Uncertainty, and Monetary Policy. Speech at the "Prospects for Growth: Reassessing the Fundamentals" 59th Annual Meeting of the National Association for Business Economics, Cleveland, Ohio.

CHAPTER 5

Output Growth and Inflation Responses to Single and Double Credit Growth Threshold Effects in South Africa

Research Questions Explored

- Establish whether a single threshold (which is equivalent to a point threshold) is more restrictive compared to a double threshold (which is equivalent to a double band or range of thresholds).
- Estimate where the credit growth thresholds for aggregate credit growth, credit growth to the household and corporate sectors, and mortgage advances credit growth occur.
- Explore whether the credit growth thresholds for aggregate credit growth, credit growth to the household and corporate sectors, and mortgage advances credit growth exert asymmetric credit growth effects on the responses of inflation and economic activity.

5.1 Introduction

The 2007 global financial crisis demonstrated how important credit and financial conditions are. Adverse credit and financial shocks can cause large and persistent recessions. The existence of frictions due to information asymmetries and contractual rigidities implies that credit markets can act as non-linear propagators of aggregate shocks on economic activity. Earlier chapters showed that the tightening of credit conditions, lending standards, house prices and the monetary policy stance have a disproportionate effect on the household sector compared to the corporate sector.

N. Gumata, E. Ndou, *Achieving Price, Financial and Macro-Economic Stability in South Africa*,
https://doi.org/10.1007/978-3-030-66340-7_5

Furthermore, tighter credit conditions exert non-linear effects on GDP growth and the effects were accentuated post-2008Q4. Tight credit conditions neutralise the effects of the R/US$ exchange rate depreciation shock on inflationary pressures. Hence, in the absence of credit-driven demand pressures on inflation, tight credit conditions and muted GDP growth have a significant impact on the pace and magnitude of the repo rate responses to inflation. These findings pose several policy trade-offs for policy makers. Which is why this chapter explores whether a single credit growth threshold (which is equivalent to a point threshold) is more restrictive compared to a double credit growth threshold (which is equivalent to a double band of thresholds). This question is critical in the context of designing tools and policy responses within the mandates of price stability, maximum employment and financial stability.

Recent theoretical models and empirical evidence show that financial markets and institutions can be sources of shocks and vehicles transmitting shocks domestically and across borders. For instance, Eickmeier and Ng (2011) find that US credit supply shocks have a substantial effect on global GDP growth. US credit supply shocks are propagated by foreign credit and equity markets and produce a distinct global financial cycle. Boivin et al. (2013) show that an unexpected tightening of the credit conditions causes a significant unexpected increase in the external finance premium, which results in a persistent economic slowdown. Furthermore, Balke (2000), Calza and Sousa (2005) and Avdjiev and Zeng (2014) establish evidence that credit conditions exert threshold and asymmetric effects on macro-economic responses over the lending cycle. These studies establish a non-linear relationship between credit market conditions, monetary policy and real economic activity. They show that the impact of credit growth shocks on economic activity tends to be substantially larger when the economy is in a tight credit growth regime than when it is in a normal credit growth regime. Furthermore, Avdjiev and Zeng (2014) extend empirical evidence of asymmetric effects of shocks over the business cycle by estimating two-thresholds or a three-regime threshold model. They argue that single-threshold models tend to be too restrictive and cannot capture all the non-linearities in the data.

First, this chapter explores where the credit growth thresholds for aggregate credit growth, credit growth to the household and corporate sectors, and mortgage advances credit growth occur and whether they exert asymmetric credit growth effects on the responses to inflation and economic activity in South Africa. Second, aggregate credit growth and mortgage credit growth are the main counterparts of money growth and convey important information about the state of the economy. Data shows that almost more than ten years after the global financial crisis, key macroeconomic variables such as output growth, credit growth, money supply growth and household consumption growth have not returned to their pre-financial crisis trends. Hence, the role of aggregate credit growth, sectorial credit growth and mortgage credit growth threshold effects and non-linearities in GDP growth and inflation is important to explore.

Third, in view of the assertion that a single threshold is too restrictive to fully capture all the non-linearities in the data, this chapter establishes the levels at which the lower and upper thresholds for aggregate credit growth, sectorial credit growth and mortgage credit growth occur. We argue that it is possible that the thresholds for aggregate credit growth are different from those of sectorial credit growth (household and corporate sectors) and mortgage credit growth. Establishing the sectorial credit growth rates contributes to the design of the macro-prudential tools aimed at dealing with sectorial capital requirements as envisaged by the countercyclical capital buffer (CCyB). For instance, the Bank of Ireland (2014) shows that while the CCyB increases the banks' capacity to absorb losses in a downturn, it does not specifically target household's resilience or indebtedness.[1] The CCyB falls short of directly addressing household demand for credit or the household sector's financial resilience and indebtedness. The establishment of sectorial credit growth thresholds contributes towards filling this existing policy gap and assists in setting the guidelines on targeted tools such as loan-to-value (LTV) ratios and repayment-to-income (RTI) ratios over the credit cycle.

Gumata and Ndou (2017) show that the aggregate credit growth threshold can be used as a complementary indicator to the credit-gaps that are proposed to be used to calibrate a CCyB for regulatory purposes. They provide empirical analysis based on the aggregate credit growth threshold, which shows that inflation is bad for economic growth, irrespective of credit growth regimes. The negative effects of inflation are not constrained by credit growth regimes. Even in low credit growth regimes, high inflation exerts disproportionately negative effects on GDP growth.

[1] We explore the interactions of the CCyB, liquid asset holdings of banks, risk-weighted assets, mortgage market credit conditions (MMCI), labour market conditions (LMCI), non-performing loans, the repo rate and the deposit and lending rate margins in later chapters of the book.

Furthermore, the authors establish that contractionary monetary policy reinforces the bank risk channel, particularly if the lending spreads capture risk taking by banks. Raising the policy rate reduces risk taking and this may lessen the burden on the use of macro-prudential tools. Therefore, monetary policy is not neutral from a financial stability perspective.

Furthermore, prudential policies spill-over into the price stability mandate and affect inflation expectations. Three macro-prudential tools aimed at the household sector and aspects of the housing market, namely, the National Credit Act, LTV ratios and the RTI ratios, reinforce the effects of the repo rate. Positive repo rate shocks lead to pronounced contractions in output growth and credit growth compared to the LTV ratio tightening shock. In addition, although these prudential tools are mainly for financial stability purposes, the authors find that they have beneficial spill-overs to price stability. Hence, financial regulatory and macro-prudential tools tend to complement each other over the business and credit cycles—thus, calling for concerted efforts for greater policy co-ordination, as this will assist in achieving the desired effects on their own targets.

This chapter fills various academic and policy research gaps by establishing whether a single credit growth threshold (which is equivalent to a point threshold) is more restrictive compared to a double credit growth threshold (which is equivalent to a band or a range of thresholds). In addition, we establish where the credit growth thresholds for aggregate credit growth, credit growth to the household and corporate sectors, and mortgage advances credit growth occur. Lastly, we establish whether the credit growth thresholds for aggregate credit growth, credit growth to the household and corporate sectors, and mortgage advances credit growth exert asymmetric credit growth effects on the responses to inflation and economic activity.

5.2 Brief Literature Review of Linear and Non-linear Models with Financial Frictions

Literature estimates the role of financial frictions within linear and non-linear models. Silvestrini and Zaghini (2015) show that the difference is that in linear time series models the temporal dependence between random variables in the model is determined by their (auto) covariance structure, which is assumed to be constant over time. This contrasts with non-linear time series models, in which this dependence takes a more general functional form and changes over time.

Within non-linear univariate and multivariate time series models, a distinction between threshold and Markov-switching models can be made. The estimation of regimes in Markov-switching models is governed by an unobservable Markov process. On the other hand, in threshold models, observable time series thresholds determine the regimes for the whole system.

5.2.1 The Non-linear Effects of Money and Credit Growth

Vast models in empirical literature assume imperfect capital markets. In these models, credit plays an important role in the non-linear propagation of shocks in the form of asymmetry and regime switching. Blinder (1987) shows that monetary policy shocks exert different effects when credit-rationing regimes have aggregate supply effects. Bernanke and Gertler (1989) find that in the presence of credit frictions, changes in the balance sheet condition of firms via the financial accelerator mechanism amplify fluctuations in output. Furthermore, exogenous technology shocks exert asymmetric effects on economic activity. Therefore, negative shocks are likely to have a greater effect than positive shocks. In Azariadis and Smith (1998), the presence of credit markets give rise to endogenous fluctuations. In addition, they establish that the economy can switch between the equilibrium regime and a credit-rationing regime characterised by binding credit constraints.

Recent studies use non-linear VAR models to study the asymmetric behaviour of macro-economic variables over the different phases of the credit and business cycles. The threshold models of McCallum (1991), Galbraith (1996), Balke (2000), Atanasova (2003) and Calza and Sousa (2005) conclude that there is significant evidence of threshold effects in the relationship between economic activity, money and credit. The technique adopted in these studies is that of splitting the sample endogenously into tight and loose credit regimes. Thereafter, they search for evidence of asymmetric responses of real economic variables to shocks in the identified regimes.

Weise (1999) uses a logistic smooth transition vector autoregression (LSTVAR) model and shows that increasing money supply is more effective in stimulating output during an economic bust than during an economic boom. Using a Markov regime-switching model, Garcia and Schaller (2002) and Peersman and Smets (2001) find that the effects of monetary policy actions tend to be larger during recessions than during expansions.

Avdjiev and Zeng (2014) use a three-regime threshold vector autoregression (TVAR) approach to examine how the non-linear interactions between credit market conditions, monetary policy and real economic activity change as the economy moves through three different phases of the business cycle. The three regimes roughly correspond to sub-par economic growth, moderate economic growth and high economic growth. In their model, the relevant threshold variable is output growth and describes the state of economic activity rather than the state of the credit markets. However, because the thresholds are determined endogenously, they can examine how macro-economic, monetary policy and credit shocks affect the probability of regime switching.

They find that the dynamics of the interactions among credit market conditions, monetary policy and economic activity change considerably as the economy moves from one stage of the business cycle to another. Shocks to real output and credit growth tend to have the largest impact in the sub-par growth regime. They also show that compared to positive shocks, negative output shocks have larger and more persistent effects on credit quantities and credit spreads. Furthermore, their results reveal that the response of output to monetary policy shocks is largest when economic growth is below par, suggesting that the degree of effectiveness of monetary policy varies over the business cycle.

On sectorial credit, Serwa (2011) estimates the dynamic panel data models using the bootstrap-corrected least squares dummy variable method to identify normal and boom regimes in credit to households. They find that a one percentage point increase in the loan-deposit interest rate spread lowers the equilibrium level of credit to households by 4.5 per cent. In addition, shocks that shift household credit away from the equilibrium tend to have persistent effects. On the other hand, Coricelli et al. (2006) estimate an aggregate consumption function and assume that households face liquidity constraints. Their result shows that household credit markets are very responsive to credit supply shocks that relax the liquidity constraints. In turn, loose credit market conditions have sizable effects on consumption, which can create macro-economic imbalances that manifest via large current account deficits and inflationary pressures.

5.3 Methodology

Literature shows that filtering techniques are not based on any economic foundations and therefore can be less informative about the fundamentals driving credit growth. In addition, linear error correction models tend to be biased and understate deviations associated with boom episodes in favour of correcting towards to the long-run equilibrium. Furthermore, studies using standard linear time series techniques can have difficulty distinguishing the separate effects of shocks and the propagation mechanism. Hence, this chapter uses three econometric approaches, namely: (i) the Tsay (1989) approach to formally test for the presence of threshold, (ii) the Balke (2000) approach and (iii) the Kilian and Vigfusson (2011) approach to test for the asymmetric transmission of credit growth shocks.

First, we use the Balke (2000) approach to establish the double credit growth thresholds, which allows us to estimate the three-regime-dependent and non-linear impulse responses. The established credit growth thresholds delineate between three credit market regimes: (i) sub-par and moderate credit growth regime, when credit growth is below the lower threshold, (ii) normal credit growth regime, when credit growth is at or above the lower threshold, and (iii) high credit growth regime, when credit growth is above the upper credit threshold. Thereafter, we use the estimated thresholds as inputs in the threshold VAR (TVAR) to estimate the regime-dependent impulse responses and non-linear responses induced by the credit growth thresholds. The regime-dependent impulse responses and non-linear impulse responses assess whether the credit growth threshold effects exert asymmetric or non-linear propagation of shocks across regimes. However, even though the switching of credit growth regimes becomes consistent with the role for credit growth as the propagator of shocks, Balke and Chih-Ping (1995) show that non-linear impulse responses fail to account for the effects of different magnitudes of shocks.

Finally, for robustness analysis of the asymmetric responses to the size of the shocks, we use the Kilian and Vigfusson (2011) approach. The Kilian and Vigfusson (2011) approach is an empirical methodology aimed at establishing and quantifying asymmetries of the response of the variables of interest depending on the sign and size of the shocks. For instance, Balke and Chih-Ping (1995) and Balke (2000) argue that it is possible that a sufficiently large shock can result in the economy repeatedly switching between two regimes. In this case, non-linear impulse responses are better able to capture involved asymmetries since they do not bind the system to remain within the regime prevailing at the time of the initial shock. Hence, we use this approach to assess for robustness analysis and contribute to existing literature on the non-linearities.

5.3.1 *Data and Stylised Facts*

The chapter uses quarterly data spanning 1980Q1 to 2015Q4 for GDP growth, CPI inflation, repo rate, total credit growth, M3 money supply growth, credit growth to households and companies, mortgage advances credit growth, house price growth and gross fixed capital formation growth for the residential sector. All growth rates are at an annual rate. The data is sourced from the South African Reserve Bank database. The analysis starts by showing the relationship between GDP growth, credit growth and inflation during the period 2000Q1 to 2014Q4 in Fig. 5.1. The scatterplots show that the relationship between GDP growth and credit growth is positive and strong whereas it is positive but very weak between inflation and credit growth. The lead lag relationships also show that credit growth increases more when it is preceded by strong GDP growth. Similarly, inflation increases more when it is preceded by strong credit growth.

What do the stylised relationships tell us about the associations between (i) inflation and GDP growth and (ii) house price growth and credit growth? Figure 5.2 establishes a negative relationship between inflation and GDP growth. The negative relationship is much stronger when

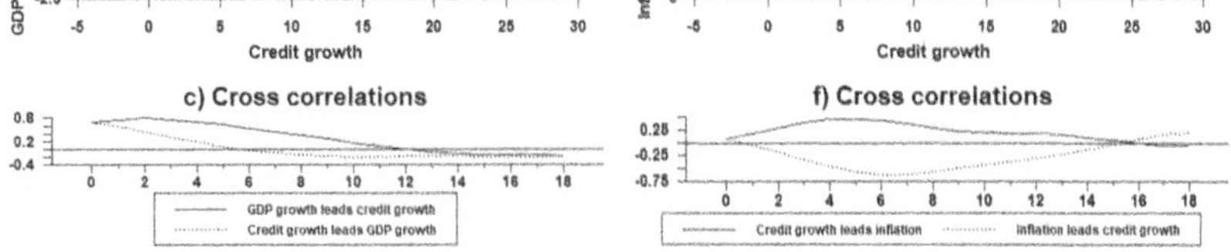

Fig. 5.1 GDP growth, credit growth and inflation. (Source: Authors' calculations)

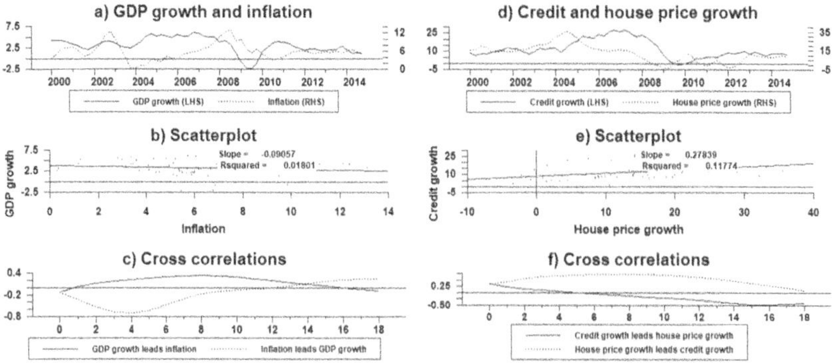

Fig. 5.2 Inflation, GDP growth, house price growth and credit growth. (Source: Authors' calculations)

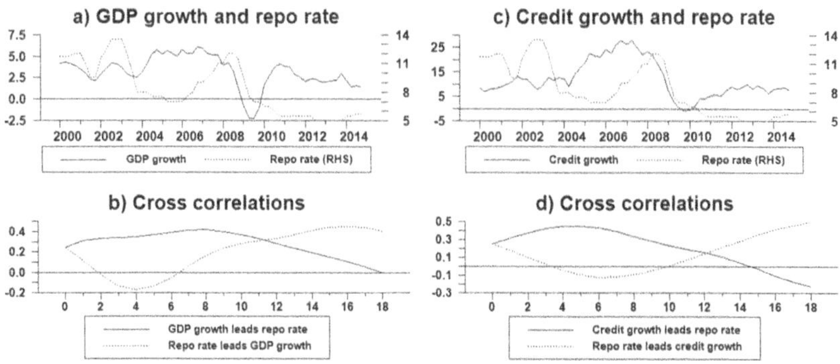

Fig. 5.3 Repo rate, GDP growth and credit growth. (Source: Authors' calculations)

inflation leads GDP growth. On the other hand, credit growth and house price growth are positively related and credit growth is much stronger when it is preceded by house price growth.

What about the policy rate? Figure 5.3 shows that GDP growth declines when the repo rate increases and that the reverse is true. The same negative relationship holds between credit growth and the repo rate.

5.3.2 *Non-linearity Tests*

This section starts by determining whether there is a break in the aggregate credit growth, sectorial credit growth and mortgage advances credit growth series. We apply three tests—the arranged autoregression test, the Hansen threshold test and the smooth transition autoregression (STAR) test—to determine whether there is a break in the credit series. We use different test statistics to assess whether these tests converge and arrive at the same conclusion. The credit equation used to test for the existence of a break point is specified such that the credit growth rate depends on a constant and its two lags by the Akaike information criterion (AIC) required for estimation. The results are shown in Table 5.1.

All the tests in Table 5.1 suggest that there exists a breakpoint in the aggregate credit growth series. The Hansen test also shows that there is a threshold value, although it does not determine whether the credit growth effects should be estimated in a linear or non-linear way. The STAR test indicates that the credit growth process should be estimated in a non-linear way. In all instances, we reject the null hypothesis that there is no credit growth threshold.

5.3.3 *Does the Sectorial Credit Growth Threshold Follow a Non-linear Process?*

We conduct the threshold and non-linearity tests for sectorial credit growth and mortgage advances credit growth. On average, credit growth to the household sector accounts for 56 per cent of total credit growth to private sector for the period 1994Q1 to 2014Q4. On the other hand, credit growth to the corporate sector accounts for 44 per cent of total credit growth to private sector for the same period. Mortgage advances credit growth accounts for 47 per cent of total credit growth to the private sector and 84 per cent of credit growth to the household sector

Table 5.1 Tests for non-linearity in the aggregate credit growth series

Test	*Null hypothesis*	*F-value*		*Decision*
Arranged autoregression test	No break	35.00	(0.00)**	Break
Hansen threshold test	No threshold	53.81	(0.00)**	Threshold
STAR test	Linearity	18.0	(0.00)*	Non-linearity

Source: Authors' calculations

Note: The numbers in (.) denote the *p*-value; * denotes significance at 1 per cent; ** denotes significance at 10 per cent

Table 5.2 Tests for non-linearity in the household credit growth

Test	*Null hypothesis*	*F-value*		*Decision*
Arranged autoregression test	No break	32.67	(0.00)**	Break
Hansen threshold test	No break	30.51	(0.00)**	Threshold
STAR test	Linearity	17.97	(0.00)*	Non-linearity

Source: Authors' calculations

Note: The numbers in (.) denote the *p*-value; * denotes significance at 1 per cent; ** denotes significance at 10 per cent

for the period 1994Q1 to 2014Q4. The results in Tables 5.2, 5.3 and 5.4 show that all the series follow a non-linear process and have thresholds.

5.3.4 *Credit Growth Threshold Levels*

The preceding section established that growth in aggregate credit, sectorial credit and mortgage credit should be modelled in non-linear way. This section establishes the actual threshold values using the Balke (2000) approach. The Balke (2000) threshold test choses the threshold value based on the lowest AIC test. But as suggested by Avdjiev and Zeng (2014), we consider the existence of more than one threshold. This means that we test for non-linearity in three regimes, which will be delineated by the established credit growth thresholds.

We estimate the best point and upper threshold levels and we use them to identify the non-linear credit growth shock effects in three different phases: (i) below the best point credit growth threshold, (ii) in between the best point and upper credit growth threshold, and (iii) above the upper credit growth threshold. The thresholds are based on a VAR with GDP growth, aggregate credit growth or household credit growth or credit growth to companies or mortgage advances credit growth, lending rate and inflation for the period 1995Q1 to 2015Q4. This is because data for credit growth to the household sector and companies is only available from 1994Q1. We also included nominal house price growth in the estimation of the thresholds in different VAR models to assess the robustness of the estimated thresholds.

Table 5.5 shows the estimated best and upper credit growth threshold values for aggregate credit growth, household credit growth, credit growth to corporates and mortgage credit growth.

Table 5.3 Tests for non-linearity in corporate credit growth

Test	*Null hypothesis*	*F-value*		*Decision*
Arranged autoregression test	No break	26.36	(0.00)**	Break
Hansen threshold test	No break	15.61	(0.00)**	Threshold
STAR test	Linearity	5.56	(0.00)*	Non-linearity

Source: Authors' calculations

Note: The numbers in (.) denote the *p*-value; * denotes significance at 1 per cent; ** denotes significance at 10 per cent

Table 5.4 Tests for non-linearity in mortgage credit growth

Test	*Null hypothesis*	*F-value*		*Decision*
Arranged autoregression test (Tsay 1998)	No break	86.09	(0.00)**	Break
Hansen threshold test	No break	42.00	(0.00)**	Threshold
STAR test	Linearity	7.80	(0.00)*	Non-linearity

Source: Authors' calculations

Note: The numbers in (.) denote the *p*-value; * denotes significance at 1 per cent; ** denotes significance at 10 per cent

The best threshold values for aggregate credit growth and various components are all below 10 per cent and the upper credit growth thresholds are below 13 per cent indicating that there is convergence in terms of points at which the non-linear credit growth threshold values occur. Figure 5.4 shows aggregate credit growth, household credit growth, credit growth to companies and mortgage credit growth together with the estimated thresholds over the business cycles phases. The evolution of the various credit growth series relative to the estimated thresholds indicates that post-2009, aggregate credit growth, household credit growth and mortgage advances credit growth have persistently grown below the lower thresholds indicating sub-par growth for these credit categories.

On the other hand, credit growth to the corporate sector recovered post-2009 and has been briefly above the upper threshold. Of importance, the trends in Fig. 5.4 show that it is not a one-size-fits-all and that observing aggregate credit growth alone conveys misleading information about the sectorial credit growth developments. Mortgage credit growth has been a drag on aggregate credit growth and household credit growth

Table 5.5 Estimated best and upper credit growth threshold values

Balke (2000)	*Best-point threshold*	*Upper threshold*
Aggregate credit growth	9.50	12.70
Household credit growth	9.60	12.45
Corporate credit growth	9.20	12.60
Mortgage credit growth	9.45	11.90

Source: Authors' calculations

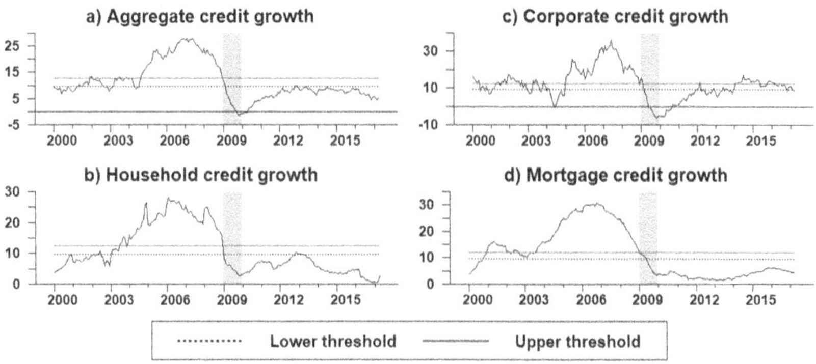

Fig. 5.4 Aggregate, household, corporate and mortgage credit growth, and the estimated threshold values. (Source: South African Reserve Bank and authors' calculations)

post-2009 despite the significant recovery in corporate credit growth. Hence, there is a good case to assess the threshold effects of sectorial credit growth over and above aggregate credit growth.

In the empirical section we use the estimated threshold values to delineate three credit growth regimes, which correspond to (i) sub-par credit growth, (ii) moderate credit growth and (iii) high credit growth. We estimate separate models with different specifications and the threshold levels to assess the different responses in the specific credit regimes.

5.4 Empirical Analysis

The empirical analysis uses a recursive Cholesky ordering identification scheme where GDP growth comes first, followed by CPI inflation, house price growth, aggregate credit growth or household credit growth or corporate credit growth or mortgage advances credit growth and the lending rate. Like Balke (2000) and Calza and Sousa (2005), the ordering scheme followed in the study implies that shocks to GDP growth affect all the other variables in the system contemporaneously. The positioning of the real sector variables before those related to credit and housing markets is standard in the empirical literature and is informed by the assumption that financial markets adjust simultaneously to macro-economic shocks. On the other hand, the real sector reacts sluggishly to shocks to financial variables.

In the estimations, the impulses are responses to a one standard deviation shock to aggregate credit growth or household credit growth or corporate credit growth or mortgage advances credit growth. Shocks to the credit growth variables affect the other variables in the model with a delay of one quarter. The TVAR was estimated with two lags chosen by the AIC and Hannan–Quinn information criterion (HIC) and 10,000 bootstrap draws. The sample spans the period 1995Q1 to 2015Q4 and the data is sourced from the South African Reserve bank database. All growth rates are at annual rate. The empirical analysis is specifically interested in the responses of GDP growth and inflation in different credit regimes for aggregate credit growth, household credit growth, corporate credit growth and mortgage advances credit growth. The impulses denote the 16th and 84th percentile confidence bands.

5.4.1 *Aggregate Credit Growth Regime-Dependent Impulse Responses*

This section starts by estimating a VAR model to assess the responses of GDP growth and inflation, subject to different aggregate credit growth regimes. To facilitate the comparison of the impulse responses, we present the results generated from four models estimated separately: (i) no credit growth regimes, (ii) sub-par or moderate credit growth, to capture responses when credit growth is below 9.5 per cent, (iii) normal credit growth, when credit growth is above 9.5 per cent but below 12.7 per cent, and (iii) high credit growth, for responses when credit growth is above 12.7 per cent.

Figure 5.5 shows the comparison of GDP growth and inflation responses to a positive credit growth shock in different credit growth regimes. The results show that there are differences in the responses of these macro-economic variables in different credit growth regimes. As expected, in Fig. 5.5, GDP growth increases more due to credit shocks when there are no credit growth regimes and when aggregate credit

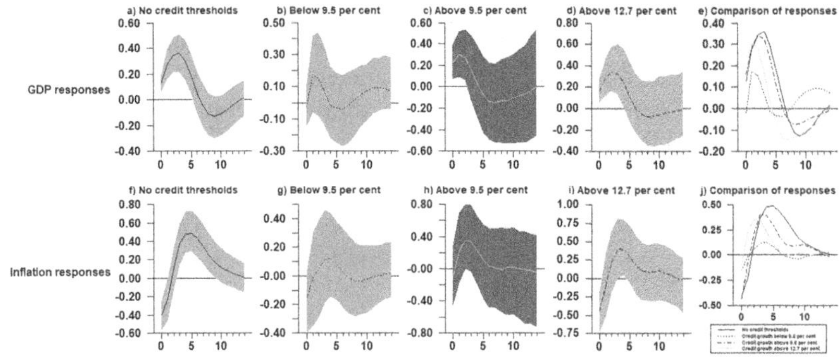

Fig. 5.5 GDP growth and inflation responses to aggregate credit growth thresholds. (Source: Authors' calculations)

growth is above 9.5 per cent and 12.7 per cent compared to when credit growth is below 9.5 per cent. But the flipside to the impulse response is that the GDP growth slowdown is shallower and recovers faster in the low credit growth regime (when credit growth is below 9.5 per cent). The GDP growth slumps, or downturns associated with credit growth in the high credit regimes are more severe and take longer to recover.

On the other hand, Fig. 5.5 shows that inflation increases with a delay across credit growth regimes. Periods characterised by no credit growth regimes, credit growth above 9.5 per cent and 12.7 per cent tend to have high peak levels for inflation compared to when credit growth is below the 9.5 per cent threshold. The distinction in the inflation response across regimes is evident, particularly in the credit growth regime when credit growth is persistently below 9.5 per cent. Inflation peaks at more than double the level when there are no credit regimes, credit growth is above 9.5 per cent and 12.7 per cent compared to the when credit growth is below 9.5 per cent. Furthermore, inflation persists at higher levels when there are no credit growth regimes, credit growth is above 9.5 per cent and 12.7 per cent compared to when credit growth is below 9.5 per cent.

Overall, the results presented in this section suggest that credit growth above 9.5 per cent contributes to accentuated business cycle phases and credit demand driven inflationary pressures, which tend to be highly persistent. These findings are in line with literature showing that periods of excessively high credit growth tend to be associated with boom-and-bust episodes with persistent real economic costs. The results in this section concur with the rationale put forward for the use of the CCyB to moderate the impact of the credit cycles on the business cycles as shown in later chapters in the book.[2] The policy implication is that macro-prudential tools, by moderating the credit cycle and credit demand driven booms, have benefits for monetary policy tools as they neutralise inflationary pressures and result in low inflation regimes.

5.4.2 *Are the Responses Different When Considering Sectorial Credit Growth?*

This section tests whether the results change when we consider sectorial credit growth. We consider the role of credit shocks in sectorial credit growth and the threshold effects on the responses of GDP growth and inflation. Like the previous sections we estimate different TVAR models based on the estimated sectorial credit growth thresholds. We start by discussing the responses to household credit growth thresholds in Fig. 5.6.

The results show that in cases where there are no credit growth regimes accounted for and when household credit growth is below 9.6 per cent, GDP growth tends to peak at higher rate compared to when it is above 9.6 per cent. Like earlier results in relation to aggregate credit growth, when household credit growth is above 9.6 per cent and 12.5 per cent, the decline in GDP growth is much more severe and tends to be persistently

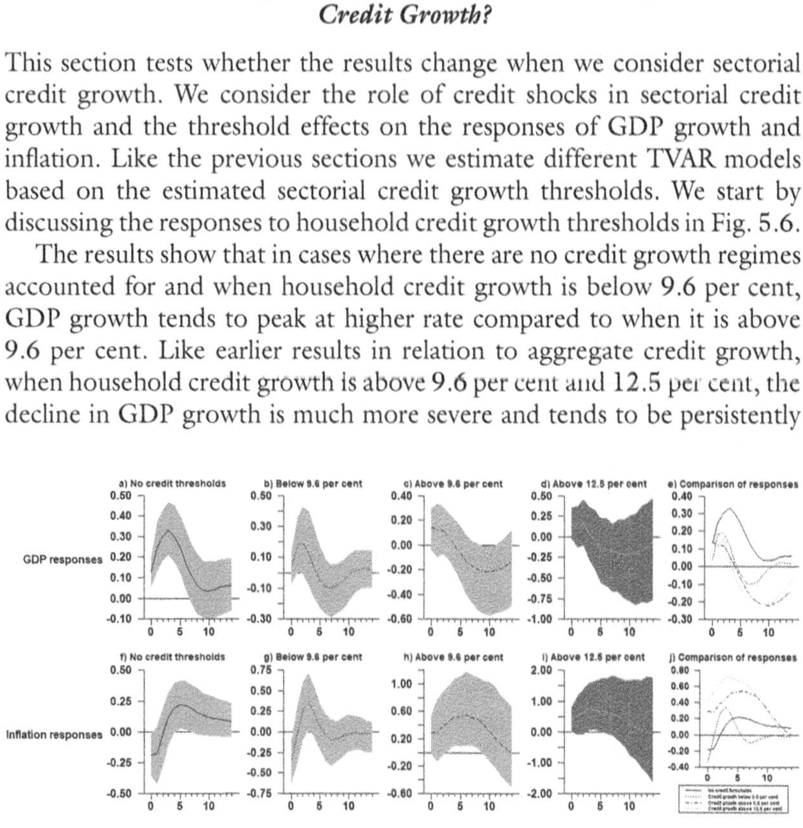

Fig. 5.6 GDP growth and inflation responses to household credit growth thresholds. (Source: Authors' calculations)

[2] Later chapters in the book assess the interactions of the countercyclical capital buffer (CCyB), mortgage market credit conditions (MMCI) and labour market conditions (LMCI). Changes to the CCyB are mainly targeted at influencing the risk-taking behaviour of banks.

weak for longer periods. Furthermore, the GDP growth responses to household credit growth in different regimes suggest the presence of significant asymmetries. For instance, it is evident that household credit growth above 9.6 per cent and 12.6 per cent does not necessarily result in a high level of GDP growth response compared to credit growth below 9.6 per cent although the declines are more severe following high credit growth. The policy implication is that additional credit growth above 9.6 per cent and 12.6 per cent does not necessarily result in accelerated and incremental GDP growth, but rather may, as suggested by the responses of inflation to credit growth above 9.6 per cent and 12.5 per cent, lead to heighted inflationary pressures. Inflation increases by more than double at peak response in the high credit growth regimes compared to periods when household credit growth is below 9.6 per cent.

Are there discernible differences due to corporate credit growth regimes? Figure 5.7 suggests that GDP growth responds more to corporate credit growth below 9.3 per cent although the increase tends to be highly transitory compared to above 12.6 per cent.

On the other hand, the inflation responses tend to be lower and insignificant when corporate credit growth is below 9.3 per cent compared to the high credit growth regimes. The results in this section imply that sectorial credit growth thresholds and regimes exert non-linear GDP growth and inflation responses. Periods of high credit growth regimes are characterised by high inflationary pressures and do not necessarily result in persistently higher GDP growth. Furthermore, this evidence corroborates earlier findings that credit growth busts associated with high credit

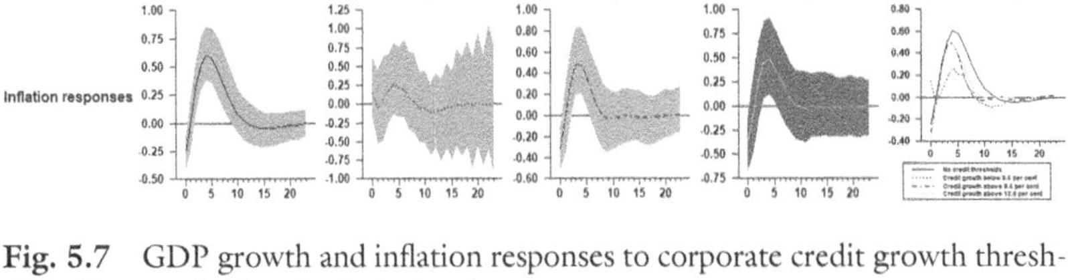

Fig. 5.7 GDP growth and inflation responses to corporate credit growth thresholds. (Source: Authors' calculations)

growth regimes tend to exert persistent costs on GDP growth. The implication is that additional aggregate credit growth and sectorial credit growth does not necessarily result in incrementally higher GDP growth but exerts heightened inflationary pressures.

5.4.3 *Do Mortgage Credit Growth Regimes Exert Different GDP Growth and Inflation Responses?*

The period preceding the global financial crisis was characterised by a housing boom. Vast empirical literature shows that housing credit growth and house price growth mainly via the wealth and collateral channels resulted in robust GDP growth. What the evidence suggests is the case for the South African economy. This section estimates regime-dependent impulse response for GDP growth and inflation in different mortgage credit growth regimes based on the credit growth thresholds shown in Table 5.5. Figure 5.8 shows that mortgage credit growth regimes result in persistently higher GDP growth responses when mortgage credit growth is above 9.45 per cent compared to above 11.9 per cent and below 9.45 per cent. Credit growth shocks when mortgage credit growth is below 9.45 per cent do not contribute much to GDP growth.

Similarly, mortgage credit growth above 9.45 per cent and 11.9 per cent results in higher inflationary pressures and peak responses suggesting that credit growth above the established thresholds tends to generate more inflationary pressures that are not accompanied by persistently higher GDP growth. At the same time, mortgage credit growth below 9.45 per cent contributes to subdued inflationary pressures.

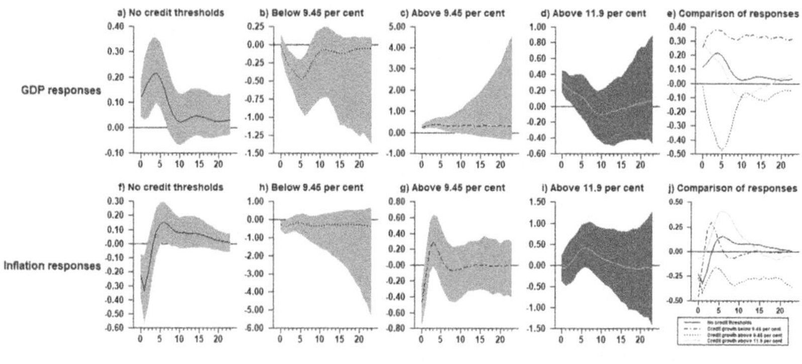

Fig. 5.8 GDP growth and inflation responses to mortgage credit growth thresholds. (Source: Authors' calculations)

5.5 Robustness Analysis: Sensitivity to Model Size

This section assesses the robustness of the TVAR model to the increase in the model size by including household consumption expenditure growth and gross fixed capital formation. We analyse the responses of household consumption expenditure growth to shocks to household credit growth and mortgage credit growth. This is because it is possible that the aggregation in total private sector credit growth masks the sensitivity of sectors to credit growth categories.

5.5.1 Household Consumption Expenditure Growth and Credit Growth Thresholds

We estimate different TVAR models subject to the household credit growth and mortgage credit growth thresholds separately. Figure 5.9 shows the responses of GDP growth, inflation and household consumption expenditure growth to credit growth shocks in different credit growth regimes. Evidence suggests that the responses of GDP growth and inflation are robust to changes in the model size and specification. Aggregate credit growth above 9.5 per cent results in a higher level of GDP growth and inflation compared to credit growth above 12.7 per cent. Similarly, household consumption expenditure growth responds more when credit growth is above 9.5 per cent compared to when it is

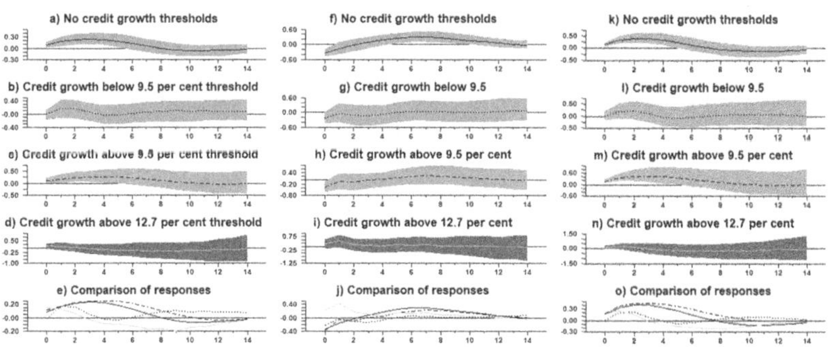

Fig. 5.9 GDP growth, inflation and household consumption growth responses to aggregate credit growth thresholds. (Source: Authors' calculations. Note: HH cons. = household consumption)

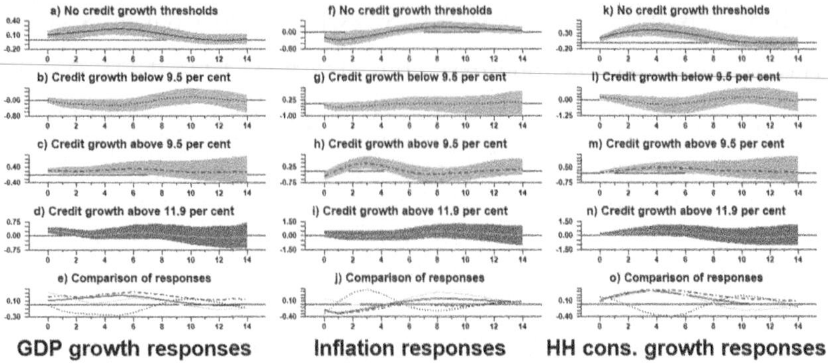

Fig. 5.10 GDP growth, inflation and household consumption growth responses to aggregate credit growth thresholds. (Source: Authors' calculations. Note: HH cons. = household consumption)

above 12.7 per cent. The implication is that credit growth above 9.5 per cent does not have additional incremental positive effects but exerts more inflationary pressures.

In the specification for the results generated in Fig. 5.10, we replaced aggregate credit growth with mortgage credit growth. The results in Fig. 5.10 suggest that mortgage credit growth below 9.5 per cent benefits GDP growth and inflationary pressures as inflation remains subdued compared to when mortgage credit growth is above 9.5 per cent. This may be because household consumption expenditure growth increases transitorily and remains subdued thereafter when credit growth is below 9.5 per cent and this helps to contain inflationary pressures. Thus, the results are robust to changes in the specification of sectorial credit growth. Credit growth below the normal credit growth threshold helps to contain inflationary pressures and is consistent with price and financial stability to the degree that excessive credit and debt-driven household consumption growth is contained.

5.6 Non-Linear Impulse Responses to Credit Growth Regimes

We have established that the regime-dependent impulse responses in the previous sections suggest that the credit growth thresholds exert non-linear responses across credit growth regimes. The GDP growth slowdown is more severe following periods of high credit growth meaning that the corrections from episodes of severe credit growth have long-lasting effects on the business cycles. Furthermore, credit growth above 9.5 per cent elicits more responses on inflation compared to GDP growth and household consumption growth.

This section concludes the analysis of the non-linear and symmetries exerted by credit growth regimes by estimating the Balke (2000) threshold VAR approach. For the analysis of asymmetric responses, we assess the impact of: (i) positive (+) and negative (-) credit growth regime shock effects and the impact of the magnitudes of the shocks, and (ii) small (one standard deviation) and large (two standard deviation) unexpected credit growth shocks. We compare the responses of GDP growth, inflation and household consumption growth to positive and negative one and two standard deviation shocks to aggregate credit growth when credit growth is below 9.5 per cent and above 12.7 per cent. The intention is to gauge the degree of the asymmetric effects exerted by the different credit growth regimes.

Figure 5.11 shows that there are significant and large asymmetric responses in different credit growth regimes. For instance, GDP growth and household consumption growth increase more when credit growth is below 9.5 per cent and evidence shows that credit growth above 12.7 per cent does not result in significantly higher GDP growth.

On the other hand, inflation increases more when credit growth is above 12.7 per cent compared to when it is below 9.5 per cent. The non-linear responses in inflation when credit growth is above 12.7 per cent are almost double at peak compared to when credit growth is below 9.5 per

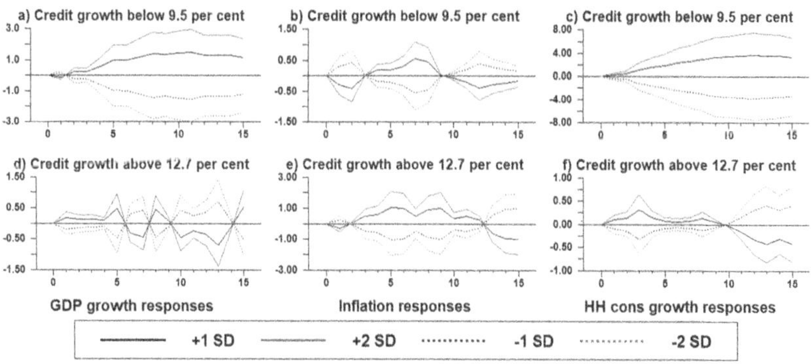

Fig. 5.11 GDP growth, inflation and household consumption growth non-linear responses to aggregate credit growth thresholds. (Source: Authors' calculations)

cent. This means that the larger magnitudes of credit growth shocks when credit growth is already growing above 12.7 per cent result in magnified inflation responses.

5.6.1 *Robustness on Non-Linearities Exerted by Credit Growth Regimes*

To conclude the robustness analysis on the non-linearities exerted by credit growth regimes, this section looks at the robustness of the non-linear responses to changes in the technique used to generate the impulse responses. We use the Kilian and Vigfusson (2011) approach to test for the asymmetric transmission of aggregate credit growth and corporate credit growth shocks on GDP growth and household consumption growth. The analysis looks at the responses of GDP growth and household consumption growth to positive one, two and four standard deviation shocks to aggregate credit growth and corporate credit growth. Figure 5.12 shows that smaller magnitudes of positive credit growth shocks result in the smaller and transitory increases in GDP growth and household consumption growth.

5.7 Conclusion and Policy Implications

The chapter tested for the credit growth threshold effects of the double credit growth thresholds on aggregate credit growth, sectorial credit growth and mortgage credit growth. Do the double credit growth thresholds exert asymmetric effects on GDP growth, inflation and household

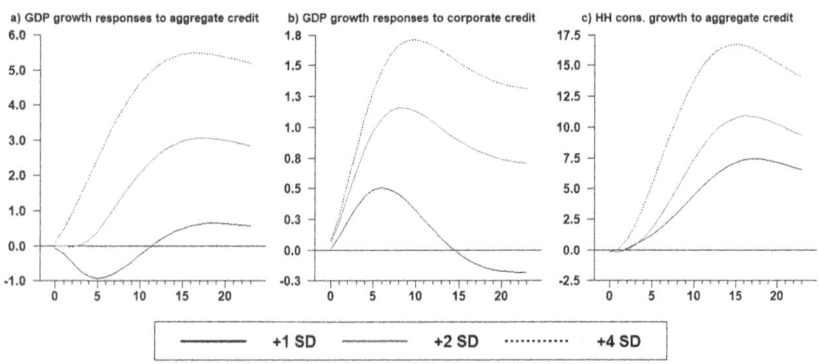

Fig. 5.12 GDP growth and household consumption growth non-linear responses to credit growth thresholds. (Source: Authors' calculations)

consumption growth? We establish that lower and upper credit growth threshold levels for aggregate credit growth, sectorial credit growth and mortgage credit growth occur around 9.2 per cent and 12.7 per cent respectively. We use these credit growth thresholds to classify credit growth regimes as: (i) sub-par or moderate credit growth, to capture responses when credit growth is below the lower credit threshold, (ii) normal credit growth, when credit growth is at or above the lower credit threshold, and (iii) high credit growth, for responses when credit growth is above the upper credit threshold.

We establish that there are significant differences in the GDP growth, inflation and household consumption growth below the lower thresholds and above the upper threshold. Consistent with literature on financial boom-and-bust effects, evidence shows that there are significant differences in the GDP growth, inflation and household consumption growth in the three credit growth regimes. GDP growth increases more due to credit growth shocks when there are no credit growth regimes and when aggregate credit growth is above 9.5 per cent and 12.7 per cent compared to when credit growth is below 9.5 per cent. But the GDP growth slowdown is shallower and recovers faster in the low credit growth regime. The GDP growth slumps, or downturns associated with credit growth in the high credit regimes are more severe and take longer to recover. Similarly, inflation peaks at more than double and is more persistent when credit growth is above 9.5 per cent and 12.7 per cent compared to the low credit growth regime.

Furthermore, we establish that sectorial credit growth above moderate credit growth does not necessarily result in a high level of GDP growth and household consumption growth. The policy implication is that additional credit growth above the normal and high credit growth regimes does not necessarily result in accelerated and incremental GDP growth and household consumption growth, but rather induces higher inflation responses, meaning that credit growth above the normal credit growth regime results in higher inflationary pressures. Aggregate credit growth, sectorial credit growth and mortgage credit growth above the normal credit growth thresholds tend to generate more inflationary pressures that are not accompanied by higher GDP growth and household consumption growth.

Moreover, credit growth below the normal credit growth helps to contain inflationary pressures and is consistent with the price and financial stability mandates to the degree that excessive credit and debt-driven household consumption growth is contained. Thus, the established credit growth thresholds contribute to the design of the macro-prudential tools aimed at dealing sectorial capital requirements under the CCyB in as far as they complement policies aimed at increasing the household's sector financial resilience during economic slumps. In addition, the findings in the chapter indicate that periods of excessively high credit growth tend to be associated with boom-and-bust episodes with persistent real economic costs. Hence, the results concur with the rationale put forward for the use of the CCyB to moderate the impact of the credit cycles on business cycles. The policy implication is that macro-prudential tools, by moderating the credit cycle and credit demand driven booms, have benefits for monetary policy tools as they neutralise inflationary pressures and result in low inflation regimes. Therefore, macro-prudential tools by moderating credit growth regimes and credit demand driven booms complement monetary policy tools.

References

Atanasova C. 2003. 'Credit Market Imperfections and Business Cycle Dynamics: A Nonlinear Approach', Studies in Nonlinear Dynamics and Econometrics, 7(4), pp. 516–536.

Avdjiev F, and Zeng Z. 2014. Credit Growth, Monetary Policy, and Economic Activity in a Three-Regime TVAR Model. BIS Working Papers No. 449.

Azariadis C, and Smith B. 1998. 'Financial Intermediation and Regime Switching in Business Cycles', American Economic Review, 88(3), pp. 516–536.

Balke N S. 2000. 'Credit and Economic Activity: Credit Regimes and Nonlinear Propagation of Shocks', The Review of Economics and Statistics, MIT Press, 82(2), pp. 344–349.

Balke N S, and Chang Chih-Ping. 1995. Credit and Economic Activity: Shocks or Propagation Mechanism? Federal Reserve Bank of Dallas.

Bernanke B S, and Gertler M. 1989. 'Agency Costs, Net Worth, and Business Fluctuations', American Economic Review, 79(1), pp. 14–31.

Blinder A S. 1987. 'Credit Rationing and Effective Supply Failures', Economic Journal, 97(386), pp. 327–352.

Boivin J, Giannoni M P, and Stevanović D. 2013. Dynamic Effects of Credit Shocks in a Data-Rich Environment. Federal Reserve Bank of New York Staff Report No. 615.

Calza A, and Sousa J. 2005. Output and Inflation Responses to Credit Shocks: Are There Threshold Effects in the Euro Area? Studies in Nonlinear Dynamics & Econometrics 10 (Issue 2, Article 3).

Central Bank of Ireland. 2014. Financial Stability Review.

Coricelli F, Mucci F, and Revoltella D. 2006. Household Credit in the New Europe: Lending Boom or Sustainable Growth? CEPR Discussion Paper 5520.

Eickmeier S, and Ng T. 2011. How Do Credit Supply Shocks Propagate Internationally? A GVAR Approach. Deutsche Bundesbank Discussion Paper Series 1: Economic Studies No. 27/2011.

Galbraith J.W. 1996. 'Credit rationing and threshold effects in the relation between money and output'. Journal of Applied Econometrics, 11(4), pp. 416–429.

Garcia R, and Schaller H. 2002. 'Are the Effects of Interest Rate Changes Asymmetric?', Economic Inquiry, 40, pp. 102–119.

Gumata N, and Ndou E. 2017. Bank Credit Extension and Real Economic Activity in South Africa: The Impact of Capital Flow Dynamics, Bank Regulation and Selected Macroprudential Tools. Palgrave Macmillan. ISBN 978-3-319-43550-3.

Kilian L and Vigfusson R J. 2011. Are the Responses of the U.S. Economy Asymmetric in Energy Price Increases and Decreases? Quantitative Economics, 2(4), pp. 419–453.

McCallum, J. 1991. 'Credit rationing and the monetary transmission mechanism'. American Economic Review, 81(4), pp. 946–951.

Peersman G, and Smets F. 2001. Are the Effects of Monetary Policy in the Euro Area Greater in Recessions than in Booms? European Central Bank Working Paper No. 52.

Serwa D. 2011. Identifying Multiple Regimes in the Model of Credit to Households. National Bank of Poland Working Paper No. 99.

Silvestrini A and Zaghini A. 2015. Financial shocks and the real economy in a nonlinear world: a survey of the theoretical and empirical literature. Bank of Italy Ocassional Paper No. 255.

Tsay R S. 1989. Testing and modelling threshold autoregressive processes, Journal of the American Statistical Association 84, 231–240.

Tsay R S. 1998. Testing and modelling multivariate threshold models, Journal of the American Statistical Association 93, 1188–1202.

Weise C L. 1999. 'The Asymmetric Effects of Monetary Policy: A Nonlinear Vector Autoregression Approach', Journal of Money, Credit and Banking, 31(1), pp. 85–108.

CHAPTER 6

Do Contractionary Fiscal Policy Shocks Transmitted via GDP Growth Dampen Credit Growth?

Research Questions Explored

- Show whether contractionary fiscal policy is transmitted via GDP growth to impact credit growth.
- Establish the impact of persistent and non-persistent contractionary fiscal policy shocks on credit growth.
- Examine the transmission of the effects of positive shocks to taxes on goods and services, income, and company taxes on credit growth.

6.1 Introduction

Gumata and Ndou (2017) established that contractionary fiscal policy shocks dampen GDP growth. Is it possible that this is another channel through which contractionary fiscal policy shocks affects credit growth? The main hypothesis tested in this chapter is whether contractionary fiscal policy shocks exert pronounced effects on credit growth when GDP growth is constrained. Figure 6.1 shows the theoretical link between fiscal policy effects and credit markets based on the new classical theory.

The theoretical predictions of the new classical view about expansionary fiscal policy is that individuals will link expansionary fiscal policy with high future taxes thus leading them to decrease current consumption and consequently increasing savings. Therefore, when individuals anticipate

N. Gumata, E. Ndou, *Achieving Price, Financial and Macro-Economic Stability in South Africa*,
https://doi.org/10.1007/978-3-030-66340-7_6

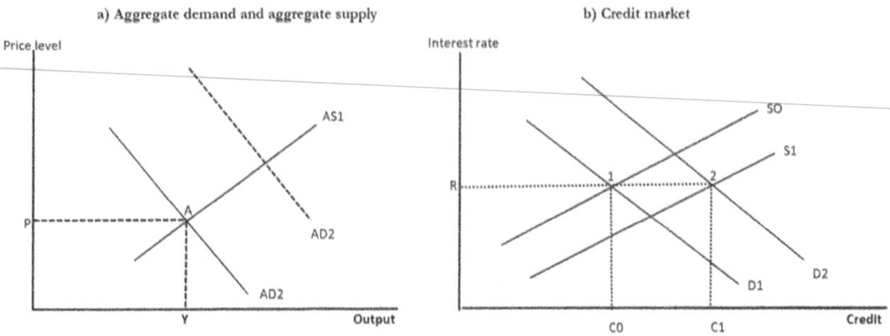

Fig. 6.1 New classical view of expansionary fiscal policy effects. (Source: Authors' drawing)

higher future taxes from high expansionary fiscal policy, the aggregate demand curve will not shift upwards. The decrease in consumption prevents the aggregate demand curve from shifting rightward from AD1 to AD2 (Fig. 6.1). This means that expansionary fiscal policy is not stimulatory.

Furthermore, because expansionary fiscal policy leads to a deficit which requires financing, this results in the demand for loanable funds shifting the demand curve to the rightward from D1 to D2. At the same time, individuals perceive the deficit in terms of higher future taxes and increase their savings enough to offset those tax increases. The increased savings lead to the rightward shift in the loan supply curve from S_0 to S_1. The main implication is that anticipated expansionary and contractionary fiscal policy neither affect real GDP, unemployment, the price level nor the interest rates but impacts the demand for credit.

The chapter fills academic and policy research gaps by showing that contractionary fiscal policy, in the form of tax increase and spending cut shocks, exerts different effects on credit growth and GDP growth. Furthermore, we establish the impact of persistent and non-persistent contractionary fiscal policy shocks on credit growth. We also examine the impact of treating GDP growth as an exogenous and endogenous variable in the estimations. We conclude by exploring the transmission of the effects of positive shocks to taxes on goods and services, income, and company taxes on credit growth. All these research aspects have not been explored in South Africa.

6.2 Evidence from the Endogenous–Exogenous Model

This section begins the analysis by examining the role of GDP growth in transmitting contractionary fiscal policy shocks to credit growth. We use a VAR model with fiscal variables, inflation and credit growth. In the estimation of different models, GDP growth is used as an endogenous as well as an exogenous variable in different estimated models. The fiscal variables used in the model include government spending, personal income tax, company income tax and taxes on goods and services. The fiscal variables are expressed in annual growth rate and as ratios of GDP in some models. The sample spans the period 2000Q1 to 2015Q4. The data is sourced from the South African Reserve Bank. All growth rates are at an annual rate. The VAR model is estimated using two lags and 10,000 Monte Carlo draws. The shock refers to one standard deviation shock.

First, we use GDP growth as an exogenous variable in one model and an endogenous variable in another model to assess the amplification effects of contractionary fiscal policy shocks via the GDP growth channel. Figure 6.2(a) shows that a positive tax shock has an adverse effect on credit growth. Credit growth declines more when GDP growth is an endogenous variable in the model than when it is an exogenous variable. The peak decline in credit growth is more than double when GDP growth is endogenous. In addition, Fig. 6.2(b) shows that a positive tax shock induces more fluctuations in credit growth when GDP growth is an endogenous variable than when it is an exogenous variable in the model.

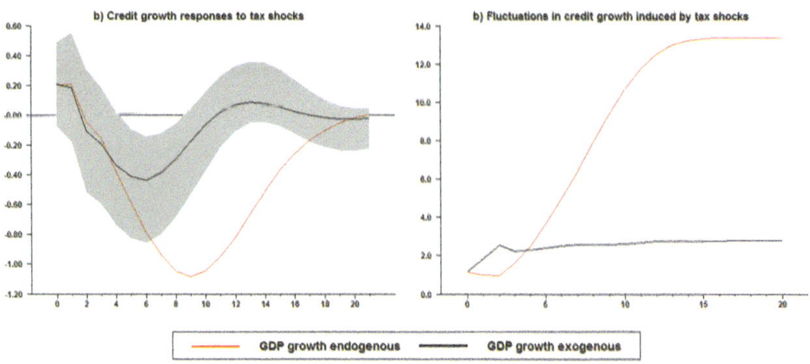

Fig. 6.2 Effects of a positive tax shock on credit growth. (Source: Authors' calculations)

Does it matter whether the contractionary fiscal policy shock is in the form of a tax increase or spending cut shocks? Figure 6.3(a) shows that the credit growth responses to spending cut shocks are larger compared to tax increase shocks. This means that spending cuts exert pronounced adverse effect on credit growth when GDP growth is an endogenous variable in the model. In addition, the spending cut shock induces more fluctuations in credit growth when GDP growth is an endogenous variable in the model.

This evidence shows that contractionary fiscal policy shocks have adverse effects on credit growth. A one standard deviation fiscal spending cut shock reduces credit growth by nearly 1.75 percentage points at peak when GDP growth is an endogenous variable in the model, which exceeds the 1 percentage point decline due to a positive tax shock. In addition, fiscal spending cut shocks in the long run explain about 60 per cent of fluctuations in credit growth, which exceeds the 14 per cent due to positive tax shocks when GDP growth is an endogenous variable in the model.

Furthermore, Fig. 6.4 shows that persistent and non-persistent contractionary fiscal policy shocks result in different effects on credit growth. The trajectories depicting the persistent and non-persistent contractionary fiscal policy shocks are shown in Fig. 6.4(a). On the other hand, Fig. 6.4(b and c) shows that credit growth declines more when GDP growth is an endogenous variable in the model due to both persistent and non-persistent shocks. But persistent contractionary fiscal policy shocks result in a prolonged slump in credit growth.

Similarly, evidence in Fig. 6.5 indicates that a positive tax shock leads to a large decline in credit growth when GDP growth is an endogenous variable in the model, irrespective of whether the contractionary fiscal policy shocks are persistent and non-persistent.

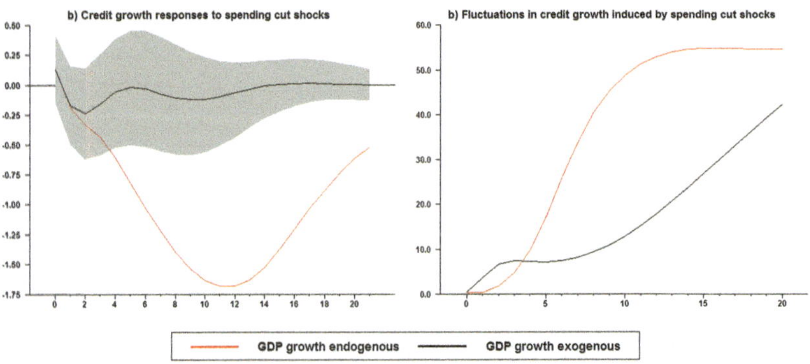

Fig. 6.3 Effects of spending cut shocks on credit growth. (Source: Authors' calculations)

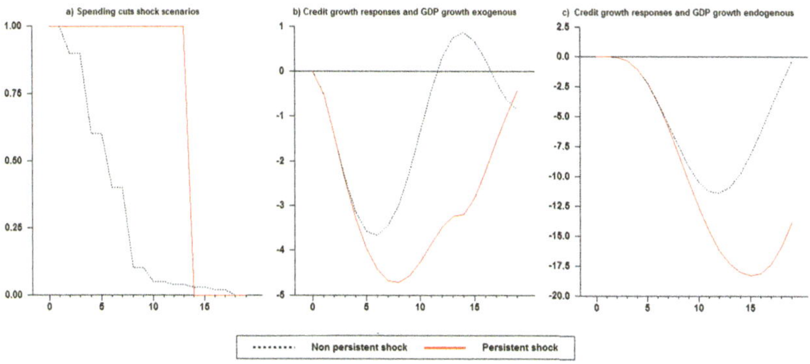

Fig. 6.4 Credit growth responses to persistent and non-persistent spending cut shocks. (Source: Authors' calculations)

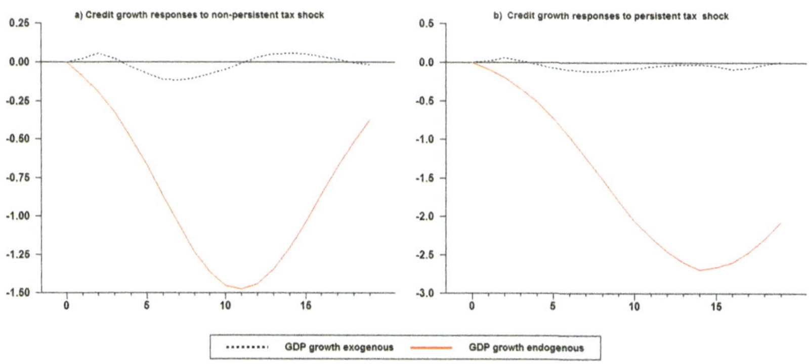

Fig. 6.5 Credit growth responses to persistent and non-persistent positive tax shocks. (Source: Authors' calculations)

This shows that allowing for feedback effects of GDP growth in the model leads to the worsening of the decline in credit growth due to contractionary fiscal policy shocks. In addition, the results show that GDP growth plays an important role in the transmission of spending cut and positive tax shocks in credit dynamics.

6.3 Evidence from the Counterfactual VAR Analysis Approach

This section applies a counterfactual VAR model to determine the robustness of the preceding findings. We focus on assessing the role of GDP growth in amplifying credit growth responses to contractionary fiscal policy shocks. Figure 6.6 shows that actual credit growth declines more than the counterfactual responses due to positive tax and spending cut shocks. This evidence confirms that GDP growth amplifies the reaction of credit growth to contractionary fiscal policy shocks.

The size of the amplifications by GDP growth in Fig. 6.7 shows that GDP growth worsens the decline in credit growth more due to the spending cut shocks compared to positive tax shocks. This could be explained by the pronounced decline in GDP growth due to spending cut shocks in Fig. 6.7(b).

6.3.1 *Do Different Tax Components Exert Different Effects?*

Figure 6.8 compares the responses of credit growth due to positive income tax and taxes on goods and services shocks.

The results show that credit growth declines in response to all positive tax shocks. Like earlier sections, the role of GDP growth is potent as credit growth declines more when it is included in the model, especially due to

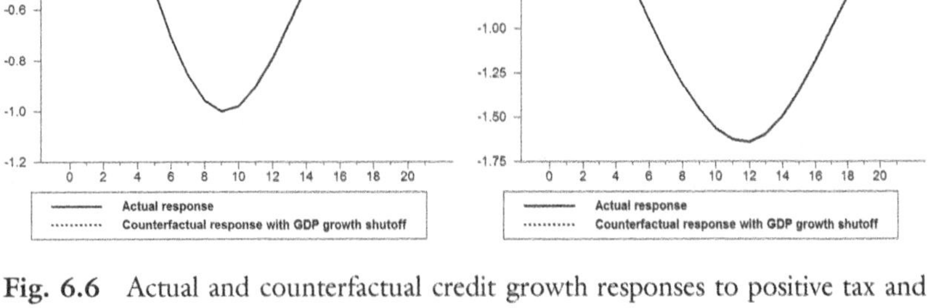

Fig. 6.6 Actual and counterfactual credit growth responses to positive tax and spending cut shocks. (Source: Authors' calculations)

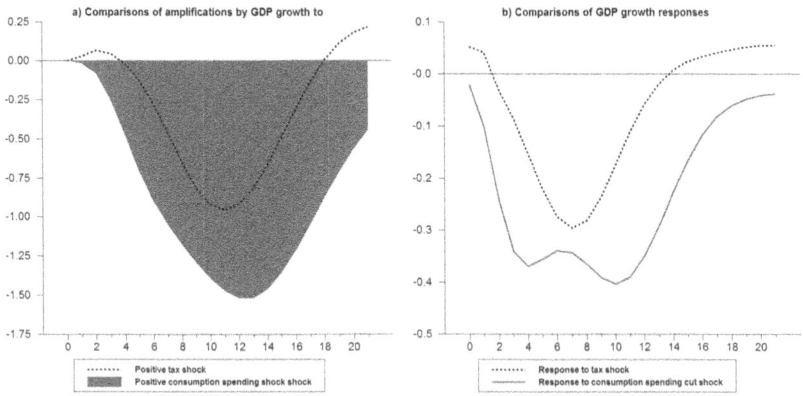

Fig. 6.7 Credit growth responses to spending cut and positive tax shocks. (Source: Authors' calculations)

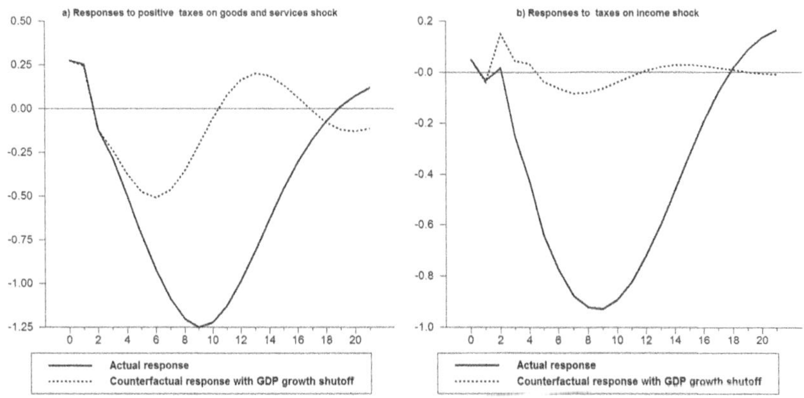

Fig. 6.8 Credit growth responses to positive taxes on goods and services and taxes on income shocks. (Source: Authors' calculations)

taxes on goods and services compared to an increase in taxes on income. At peak, taxes on goods and services result in a decline of 1.25 percentage points compared to 0.9 percentage points due to increases on income taxes.

The comparison of the amplification effects in Fig. 6.9(a) shows that GDP growth leads to larger credit growth contraction due to a positive tax on goods and services shock than to taxes on income shock. This may be

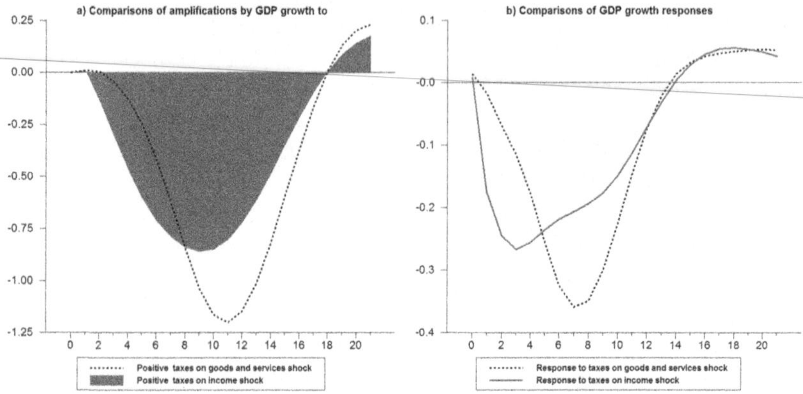

Fig. 6.9 Amplification of credit growth responses to positive income tax and taxes on goods and services shocks by the GDP growth channel. (Source: Authors' calculations)

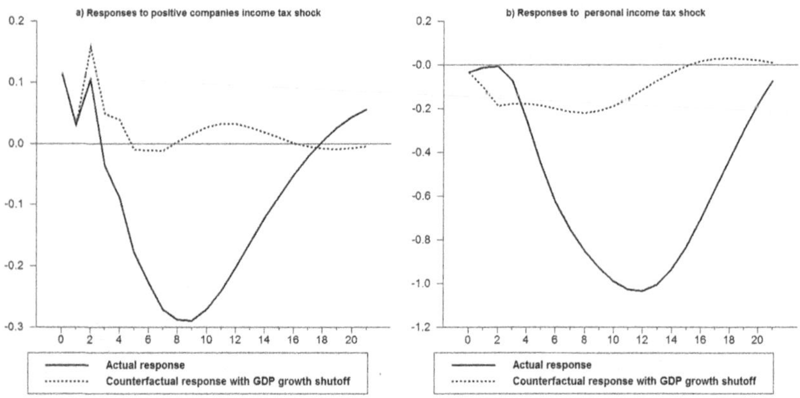

Fig. 6.10 Credit growth responses to positive personal income tax and company tax shocks. (Source: Authors' calculations)

linked to a larger decline in GDP growth at peak in Fig. 6.9(b) due to a positive tax on goods and services shock.

What about the effects of positive personal and company income tax shocks? Figure 6.10 shows that a positive income tax shock leads to a decline in credit growth even when GDP growth is shut-off in the model compared to a positive shock to company tax. At peak, credit growth

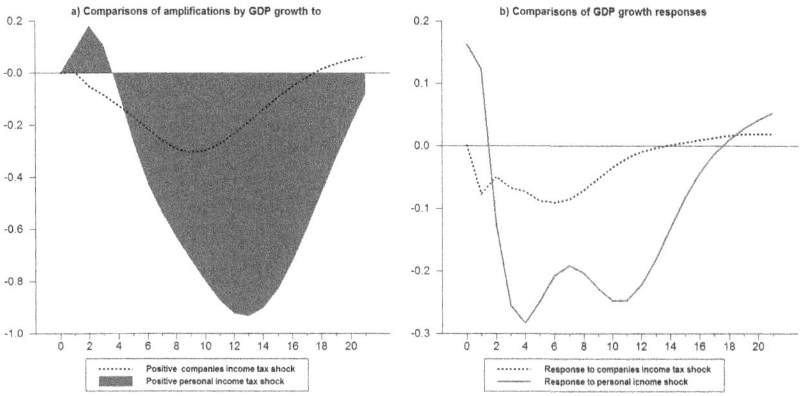

Fig. 6.11 Amplification of credit growth responses to positive personal income tax and company income tax shocks by the GDP growth channel. (Source: Authors' calculations)

declines by 1.1 percentage points due to a positive income tax shock and is more than double compared to the 0.3 percentage points due to a positive company tax shock.

Furthermore, the comparisons of amplifications in Fig. 6.11 show that GDP growth propagates the decline in credit growth more due to a positive personal income tax shock compared to a company income tax shock. This difference could be attributed to a pronounced decline in GDP growth due to a positive personal income tax shock in Fig. 6.11(b).

6.4 Conclusion and Policy Implications

This chapter examined whether the GDP growth channel amplifies the effects of contractionary fiscal policy shocks on credit growth. Evidence shows that a positive tax shock has an adverse effect on credit growth. Credit growth declines more than double due to a positive tax shock when GDP growth is an endogenous variable in the model. In addition, a positive tax shock induces more fluctuations in credit growth when GDP growth is an endogenous variable in the model. However, does it matter whether the contractionary fiscal policy shock is in the form of tax or spending cut shocks? Evidence shows that credit growth responses to spending cut shocks are larger and that spending cut shocks induce more fluctuations in credit growth. A one standard deviation fiscal policy spending cut shock reduces credit growth by nearly 1.75 percentage point at peak effects when GDP growth is an endogenous variable in the model. This magnitude exceeds the 1 percentage points due to a positive tax shock.

Furthermore, spending cuts exert pronounced adverse effects on credit growth when GDP growth is an endogenous variable in the model. Fiscal spending cut shocks in the long run explain about 60 per cent of fluctuations in credit growth, which exceeds the 14 per cent due to positive tax shocks. Thus, allowing for feedback effects of GDP growth in the model leads to the worsening of the decline in credit growth due to contractionary fiscal policy shocks. In addition, the results show that GDP growth plays an important role in the transmission of spending cut and positive tax shocks in credit dynamics. GDP growth amplifies the reaction of credit growth to contractionary fiscal policy shocks. This is because GDP growth declines more due to spending cut shocks compared to positive tax shocks and this is transmitted into credit growth. Hence, we conclude that the GDP growth channel is a potent channel through which the contractionary fiscal policy shocks are transmitted to credit growth.

Evidence also shows that credit growth declines more especially due to positive shocks to taxes on goods and services and personal income tax compared to an increase in company taxes. At peak effect, taxes on goods and services and personal income tax shocks result in a decline of 1.25 percentage points and 1.1 percentage points, respectively, compared to 0.3 percentage points due to increases on company taxes. This is because GDP growth leads to a larger credit growth contraction due to positive tax shocks on goods and services and personal income tax shocks compared to company tax shocks. This may be linked to the larger propagation effects of the decline in GDP growth at peak due to positive goods and services and personal income tax shocks.

Reference

Gumata N, and Ndou E. 2017. Labour market and Fiscal Policy Adjustments to shocks: The role and implications for price and financial stability in South Africa. Palgrave Macmillan ISBN 978-3-319-66519-1.

CHAPTER 7

Do Synchronised Credit Growth and House Price Growth Booms Impact the Monetary Policy Reaction to Inflationary Pressures?

Research Questions Explored

- Assesses the extent to which the synchronicity of credit growth and house price growth boom episodes impacts the policy response to inflationary pressures.
- Test whether house prices growth and mortgage market credit conditions have pronounced effects on credit growth and GDP growth via the collateral and wealth effects.
- Examine whether periods of a simultaneous occurrence of credit growth and house price growth booms propagate inflationary shocks and repo rate responses differently compared to synchronised non-boom episodes.
- Examine whether the 6 per cent inflation threshold affects the way in which synchronised boom and non-boom episodes propagate shocks.

7.1 Introduction

Claessens et al. (2011) show that credit growth, house price growth and equity price growth cycles, collectively referred to as the financial cycle, tend to be long. In addition, busts in house prices growth and equity price growth following periods of high credit growth lead to deeper and

N. Gumata, E. Ndou, *Achieving Price, Financial and Macro-Economic Stability in South Africa*,
https://doi.org/10.1007/978-3-030-66340-7_7

more protracted recessions. Against this background, this chapter assesses the extent to which the synchronicity of credit growth and house price growth boom episodes impact the policy response to inflationary pressures. Recent evidence shows that indeed financial cycles matter but the synchronised occurrence of boom episodes in the constituents of the financial cycle matters as well. First, we identify and date boom and non-boom episodes for house price growth and credit growth. Thereafter, we test the hypothesis that house price growth and the mortgage market credit conditions have pronounced effects on credit growth and GDP growth via the collateral and wealth effects.[1] In particular, we apply the counterfactual approach to examine whether periods of simultaneous occurrence of credit growth and house price growth booms propagate inflationary shocks and thus influence the repo rate responses differently compared to synchronised non-boom episodes. Moreover, do synchronised boom and non-boom episodes propagation effects differ when inflation exceeds 6 per cent?

This chapter fills the academic and policy research gaps by assessing the extent to which the synchronicity of credit growth and house price growth boom episodes impacts the policy response to inflationary pressures. We identify and date boom and non-boom episodes for house price growth and credit growth. Furthermore, we test whether house price growth and mortgage market credit conditions have pronounced effects on credit growth and GDP growth via the collateral and wealth effects. We examine whether periods of simultaneous occurrence of credit growth and house price growth booms propagate inflationary shocks. Furthermore, we explore whether the repo rate responds differently to synchronised boom and non-boom episodes. Last, we fill research policy gaps by examining whether the 6 per cent inflation threshold affects the way in which synchronised boom and non-boom episodes propagate shocks.

7.2 In Which Periods Did Boom and Non-boom Episodes in Credit Growth and House Price Growth Occur?

This section uses three techniques to identify (i) the financial cycle boom and bust episodes, and (ii) the duration, amplitude and slopes of the financial cycles. First, we use the filtering techniques, the Hodrick-Prescott and

[1] The methodology of estimating the mortgage market credit condition indices is discussed in later chapters of this book.

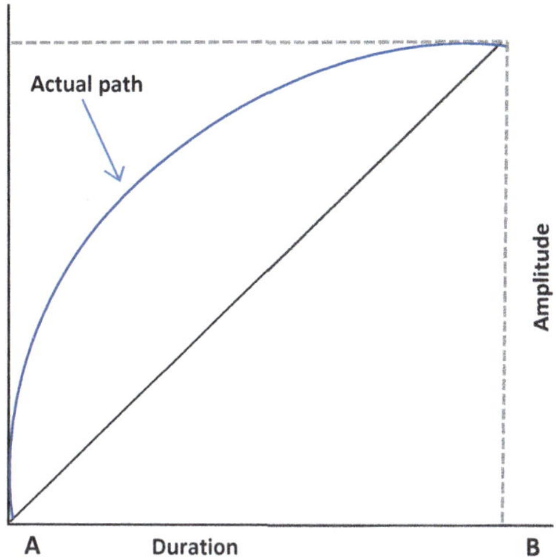

Fig. 7.1 Key features of the cyclical phases. (Source: Adapted from Harding and Pagan (1999))

extended Kalman filtering techniques, to establish boom and bust episodes based on deviations from trend. Second, the threshold approaches, namely the Fatas et al. (2009) and Borgy et al. (2009) approaches, are used to date boom and non-boom episodes based on certain threshold values. Last, the Pagan Harding (1997) approach is used to date the duration, amplitude and slopes of the financial boom and non-boom episodes shown in Fig. 7.1.

In Fig. 7.1, the duration for recessions (downturns) is defined as the number of quarters (months) between the peak and the trough. The duration for upturns is the time it takes to attain the level at the previous peak after the trough. The amplitude is the absolute distance between the trough (peak) and peak (trough). To estimate the financial cycles, we use data spanning the sample period 1980Q1 to 2015Q4. The data is sourced from the South African Reserve Bank database. All growth rates are at annual rate.

Figure 7.2 presents the financial and growth cycles since 1980Q1, defined as episodes of rapid or excess growth when the deviation from trend is greater than 1.5 times its standard deviation.[2] The periods of positive deviations greater than 1.5 times deviations from trend are shaded in grey. It is evident that periods of excess positive deviation are similar between the variables although the magnitudes of peaks and durations of the excesses differ.

[2] See Dell'Ariccia et al. (2012) for further details.

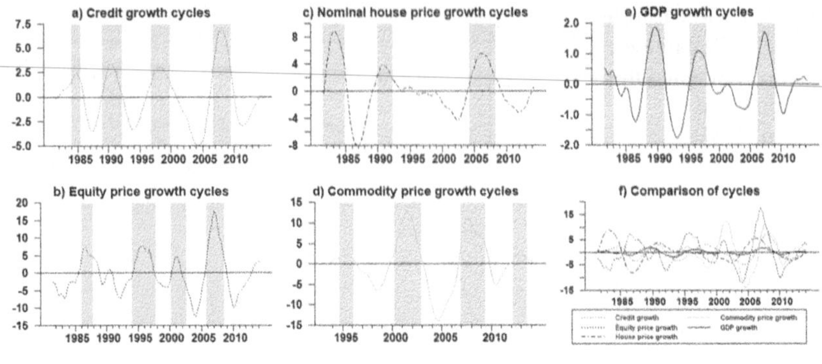

Fig. 7.2 The financial and output growth cycles. (Source: Authors' calculations)

The credit growth cycle, GDP growth, equity price growth and commodity price growth in Fig. 7.2a, b, d and e have four periods of excess positive deviation over the sample. Nominal house price growth cycles in Fig. 7.2b have three periods of excessive positive deviation. Across all variables, the excess positive deviation in 2004–2008 was the highest in amplitude and longest in duration in recent history. In line with vast empirical literature,[3] the comparison of the cyclical properties of the various variables in Fig. 7.2f shows that indeed GDP growth tends to have low-frequency cycles compared to the financial cycles. Furthermore, it is evident that the real and financial cycles have become more synchronised post-2000.

For the threshold techniques, we use the thresholds of ±15 per cent and ±20 per cent set by Fatas et al. (2009) and Borgy et al. (2009) to establish the boom and bust episodes. We assess the boom and bust episodes for nominal and real house price growth, and aggregate, household and corporate credit growth. Figure 7.3 shows the periods of booms identified by the cut-offs of +15 per cent and +20 per cent, which are shaded in light grey. The identified booms are comparable to those identified using the filtering techniques. We establish five episodes of booms for aggregate credit growth, two episodes for credit growth to households and companies, four boom episodes for nominal house price growth compared to two boom episodes for real house price growth.

[3] See Borio and Lowe (2002), Drehmann et al. (2012), Claessens et al. (2011), Borio (2014) and Claessens and Kose (2018), who show that since the early 1980s, financial cycles appear to have grown in amplitude and length (duration).

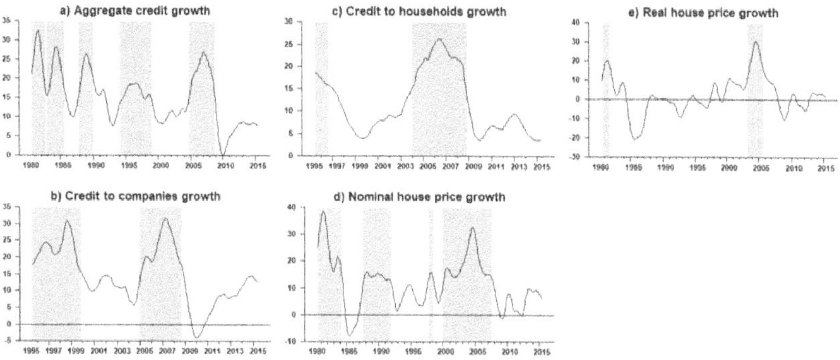

Fig. 7.3 Total and sectorial credit growth, nominal and real house price growth boom episodes. (Source: Authors' calculations)

However, of note is that we fail to identify episodes of busts or severe contraction in aggregate and household credit growth. Second, evidence shows that credit to companies was the key driver of the 1995–1999 credit growth boom as credit growth to the household sector was on a decline. However, it is evident that the household credit growth contributed to the prolonged duration of aggregate credit growth during the recent credit growth boom whereas credit growth to companies contributed more to the amplitude of the boom. At the same time, evidence in Fig. 7.3d shows that the duration and amplitude of the nominal house price growth also played a significant role in the recent credit growth boom. Furthermore, we are unable to identify a bust episode for the nominal house price growth over the entire samples as opposed to real house price growth. The decline during 1984–1987 does not qualify to be classified as a bust based on the threshold techniques we use in this chapter. This contrasts with real house price growth which declined by more than 20 per cent during the same period in October 1984 to December 1986.

7.2.1 How Long Is the Duration of Financial Downturns on Average over the Sample Period?

To answer the question asked in this section, we use the Bry-Boschan algorithm to date the troughs, peaks, durations of upturns and downturns, and the amplitude. We define the duration of financial downturns as the number of quarters between the peak and trough. Thus, the duration for financial upturns is defined as the time it takes to attain the level at the

Table 7.1 Peaks, troughs, duration and amplitudes of total credit growth

Peaks	*Troughs*	*Duration of downturns*	*Amplitude*
1981 July	1983 February	19	20.67
1984 May	1987 February	33	31.50
1988 October	1990 October	24	27.10
1991 October	1992 October	12	6.39
1996 October	1998 January	15	14.41
1998 August	2000 June	22	13.31
2001 December	2002 December	12	7.22
2003 November	2004 June	7	4.35
2007 February	2009 November	33	24.52
2012 December	2013 December	12	5.97
2014 July	2015 June	11	5.76

Source: Authors' calculations

Table 7.2 Peaks, troughs, duration and amplitudes of credit growth households

Peaks	*Troughs*	*Duration of downturn*	*Amplitude*
1995 May	1999 November	54	33.38
2002 June	2002 December	6	2.20
2006 February	2009 November	45	40.50
2011 January	2011 September	8	2.45
2011 November	2015 May	30	18.98

Source: Authors' calculations

previous peak after the trough as shown in Fig. 7.1. The amplitude is defined as the absolute distance between the trough (peak) and peak (trough). To simplify the analysis in this section, we present the results on the cyclical downturns only.

The results in Table 7.1 suggest that on average aggregate credit growth downturns last 18 months. The longest downturns occurred in 1984 May to 1987 February; and recently in 2007 February to 2009 November. But the amplitude for 2007 February to 2009 November saw aggregate credit growth decline by 24.5 per cent which is lower than 31.5 per cent during 1984 May to 1987 February.

The characteristics of sectorial credit growth in Tables 7.2 and 7.3 show that the duration of the downturn for credit growth to households lasts longer than that of credit growth to companies. On average, the duration of downturns of credit growth to households lasts for 27 months

Table 7.3 Peaks, troughs, duration and amplitudes of credit growth to companies

Peaks	*Troughs*	*Duration of downturn*	*Amplitude*
1996 October	1997 November	13	13.53
1998 November	2000 December	25	19.57
2001 December	2004 June	30	14.68
2005 May	2006 January	8	8.47
2007 June	2009 November	29	16.37
2012 March	2013 February	11	3.63
2014 July	2015 June	11	8.79

Source: Authors' calculations

Table 7.4 Peaks, troughs, duration and amplitudes of mortgage credit growth

Peaks	*Troughs*	*Duration of downturn*	*Amplitude*
1981 April	1982 August	16	13.04
1984 March	1986 January	22	24.83
1988 December	1990 December	24	25.63
1991 November	1992 August	9	10.79
1995 January	1999 October	57	42.18
2001 May	2002 December	19	15.18
2006 January	2013 June	80	51.37

Source: Authors' calculations

compared to 18 months for credit growth to companies which is comparable to that of total credit growth.

The amplitudes of credit growth to household downturns are more severe. For example, the absolute decline in household credit growth during the recent downturn in 2006 February to 2009 November was 10.5 per cent. At the same time, the downturn for credit growth to companies occurred between 2007 June to 2009 November and the amplitude was 16.37 per cent. Furthermore, the dates of troughs and downturns for the credit growth cycle tend to coincide with those of credit growth to companies.

On the other hand, the characteristics of the mortgage advances credit growth cycle in Table 7.4 reveal that the recent downturn during 2006 January and 2013 June was the longest and most severe on record with amplitude of 51.37 per cent. The downturn for mortgage advances credit growth on average lasts 32 months, which is longer than that of total credit growth and credit growth to companies.

It is also interesting to observe that the mortgage advances credit growth cycles do not necessarily occur at the same time as those in total

Table 7.5 Characteristics of the nominal house price growth cycle

Peaks	*Troughs*	*Duration of downturn*	*Amplitude*
1981 May	1982 November	18	22.89
1983 November	1985 July	20	-8.47
1988 January	1989 January	12	11.09
1989 June	1991 April	22	20.60
1991 November	1992 September	10	-1.78
1994 July	1996 June	23	9.011
1998 February	1999 September	19	8.06
2000 October	2001 December	14	13.96
2004 October	2006 September	23	25.04
2007 October	2009 May	26	-2.28
2010 April	2012 April	24	-2.84
2013 April	2014 February	10	13.18

Source: Authors' calculations

and sectorial credit growth. But when they occur, they persist. Similarly, the characteristics of the nominal house price growth cycle in Table 7.5 are not necessarily linked to mortgage advances credit growth.

The nominal house price growth downturns last 18 months on average compared to an average of 24 months for real house price growth. The amplitudes of real house price growth cycles are severe compared to those of nominal house price growth. Overall, the characteristics of the credit growth and housing cycles presented so far indicate that downturns in credit growth and house price growth cycles tend to be severe and last longer compared to upturns.

7.3 Does the Mortgage Credit Growth Boom Matter for the Transmission of House Price Growth Boom Shocks to Credit Growth and GDP Growth?

To analyse the propagation effects of mortgage boom in transmitting house price growth boom shocks on credit growth and GDP growth, this section estimates various VAR models, which include GDP growth, credit growth, the house price growth boom and mortgage credit growth boom episodes identified in the earlier section. We use dummy variables for the mortgage credit growth and house price growth booms, which refer to the dummy variables that capture periods during which mortgage advances credit growth and house price growth are in a boom episode and zero otherwise. The propagation or restraining (stifling) abilities of the housing

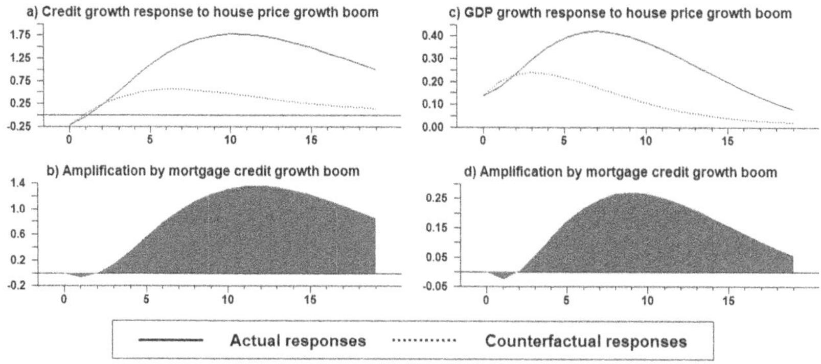

Fig. 7.4 Propagation effects of house price growth boom shocks on credit growth and GDP growth. (Source: Authors' calculations)

credit growth or house price growth channel are determined by the gap between actual and counterfactual responses when the variable is active and shut-off in the model. The VAR models are estimated for the period 2000Q1 to 2015Q4 and have two lags chosen by the AIC and the impulses are generated from 10,000 Monte Carlo draws.

Figure 7.4 shows that mortgage credit growth plays a significant role in propagating the boom episodes in house price growth. In the absence of mortgage credit growth, the house price growth boom episode shock has a positive impact on credit growth and GDP growth, but these effects are magnified or propagated by mortgage credit growth as a conduit for house price growth. The magnifying effects of house price growth booms increase credit growth by 1.4 percentage points and GDP growth by 1.3 percentage points at peak.

7.3.1 Does the Synchronicity of House Price Growth and Credit Growth Booms Impact the Policy Responses to Positive Inflation Shocks?

The preceding section shows evidence of the asset price growth channel and probably the collateral channel but is silent on how synchronised boom and non-boom episodes impact the response of monetary policy to inflationary pressures. To assess for the impact of synchronised boom and non-boom episodes, we distinguish the repo rate responses to positive inflation shocks during synchronised house price growth and credit growth boom and non-boom periods. To capture the differential effects, we separate the boom and non-boom episodes and create dummy variables to identify these episodes individually. We define a boom (non-boom) dummy as the dummy variable that captures the periods in which house price growth and credit growth booms (non-booms) occur at the same time, and zero otherwise. We control for the recession effects beginning in 2009M1 by creating a dummy variable for the recession. The recession dummy variable is equal to one for the period 2009M1 to 2009M12 and zero otherwise.

Like the earlier section, we estimate a three-variable VAR model, which includes inflation, repo rate and a dummy variable for the boom or non-boom period. The VAR models are estimated using monthly data from 2000M1 to 2015M12. We include lending rate spreads relative to the repo rate and manufacturing production growth to assess for the robustness of the results. The role of the synchronised boom and non-boom periods is given by the gap between the actual repo rate responses when the boom or non-boom periods are included and shut-off in the model. The VAR model is estimated using three lags chosen by the AIC and the impulse responses are generated from 10,000 Monte Carlo draws.

Figure 7.5 shows that the responses of the repo rate are different during periods when the house price growth and credit growth boom are synchronised compared to those of non-boom periods. Synchronised boom episodes propagate inflationary pressures and result in pronounced increases in the repo rate.

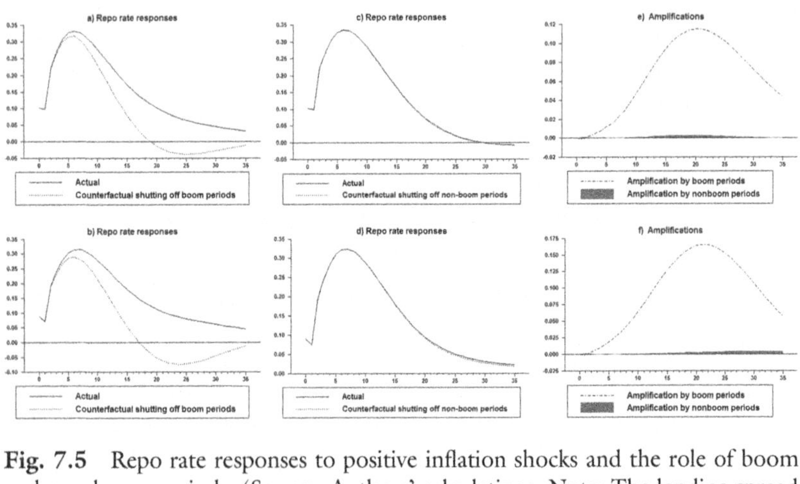

Fig. 7.5 Repo rate responses to positive inflation shocks and the role of boom and non-boom periods. (Source: Authors' calculations. Note: The lending spread is included in Row 1. Manufacturing production growth is included in Row 2)

Thus, the coccurrence of house price growth and credit growth boom periods amplifies the repo rate responses to positive inflation shocks. The amplification due to house price growth and credit growth boom is enormously higher than that induced by non-boom periods. This finding is robust to the inclusion of the lending spread and manufacturing activity in the model.

7.3.2 What Are the Implications of Boom and Non-boom Episodes When Inflation Is Above 6 Per Cent?

How do boom and non-boom episodes transmit inflation shocks to the policy rate, especially when inflation exceeds the 6 per cent threshold? To answer this question, we create a dummy variable for the periods when inflation exceeds the 6 per cent threshold and zero otherwise. The inflation threshold dummy is included in the VAR model to estimate the amplification effects of the boom and non-boom episodes when inflation exceeds the 6 per cent threshold. Figure 7.6 shows evidence that the synchronised house price growth and credit growth booms result in aggressive repo rate tightening to inflationary pressures. On the other hand, synchronised non-boom episodes have very little effect on the amplification of the policy rate responses to positive inflation when inflation is above 6 per cent.

Would the conclusion differ when the VAR model size is increased to include more variables? To test for this, we estimate a four-variable VAR model and include the lending rate-repo rate spread and manufacturing production growth. These variables are included individually in the VAR

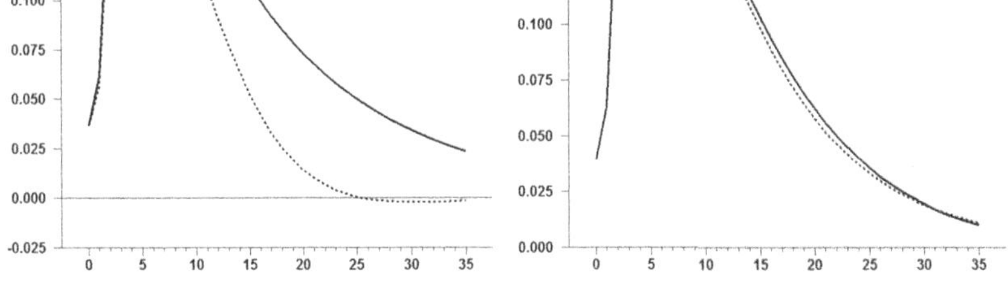

Fig. 7.6 Repo rate responses to positive inflation shocks when inflation is above 6 per cent. (Source: Authors' calculations)

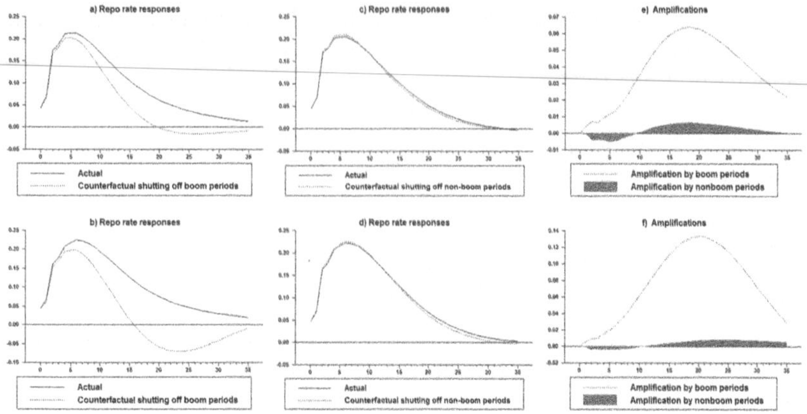

Fig. 7.7 Repo rate responses to positive inflation shocks when inflation is above 6 per cent. (Source: Authors' calculations. Note: The lending spread is included in Row 1. Manufacturing production growth is included in Row 2)

estimations. Evidence in Fig. 7.7 concurs with earlier results that the synchronised house price growth and credit growth booms amplify inflationary pressures and the rate at which the repo rate responds.

7.4 Conclusion and Policy Implications

This chapter explored the extent to which synchronised credit growth and house price growth boom episodes impact the policy response to inflationary pressures. First, we establish that the credit cycle, GDP growth, equity price growth and commodity price growth have four periods of excess positive deviation over the sample period 1980Q1 to 2015Q4 compared to three cycles for nominal house price growth. Across all variables, the excess positive deviation in 2004–2008 was the highest in amplitude and longest in duration in recent history. In addition, the comparison of the cyclical properties of the various variables shows that indeed GDP growth tends to have low-frequency cycles compared to the financial cycles. Furthermore, the real and financial cycles have become more synchronised post-2000.

However, we fail to identify episodes of busts or severe contraction in aggregate and household credit growth. In addition, evidence shows that household credit growth contributed to the prolonged duration of aggregate credit growth during the recent credit boom whereas credit growth to companies contributed more to the amplitude of the boom. At the same time, the duration and amplitude of nominal house price growth also played a significant role in the recent credit growth boom. But the duration of the downturn for credit growth to households lasts longer compared to that of credit growth to companies. On average, the duration of downturns for credit growth to households lasts for 27 months compared to 18 months for credit growth to companies, which is comparable to that of total credit growth. Similarly, the mortgage advances credit growth cycle tends to be long and severe. The downturn for mortgage advances credit growth on average lasts 32 months, which is longer than that of total credit growth and credit growth to companies. Nonetheless, the mortgage advances credit growth cycles do not necessarily occur at the same time as those in total and sectorial credit growth. Similarly, the characteristics of the nominal house price growth cycle are not necessarily linked to mortgage advances credit growth. Overall, the characteristics of the credit growth and housing cycles indicate that downturns in credit growth and house price growth cycles tend to be severe and last longer compared to upturns.

Evidence in this chapter also shows that mortgage credit growth plays a significant role in propagating the house price growth boom episodes. Mortgage credit growth magnifies the effects of house price growth booms and this contributes to an increase of 1.4 percentage points in credit growth and 1.3 percentage points in GDP growth at peak response, respectively. The implication is that mortgage credit growth is an important conduit through which house price growth boom episode shocks are transmitted to credit growth and GDP growth.

Do synchronised boom and non-boom episode propagation effects differ when inflation exceeds 6 per cent? Evidence shows that the repo rate responds differently during periods when the house price growth and credit growth boom episodes are synchronised compared to those of non-boom periods. Synchronised boom episodes propagate inflationary pressures and result in pronounced increases in the repo rate. Thus, the coccurrence of house price growth and credit growth boom periods amplifies the repo rate responses to positive inflation shocks. The amplification due to house price growth and credit growth booms is enormously higher compared to that induced by non-boom periods. In addition, evidence showed that the synchronised house price growth and credit growth boom episodes result in aggressive repo rate tightening to inflationary pressures when inflation exceeds the 6 per cent threshold. The synchronised non-boom episodes have very little effect in the amplification of the policy rate responses to positive inflation when inflation is above 6 per cent.

The policy implication of the findings in this chapter is that asset price growth and credit growth boom and non-boom episodes spill over into the real economy, have an impact on inflationary pressures and the rate at which the policy rate responds. Developments in credit markets are conduits through which asset price developments are transmitted into real economic activity. Hence, macroprudential tools, to the degree they influence asset prices, credit growth and financial cycles, have an impact on inflationary pressures and thus complement monetary policy tools. These findings further advance the case for the co-ordination of financial regulation, and macroprudential and monetary policy tools.

References

Borgy V, Clerc L, and Renne Jean-Paul. 2009. Asset-Price Boom-Bust Cycles and Credit: What is the Scope of Macro-Prudential Regulation? Banque de France Working Paper No. 263.

Borio C. 2014. "The financial cycle and macroeconomics: What have we learnt?", Journal of Banking & Finance, vol. 45, pp. 182–198, August. Also available as BIS Working Papers, no. 395, December 2012.

Borio C and Lowe P. 2002. "Asset prices, financial and monetary stability: Exploring the nexus", BIS Working Papers, no. 114, July.

Claessens S, and Kose M. 2018. "Frontiers of macrofinancial linkages", BIS Papers, no. 95, January.

Claessens S, Kose M, and Terrones M. 2011. "Financial cycles: What? How? When?", IMF Working Papers, WP/11/76.

Dell'Ariccia G, Igan D, Laeven L, and Tong H, Bakker B, and Vandenbussche J. 2012. Policies for Macrofinancial Stability: How to Deal with Credit Booms. IMF Staff Discussion Note SDN/12/06.

Drehmann et al. 2012. "Characterising the financial cycle: Don't lose sight of the medium term!", BIS Working Papers, no. 380, June.

Fatas A, Kannan P, Rabanal P, and Scott A. 2009. Lessons from Asset Price Fluctuations for Monetary Policy. World Economic Outlook, International Monetary Fund, September 2009.

Gumata N and Ndou E. 2017. Bank Credit Extension and Real Economic Activity in South Africa: The Impact of Capital Flow Dynamics, Bank Regulation and Selected Macroprudential Tools. Palgrave Macmillan. ISB 978-3-319-43550-3.

Harding D. 1997. The Definition, Dating, and Duration of Cycles. Paper presented to the Melbourne Institute conference on Business Cycles: Policy and Analysis.

Harding D, and Pagan A. 1999. Dissecting the Cycle. Melbourne Institute Working Paper No. 13/99.

Lautenschläger S. 2018. A stable financial system—More than the sum of its parts. Keynote speech at the Dutch Banking Day 2018, Amsterdam, 15 February 2018.

CHAPTER 8

Do Synchronised Boom and Non-boom Episodes in Credit Growth, Commodity and Equity Prices Impact the Response of the Repo Rate to Positive Inflation Shocks?

Research Questions Explored

- Explore the extent to which synchronised equity price, commodity price and credit growth boom and non-boom episodes impact the reaction of repo rate to positive inflation shocks.
- Establish whether the effects of synchronised non-boom equity price growth, commodity price growth and credit growth episodes differ between credit to companies and households.
- Assess the role of synchronised boom and non-boom episode effects in the transmission to inflation shock and the monetary policy response.

8.1 Introduction

Earlier chapters established that synchronised booms and non-boom episodes in house price growth and credit growth impact inflationary pressures and the rate at which the repo rate responds to positive inflation shocks. This chapter extends the analysis on the impact of boom and non-boom episodes on asset prices by exploring the extent to which synchronised (i) commodity price growth and credit growth non-boom episodes and (ii) equity price growth and credit growth boom and non-boom episodes

N. Gumata, E. Ndou, *Achieving Price, Financial and Macro-Economic Stability in South Africa*,
https://doi.org/10.1007/978-3-030-66340-7_8

impact the reaction of repo rate to positive inflation shocks. Alternatively put, is the enforcement of the price stability mandate impacted by synchronised non-boom equity price growth, commodity price growth and credit growth episodes? Furthermore, do the effects of synchronised non-boom episodes differ between credit to companies and households?

This chapter fills several academic and policy research gaps. The gaps include exploring the extent to which synchronised equity price growth, commodity price growth and credit growth boom and non-boom episodes impact the response of the repo rate to positive inflation shocks. In addition, we establish whether the effects of synchronised non-boom equity price growth, commodity price growth and credit growth episodes differ between credit growth to companies and households. Furthermore, we assess the role of synchronised boom and non-boom episode effects in the transmission to inflation shocks and the monetary policy response.

8.2 The Identification of Cycles and Boom Episodes

This section starts by identifying cycles and episodes of booms and non-booms using the techniques discussed in earlier chapters. Figure 8.1 shows that post-2000 all the variables experienced a boom episode albeit with differing amplitudes and durations. The equity prices growth, commodity

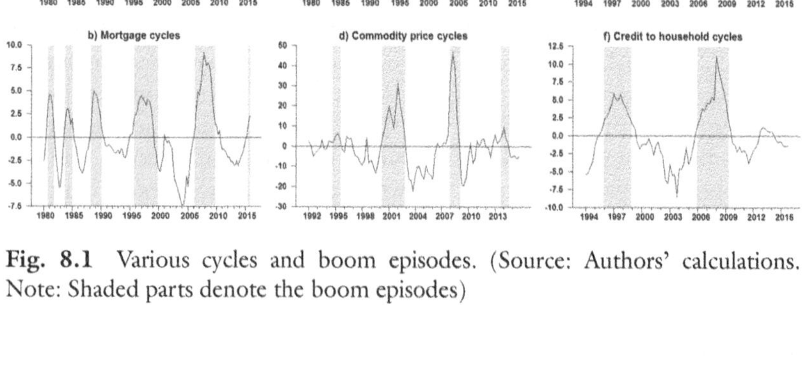

Fig. 8.1 Various cycles and boom episodes. (Source: Authors' calculations. Note: Shaded parts denote the boom episodes)

prices growth, the credit growth cycle and its components experienced a boom episode during 2005, which bust post-2009. On the other hand, the commodity price growth boom experienced a short-lived recovery during 2013, but the recovery was not synchronised with the credit growth cycle and its components. Hence the period post-2009 was characterised as non-synchronised booms in various financial variables.

8.3 Do Synchronised Boom Episodes Matter for Monetary Policy Responses to Positive Inflation Shocks?

To answer this question, this section performs a counterfactual VAR analysis and shuts off the synchronised boom episodes to estimate the counterfactual repo rate, and determines the size of the amplification effects of the boom episodes. The estimated counterfactual VAR model includes the GDP growth, CPI inflation, repo rate, R/US$ exchange rate changes and the boom episode variable. The boom episodes are for the (i) credit growth and equity growth and (ii) mortgage credit growth and equity growth. The boom dummy variables takes one when the boom episodes in these variables coincide and zero otherwise. The counterfactual repo rate response is the reaction of the repo rate to shocks when the synchronised boom episodes indicator variable is shut-off from transmitting the shock to repo rate in the model. The data is sourced from the South African Reserve Bank database. All growth rates are at an annual rate. The model uses quarterly (Q) data spanning 1995Q1 to 2015Q4. The model is estimated using two lags and 10,000 Monte Carlo draws. The main aim of this section is to show the sizes of the amplification related to synchronised equity market or commodity price growth and credit growth boom and non-boom in transmitting inflation shock to the repo rate. How relevant are the identified boom episodes in the amplification of the repo rate responses to positive inflation shocks?

Figure 8.2 shows the actual and counterfactual repo rate responses, and the gap between these responses measures the size of the amplification effects. We begin by showing the cumulative responses of the repo rate to positive inflation shocks and the role of synchronised (i) credit growth and equity price growth boom episodes (*Credit_equity*) and (ii) mortgage credit growth and equity equity price growth (*Mortgage_equity*) boom episodes.

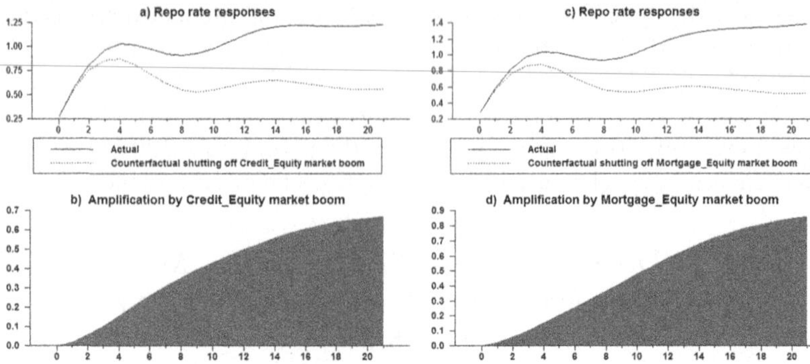

Fig. 8.2 Cumulative responses to positive inflation shocks and the role of synchronised equity price growth and credit growth boom episodes. (Source: Authors' calculations)

The cumulative actual repo rate response exceeds that of the counterfactual, indicating that the synchronised boom episodes lead to larger repo rate changes than what the counterfactual suggests. The positive amplification magnitudes in Fig. 8.2(b and d) indicate that synchronised booms lead to aggressive tightening in the repo rate due to positive inflation shocks than the level that would prevail in their absence. The implication is that synchronised (i) credit growth and equity price growth boom episodes (*Credit_equity*) and (ii) mortgage credit growth and equity price growth (*Mortgage_equity*) boom episodes propagate the inflationary pressures and result in aggressive repo rate tightening to curb the overheating effects. These results corroborate the findings in earlier chapters that credit-driven demand inflationary pressures underpinned by synchronised asset price growth and credit growth boom episodes tend to result in the aggressive tightening of the repo rate.

8.3.1 *Do Synchronised Non-booms Matter for the Monetary Policy Responses to Positive Inflation Shocks?*

This section continues the analysis using the model estimated in the earlier section but replaces the boom episodes variable with the non-boom episodes variable. Like the previous section, we focus on the synchronised non-boom episodes in equity price growth and credit growth categories. The results in Fig. 8.3(a and e) show that the counterfactual repo rate

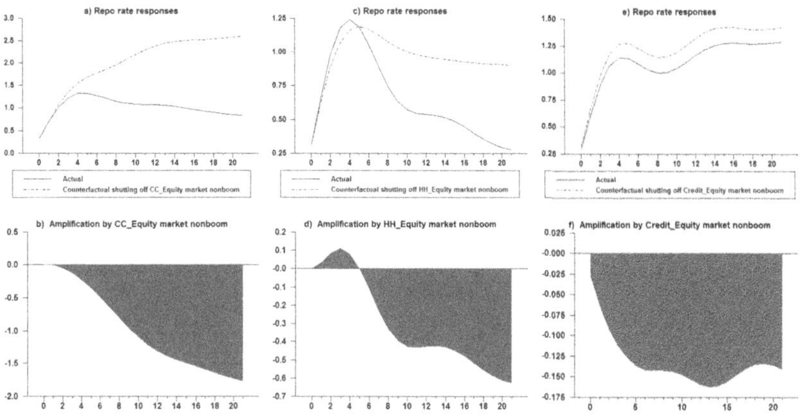

Fig. 8.3 Cumulative responses to positive inflation shocks and the role of synchronised equity price and credit growth non-boom episodes. (Source: Authors' calculations)

exceeds the actual repo rate. This indicates that synchronised non-boom episodes in aggregate credit and credit to companies with equity price growth exert downward pressure on the magnitude and pace of the repo rate tightening towards curbing inflationary pressures. The dampening effects of the non-boom episodes are larger when considering the effects of synchronised non-boom episodes on credit to companies and equity markets.

8.3.2 Do Synchronised Commodity Price Growth and Credit Growth Non-booms Matter for the Monetary Policy Responses to Positive Inflation Shocks?

This section extends the analysis of the role of synchronised commodity price growth and credit growth non-booms in the repo rate responses to positive inflation shocks. We find in Fig. 8.4(a and c) that the actual repo rate rises less than the counterfactual responses, which suggests that synchronised (i) credit growth to the corporate sector and the commodity price growth (*CC_commodity*) non-boom episodes and (ii) aggregate credit growth and the commodity price growth (*Credit_commodity*) non-boom episodes dampened the transmission of inflationary pressures to the repo rate responses. However, the synchronised commodity

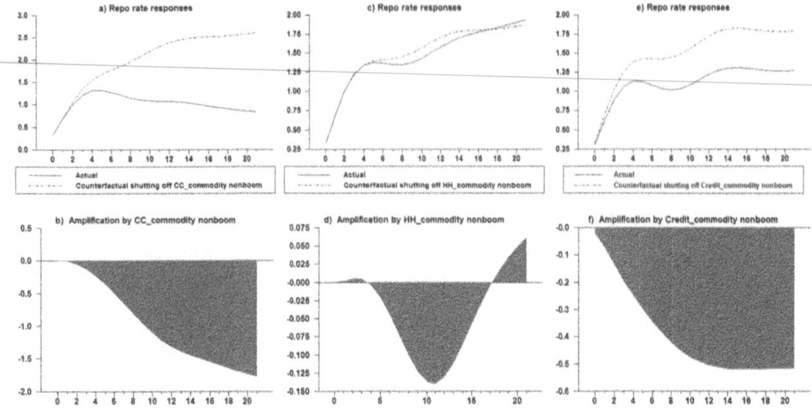

Fig. 8.4 Cumulative responses to positive inflation shocks and the role of synchronised commodity price growth and credit growth non-boom episodes. (Source: Authors' calculations)

price growth and credit growth to the household sector (*HH_commodity*) non-boom in Fig. 8.4(b) have little dampening effect on the transmission of inflation shocks to the repo rate responses.

Evidence shows that synchronised commodity price growth and credit growth to the corporate sector non-boom episodes have a larger dampening impact on the transmission of positive inflation shocks to the repo rate than the synchronised non-boom episodes in commodity price growth and credit growth to the household sector.

In addition, to test for the robustness of the earlier findings, we estimate a VAR model. We make endogenous–exogenous assumptions regarding the role of synchronised non-boom episodes in commodity price growth and aggregate credit growth (*CC_commodity*) or credit growth to the corporate sector (*Credit_commodity*). The evidence in Fig. 8.5 indicates that the results are robust, whether we include the non-boom episodes as endogenous or exogenous variables in the model. Synchronised commodity price growth and credit growth to the corporate sector non-boom episodes have a larger dampening impact on the transmission of inflation shocks to the repo rate compared to the propagation effects exerted by synchronised non-boom episodes on commodity price growth and credit growth to the household sector.

We conclude the analysis by performing a comparison of the (i) commodity price growth boom episodes and aggregate credit growth

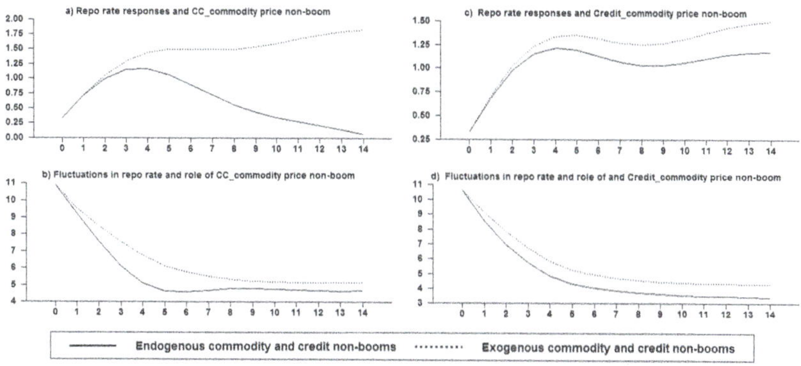

Fig. 8.5 Cumulative responses to positive inflation shocks and the role of synchronised commodity price growth and credit growth non-boom episodes in the endogenous-exogenous model. (Source: Authors' calculations)

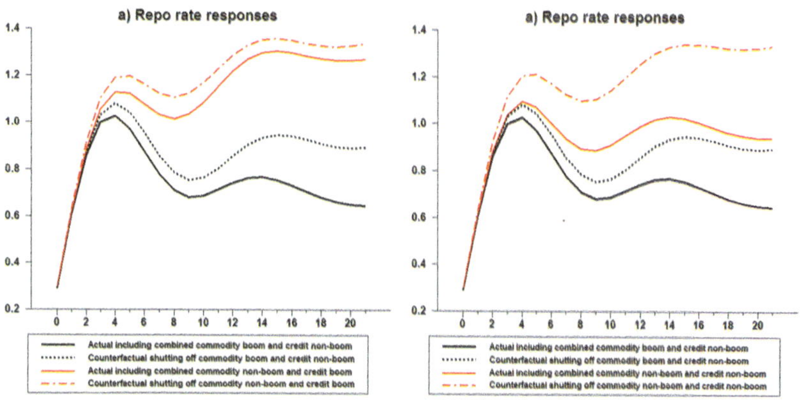

Fig. 8.6 Cumulative responses to positive inflation shocks and the role of synchronised commodity price growth and credit growth booms and non-booms. (Source: Authors' calculations)

non-boom episodes versus commodity price growth boom and aggregate credit growth boom episodes; and (ii) commodity price growth boom episodes and aggregate credit growth non-boom episodes versus aggregate credit growth and commodity price growth non-boom episodes. Evidence in Fig. 8.6 shows that the cumulative repo rate response would be much lower during periods of commodity price growth booms and credit growth non-booms. In contrast, the repo rate is aggressively tightened during periods of commodity price growth non-boom episodes and aggregate credit growth boom episodes. This shows that credit growth boom episodes have a bigger influence on the magnitude and pace of the repo rate tightening to positive inflation shocks.

8.4 Conclusion and Policy Implications

This chapter explored whether synchronised boom episodes in credit growth, commodity price growth and equity price growth impact the response of the repo rate to positive inflation shocks. Evidence shows that they do. The synchronised boom episodes lead to larger repo rate changes than what the counterfactual responses suggest. The positive amplification magnitudes indicate that synchronised booms lead to aggressive tightening in the repo rate due to positive inflation shocks than the level that would prevail in their absence. The implication is that synchronised (i) credit growth and equity price growth boom episodes and (ii) mortgage credit growth and equity price growth boom episodes propagate the inflationary pressures and result in aggressive repo rate tightening to curb the overheating effects.

On the other hand, evidence shows that synchronised non-boom episodes in equity price growth and credit growth, and credit growth to the corporate sector, exert downward pressure on the magnitude and pace of the repo rate tightening towards curbing inflationary pressures. The dampening effects of the non-boom episodes are larger when considering the effects of synchronised non-boom episodes on credit growth to the corporate sector and equity markets. Furthermore, synchronised commodity price growth and credit growth to the corporate sector non-boom episodes have a larger dampening impact on the transmission of positive inflation shocks to the repo rate compared to the propagation of synchronised non-boom episodes in commodity price growth and credit growth to the household sector.

But a comparison between the propagation effects of (i) commodity price growth boom episodes and aggregate credit growth non-boom episodes versus (ii) commodity price growth boom and aggregate credit growth boom episodes shows that the repo rate is aggressively tightened. This shows that credit growth boom episodes have a bigger influence on the magnitude and pace of the repo rate tightening to positive inflation shocks. Thus, the boom and non-boom episodes in credit growth, equity price growth and commodity price growth matter for positive inflation shocks and the rate at which the repo rate responds to inflationary pressures.

References

Borio C. 2014. "The financial cycle and macroeconomics: what have we learnt?", Journal of Banking & Finance, vol 45, pp 182–98, August. Also available as BIS Working Papers, no 395, December 2012.

Claessens S, and Kose M. 2018. "Frontiers of macrofinancial linkages", BIS Papers, no 95, January.

Claessens S, Kose M, and Terrones M. 2011. "Financial cycles: What? How? When?", IMF Working Papers, WP/11/76.

Gumata N, and Ndou E. 2017. Bank Credit Extension and Real Economic Activity in South Africa: The Impact of Capital Flow Dynamics, Bank Regulation and Selected Macroprudential Tools. Palgrave Macmillan. ISB 978-3-319-43550-3.

Harding D, and Pagan A. 1999a. Dissecting the Cycle. Melbourne Institute Working Paper No. 13/99.

Harding D, and Pagan A. 1999b. Dissecting the Cycle. Melbourne Institute Working Paper No. 13/99.

CHAPTER 9

To What Extent Do Capital Inflows Impact the Response of South African Economic Growth to Positive SA-US Interest Rate Differential Shocks?

Research Questions Explored

- Explore whether capital inflows impact the response of domestic output growth to positive South Africa-United States SA-US interest rate differential shocks.
- Assess whether the impact of equity capital inflows differs from that of debt capital inflows.
- Test whether the application of the interest rate parity condition has weakened post the recent global financial crisis.
- Understand the importance of the interest rate differentials during periods of asynchronised output growth.

9.1 Introduction

The United States of America Federal Reserve Bank (US Fed) tightened its monetary policy about four times during 2018. This is not surprising given that the economic fundamentals supported the US Fed policy stance. The fundamentals include high US GDP growth, the decline in the unemployment rate to post-2007 historic low levels and inflation remains below the targeted level. The tightening of the US monetary policy stance could lead to elevated exchange rate volatility of the emerging market economies' (EMEs) exchange rates due to capital outflows to the

N. Gumata, E. Ndou, *Achieving Price, Financial and Macro-Economic Stability in South Africa*,
https://doi.org/10.1007/978-3-030-66340-7_9

US. This chapter explores the extent to which capital inflows impact the response of the South African output growth due to positive SA-US interest rate differential (margin) shocks.

The Mundell-Fleming model predicts that the Rand exchange rate to the US$ (R/US$) denoted by (E) in Fig. 9.1 will depreciate following an unexpected US monetary policy tightening. The exchange rate depreciates from E0 to E1. The exchange rate depreciation is expected to shift the IS(E0) to IS(E1) in Fig. 9.1. All else equal, the R/US$ exchange rate depreciation should raise the domestic net trade balance to point B relative to what it would be at point A. Three important aspects arise in this setting. First, the monetary policy tightening by the US Fed will lead to capital outflows from EMEs such as South Africa (SA), thus leading to the R/US$ exchange rate depreciation. Second, the US contractionary (tight) monetary policy will be helpful to the South African exports. Hence, the South African income is expected to rise when net exports increase following the R/US$ exchange rate depreciation, *ceteris paribus*. Third, the increase in the domestic income should increase the transactions demand for money, thus putting upward pressure on the domestic interest rates to rise. The money demand increases as income rises. The increase in the SA policy rate to curb the increase in money demand should attract capital

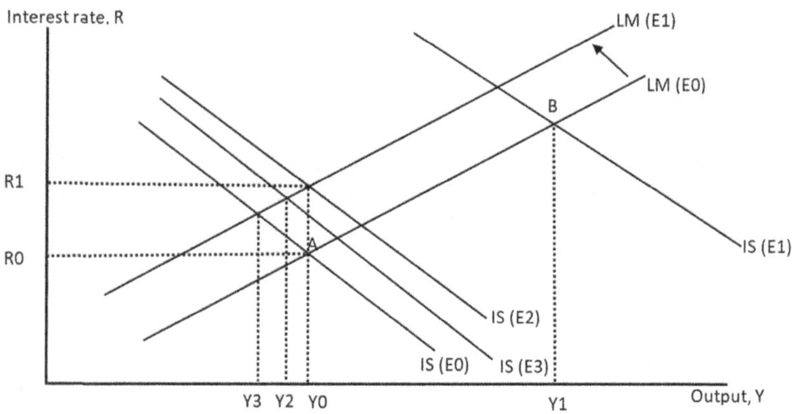

Fig. 9.1 Stylised expected responses of the domestic economy following a tight US monetary policy shock under the Mundell-Fleming model. (Source: Authors' drawing)

inflows, which in turn appreciates the R/US$ exchange rate. The R/US$ exchange rate appreciation erodes the initial exports competitiveness.

Thus, depending on the magnitude of the capital inflows and the R/US$ exchange rate appreciation, it is possible for the IS curve to shift all the way from IS(E1) to either IS(E2) or IS(E3) or IS(E0) in Fig. 9.1. The intersection of these curves with LM(E1) indicates the possibility that output may be lower than the original output (Y0) or return to the initial level as the R/US$ exchange rate appreciation erodes exports competitiveness.

This chapter fills the following academic and policy research gaps. First, we explore whether capital inflows impact the response of domestic GDP growth due to positive SA-US interest rate differential shocks. Second, we test whether the equity capital inflows shock differs from that due to debt capital inflows shock. Third, we examine whether the application of the interest rate parity condition has weakened since the recent global financial crisis. Fourth, we explore the importance of the SA-US interest rate differentials during periods of asynchronised output growth.

9.2 Why Is the Focus on the Capital Inflow Dynamics Important for This Study?

1. A surge in capital outflows from SA will lead to a sharp R/US$ exchange rate depreciation following the US monetary policy tightening.
2. An increase in the domestic policy rate should attract capital inflows. This is expected to appreciate the R/US$ exchange rate and erode the initial exports competitiveness.
3. Vast empirical evidence reveals that a surge in capital inflows significantly raises output growth. However, the analysis in most of these studies does not necessarily consider the role of the interest rate differentials. The impact of a surge in capital inflows can have the following effects: (a) output can decline below the initial level of output because of the R/US$ exchange rate appreciation effects on exports competitiveness; and (b) output can return to the initial level.

Given these possible outcomes, it is important to explore the extent to which an increase in capital inflows impacts the response of the domestic output growth due to positive SA-US interest rate differential (*hereafter referred to as the interest rate differential*) shocks. We pose the question:

Does the role of an increase in capital inflows vary depending on whether the increase is largely driven by equity capital inflows or debt capital inflows shocks?

This study is motivated by three reasons. First, we are of the opinion that the application of the interest rate parity condition may have been weakened post the recent global financial crisis. This is because the US and SA output growth rates used to be highly synchronised or highly correlated before the onset of the global financial crisis in 2007. The high correlation between the output growth has weakened in recent years, as the US output growth has been robustly rising while SA has been experiencing a prolonged period of low and volatile growth, which, at times, has entered recessionary territory. We think that the synchronised business cycles pre-global financial crisis in 2007 have rendered the implications of the output growth repercussions theory pre-2007 financial crisis understandable in explaining the increase in the SA-US interest rate differentials. According to the repercussions theory, an increase in US output growth should lead to increased demand for goods from other economies, including SA. This will lead to synchronised or correlated output growth cycles. In turn, this raises the likelihood that actual output levels can exceed potential output in both economies, also resulting in synchronised output-gaps. The synchronised output-gaps should also lead to synchronised inflationary pressures, that is, if the Philips curve holds. In return, high inflation will raise the demand for money. The rise in the money demand will then lead to synchronised interest rate movements, instantaneously or with a lag, thus curbing actual and expected inflationary pressures.

The second motivation is based on the policy implications of the asynchronised output growth between South Africa and the US post-2009. South Africa had volatile and subdued GDP growth post-2009, whereas the US has had high output growth. Given the SA economic growth challenges, have the predictions of international macroeconomics theory evolved with time to offer guidance on how the interest rate parity condition should be applied? This is because empirical studies have shown that the size of the exchange rate pass-through (ERPT) coefficients in SA has weakened over time and has become smaller.[1] This has occurred despite the fact that the SA-US interest rate differential has narrowed and the R/US$ exchange rate has depreciated persistently post-2009. Third, we are

[1] See, for instance, Ndou et al. (2018) and Kabundi and Mlachila (2018).

of the opinion that there is a need to understand the optimal interest rate differential (margin), which should indicate what happens to capital inflows before reaching this threshold, at peak of this threshold and after the threshold point is passed. It is important to understand the interest rate differential and capital flow dynamics especially as the US economic fundamentals keep on improving while the SA economic fundamentals weaken and even take longer to improve. Such an exploration is also important as we borrow from the implications of the Laffer curve which shows that increases in tax rates will lead to falling revenues after some optimal tax rate. Can a similar pattern be observed for the influence of the interest rate differential on capital inflows?

Figure 9.2 links the relationship between the size of capital inflows and the interest rate differential. It shows that there is an interest rate differential (margin) threshold such that above this optimal limit, the size of capital inflows should start declining or there is an increase in capital outflows. On the other extreme, there will be no capital inflows at zero interest rate differentials. As the interest rate differential rises, there is an increase in capital inflows until an optimal interest rate differential is reached. Beyond the optimal interest rate differential, capital inflows may recede, and

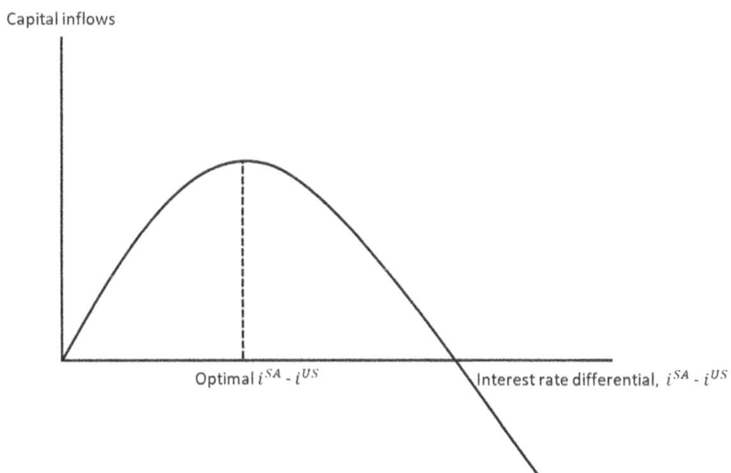

Fig. 9.2 Capital inflows and the interest rate differential. (Source: Authors' drawing)

capital outflows may be triggered. This is because investors begin to weigh the adverse effects of policy rate increases on the evolution of other capital flow pull factors such as business confidence, consumer confidence, GDP growth, investment spending growth and consumption expenditure growth. It is an undisputable fact that high GDP growth is also an important pull factor in attracting capital inflows.

In addition, it is reasonable to assume that the optimal interest rate differential (margin) is much lower in a subdued output growth environment compared to that in high output growth regimes. Hence, the worsening in output growth may lead to capital outflows despite the prevailing high interest rate differential. This happens if output growth has a higher weight on the choices of inputs in the compilation of the investor portfolios.[2] If other factors dominate the influence of the interest rate differential (margin), this offers policymakers an opportunity to adopt alternative policy options which may have less adverse effects on economic growth. It thus becomes important that the importance attached to the interest rate differentials (margins) during periods of asynchronised output growth is considered.

9.3 Empirical Results

This section estimates the role of the capital inflow channel in transmitting the positive SA-US interest rate differential shock into domestic output growth. We establish these channels of transmission by estimating various counterfactual VAR models. In all instances, the counterfactual responses are those in which the role of the capital inflow channel in transmitting a positive one standard deviation SA-US interest rate differential shock into domestic output growth is shut-off. The shock denotes approximately a 100-basis point increase in the SA-US interest rate differential. This analysis uses quarterly (Q) data spanning 1990Q1 to 2007Q2. All models are estimated using two lags and include a dummy variable for the adoption of the inflation-targeting framework in South Africa. The inflation-targeting dummy variable takes on the values of one during the period of inflation targeting, and zero otherwise.

[2] This is supported by literature which indicates the non-linear effect of the policy rate on economic growth.

9.3.1 *Evidence from a Three-Variable Counterfactual VAR Model*

The empirical analysis begins by estimating a baseline counterfactual VAR model with three variables, namely, the SA-US interest rate differential, SA output growth and portfolio inflows to SA as a per cent of GDP. The results in Fig. 9.3 show that the counterfactual output growth declines more than the actual output growth response. This evidence suggests that the portfolio inflow channel does not fully offset or neutralise the decline in output growth from an unexpected increase in the SA-US interest rate differential.

We determine the robustness of the role of the portfolio inflow channel in the preceding model by replacing this channel with aggregated capital inflow data as a variable. Figure 9.4(a) shows that the counterfactual output growth declines more than the actual suggests. This implies that increased capital inflows do not fully offset or neutralise the decline in output growth following an unexpected increase in the SA-US interest rate differential. Thus, we conclude that the results of the effects of the SA-US interest rate differential are robust to the changes in the specification of the model. The portfolio inflow channel and the aggregated capital inflow channel are unable to fully offset the effects of a positive SA-US interest rate differential shock on the domestic output growth.

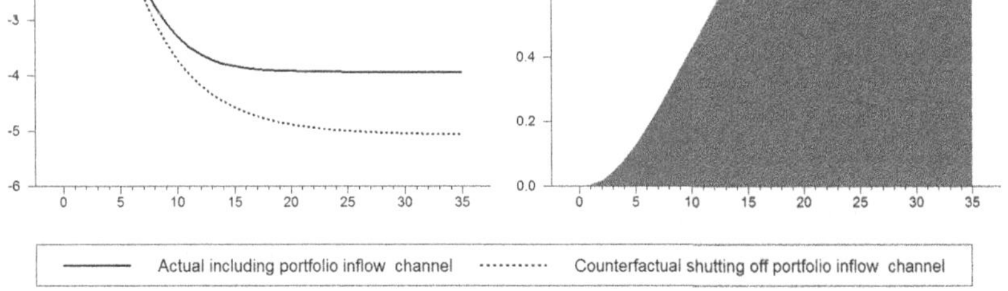

Fig. 9.3 Cumulative responses to a positive interest rate differential shock and the role of the portfolio inflow channel. (Source: Authors' calculations)

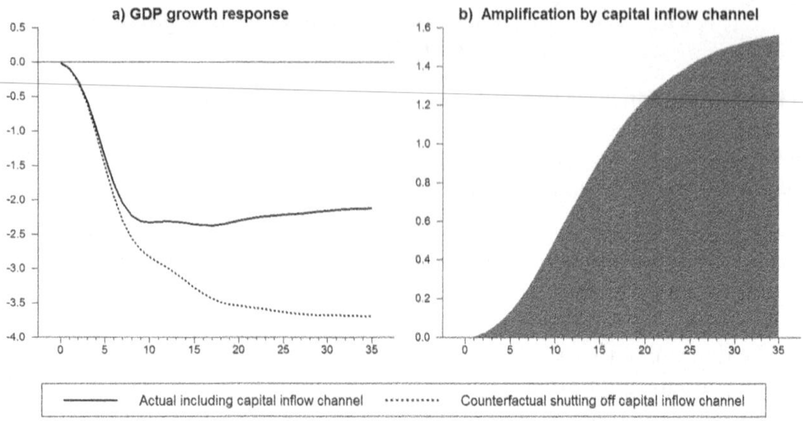

Fig. 9.4 Cumulative responses to a positive interest rate differential shock and the role of the aggregate capital inflow channel. (Source: Authors' calculations)

9.3.2 *Evidence from the Four-Variable Counterfactual VAR Model*

The analysis in this section conducts further robustness tests of the results in the preceding section by estimating an augmented baseline counterfactual VAR model. The augmented model includes the SA-US interest rate differential, SA output growth, SA consumer price inflation and either portfolio or aggregate capital inflows to SA as a per cent of GDP. The results in Fig. 9.5 show that the counterfactual output growth declines more than the actual output growth response. This indicates that both the portfolio and aggregated capital inflow channels do not fully offset decline in economic growth from an unexpected increase in the SA-US interest rate differential. The results are robust to using the aggregated capital inflow channel as shown in Fig. 9.5(c and d).

9.3.3 *Evidence Based on a Five-Variable VAR Model*

This section conducts further robustness tests by estimating an augmented counterfactual VAR model, which includes domestic consumer price inflation, the domestic nominal effective exchange rate (NEER) changes, the SA-US interest rate differential, domestic output growth and portfolio and aggregated capital inflows to SA as per cent of GDP. The exogenous

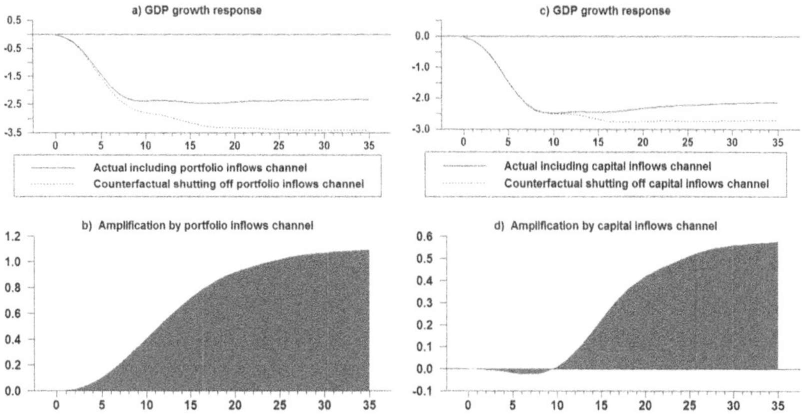

Fig. 9.5 Cumulative responses to a positive interest rate differential shock and the role of the capital inflow channel. (Source: Authors' calculations)

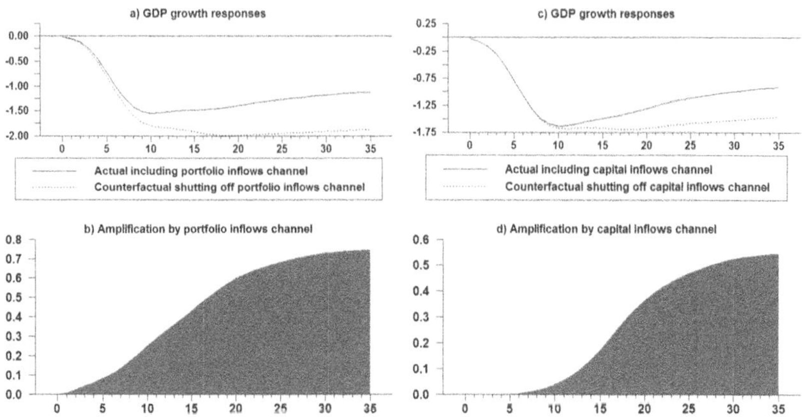

Fig. 9.6 Cumulative responses to a positive interest rate differential shock and the role of the portfolio inflow and capital inflow channels. (Source: Authors' calculations)

variables in the model include the US output growth, US consumer price inflation and changes in the All-shares price index. All growth rates (changes) are at annual rate. The results in Fig. 9.6 show that the counterfactual output growth declines more than the actual output growth response. This suggests that the portfolio and aggregated capital inflow channels do not fully neutralise the decline in output growth due to a positive SA-US interest rate differential shock. The results are robust to using R/US$ exchange rate and real effective exchange rate changes.

9.3.4 *Does the Role of the Capital Inflow Channel Vary Depending on Whether It Is Equity Capital Inflows or Debt Capital Inflows?*

We conclude the analysis in this chapter by establishing whether the different components of capital inflows differ in transmitting the positive SA-US interest differential shocks to SA output growth. For this exercise, the capital inflow channel is separated into debt capital inflows and the equity capital inflows channels. The debt capital inflows and the equity capital inflows to SA are expressed as per cent of GDP. The counterfactual VAR model estimated in this section includes the SA-US interest rate differential, SA output growth and either debt capital inflows or equity capital inflows to SA as per cent of GDP. The debt capital inflows and equity capital inflows channels are shut-off to calculate the counterfactual output growth responses. In Fig. 9.7, the counterfactual output growth declines more than the actual output growth response when considering the debt capital inflows channels. This evidence suggests that the debt capital

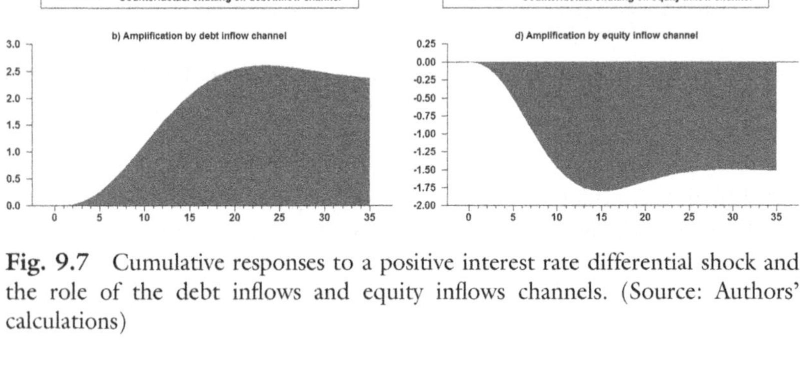

Fig. 9.7 Cumulative responses to a positive interest rate differential shock and the role of the debt inflows and equity inflows channels. (Source: Authors' calculations)

inflows channel mitigates the decline in economic growth from the increase in the SA-US interest rate differential. In contrast, actual output growth responses decline more than the counterfactual when including the role of equity capital inflows channel. This suggests that the equity capital inflows channel exacerbates the decline in output growth following a positive SA-US interest rate differential shock.

9.4 Conclusions and Policy Implications

To what extent do capital inflows impact the response of SA GDP growth to positive SA-US interest rate differential shocks? Evidence in this chapter reveals that an unexpected increase in the SA-US interest rate differential lowers SA economic growth. The actual decline in economic growth is lower than that suggested by the counterfactual response. This implies that the increase in the capital inflows following an unexpected increase in the SA-US interest rate differential does not fully prevent the decline in economic growth. This suggests that capital inflows due to an unexpected increase in the SA-US interest rate differential are not large enough to raise economic growth to fully neutralise the adverse effects of a tight monetary policy stance. An effective outcome is achieved when the adverse effects of the interest rate shocks on growth are fully offset by the beneficial effects of capital inflows in stimulating economic growth. These results imply that, first, it is important to quantify the extent to which the interest rate differential compares to other pull factors in attracting capital inflows. If other factors dominate the influence of the interest rate differential, this offers policymakers the opportunity to adopt alternative policy options, which may have less adverse effects on economic growth. Second, there is a need to understand how the optimal interest rate differential threshold, which indicates what happens to capital inflows before reaching this limit, at peak and after this threshold point, affects domestic output growth. This requires determining whether the SA-US interest rate differential threshold differs between the high economic growth scenarios compared to that in very low growth or recessionary environment. The non-consideration of the SA-US interest rate threshold effects in policy discussions weakens the importance attached to the interest rate differential in periods of asynchronous economic growth.

References

Kabundi A, and Mlachila M. 2018. Monetary policy credibility and exchange rate pass through in South Africa, IMF Working Paper No. 4 WP/18/04.

Ncube M, Ndou E, and Gumata N. 2016. Global Growth and Financial Spillovers and the South African Macro-economy, Palgrave Macmillan. ISBN 978-1-137-51296-3.

Ndou E, Gumata N, and Tshuma M M. 2018. Exchange rate pass through, second round effects and inflation process, Evidence from South Africa. Palgrave Macmillan. ISBN 978-3-030-13932-2.

PART II

The Interaction of the South African Reserve Bank, Public Investment Corporation and Private Banks' Balance Sheets: Effects on Fiscal and Monetary Policy Tools

CHAPTER 10

Is There a Compelling Case to Increase the SARB Holdings of Government Securities to Supplement Interest Income and Neutralise Losses Due to Foreign Investments and Foreign Currency Reserves Accumulation?

Research Questions Explored

- Explore whether there is a compelling case for the South African Reserve Bank (SARB) to increase its holdings of government securities to supplement interest income and neutralise losses due to foreign investments and foreign currency reserves accumulation (forex reserves accumulation).
- Assess the channels through which the effects of an increase in the SARB balance sheet are transmitted through, such as the supply-induced and reserve-induced portfolio balance effects and the re-anchoring channel.
- Establish the impact of SARB asset purchases on government bond yields, short-term interest rates, R/US$ exchange rate, inflation outcomes and expectations, output growth, employment growth, the unemployment rate and income inequality (Gini coefficient).

N. Gumata, E. Ndou, *Achieving Price, Financial and Macro-Economic Stability in South Africa*,
https://doi.org/10.1007/978-3-030-66340-7_10

10.1 Introduction

Is there a compelling case for the SARB to increase its holdings of government securities on the balance sheet, alternatively, to embark on large-scale asset purchases (LSAPs) of government securities, to supplement interest income and neutralise losses due to foreign investments and foreign currency reserves accumulation? This question arises because the costs associated with forex reserves accumulation and the sterilisation of Rand liquidity created in the process have resulted in the SARB incurring persistent losses post-2009. Foreign currency reserves constitute 90 per cent of the SARB balance sheet and in the period post-2009, which was associated with very low global interest rates and yields, the returns on foreign investments have been insufficient for the SARB's operational costs.[1] For instance, Fig. 10.1 shows that post-2009, as the policy rates in the United States (US) hit the lower bound, the Treasury Bill (TB) rates and the ten-year government bond yields declined, negatively affecting the returns on these assest classes.

In addition, during this period, the interest rate differentials widened in favour of South African (SA) assets, as shown in Fig. 10.1. The widening in the interest rate differentials means that an asset allocation strategy that

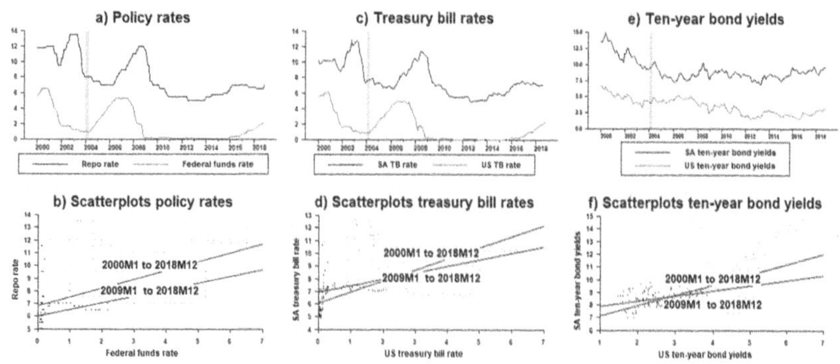

Fig. 10.1 SA and US policy rates and government yields. (Source: South African Reserve Bank, Fred data and authors' calculations)

[1] See various annual reports post-2009 for detailed reporting on the financial performance of the Bank. https://www.resbank.co.za/Lists/News%20and%20Publications/Attachments/6293/Annual%20Financial%20Statements%2031%20March%202014.pdf.

sought to increase the share of South African assets on the SARB's balance sheet would have greatly neutralised losses due to foreign investments. The trends in Fig. 10.2 show that whereas foreign investments were earning less than 2 per cent depending on the maturities of the investments, local currency investments were consistently recording returns above 5 per cent and these were not associated with the exchange rate valuation risks.

It is against this background that this chapter explores whether there is a compelling case to increase the SARB holdings of government securities, alternatively, to embark on LSAPs to supplement interest income and neutralise losses due to foreign investments and foreign currency reserves accumulation.[2] Large-scale asset purchases of government securities, or quantitative easing (QE), is defined as the outright purchase of government and other securities funded by the creation of central bank reserves.[3] Since the 2007 global financial crisis, central bank balance sheet expansions have

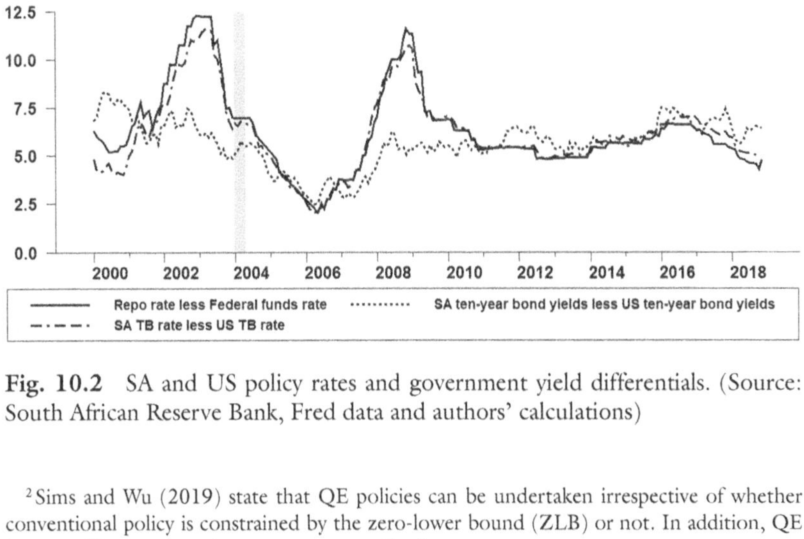

Fig. 10.2 SA and US policy rates and government yield differentials. (Source: South African Reserve Bank, Fred data and authors' calculations)

[2] Sims and Wu (2019) state that QE policies can be undertaken irrespective of whether conventional policy is constrained by the zero-lower bound (ZLB) or not. In addition, QE is more effective when short-term rates are fixed.

[3] The policy of QE or central bank expansion is different to that of changing the composition of the central bank's balance sheet, which is often referred to as credit easing, alternatively, comprehensive credit easing. In such instances, the central bank shifts between short-maturity and longer-maturity government bonds or shifts into riskier private assets, such as corporate bonds or equities. Ito (2014) states that at its core, comprehensive credit easing is aimed at purchasing assets of dysfunctional markets, while QE is aimed at expanding the monetary base to stimulate demand.

taken on an explicit monetary policy objective, leading to a substantial increase in central banks' balance sheets relative to nominal GDP and to the stock of outstanding government debt.[4] The size of the balance sheet became a major monetary policy tool to complement the policy rates as monetary policy tools. Central banks in advenced economies such as the the US, Europe, United Kingdom (UK) and Japan embarked on LSAPs or QE and purchased trillions of dollars of assets to reinforce accommodative monetary policy and stimulate their economies, as policy rates were constrained at the zero-lower bound.

However, while it is widely accepted that QE has helped reduce long-term interest rates, increased other asset prices and supported real economic activity, the proper identification and understanding of the channels of transmission to long-term yields, other asset prices and real economic activity remains partial, theoretically as well as empirically. For instance, Christensen and Krogstrup (2016) argue that central bank asset purchases can result into (i) supply-induced portfolio balance and (ii) reserve-induced portfolio balance effects, as was the case in the QE conducted by the United States Federal Reserve Bank (US Fed), Bank of England (BoE), European Central Bank (ECB) and the Bank of Japan (BoJ). These central banks conducted QE predominantly via the purchase of long-term bonds. On the other hand, the Swiss National Bank (SNB) conducted a QE programme without any purchase of long-term assets but managed to lower long-term yields.

The key channel of transmission of QE is the portfolio balance effect and can be decomposed into (i) the traditional supply-induced portfolio balance effect associated with the decrease in yields due to the shortage (reduction in supply) of long-term bonds[5] and (ii) the reserve-induced portfolio balance effect, which occurs due to the increase in the supply of bank reserves that accompanies asset purchases. Against this background, this chapter asks: Is there a compelling case to increase for the SARB the holdings of government securities on its balance sheet to supplement the interest income and neutralise losses due to foreign investments and foreign currency reserves accumulation? Contrary to the intentions of QE in advanced economies, which was to reinforce or propagate the impact of

[4] Haldane et al. (2016) state that in previous centuries, monetary policy injections through the central bank balance sheets were associated with the financing of wars or the bail-out of banking systems, rather than operating as a monetary policy tool.

[5] In the case of the traditional supply-induced portfolio balance effect, literature shows that the decline in the supply of long-term securities occurs through the signalling channel and when central banks conduct QE through the purchase of long-term securities.

monetary policy accommodation on financial markets and real economic activity,[6] we argue that there is a case for the SARB to increase its holdings of government securities to supplement interest income and neutralise losses due to foreign investment and the foreign currency reserves accumulation programme. In this regard, our motivation is intricately linked to that of the Swiss National Bank.[7]

However, the fact that our motivation for the SARB to embark on LSAPs differs from that of major advanced central banks does not mean that the LSAPs by the SARB will not have a positive effect of lowering inflation, increasing output growth and employment growth and lowering the unemployment rate. In fact, we show that as part of monetary policy tools, even with a different motive, embarking on LSAPs operates through the same channels of transmission as those that would be active and potent in the case of dealing with financial market dislocations, depressed economic activity and subdued inflationary pressures, as was the case in advanced economies. Furthermore, considering the effects of QE on yields and the exchange rate, we argue that can it help in anchoring inflation expectations.

This chapter contributes to literature in this area in various ways. First, we assess the impact of LSAPs by the SARB on government bond yields and government interest costs, financial asset prices, the exchange rate, inflation, output growth and employment growth, the unemployment rate and the Gini coefficient (income inequality). Alternatively, we assess whether embarking on LSAPs by the SARB is consistent with the mandates of price, financial and macro-economic stability. Second, we use different approaches to identify and estimate the impact of QE on the financial and real economic sectors. In this case, we address the well-documented weaknesses of 'event studies' in assessing the impact of QE.[8] We use time

[6] See Gagnon et al. (2010) for further reading.

[7] See Christensen and Krogstrup (2016) for further reading.

[8] See, for instance, Li and Wei (2013) who show that results based on event studies are known to be sensitive to the selection of event windows. The event-study method involves focusing on the reaction of market prices over a fairly narrow interval after the QE-related news is released, with the aim of capturing the market's direct reaction to the news, abstracting from other factors that may also have been affecting asset prices. One judgement is how large to make the time interval (window) for comparison. This is because a very short window implies that there are risks of missing the full market reaction, as it may take time for the market to evaluate the news. On the other hand, if a very long window is chosen, the risks are that the estimated reaction can be contaminated by other news events not related to the announcement of QE. On the other hand, time-series regressions used in studies exploring

series methods, historical decompositions and counterfactual VAR approaches to assess the financial and macro-economic impact of LSAPs by the SARB.

10.2 The Main Channels of Transmission of Balance Sheet Policy

Haldane et al. (2016) indicate that as monetary policy tools, central bank asset purchases can be used for a variety of price, financial and macro-economic stability objectives. First, these tools can be used to provide liquidity support to the banking sector and improve the functioning of the monetary policy transmission mechanism. This was the case in the early stages of the recent global financial crisis when the US Fed, BoE and the ECB expanded their balance sheets using repurchase programmes. Second, the balance sheet tools can be used to influence credit and duration risk[9] in the private sector in cases where the central bank conducts outright purchases of long-maturity government debt funded by the creation of central bank reserves. The creation of central bank reserves is essentially at no (zero) credit risk and no (zero) duration risk. This is because in the case of government debt purchases, the extent of credit risk transfer is minimal since most government debt is perceived as low risk.

Haldane et al. (2016) identified several potential channels through which unconventional monetary policy tools (UMPT) or actions might operate, as shown in Fig. 10.3. First, the asset purchases by the central bank work via monetary policy signalling, where QE conveys extra information about the future path of short-term interest rates.[10] The signalling channel is largely through the communication of policy actions by the central bank, alternatively, the announcements of future balance sheet operations by the central bank. The balance sheet operations

the effects of LSAPs are likely to be susceptible to the small-sample bias, given the high persistence of supply variables and endogeneity problems. This is because changes in the supply of government securities are likely to be correlated with other factors driving the yield curve.

[9] During the 2007 global financial crisis, central banks went further along the credit risk spectrum by purchasing private sector assets through 'credit easing'. See Haldane et al. (2016) for further reading.

[10] According to Joyce et al. (2010), the signalling channel of central bank asset purchase captures news about the expected future policy rates. But it can be defined more broadly to include perceptions of the risks around the path of future short rates, which includes revisions to the term premia.

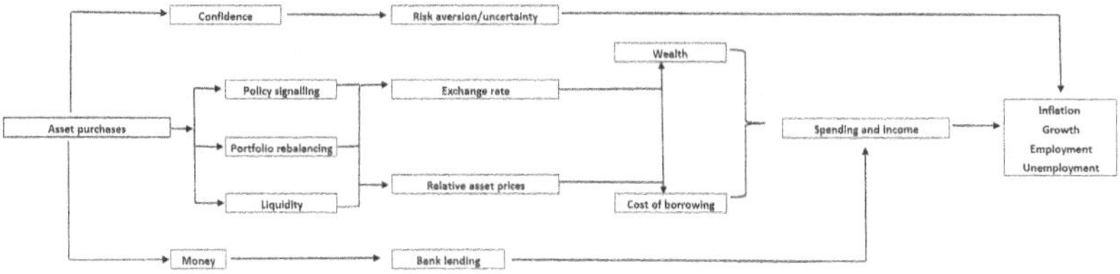

Fig. 10.3 The channels of transmission of central bank asset purchases. (Source: Adapted from Haldane et al. [2016])

undertaken by the central bank, or their communication, influence the public expectations about the key factors that underpin asset market valuation. These factors include expectations regarding the future course of policy, relative scarcities of different assets, their risk and liquidity profiles. It for this reason that the signalling effects of the asset purchase programmes (APPs) can lower government bond yields by influencing the two main components that shape long-term interest rates, namely expectations of future short-term rates and the term premium. Asset purchases by the central bank compress the term premia by removing duration risk from the market.

Recent empirical evidence shows that QE announcements have lowered yields on long-term government debt. For instance, Cœuré (2018) shows that there are sizeable announcement effects related to the stock of asset purchases. These effects occur whenever financial market participants receive new information about the parameters and timing of the central bank purchase programme. The parameters of the central bank asset purchase programme include its size, duration and composition. To this effect, evidence shows that the persistence of the effects of the central bank asset purchases matters. However, it is also true that the amount of central bank asset purchases needed to deliver a certain amount of the compression of the term premium falls over time as the acquired stock of assets increases. Along similar lines, Cœuré (2018) argues that central bank asset purchases in principle also have a signalling effect for the expected policy rate path because financial market participants generally do not expect the central banks to start raising the policy rate while still buying assets. Thus, the signalling effect of asset purchases is also likely to depend on the degree of uncertainty that investors have about the policy rate outlook.

Furthermore, empirical evidence shows that financial market participants generally want to see a clear commitment by the central bank to counter the downside risks. They want central banks to 'put their money where their mouth is'. To this effect, vast empirical evidence shows that the speech and commitment by Draghi, where he pledged to 'do whatever it takes' to preserve the euro, is seen as a turning point, to the degree that it removed the tail risks of a Eurozone breakup and thus narrowed the interest rate spreads of the countries that were severely affected by the sovereign debt crisis.[11]

Second, central bank asset purchases work through the portfolio rebalancing channel. In this case, QE induces a switch into longer duration or higher-risk assets. The portfolio rebalancing channel works though changes in the composition of private sector portfolios. When assets (and liabilities) are imperfect substitutes, changes in the relative supplies of financial securities brought about by the central bank operations can significantly affect the composition of portfolios, alter the behaviour of financial market participants and induce an adjustment in relative yields and asset prices. Andrade et al. (2016) argue that because the portfolio rebalancing channel involves a central role for changes in the valuation of expected future returns, it can also be referred to as the asset valuation channel.[12] Evidence shows that central bank QE interventions are associated with changes in other asset prices, such as equities, corporate bonds and exchange rates. These effects are transmitted via the exchange rate and relative asset price channels as QE lowers the price of domestic assets relative to overseas assets. Andrade et al. (2016) show that the portfolio rebalancing transmission channel also encompasses the (i) *duration risk channel*, which emphasises the importance of purchasing long-maturity bonds, and the (ii) *capital relief channel*, because the increase in asset prices that are generated by the asset purchase programmes are synonymous to a capital injection for leverage-constrained institutions.

[11] See, for example, how the ECB launched a landmark programme to purchase distressed debt in countries facing the burden of debt repayments and how potential liquidity persistently lowered the sovereign debt yield spreads. https://www.ft.com/content/45de9cca-fda7-3191-ae70-ca5daa2273ee.

[12] As the central bank purchases government securities, this reduces the supply of longer-term government securities, financial market participants rebalance their portfolios and this results in the increase in the price of the purchased security, lowering the yield of the asset concerned and those of close substitutes.

Third, central bank asset purchases work through the liquidity effects, bank lending channel and cost of borrowing. These effects occur as QE squeezes the liquidity premium on various assets, and the liquidity injected through QE into the economy in return for other assets increases the liquidity of the private sector balance sheets. Gagnon et al. (2010) show that LSAPs by the US Fed were transmitted through the risk premium on the asset being purchased, whereas the reduction in the long-term yields came through the narrowing in the risk premiums. The LSAPs removed a significant amount of assets with high duration from the markets thereby lowering the most important component of the risk premium, namely, the term premium.[13] Borio and Disyatat (2009) show that by providing funding at more attractive terms and larger quantities than market participants would have provided, the central bank can boost the volume of lending and asset prices.

In addition, Joyce et al. (2010) show that the presence of the central bank in the market as a significant buyer of assets can lead to the improvement in the market functioning and thus reducing the risk premium for illiquidity through the liquidity premium channel effect. The central bank's purchases may make it easier for financial market participants to sell assets when required, especially in stressed financial conditions when the illiquidity risk premium is significant. Improved trading opportunities and conditions could reduce the liquidity risk premiums embedded in asset prices and thus lower their yields. Gagnon et al. (2010) show that the liquidity channel of transmission was important in the early stages of the LSAPs programmes for certain types of assets. The combined effects of the LSAPs through the portfolio balance effects and the market functioning effects were the potent channels in the early stages of the financial crisis. Along similar lines, Bernanke (2018) provides evidence that the unusual severity of the 2008 recession was primarily due to the

[13] Gagnon et al. (2010) indicate that the high term premiums largely reflect the reluctance of financial market participants to bear the interest rate risk associated with holding an asset that has a long duration. Thus, by removing duration, LSAPs compressed the term premium across all asset classes. In addition, the purchase of mortgage-backed securities (MBS) reduced the amount of prepayment risk, causing the duration of MBS to shrink. Andrade et al. (2016) show that as the central bank eliminates some risk from the market through asset purchases, this induces a relaxation of the value-at-risk constraint, which translates in a reduction of the market price of risk. However, the reallocation and transfer of risks to the central bank's balance sheet is not neutral. But the central bank does not face any funding constraints and a value-at-risk constraint.

panic in funding and securitisation markets, which disrupted the supply of credit. This evidence underscores why financial stresses are economically costly. Nonetheless, the deterioration of household balance sheets and the associated deleveraging also contributed to the initial economic downturn and the slowness of the recovery.

Furthermore, central bank asset purchases can alter investor risk preferences and risk tolerance through the risk-taking channel, as identified by Borio and Zhu (2008). The authors show that easier funding conditions or the removal of risky assets from private sector portfolios can reduce the perceived risks and induce higher risk-taking. This effect also interacts with the ***search-for-yield*** behaviour associated with lower yields on benchmark assets. Changes in investor risk preferences also affect the exchange rate. Glick and Leduc (2012, 2015) and Neely (2015) find that the US asset purchases affected the US dollar.[14] In addition, Andrade et al. (2016) and Gertler and Karadi (2011, 2013) show that when banks face funding constraints that arise endogenously as a consequence of the banks' capital position, the mechanisms which activate changes in asset valuations activate the ***asset valuation channel***. The asset purchases by central banks replace long-term and/or riskier assets with short-term and safe central bank reserves. This mitigates the riskiness of banks' portfolios and allows banks to increase risky loans and reduce lending rates. The central bank asset purchases under this channel become more effective through the purchases of 'riskier' assets, that is, those with higher duration, higher liquidity or counterparty risk. This effect eases the banks' funding constraints and results in more potent macro-economic effects.

The confidence, risk aversion and uncertainty channel of transmission is activated as QE reduces the amount of volatility in markets or uncertainty about the outlook. Under this channel of transmission, QE is expected to affect the risk premia more broadly.[15] Borio and Disyatat (2009) show that this is because the announcement that the central bank is prepared to engage in operations involving illiquid assets may in itself boost investor activity in that market segment, thus reducing the liquidity premium and stimulating trading activity.

[14] See also Gumata and Ndou (2017) on the impact of various rounds of US QE on the US$/R exchange rate and the inverse transmission of positive global liquidity shocks into the South African economy.

[15] See Dale (2010).

The transmission of QE also works through the re-anchoring of expectations channel. Andrade et al. (2016) show that the uncertainty channel also affects the *re-anchoring channel*, which refers to the ability of the central bank implementing QE to reassure the private sector of its ability to anchor inflation expectations to levels consistent with the price stability mandate. If the private sector has doubts about the credibility of the central bank's medium-term inflation objective, it can try to infer any changes in the objective by using currently available information. Persistent upward deviations of inflation from the inflation objective that are not accompanied by sufficiently forceful countervailing policy actions affect the central bank credibility[16] and de-anchor inflation expectations.

All the channels discussed earlier are transmitted into the real economy and affect wealth, spending and investment decisions, output growth and employment growth, inflation, the unemployment rate and income inequality. Results from various studies show that greater liquidity injected through QE can push up the asset prices, which, in turn, reduces the cost of borrowing, and encourages higher consumption by households and investment spending by firms. Higher asset prices work via the wealth effects of asset holders to boost spending. For instance, recent literature shows that QE in the euro area through the ECB's asset purchase programme (APP) by stimulating economic activity and asset prices, affected income and wealth inequality among households. Ampudia et al. (2019) find that the ECB's asset purchase programme decreased income inequality, mostly by reducing the unemployment rate for poorer households and to a lesser extent by increasing the wages of the employed. They find that the indirect income channel has an overwhelming importance, especially for households holding few or no liquid assets. The indirect income channel is also a substantial driver of changes in consumption expenditure at the aggregate level. The effects of QE can mostly be ascribed due to the disproportionately large drop in the unemployment rate of low-income households produced by the APP. Furthermore, the authors find that QE has also helped to reduce net wealth inequality slightly through its positive impact on house prices.

However, it is also worth noting that all these channels also operate when using conventional interest rate instruments. But Haldane et al. (2016) note that the portfolio balance and liquidity channels are specific,

[16]See Ndou et al. (2019) on empirical evidence on the SARB credibility of monetary policy conduct.

if not unique, to QE. Similarly, Harrison (2017) argues that the portfolio balance mechanism is the predominant channel through which QE affects asset prices and the wider economy. In addition, Joyce et al. (2010) show that QE can be effective only if it changes expectations regarding the path of future policy rates and/or inflation. When financial frictions such as credit constraints or distortionary taxes or incomplete markets with imperfect substitutability between different assets are present, QE can also affect asset prices by changing the relative supplies of different assets.

10.3 Stylised Facts on Selected Central Bank Balance Sheet and Government Debt Indicators

This section starts by conducting some stylised facts on the SARB balance sheet and government debt. The intention is to assess the key characteristics of the SARB balance sheet. First, Fig. 10.4 shows that the SARB balance sheet increased post-2004 in line with the objective of increasing the level of foreign currency reserves.[17]

Second, Fig. 10.4(b) shows that foreign currency reserves constitute almost 90 per cent of the SARB's balance sheet. Third, the SARB holds less than 2 per cent of government bonds on its balance sheet. Alternatively,

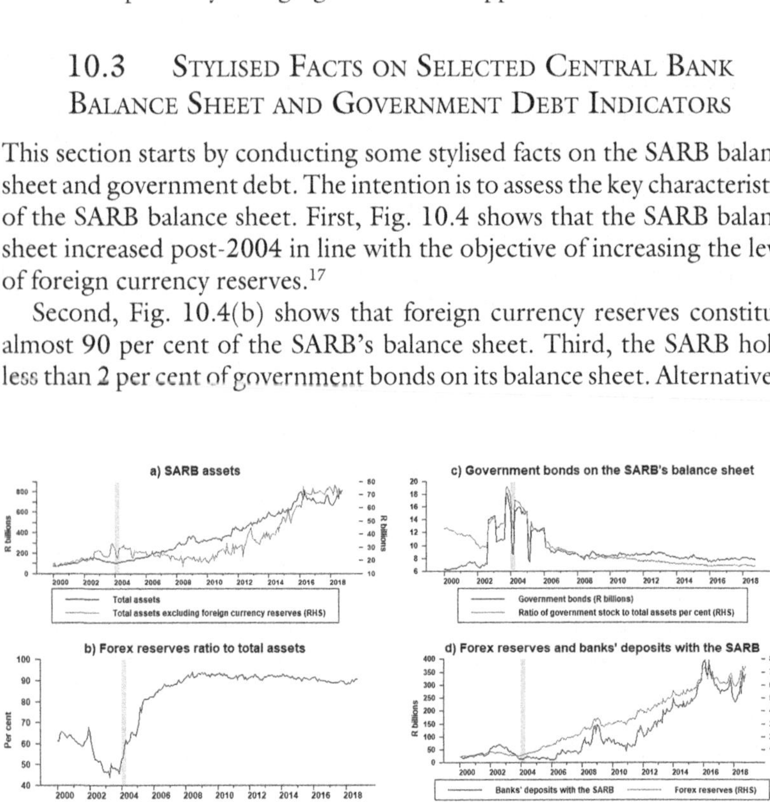

Fig. 10.4 Key characteristics of the central bank balance sheet. (Source: South African Reserve Bank and authors' calculations)

[17] Foreign exchange reserves accumulation is part and parcel of balance sheet policies, alternatively, monetary policy interventions. Analytically, it is a subset of balance sheet policies (Borio and Disyatat 2010).

of the R2.1 trillion outstanding government bonds shown in Fig. 10.4(b), the SARB holds around R7 billion as shown in Fig. 10.4(c). Fourth, Fig. 10.4(d) shows that the process of forex reserves accumulation has been associated with an increase in banks' sterilisation deposits with the SARB, which is on account of the sterilisation of Rand liquidity created in the process of reserves accumulation. As a result, the ratio of banks' deposits on the SARB's balance sheet to total assets has increased gradually and constituted more than 40 per cent at the end of 2018. Whereas government deposits with the SARB in Fig. 10.5(c) also increased from almost zero in 2004 to above 20 per cent in 2018.

On the other hand, the share of notes and coin in circulation in Fig. 10.5(d) has been on a persistent declining trend from above 40 per cent since 2004 to just below 20 per cent in 2018. This is because annual growth in notes and coin in circulation (cash in circulation) has also been on declining trend in line with subdued inflationary pressures as shown in Fig. 10.19 in the Appendix. Collectively, government deposits, banks' deposits and notes and coin in circulation constitute around 85 per cent of total SARB liabilities, as shown in Fig. 10.5(e).

A further disaggregation of the institutional holdings of government debt in Fig. 10.6 shows that on a comparative basis, the SARB holds less than 1 per cent of Treasury Bills, and short- and long-term government bonds.[18] On the other hand, banks hold the largest share of Treasury Bills

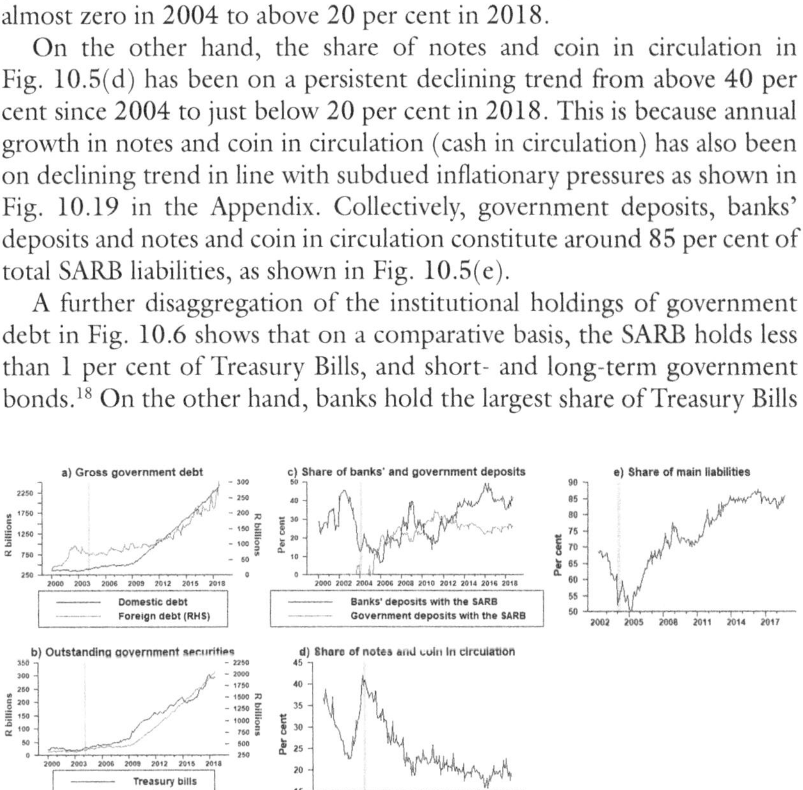

Fig. 10.5 Main characteristics of the central bank balance sheet and government debt. (Source: South African Reserve Bank and authors' calculations)

[18] See Fig. 10.20 in the Appendix for the institutional breakdown based on R billions.

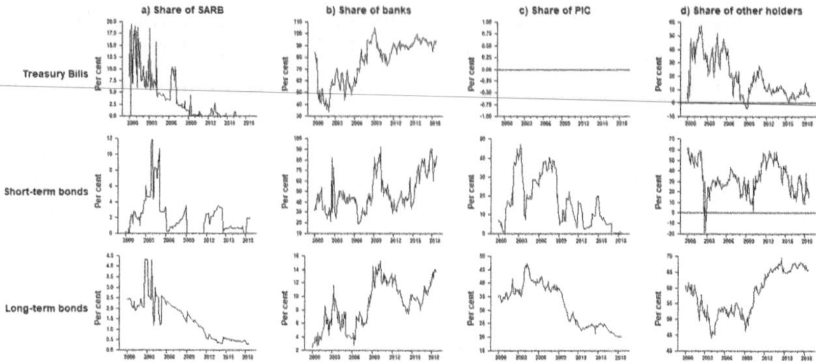

Fig. 10.6 Proportions of holdings of disaggregated government debt. (Note: PIC = Public Investment Corporation. Other holders include other pension funds, insurers, other financial institutions and non-residents. Source: South African Reserve Bank and authors' calculations)

and short-term government bonds.[19] The Public Investment Corporation (PIC) holds no Treasury Bills, has reduced its holdings of short-term government bonds to zero and long-term government bonds from 45 per cent in 2004 to just 20 per cent in 2018.

Other institutional holders of government securities hold a larger proportion of long-term government bonds and account for almost 70 per cent since 2015. The increase in the holdings of long-term government bonds by other counterparties coincides with the increase in government debt in 2009 and the inclusion of South African government bonds in the World Global Bond Index (WGBI) in October 2012.[20] Further disaggregation of government debt instruments by maturity in Fig. 10.7(a) shows that government has lengthened the maturity of outstanding TBs by issuing more long-term TBs since 2009 whilst decreasing the share of short-term TBs from almost 90 per cent of total outstanding TBs in the early 2000s to less than 10 per cent in 2018.

On the other hand, Fig. 10.7(b) shows that a large proportion of outstanding bonds is made up of fixed-rate bonds and inflation-linked bonds.

[19] These holdings are largely on account of banks' excess liquid asset holdings, which we explore in later chapters in the book.

[20] We explore the effects of LSAPs on non-resident purchases of South African securities and the R/US$ exchange rate in later chapters in the book.

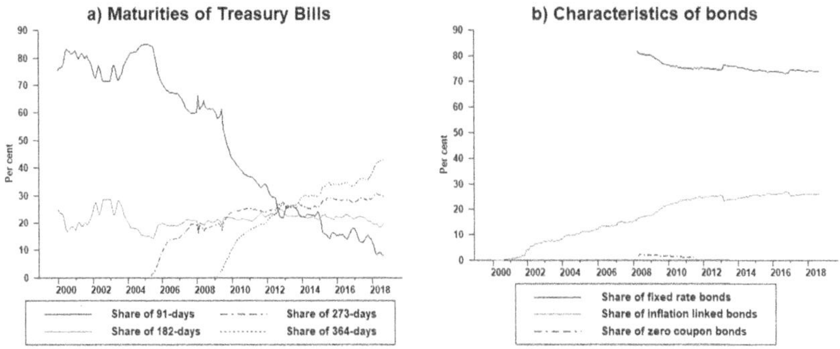

Fig. 10.7 Maturities of Treasury Bills and characteristics of outstanding bonds. (Source: South African Reserve Bank and authors' calculations)

10.4 SARB Balance Sheet, Selected Financial and Macro-economic Variables

What is the ratio of the Banks' balance sheet to GDP and how has it evolved over time? Figure 10.8 shows that the ratio of the SARB assets relative to nominal GDP increased in line with the accumulation of foreign currency reserves in 2004. The SARB assets increased from 8 per cent of GDP to 16 per cent in 2018.

Nonetheless, Fig. 10.9 shows that the SARB balance sheet as a ratio of outstanding government debt declined post-2009 as government debt increased at a faster pace compared to SARB assets. We show in later chapters in the book that the slowdown in the growth of the SARB balance sheet is largely explained by the halt in the forex reserves accumulation programme post-2009. Thus, the accelerated pace of government debt and the halting of forex reserves accumulation largely resulted in the decline in the ratio of the SARB balance sheet relative to outstanding government debt.

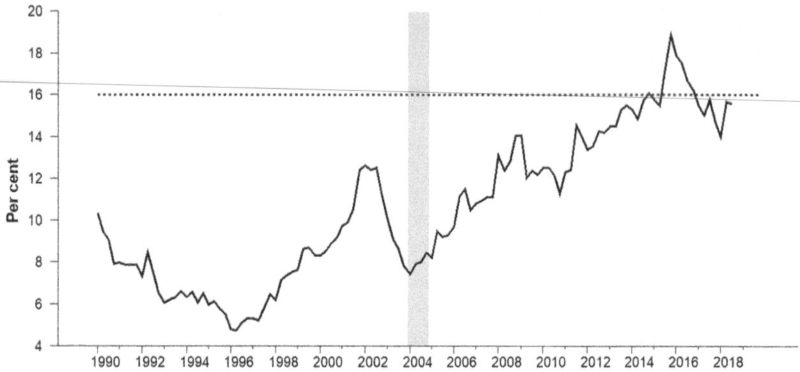

Fig. 10.8 SARB balance sheet as a ratio of nominal GDP. (Source: South African Reserve Bank and authors' calculations)

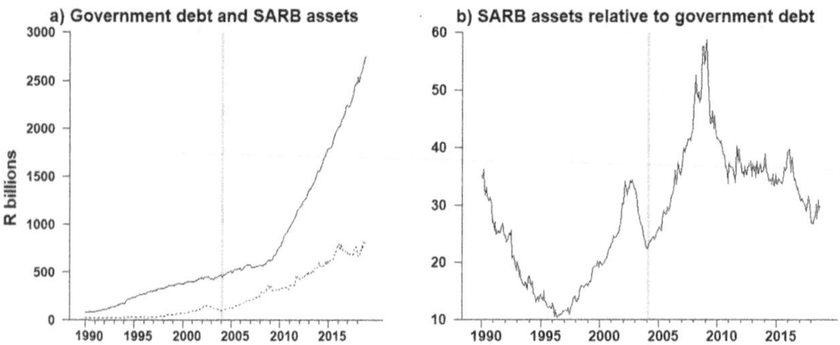

Fig. 10.9 Government debt and SARB assets. (Source: South African Reserve Bank and authors' calculations)

10.5 What Is the Impact of Positive Shocks to the SARB Balance Sheet on Ten-Year Yields, Term Spread and Weighted Government Debt Costs?

To answer this question, we start by exploring the nature of the association between the (i) SARB assets as a ratio of GDP with TB rates and ten-year government bond yields, and the (ii) repo rate, ten-year yields and the weighted cost of government debt. What happens to Treasury Bills and ten-year yields when the SARB assets-to-GDP ratio increases? Figure 10.10(b and e) shows that there is a negative association between

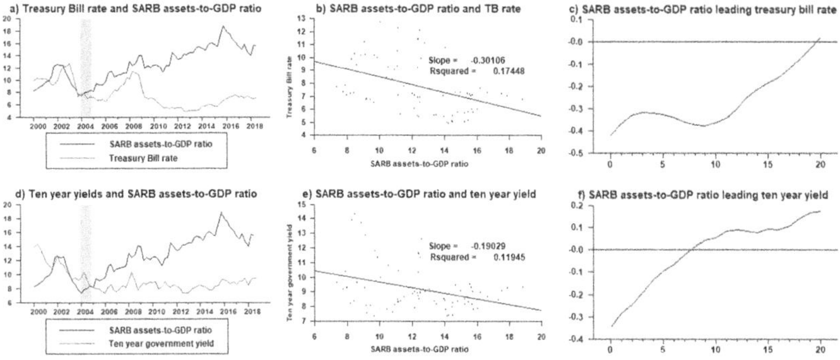

Fig. 10.10 SARB assets, Treasury Bill rate and ten-year yields. (Source: South African Reserve Bank and authors' calculations)

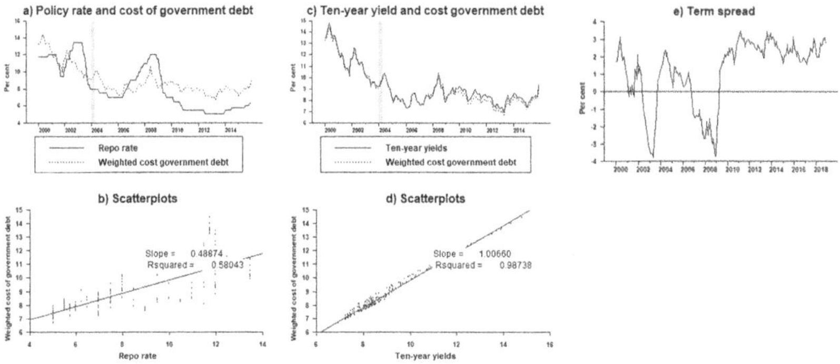

Fig. 10.11 Government weighted cost of debt, repo rate and ten-year bond yield. (Source: South African Reserve Bank and authors' calculations)

the SARB assets to GDP ratio, TB rates and the ten-year government bond yield. Furthermore, the TB rate and ten-year government bond yield decline when they are preceded by an increase in the SARB assets-to-GDP ratio in Fig. 10.10(c and f). Thus, the negative association between the SARB assets-to-GDP ratio, TB rate and ten-year government bond yield is robust. This means that an increase in the share of government securities on the SARB's balance sheet will exert downward pressure on interest rates and yields on government securities.

On the other hand, Fig. 10.11 shows how the term spread has evolved over time and that there is almost 100 per cent association between the government weighted cost of debt and the ten-year government bond yields and 60 per cent positive association with the repo rate. These stylised facts indicate that movements in the repo rate and government bond yields have large bearing on government debt costs and that policy interventions (factors) that lower the repo rate and the levels of government bond yields will also have a direct impact on lowering the cost of government debt.

We conduct further robustness tests and assess whether there are asymmetric responses associated with different shock sizes to positive shocks to SARB assets growth. We use the modified Kilian and Vigfusson (2011) approach to assess for the effects of one, four, six and ten positive standard deviations to SARB assets growth on TB rates and ten-year government yields. What are the implications for the monetary policy stance? Alternatively, what are the responses of the repo rate to an increase in asset purchases? We examine this question given the fact that the repo rate is an important anchor for the yield curve, Treasury Bills, other money market interest rates and the yield curve rates are priced off the repo rate.

The bivariate VAR models are estimated for the sample period 2000Q1 to 2018Q4. The models include growth in SARB assets growth, the interest rates indicator and the weighted cost of government debt. The interest rates indicators are the repo rate, three-month TB rate, ten-year yields and term spread. The repo rate, three-month TB rate, ten-year yields, term spread and the weighted cost of government debt enter the model separately. The growth rates are at an annual rate. The term spread is calculated as the difference between the ten-year yields and the repo rate. The model is estimated using 10,000 Monte Carlo draws and 2 lags. The results in Fig. 10.12 and Fig. 10.13 indicate that different sizes of positive (increase) shocks to SARB assets growth result in a decline in the repo rate, TB rate, government bond yields, term spread and costs on government debt.

The results concur with those in literature that show that LSAPs helped reduce long-term interest rates. For instance, Joyce et al. (2010) find that QE may have depressed gilt yields by about 100 basis points and that the largest part of the impact of QE came through the portfolio rebalancing channel, suggesting that the term premium effect has broadly coincided with the portfolio rebalancing effect. Furthermore, Andrade et al. (2016) show that for given amount of assets purchased, the macro-economic benefits are larger the higher the duration of the targeted assets. They argue that this evidence shows the direct implication of the duration risk channel.

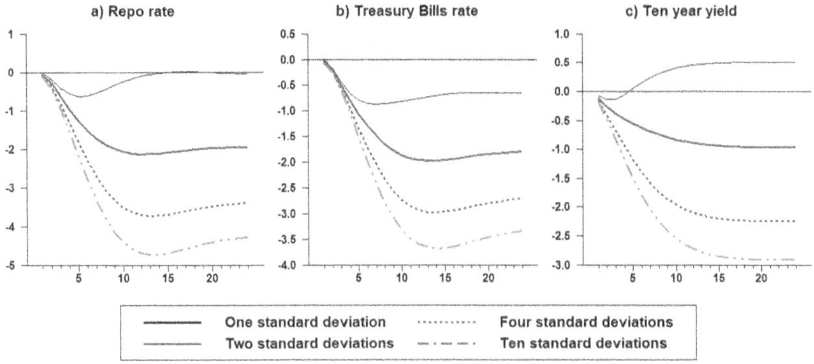

Fig. 10.12 Accumulated responses of the repo rate, Treasury Bill rates and ten-year government bond yields to positive shocks to SARB assets growth. (Source: Authors' calculations)

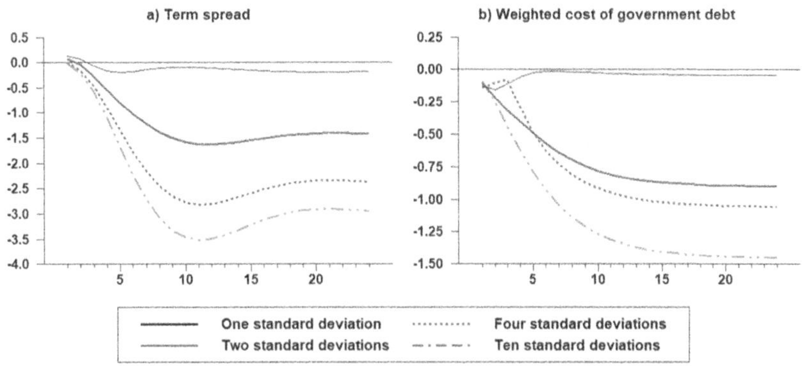

Fig. 10.13 Accumulated responses of the term spread and cost on government debt to positive shocks to SARB assets growth. (Source: Authors' calculations)

In addition, Joyce et al. (2010) find that the effects of QE also spilled over to other asset prices. They find that corporate yields also declined, liquidity in the corporate bond markets improved and net equity and corporate bond issuance increased after the implementation of QE. Similarly, Gagnon et al. (2010) establish evidence that large-scale asset purchases by the Fed led to significant, economically meaningful and a long-lasting decline in long-term interest rates on a range of securities, including securities that were not included in the central bank asset purchase programmes. The decline in interest rates primarily reflects lower risk premiums, including term premiums. Gagnon et al. (2010) estimate that the overall decline in the ten-year term premium on US Treasuries in response to the Fed's purchase programme was somewhere between 30 and 100 basis points. In addition to this effect, they find an even more powerful effect on agency debt and agency mortgage-backed securities. In the case of Japan, Ito (2014) finds that various rounds[21] of QE, coupled with forward guidance, lowered long-term interest rates and flattened the yield curve significantly and persistently.

Furthermore, Motto et al. (2015) find that euro area asset purchases had a sizeable effect on asset prices although the programme was announced at a time of low financial distress. These findings contradict existing literature that finds a large impact of asset purchases only in periods of high financial distress. Andrade et al. (2016) and Motto et al. (2015) find that large-scale asset purchases reinforced other channels due to the interaction between large-scale asset purchases and the asset composition of the asset purchases programme. Targeting assets at long maturities supported the duration channel and the credit channel. The authors find that euro area sovereign ten-year bond yields fell by 30–50 basis points. At the same time, the low degree of financial stress, prevailing at time of the announcement of the programme, weakened the local supply channel and facilitated spill-overs to non-targeted assets.

Evidence in this section is consistent with the effects of LSAPs on the duration risk channel, which posits that the bond risk premium increases the exposure of bond holders to the risk of unexpected future changes in policy interest rates. Long-duration bonds are riskier because they are more sensitive to interest rate risk. Thus, by reducing private sector holdings of such bonds, central bank purchases reduce exposure to duration risk and thus lead to a decline in yields. In addition, the announcement of the LSAPs exert downward pressure on market expectations of future short-term interest rates. The downward shift in the yield curve also reflects an improvement in the outlook for output growth. These effects on bond yields and the yield curve are consistent with the signalling channel.

[21] The first QE was introduced by the Bank of Japan (BoJ) in 2001 and maintained until 2006. The Bank of Japan adopted a new QE, termed QQE, under the comprehensive easing in October 2010.

10.6 Do Positive Shocks to SARB Assets Growth Exert Asymmetric Effects on the Rand/US$ Exchange Rate and Inflation?

The results in the earlier section indicated that the repo rate along with the TB rate and the ten-year yields decline in response to positive shocks to the SARB assets. Nonetheless, we are aware that the repo rate as a monetary policy tool is primarily aimed at responding to inflationary pressures. So, what is the effect of positive shocks to SARB assets growth on the R/US$ exchange rate, inflation outcomes and expectations? Like the earlier sections, we estimate several bivariate VAR models using the modified Kilian and Vigfusson (2011) approach. The models include SARB assets growth and one macroeconomic indicator. The macroeconomic indicators are the R/US$ exchange rate changes and headline CPI inflation. The indicators are included separately in the model. The models are estimated using two lags and 10,000 Monte Carlo draws. All growth rates are at an annual rate. For the R/US$ exchange rate changes, positive (negative) changes imply depreciation (appreciation).

The results in Fig. 10.14 show that the R/US$ exchange rate appreciates in response to an increase in the SARB assets growth (large-scale asset purchases) and inflation declines. These responses in part explain why the repo rate declines in response to LSAPs.

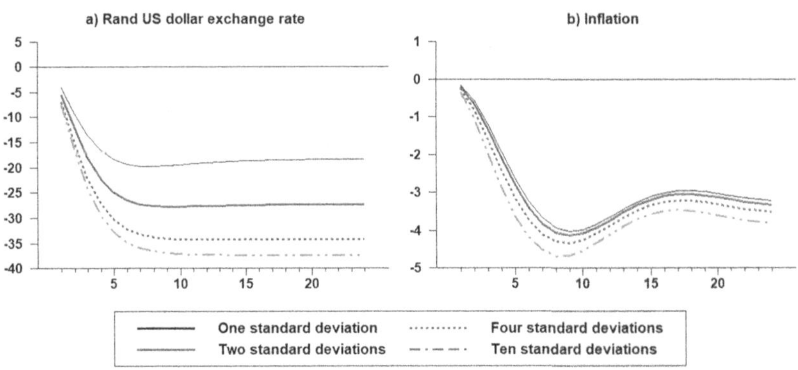

Fig. 10.14 Accumulated responses of inflation and the R/US$ exchange rate to positive shocks to SARB assets growth. (Source: Authors' calculations)

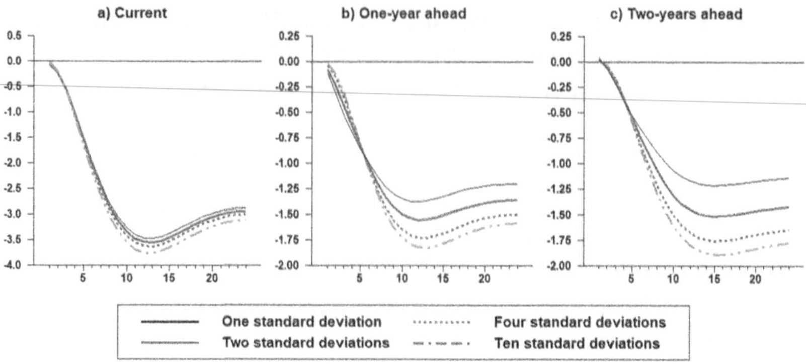

Fig. 10.15 Accumulated responses of inflation expectations to positive shocks to SARB assets growth. (Source: Authors' calculations)

In addition, the results in Fig. 10.15 indicate that inflation expectations across maturities decline. These results concur with evidence in Andrade et al. (2016) showing that the introduction of the asset purchases programme helps policy makers to guide long-term inflation expectations closer to the price stability objective. The authors refer to this effect as the 're-anchoring' channel. This is because LSAPs in part induce some form of certainty to the private sector about the length of the horizon over which price stability will be restored. As such their results provide evidence for the signalling channel and the re-anchoring channel at the time of the asset purchase programme (APP) announcement.

10.7 What Are the Effects of SARB LSAPs on Employment Growth, Unemployment Rate, Inequality and Other Key Macro-economic Variables?

Literature shows that QE in the US, the UK and the euro area stimulated economic activity and asset prices, affecting income and wealth inequality among households. Evidence shows that QE has decreased income inequality, mostly by leading to the decline in the unemployment rate for poorer households. The decline in income inequality through the increase in the wages of the employed was limited.[22] Furthermore, QE also helped to reduce net wealth inequality slightly through its positive impact on house prices. Luck and Zimmermann (2018) show that LSAPs, similar to interest rate cuts in times of conventional monetary policy, are transmitted into the real economy through the bank lending channel. To assess the effects of QE on employment growth, unemployment rate, inequality and other key macro-economic variables, we estimate various bivariate VAR models using the modified Kilian and Vigfusson (2011) approach. The models include SARB assets growth and one macroeconomic indicator. The macroeconomic indicators are GDP growth, investment growth, employment growth, the unemployment rate, Gini coefficient, household financial wealth and consumption. All growth rates are at an annual rate. The macroeconomic indicators are included separately in the model.

The results in Fig. 10.16 show that larger shocks to SARB assets growth exert larger increases in GDP growth, investment growth, employment growth and the unemployment rate. Similarly, the Gini coefficient declines more whereas household financial assets and consumption growth increase more due to larger positive shocks to SARB assets growth in Fig. 10.17. The results are robust to using the Gini coefficient in levels and household financial assets, as shown in Fig. 10.21 in the Appendix. Fig. 10.18 shows that, in part, the channels through which

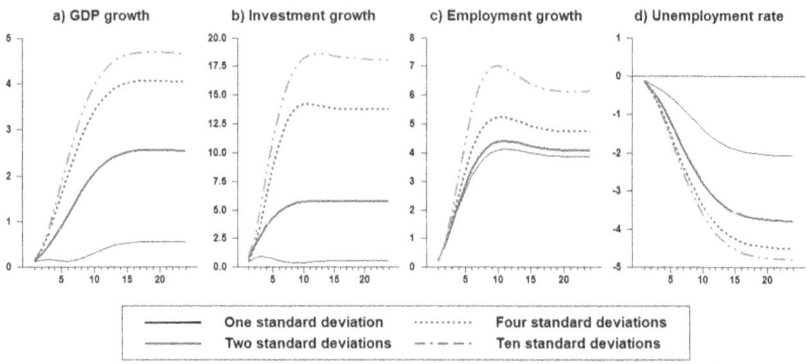

Fig. 10.16 Accumulated responses of GDP growth, investment growth and employment growth and the unemployment rates to positive shocks to SARB assets growth. (Source: Authors' calculations)

[22] See Lenza and Slacalek (2019), Ampudia (2019) and Constâncio (2017).

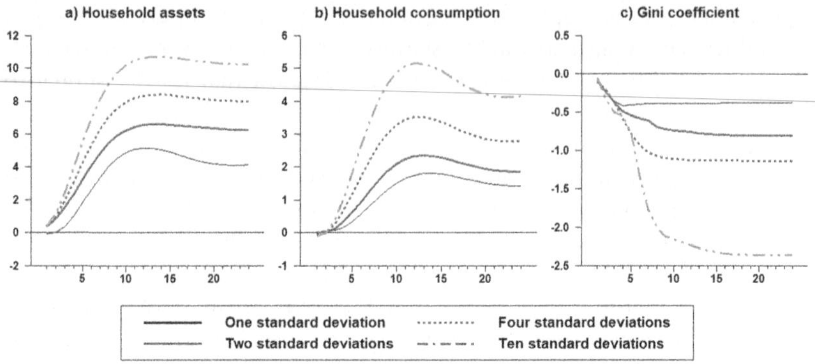

Fig. 10.17 Accumulated responses of the Gini coefficient, household assets and consumption to positive shocks to SARB assets growth. (Source: Authors' calculations)

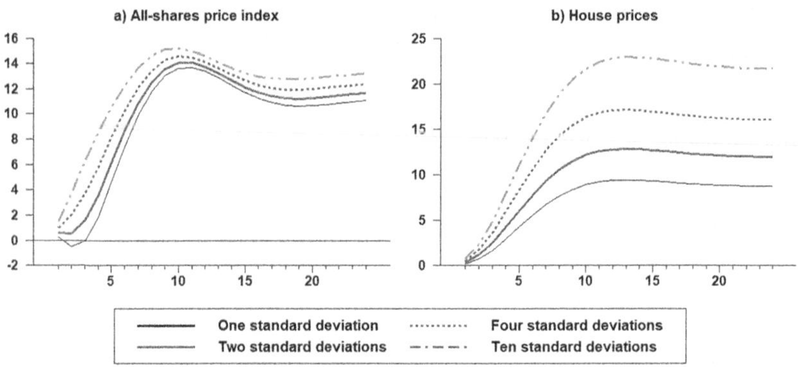

Fig. 10.18 Accumulated responses of equity and house prices to positive shocks to SARB assets growth. (Source: Authors' calculations)

household financial wealth and consumption growth respond to positive shocks to SARB assets growth are through increases in the All-shares price index and house prices.

These channels encompass what Andrade et al. (2016) refer to as the capital relief channel, which suggests that the higher prices of sovereign bonds induced by the APP benefited banks through the ensuing increased valuation of their bond holdings. This mechanism is referred to as the capital relief channel because it is analogous to a capital injection.

Their results show that the equity prices of banks holding a larger portfolio share of government bonds benefited more from the increase in bond prices. We explore the impact of LSAPs by the SARB on private banks' balance sheets in later chapters of the book.

Nonetheless, Andrade et al. (2016) indicate that there are financial stability risks associated with LSAPs. For instance, financial stability risks arise from the compression in spreads induced by LSAPs, which in the short run tends to reduce profits for banks and other financial institutions. However, their results suggest that this effect was probably more than compensated (neutralised) by the capital relief channel. In addition, risks of capital losses to central banks are less likely to materialise. This is because the more the LSAPs are successful in strengthening the economic and labour market recovery and in ensuring a faster return towards inflation levels consistent with the monetary policy definition of price stability, the lesser are the risks of capital losses to central banks, which can be prudently managed.

10.8 Conclusion and Policy Implications

Is there a compelling case to increase the SARB holdings of government securities to supplement interest income and neutralise losses due to foreign investments and foreign currency reserves accumulation? Evidence in this chapter establishes that there is. We find that an increase in SARB holdings of government securities exerts downward pressure on the repo rate, TB rate, ten-year yields, the term spread and government debt costs. An increase in the SARB holdings of government securities lowers domestic government bond yields and risk, and loosens the domestic financial conditions and the fiscal constraints. Evidence shows that an increase in the SARB holdings of government securities results in the appreciation of the R/US$ exchange rate, and lower inflation outcomes and expectations. These factors assist the SARB in achieving its price stability mandate of reducing inflation and inflation expectations. Furthermore, positive shocks to the SARB balance sheet assist in achieving macro-economic stability as they result in an increase in GDP growth, investment growth and employment growth and a decline in the unemployment rate and the Gini coefficient. Positive shocks to the SARB balance sheet are transmitted via the supply-induced, reserve-induced portfolio signalling effect and the re-anchoring channels. Increasing the holdings of government bonds on the SARB balance sheet is consistent with its primary mandate of price stability and macro-financial stability. The size of the SARB balance sheet is another major monetary policy tool to complement interest rates as monetary policy tool.

Appendix

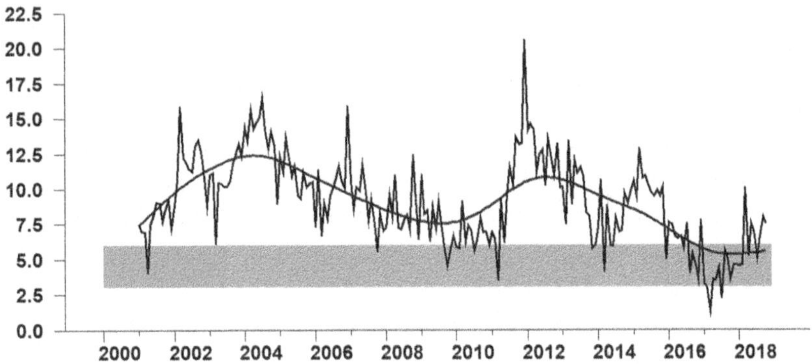

Fig. 10.19 Notes and coin in circulation. (Source: South African Reserve Bank and authors' calculations)

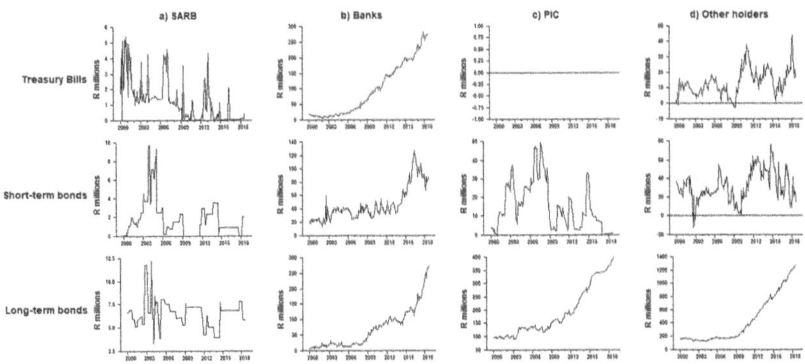

Fig. 10.20 Holdings of disaggregated government debt. (Source: South African Reserve Bank and authors' calculations)

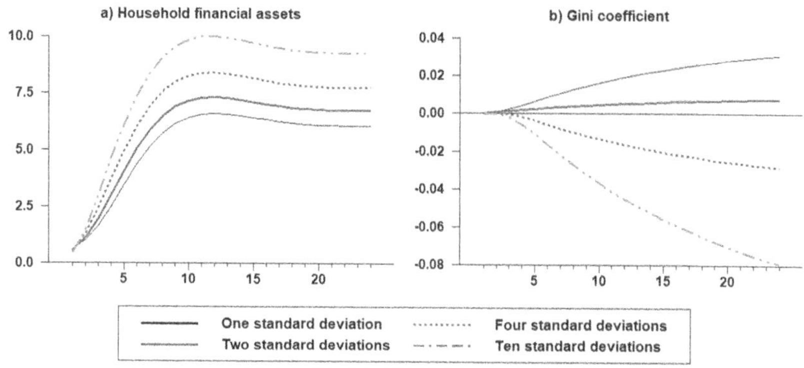

Fig. 10.21 Responses of the Gini coefficient, household assets and consumption to positive shocks to SARB assets. (Source: Authors' calculations)

References

Altavilla C, Carboni G, and Moot R. 2015. "Asset purchase programmes and financial markets: lessons from the euro area". ECB Working Paper 1864. https://www.ecb.europa.eu/pub/pdf/scpwps/ecbwp1864.en.pdf.

Ampudia M, Georgarakos D, Slacalek J, Tristani O, Vermeulen P, Violant G L. 2019. Monetary policy and household inequality. ECB Working Paper No 2170 / July 2018. https://www.ecb.europa.eu/pub/pdf/scpwps/ecb.wp2170.en.pdf?utm_source=ecb_twitter&utm_medium=social&utm_campaign=20181227_end_of_year_thread&utm_term=July_inequality.

Andrade P, Breckenfelder J, De Fiore F, Karadi P, and Tristani O. 2016. "The ECB's asset purchase programme: an early assessment". ECB Working Paper 1956. https://www.ecb.europa.eu/pub/pdf/scpwps/ecbwp1956.en.pdf.

Bernanke B. 2018. The real effects of the financial crisis. BPEA Conference Draft Fall September 13–14, 2018. https://www.brookings.edu/wp-content/uploads/2018/09/BPEA_Fall2018_The-real-effects-of-the-financial-crisis.pdf.

Bernanke B, Reinhart V, and Sack B. 2004. "Monetary policy alternatives at the zero bound: An empirical assessment," Brookings Papers on Economic Activity, 2, pp 10–77. https://www.federalreserve.gov/pubs/feds/2004/200448/200448pap.pdf.

Borio C, and Disyatat P. 2009. Unconventional monetary policies: an appraisal. BIS Working Papers No 292. https://www.bis.org/publ/work292.pdf.

Borio, C, and Disyatat P. 2010. "Unconventional monetary policies: an appraisal", The Manchester School, 78(s1), pp 53–89, September. Also available as BIS Working Papers, no 292, November 2009.

Borio C, and Zabai A. 2016. Unconventional monetary policies: a re-appraisal. BIS Working Papers No 570.

Borio C and Zhu H. 2008. Capital regulation, risk-taking and monetary policy: a missing link in the transmission mechanism? BIS Working Papers No 268.

Broadbent B. 2018. Discussion of "Unconventional Monetary Policies in the Euro Area, Japan and the United Kingdom." https://www.brookings.edu/wp-content/uploads/2018/09/5-Broadbent.pptx.

Christensen, Jens H E, and Krogstrup Signe. 2016. "Transmission of Quantitative Easing: The Role of Central Bank Reserves." Federal Reserve Bank of San Francisco Working Paper 2014-18. http://www.frbsf.org/economicresearch/publications/working-papers/wp2014-18.pdf.

Christophe C, Julien M, Jean-Guillaume S. 2017. Assessing the Macroeconomic Effects of LTROs During the Great Recession. Journal of Money, Credit and Banking, 49(7), pp. 1443–1482.

Churm R, Joyce M, Kapetanios G, and Theodoridis K. 2015. Unconventional monetary policies and the macroeconomy: the impact of the United Kingdom's QE2 and Funding for Lending Scheme. Bank of England Staff Working Paper No. 542.

Clouse J, Henderson A, Orphanides A, Small D, and Tinsley P. 2000. "Monetary policy when the nominal short-term interest rate is zero," Board of Governors of the Federal Reserve System Working Paper No 00-51, November. https://www.federalreserve.gov/pubs/feds/2000/200051/200051pap.pdf.

Cœuré B. 2018. The persistence and signalling power of central bank asset purchase programmes. Speech at the 2018 US Monetary Policy Forum, New York City, 23 February 2018. https://www.ecb.europa.eu/press/key/date/2018/html/ecb.sp180223.en.html.

Constâncio V. 2017. Inequality and macroeconomic policies. Speech at the Annual Congress of the European Economic Association Lisbon, 22 August 2017. https://www.ecb.europa.eu/press/key/date/2017/html/ecb.sp170822.en.html.

Daines M, Michael A S, Joyce M A S, and Matthew Tong M. 2012. QE and the gilt market: a disaggregated analysis. Bank of England Working Paper No. 466. https://www.bankofengland.co.uk/working-paper/2012/qe-and-the-gilt-market-a-disaggregated-analysis.

Dale, S. 2010. QE—one year on, Remarks at the CIMF and MMF Conference, Cambridge, 12 March. https://www.bis.org/review/r100316i.pdf.

De Grauwe P, and Polan M. 2005. "Is inflation always and everywhere a monetary phenomenon?", Scandinavian Journal of Economics, 107(2), pp. 239–259.

Diez de los Rios A, and Shamloo M. 2017. Quantitative Easing and Long-Term Yields in Small Open Economies. Bank of Canada Working Paper 2017-26. https://www.bankofcanada.ca/wp-content/uploads/2017/07/swp2017-26.pdf.

Dudley W C. 2018. Comments on "A Skeptical View of the Impact of the Fed's Balance Sheet." Remarks at the 2018 US Monetary Policy Forum, New York City, 23 February 2018a.

Dudley W C. 2018b. Comments on "A Skeptical View of the Impact of the Fed's Balance Sheet" at the US Monetary Policy Forum. Federal Reserve Bank of New York.

Eggertsson G B, Juelsrud R E and Wold E G. 2017. Are Negative Nominal Interest Rates Expansionary? NBER Working Paper No. 24039

Eggertsson G B, Juelsrud R E, Summers H L, and Wold E G. 2019. Negative Nominal Interest Rates and the Bank Lending Channel NBER Working Paper No. 25416.

Gagnon, J, Raskin, M, Remache, J, and Sack, B. 2010. Large-scale asset purchases by the Federal Reserve: did they work? Federal Reserve Bank of New York, Staff Report No, 441. https://www.newyorkfed.org/research/staff_reports/sr441.html.

Gertler, Mark, and Peter Karadi. 2011. A model of unconventional monetary policy. Journal of monetary Economics, 58(1), pp. 17–34.

Gertler M, and Karadi P. 2013. QE 1 vs. 2 vs. 3...: A Framework for Analyzing Large-Scale Asset Purchases as a Monetary Policy Tool. International Journal of Central Banking 9(2), pp. 6–53.

Glick R, and Sylvain Leduc S. 2012. Central Bank Announcements of Asset Purchases and the Impact on Global Financial and Commodity Markets. Journal of International Money and Finance, 31(8), 2078–2101.

Glick R, and Leduc S. 2015. Unconventional Monetary Policy and the Dollar: Conventional Signs, Unconventional Magnitudes." Federal Reserve Bank of San Francisco Working Paper 2015–18.

Greenlaw D, Hamilton J D, Harris E S, and West K D. 2018. A Skeptical View of the Impact of the Fed's Balance Sheet. http://econweb.ucsd.edu/~jhamilto/USMPF_2018.pdf.

Grisse C, and Silvio Schumacher S. 2017. The response of long-term yields to negative interest rates: evidence from Switzerland. Swiss National Bank Working Paper 10/2017. https://www.snb.ch/n/mmr/reference/working_paper_2017_10/source/working_paper_2017_10.n.pdf.

Gumata N, and Ndou E. 2017. Bank Credit Extension and Real Economic Activity in South Africa: The Impact of Capital Flow Dynamics, Bank Regulation and Selected Macroprudential Tools. Palgrave Macmillan. ISBN 978-3-319-43550-3.

Haldane A G, Roberts-Sklar M, Wieladek T, and Young C. 2016. QE: the story so far. Bank of England Staff Working Paper No. 624. https://www.bankofengland.co.uk/working-paper/2016/qe-the-story-so-far.

Hamilton J. 2018. The effectiveness of large-scale asset purchases. VOX CEPR Policy portal. https://voxeu.org/article/effectiveness-large-scale-asset-purchases#.W8BF-kR0x0U.twitter.

Harrison R. 2017. Optimal Quantitative Easing. Bank of England Working Paper No. 678.

Ito T. 2014. "We Are All QE-sians Now", IMES Discussion Paper Series 2014-E-5, Bank of Japan.

Jens H. E. Christensen J H E and Krogstrup S. 2018. "A Portfolio Model of Quantitative Easing." Federal Reserve Bank of San Francisco Working Paper 2016-12. https://doi.org/10.24148/wp2016-12.

Joyce M, Lasaosa A, Stevens I, and Tong M. 2010. The financial market impact of quantitative easing. Bank of England Working Paper No. 393. https://www.bankofengland.co.uk/working-paper/2010/the-financial-market-impact-of-quantitative-easing.

Kilian L, and Vigfusson R J. 2011. Are the Responses of the U.S. Economy Asymmetric in Energy Price Increases and Decreases? Quantitative Economics, 2(4), pp. 419–453.

Krogstrup S, Reynard S, and Sutter B. 2012. Liquidity Effects of Quantitative Easing on Long-Term Interest Rates. Swiss National Bank Working Paper 2012-2.

Lenza M, and Slacalek J. 2019. Quantitative easing did not increase inequality in the euro area. ECB Research Bulletin No. 54. https://www.ecb.europa.eu/pub/economic-research/resbull/2019/html/ecb.rb190129.en.html.

Li C, and Wei M. 2013. Term Structure Modeling with Supply Factors and the Federal Reserve's Large-Scale Asset Purchase Programs. International Journal of Central Banking March 2013. https://www.ijcb.org/journal/ijcb13q1a1.pdf, https://www.ijcb.org/journal/ijcb13q1a1.htm.

Luck S, and Zimmermann T. 2018. Employment Effects of Unconventional Monetary Policy: Evidence from QE (October 9, 2018). Available at SSRN: https://ssrn.com/abstract=3002047 or https://doi.org/10.2139/ssrn.3002047.

Meier, A. 2009. "Panacea, curse, or nonevent? Unconventional monetary policy in the United Kingdom," IMF Working Paper, WP/09/163. https://www.imf.org/external/pubs/ft/wp/2009/wp09163.pdf.

Motto R, Altavilla C, and Carboni G. 2015. Asset purchase programmes and financial markets: lessons from the euro area. Working Paper Series 1864, European Central Bank.

Neely C J. 2015.Unconventional monetary policy had large international effects. Journal of Banking & Finance 52, pp. 101–111.

Ndou E, Gumata N, and Tshuma M M. 2019. Exchange Rate, Second Round Effects and Inflation Processes: Evidence From South Africa. Pagrave Macmillan. ISBN 978-3-030-13932-2.

Praet P. 2018. Assessment of quantitative easing and challenges of policy normalization. Speech at The ECB and Its Watchers XIX Conference, Frankfurt am Main, 14 March 2018. https://www.ecb.europa.eu/press/key/date/2018/html/ecb.sp180314_2.en.html.

Saiki Ayako, and Frost Jon. 2014. "How does unconventional monetary policy affect inequality? Evidence from Japan," DNB Working Papers 423, Netherlands Central Bank, Research Department. https://www.cepweb.org/wp-content/uploads/CEP_WP_Unconventional_Monetary_Policy_and_Inequality.pdf.

Samuel Reynard S. 2018. Negative Interest Rate, QE and Exit. SNB Working Papers 19/2018. https://www.snb.ch/n/mmr/reference/working_paper_2018_19/source/working_paper_2018_19.n.pdf?mod=djemRTE_h.

Shirai S. 2018. The effectiveness of the Bank of Japan's large-scale stock-buying programme. VOX CEPR Policy portal. https://voxeu.org/article/effectiveness-bank-japan-s-large-scale-stock-buying-programme.

Sims E, and Wu J C. 2019. Evaluating Central Banks' Tool Kit: Past, Present, and Future. https://www.chicagofed.org/~/media/others/events/2019/monetary-policy-conference/monetary-policy-tools-sims-wu-pdf.pdf#page44.

Draghi M. 2012. Speech at the Global Investment Conference in London 26 July 2012. https://www.ecb.europa.eu/press/key/date/2012/html/sp120726.en.html.

Vlieghe G. 2018. The yield curve and QE. Speech given at the Imperial College Business School, London. Bank of England. https://www.bankofengland.co.uk/speech/2018/gertjan-vlieghe-imperial-college-business-school-london.

Werner R A. 2014. Can banks individually create money out of nothing? The theories and the empirical evidence. International Review of Financial Analysis. Volume 36, July 2016, Pages 1–19. https://ac.els-cdn.com/S1057521914001070/1-s2.0-S1057521914001070-main.pdf?_tid=82bd9284-1afa-4fa9-af15-a9bb9e93f096&acdnat=1551942094_60f15be9ed1d974197c90e3609be9e93.

Werner R A. 2016. A lost century in economics: Three theories of banking and the conclusive evidence. International Review of Financial Analysis. Volume 46, July 2016, Pages 361–379. https://ac.els-cdn.com/S1057521915001477/1-s2.0-S1057521915001477-main.pdf?_tid=02ee9dcc-655e-4f71-a8d0-4d6001b87560&acdnat=1551941511_9ccf23770609ab0cb5cf6938819dcab2.

CHAPTER 11

Are the Amplification Effects of Positive Shocks to SARB Assets Growth and Forex Reserves Accumulation on Long-Term Yields Dependent on Government Debt Growth Regimes?

Research Questions Explored

- Explore whether the association between government debt growth and ten-year yields has changed over time.
- Examine the dynamic relationship between long-term yields and government interest costs over time.
- Assess whether the amplification effects of positive shocks to South African Reserve Bank assets and foreign currency reserves (forex reserves) on long-term yields are dependent on government debt growth regimes.
- Understand the effects of government debt growth thresholds on the R/US$ exchange rate and inflation.
- Examine whether the fiscal policy stance as measured by government debt growth regimes interacts with the monetary policy balance-sheet tools to amplify the effects of government debt growth regimes on the R/US$ exchange rate and inflation.

N. Gumata, E. Ndou, *Achieving Price, Financial and Macro-Economic Stability in South Africa*,
https://doi.org/10.1007/978-3-030-66340-7_11

11.1 Introduction

Earlier chapters explored the impact of large-scale asset purchases (LSAPs) by the South African Reserve (SARB) and their impact on various financial and macro-economic variables including government bond yields, the term spread and the cost of government debt. We found that LSAPs exert downward pressure on bond yields, the term spread and the cost of government debt. But do government debt growth regimes impact the effects of LSAPs? This chapter explores whether government debt growth regimes affect the potency of LSAPs. Do government debt growth regimes dampen or amplify the effects of LSAPs on bond yields and government debt costs?

Theory suggests that government debt impacts the economy through several channels. An increase in government debt, which raises interest rates, would lower investment, consumption expenditure on interest-rate-sensitive components of household consumption and the value of household assets. The decline in household wealth asset dampens household consumption spending via the wealth channel. Hubbard (2012) and Liaaqat (2019) indicate that the negative effects of increased government debt depend on the extent to which the interest rates rise, and there are mixed results in the link between government debt and interest rates. Some studies find no relationship between government debt and interest rates (Elmendorf and Mankiw (1999), Gale and Orszag (2003); Engen and Hubbard (2004)). Blanchard (2019) shows that in cases where safe interest rates are low and expected to remain below GDP growth rates for a long time, as is currently the case in the US, debt rollovers[1] may well be feasible. Alternatively, public debt may have no fiscal cost. Furthermore, in such cases, welfare costs associated with public debt may be smaller than typically assumed because if the safe rate[2] is lower than the GDP growth rate, this means that the risk-adjusted rate of return on capital is in fact low.

According to the new Keynesian theory, when higher debt is brought about by tax cuts or spending increases, this results in an increase in aggregate demand and income levels.[3] When negative public savings are not fully offset by capital inflows and rising private savings, interest rates may rise. Such a rise in interest rates will crowd out capital formation and lower output growth. Hubbard (2012) shows that increasing government debt

[1] That is the issuance of debt without a later increase in taxes, alternatively, the issuing of debt whilst achieving a decreasing debt-to-GDP ratio without the possibility of having to raise taxes later.

[2] This is the risk-adjusted rate of return on capital.

[3] The conventional view is that government borrowing is expansionary in the short run but contractionary in the long run (Elmendorf and Mankiw 1999).

reduces investment by tightening the credit constraints faced by firms.[4] Liaqat (2019) found evidence of the crowding-out effect of government debt on investment, leading to a significant decline in income. The results were robust for various model specifications and proxies of government debt and capital formation.

In earlier chapters, we argued that the concurrence of LSAPs and the accumulation of forex reserves reinforce each other and contribute to lower government bond yields, appreciation of the R/US$ exchange and lower inflation. As such, these monetary policy interventions and tools contribute towards the attainment of the price stability mandate. This chapter explores the interaction and role of LSAPs, forex reserves accumulation and government debt growth regimes. Do low government debt regimes[5] interact with LSAPs and forex reserves accumulation to lower government bond yields? What are the effects on the R/US$ exchange rate and inflation?

This chapter contributes to literature by exploring the role of government debt growth regimes on the ten-year government bond yields, government interest costs, R/US$ exchange rate and inflation. We use several quantitative techniques to assess whether government debt growth regimes dampen or amplify the impact of LSAPs and forex reserves accumulation on the ten-year government bond yields, government interest costs, R/US$ exchange rate and inflation. The results in this chapter enhance the understanding of the interaction of monetary policy tools, especially in the form of balance sheet policy tools and fiscal policy.

Figure 11.1 shows that the relationship between growth in government debt and the ten-year yields changed from being positive for the sample period 1990M1 to 2019M12 to negative for the sample periods 2000M1 to 2019M12 and 2009M1 to 2019M12. The period 2000M1 to 2008M12 was associated with very low levels of government debt growth. Growth in government debt averaged 5.1 per cent between 2000M1 and 2008M12 compared to 14.9 per cent between 2009M1 and 2019M12 and 16.3 per cent between 1990M1 and 1999M12. Nonetheless, it is evident that the slope of the positive relationship is less steep (much gentler) for the sample period 2009M1 to 2019M12, as yields started to increase in 2013.

[4] The presence of a countercyclical fiscal policy can generate a long-run negative correlation between debt and growth, where it is low growth that causes high debt and not the other way around (Huang et al. 2018).

[5] We use the 9.62458 per cent threshold for gross government debt growth established in Gumata and Ndou (2017).

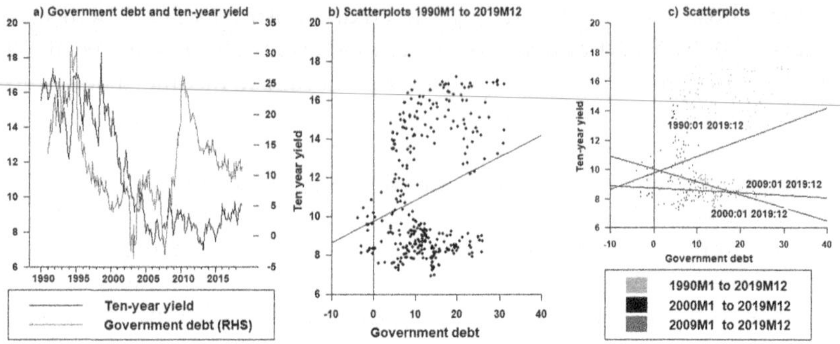

Fig. 11.1 Government debt growth and ten-year yields. (Source: South African Reserve Bank and authors' calculations)

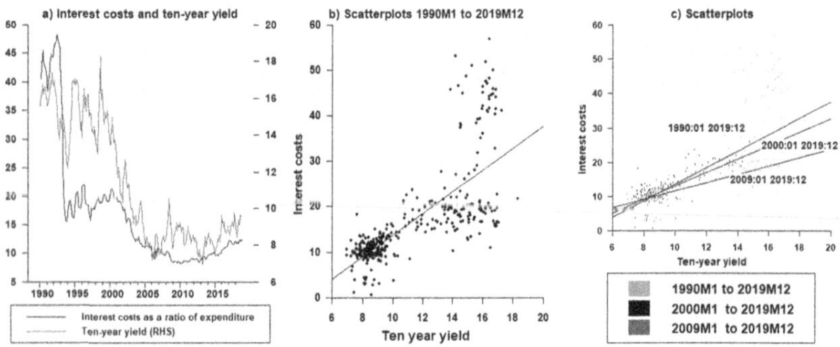

Fig. 11.2 Ten-year yields and government interest costs. (Source: South African Reserve Bank and authors' calculations)

At the same time, Fig. 11.2 shows that the interest costs as a ratio of total government spending declined from the high levels of around 45 per cent in the early 1990s to the low levels of around 8 per cent pre-2009 and have since increased to around 12 per cent in 2019. Similarly, Fig. 11.2 shows that the slope of the association between the ten-year yields and the interest costs as a ratio of expenditure gradually declined in line with changes in the ten-year yield.

The period 2009M1 to 2019M12 coincides with the steep increase in government debt growth, holdings of government bonds by non-residents and the tapering-off of LSAPs by the United States Federal Reserve Bank (US Fed). Furthermore, we showed in earlier chapters that effectively the SARB halted its forex reserves accumulation, thus also contributing to the prolonged or persistent increase in government bond yields and the R/US$ exchange-rate depreciation.

11.2 The Impact of Government Debt Growth Regimes on Long-Term Government Bond Yields

This section starts by assessing the impact of low and high government debt growth regimes on the ten-year government bond yields. We estimate a threshold VAR which includes government debt growth and the ten-year yields. The responses of the yields are delineated based on the 9.62458 per cent threshold for gross government debt growth established in Gumata and Ndou (2017). Periods where growth in government debt growth is below (above) this threshold signify low (high) government debt growth regimes. All growth rates are annual rates. The sample for the estimations starts in 1990M1 and ends in 2019M12. The VAR models are estimated using two lags and 10,000 Monte Carlo draws.

The results in Fig. 11.3 show that indeed government debt growth regimes matter for the response of the ten-year government bond yields. Long-term government bond yields increase more in response to positive shocks to government debt growth in high-debt regimes compared to the low-debt regimes. Thus, government debt growth regimes matter for the responses of long-term yields.

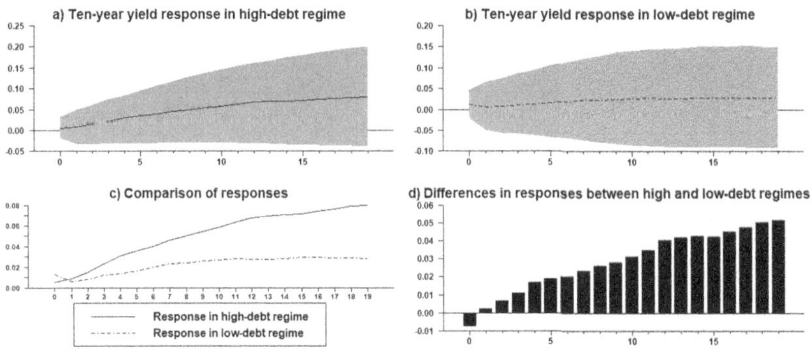

Fig. 11.3 Ten-year yield responses to government debt growth regimes. (Source: Authors' calculations. Note: The grey-shaded areas denote the 16th and 84th percentile confidence bands)

11.3 Are the Amplification Effects of Positive Shocks to SARB Assets Growth and Forex Reserves Accumulation on Long-Term Yields Dependent on Government Debt Growth Regimes?

This section assesses whether the amplification effects of positive shocks to SARB assets growth and forex reserves accumulation on long-term yields are dependent on government debt growth regimes. Like in the earlier sections, we use the 9.62458 per cent threshold for gross government debt growth established in Gumata and Ndou (2017) to delineate the low and high government debt growth regimes. We estimate a regime-dependent counterfactual VAR model which includes growth in government debt, ten-year yields, forex reserves accumulation and SARB assets growth. The forex reserves accumulation and SARB assets growth enter the VAR estimations separately. All growth rates are annual rates. The sample spans the period 2000M1 to 2019M12. The models are estimated with two lags and 10,000 Monte Carlo draws.

The results in Fig. 11.4 indicate that the ten-year government bond yields decline more in response to positive shocks to government debt growth in low-debt regimes and the forex reserves accumulation amplify the decline more compared to the high-debt regimes, as shown in Fig. 11.4(e).

What about the amplification effects of positive shocks to SARB assets growth on the long-term yields? Are they dependent on government debt growth regimes? We conclude this section by estimating a

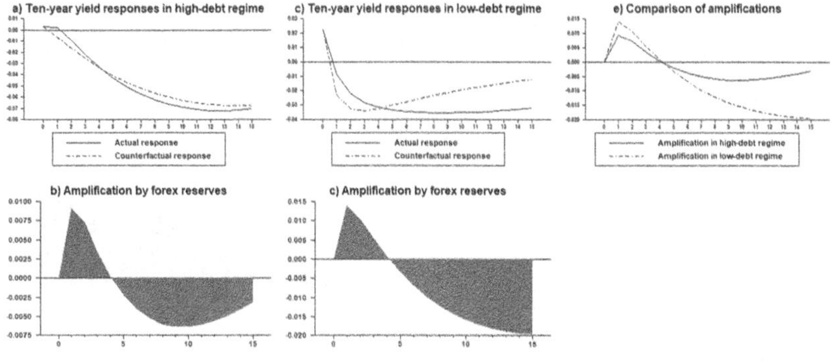

Fig. 11.4 Responses to positive government debt growth shocks in the low and high government debt growth regimes and propagation by the forex reserves accumulation channel. (Source: Authors' calculations)

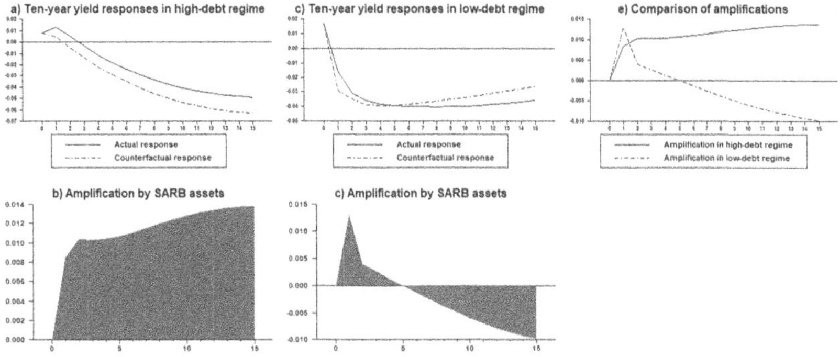

Fig. 11.5 Responses to positive government debt growth shocks in the low and high government debt growth regimes and propagation by the SARB assets growth channel. (Source: Authors' calculations)

regime-dependent counterfactual VAR model which includes growth in SARB assets growth, forex reserves accumulation, ten-year yields and government debt growth. The intention of the analysis is to assess whether the SARB assets growth amplify or dampen the positive shock effects of the forex reserves accumulation. The results in Fig. 11.5 indicate that like the effects of forex reserves, ten-year yields decline but the impact of SARB assets growth is neutralised in the high-debt regimes, as shown in Fig. 11.5(e), compared to those in the low-debt regimes.

The results imply that government debt growth regimes matter for the impact of forex reserves accumulation and SARB assets growth on government debt yields. Thus, a policy strategy that contains growth in government debt growth below 10 per cent, coupled with the forex reserves accumulation and LSAPs by the SARB, will have a positive effect on long-term government bond yields.

To conclude this section, we assess the responses of the government interest costs as a ratio of total government spending to positive shocks to long-term yields, subject to government debt growth thresholds, and whether these effects are amplified or dampened by forex reserves accumulation and SARB assets growth. In the VAR model, we replace the ten year government bond yields with the government interest costs as a ratio of total government spending. The results in Fig. 11.6 indicate that forex reserves accumulation have a dampening effect on the government interest costs in the low-government debt growth regimes compared to the high-government debt growth regimes.

Similarly, Fig. 11.7 shows that SARB assets growth have a dampening effect on government interest costs in the low government debt growth regime.

The results imply monetary policy balance sheet tools are more potent in the low government-debt growth regimes.

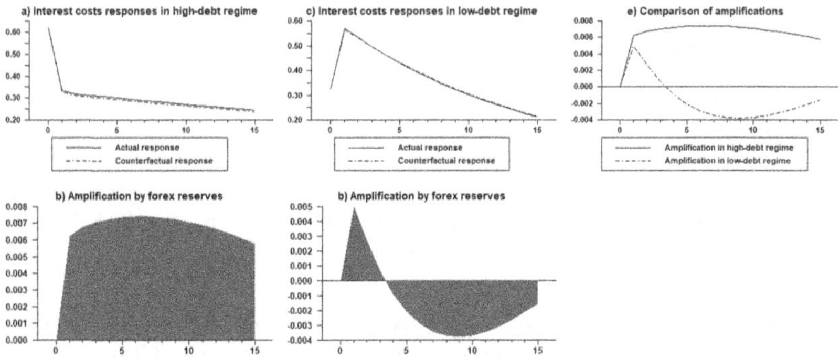

Fig. 11.6 Responses of government interest costs to positive government debt growth shocks in the low and high-debt growth regimes and propagation by the forex reserves accumulation channel. (Source: Authors' calculations)

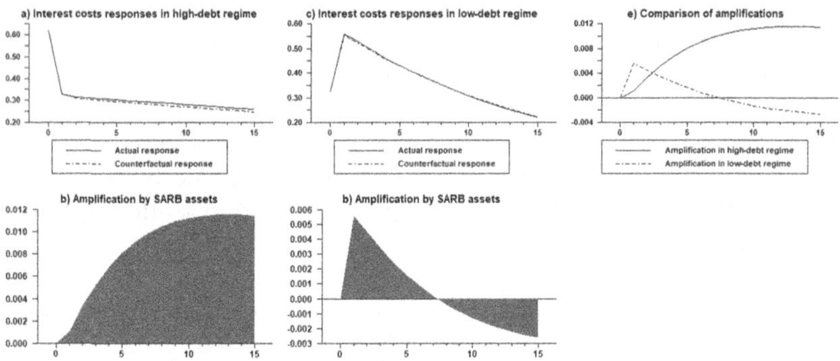

Fig. 11.7 Responses of interest costs to positive government debt shocks in low- and high-debt regimes and propagation by the SARB assets channel. (Source: Authors' calculations)

11.4 What Are the Effects of Government Debt Growth Thresholds on the R/US$ Exchange Rate and Inflation?

To conclude this chapter, we assess the impact of government debt growth regimes on the R/US$ exchange rate and inflation. We start by estimating VAR models which include growth in government debt, R/US$ exchange rate and inflation. The growth rates are annual rates. Increases (decreases) in the R/US$ exchange rate indicate a depreciation (appreciation). The models are estimated using two lags and 10,000 Monte Carlo draws. The shock is a one standard deviation shock to government debt growth.

The results in Figs. 11.8 and 11.9 indicate that government debt growth regimes matter for the R/US$ exchange rate and inflation. The R/US$ exchange rate appreciates (depreciates) in response to positive shocks to government debt growth in the low (high) government debt regimes. Similarly, inflation accelerates (decelerates) in response to positive shocks to government debt growth in the low (high) government debt growth regimes. Thus, government debt growth regimes also matter for the R/US$ exchange rate and inflation. In the same way that low government debt growth regimes enhance the effectiveness of monetary policy balance sheet tools in lowering long-term bond yields and in turn government interest costs, they are conducive for the exchange-rate appreciations and low-inflation regimes.

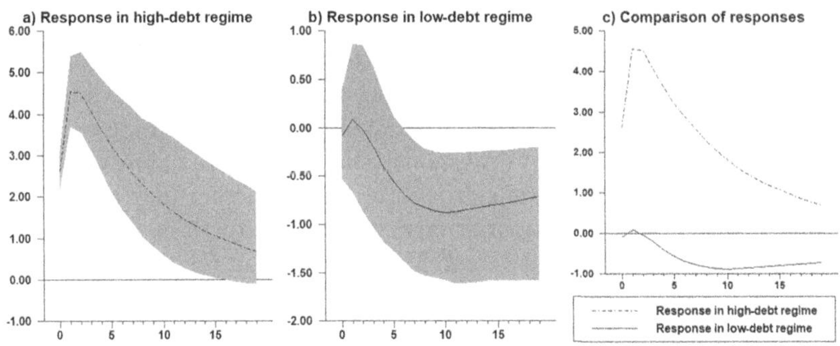

Fig. 11.8 Responses of the R/US$ exchange rate to positive government debt growth shocks in the high and low government debt growth regimes. (Source: Authors' calculations. Note: The grey-shaded areas denote the 16th and 84th percentile confidence bands)

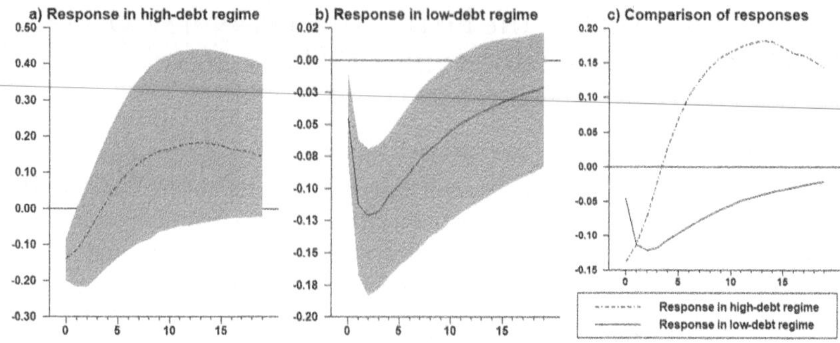

Fig. 11.9 Responses of inflation to positive government debt growth shocks in the high and low government debt growth regimes. (Source: Authors' calculations. Note: The grey-shaded areas denote the 16th and 84th percentile confidence bands)

11.5 Are the Amplification Effects of Positive Shocks to SARB Assets Growth and Forex Reserves Accumulation on Long-Term Yields Dependent on Government Debt Growth Regimes?

To conclude the analysis in this section, we estimate regime-dependent counterfactual VAR models to assess the propagation effects of the SARB assets growth and forex reserves accumulation. We estimate regime dependent VAR models, which include government debt growth, R/US$ exchange rate growth, inflation and a SARB balance sheet indicator. The SARB balance sheet indicators are SARB assets growth and forex reserves accumulation and these enter the VAR models separately during the estimations. The counterfactual VAR models shut off the role of forex reserves accumulation and SARB assets growth to assess whether they amplify or dampen the positive shocks of government debt growth in the low and high government debt growth regimes. The results in Fig. 11.10 indicate that forex reserves accumulation amplify the depreciation (appreciation) of the R/US$ exchange rate in the high (low) government debt growth regimes.

Similarly, the results in Fig. 11.11 show that inflation rises (declines) in response to positive government debt growth shocks in the high (low) government debt growth regimes. Furthermore, the forex reserves

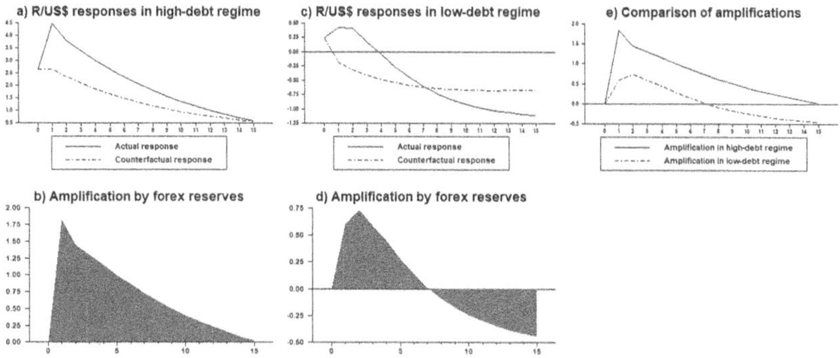

Fig. 11.10 R/US$ exchange rate responses to positive government debt growth shocks in the high and low government debt growth regimes and propagation by the forex reserves accumulation channel. (Source: Authors' calculations)

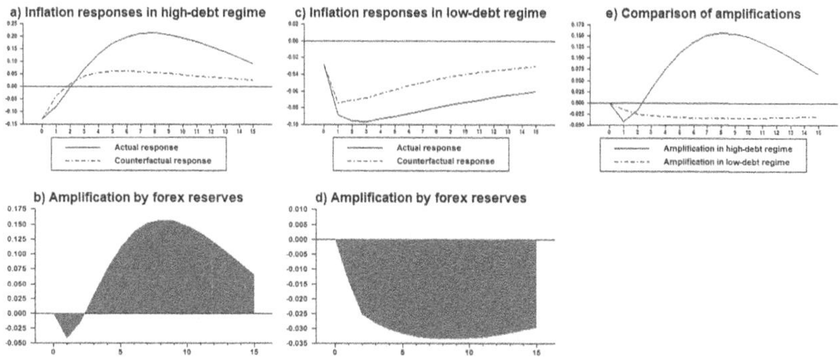

Fig. 11.11 Inflation responses to positive government debt growth shocks in the high and low debt growth regimes and propagation by the forex reserves accumulation channel. (Source: Authors' calculations)

accumulation amplify (dampen) the increase (decrease) in inflation in the high (low) government debt growth regimes. Thus, the fiscal policy stance as measured by the government debt growth regimes via its impact on the R/US$ exchange rate interacts with monetary policy through its effects on inflation (price stability).

Finally, in Figs. 11.12 and 11.13, we establish that SARB assets growth exert similar effects on the R/US$ exchange rate and inflation as those exerted by the forex reserves accumulation. The SARB assets

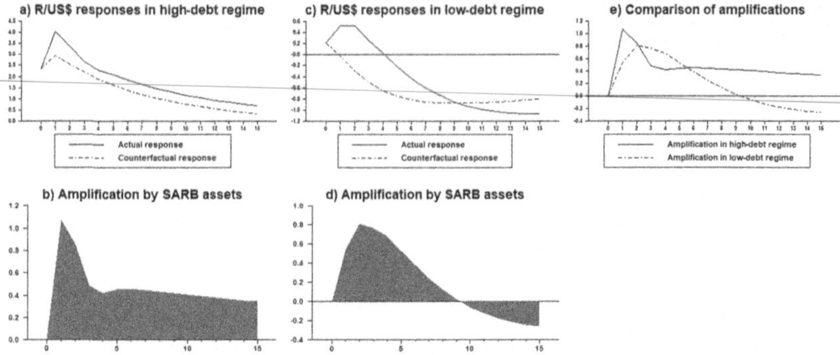

Fig. 11.12 R/US$ exchange rate responses to positive government debt growth shocks in the high and low debt growth regimes and propagation by the SARB assets growth channel. (Source: Authors' calculations)

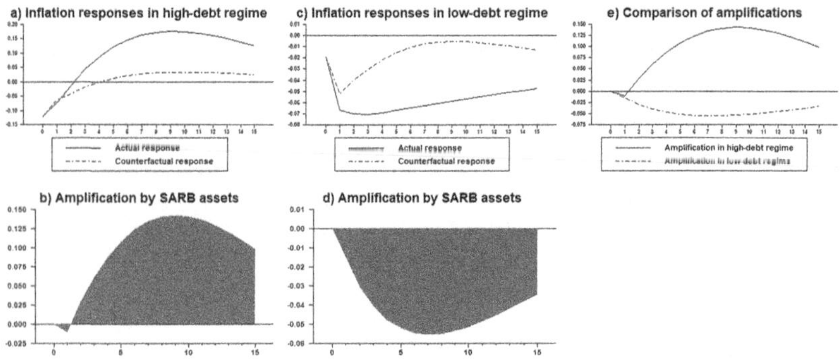

Fig. 11.13 Inflation responses to positive government debt growth shocks in the high and low debt growth regimes and propagation by the SARB assets growth channel. (Source: Authors' calculations)

growth amplify the depreciation (appreciation) of the R/US$ exchange rate in the high (low) government debt growth regimes.

Similarly, SARB assets growth amplify the increase (decrease) in inflation in the high (low) government debt growth regimes.

The fiscal policy stance as measured by the government debt growth regimes interacts with monetary policy through its effects on inflation (price stability). At the same time, the monetary policy balance sheet tools amplify the effects of the fiscal policy stance, as measured by the government debt growth regimes. These findings concur with those in Ndou et al. (2019), showing that inflation increases more due to the persistent weakening in the fiscal policy credibility shock. The authors show that a persistent increase in fiscal policy credibility is necessary to support the exchange-rate appreciations and the decline in inflation. High fiscal policy credibility dampens the pass-through of the exchange-rate depreciation shocks to inflation. In addition, the authors provide evidence showing that fiscal policy credibility directly impacts inflation expectations. Therefore, government debt growth regimes matter for the effectiveness of the monetary policy balance sheet tools on long-term government bond yields, the R/US$ exchange rate and inflation.

11.6 Conclusion and Policy Implications

Do government debt growth regimes impact the effects of LSAPs? We find that indeed government debt growth regimes matter for the response of ten-year government bond yields, government interest costs, the R/US$ exchange rate and inflation. Long-term government bond yields, government interest costs and inflation increase more in response to positive shocks to government debt growth in the high government debt growth regimes than in the low government debt growth regimes. Whereas the R/US$ exchange rate depreciates (appreciates) in the high (low) government debt growth regimes. Furthermore, we establish that the forex reserves accumulation amplify the decline in bond yields, government interest costs and inflation more in the low government debt growth regimes compared to the high government debt growth regimes. Similarly, in the high government debt growth regimes, the forex reserves accumulation dampen the appreciation of the R/US$ exchange rate.

Are the amplification effects of positive shocks to SARB assets growth and forex reserves accumulation on long-term yields dependent on government debt growth regimes? Yes, they are. We find that ten-year bond yields do decline but the impact of LSAPs is neutralised in the high government debt regimes compared to those in the low government debt growth regimes. Thus, government debt growth regimes matter for the impact of forex reserves accumulation and LSAPs on government debt yields and government interest costs. The policy implication is that a policy strategy that contains growth in government debt below 10 per cent, coupled with forex reserve accumulation and LSAPs by the SARB, will have a positive effect on long-term government bond yields and government interest costs. The fiscal policy stance, as measured by the government debt growth regimes, interacts with monetary policy through its effects on inflation (price stability). At the same time, monetary policy balance sheet tools amplify the effects of the fiscal policy stance, as measured by government debt growth regimes. Therefore, government debt growth regimes matter for the effectiveness of the monetary policy balance sheet tools on long-term government bond yields, the R/US$ exchange rate and inflation.

References

Blanchard O. 2019. Public Debt and Low Interest Rates. The American Economic Review Presidential Lecture, given in January 2019. https://www.aeaweb.org/aea/2019conference/program/pdf/14020_paper_etZgfbDr.pdf.

Elmendorf D W, and N. Mankiw G. 1999. Government Debt. In (J. B. Taylor & M. Woodford (ed.)) Handbook of Macroeconomics 1, part 3: 1615–1669.

Engen E, and R. Glenn Hubbard R G. 2004. Federal Government Debt and Interest Rates. NBER Working Paper No. 10681.

Gale, W G, and Orszag, P R. 2003. Economic Effects of Sustained Budget Deficits. National Tax Journal, 56(3), 2003.

Gumata N, and Ndou E. 2017. Labour Market and Fiscal Policy Adjustments to Shocks: The role and implications for price and financial stability in South Africa. Palgrave Macmillan. ISBN 978-3-319-66520-7.

Huang, Y, Panizza U, and Varghese, R. 2018. Does the public debt crowd out corporate investment? International evidence, Graduate institute of international and development studies, international economic department, working paper number, HEIDWP08-2018.

Hubbard G. 2012. Consequences of Government Deficits and Debt. International Journal of Central Banking, 8(S1), 203–235. January 2012.

Liaqat Z. 2019. Does government debt crowd out capital formation? A dynamic approach using panel VAR. Economics Letters, 178, 86–90.

Ndou E, Gumata N, and Tshuma M M. 2019. Exchange rate, second round effects and inflation process: Evidence from South Africa. Pagrave Macmillan. ISBN 978-3-030-13932-2.

CHAPTER 12

Does an Increase in Government Debt Threaten Economic Growth Recovery Via Tightening Credit Conditions?

Research Questions Explored

- Examine the effects of an increase in government gross loan debt to GDP shocks on credit conditions.
- Show the effects of an unexpected tightening in credit conditions on GDP, household consumption, investment, and business and consumer confidence.
- Perform a counterfactual analysis to show the role of the credit conditions channel in transmitting positive government debt shocks to GDP, investment and household consumption.

12.1 Introduction

Media commentaries and policymakers have pointed out that the weakening in South African economic growth is due to a variety of factors. One of the factors mentioned is the lack of the implementation of structural reforms. Amidst these pronouncements, there has been no quantification of how long it will take for these structural reforms to raise economic growth to levels observed before the recession in 2009. In addition, post-2009 recession, the South African economic growth did not increase as expected due to the impulses of the global economic recovery as

N. Gumata, E. Ndou, *Achieving Price, Financial and Macro-Economic Stability in South Africa*,
https://doi.org/10.1007/978-3-030-66340-7_12

predicted by the repercussion growth theory. Despite a variety of factors that economic agents may propose as the dominating explanations to weak economic growth, this analysis shows that an unexpected rise in the government debt to GDP leads to tight credit conditions, which exert adverse effects on GDP, household consumption, investment, business and consumer confidence. It is for this reason that the upward trend in domestic government debt to GDP post-2009 and its influence on credit conditions should be given more weight in explaining the weak economic growth outcomes post-2008.

In Fig. 12.1, the increase in the government debt to GDP was accompanied by the stagnation and even a reduction in the ratio of gross fixed-capital formation to GDP post-2009. These contrasting trends indicate that the increase in government debt post-2009 did not necessarily result in a conducive environment for an increase in investment growth. So, what explains this phenomenon?

The findings in this chapter indicate that the decline in GDP is due to the unexpected increase in government debt to GDP and the effects are amplified by the tightening in credit conditions. These results imply that there is a leakage in the system and transmission of positive government debt shocks to real economic activity and investment. These results are consistent with findings in Gumata and Ndou (2017), indicating that the

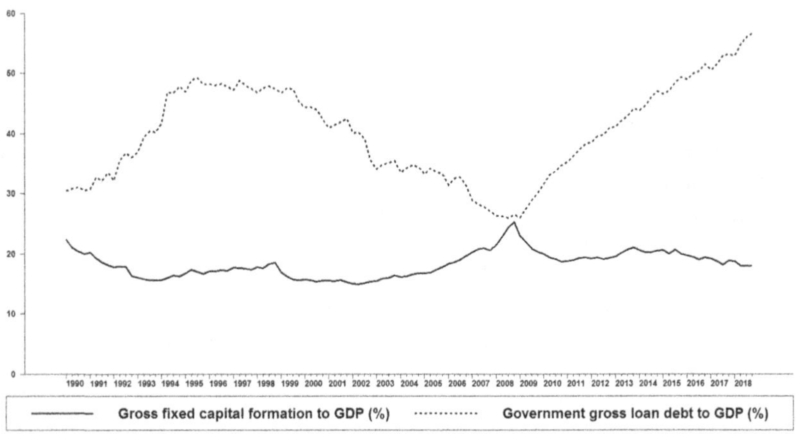

Fig. 12.1 Government debt to GDP and investment to GDP. (Source: South African Reserve Bank)

size and quality of public expenditure matters to investors. This is because the quality, efficiency and composition of public spending matters for financial markets. The results in this chapter show that an unexpected tightening in the credit conditions leads to a significant contraction in GDP, household consumption, investment, business and consumer confidence. To mitigate the adverse effects of an unexpected tightening in credit conditions, policy interventions that loosen credit conditions must be implemented.

12.2 Empirical Results

The analysis begins by examining the effects of an unexpected increase in the government debt to GDP on the credit conditions index using Vector autoregression (VAR) models. The credit conditions index (CCI) is obtained from Gumata and Ndou (2017). The study uses quarterly (Q) data from 2000Q1 to 2016Q1. The VAR model includes government debt to GDP, the log nominal effective exchange rate (NEER) and the CCI as endogenous variables. The exogenous variables in the model include the log consumer price index and repo rate. All log variables are multiplied by 100. The results of this model are shown in Fig. 12.2(a). The results shown in Fig. 12.2(b–f) are based on the four variables VAR

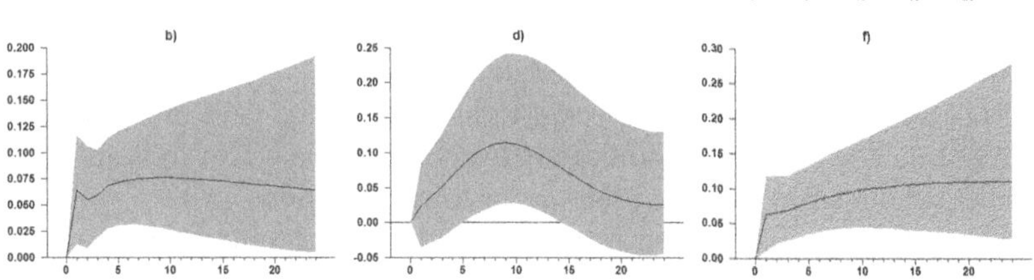

Fig. 12.2 Responses of the credit conditions index to a positive government debt to GDP shock. (Source: Authors' calculations. Note: The grey shaded error bands denote 16th and 84th percentiles confidence bands)

model which includes government debt to GDP, *real_variables*, log NEER and the CCI. The *real_variables* are log GDP, log gross fixed capital formation, log household consumption, gross fixed capital formation as percent of GDP and log business confidence index. These variables enter the model as endogenous variables and are included separately in the model. In all these models the exogenous variables include the repo rate and log consumer price index. The models are estimated using two lags and 10,000 Monte Carlo draws. The shock is a one standard deviation shock.

The results in Fig. 12.2 show that the credit conditions index tightens significantly over long horizons. The tightening in the credit conditions to positive government gross loan debt to GDP shocks is robust to different vector autoregression (VAR) model specifications and different ordering of the variables in the models.

12.2.1 The Effects of a Tight Credit Conditions Shock

This section shows the responses of log GDP, log household consumption, log gross fixed-capital formation, log consumer confidence and log business confidence to an unexpected tightening in credit conditions. The impulse responses shown in this figure are based on the four-variable VAR model which consists of the following endogenous variables: government debt to GDP, *real_variables*, log NEER and the CCI. The *real_variables* are log GDP, log gross fixed-capital formation, log household consumption, gross fixed-capital formation as a percentage of GDP, log business confidence index and log consumer confidence index. These variables are included separately in the model. In all these models, the exogenous variables include repo rate and log consumer price index. The models are estimated using two lags and 10,000 Monte Carlo draws. The shock is a one standard deviation shock. The results are robust to the different ordering of the variables in the models.

The responses to an unexpected tightening in the CCI are shown in Fig. 12.3. The CCI rises significantly over all horizons. This indicates that credit conditions will remain tighter for longer periods.

The results in Fig 12.3 show that GDP declines significantly for a long period. At the peak, GDP declines by about 0.6 per cent. This suggests that the tightening in credit conditions due to an unexpected increase in the government debt to GDP will delay the recovery of economic growth. In addition, business and consumer confidence indices decline for long

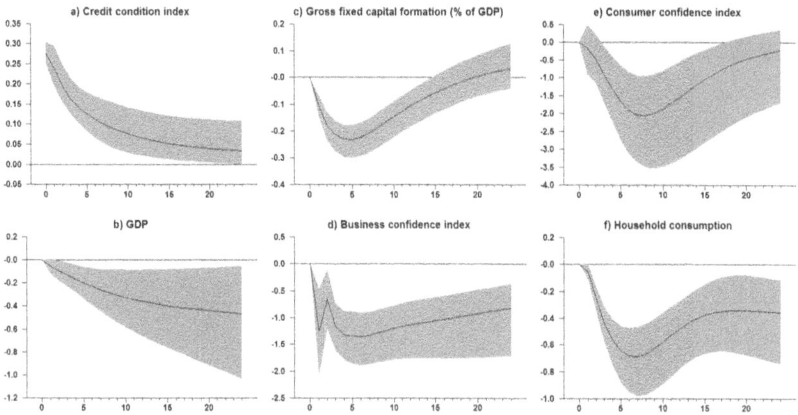

Fig. 12.3 Responses to an unexpected tightening in the credit conditions index. (Source: Authors' calculations. Note: The grey shaded error bands denote 16th and 84th percentiles confidence bands)

periods. This suggests that tightening in credit conditions dampens business and consumer confidence indicators. Therefore, it cannot be refuted that tightening credit conditions directly impact business confidence, consumer confidence, household consumption, gross fixed-capital formation and GDP. A tightening in credit conditions following an unexpected increase in the government debt to GDP requires various policy interventions that loosen credit conditions.

12.2.2 *The Role of Credit Conditions in Transmitting Positive Government Debt Shocks to GDP, Household Consumption and Gross Fixed-Capital Formation*

This section shows the responses of log GDP, log gross fixed-capital formation, gross fixed-capital formation and log household consumption to a 1 per cent positive government debt to GDP shock. The impulse responses shown in Fig. 12.4 are based on the four-variable VAR model which consists of the following endogenous variables: government gross-loan-debt to GDP, *real_variables*, log NEER and the CCI. The *real_variables* are log GDP, log gross fixed-capital formation, log household consumption and gross fixed-capital formation as a percentage of GDP. These variables are included separately in the model. In all these

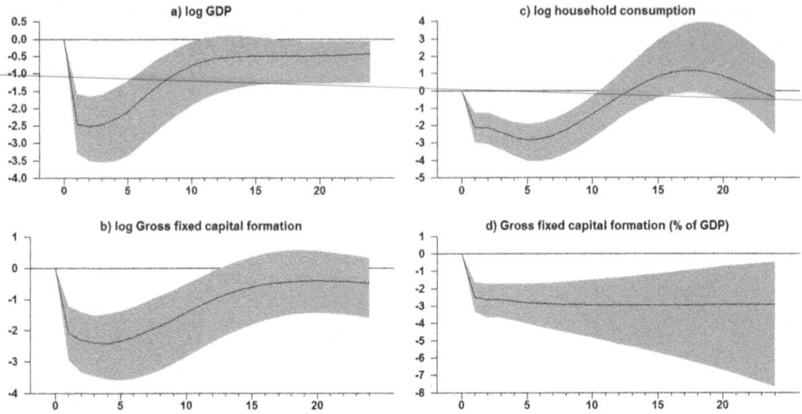

Fig. 12.4 Responses to a positive government debt to GDP shock. (Source: Authors' calculations. Note: The grey shaded error bands denote 16th and 84th percentiles confidence bands)

models, the exogenous variables include repo rate and log consumer price index. The models are estimated using two lags and 10,000 Monte Carlo draws. The shock is a one standard deviation shock. The results are robust to the different ordering of the variables in the models.

The results in Fig. 12.4. show that GDP, gross fixed-capital formation and log household consumption decline significantly to a 1 per cent positive government to GDP shock. This shows that an unexpected increase in government debt has adverse spill-over effects on the components of GDP.

We estimate a counterfactual VAR model to assess the role of the credit conditions channel in transmitting positive government gross loan debt to GDP shocks to GDP, household consumption and gross fixed-capital formation. The counterfactual refers to the responses when the indicated the CCI channel is shut off in transmitting positive shocks to government debt to GDP in the model. In the first model, the endogenous variables are government debt to GDP, log GDP and the CCI. In the second model, the endogenous variables are government debt to GDP, log household consumption and the CCI. In the third model, the endogenous variables are government debt to GDP, log gross fixed-capital formation and the CCI. All models include the log consumer price index and repo rate as exogenous variables and are estimated using two lags and 10,000 Monte Carlo draws.

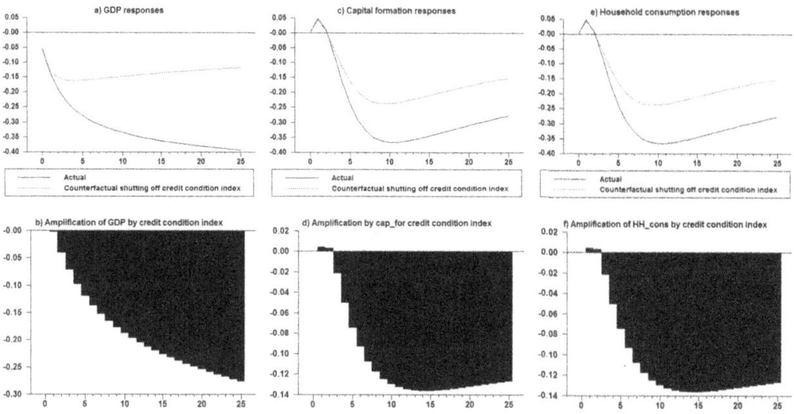

Fig. 12.5 Responses to a positive government debt to GDP shock and the role of the credit conditions channel. (Source: Authors' calculations. Note: Actual refers to the response which includes credit conditions index. Cap_form denotes gross fixed-capital formation and HH_cons denotes household consumption)

The responses of gross fixed-capital formation, GDP and household consumption to positive government debt to GDP shocks are shown in Fig. 12.5(a). In both instances, gross fixed-capital formation, household consumption and GDP decline irrespective of whether the CCI channel is operative or shut off in the model. Gross fixed-capital formation, GDP and household consumption decline more when the CCI channel is allowed to transmit positive government debt to GDP shocks than when this channel is shut off. The negative amplifications are shown in the second row in Fig. 12.5(a). GDP, household consumption and gross fixed-capital formation decline more when the CCI channel is operational than when it is shut off in the transmitting positive government debt to GDP shocks. In addition, we determine the robustness of the preceding conclusions to shocks to government debt to GDP without scaling this variable by GDP. The finding is robust to whether government debt is scaled by GDP or not. This evidence shows that the CCI is an indirect channel through which the decline in real economic activity following an unexpected increase in government debt is exacerbated.

12.3 Conclusion and Policy Implications

Evidence in this chapter reveals that a positive standard deviation increase in government debt to GDP leads to a significant tightening in credit conditions. The unexpected tightening in credit conditions leads to a significant contraction in GDP, household consumption, gross fixed-capital formation, business and consumer confidence. The counterfactual analysis shows that GDP, investment and household consumption decline more when the credit conditions channel is active in the model and transmits positive government debt to GDP shocks compared to when this channel is shut off. This suggests that the tightening in credit conditions due to an unexpected increase in government debt to GDP worsens the delay in the recovery of economic growth. This implies that there is an urgent need for policy interventions that loosen credit conditions.

Reference

Gumata N, and Ndou E. 2017. Bank Credit Extension and Real Economic Activity in South Africa: The Impact of Capital Flow Dynamics, Bank Regulation and Selected Macroprudential Tools. ISBN 978-3-319-43550-3.

CHAPTER 13

Foreign Currency Reserves: Do They Contribute to GDP Growth and Employment Growth?

Research Questions Explored

- Assess the role of foreign currency reserves (forex reserves) accumulation on the unemployment rate, GDP growth and employment growth.
- Explore whether there is scope and capacity for the South African Reserve Bank (SARB) to embark on another forex reserves accumulation programme like that post-2004.
- Assess whether large-scale asset purchases (LSAPs) by the SARB reinforce the positive effects of forex reserves accumulation on GDP growth and employment growth, and the unemployment rate.
- Examine the cumulative impact of non-persistent and persistently rising shocks to forex reserves on GDP and employment growth and the unemployment rate.

N. Gumata, E. Ndou, *Achieving Price, Financial and Macro-Economic Stability in South Africa*,
https://doi.org/10.1007/978-3-030-66340-7_13

13.1 Introduction

Foreign currency reserves accumulation is part of the balance sheet polices, alternatively monetary policy interventions.[1] The process of forex reserves accumulation or using foreign currency reserves is intricately linked to the conduct of monetary policy. Furthermore, in the process of foreign exchange intervention, the asset that is purchased is denominated in foreign currency rather than in domestic currency; hence, there is an aspect of changes in financial conditions related to the exchange rate as opposed to a set of other domestic asset prices. This chapter explores whether there is scope and capacity for the SARB to embark on another forex reserves accumulation programme like that post-2004. In addition, beyond the well-known primary objectives and motives for holding foreign currency reserves, do forex reserves contribute to lowering bond yields, inflation and the unemployment rate whilst increasing GDP growth and employment growth?

Furthermore, what is the nature of the interaction between asset purchases and the accumulation of forex reserves? William and Dudley (2018) argues that if LSAPs are not as powerful as some of the event studies imply,[2] the answer is not to simply discard the tool, but instead to look for ways to enhance its efficacy and use it more aggressively. In this respect, he argues that LSAPs work best when they are open-ended and may be helpful in reducing tail risks. Along similar lines, Cœuré (2018) argues that investors want to see a clear commitment by the central bank to counter the downside risks. They want central banks to "put their money where their mouth is". To this effect, vast empirical evidence shows that the speech and commitment by Draghi where he pledged to "do whatever it takes" to preserve the euro is seen as a turning point to the degree that it removed the tail risks of a Eurozone breakup and thus narrowed the interest rate spreads of the countries that were severely affected by the sovereign debt crisis.[3]

[1] Borio and Disyatat (2010) state that foreign exchange intervention is a subset of balance sheet policies.

[2] However, it is worth noting that the weaknesses of "event studies" in assessing the impact of QE is well documented.

[3] See, for example, how the ECB launched a landmark programme to purchase distressed debt in countries facing the burden of debt repayments and how potential liquidity persistently lowered the sovereign debt yield spreads https://www.ft.com/content/45de9cca-fda7-3191-ae70-ca5daa2273ee

Against this backdrop, we assess whether another forex reserves accumulation programme like that post-2004 propagates the effects of LSAPs in lowering bond yields, inflation and the unemployment rate whilst increasing GDP growth and employment growth. What is the nature of the interaction between LSAPs and the accumulation of forex reserves? Do they substitute or complement each other's effects on the price, financial and long-term macro-economic stability objectives? We argue that the concurrence of LSAPs and another forex reserves accumulation programme will enhance the achievement of price, financial and long-term macro-economic stability objectives.

In literature, there are several motives for holding foreign currency reserves. At the core, foreign currency reserves are accumulated (i) as a buffer against crisis, alternatively, a rainy-day fund, and (ii) to maintain confidence in the exchange-rate-centred monetary policy, alternatively, to support the exchange rate policy or serve as a stability fund.[4] But foreign currency reserves are also accumulated for non-precautionary reasons, such as to provide a stream of investment income to help finance part of the annual government budget, alternatively, for intergenerational savings or an endowment fund.[5] For instance, Menon (2019) indicates that in the case of Singapore, during the Global Financial Crisis, the forex reserves were drawn down to finance a package of measures, to preserve jobs by subsidising employers' wage bills and to help viable companies stay afloat by sharing the risk of bank lending. Furthermore, the income derived from investing the forex reserves provides an increasingly important source of revenue to fund government expenditure. As such, the role of the forex reserves as an endowment fund from which to draw a steady stream of income to finance the government budget will become even more important in the years ahead. According to the IMF (2011), this approach to reserves adequacy is broader than the balance of payments-determined definition or consideration of forex reserves assets. Such a broad approach to forex reserves accumulation complements sound macro-economic and prudential policy frameworks and limits a country's vulnerability to multiple shocks.[6]

[4] See Chang (2007) on the experiences of Brazil, Chile, Colombia and Peru foreign exchange reserves strategies and motives.

[5] See IMF (2011), Menon (2019), Olivier and Ranciere (2006).

[6] Inflation-targeting frameworks in emerging market economies (EMEs) have generally been successful. These frameworks have been combined with varying degrees of FX intervention, together with the active use of macroprudential tools. This approach reflects EMEs' response to capital flow and associated exchange rate volatility as policymakers seek to design

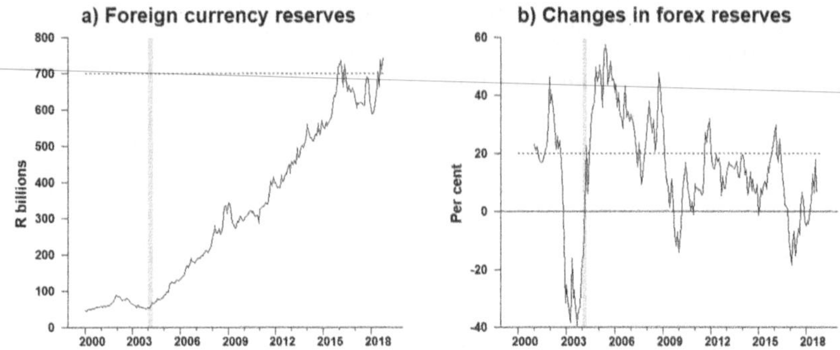

Fig. 13.1 Evolution of foreign currency reserves. (Source: South African Reserve Bank and authors' calculations)

Figure 13.1 shows the evolution of foreign currency reserves in South Africa. In Rand terms, forex reserves have increased from less than R100 billion in 2004 to just around R700 billion in 2012. At the height of the forex reserves accumulation programme between 2004 and 2010, forex reserves grew at growth rates well above 20 per cent. A similar trend is evident in Fig. 13.5(b) when assessing forex reserves in US$.

Furthermore, Fig. 13.2 shows that if we use some form of the traditional measures of reserves adequacy,[7] weeks of import cover increased from two weeks in pre-2004 to five weeks post-2004. At the same time, the ratio of forex reserves to GDP increased from 20 per cent pre-2004 to 60 per cent in 2018. These measures mainly consider the precautionary

and implement a monetary policy framework for both price and financial stability. In this way, practice has moved ahead of theory, much as it did when inflation targeting was adopted in the early 1990s by some advanced economies. https://www.bis.org/publ/arpdf/ar2019e.pdf

[7] Traditional measures of reserve adequacy include (i) import cover, which measures the number of months imports can be sustained should all inflows (such as export revenue and external financing) cease; (ii) the short-term debt (STD) as an indicator of crisis risk for market-access. The Greenspan-Guidotti rule of 100 per cent cover or one year of STD is the most widely used standard of adequacy for emerging market economies; (iii) the broad money (typically M2) indicator. The ratio of 20 per cent is normally used as the upper end of the range. This measure is based on the fact that many recent capital account crises are accompanied by outflows of deposits of domestic residents. The broad money metric is usually intended to capture this risk of capital flight; (iv) as a ratio of GDP and this is best used as a scaling factor for cross-country analysis.

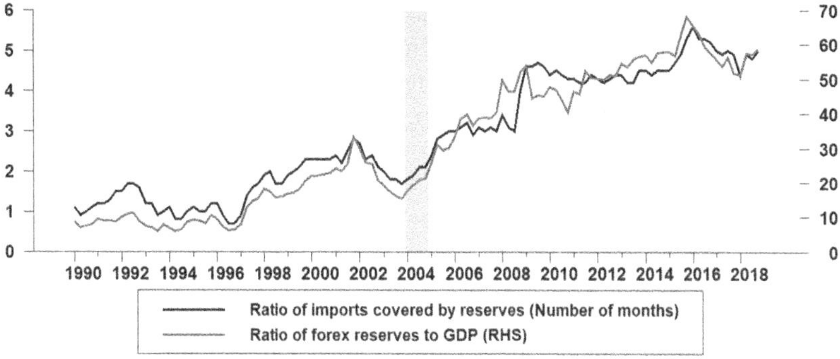

Fig. 13.2 Foreign currency reserves import cover and as a ratio of GDP. (Source: South African Reserve Bank and authors' calculations)

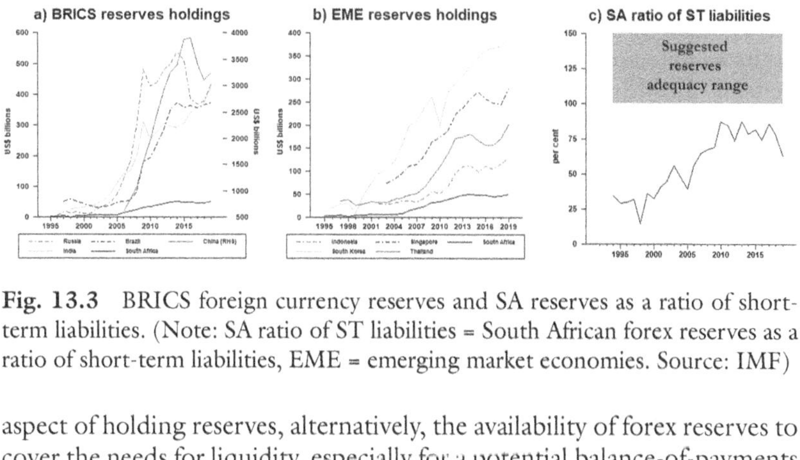

Fig. 13.3 BRICS foreign currency reserves and SA reserves as a ratio of short-term liabilities. (Note: SA ratio of ST liabilities = South African forex reserves as a ratio of short-term liabilities, EME = emerging market economies. Source: IMF)

aspect of holding reserves, alternatively, the availability of forex reserves to cover the needs for liquidity, especially for a potential balance-of-payments crisis needs. Nonetheless, the growth rates in forex reserves accumulation declined post-2009, especially in US$ terms, which characterises the role of the R/US$ exchange-rate depreciation during this period.

In addition, Fig. 13.3 shows that South Africa falls short of the reserves adequacy measure of forex reserves as a percentage of short-term liabilities. The suggested range for adequate reserves is between 100 per cent and 150 per cent. At the same time, Fig. 13.3(a) shows that at US$60 billion worth forex reserves, South Africa is way below its peers in BRIC countries. This is the case even when compared to other emerging market economies (EMEs) in Fig. 13.3(b).

Like other countries, the SARB accumulates foreign currency reserves mainly through interventions in the foreign exchange market and by taking advantage of persistent capital inflows. In the process of forex reserves accumulation, there are spill-overs to the nominal exchange rate, and this is in turn transmitted to other macro-economic variables such as inflation. In such a process, forex reserves accumulation and management tend to go beyond the financial stability objectives and assist in the price stability objective.

It is against this background that in this chapter, we explore the effects of different positive shock sizes to forex reserves and their impact on various macro-economic variables. For instance, a one standard deviation positive shock is equivalent to 8 per cent, whereas a two standard deviation shock is double that amount and the four and ten standard deviation shocks are incrementally larger. This kind of analysis gives us an indication of what the effects of such incrementally larger positive shocks to forex reserves on the macro-economy are over time. This chapter does not aim to estimate the optimal level of reserves;[8] rather we contribute to literature by assessing the benefits of embarking on another forex reserves accumulation programme.

First, we assess the stylised facts of forex reserves on the SARB balance sheet and their association with the R/US$ exchange rate, long-term government bond yields, inflation, the unemployment rate, GDP growth and employment growth. Second, for historical context, we assess the historical contributions of the forex reserves programme post-2004 to the unemployment rate, GDP growth and employment growth. We are interested in the period 2004Q1 to 2007Q4, when the SARB embarked on the forex reserves accumulation that resulted in forex reserves increasing from below US$10 billion in 2004 to US$ 50 billion in 2009. It also happens that during this period, the South African economy performed very well and whilst maintaining the price stability mandate. Such a historical decomposition analysis helps us to place the role of a policy of reserves accumulation and the exchange-rate management in context and assess its benefits to the wider macroeconomy.

Third, given the fact that the reserves accumulation programme entails an increase in the balance sheet of the SARB with similar characteristics as

[8] Literature shows that cost-benefit models aimed at identifying optimal reserves (alternatively, models that describe reserve accumulation explicitly as an optimisation problem) are very sensitive to the assumptions made about costs and benefits of holding reserves. See, for example, IMF (2011).

those explored in earlier chapters, we use the counterfactual VAR analysis to assess whether the simultaneous occurrence of a forex reserves accumulation programme and LSAPs by the SARB reinforce each other's effects on the price stability mandate, the unemployment rate, GDP growth and employment growth. To complement this exercise, we use the modified Kilian and Vigfusson (2011) approach to conduct a scenario analysis of what the impact of different sizes of positive shocks to forex reserves have on long-term yields, the R/US$ exchange rate, inflation, the unemployment rate, GDP growth and employment growth. We argue that this approach of analysing the effects of reserves accumulation is broader than just the balance of payments-determined definition or considerations. It encompasses the analysis of the benefits of forex reserves accumulation on other macro-economic objectives and the complementary role they play in the conduct of sound monetary, fiscal, prudential and macro-economic policy frameworks to limit a country's vulnerability to multiple shocks.

13.2 Stylised Facts on Foreign Currency Reserves Accumulation and Select Macro-economic Indicators

This section starts by conducting some stylised facts on the accumulation of foreign currency reserves and select macro-economic variables. First, Fig. 13.4 shows that foreign currency reserves constitute almost 90 per cent of the SARB's balance sheet. The counter-entry on the SARB balance sheet to the accumulation of foreign currency reserves which is an outcome of the sterilisation of Rand liquidity created in the process of foreign currency reserves accumulation, is banks' deposits with the SARB (sterilisation deposits). The sterilisation deposits with the SARB are almost 50 per cent of the level of foreign currency reserves and SARB's total liabilities. The sterilisation deposits with the SARB on account of the sterilisation of Rand liquidity created in the process of forex reserves accumulation are remunerated at market-related interest rates.[9]

Nonetheless, Fig. 13.5 shows that in US$ terms, forex reserves have remained stagnant around US$50 billion since 2011. Figure 13.5 shows that the forex reserves accumulation programme stopped in 2010. We argue that this halt in the forex reserves accumulation possibly explains a

[9] As such the interest paid on banks' deposits with the SARB due to sterilisation of foreign currency accumulation can be used to give an indication or estimate of a large portion of the sterilisation costs and costs associated with foreign currency accumulation.

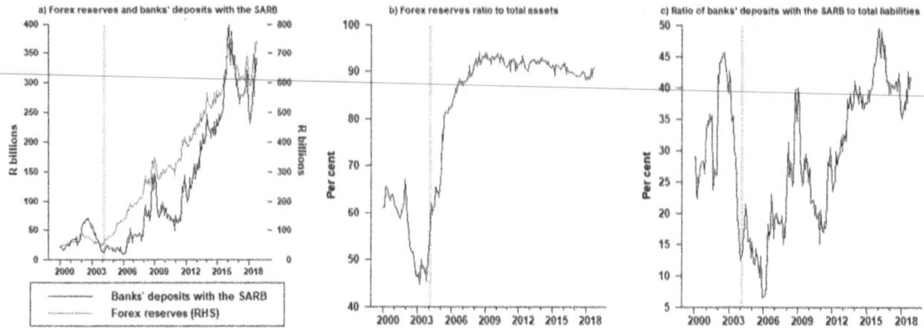

Fig. 13.4 Forex reserves and sterilisation deposits with the SARB. (Source: South African Reserve Bank and authors' calculations)

Fig. 13.5 Forex reserves in US$ terms and the R/US$ exchange rate. (Source: South African Reserve Bank and authors' calculations)

larger portion of the persistent R/US$ exchange-rate depreciation post-2010, as shown in Fig. 13.5(c) by the arrow, over and above the inflationary pressures, political and policy uncertainty that characterised this period.[10] This speaks to the much-needed policy co-ordination within the inflation-targeting framework, which includes the exchange rate stabilisation policy.

Furthermore, Chang (2007) shows that within the inflation-targeting framework, most importantly the implied exchange-rate stabilisation policy is not for its own sake but is derived from the objectives of stabilising inflation and the output gap. These are the two variables in the monetary

[10] See Ndou et al. (2017) on the transmission and role policy uncertainties into the South African economy.

policy makers' objective function, alternatively, the policy trade-off. In addition, Ndou and Gumata (2017) showed that the accumulation of foreign exchange reserves plays a role in appreciating the exchange rate, lowering permanent and overall R/US$ exchange-rate volatilities, lowers inflation and lessens the burden of adjustment on the repo rate whilst supporting the price stability mandate. Thus, concluding that a forex reserves accumulation complementary policy approach can induce additional benefits of reduced welfare costs of elevated inflation hence minimising the policy trade-off.

The growth rates in Fig. 13.5(b) show that forex reserves in US$ terms barely grew more than 10 per cent between 2004 and 2008 but declined for the most part post-2009. This means that a large portion of the increase in the level of forex reserves in Rand terms post-2009 was largely due to the depreciation of the R/US$ during this period. Alternatively, the large part of the increase in forex reserves in Rand terms was largely due to the R/US$ exchange-rate valuation effects, as shown in Fig. 13.5(c).

Figure 13.6 shows that there is a negative association between changes in the rate of foreign currency reserves accumulation and the ten-year government bond yield. The negative association is much steeper for the sub-sample 2004M1 to 2018M12 when the SARB started to accumulate foreign currency reserves at a much aggressive rate, as shown in Fig. 13.6(b). Similarly, the cross correlations in Fig. 13.6(c) show that the ten-year yields decline more when preceded by an increase in foreign currency reserves during the sub-sample 2004M1 to 2018M12 compared to 2000M1 to 2018M12.

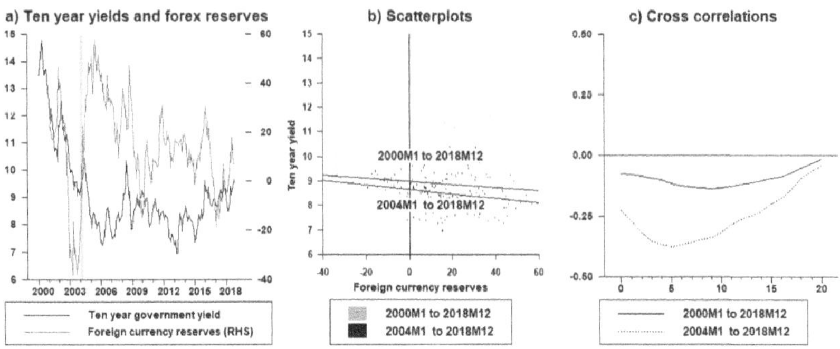

Fig. 13.6 Foreign currency reserves and ten-year yields. (Source: South African Reserve Bank and authors' calculations)

We establish the same impact when assessing the association between the banks' sterilisation deposits with the SARB and ten-year government bond yields in Fig. 13.18 in the Appendix. Similarly, we establish that there is a negative association between the increase in the foreign currency reserves, banks' sterilisation deposits with the SARB and the term spread. The term spread declines when preceded by the increase in forex reserves accumulation and the banks' sterilisation deposits with the SARB in Fig. 13.19 (b and d).

This means that the increase in reserves accumulation and the banks' sterilisation deposits with the SARB reinforce each other and lower the yield spread or the term premium. Because the results established in this section are the same as those exerted by positive shocks to SARB assets growth on yields in earlier chapters, we empirically assess whether LSAPs reinforce the effects of forex reserves on selected financial and macro-economic variables.

Therefore, these are early indications of the existence of the liquidity effect of the forex reserves accumulation on bond yields. The liquidity drained from the market via the sterilisation of the Rand liquidity created during the process of reserves accumulation does affect bond yields. Furthermore, Fig. 13.7 shows that changes in the foreign currency reserves are negatively associated with the unemployment rate and positively associated with GDP growth and employment growth. This means that an increase (accumulation) in forex reserves contributes to the decline in the unemployment rate and an increase in GDP growth and employment growth.

Finally, we show the bilateral relationship between forex reserves accumulation in US$ terms and the R/US$ exchange rate, and forex reserves

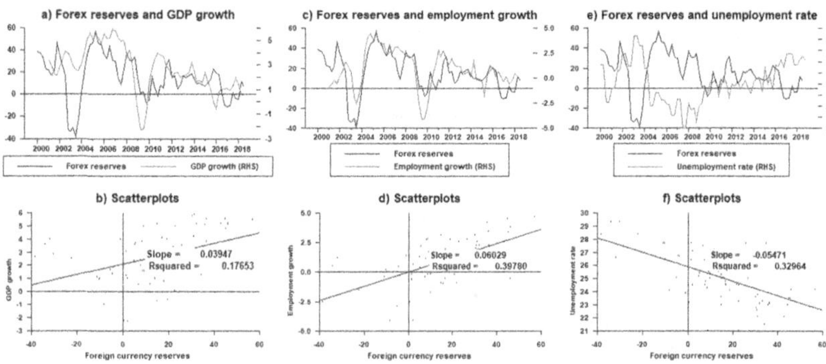

Fig. 13.7 Foreign currency reserves and selected macro-economic variables. (Source: South African Reserve Bank and authors' calculations)

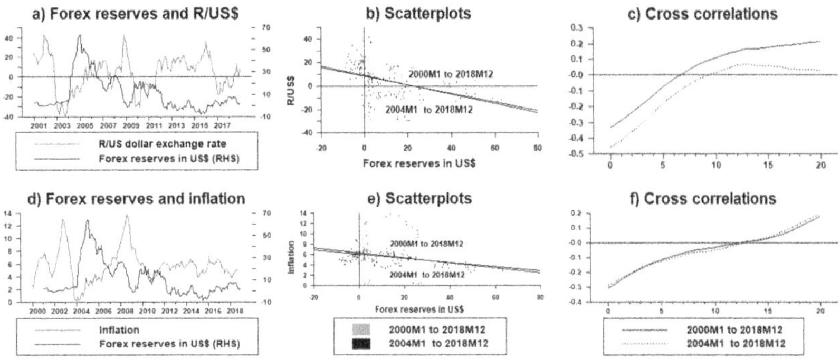

Fig. 13.8 Forex reserves in US$ terms and select macro-economic variables. (Source: South African Reserve Bank and authors' calculations)

and inflation. Figure 13.8(b) shows that there is a negative association between forex reserves and the R/US$ exchange rate and inflation. The R/US$ exchange rate appreciates and inflation declines when preceded by an increase in forex reserves accumulation. This means that the accumulation of forex reserves has the desired effects of neutralising the impact of the R/US$ exchange-rate depreciation on inflation.

13.3 The Impact of Positive Shocks to Reserves Accumulation on the Unemployment Rate, GDP Growth and Employment Growth

This section starts by estimating a four-variable VAR model to assess the impact of positive shocks to forex reserves accumulation. The VAR model includes forex reserves growth, GDP growth, employment growth and the unemployment rate. The growth rates are annual rates. The sample starts in 2000Q1 to 2018Q4. The VAR model is estimated with two lags and 10,000 Monte Carlo draws. The shock is a one standard deviation shock.

The results in Fig. 13.9 show that GDP growth and employment growth increase in response to positive shocks to forex reserves accumulation, whereas the unemployment declines. These results are robust to reverse ordering.

The variance decompositions in Fig. 13.10 show that forex reserves explain around 50 and 20 per cent of the variance in GDP growth and the unemployment rate at peak compared to 10 per cent in employment growth.

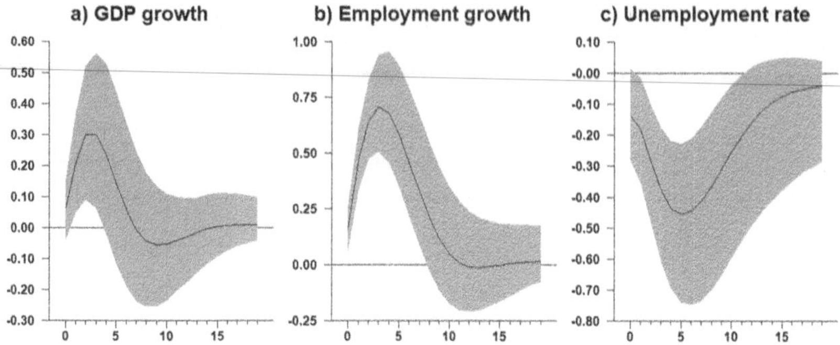

Fig. 13.9 Responses to positive forex reserves shocks. (Source: Authors' calculations)

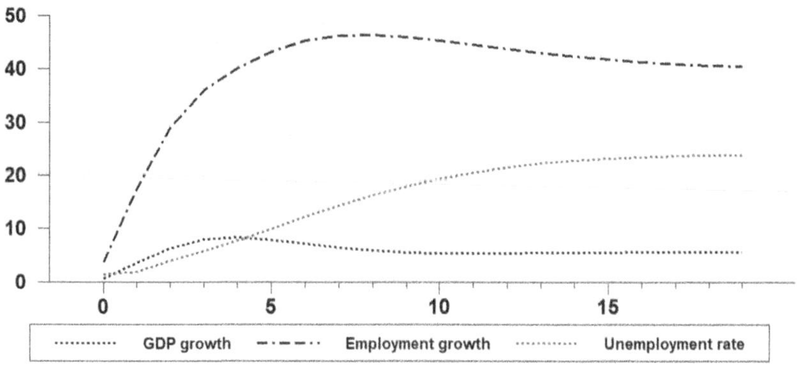

Fig. 13.10 Variance due to positive forex reserves shocks. (Source: Authors' calculations)

13.4 Historical Contributions of Positive Forex Reserves Shocks to the Unemployment Rate, GDP Growth and Employment Growth

We showed earlier that the level of foreign currency reserves has increased since 2004 but has moved sideways post-2009 and the growth rate even briefly turned negative during 2016 and 2017 but has since recovered. In addition, Fig. 13.2 showed that weeks of import cover increased from two weeks in pre-2004 to five weeks post-2004. At the same time, the ratio of forex reserves to GDP increased from 20 per cent in the period pre-2004 to 60 per cent in 2018. To further assess the validity of our hypothesis that positive shocks to forex reserves contribute positively to GDP growth and employment growth, thus lowering the unemployment rate, we show the historical contributions of a positive forex reserves shocks to these variables over time. We are interested in the period 2004Q1 to 2007Q4 when GDP growth and employment growth reached maximum levels of 5.9 per cent and 4.8 per cent respectively, and the unemployment rate declined to 21 per cent.

For this exercise, we estimate a pure-sign restricted VAR model for the period 2000Q1 to 2018Q4. The variables included in the VAR are forex reserves growth, GDP growth, employment growth and the unemployment rate. The growth rates are annual rates. The VAR model is estimated with two lags, 10,000 Monte Carlo draws and the effects of the shock last for four quarters. We impose the positive sign restrictions on the forex reserves and GDP growth variables only and leave the rest of the variables unrestricted so that they are identified by the variables in the model. We derive the counterfactual responses by closing the role of the forex reserves in the evolution of the variable of interest. The contribution of the forex reserves shock is then derived as the difference between the actual and counterfactual responses.

The results of the VAR model in Fig. 13.11 show that the forex reserves accumulation shock made positive contributions to GDP growth and employment growth during 2004Q1 and 2008Q4 and exerted downward

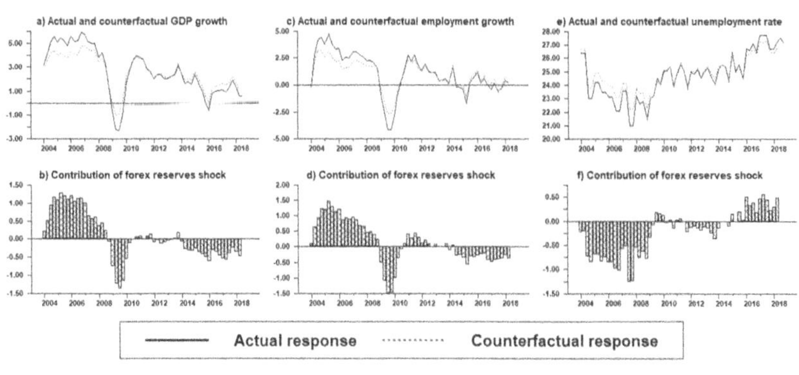

Fig. 13.11 Contributions of forex reserves shocks to GDP growth, employment growth and the unemployment rate. (Source: Authors' calculations)

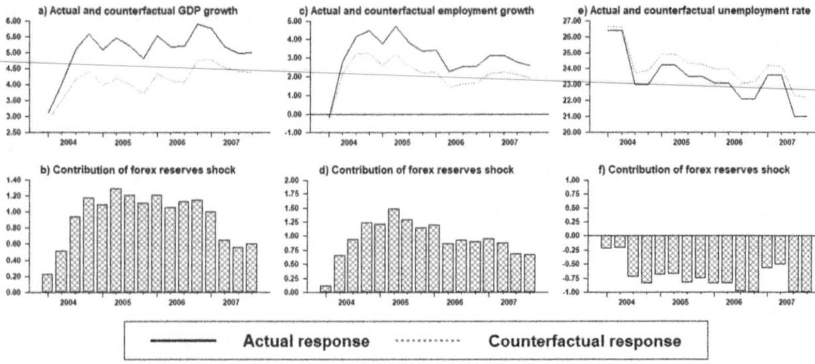

Fig. 13.12 Contributions of forex reserves shocks to GDP growth, employment growth and the unemployment rate during 2004Q1 and 2007Q4. (Source: Authors' calculations)

pressure on the unemployment rate. However, post 2009Q1, the forex reserves have largely been a drag on GDP growth and employment growth and did not help to contain the increase in the unemployment rate.

Furthermore, when we zoom into the period 2004Q1 to 2007Q4, Fig. 13.12 shows that the forex reserves shock made consistent positive contributions to GDP growth and employment growth, leading to a consistent decline in the unemployment rate. Thus, we conclude that our hypothesis that positive shocks to forex reserves contribute positively to GDP growth and employment growth, thus lowering the unemployment rate, is valid.

The accumulation of forex reserves is an important and integral aspect of tools aimed at increasing GDP growth and employment growth and lowering the unemployment rate. As such, the reserves accumulation policy contributed positively to key macro-economic variables. In the absence of the reserves accumulation shock, GDP growth and employment growth would have been 1.2 percentage points and 1.5 percentage points higher at peak response, respectively, whereas the unemployment rate would have been 1 percentage point higher during 2004Q1 to 2007Q4.

13.5 Do Large-Scale Asset Purchases by the SARB Propagate the Effects of Forex Reserves on the Unemployment Rate, GDP Growth and Employment Growth?

We stated earlier that forex reserves accumulation is part and parcel of the balance sheet polices. This section assesses whether positive shocks to reserves accumulation are propagated by positive shocks to LSAPs by the SARB. Alternatively, does the simultaneous occurrence of forex reserves accumulation and LSAPs by the SARB reinforce each other's effects on the unemployment rate, GDP growth and employment growth? To answer this question, we estimate various counterfactual VAR models which include growth in SARB assets (LSAPs), forex reserves, unemployment rate, GDP growth and employment growth. The growth rates are annual rates. The models are estimated using two lags and 10,000 Monet Carlo draws. The sample starts in 2000Q1 to 2018Q4.

The results in Fig. 13.13 indicate that LSAPs reinforce the effects of positive shocks to forex reserves on the unemployment rate, GDP growth and employment growth. In the absence of LSAPs, GDP growth and employment growth increase and the unemployment rate declines in response to positive shocks to forex reserves, but these increases are more and amplified by the presence of LSAPs, as shown in Fig. 13.13 (b, d and f). The results imply that the simultaneous occurrence of forex reserves accumulation and LSAPs by the SARB reinforce each other's effects on

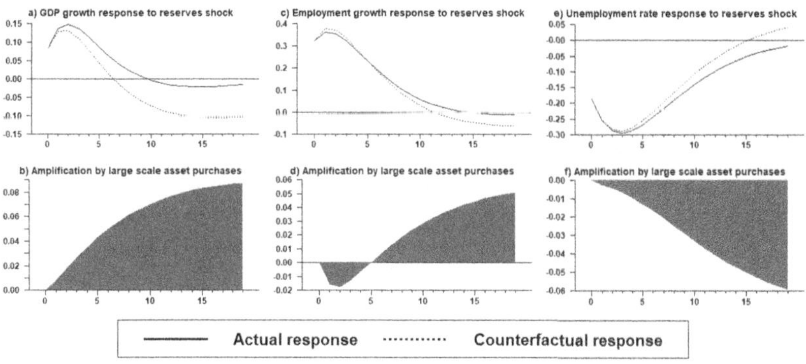

Fig. 13.13 Cumulative responses to forex reserves shocks and amplification by the large-scale asset purchase channel. (Source: Authors' calculations)

the unemployment rate, GDP growth and employment growth. As such, these two monetary policy balance sheet tools complement each other.

13.6 The Asymmetric Effects of Positive Shocks to Forex Reserves on Various Macro-economic Indicators

This section uses the modified Kilian and Vigfusson (2011) approach to assess the impact of one, two, four and ten positive standard deviation shocks to foreign currency reserves on several macro-economic variables. This exercise complements earlier analysis, in that it demonstrates how different positive shock sizes to forex reserves which are equivalent to different incremental changes in forex reserves accumulation have different effects on selected financial and macro-economic variables. For instance, a one standard deviation shock is equivalent to 8 per cent, whereas a two standard deviation shock is double that amount and the four and ten standard deviation shocks are incrementally larger. Furthermore, this exercise enables us to assess what the effects of incrementally large positive shock effects of forex reserves are. We showed in Figs. 13.1 and 13.5 that periods when forex in Rand and US$ terms were increasing at rates more than 20 per cent and 10 per cent, respectively, were associated with price and macro-economic stability.

We estimate several bivariate VAR models which test the asymmetric effects of the different sizes of forex reserves accumulation on the ten-year yields, R/US$ exchange rate, inflation, GDP growth, employment growth and the unemployment rate. The bivariate VAR models are estimated using two lags and 10,000 Monte Carlo draws. The bivariate models include the ten-year yields and another macroeconomic indicator. The macroeconomic indicators are the R/US$ exchange rate growth, inflation, GDP growth, employment growth and the unemployment rate which are included separately in the estimations. All growth rates are annual rates.

Figure 13.14 shows that ten-year yields, the R/US$ exchange rate and inflation decline at differing degrees in response to small and larger positive shocks to forex reserves. Similarly, in Fig. 13.15, we establish that larger positive shocks to forex reserves accumulation exert larger positive effects on GDP growth and employment growth, resulting in larger declines in the unemployment rate.

In the process of reserves accumulation, there are spill-overs to the nominal exchange rate, and this is in turn transmitted to other

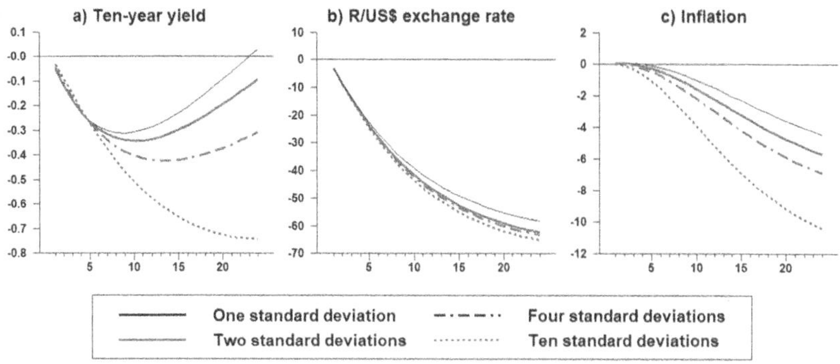

Fig. 13.14 Accumulated responses to positive shocks to forex reserves. (Source: Authors' calculations)

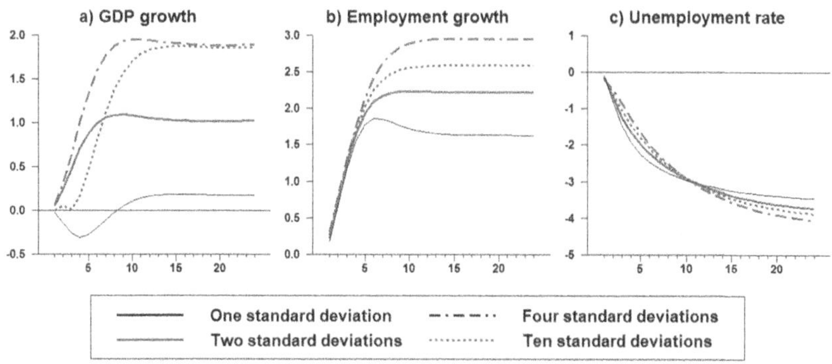

Fig. 13.15 Accumulated responses to positive shocks to forex reserves. (Source: Authors' calculations)

macro-economic variables such as inflation. In such a process, forex reserves accumulation and management tend to go beyond financial stability objectives and assist in the price stability objective.

The policy implications of the results in this section are that a forex reserves accumulation programme that increases South Africa's forex reserves by a minimum of 8 per cent will complement other policies aimed at enforcing a stable exchange rate, a moderate increase in government funding costs and macro-economic stability in the form of a lower unemployment rate, robust GDP growth and employment growth. Incrementally larger increases in forex reserves result in better outcomes in these selected financial and macro-economic variables. Furthermore, all these outcomes are consistent with the central bank mandates of price, financial and macro-economic stability. Thus, there is scope and capacity for the SARB to embark on another forex reserves accumulation programme like that post-2004.

13.7 The Impact of Transitory and Permanent Shocks to Foreign Currency Reserves Accumulation

Because the process of reserves accumulation inherently implies that the trajectory of the increase in the level of forex reserves can differ over time, this section assesses the impact of a transitory (one-off) and persistently rising positive shock to forex reserves. We estimate a number of VAR models to assess the impact of transitory and persistently rising positive shocks to forex reserves on the unemployment rate, GDP growth and employment growth. The VAR model is estimated using two lags and 10,000 Monte Carlo draws.

The results in Fig. 13.16 show that persistently rising positive shocks to forex reserves result in a larger increase in GDP growth and employment growth and thus a larger decline in the unemployment rate. This is evident in the cumulative effects shown in Fig. 13.17, which show the difference between the effects of persistently rising and non-persistent shocks on the unemployment rate, GDP growth and employment growth.

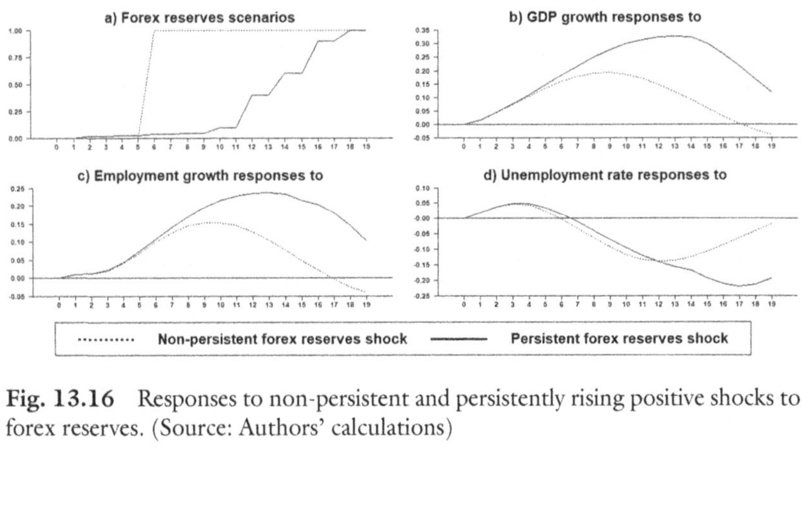

Fig. 13.16 Responses to non-persistent and persistently rising positive shocks to forex reserves. (Source: Authors' calculations)

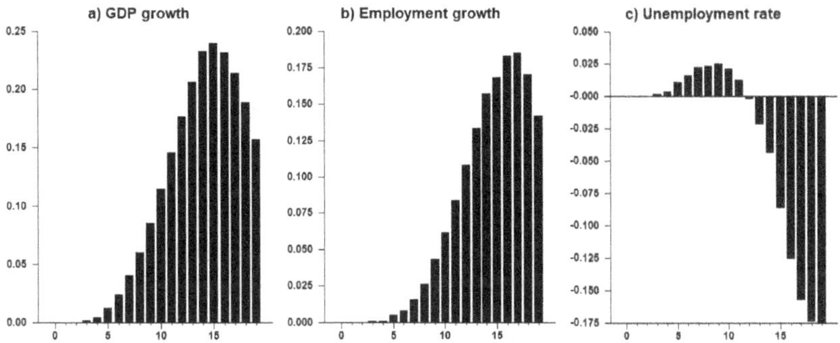

Fig. 13.17 Cumulative effects of persistently rising positive forex reserves shocks. (Source: Authors' calculations)

Thus, beyond the traditional and well-known primary objectives and motives for holding forex reserves, persistently rising positive shocks forex reserves contribute to increasing GDP growth and employment growth whilst lowering the unemployment rate. There is, therefore, a case for the accumulation of forex reserves beyond the precautionary risks associated with the balance of payments and sudden stops of capital inflows.

13.8 Conclusion and Policy Implications

This chapter assessed whether forex reserves accumulation programmes contribute to GDP growth and employment growth. Evidence shows that GDP growth and employment growth increase in response to positive shocks to forex reserves accumulation, whereas unemployment declines. In addition, the counterfactual historical contributions for the period 2004Q1 to 2007Q4 show that forex reserves accumulation shocks made consistent positive contributions to GDP growth and employment growth, leading to a consistent decline in the unemployment rate. In the absence of positive forex reserves shocks, unemployment would have been higher, whereas GDP growth and employment growth would have been lower. Furthermore, we establish that the simultaneous occurrence of forex reserves accumulation and LSAPs by the SARB reinforce each other's effects on the unemployment rate, GDP growth and employment growth. We find that in the absence of LSAPs, the impact of forex reserves accumulation on the unemployment rate, GDP growth and the employment rate is much lower. Thus, these two monetary policy balance sheet tools complement each other.

Is there scope and capacity for the SARB to embark on another forex reserves accumulation programme like that post-2004? Yes, the results establish that there is. We find that larger shocks to forex reserves accumulation exert larger positive effects on GDP growth and employment growth, resulting in larger declines in the unemployment rate. Furthermore, persistently rising positive shocks to forex reserves have cumulatively larger effects on GDP growth and employment growth and the unemployment rate. The policy implications of these results are that a forex reserves accumulation programme that increases South Africa's forex reserves by a minimum of 8 per cent will complement other policies aimed at enforcing a stable exchange rate, a moderate increase in government funding costs and macro-economic stability in the form of a lower unemployment rate, robust GDP growth and employment growth. Incrementally larger increases in forex reserves result in better outcomes in these selected financial and macro-economic variables. Furthermore, all these outcomes are consistent with the SARB mandates of price, financial and macro-economic stability. Such a broad approach to reserves accumulation complements sound macroeconomic and prudential policy frameworks and limits a country's vulnerability to multiple shocks. This speaks to the much-needed policy co-ordination within the inflation-targeting framework, which includes the exchange-rate stabilisation policy.

Appendix

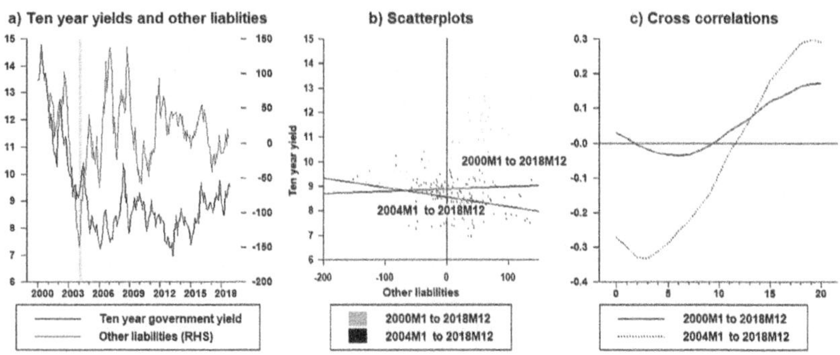

Fig. 13.18 Sterilisation deposits and the ten-year yields. (Source: South African Reserve Bank and authors' calculations)

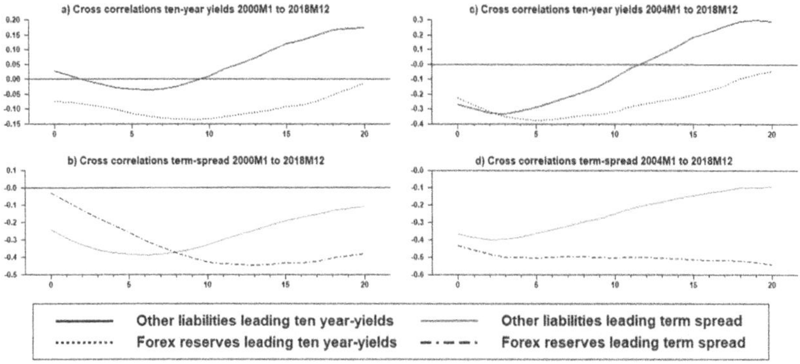

Fig. 13.19 The effects of sterilisation deposits and forex reserves accumulation on the ten-year yields. (Source: South African Reserve Bank and authors' calculations)

References

Borio C, and Disyatat P. 2010. Unconventional Monetary Policies: An Appraisal. Manchester School, University of Manchester, 78(s1), pp. 53–89, September.

Cœuré B. 2018. The persistence and signalling power of central bank asset purchase programmes. Speech at the 2018 US Monetary Policy Forum, New York City, 23 February 2018.

Menon M. 2019. How Singapore manages its reserves. Keynote speech at the National Asset-Liability Management Europe Conference, Singapore, 13 March 2019. https://www.bis.org/review/r190313b.pdf

IMF Assessing Reserve Adequacy. https://www.imf.org/external/datamapper/ARA/index.html

IMF. 2011. Assessing Reserve Adequacy. Third IMF Roundtable of Sovereign Asset and Reserves Managers. https://www.imf.org/external/np/pp/eng/2011/021411b.pdf

Kilian L, and Vigfusson R J. 2011. Are the Responses of the U.S. Economy Asymmetric in Energy Price Increases and Decreases? Quantitative Economics, 2(4), pp. 419–453.

Lane T. 2019. Taking Precautions: The Canadian Approach to Foreign Reserves Management. Remarks at the Peterson Institute for International Economics, Washington, D.C. February 6, 2019. https://www.bankofcanada.ca/2019/02/taking-precautions-canadian-approach-foreign-reserves-

management/?utm_source=twitter&utm_medium=social&utm_campaign=SPTL190206
Ndou E, Gumata N, and Ncube M. 2017. Global Economic Uncertainties and Exchange Rate Shocks: Transmission Channels to the South African Economy. Palgrave Macmillan. ISBN 978-3-319-62280-4.
Olivier J, and Ranciere R. 2006. "The Optimal Level of International Reserves for Developing Countries: Formulas and Applications". IMF Working Paper 06/229. https://www.imf.org/external/pubs/ft/wp/2006/wp06229.pdf
Rodrik D. 2006.The Social Cost of Foreign Exchange Reserves Dani Rodrik NBER Working Paper No. 11952 January 2006 JEL No. F3. https://www.nber.org/papers/w11952.pdf
Chang R. 2007. Inflation Targeting, Reserves Accumulation, and Exchange Rate Management in Latin America. Papers and Proceedings—Inflation Targeting. http://www.banrep.gov.co/sites/default/files/publicaciones/archivos/borra487.pdf
Ndou E, and Gumata N. 2017. Inflation Dynamics in South Africa: The Role of Thresholds, Exchange Rate Pass-through and Inflation Expectations on Policy Trade-offs. Palgrave Macmillan. ISBN 978-3-319-46702-3.
Arce A, Bengui J, and Bianchi J A. 2019. Macroprudential Theory of Foreign Reserve Accumulation. Bank of Canada staff Working Paper 2019-43. https://www.bankofcanada.ca/wp-content/uploads/2019/10/swp2019-43.pdf
William C, Dudley C W. 2018. A Skeptical View of the Impact of the Fed's Balance Sheet. Speech at the 2018 U.S. Monetary Policy Forum, New York City, February 23, 2018.

CHAPTER 14

What Is the Impact of Large-Scale Asset Purchases and Private Banks' Balance Sheets?

Research Questions Explored

- Assess the threshold effects of large-scale asset purchases (LSAPs) by the South African Reserve Bank (SARB) on banks' balance sheets.
- Assess whether LSAPs of government securities by the SARB curb the excess liquid asset holdings (LAH) of banks.
- Assess the transmission channels through which LSAPs of government securities by the SARB are transmitted to the banks' deposit and lending rates.
- Explore whether LSAPs of government securities by the SARB affect the interest rate pass-through, bank loan intermediation mark-up and credit conditions.
- Assess whether increasing the share of banks' funding via the discount window complements or propagates or dampens the effects of LSAP

14.1 Introduction

What is the impact of large-scale asset purchases (LSAPs) by the South African Reserve Bank (SARB) on private banks' balance sheets? In earlier chapters, we showed that banks hold almost 90 per cent of Treasury Bills

N. Gumata, E. Ndou, *Achieving Price, Financial and Macro-Economic Stability in South Africa*,
https://doi.org/10.1007/978-3-030-66340-7_14

(TBs), 80 per cent of short-term government bonds and 14 per cent of long-term government bonds. For bank liquidity regulatory purposes, government securities form part of liquid assets. On the other hand, reserves requirements are held for three main purposes: (i) prudential, (ii) monetary control and (iii) liquidity management purposes. For prudential purposes, required reserves (RR) provide some protection against liquidity and solvency risks. With respect to monetary control, RR can restrict the commercial bank balance sheet growth and the central bank can vary the level of unremunerated RR in a way that is intended to influence the spread between deposit and lending rates. This is in turn expected to impact the growth of monetary aggregates and thus inflation. For liquidity management purposes, RR can be used actively or passively. Actively used by the central bank, RR can be adjusted to neutralise the impact of surplus reserves on bank behaviour so that it does not result in inflationary pressures or the depreciation of the exchange rate. Similarly, RR can be used passively through the averaging approach to manage the commercial banks' short-term liquidity and in turn a reduction in the short-term interest rate volatility (Gray 2011). In the South African case, RR are managed passively.[1]

Figure 14.1 shows that banks hold R350 billion, alternatively, almost 60 per cent of government securities, in excess of the minimum required

Fig. 14.1 Banks' liquid asset holdings and breakdown by asset type. (Source: South African Reserve Bank and authors' calculations)

[1]We explore the role of RR in the banking system and their interaction with the liquid asset holding of banks and the accumulation of foreign currency reserves in later chapters in the book.

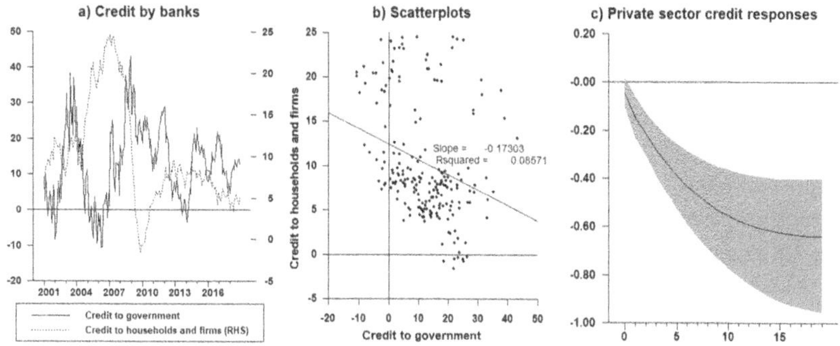

Fig. 14.2 Credit to government and the private sector. (Note: The grey shaded areas in part (c) denote the 16th and 84th percentile confidence bands. Source: South African Reserve Bank and authors' calculations)

liquid assets in Fig. 14.1 (c and d). Of the total current liquid asset holdings, Treasury Bills and government bonds constitute almost 50 per cent of the total, respectively in Fig. 14.1(b). This resulted in an increase in the share of bank credit to the government from around 6 per cent to 22 per cent in Fig. 14.1(e), at the end of 2018. At the same time, Fig. 14.2 shows that during this period, credit to government increased at a faster rate compared to credit to households and companies. Furthermore, there is a negative association between credit to government and the private sector. Credit to the private sector declines in response to positive shocks to credit to government in Fig. 14.2(c). Thus, an increase in bank credit to government tends to depress credit to the private sector.

So, what are the effects of LSAPs of government securities by the SARB on private banks' balance sheets? Do LSAPs of government securities by the SARB curb excess LAH by banks? How are LSAPs of government securities by the SARB transmitted to the banks' deposit and lending rates? Do LSAPs of government securities by the SARB affect the interest rate pass-through, bank loan intermediation mark-up and credit conditions?

Recent literature on the effects of LSAPs by central banks shows that they affect private banks' balance sheets. For instance, ECB (2015)[2] shows that the credit easing package, focusing on the targeted longer-term

[2] See https://www.ecb.europa.eu/pub/pdf/other/eb201507_article01.en.pdf

refinancing operations (TLTROs),[3] and the expanded asset purchase programme (APP), focusing on the public sector purchase programme (PSPP),[4] significantly lowered yields in a broad set of financial market segments. The significance of these effects was generally different depending on the maturity and riskiness of assets involved. These non-standard programmes also contributed to a reduction in the banks' funding costs, which in turn incentivised banks to pass on the cost relief to final borrowers by granting more credit at better conditions.

Haldane et al. (2016) indicate that as monetary policy tools, LSAPs can be used to provide liquidity support to the banking sector and improve the functioning of the monetary policy transmission mechanism. Andrade et al. (2016) show that this transmission channel of LSAPs also encompasses the (i) "*duration risk channel*", which emphasises the importance of purchasing long-maturity bonds; and the (ii) "*capital relief channel*", because the increase in asset prices that are generated by the asset purchase programme are synonymous with a capital injection for leverage-constrained institutions. Furthermore, ECB (2017) shows that through the portfolio rebalancing channel, non-standard ECB programmes affected financial assets and incentivised banks to improve credit conditions for households and nonfinancial corporations alike. The study established that different non-standard measures have had a mutually reinforcing impact on bank lending conditions. For instance, on the liability side, the TLTROs have brought funding relief for banks participating in the central operations. At the same time, the APP and policy rate cuts have led to a compression of funding costs for the banking system as a whole.

On the asset side, the negative interest rates on excess liquidity (excess reserves balances) have reinforced portfolio rebalancing effects.[5] This is because the implicit charge applied on excess reserves has increased the velocity of circulation of excess reserves in the money market, and thus has improved the relative attractiveness for banks of granting loans or holding securities with a higher return. However, the precise patterns of the resultant improvements in credit conditions have varied across different types of banks and/or across countries. On the other hand, in Sweden, evidence

[3] See on the definition and purpose of TLTROs https://www.ecb.europa.eu/mopo/implement/omo/tltro/html/index.en.html

[4] See on the details of various asset purchase programmes conducted by the ECB https://www.ecb.europa.eu/mopo/implement/omt/html/index.en.html

[5] We explore the threshold effects of excess reserves and their role on inter-bank rate volatility in later chapters of the book.

shows that negative interest rates are not harmful to the economy. Negative interest rates do not impede lending growth and are transmitted to actual lending rates.[6]

This chapter contributes to literature by assessing the impact of LSAPs on the private banks' balance sheets. We explore the impact of LSAPs on banks' excess LAH. The implication of the trends in Fig. 14.1 is that the SARB can shave off or buy the excess 50 per cent of government securities without disrupting or inducing undue distortions in the money market. We test whether there are asymmetric effects introduced by lowering the excess LAH from the current 60 per cent to 10 per cent. Guidance for this demarcation and threshold is derived from the trend since 2009, shown in Fig. 14.1(c and d). In addition, we assess how LSAPs are transmitted to banks' credit conditions, lending and deposit rates, and whether LSAPs propagate the impact of the repo rate to these variables.

The National Development Plan (NDP) has set an objective to move the unemployment rate to single digits by 2030. Small-, micro- and medium-sized enterprises (SMMEs) have been earmarked as one of the key sectors that will contribute meaningfully to reach this target. As such, the NDP projects that more than 90 per cent of new employment opportunities, alternatively, at least 11 million of new employment opportunities, will be created by (SMMEs) by 2030. It is estimated that for this to happen, South Africa needs over 49,000 SMMEs growing at a rate of 20 per cent per annum and roughly 8.2 million micro-enterprises.[7] The NDP identified easing access to finance to SMMEs as one critical policy intervention to deal with the reluctance of lenders to lend to this sector. Furthermore, the NDP calls for urgent measures to reform the mandates and operations of development finance institutions, in line with initiatives to bring services to this sector.[8]

Against this backdrop and largely based on the experience of the ECB with TLTROs, we also assess whether there is a case for increasing the rate at which banks borrow at the SARB discount window whilst increasing the

[6] See https://www.bloomberg.com/news/articles/2019-01-16/summers-is-rebutted-in-sweden-after-criticizing-negative-rates

[7] See https://www.biznews.com/transformation/2015/05/05/ndp-aims-high-target-of-11mln-jobs-by-2030-needs-49-000-smes-at-growth-of-20-pa

[8] Part of the reluctance of credit providers to lend in this market arises from high costs of additional monitoring, advisory and support services that are required to manage the risk of default. See pages 117 to 120 of the NDP https://www.gov.za/sites/default/files/gcis_document/201409/ndp-2030-our-future-make-it-workr.pdf

maturities of the repurchase agreements on offer by the SARB. What are the effects of increasing the share of banks' funding via the discount window (repo accommodation) on credit conditions, lending and deposit rates? Does increasing the share of banks' funding via the discount window complement or dampen the effects of LSAPs of government securities?

Over and above the positive financial and macro-economic effects of increasing the rate at which banks borrow at the SARB discount window by lengthening the maturities of the repurchase agreements, we argue that such a strategy will neutralise the impact of sterilisation and other costs associated with the forex reserves accumulation programme recommended in earlier chapters.

We use three econometric techniques to answer the questions posed in this chapter. First, we use the modified Kilian and Vigfusson (2011) approach to assess the impact of the LSAPs on banks' credit conditions, and various lending and deposit rates. Second, we use the threshold VAR approach to explore the implication of the SARB shaving off or buying the excess 50 per cent of government securities, as shown in Fig. 14.1(c and d). We use the threshold VAR approach to test the asymmetric effects introduced by lowering the excess LAH from the current 60 per cent to 10 per cent. Guidance for this demarcation and threshold is derived from the trend since 2009, as shown in Fig. 14.1(c and d). Third, we use the counterfactual VAR approach to assess whether LSAPs propagate or dampen the effects of the repo rate on credit conditions, and various lending and deposit rates.

In addition, Andrade et al. (2016) and Gertler and Karadi (2011 and 2013) show that when banks face funding constraints that arise endogenously as a consequence of banks' capital position, the mechanisms which activate changes in asset valuations activate the "asset valuation channel". The asset purchases by central banks replace long-term and/or riskier assets with short-term and safe central bank reserves. This mitigates the riskiness of banks' portfolios and allows them to increase risky loans and to reduce lending rates. The asset purchases under this channel become more effective through the purchases of "riskier" assets (i.e. those with higher duration, higher liquidity or counterparty risk). This eases the banks' funding constraints and results in more potent macro-economic effects.

14.2 Private Banks' Balance Sheets, Deposit Breakdown and Money Market Rates

This section starts by exploring the various relationships between the repo rate, credit conditions, and lending and deposit rates. The credit conditions index used in this chapter was estimated in Gumata and Ndou (2017).[9] Negative (positive) values of the credit conditions index imply loose (tight) bank credit conditions. Figure 14.3(a) shows that the repo rate is bounded by the lending and deposit rates. At the same time, there is a negative association between the repo rate and the bank credit conditions in Fig. 14.3(c). This means that increases (decreases) in the repo rate lead to tight (loose) bank credit conditions.

Literature shows that central bank LSAPs also affect private banks' balance sheets by influencing their balance sheet developments, funding conditions and risk-bearing capacity. The ECB (2015) indicates that as an attractive source of long-term funding, the TLTROs are intended to allow banks to replace more costly sources of funding and extend the maturity of their liabilities in order to better match that of the lending targeted by the measure. Furthermore, evidence shows that the funding substitution took place because of the TLTROs and resulted in a significant extension of the maturity of bank funding. The extension of maturity provides banks

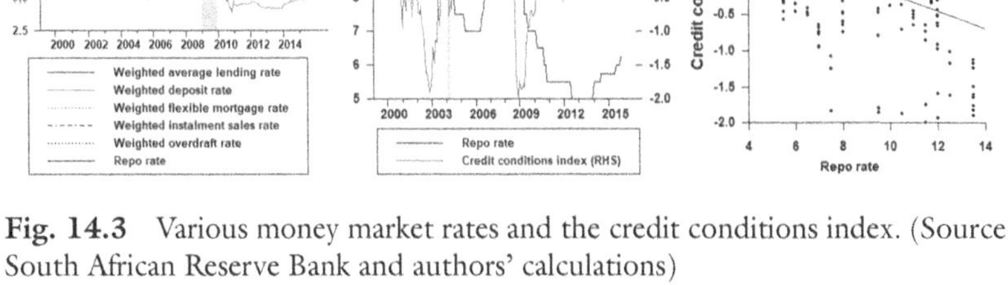

Fig. 14.3 Various money market rates and the credit conditions index. (Source: South African Reserve Bank and authors' calculations)

[9] See Gumata and Ndou (2017) for details on the methodology followed to construct the credit conditions index.

with funding certainty over a longer period and allows them to better match the maturity of their liabilities with that of assets such as loans to households and firms. Evidence also shows that TLTRO borrowers also reduced their recourse to wholesale funding, that is, issuance of debt securities and interbank borrowing.

Figure 14.4 shows the long-term structure of the South African banks' asset and liabilities. It is evident that banks largely source their funding from deposits, the interbank and debt securities markets.

On the asset side, banks largely transform these deposits and funds to credit to the households and firms. For a shortage-based refinancing system[10] such as in South Africa, Fig. 14.4 shows that banks only use about 2 per cent of funds sourced at the repurchase agreement market to fund themselves. The trends in Fig. 14.4 indicate that banks largely fund themselves in the retail, wholesale, interbank and debt securities markets, as opposed to the the discount window. This aspect of the banks' balance sheets speaks directly to the ability of banks to transmit changes in the repo rate to the economy at large. Put differently, Fig. 14.5(a) shows that on average, deposit rates are priced below the repo rate when considering

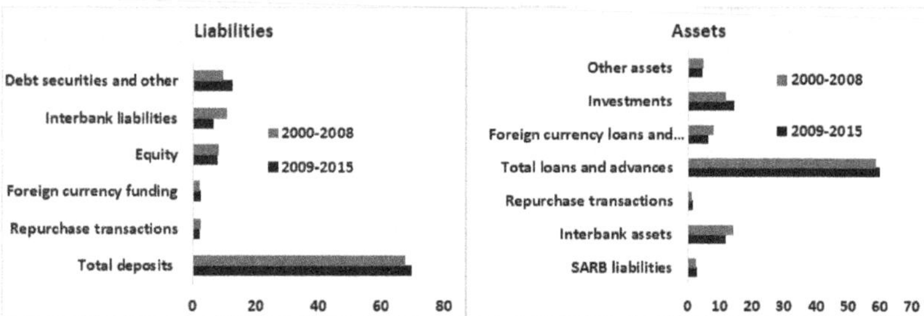

Fig. 14.4 Banks' assets and liabilities. (Source: South African Reserve Bank and authors' calculations)

[10] In a shortage-based accommodation system, the central bank creates a liquidity shortage in the market by withdrawing excess liquidity, thus compelling banks to fund the liquidity shortage at the accommodation window. In earlier chapters, we showed that one of the mechanisms the SARB uses to control money market liquidity is the sterilisation of its foreign currency reserve accumulation. During the course of foreign currency reserve accumulation, banks are required to deposit the Rand liquidity created with the SARB, thus draining the Rand liquidity created and controlling the money supply. These money market operations contribute to the creation (level) of the liquidity shortage in the money market.

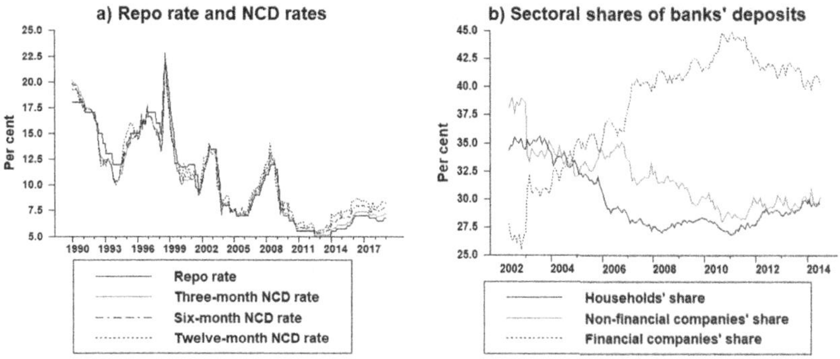

Fig. 14.5 Sectoral breakdown of banks' deposits and Nonnegotiable Certificates of Deposit (NCD) rates. (Source: South African Reserve Bank and authors' calculations)

the average weighted deposit rate, whereas lending rates are priced at a minimum of 300 basis points above the repo rate.

However, when considering the fact that financial companies[11] constitute more than 40 per cent of deposits with banks, as shown in Fig. 14.5(b), compared to almost 30 per cent of households and non-financial companies, it is also appropriate to consider the NCD rates relative to the repo rate. Figure 14.3 shows that compared to the average weighted deposit rate shown in Fig. 14.5(a), the NCD rates are priced a few basis points above the repo rate. These trends also indicate that retail (household) deposits constitute a smaller share as opposed to wholesale deposits as a key source of funding for banks.

14.3 Banks' Liquidity Requirement, Repo Rate and Other Money Market Rates

We showed in Fig. 14.4 that banks use about 2 per cent of funds sourced at the discount window to fund themselves. What are the implications of LSAPs for banks' balance sheets in such an accommodation system? Alternatively, what are the effects of increasing the share of the banks' funding via the discount window on credit conditions, lending and deposit

[11] This category is largely made up of insurers, pension funds and other financial corporations. See Fig. 14.16 in the appendix for the breakdown of financial companies' deposits with banks.

rates? Does increasing the share of banks' funding via the discount window complement or propagate or dampen the effects of LSAPs ?

The intention of exploring these questions is to assess whether a change to the accommodation system (discount window) to increase the share of banks' funding sourced from repurchase agreements will enhance the monetary policy transmission mechanism. Recent literature, especially from the euro area, indicates that innovations to banks' accommodation system via instruments such as TLTROs had the desired positive effects in enhancing the transmission of monetary policy actions and reinforcing the accommodative monetary policy stance. Currently, the SARB accommodation system operates on short-dated (maturity) repurchase agreements on a weekly basis (six days) financed at the repo rate. As such, is there a case for augmenting the current accommodation system by introducing longer-dated (maturity) accommodation window instruments? What are the implications of such an augmentation in the accommodation system?

As a preliminary exercise to the empirical assessment of the impact of the increase in the banks' liquidity requirements (funding at the accommodation window), we assess the association between changes in the banks' liquidity requirements (banks' funding at the discount window), repo rate, NCD rate, deposit and lending rates. In Fig. 14.6 the scatterplots indicate that there is a negative association between the banks' liquidity requirements, repo rate, NCD rate, deposit and lending rates. This means that an increase (decline) in the bank's liquidity requirement

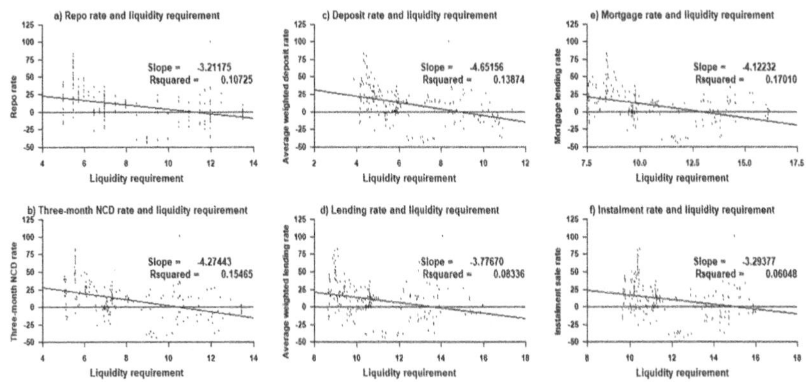

Fig. 14.6 Banks' liquidity requirement and various interest rates. (Source: South African Reserve Bank and authors' calculations)

results in a decline (increase) in the repo rate, NCD rate, deposit and lending rates. The increase in the liquidity requirements of banks is equivalent to the increase in the money market shortage and an injection of liquidity in the money market via an increased usage of the discount window. The increase in the money market shortage effectively enhances the use of the discount window and the effectiveness of the transmission of the repo rate to the money market rates and the real economy.

Further, to establish the responses of various money market rates to positive shocks to the banks' liquidity requirements, we estimate various bilateral VAR models. The bilateral VAR models include changes in the banks' liquidity requirements, and the interest rate. The interest rate is captured by the repo rate and other money market interest rates. The other money market interest rates are the three-month NCD rate, average weighted lending rate and mortgage rate. The money market rates enter the VAR model separately. The VAR models include M3 growth as an exogenous variable. The growth rates are annual rates. The sample for the estimations spans the period 2000M1 to 2018M12. The VAR models are estimated using two lags and 10,000 Monte Carlo draws. The shock is a one standard deviation shock.

The results in Fig. 14.7 indicate that all money market rates decline in line with the repo rate in response to a positive shock to the banks' liquidity requirements. A comparison of the peak responses in Fig. 14.7(f) shows that the three-month NCD rate declines more, followed by the

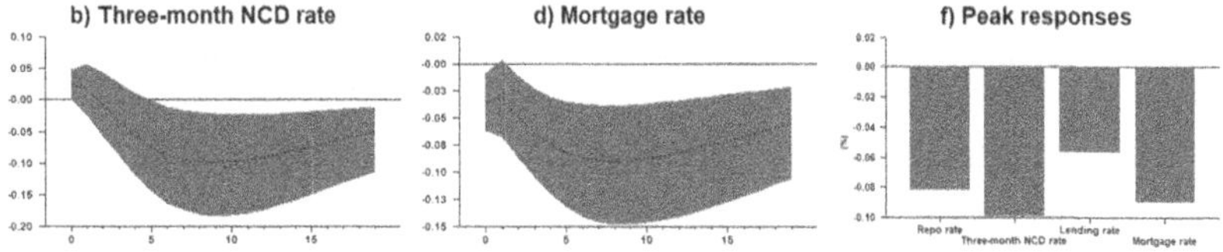

Fig. 14.7 Responses to positive shocks to the banks' liquidity requirements. (Note: The grey shaded areas denote the 16th and 84th percentile confidence bands. Source: Authors' calculations)

mortgage lending rate. These results indicate that indeed increasing the money market shortage and the rate at which banks lend at the discount window leads to a decline in the funding rates and this is transmitted to the lending rates. How robust are these results to changes in the estimation technique and model specification? To assess for robustness, we use the modified Kilian and Vigfusson (2011) approach. Furthermore, the modified Kilian and Vigfusson (2011) approach assists us in exploring the asymmetries induced by shocks of different magnitudes to the banks' liquidity requirements. Exploring the impact of different magnitudes of shocks to the banks' liquidity requirements also gives us a good estimation and indication of what the impact of increasing the repurchase agreements as a source of funding for banks from the current 2 per cent to, for example, 10 per cent, 20 per cent and 30 per cent over time. We estimate a modified version of the asymmetric VAR using the modified Kilian and Vigfusson (2011) approach for the period 2000M1 to 2018M12. We create a dummy variable to capture the effects on an increase in the banks' liquidity requirements only. This dummy takes on all the positive values of banks' liquidity requirements and zero otherwise. The bilateral VAR model includes changes in banks' liquidity requirements and interest rate. The interest rate variables are the repo rate, three-month NCD rate, average weighted lending rate and mortgage rate. The money market rates enter the VAR model separately. The growth rates are annual rates. The model is estimated using four lags and 1000 Monte Caro draws.

The results in Fig. 14.8 indicate that the decline in the repo rate, and other money market and lending rates is robust to changes in the estimation technique and the specification of the model. Nonetheless, the asymmetry induced by different sizes of shocks to the banks' liquidity requirements is not very pronounced.

Thus, the results indicate that the lengthening of the maturities of funding options available at the discount window can result in the substitution of funding sources by banks on the liabilities side of their balance sheets and the cost of funding. Most importantly, long-term repurchase agreements will also affect the way banks price lending on the asset side. As such, lengthening of the maturities of funding options available at the discount window can loosen the funding constraints experienced by banks and this will spill over to the funding of important markets such as the housing sector and SMMEs.[12] Furthermore, from a policy and regulatory

[12] The ECB indicates that the TLTROs are targeted operations. The amount that banks can borrow is linked to their loans to non-financial corporations and households. Moreover,

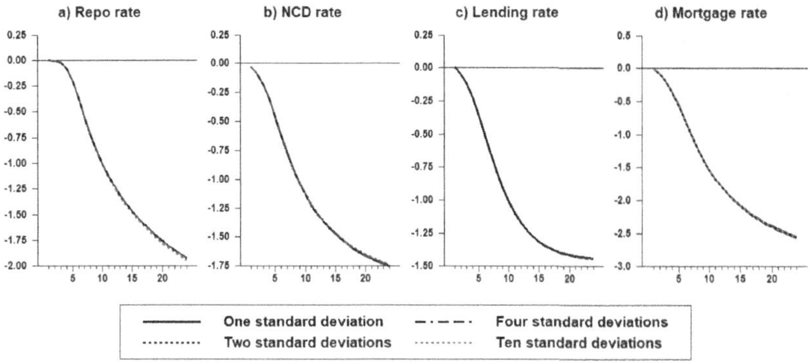

Fig. 14.8 Accumulated responses to positive shocks to the banks' liquidity requirements. (Source: Authors' calculations)

perspective, the lengthening of the maturity of the funding options for banks is especially important given the longstanding regulatory concern of the maturity mismatch risks induced by funding long-term assets, such as housing, using deposits which are of a short duration.

14.4 Does the Increase in the Banks' Liquidity Requirements Propagate the Effects of an Accommodative Monetary Policy Stance?

The earlier section showed that a positive (increase) shock to the banks' liquidity requirements results in a decline in the repo rate, and other funding and lending rates. This section extends the analysis by assessing whether positive shocks to the banks' liquidity requirements propagate the effects of an accommodative monetary policy stance (decline in the repo rate) on other money market (funding) rates and lending rates.

We estimate several counterfactual VAR models, which include three variables in the baseline VAR model. The models include the repo rate, the three-month NCD rate, the average weighted lending rate, the mortgage

under the TLTRO II scheme, the interest rate applied was linked to the participating banks' lending patterns. The more loans that participating banks issue to non-financial corporations and households (except loans to households for house purchases), the more attractive the interest rate on their TLTRO II borrowings becomes. See for further details https://www.ecb.europa.eu/mopo/implement/omo/tltro/html/index.en.html

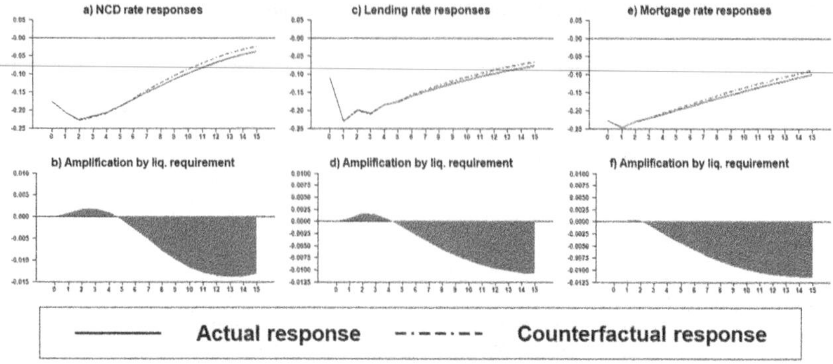

Fig. 14.9 Responses to positive shocks to the repo rate and propagation by the banks' liquidity requirements channel. (Note: Liq. requirement = banks' liquidity requirement. Source: Authors' calculations)

rate and growth in the banks' liquidity requirements. Growth in M3 money supply enters the VAR mode as an exogenous variable. The counterfactual VAR model calculates the responses of the various money market and lending rates to the decline in the repo rate in the presence (when the variable is active in the model) and absence (counterfactual) of the banks' liquidity requirements. Thus, we shut off the banks' liquidity requirements channel to calculate the counterfactual response. The growth rates are annual rates. The sample spans the period 2000M1 to 2018M12. The VAR models are estimated using two lags and 10,000 Monte Carlo draws. The results in Fig. 14.9 show that the three-month NCD, average weighted lending and mortgage interest rates decline in response to a decline in the repo rate and that the banks' liquidity requirements propagate the decline in the money market and lending rates across the board.

14.5 Do Large-Scale Asset Purchases of Government Securities by the SARB Exert Similar Effects to Positive Shocks to the Banks' Liquidity Requirements, the Repo Rate, and the Money Market and Lending Rates?

We stated earlier that in intervening via non-standard monetary policy, central banks used the credit easing package that (i) focused on easing tensions in the interbank markets so as to unblock the transmission of policy interventions and (ii) engaged in asset purchases. Evidence shows that these interventions significantly lowered yields and rates in a broad set of financial market segments. To complement the results in the previous section and earlier chapters, this section assesses whether positive shocks to LSAPs by the SARB exert the same downward pressure on the repo rate, and other money market and lending interest rates. We use the modified Kilian and Vigfusson (2011) approach for the period 2000M1 to 2018M12. The bivariate VAR models include growth in SARB assets and other variables. The other variables are, the credit conditions index, mortgage market credit conditions,[13] the repo rate, the three-month NCD rate, the average weighted lending rate and the average weighted mortgage lending rate. The credit conditions index, mortgage market credit conditions, the repo rate, the three-month NCD rate, the average weighted lending rate and the average weighted mortgage lending rate enter the VAR estimations separately. All the growth rates are annual rates. The models are estimated using four lags and 10,000 Monte Carlo draws.

The results in Fig. 14.10 show that positive shocks to SARB assets growth induce similar responses as those due to the banks' liquidity requirements. Thus, evidence indicates that positive shocks to the banks' liquidity requirements and an increase in SARB assets growth push the repo rate, the money market rates and other lending rates in the same

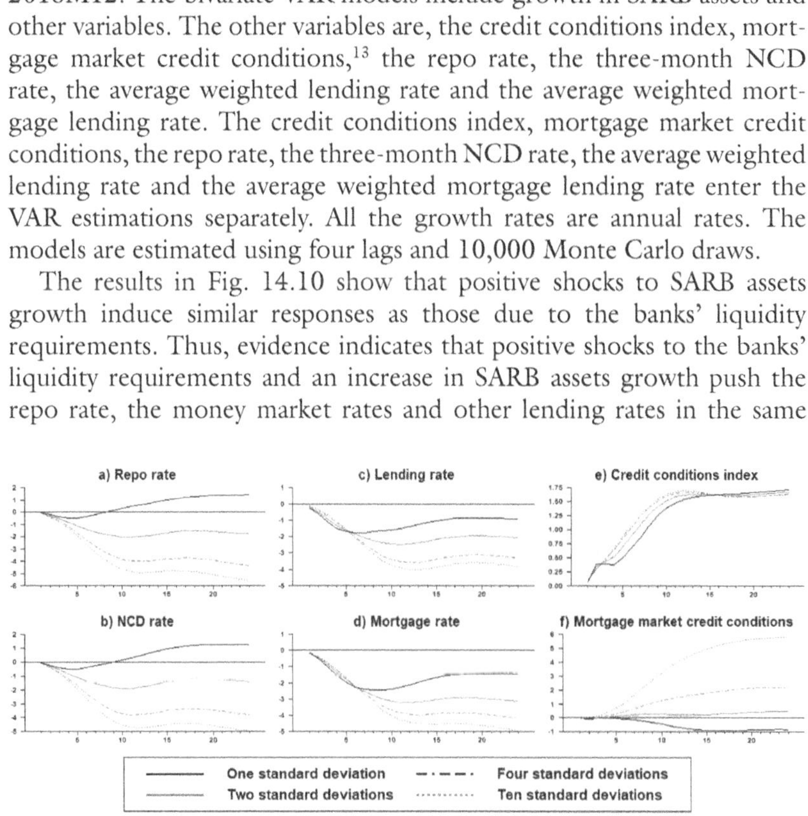

Fig. 14.10 Accumulated responses to positive shocks to SARB assets growth. (Source: Authors' calculations)

[13]The construction of the mortgage market credit condition is discussed in later chapters in the book.

direction. On the other hand, evidence in Fig. 14.10(e and f) shows that an increase in SARB assets growth loosens the mortgage market and overall credit conditions. As such, it is possible that these monetary policy tools reinforce each other's effects. We explore whether these balance sheet tools reinforce or dampen each other's effects on the interest rate pass-through and bank loan intermediation mark-up in the next section.

14.6 Do LSAPs and an Increase in the Banks' Liquidity Requirements Affect the Interest Rate Pass-Through and Bank Loan Intermediation Mark-Up?

We stated earlier that part of the motivation for unconventional monetary policy interventions is to enhance the transmission of monetary policy decisions, to loosen the funding costs for banks and to make sure that the easy monetary and funding conditions are transmitted to the real economy. Earlier sections indicated that indeed an increase in the banks' liquidity requirements and LSAPs loosen the banks funding constraints and credit conditions. We extend the analysis in this section to assess how LSAPs by the SARB and an increase in the banks' liquidity requirements affect the interest rate pass-through (IRPT) and the bank loan intermediation mark-up. The IRPT and the bank loan intermediation mark-up are sourced from Ndou et al. (2019).[14]

Like in the earlier sections, we use the modified Kilian and Vigfusson (2011) approach for the period 2000M1 to 2017M12. The bivariate VAR models include changes in the banks' liquidity requirements and other variables. The other variables are, SARB assets growth, the IRPT and the bank loan intermediation mark-up. The SARB assets growth, the IRPT and the bank loan intermediation mark-up enter the bivariate VAR models separately. Similar to the earlier sections, to test for the robustness of the results to changes in the model specification and measurement of variables, we create a dummy variable to capture the effects on an increase in the banks' liquidity requirements only. This dummy takes on all the positive values of the banks' liquidity requirements and zero otherwise. This approach is meant to assess the robustness of the results using positive shocks to SARB assets. All the growth rates are annual rates. The model is

[14] See Ndou et al. (2019) for the details of how these are estimated.

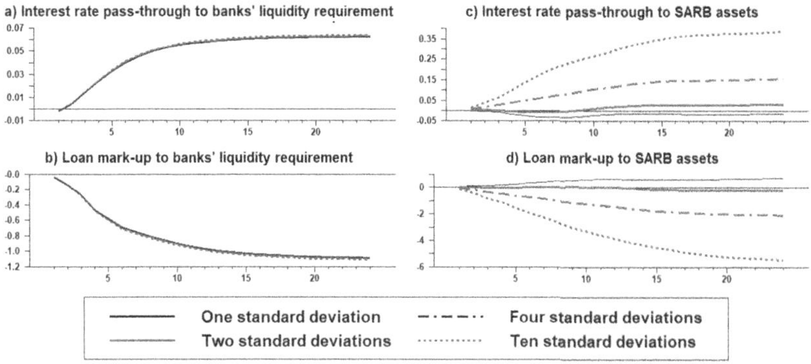

Fig. 14.11 Asymmetric responses of the IRPT and loan mark-up to positive shocks to the banks' liquidity requirements and SARB assets growth. (Source: Authors' calculations)

estimated using four lags and 1000 Monte Carlo draws. The sample spans the period 2002M3 to 2017M6 due to the availability of data for the IRPT and the loan intermediation mark-up.

The results in Fig. 14.11 show that positive shocks to the banks' liquidity requirements and SARB assets growth push the IRPT and the loan intermediation mark-up in different directions. The IRPT increases and the loan mark-up declines, and this is especially the case with respect to larger shocks to SARB assets growth. Nonetheless, it is evident that different sizes of positive shocks to the banks' liquidity requirements do not induce much asymmetry to the IRPT and the loan intermediation mark-up.

To conclude this section, we assess whether an increase in the banks' liquidity requirements propagates or dampens the effects of positive shocks to SARB assets growth on the IRPT and the loan mark-up. We use the counterfactual VAR approach where we assess the impact of positive shocks to SARB assets growth when the banks' liquidity requirements are allowed (not allowed) to transmit shocks in the model. The difference between the actual and the counterfactual responses indicates the degree to which the banks' liquidity requirements amplify or dampen the effects of positive shocks to SARB assets growth. The estimated counterfactual VAR model includes growth in SARB assets, banks' liquidity requirements, the IRPT and the loan mark-up. The broad M3 money supply growth enters the VAR as an exogenous variable. The role of the banks' liquidity requirement channel is shut off in the model to assess

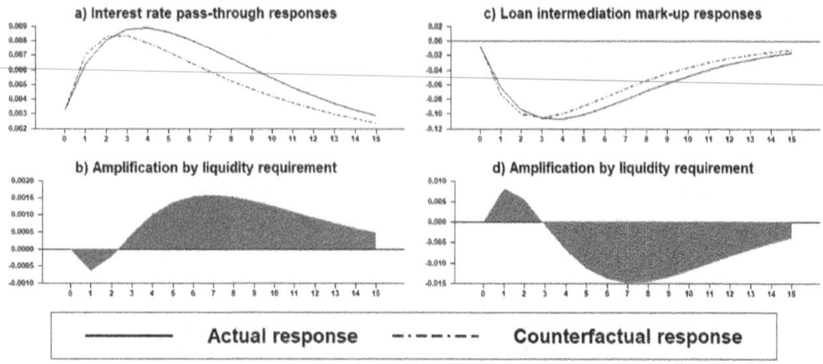

Fig. 14.12 IRPT and loan mark-up responses to positive shocks to SARB assets growth and propagation by the banks' liquidity requirements channel. (Source: Authors' calculations)

whether it amplifies or dampens the impact of positive shocks to SARB assets growth on the IRPT and the loan intermediation mark-up.

The results in Fig. 14.12 show that the IRPT increases and the loan intermediation mark-up declines in response to positive shocks to the LSAPs. In addition, Figs. 14.12(b and d) indicate that the IRPT increases more, whereas the loan intermediation mark-up declines more in the presence of the banks' liquidity requirements.

Thus, we conclude that the positive shocks to LSAPs and the banks' liquidity requirements reinforce each other's effects on the balance sheets of private banks, and this influences the IRPT and the loan intermediation mark-up.

14.7 Do LSAPs Curb Excess Liquid Asset Holdings by Banks?

We argued earlier that largely due to the excessively high level of LAH by banks, the SARB can shave off or buy the excess 50 per cent of government securities without disrupting or inducing undue distortions in the money market. Shaving off or buying the excess 50 per cent of government securities means that banks will hold an excess of 10 per cent above the minimum required liquid assets. Guidance for this demarcation and threshold is derived from the trend since 2009, as shown in Fig. 14.1(c and d).

First, we test whether there are significantly different effects induced by the decline in excess LAH from 60 per cent to 10 per cent of the minimum required LAH. We use a threshold VAR (TVAR) where we compare the responses of the banks' select balance sheet items to a model where there are (i) no thresholds and (ii) when excess LAH ranges between 5 per cent and 10 per cent. Second, we assess whether there are asymmetric effects introduced by different sizes of shocks to excess LAH on the banks' select balance sheet items. The different size shocks test what the incremental effects of decreasing excess LAH by banks. In this instance, for example, a one standard deviation shock is equivalent to 8 per cent and the sizes of the shocks increases as we assess higher levels of standard deviation shocks to a decline in the excess LAH.

We start the discussion on the results in this section, by showing the responses of excess LAH by banks to an increase in LSAPs by the SARB. This is because we argued that the increase in the LSAPs by the SARB will taper the excess LAHs by banks and will have no significant impact on the banks' balance sheets. Figure 14.13 shows that indeed excess LAH declines in response to positive shocks to LSAPs. This is the case whether we measure excess LAH as a ratio of the minimum required LAH in Fig. 14.13(a) or as annual changes in Fig. 14.13(b). In addition, the results show that large shocks to LSAPs result in a larger decline in excess LAH as a ratio of the minimum required LAH in Fig. 14.13(c) and annual changes in Fig. 14.13(d).

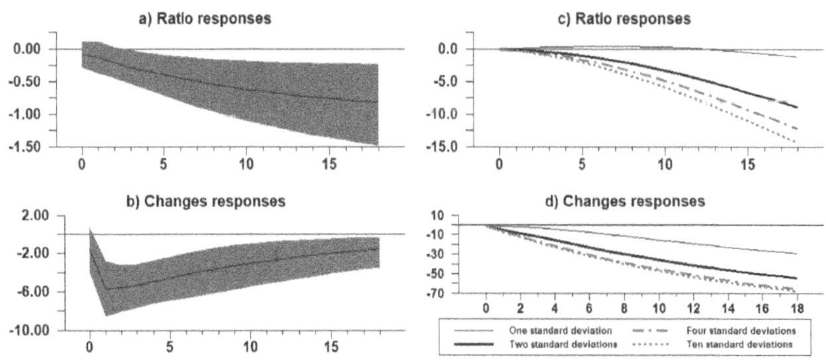

Fig. 14.13 Excess LAH responses to positive shocks to LSAPs. (Source: Authors' calculations)

To conclude this section, we assess the impact when excess LAH is decreased to 10 per cent and below on selected the banks' balance sheet items. We use data sourced from the banks' income statements to see how the selected indicators such as interest earned, return on assets, non-performing loans, banks' holdings of government securities, credit to the private sector and government respond to a decrease in the banks' excess LAH. This is because banks earn interest from several instruments on their balance sheets. Although interest earned from items related to their core lending business activity to households and companies will be largely unaffected by the LSAPs of government securities and trimming of excess LAH, their lending business to government via their purchases of government securities and in turn the interest earned will be most affected. We have already shown in Fig. 14.2 that there is an inverse relationship between bank credit to government and the private sector.

For this section, we estimate two VAR models to capture the role of the 10 per cent threshold for excess LAH. We then assess the responses of credit to the private sector, banks' holdings of government securities, credit to government, banks' interest income and return-on-assets in a TVAR with excess LAH below and above the 10 per cent threshold to assess the impact.

The results in Fig. 14.14 show that there is indeed a differential impact of positive shocks to excess LAH in the regimes below and above the 10 per cent threshold. Evidence shows that interest income and return-on-assets decline but remain positive in the low excess LAH regime. Similarly,

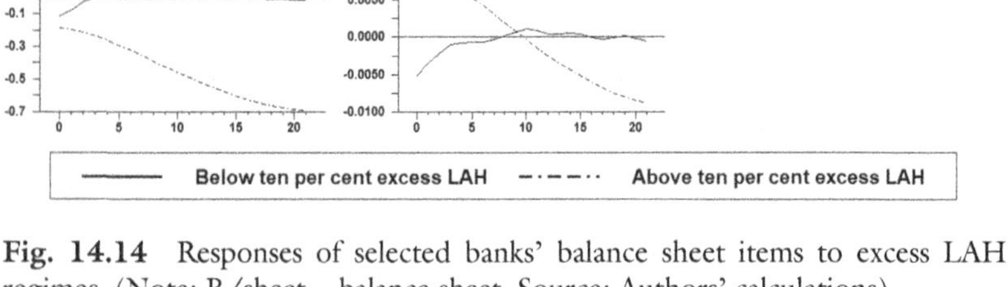

Fig. 14.14 Responses of selected banks' balance sheet items to excess LAH regimes. (Note: B/sheet = balance sheet. Source: Authors' calculations)

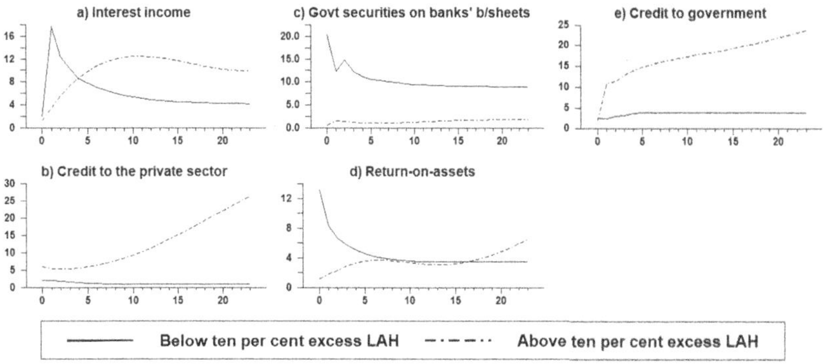

Fig. 14.15 Variance decompositions of selected banks' balance sheet items to excess LAH regimes. (Note: B/sheet = balance sheet. Source: Authors' calculations)

credit to government and government securities on banks' balance sheets decline, but this is offset by the increase in credit to the private sector. Furthermore, the results in Fig. 14.15 indicate that positive shocks to excess LAH in the low regime explain less variation in these banks' balance sheet items compared to the high regime. We therefore conclude that LSAPs that reduce excess LAH to 10 per cent will not lead to disruptions in credit markets, nor will they compromise the high-quality collateral requirements under the liquidity coverage ratio.

14.8 Conclusion and Policy Implications

This chapter assessed whether LSAPs of government securities by the SARB curb excess LAH by private banks. Using a TVAR model, we find that LSAPs by the SARB result in a decline in the excess LAH by banks. In addition, evidence shows that bank credit to government declines. Thus, lowering excess LAH by banks via LSAPs will not compromise the high-quality collateral requirements under the liquidity coverage ratio. How are LSAPs of government securities by the SARB transmitted to banks' deposit and lending rates? Evidence shows that LSAPs result in loose (accommodative) credit conditions, an increase in the interest rate pass-through and a decline in the bank loan intermediation mark-up.

The NDP identified easing access to finance to SMMEs as one critical policy intervention to deal with the reluctance of lenders to lend to this sector. Furthermore, the NDP calls for urgent measures to reform the mandates and operations of development finance institutions, in line with initiatives to bring services to this sector. Against this backdrop, we also assess whether there is a case for increasing the rate at which banks borrow at the SARB discount window whilst increasing the maturities of the repurchase agreements on offer by the SARB. The results indicate that lengthening of the maturities of funding options available at the accommodation can result in the substitution of funding sources by banks on their liabilities side of the balance sheets and the cost of funding. Most importantly, long-term repurchase agreements will also affect the way banks price lending on their asset side.

As such, lengthening of the maturities of funding options available at the discount window can loosen the funding constraints experienced by banks and this will spill over to the funding of important markets such as the housing sector and SMMEs. In addition, from a policy and regulatory perspective, the lengthening of the maturity of the funding options for banks is especially important given the longstanding regulatory concern of the maturity mismatch risks induced by funding long-term assets, such as housing, using deposits which are of a short duration. At the same time, such a strategy will neutralise the impact of sterilisation and other costs associated with the forex reserves accumulation programme.

Appendix

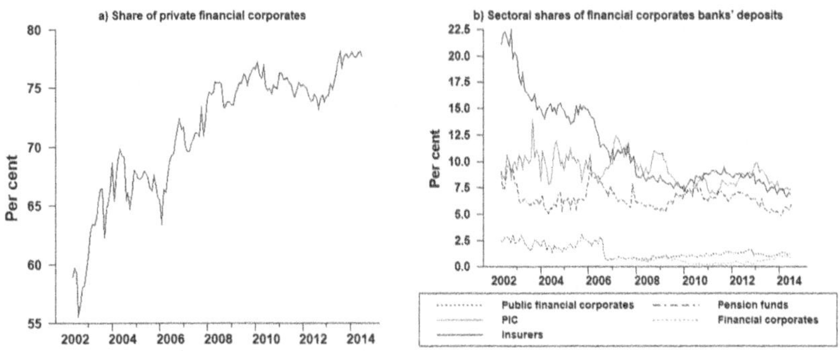

Fig. 14.16 Share of financial companies' deposits with banks. (Source: South African Reserve Bank and authors' calculations)

References

Andrade P, Breckenfelder J, De Fiore F, Karadi P, and Tristani O. (2016). "The ECB's asset purchase programme: an early assessment". ECB Working Paper 1956.

The transmission of the ECB's recent non-standard monetary policy measures. 2015. ECB Economic Bulletin, Issue 7. https://www.ecb.europa.eu/pub/pdf/other/eb201507_article01.en.pdf

Gertler M, and Karadi P. 2011. A Model of Unconventional Monetary Policy. Journal of Monetary Economics, 58(1), pp. 17–34.

Gertler M, and Karadi P. 2013. Qe 1 vs. 2 vs. 3...: A framework for analyzing large-scale asset purchases as a monetary policy tool. International Journal of central Banking, 9(1), pp. 5–53.

Gumata N, and Ndou E. 2017. Bank Credit Extension and Real Economic Activity in South Africa: The Impact of Capital Flow Dynamics, Bank Regulation and Selected Macroprudential Tools. Palgrave Macmillan. ISBN 978-3-319-43550-3.

Haldane A, Roberts-Sklar M, Wieladek T and Young C. 2016. QE: The Story so far. Bank of England working papers 624, Bank of England.

Impact of the ECB's non-standard measures on financing conditions: taking stock of recent evidence. 2017. ECB Economic Bulletin, Issue 2. https://www.ecb.europa.eu/pub/pdf/other/eb201702_focus03.en.pdf

Kilian L and Vigfusson R J. 2011. Are the Responses of the U.S. Economy Asymmetric in Energy Price Increases and Decreases? Quantitative Economics, 2(4), 419–453.

Lonergan E. 2019. It's time for the ECB to use its monetary power. Blog post 28th March 2019. https://www.philosophyofmoney.net/time-ecb-use-monetary-power/

Ndou E, Gumata N, and Tshuma M M. 2019. Exchange Rate, Second Round Effects and Inflation Processes: Evidence From South Africa. Palgrave Macmillan. ISBN 978-3-030-13932-2.

IMF. 2011. Assessing Reserve Adequacy. Third IMF Roundtable of Sovereign Asset and Reserves Managers. https://www.imf.org/external/np/pp/eng/2011/021411b.pdf

Heider F, Saidi F, and Schepens G. 2018. Life Below Zero: Bank Lending under Negative Rates. ECB second annual conference. https://www.ecb.europa.eu/pub/conferences/shared/pdf/20170925_2nd_ecb_annual_research_conference/03_Glenn_Schepens_paper.pdf

Gray S. 2011. Central Bank Balances and Reserve Requirements. IMF Working Paper WP/11/36. https://www.imf.org/external/pubs/ft/wp/2011/wp1136.pdf

Draghi M. 2019. Twenty Years of the ECB's monetary policy. Speech at the ECB Forum on Central Banking, Sintra, 18 June 2019. https://www.ecb.europa.eu/press/key/date/2019/html/ecb.sp190618~ec4cd2443b.en.html

CHAPTER 15

Is the Interest Rate Corridor an Effective Instrument to Dampen the Accumulation of Excess Reserves and the Inter-bank Rate Volatility?

Research Questions Explored

- Explore the impact of monetary policy tightening and loosening, the R/US$ exchange rate appreciation and depreciation on excess reserves.
- Examine whether monetary policy tightening and the R/US$ exchange rate depreciation shocks propagate each other's effects on excess reserves.
- Establish the relationship between excess reserves and the policy interest rate corridor.
- Estimate the transition function for inter-bank interest rates from low to high excess reserves regimes within the policy interest rate corridor.
- Assess whether there are asymmetrical excess reserves threshold effects on the inter-bank interest rate volatilities.

15.1 Introduction

In earlier chapters, we showed that banks hold liquid assets of 60 per cent in excess of the minimum requirement. We showed that large-scale asset purchases (LSAPs) can be successfully used to curb this excess to 10 per

N. Gumata, E. Ndou, *Achieving Price, Financial and Macro-Economic Stability in South Africa*,
https://doi.org/10.1007/978-3-030-66340-7_15

cent without compromising the high-quality collateral requirements under the liquidity coverage ratio (LCR) and the functioning of the banking sector. This chapter extends the analysis of the banking sector excess liquidity by exploring the transition of the inter-bank rates or short-term interest rates from different states of the banks' excess reserves. How do inter-bank or short-term interest rates transition from the low to the high bank excess reserves regimes? Is the policy rate interest rate corridor effective in managing banks' excess reserves and the inter-bank rate volatilities?

We explore these questions because trends from central banks that have conducted LSAPs show that these policy interventions are also associated with an increase in banks' excess reserves with central banks. Contrary to the United States Federal Reserve Bank (US Fed) and the European Central Bank (ECB) as shown in Fig. 15.2, banks' excess reserves in South Africa are mainly on account of the programme of foreign currency reserves accumulation and the R/US$ exchange rate fluctuations. In this sense, the South African case explored in this chapter is like that of the Swiss National Bank (SNB). It is for this reason that we also briefly explore the arrangements adopted by the SNB to deal with excess reserves.

Furthermore, Christensen and Krogstrup (2016) show that central bank asset purchases can result in supply-induced portfolio balance and (ii) reserve-induced portfolio balance effects as was the case in the quantitative eqaing (QE) conducted by the US Fed, the Bank of England (BoE), the ECB and the Bank of Japan (BoJ). These central banks conducted QE predominantly via the purchase of long-term government bonds. On the other hand, the SNB conducted a QE programme without any purchase of long-term assets but managed to lower long-term yields.

For instance, Fig. 15.1 shows that in the US and the ECB banks' excess reserves increased post-2009 coinciding with LSAPs. For the ECB, the amount of excess reserves, was standing at the beginning of 2018 above 1 trillion euro. However, in the US, as the US Fed has scaled back its LSAPs, the level of excess reserves has declined. As the US Fed balance sheet grew to an unprecedented size, the Open Market Desk at the New York Fed found it increasingly difficult to achieve the Federal Open Market Committee (FOMC)'s target funds rate. In October 2008, the US Fed began paying interest on required reserves and excess reserve balances.[1] This interest rate was expected to establish a floor under the federal

[1] The interest rate on required reserves rate (IORR) is intended to eliminate the implicit tax that reserve requirements impose on depository institutions. On the other hand, the interest rate on excess reserve (IOER) is meant to give the Federal Reserve an additional tool

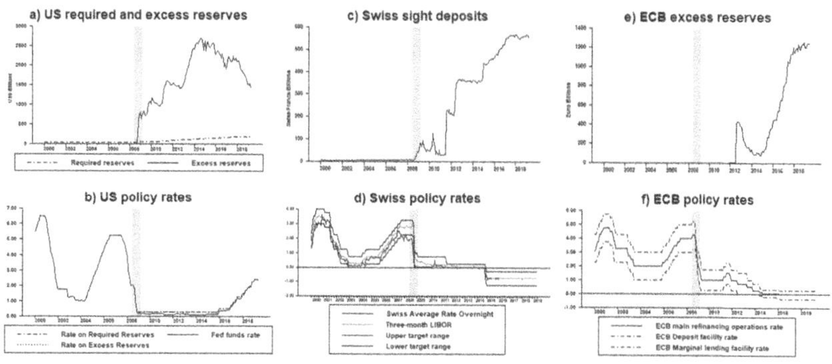

Fig. 15.1 Required reserves and policy rates in the US, Switzerland, and euro area. (Source: Fred data, Swiss National Bank, ECB data warehouse and authors' calculations)

funds rate, whereas the discount rate, which since January 2003 has been set as a penalty rate above the funds rate target, was expected to limit upward pressure on the funds rate. According to Kahn (2010), with these changes, the Federal Reserve's operating framework incorporated the essential elements of a 'channel' or 'corridor' system.

Contrary to the US Fed, the ECB, faced with a build-up of excess reserves, opted to use a negative interest rate policy (negative deposit rate facility).[2] In the case of the ECB, the negative rate applies also to average reserve holdings in excess of the minimum reserve requirements and all other deposits held with the Eurosystem. The negative deposit facility interest rate also applies to (i) banks' average reserve holdings in excess of

for the conduct of monetary policy. Both rates are determined by the Board. This approach also provides an important "exit strategy" tool, which will allow the Fed to better control the level of excess reserves when it begins to remove monetary policy stimulus.

See for further reading https://www.federalreserve.gov/monetarypolicy/reqresbalances.htm and https://www.frbsf.org/education/publications/doctor-econ/2013/march/federal-reserve-interest-balances-reserves/

https://www.frbsf.org/education/publications/doctor-econ/2013/march/federal-reserve-interest-balances-reserves/

[2] See for further reading https://www.ecb.europa.eu/press/pr/date/2014/html/pr140605_3.en.html

The 2014 decision by the ECB to push the relevant policy rate (the deposit facility rate) into negative territory was a crucial policy innovation.

https://www.ecb.europa.eu/press/key/date/2019/html/ecb.sp190701~0c1fa3c8fc.en.html

the minimum reserve requirements; (ii) government deposits held with the Eurosystem that exceed certain thresholds; (iii) Eurosystem reserves management services accounts if not currently remunerated; (iv) participants' account balances in TARGET2; (v) non-Eurosystem NCB balances (overnight deposits) held in TARGET2; and (vi) other accounts held by third parties with Eurosystem central banks when stipulated that they are not currently remunerated or are remunerated at the deposit facility rate.

With respect to the SNB, as the central bank increased its interventions in the currency markets, so did the sight deposits of banks, as shown in Fig. 15.1.[3] At the same time, the SNB implements its monetary policy by fixing a target range for the reference interest rate, the London Interbank Offered Rate (Libor) for three-month interbank loans in Swiss francs. Nonetheless, on 13 June 2019,[4] the SNB introduced the Swiss Average Rate Overnight (Saron) as a new monetary policy tool replacing the Libor. As shown in Fig. 15.1(d), the Saron and the Libor move in tandem. The SNB steers the Libor/Saron into the defined target range through its monetary policy operations, as shown in Fig. 15.1(d). As a rule, the SNB maintains the Libor/Saron in the middle of the defined range. Like the ECB, as excess reserves continued to accumulate, the SNB decided to impose negative interest rates on sight deposit account balances. Since January 2015, the SNB has applied negative interest rates within a target range of -1.25 per cent and -0.25 per cent.

Within this context, this chapter asks: How do inter-bank or short-term interest rates transition from low to high bank excess reserves regimes? Is the policy rate interest rate corridor effective in managing banks' excess reserves and the volatility of inter-bank interest rates? Furthermore, we assess whether there are asymmetrical excess reserves threshold effects on inter-bank interest rate volatilities. We contribute to literature in this area by using several approaches to answer questions posed in this chapter. First, we use the Choleski VAR and historical decomposition approach to assess the impact of (i) monetary policy tightening and loosening; and (ii) R/US$ exchange rate appreciation and depreciation on banks' excess reserves. We are interested in the historical contributions of changes in the monetary policy stance and the R/US$ exchange rate on the evolution of banks' excess reserves post-2010. Second, we use the logistic smooth

[3] Sight deposits are the most important means of financing SNB currency purchases. See for further details https://snbchf.com/snb/snb-sight-deposits-debt/

[4] See for further reading https://www.snb.ch/en/mmr/reference/pre_20190613/source/pre_20190613.en.pdf

transition autoregressive (LSTAR) models to estimate the nature of the relationship between the inter-bank rate and the banks' excess reserves and how it transitions between high and low excess bank reserves. Through the LSTAR models we establish the threshold at which inter-bank rates transition from low to high excess bank reserves. Third, we use the generalised autoregressive conditional heteroskedasticity (GARCH) models to estimate the volatilities of the inter-bank rates. Fourth, we use the estimated volatilities and the threshold in the threshold VAR (TVAR) models to estimate the responses of the inter-bank volatilities in different banks' excess reserves regimes.

15.2 What Are the Key Features of the SARB Operational Framework for Monetary Policy?

The SARB conducts monetary policy operations within the interest rate corridor system guided by the standing facilities. The standing facilities determine the floor and ceiling (interest rate corridor) for the repurchase rate (policy rate) and other inter-bank market interest rates, as shown in Fig. 15.2.[5] Since August 2010, the SARB has operated monetary policy within the interest rate corridor of a 100 basis points on either side of the repo rate. The spread between the rates for the standing facilities and the repurchase rate was widened from 50 basis points to 100 basis points below and above the prevailing repurchase rate. In addition, the scatterplots in Fig. 15.2(b and d) show that there is an inverse relationship between the South African overnight rate (Sabor), the overnight forex rate and the excess reserves bank balances.[6] Thus, the policy rates within the

[5] Standing facilities in the form of supplementary repurchase agreements auctions were initially introduced in April 2001 as daily square-off operations. The standing facilities are used to provide liquidity instances where the banking sector ends up having unexpected long or short cash positions. These auctions were used at the SARB's discretion and in exceptional circumstances. In August 2010, the SARB discontinued the use of these square-off operations. As a result, the marginal lending rate or SAMOS penalty rate facility priced at the repo rate plus 500 basis points was abolished. See the following links for further reading.

https://www.resbank.co.za/Lists/News%20and%20Publications/Attachments/7264/FMD%20April%202016.pdf

https://www.resbank.co.za/Lists/News%20and%20Publications/Attachments/3640/Quarterly%20Economic%20Review.pdf

[6] The benchmark overnight funding rates, namely, the South African Overnight Inter-bank Average (Saonia and Saonia+), the foreign-exchange forward rate and the carry rate were discontinued on 27 March 2007. They were replaced with the South African Benchmark

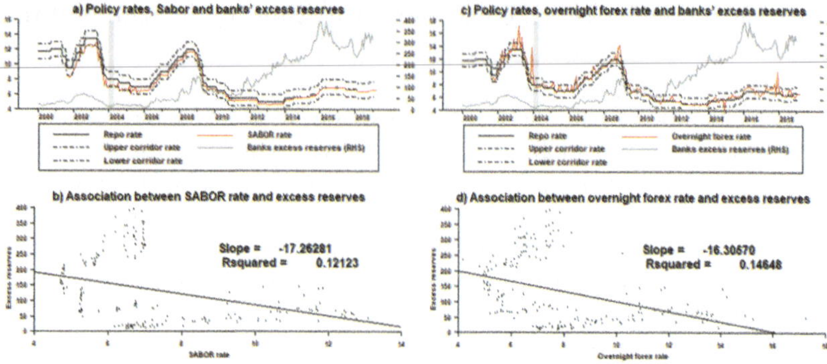

Fig. 15.2 Policy rates, SABOR/SAONIA rate and banks' excess reserves. (Source: Authors' calculations)

interest rate corridor can be used to influence the level of banks' excess balances.

The negative association between the Sabor, the overnight forex rate and the level of excess reserves in Fig. 15.2(b and d) is also characteristic of the assumption in Veyrune et al. (2018). The authors assume that the relationship between the inter-bank or short-term interest rates and excess reserves can be modelled as a bivariate logistic function, which is defined in such a way that inter-bank or short-term rates (i) converge to the top of the interest rate corridor when excess reserves are increasingly positive, (ii) converge to the bottom of the corridor when the excess reserves decline and (iii) take the value 0.5 when there are no excess reserves. The interest rate corridor is defined by the interest rates of the central bank's standing facilities as shown in Fig. 15.3. It is the outcome of an approach adopted by the central bank to steer short-term rates, for example: (i) the interest rates at which reserves are supplied or withdrawn via open market operations; (ii) the interest rate at which excess reserves are remunerated; and (iii) the interest rate for the main refinancing operations. In an interest rate

Overnight Rate on Deposits (Sabor) and the overnight foreign exchange rate. See, for further reading on how the Sabor and the overnight foreign exchange rate are calculated https://www.resbank.co.za/Lists/News%20and%20Publications/Attachments/4085/Quarterly%20Economic%20Review.pdf

https://www.resbank.co.za/Markets/Domestic/SABOR/Documents/SaborDiscPaper.pdf

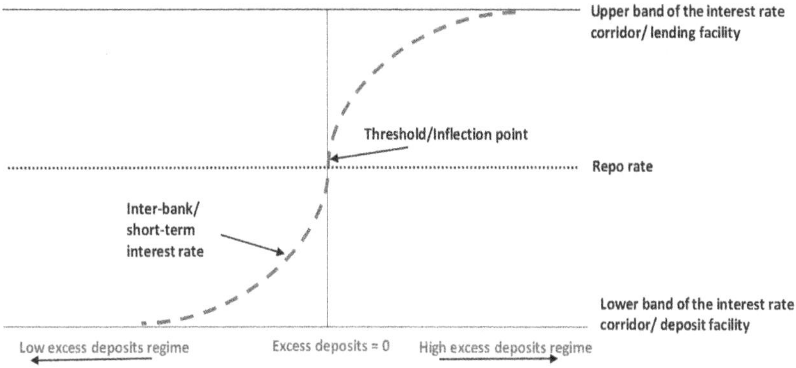

Fig. 15.3 Stylised logistic representation of the inter-bank/short-term interest rates in an interest rate corridor. (Source: Authors' drawing and adapted from Veyrune et al. 2018)

corridor system, as is the case in the traditional monetary policy framework, the central bank chooses the policy rate that is consistent with its price and financial stability mandates.

The stylised representation of the policy rate corridor depicted in Fig. 15.3 is according to Veyrune et al. (2018),[7] best captured via the logistic transition function. The logistic transition function of the inter-bank/short-term interest rates in Fig. 15.3 incorporates these main characteristics:

(i). Inter-bank or short-term interest rates are bounded between the standing facility rates which are the upper range or the lending facility rate and the lower range or the deposit facility rate. The demand schedule for reserves balances at the repo rate is perfectly elastic (horizontal). This is because no depository institution would be willing to borrow funds in the inter-bank market at a higher rate than what the central bank is charging. The demand schedule is also perfectly elastic at the interest rate on excess reserves because no institution would be willing to loan overnight funds in the inter-bank market at a lower rate than what the central bank is offering to pay.

[7] See also Kahn (2010), Bech, and Monnet (2015) and Vari (2016) amongst others.

(ii). In the area between the mid-point of the interest rate corridor and the upper end, the demand schedule is downward sloping. This is because depository institutions balance the potential costs of falling short of their reserve or settlement requirements (i.e. having to borrow in the inter-bank market) against the cost of having excess reserves. As the rate on overnight funds falls, the opportunity cost of holding excess reserves as a precaution against a shortfall of reserves falls.

(iii). The interest rate is set above the target policy rate to impose a penalty on depository institutions that borrow from the central bank rather than in the inter-bank market. First, it could be viewed as a standing facility in which depository institutions can deposit their excess reserves overnight at a fixed interest rate. Analogous to the discount rate, the deposit rate would be set below the target policy rate to provide an incentive for the depository institution to invest surplus funds in the overnight inter-bank market instead of parking them at the central bank.

(iv). Depending on the level of excess liquidity, the inter-bank or short-term rates can be anchored at the upper bound or lending facility rate, lower bound or deposit facility rate or the midpoint of the corridor, which is the repo rate for the main repurchase auctions. In such a corridor approach, high excess reserves should anchor the inter-bank or short-term rates to the deposit facility. On the other hand, a neutral allotment policy should keep inter-bank or short-term rates near the middle of the interest rate corridor, whereas a reserve shortage[8] should anchor inter-bank or short-term rates to the lending facility rate.

(v). The threshold or inflection point represents the level of excess reserves above which inter-bank or short-term rates decrease and below which short-term rates increase. In the stylised logistic function this level is assumed to occur at zero. But it will be empirically estimated in later sections.

[8] This is a scenario where the central bank regularly supplies via regular refinancing operations fewer reserves than needed.

Thus, an interest rate corridor operating framework can help a central bank achieve a target policy rate in an environment in which reserve requirements are not binding. This is due either to low or non-existent reserve requirements or the use of the central bank's balance sheet as a policy instrument independent of the policy interest rate. In practice, the corridor system has effectively stabilised the policy rate near its target in several countries. In the US, however, the potential effectiveness of the corridor system is yet to be established since it has not been fully implemented. In addition, central banks provide standing facilities that can be accessed, in principle, at any point in time by the commercial banks for potentially unlimited amounts. The interest rate corridor avoids excessively large jumps in short-term rates in the event of unexpected autonomous factor developments.

A corridor is defined as one that limits fluctuations in the overnight policy rate such that regardless of the supply of reserves, the central bank can tightly control the interest rate on overnight funds. As such, positions on either side of the vertical line where excess reserves are zero are determined by the deposit rate or the rate on excess reserves. Conducting monetary policy in the region of zero excess reserves (where the demand curve is a variant of the corridor system) is referred to as a floor operating system. In a floor system, the interest rate on reserves becomes the target rate for monetary policy. On the contrary, in a corridor system, the central bank can change the target policy rate by simply announcing a change in the floor and ceiling of the corridor. The corridor system also allows the central bank to change the supply of reserves while maintaining control over the policy rate. As shown in Fig. 15.4, when the central bank increases the supply of reserves, the supply curve shifts to the right, from S1 to S2 and S3.

In the traditional framework, such an increase in reserves would cause the policy rate to decline along a continuously downward-sloping demand curve. Within the traditional framework, the steady increase in the supply of reserves would result in the policy rate eventually falling to the zero-lower bound. However, in the interest rate corridor system, the decline in the policy rate is constrained by the floor of the corridor (the deposit rate or the interest rate on excess reserves). As the supply of reserves increases from S1 to S2 to S3, the policy rate remains anchored and bounded by the interest rate on reserves (ir). It is for this reason that Kahn (2010) states that the interest rate corridor floor allows the central bank to separate the interest rate policy (monetary policy stance) from the liquidity policy. This

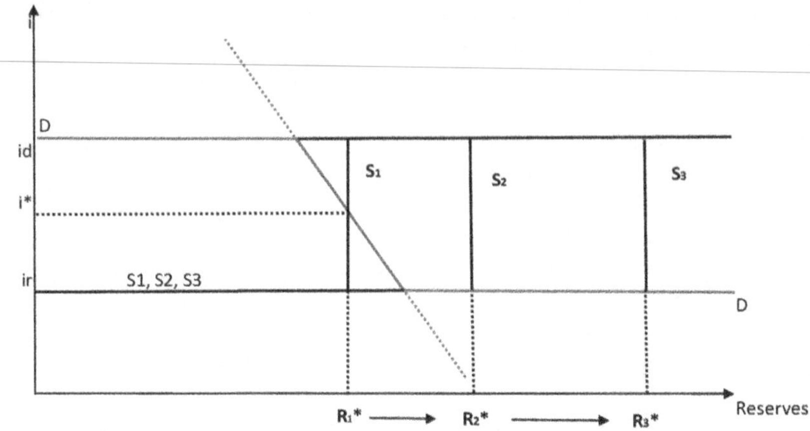

Fig. 15.4 Stylised representation of a change in the supply of reserves without a change in the policy rate within the interest rate corridor. (Source: Authors' drawing and adapted from Kahn 2010)

separation can be important in a liquidity crisis when the central bank might need to pump an unusually large quantity of reserves into the banking system. Without the interest rate floor established by the corridor, such an injection of reserves could push the policy rate well below its target.[9]

To complete the discussion on the interest rate corridor, Fig. 15.5 shows the role played by the interest rate corridor when the central bank normalises its balance sheet and policy rates. In Fig. 15.5, to re-normalise the policy settings, the central bank can increase the overnight inter-bank rate by announcing an increase in the interest rate on reserves. This action can be implemented without a reduction in the supply of reserves, thus allowing the central bank to independently determine the appropriate speed with which to shrink its balance sheet. In this set up, the payment of interest on reserves allows the central bank to eventually renormalise monetary policy. Once the supply of reserves has fallen within the range of the downward-sloping portion of the demand curve for reserves (moving from R2* to R1*), monetary policy can potentially operate under a pure corridor system.

[9] In the case of the U.S., the increase in the supply of reserves initially led to the funds rate falling below its target rate. The introduction of interest on reserves in October 2008 eventually helped anchor the funds rate near the FOMC's target rate, Kahn (2010).

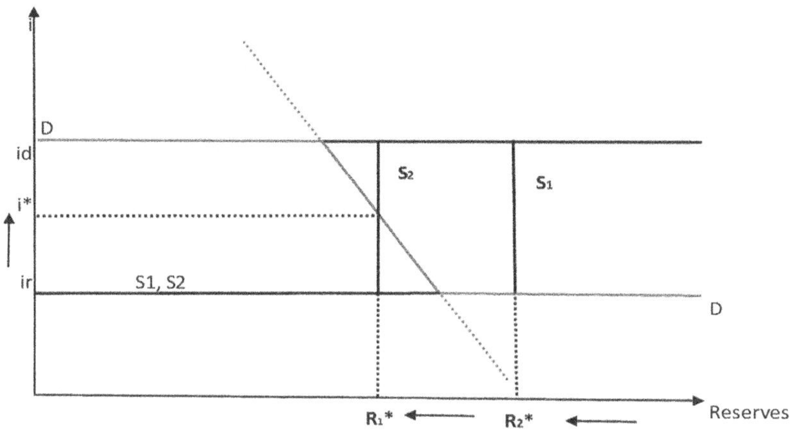

Fig. 15.5 Stylised representation of re-normalisation of monetary policy within the interest rate corridor. (Source: Authors' drawing and adapted from Kahn 2010)

15.3 What Are the Key Features of the Market of the South African Reserve Bank Balances?

The South African monetary policy framework operates on a liquidity shortage approach. This means that the central bank manages the money market liquidity in such a way that the banks have a shortage and can always be active at the discount window to access additional liquidity from the central bank. Furthermore, the SARB open market operations (OMO) operate on the approach of full allotment, that is, the central bank provides the exact amount of refinancing necessary to fulfil the banks' demand at the refinancing window. Figure 15.6 summarises the key variables that form part of the market for banks' balances at the central bank. Figure 15.6(b) shows that banks hold almost R350 billion worth of deposits on account of the sterilisation of the foreign currency reserves accumulation. These deposits are remunerated.

Secondly, banks hold a minimum of 2.5 per cent of their liabilities with the public as required reserve deposits with the SARB, as shown in Fig. 15.6(a). The reserve requirements (RR) deposits in South Africa are not remunerated. Theoretically, RR are held for three main purposes, namely, for (i) prudential, (ii) monetary control and (iii) liquidity

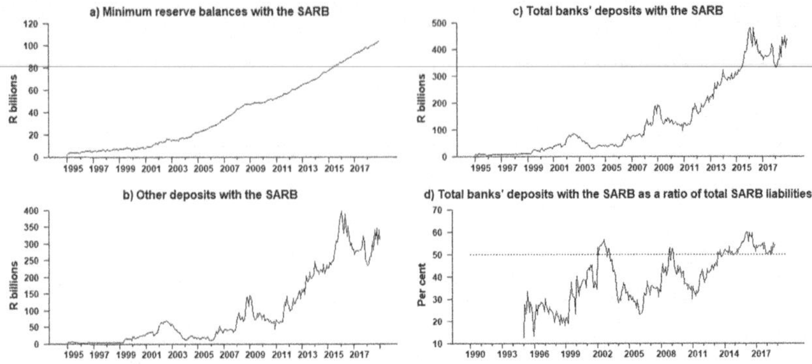

Fig. 15.6 Banks' deposits with the SARB. (Source: South African Reserve Bank and authors' calculations)

management purposes. For prudential purposes, the RR provide some protection against liquidity and solvency risks. With respect to monetary control, the RR can restrict the commercial bank balance sheet growth and the central bank can vary the level of unremunerated RR in a way that is intended to influence the spread between the deposit and lending rates. This is, in turn, expected to impact the growth of monetary aggregates and thus inflation. For liquidity management purposes, the RR can be used actively or passively. Actively used by the central bank, the RR can be adjusted to neutralise the impact of surplus reserves on bank behaviour, so that it does not result in inflationary pressures or the depreciation of the exchange rate. Similarly, the RR can be used passively through the averaging approach to manage commercial banks' short-term liquidity and in turn a reduction in short-term interest rate volatility[10] (Gray 2011).

In the South African case, the RR are managed passively.[11] Although the RR are not remunerated, banks can use them to bridge their liquidity needs during the maintenance period. This approach to managing the RR is also known as the averaging of minimum cash reserve holdings during

[10] We explore the role of excess reserves on money market interest rates in later chapters of the book.

[11] The required reserves are a dormant (passive) monetary policy tool as they have barely changed from 2.5 per cent of banks' total liabilities to the public since 1998.

the maintenance period.[12] In total, banks hold R500 billion worth of deposits with the SARB, as shown in Fig. 15.6(c). Furthermore, Fig. 15.2 (d) shows that banks' total deposits on the SARB's balance sheet as a ratio of the SARB's total assets has increased gradually and constituted more than 50 per cent at the end of 2018. The size of banks' deposits with the SARB is an indication of how cash flush the banking sector is, alternatively an indicator of excess bank reserves. In addition, excess bank reserves are partly an indication of the weakness of the current money market shortage system and contribute to the dysfunction in the inter-bank money market.

15.4 What Is the Nature of the Association Between the Repo Rate and Banks' Deposits with the SARB?

This section assesses whether the excess bank balances with the SARB are in anyway associated with the repo rate and the money market liquidity requirement. Figure 15.7(b) shows that the level of banks' deposits with the SARB is positively associated with the R/US$ exchange rate, and the

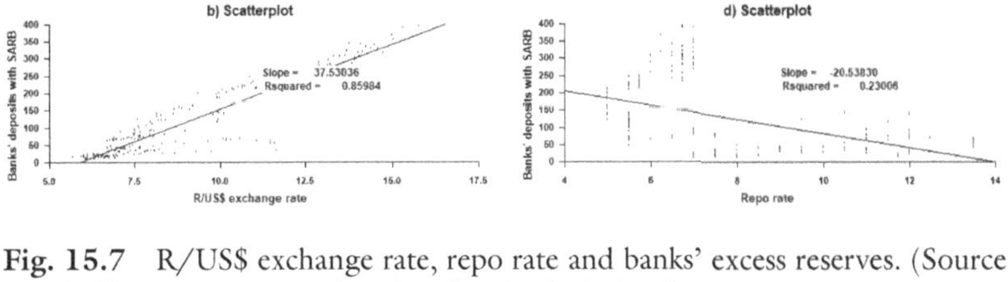

Fig. 15.7 R/US$ exchange rate, repo rate and banks' excess reserves. (Source: South African Reserve Bank and authors' calculations)

[12] Reserve requirement averaging can be allowed over a long enough maintenance period, that is, the period during which the reserve requirement should be fulfilled on average. This approach is designed to help banks better manage their daily liquidity positions and to absorb the central bank liquidity forecast errors. We explore the role of reserve requirement tightening shocks on bank liquidity in later chapters of the book.

exchange rate explains almost 86 per cent of the variation in the level of these deposits. These results concur with the findings in earlier chapters of the book showing that the increase in banks' excess reserves coincides with the prolonged R/US$ exchange rate depreciation. Nonetheless, it is also evident in Fig. 15.7(d) that these deposits are negatively associated with the repo rate. This means that the tightening (loosening) in the repo rate results in an increase (decline) in the level of these deposits. These results indicate that although the R/US$ exchange rate dominates the direction of the level of these deposits, the changes in the repo rate also play a role, albeit marginal compared to that of the R/US$. Thus, changes in the monetary policy stance do affect these balances. This might in part be explained by the fact that they are always remunerated at some positive margin to the repo rate. Similarly, Bowman et al. (2011) indicate that in most cases when central banks tightened monetary policy, they increase the rates of interest paid on balances held at the central bank, and notably, such tightening was not accompanied by decreases in aggregate balances.

With the background of the relationships established, what is the nature of the association between the money market shortage created (banks' liquidity requirement) via the OMO and the repo rate? Figure 15.8 shows that the liquidity requirement of banks increased persistently since 2010 in line with banks' balances with the SARB, as shown in Fig. 15.8(a). However, at R60 billion, it is less than 1 per cent as a ratio of deposits with the SARB, as shown on Fig. 15.8(c). In addition, we showed in earlier chapters that banks rely for a mere 2 per cent on the SARB discount

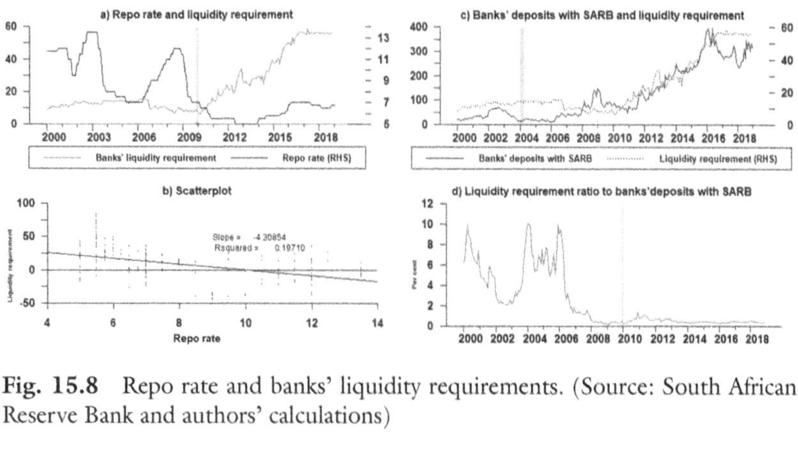

Fig. 15.8 Repo rate and banks' liquidity requirements. (Source: South African Reserve Bank and authors' calculations)

window for their funding needs. Given that this funding is short-term in nature, we argued that there is a compelling case to lengthen the maturities of repurchase agreements.[13]

Like Fig. 15.6(b), we establish that there is a negative association between the increase in the banks' liquidity requirements and the repo rate, albeit weak. Thus, the money market shortage created via banks' balances with the SARB does indeed result in an increase in the use of the SARB discount window, rendering the repo rate somewhat effective. In addition, the implication is that the forex reserves accumulation and the R/US$ exchange rate have a significant effect on the SARB money market operations, as shown in Fig. 15.8(d).

15.5 To What Extent Do Aggregate Balances Change When Monetary Policy Is Adjusted?

The earlier sections have established a negative association between the repo rate and excess balances with the SARB; and a positive association between the R/US$ exchange rate changes and excess balances with the SARB. We extend the analysis by conducting an empirical analysis of the responses of banks' excess reserves to changes in the monetary policy stance. This section estimates several bilateral VAR models, which include changes in banks' excess deposits and the dummy variables. The dummy variables are for (i) the repo rate changes and (ii) R/US$ exchange rate changes. The repo rate dummy variable take on the values of an increase (decrease) in the repo rate to signify monetary policy tightening (loosening) and zero otherwise. The dummy variable for the exchange rate denotes the R/US$ exchange rate increase (decrease) to signify the exchange rate depreciation (appreciation) and zero otherwise. Each dummy for each variable is included separately in the model. The models are estimated for the sample period 2000M1 to 2018M12. The VAR models are estimated using two lags and 10,000 Monte Carlo draws. All growth rates are annual rates.

The results in Fig. 15.9 show that monetary policy tightening and loosening; and the R/US$ exchange rate depreciation and appreciation push banks' excess reserves in opposite directions. A tight monetary policy stance and the R/US$ exchange rate depreciation increase banks' excess

[13] See earlier chapters of the book for the motivation and findings.

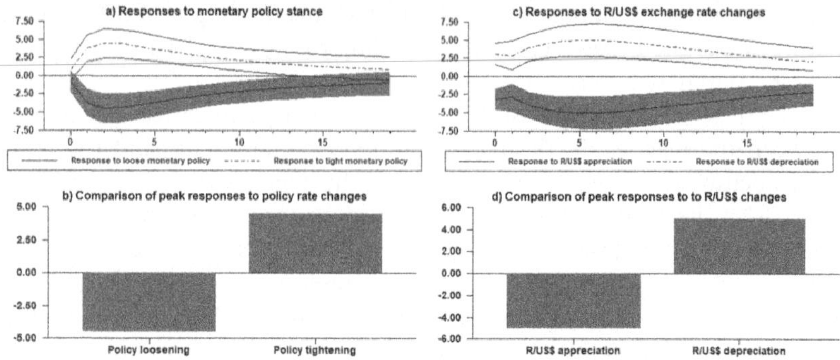

Fig. 15.9 Excess reserve responses to the repo rate and R/US$ exchange rate changes. (Note: The grey shaded areas denote the 16th and 84th percentile confidence bands. Source: Authors' calculations)

reserves, whereas a loose monetary policy stance and the exchange rate appreciation result in a decline.

So, if a tight monetary policy stance and the R/US$ exchange rate depreciation result in an increase in excess reserves, does it mean that the concurrence of these factors reinforces each other? To test whether monetary policy tightening and R/US$ exchange rate depreciation propagate and reinforce each other's effects on banks' excess reserves, we estimate a counterfactual VAR model. The counterfactual model estimates the role of the R/US$ exchange rate depreciation channel in propagating the effects of tight monetary policy on banks' excess reserves. The counterfactual VAR models include changes in banks' excess reserves, the R/US$ exchange rate changes and the repo rate. We create four dummy variables one that takes on the values of (i) the R/US$ exchange rate depreciation, and zero otherwise (ii) exchange rate appreciation and zero otherwise, (iii) one that takes on the values of monetary policy tightening, and zero otherwise (iv) monetary policy loosening and zero otherwise . The dummy variables enter the VAR models separately. The models are estimated with two lags and 10,000 Monte Carlo draws. The changes are at an annual rate. The results in Fig. 15.10a and b show that excess reserves increase in response to positive shocks to the repo rate and that the exchange rate depreciation channel amplifies the increase. Similarly, in Fig. 15.10 c and d, excess reserves increase in response to positive shocks to the exchange rate changes and the repo rate tightening channel amplifies the increase.

The results in Fig. 15.11 show that the R/US$ exchange rate depreciation and the repo rate tightening shocks propagate each other's effects on

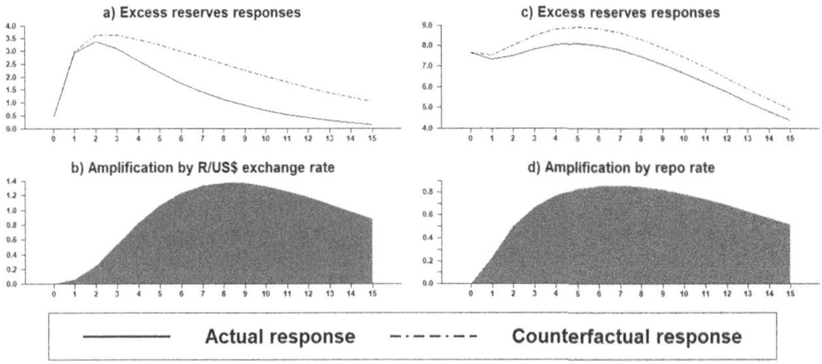

Fig. 15.10 Accumulated responses to shocks and amplification by the repo rate tightening and R/US$ exchange rate depreciation channels. (Source: Authors' calculations)

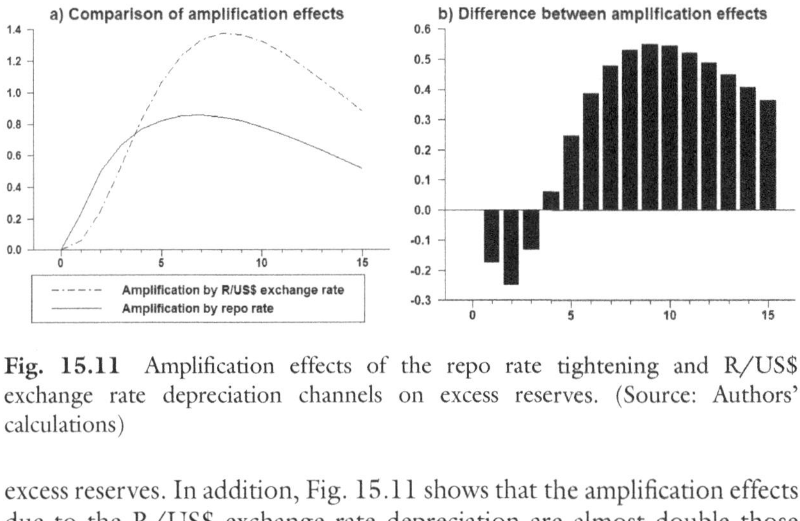

Fig. 15.11 Amplification effects of the repo rate tightening and R/US$ exchange rate depreciation channels on excess reserves. (Source: Authors' calculations)

excess reserves. In addition, Fig. 15.11 shows that the amplification effects due to the R/US$ exchange rate depreciation are almost double those due to the repo rate tightening.

If monetary policy tightening and R/US$ exchange rate depreciations propagate and reinforce each other's effects on banks' excess reserves, then which variable contributed more to the historical developments in banks' excess reserves? To answer this question, we estimate a historical counterfactual VAR model, which includes changes in the R/US$ exchange rate, excess reserves and the repo rate. For the historical contributions, we are particularly interested in the dynamics in the period after

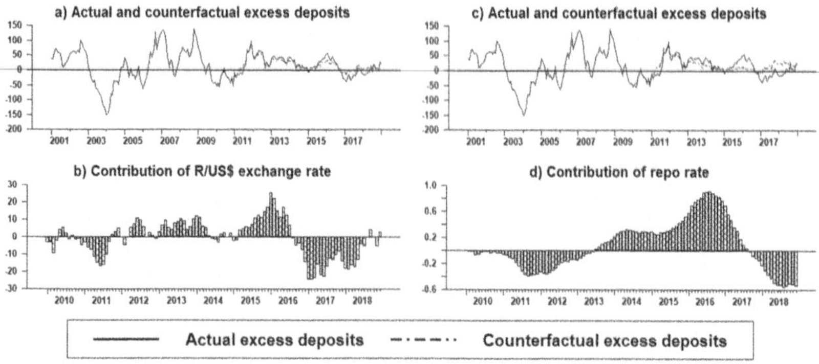

Fig. 15.12 Historical contributions of the R/US$ exchange rate and repo rate to excess reserves. (Source: Authors' calculations)

2010 when the R/US$ depreciated for a prolonged period and the repo rate was tightened between 2013 and 2017.

The results in Fig. 15.12 show that between 2012 and 2016, the R/US$ exchange rate depreciation contributed to the increase in excess reserves but the R/US$ appreciation since 2017 has dampened the rate of increase in excess reserves. Similarly, the 2014 and 2017 repo rate tightening phase resulted in an increase in excess reserves but the mild loosening since 2018 has contributed to the dampening in the excess reserve rate of increase.

Nonetheless, it is evident that the contributions of the R/US$ exchange rate depreciation far outweigh those of a tight monetary policy stance. Thus, the SARB reserve accumulation programme has a significant influence over the supply of excess reserves or how excess reserves evolve. These effects are over and above the effects of the R/US$ exchange rate depreciation.

15.6 How Effective Is the South African Policy Rate Corridor System for Inter-bank Rates?

Bowman et al. (2011) state that the effectiveness of the central bank interest rate as a floor for inter-bank or short-term money-market rates: (i) largely depends on the ability and willingness of institutions with access to borrow from institutions without access; and (ii) on the competitive pressures to arbitrage any differences between the rates available at the central bank rate and in the market. Accordingly, unless all institutions that borrow and lend overnight funds are allowed to have deposits at the central bank and to earn interest on those deposits, there will be some scope for the overnight market rate to trade below the policy rate floor. Such scope may not be captured in measures of market rates that exclude important segments of the market, because they do not provide any indication of the rates the excluded institutions are receiving relative to the rate paid by the central bank.

How often does the Sabor and the Johannesburg inter-bank agreed rate (Jibar) fall below policy rate floors?[14] Bowman et al. (2011) indicate that this is one simple test to assess the extent to which policy rate floors are effective in constraining declines in market rates. Nonetheless, they caution that in some of these cases, this simple test may have less to say about the permeability of the policy rate floor than about the efficacy of open-market operations. Furthermore, if central banks manage bank balances to keep market rates off the policy rate floor, then the market rate spread over the policy rate is likely to be positive whether or not the policy rate floor would actually constrain the market rate.[15]

Figure 15.13 shows that the Sabor rate has been persistently below the repo rate for the entire sample period. On the other hand, the one-month Jibar rate moves at some positive margin above the repo rate, except for a brief period during 2000 and since 2013. Nonetheless, the margin between the repo rate and the Jibar has been persistently declining since 2000 and has been negative since 2013. This means that the Jibar rate has been slightly above the repo rate. On the other hand, the margin with the

[14] We are aware that the one-month Jibar rate is not an overnight rate. We use it to illustrate the relationship with the repo as it is one of the benchmark interbank rates.

[15] For example, by targeting a rate in the centre of the policy rate corridor. Bowman et al. (2011) show that this is the case for the Reserve Bank of Australia, the Reserve Bank of New Zealand and the Riksbank, because those central banks have managed market rates throughout our sample period to keep them strictly above policy rate floors. Five of these eight central banks, namely, the European Central Bank (ECB), Bank of Japan, Bank of England, Bank of Canada, and Norges Bank operate what might be described as a "floor system". In addition, the ECB and the Bank of Japan monitor a market rate corresponding entirely to participants with access to interest on central bank balances, which suggests that in principle, the policy rate floors of these central banks should provide an effective lower bound for market lending rates.

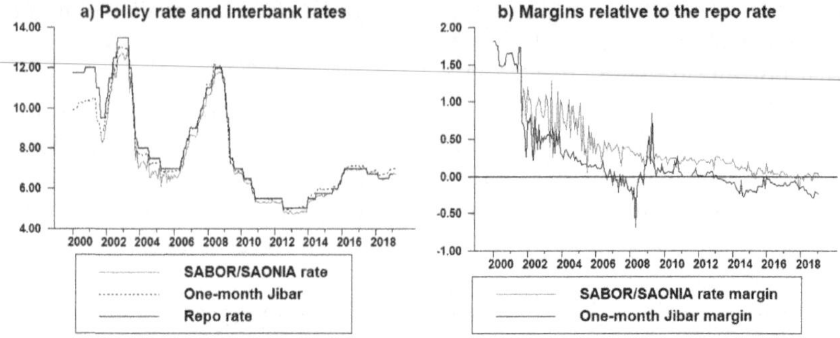

Fig. 15.13 Repo, Sabor and Jibar rates. (Source: South African Reserve Bank and authors' calculations)

Sabor rate has recently stabilised around zero. This means that effectively the overnight inter-bank market trades at the same rate as the repo rate.

However, it is evident that the margins of both rates relative to the repo rate are very volatile, particularly before 2008. This is especially the case for the Sabor rate. Veyrune et al. (2018) argue that from a monetary policy transmission perspective, inter-bank or short term rate volatility and the uncertainty regarding the level of inter-bank and short-term rates is undesirable as it increases the liquidity premium, which is in turn transmitted to the cost of funding in the economy via the interest rate term structure. Figure 15.14 shows that there is a negative relationship between the Sabor and Jibar rate spreads and excess reserves.[16]

We explore whether there are excess reserves threshold effects on the volatility of the inter-bank rates in later sections.

[16] Nonetheless, Fig. 15.21 in the appendix shows that shows that the relationship between Sabor rate margin and excess deposits has changed during the sample period 2000M1 to 2018M12. Whereas the association between the Sabor and excess deposits is negative for the sample period 2000M1 to 2018M12 it became positive during the sample period 2007M1 to 2018M12. This is the case whether we use excess or total banks' deposits as shown in Fig. 15.6(c). We establish the same pattern with respect to the one-month Jibar rate margin to the repo rate, although the relationships are somewhat flat compared to those with the Sabor rate margin. This might be because the one-month Jibar rate is not necessarily a pure overnight interbank benchmark rate per ser. These stylized facts imply that changes in the banks' deposits with the SARB generally exert downward pressure on the interbank rates margin with the repo rate. However, this relationship has changed since 2007 as there is a positive association between the margins and the banks' deposits with the SARB.

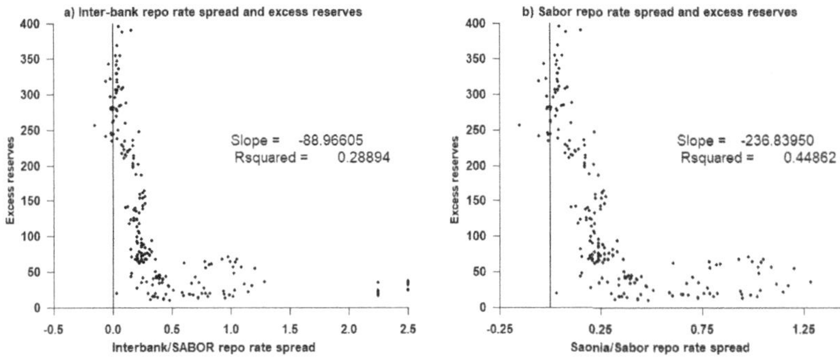

Fig. 15.14 Inter-bank spreads to the repo rate and banks' excess reserves. (Source: Authors' calculations)

15.7 Where Does the Excess Reserves Lie Within the Interest Rate Corridor System?

The earlier section showed that an inverse relationship exists between the policy rate (repo rate) and excess reserves bank balances. But from this linear association, it is unclear as to how inter-bank rates transition and whether there are any asymmetrical threshold effects exerted by excess reserves within the interest rate corridor. This section models the negative association between the Sabor and overnight forex rates and the level of excess reserves within the bivariate logistic function model, as shown in Fig. 15.3. Like Veyrune et al. (2018), we assume that the relationship between short-term interest rates and excess reserves can be modelled as a bivariate logistic function, as discussed in earlier sections.

According to Veyrune et al. (2018), the estimated logistic function enables researchers to determine for which level of excess reserves short-term rates are anchored to one of the three characteristic points of the logistic function, namely, (i) higher edge; (ii) mid-corridor; or (iii) lower edge, or are 'un-anchored'. Short-term rates become 'un-anchored' when they diverge from the main policy rates and fluctuate in the interest rate corridor between one of the corridors, the higher edge and the mid-point or the lower edge. From a monetary policy transmission perspective, the 'un-anchoring' of short-term interest rates within the interest rate corridor is undesirable because the policy stance conveyed via a policy rate in normal circumstances becomes less precisely defined as short-term rates fluctuate in the corridor. Thus, the logistic function contributes to the understanding of the inter-bank and short-term interest rates' reaction function as excess reserves vary. As such, it may help policymakers to predict the excess reserves ranges in which inter-bank and short-term interest rates become "un-anchored". Furthemore, it can help policy makers to avoid the negative consequences of 'un-anchored' inter-bank and money market interest rates. It can also inform the decision to tier the rate at which excess reserves are remunerated.

Following Veyrune et al. (2018), we estimate a bivariate logistic relationship between excess reserves, Sabor and the overnight forex rates in a symmetric interest rate corridor to assess the role of the level of excess reserves in determining and predicting the position of short-term rates within the interest rate corridor. The bivariate logistic function allows the position of short-term rates in the interest rate corridor to be determined and predicted depending on the level of excess reserves.

Furthermore, the logistic function demonstrates how the anchoring of inter-bank and short-term interest rates transitions from one state to another. The estimated LSTAR model includes the Sabor, the overnight forex rate and banks' excess reserves. The sample spans 2001M9 to 2018M12. For robustness tests, we extend the sample and start it in 1995M1, and use the inter-bank rate for the period 1995M1 to 2001M12 and the Sabor rate thereafter. The intention is to assess whether the excess reserves threshold (inflection point) effects for the inter-bank rate occurs at the same level of excess reserves when we adjust the sample size.

The results in Figs. 15.15, 15.16, and 15.17 show that that there is not much of a difference in terms of where the excess reserve threshold

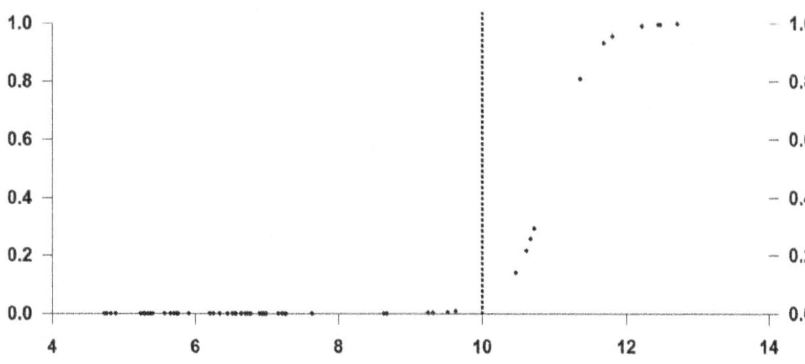

Fig. 15.15 Transition function for the Sabor rate and banks' excess reserves 2001M9 to 2018M12. (Source: Authors' calculations)

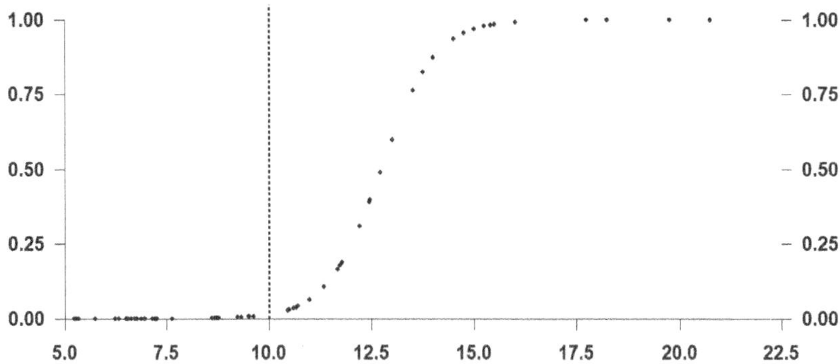

Fig. 15.16 Transition function for the Sabor rate and banks' excess reserves 1995M1 to 2018M12. (Source: Authors' calculations)

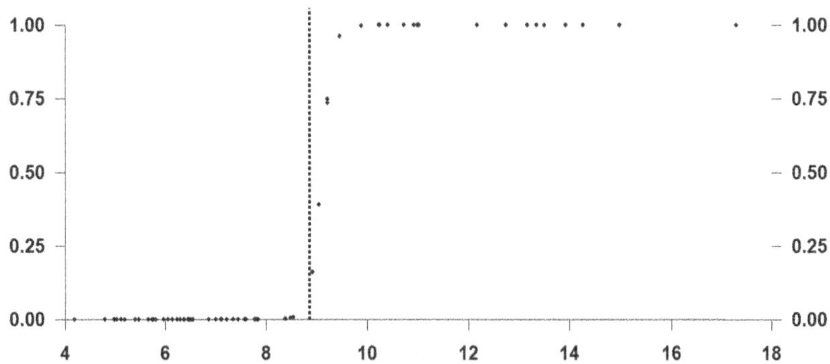

Fig. 15.17 Transition function for the overnight forex rate and banks' excess reserves 2001M9 to 2018M12. (Source: Authors' calculations)

(inflection) effects occur. The excess reserve thresholds (inflection point) occur around R90 billion and R100 billion of excess reserves.

Thus, we conclude that there is robust evidence that the excess reserves threshold effects occur at around R100 billion for the lower band of the interest rate corridor, whilst it peaks around R12.5 billion for the mid-point of the interest rate corridor. The policy implication is that the R100 billion excess reserves can be used as the threshold to guide the tiering of excess reserves and how they can be remunerated between the mid-point and the lower part of the interest rate corridor.

15.8 Is the Sabor and Overnight Forex Rate Volatility in Anyway Associated with Banks' Excess Deposits at the SARB?

This section concludes the analysis in this chapter by estimating the responses of the Sabor and the overnight forex rate volatilities to banks' excess reserves. We estimate several bilateral VAR models, which include the volatilities indicator and the banks' excess reserves growth. The volatilities indicators are for the Sabor and the overnight forex rate volatilities. The Sabor and the overnight forex rate volatilities are estimated using the Garch (1,1) model. The estimated Sabor and the overnight forex rate volatilities enter the VAR separately. The models are estimated for the sample period 2001M9 to 2018M12. The VAR models are estimated using two lags and 10,000 Monte Carlo draws. The results in Fig. 15.18 show that the Sabor and overnight forex rate volatilities increase in response to positive shocks to banks' excess reserves. Furthermore, it is evident in Fig. 15.18(c) that the overnight forex rate volatility increases more compared to the Sabor rate. At the same time, positive shocks to banks' excess reserves explain a larger variance in the overnight forex rate volatility compared to the Sabor rate volatility.

What is the role of the estimated threshold of R100 billion excess bank reserves on the volatility of the Sabor and overnight forex rates? To answer this question, we use the estimated volatility in the bilateral TVAR models to estimate the impact of banks' R100 billion of excess reserves. We use the R100 billion threshold to assess the impact of banks' low (high) excess reserve regimes on the Sabor and overnight forex rate volatilities.

We estimate two TVAR models where the R100 billion threshold is used to demarcate banks' high and low excess reserves regimes. The models are estimated from 2001M9 to 2018M12 using two lags and 10,000 Monte Carlo draws. The results in Fig. 15.19 show that there is indeed a difference between the high and low bank excess reserves as demarcated by the R100 billion threshold. The Sabor rate volatility declines in response to a positive shock to banks' excess reserves in the low excess reserves regime compared to the high excess reserves regime in Fig. 15.20(c). Similarly, shocks to banks' excess reserves explain a larger variation in the Sabor rate volatility in the high excess reserves regime compared to the low excess reserves regime in Fig. 15.20(d).

On the other hand, the results for the overnight forex rate volatility in Fig. 15.20 indicate that the volatility increases less in the low excess reserves regime compared to the high excess reserves regime. Furthermore,

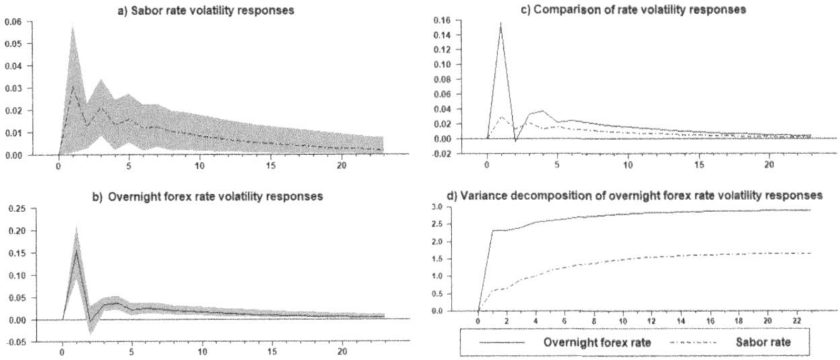

Fig. 15.18 Responses of the Sabor and overnight forex rate volatility to banks' excess reserves (model without thresholds). (Source: Authors' calculations)

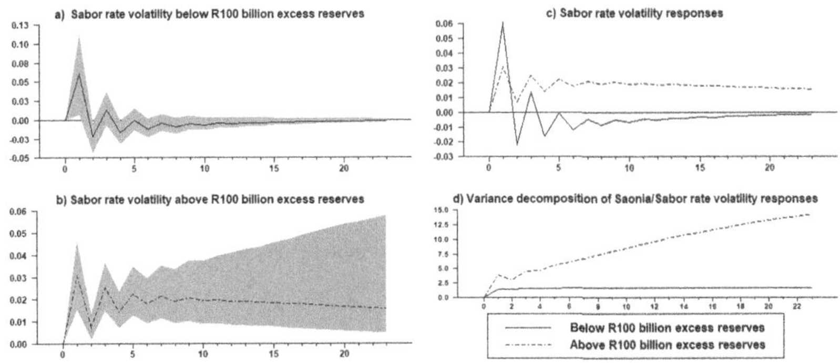

Fig. 15.19 The threshold effects of banks' excess reserves on the Sabor rate volatility. (Source: Authors' calculations)

excess reserves above the threshold explain a larger proportion of the volatility in the overnight forex rate. Thus, the results imply that the banks' R100 billion of excess reserves have statistical and economic significance in the response of the inter-bank rates and their volatility. There is a direct relationship between the level of excess reserves and the inter-bank rate volatility. Lowering the level of excess reserves to levels below the R100 billion threshold will assist in lowering the volatility in the Sabor and overnight forex rates. In addition, policymakers can gradually phase in the autonomous use of the deposit rate to manage bank liquidity or excess reserves. This gradual phasing in of the autonomous use of the deposit

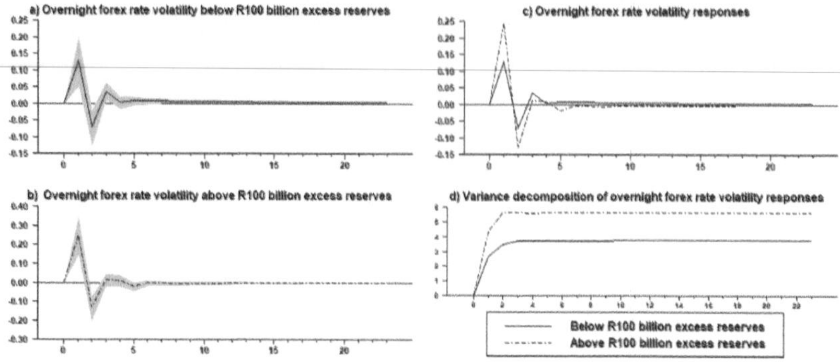

Fig. 15.20 The threshold effects of banks' excess reserves on the overnight forex rate volatility. (Source: Authors' calculations)

rate to manage bank liquidity or excess reserves can take the approach of tiering excess reserves and use the estimated threshold as a guideline. Remunerating reserves more than R100 billion at the corridor between the repo (mid-point) and the deposit rate.[17] This is especially important, given the recommendations of embarking on another forex reserves accumulation programme and LSAPs by the SARB in the previous chapters. In this way, the SARB will partly avoid the drawback posed by the accumulation of banks' excess reserves associated with the LSAPs and another large programme of forex reserves accumulation.

15.9 Conclusion and Policy Implications

Is the interest rate corridor an effective instrument to dampen the accumulation of excess reserves and inter-bank rate volatility? Yes, we find that the inter-bank rate volatility is dependent on excess reserves regimes. The overnight forex rate volatility increases more compared to the Sabor rate in response to positive shocks to banks' excess reserves. Positive shocks to banks' excess reserves explain a larger variance in the overnight forex rate volatility compared to the Sabor rate volatility. In addition, the estimated excess reserves of R100 billion have statistical and economic significance

[17] Tiered remuneration of excess reserves tiered remuneration is part of the operational framework in Switzerland, ECB, Sweden, and Denmark. See https://www.bis.org/publ/qtrpdf/r_qt1603e.pdf

in the response of the inter-bank rates and their volatility. The Sabor and overnight forex rate volatilities decline in the low excess reserves regime compared to the high excess reserves regime. Thus, there is a direct relationship between the level of excess reserves and the inter-bank rate volatility. Lowering the level of excess reserves to levels below the R100 billion threshold will assist in lowering the volatility in the Sabor and overnight forex rates.

Furthermore, the results of the transition function imply that the interest rate corridor floor allows the central bank to separate the interest rate policy (monetary policy stance) from the liquidity policy. This means that policymakers can gradually phase in the autonomous use of the deposit rate to manage bank liquidity or excess reserves. This gradual phasing in of the autonomous use of the deposit rate to manage bank liquidity or excess reserves can take the approach of tiering excess reserves and use the estimated threshold as a guideline. Remunerating reserves more than R100 billion at the corridor between the repo (mid-point) and the deposit rate. This is especially important given the recommendations of embarking on another forex reserves accumulation programme and LSAPs by the SARB in the previous chapters. In this way, the SARB will partly avoid the drawback posed by the accumulation of banks' excess reserves associated with the LSAPs and another large programme of forex reserves accumulation.

Evidence shows that monetary policy tightening and loosening; and the R/US$ exchange rate depreciation and appreciation push banks' excess reserves in opposite directions. A tight monetary policy stance and the R/US$ exchange rate depreciation increase banks' excess reserves, whereas a loose monetary policy stance and the exchange rate appreciation result in a decline. Thus, monetary policy tightening and the R/US$ exchange rate depreciations propagate and reinforce each other's effects on banks' excess reserves. The historical contributions show that between 2012 and 2016, the R/US$ exchange rate depreciation contributed to the increase in excess reserves, but the R/US$ appreciation since 2017 has dampened the rate of increase in excess reserves. Similarly, the 2014 and 2017 repo rate tightening phase resulted in an increase in excess reserves, but the mild loosening since 2018 has contributed to the dampening in the excess reserves rate of increase. Nonetheless, the contributions of the R/US$ exchange rate depreciation far outweigh those of a tight monetary policy stance. Therefore, the forex reserves accumulation and the R/US$ exchange rate movements have a significant effect on the SARB's money market operations.

Appendix

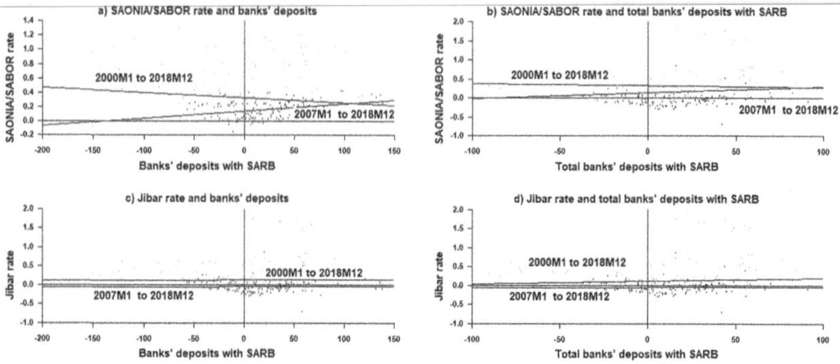

Fig. 15.21 Sabor and Jibar margins to the repo rate and banks' excess reserves. (Source: Authors' calculations)

References

Gray S. 2011. Central Bank Balances and Reserve Requirements. IMF Working Paper WP/11/36. https://www.imf.org/external/pubs/ft/wp/2011/wp1136.pdf

Amstad M, and Antoine M. 2011. Monetary Policy Implementation: Common Goals but Different Practices. Current Issues in Economics and Finance 7(7), Federal Reserve Bank of New York. https://www.newyorkfed.org/research/current_issues/ci17-7.html

David B, Gagnon E, and Leahy M. 2010. Interest on Excess Reserves as a monetary policy Instrument: The Experience of Foreign Central banks. International Financial Discussion Papers 996. Board of Governors of the Federal Reserve System. https://www.federalreserve.gov/monetarypolicy/files/FOMC20100121memo01.pdf

South African Reserve Bank. 2006. Intended replacement of the South African Overnight Interbank Average (Saonia) rate with an improved benchmark call rate. Discussion paper. https://www.resbank.co.za/Markets/Domestic/SABOR/Documents/SaborDiscPaper.pdf

South African Reserve Bank. 2018. Consultation paper on selected interest rate benchmarks in South Africa. https://www.resbank.co.za/Lists/News%20and%20Publications/Attachments/8722/Consultation%20Paper%2028-08-2018.pdf

South African Reserve Bank. 2019. Report on stakeholder feedback on the reform of interest rate benchmarks in South Africa. https://www.resbank.co.za/Markets/MPG/Documents/Feedback%20Report%20Interest%20Rate%20Reforms.pdf

Bech M., and Monnet C. 2015. "A search-based model of the interbank money market and monetary policy implementation," BIS Working Paper No. 529. https://www.bis.org/publ/work529.htm

Vari M. 2016. "Monetary policy transmission with interbank market fragmentation," CEPREMAP Working Paper No. 1516. https://www.parisschoolofeconomics.eu/IMG/pdf/jobmarket-paper-vari-pse.pdf

Kahn G A. 2010. Monetary policy under a corridor operating framework. Economic Review, Federal Reserve Bank of Kansas City, 95(Q IV), pp. 5–34.

Osborne M. 2016. Monetary policy and volatility in the sterling money market. Staff Bank of England Working Paper No. 588. https://www.bankofengland.co.uk/-/media/boe/files/working-paper/2016/monetary-policy-and-volatility-in-the-sterling-money-market

TengTeng Xu, Hu K, and Das U S. 2019. Bank Profitability and Financial Stability. IMF Working Paper WP/19/5. https://www.imf.org/~/media/Files/Publications/WP/2019/wp1905.ashx

Veyrune R, Della Valle G, and Guo S. 2018. Relationship Between Short-Term Interest Rates and Excess Reserves: A Logistic Approach. IMF Working Paper WP/18/80. https://www.imf.org/en/Publications/WP/Issues/2018/04/09/Relationship-Between-Short-Term-Interest-Rates-and-Excess-Reserves-A-Logistic-Approach-45789

ECB Bulletin. January 2014. "Recent Developments in Excess Liquidity and Money Market Rates." https://www.ecb.europa.eu/pub/pdf/other/art2_mb201401en_pp69-82en.pdf?b42b63982fb8fcfabe52dbecf9c7304b

Werner R A. 2014. Can banks individually create money out of nothing?—The theories and the empirical evidence. International Review of Financial Analysis 36 1–19. https://www.sciencedirect.com/science/article/pii/S1057521914001070

Demiralp S, Eisenschmidt J, and Vlassopoulos T. 2019. Negative interest rates, excess liquidity and retail deposits: banks' reaction to unconventional monetary policy in the euro area. ECB Working Paper Series No 2283. https://www.ecb.europa.eu/pub/pdf/scpwps/ecb.wp2283~2ccc074964.en.pdf?95f071e362a63d1017bf9ca55d065375

Altavilla C, Burlon L, Giannetti M, and Holton S. 2019. Is there a zero-lower bound? The effects of negative policy rates on banks and firms. ECB Working Paper Series No 2289. https://www.ecb.europa.eu/pub/pdf/scpwps/ecb.wp2289~1a3c04db25.en.pdf?e0c348b9bd29608f0dc3854a26f2464f

Christensen J H E, and Krogstrup S. 2016. A Portfolio Model of Quantitative Easing. Working Paper Series 2016-12, Federal Reserve Bank of San Francisco.

Bowman D, Fang C, Sally M D, and Kamin S B. 2011. Quantitative easing and bank lending: evidence from Japan," International Finance Discussion Papers 1018. Board of Governors of the Federal Reserve System (U.S.).

CHAPTER 16

Is the Impact of an Unexpected Positive Required Reserves Ratio Shock on Inflation Expectations Different from That Due to Positive Excess Liquid Asset Holdings and Forex Reserves Shock?

Research Questions Explored

- Assess the role of the tightening shocks in the banks' required reserves (RR) ratio, banks' excess liquid asset holdings (LAH) and the accumulation of foreign currency reserves on inflation expectations.
- Explore whether the tightening shocks in the banks' RR ratio, banks' excess LAH and the accumulation of foreign currency reserves propagate each other's effects on inflation expectations.
- Test the role of the exchange rate in transmitting the tightening shocks in the banks' RR ratio , banks' excess LAH and the accumulation of foreign currency reserves (forex reserves) on inflation expectations.

16.1 Introduction

This chapter continues on the theme of the interaction of the South African Reserve Bank (SARB), private banks' balance sheets, various macro-prudential tools and their effects on the macro-economy. Evidence

N. Gumata, E. Ndou, *Achieving Price, Financial and Macro-Economic Stability in South Africa*,
https://doi.org/10.1007/978-3-030-66340-7_16

in earlier chapters showed that an increase in the banks' excess (LAH results in an increase in credit to government at the expense of a decline in credit to the private sector. At the same time, evidence in previous chapters showed that an unexpected increase (tightening shock) in the RR ratio of banks results in a decline in economic growth via credit growth, consumption growth, exports growth and inflation channels, amongst others. Earlier chapters also showed that positive shocks to forex reserves contribute to an increase in GDP growth, employment growth, a decline in inflation and the unemployment rate. This chapter assesses the role of the tightening in RR ratio, excess LAH and the accumulation of forex reserves on inflation expectations. Is the impact of the unexpected positive (tightening) RR ratio shock on inflation expectations different from those due to positive excess LAH and forex reserve accumulation shocks?

This chapter fills policy and academic research gaps by showing the spill-over effects of these monetary and macro-prudential tools on the price stability mandate via the inflation expectations channel. We show the responses of inflation expectations to the tightening in the RR ratio and compare them to the effects of positive shocks to excess LAH and the accumulation of forex reserves. In addition, we fill policy and academic research gaps by determining whether these monetary and macro-prudential tools complement or propagate each other's effects on inflation expectations.

16.2 Empirical Evidence

We start the empirical analysis by estimating VAR models, which include either changes in the RR ratio or excess LAH or forex reserves, and either current (*current_exp*), or one-year-ahead *(one year ahead_exp)* or two-year-ahead *(two year ahead_exp)* inflation expectations for the period 2002Q3 to 2016Q1. These variables are included individually in the model. The model is estimated using two lags and 10,000 Monte Carlo draws. The growth rates (changes) are annual rates. The three shocks explored pertain to an unexpected increase (tightening) in the RR ratio, an increase in excess LAH and an increase in forex reserves accumulation.

Figure 16.1 shows that a positive shock to the RR ratio lowers inflation expectations. The decline is more pronounced on current inflation expectations and one-year-ahead inflation expectations. In contrast, the two-year-ahead inflation expectations decline insignificantly. On the other hand, a positive excess LAH shock has a significant but transitory negative

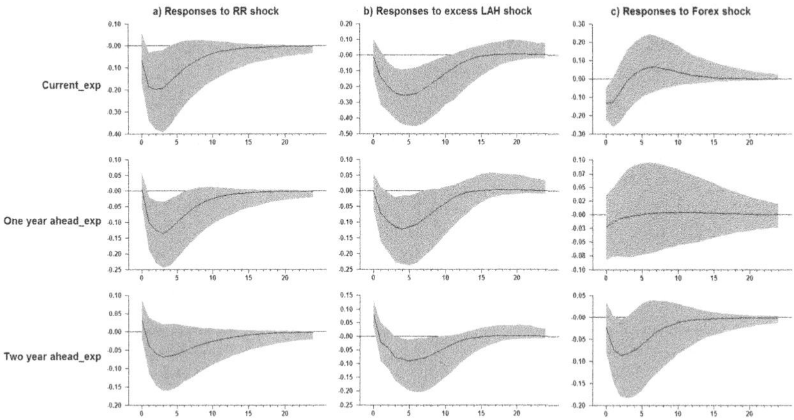

Fig. 16.1 Responses of inflation expectations to various shocks. (Source: Authors' calculations)

impact on inflation expectations and a positive forex reserves accumulation shock also lowers inflation expectations. Thus, all the shocks result in a decline in inflation expectations across maturities albeit at varying degrees.

16.3 How Robust Is the Evidence of the Decline in Inflation Expectations? Evidence from the Inclusion of the Exchange Rate in the Model

We perform additional estimations to determine the robustness of the responses of inflation expectations to a positive shock to the RR ratio, excess LAH and forex reserves accumulation. We use different techniques to determine the sensitivity of the evidence to changes in the model size, specification and econometric technique. The first robustness analysis includes assessing whether the inclusion of changes in the R/US$ exchange rate impact the direction of the inflation expectation responses. How robust are the findings to the inclusion of annual changes in the R/US$ exchange rate? The impulse responses in Fig. 16.2 show that the current inflation expectations decline more than the one-year-ahead and two-year-ahead inflation expectations due to positive RR ration and excess LAH shocks.

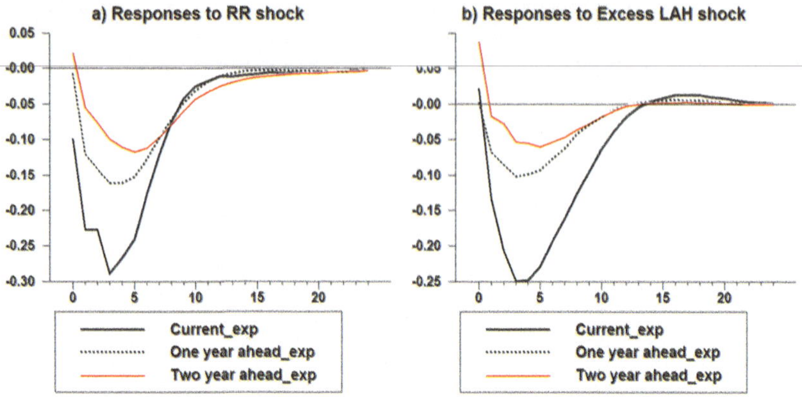

Fig. 16.2 Responses to positive RR ratio and excess LAH shocks in the model including the R/US$ exchange rate. (Source: Authors' calculations)

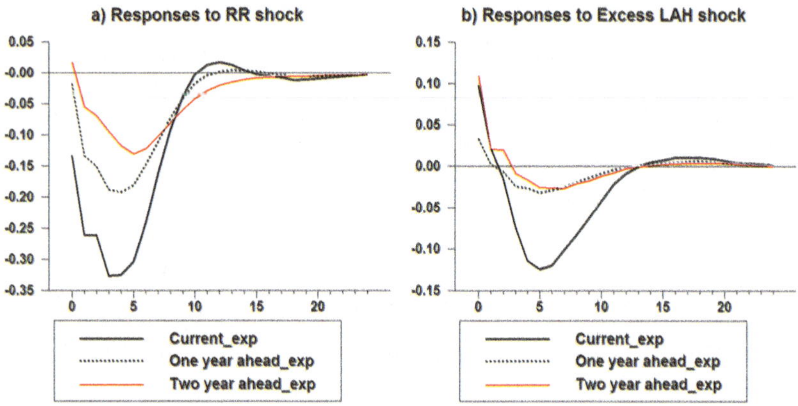

Fig. 16.3 Responses to positive RR ratio and excess LAH shocks in the model including the NEER. (Source: Authors' calculations)

Figure 16.3 shows that the responses of inflation expectations are robust to the change in the specification of the model. The results are generated from a model that replaces the R/US$ exchange rate changes with the nominal effective exchange rate (NEER) changes.

Evidence shows that even when including the NEER changes, current inflation expectations decline more than the one-year-ahead and two-year inflation expectations due to a positive RR ratio and excess LAH shock. This confirms that the results are robust to the changes in the specification of the model.

16.3.1 *Evidence from a VAR Model with the Required Reserves Ratio as an Exogenous Variable*

The second robustness test applies an exogenous VAR model. The model uses inflation expectations and annual changes in the R/US$ exchange rate in the model as endogenous variables, while annual changes in the RR ratio are an exogenous variable. The various categories of inflation expectations are included separately in the model. Figure 16.4 shows that inflation expectations decline significantly due to a positive shock to the RR ratio, but the durations of the decline differ according to the inflation expectations category. The peak decline in current inflation expectations exceeds that of the one-year-ahead and two-year-ahead inflation expectations. The R/US$ exchange rate appreciates significantly for nearly a year. Overall, the findings are robust to the inclusion of different inflation expectations categories in the model.

To assess the robustness of the results to the change in the model specification, we replace the RR ratio with annual changes in excess LAH. The VAR model is as specified in the preceding section, and the excess LAH

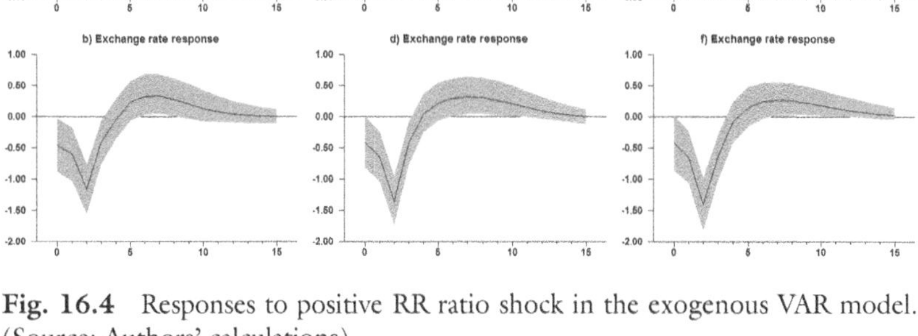

Fig. 16.4 Responses to positive RR ratio shock in the exogenous VAR model. (Source: Authors' calculations)

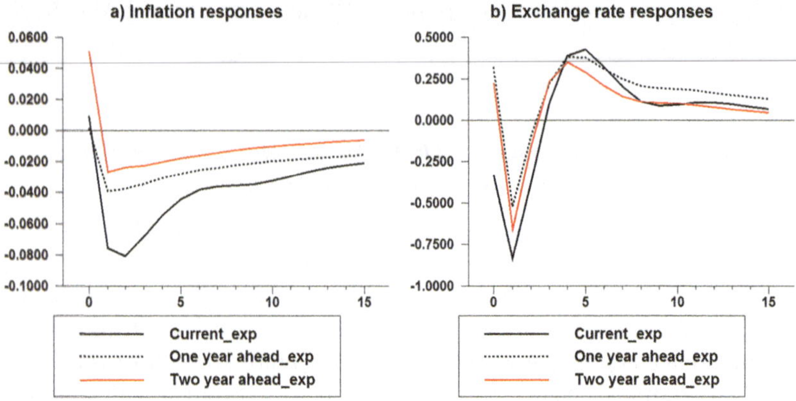

Fig. 16.5 Responses to positive excess LAH shocks in the exogenous VAR model. (Note: Current_exp refers to current inflation expectations, one-year ahead_exp refers to one-year-ahead inflation expectations and two-year ahead_exp refers to two-year-ahead inflation expectations. Source: Authors' calculations)

shock is an exogenous variable. Like earlier findings, evidence shows that inflation expectations decline following a positive excess LAH shock.

The current inflation expectations decline more than the one-year-ahead and two-year-ahead inflation expectations. In addition, Fig. 16.5(b) shows that the exchange rate appreciates following a positive excess LAH shock irrespective of the inflation expectations variable included in the model.

16.3.2 Evidence from a Modified Pentecôte and Rondeau (2015) Model

We apply a third technique to test for the robustness that inflation expectations decline due to positive shocks in the RR ratio. We use the modified Pentecôte and Rondeau (2015) and Cerra and Saxena (2008) approaches to determine the inflation expectations responses to positive RR ratio, excess LAH and forex reserves accumulation shocks using Eq. (16.1). The shocks (*Shock*$_i$) are included separately in the model. The three inflation expectations categories are included separately in the estimation for each shock.

$$Inflation\,expectation_t = Constant + \sum_{i=1}^{4} d_i Inflation\,expectation_{t-i}\ \sum_{i=0}^{4} c_i Shock_i + \varepsilon_t \tag{16.1}$$

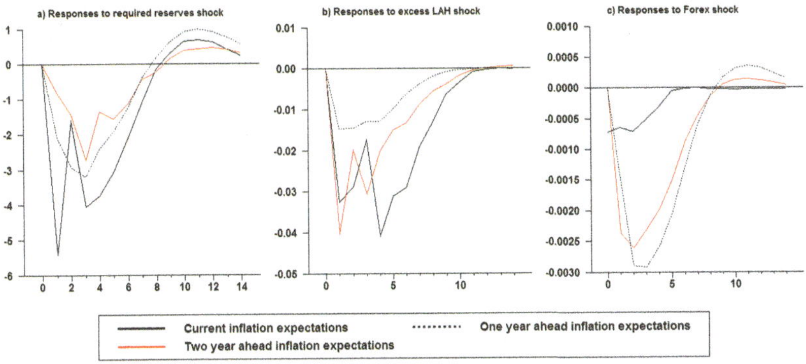

Fig. 16.6 Responses to the RR ratio, excess LAH and forex reserves accumulation shocks. (Note: The impulse responses are derived as per the specification in Eq. 16.1. Source: Authors' calculations)

The results in Fig. 16.6 show that current inflation expectations remain more depressed for longer periods than the one-year-ahead and two-year-ahead inflation expectations. The impulse responses in Fig. 16.6 show that in general, all the inflation expectations decline and revert to pre-shock periods.

All the three shocks lower the inflation expectations in Fig. 16.6 and the peak decline in current inflation expectations exceeds that from the one-year-ahead and two-year-ahead inflation expectations.

16.3.3 Evidence from the Counterfactual Analysis

We conclude the analysis by looking at the role of the R/US$ exchange rate in transmitting the positive RR ratio shocks to inflation expectations. We estimate a counterfactual VAR and shut off the role of the R/US$ exchange rate. The model uses the annual changes in the RR ratio, inflation expectations and annual changes in the R/US$ exchange rate. The model is estimated using two lags and 10,000 Monte Carlo draws. The counterfactual impulse responses refer to the specific inflation expectations category responses when the R/US$ exchange rate is shut off in the model.

Figure 16.7 shows that inflation expectations decline due to an unexpected increase in the RR ratio, but the decline is much more pronounced due to the role of the R/US$ exchange rate. The actual responses decline more than the counterfactual suggesting that the appreciation in the

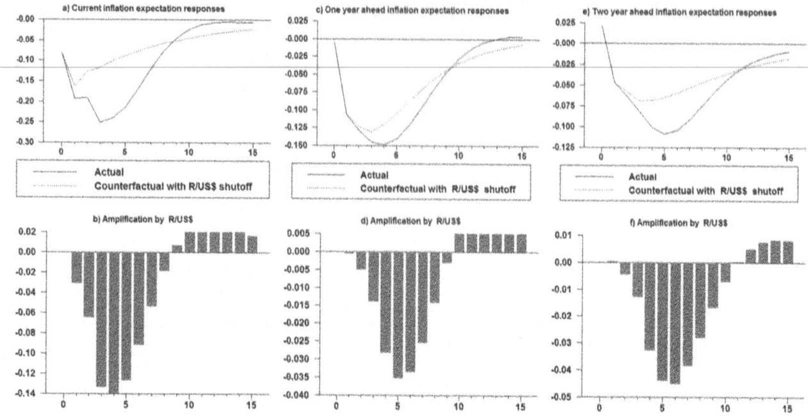

Fig. 16.7 Actual and counterfactual inflation expectations responses to positive RR ratio and the role of the exchange rate channel. (Source: Authors' calculations)

R/US$ exchange rate following a positive RR ratio shock leads to a bigger decline in inflation expectations. The size of the amplification due to the R/US$ exchange rate is shown in the second row of Fig. 16.7. The peak amplification of the decline in inflation expectations due to the R/US$ exchange rate on current inflation expectations is more than three times the peak of one-year-ahead and two-year-ahead inflation expectations.

Similarly, even if the specification of the model is changed and we replace the R/US$ exchange rate annual changes with the nominal effective exchange rate (NEER) annual changes to assess the role of the exchange rate in transmitting positive RR ratio shocks to inflation expectations in Fig. 16.8, we find that actual inflation expectations decline more than the counterfactuals. This suggests that the exchange rate appreciation leads to a pronounced decline in inflation expectations.

Figure 16.9 shows that the NEER plays a role in transmitting the positive excess LAH shocks to inflation expectations. The excess LAH shock does lower inflation expectations but the propagation effects of the NEER are much smaller compared to those established for the RR ratio shocks. Thus, we conclude that the exchange rate plays a limited role in transmitting the excess LAH shock to inflation expectations.

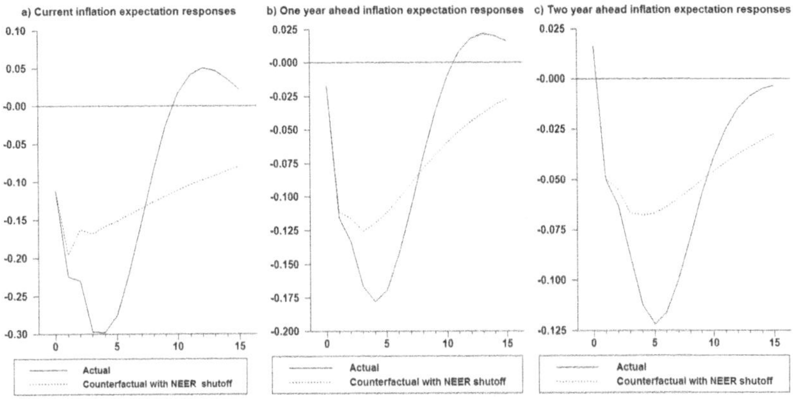

Fig. 16.8 Actual and counterfactual inflation expectations responses to positive RR ratio and the role of the NEER channel. (Source: Authors' calculations)

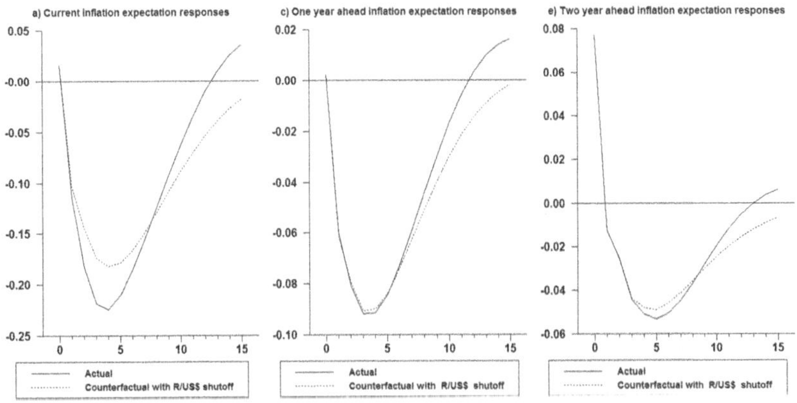

Fig. 16.9 Inflation expectations responses to positive excess LAH shocks. (Source: Authors' calculations)

16.4 Conclusion and Policy Implications

This chapter explored the interaction of various monetary and macro-prudential tools and their effects on the macro-economy and the price stability mandate. We assessed how the effects of the tightening in the banks' RR ratio, an unexpected increase in excess LAH and the forex reserves accumulation on inflation expectations differ. The chapter also assessed whether these monetary and macro-prudential tools complement or propagate each other's effects on inflation expectations in the same direction.

Evidence shows that positive RR ratio, excess LAH and forex reserves accumulation shocks lower inflation expectations across all maturities. Nonetheless, the decline is more pronounced in current inflation expectations compared to the one-year-ahead and two-year-ahead inflation expectations. The R/US$ exchange rate and the NEER play a significant role in transmitting the positive shocks to the RR ratio, excess LAH and forex reserves accumulation on inflation expectations. But inflation expectations decline more due to an unexpected increase in the RR ratio compared to the positive excess LAH shock. We conclude that all three shocks complement and propagate each other's shock on inflation expectations in the same direction. But the RR ratio tightening shocks exert the most potent shock effects on current inflation expectations and the R/US$ exchange rate plays a meaningful role in propagating these tightening effects. This is because the RR ratio tightening shock dampens credit-demand-driven inflation shocks.

References

Cerra V, and Saxena C S. 2008. Growth Dynamics: The Myth of Economic Recovery. American Economic Review. VOL. 98, NO. 1, March 2008 (pp. 439–57).

Glocker C and Towbin P. 2015. Reserve requirements as a macro-prudential instrument: Empirical evidence from Brazil. Journal of Macroeconomics. Volume 44, Pages 158–176

Pentecôte J-S, and Rondeau F. 2015. Trade spillovers on output growth during the 2008 financial crisis. International Economics, CEPII research center, issue 143, pages 36–47.

CHAPTER 17

How Potent Is the Required Reserves Tightening Shock Impact on Funding and Consumer Interest Rates?

Research Questions Explored

- Understand the impact of a required reserves (RR) ratio tightening shock as a macro-prudential tool.
- Assess whether the banks' excess liquid asset holdings (LAH) transmit the RR ratio shocks into funding and consumer interest rates.
- Explore whether the RR ratio tightening shock imposes a cost on bank intermediation via altering the retail deposit, wholesale deposit and inter-bank rates.
- Test whether the banks' excess LAH is a propagator of the RR ratio tightening shock via the bank liquidity channel.

17.1 Introduction

Subsequent to the global financial crisis, central banks explicitly adopted the financial stability as a policy mandate. As a result, research and policy discussions in this area have been pre-occupied with investigating the effectiveness and interaction of various macro-prudential tools with each other and with monetary policy tools. This focus included looking at the role of the RR ratio. Equation (17.1) shows that the total amount of reserves in a banking system can be decomposed into RR and excess

N. Gumata, E. Ndou, *Achieving Price, Financial and Macro-Economic Stability in South Africa*,
https://doi.org/10.1007/978-3-030-66340-7_17

reserves (ER). Changes in these reserves have an impact on credit creation from deposits, and credit volumes in turn impact the price of credit.

$$\text{Total amount of reserves in banking sytem} = \text{Required reserves} + \text{Excess reserves} \qquad (17.1)$$

This chapter examines the impact of the RR tightening shock as a macro-prudential tool. In addition, we determine whether the banks' LAH transmits the RR ratio shocks into funding and consumer interest rates. From Eq. (17.1) ceteris paribus, an increase in the RR ratio should be accompanied by an equivalent change in excess reserves to maintain a given total amount of reserves in the banking system. Does the RR ratio tightening shock impose a cost on bank intermediation via altering the retail deposit, wholesale deposit and inter-bank rates? In addition, all these money market interest rates are sources of bank funds, which represent the same channels impacted by a monetary policy tightening shock. The cost channel of the RR is defined as the cost or an implicit tax on the banking system induced by the increase in the RR, which also affects financial bank intermediated funds (credit extension). Is Hypothesis 17.1 applicable in the South African banking system?

Hypothesis 17.1
As long as the central bank credit (funding from the central bank *via* ***the accommodation system) and bank deposits from the public are close substitutes as alternative sources of bank funding, an increase in the RR ratio will result in a decline in the deposit interest rates but leave lending rates unchanged.***

To the best of our knowledge, no South African study has explored the efficacy of the RR ratio as a potential active macro-prudential tool. Internationally, Koray et al. (2016) show that the tightening by increasing the RR ratio affects banks' funding needs and liquidity position, resulting in a significant impact on the banks' lending behaviour. Furthermore, Basci and Kara (2011) show that the interest rate is considered the main instrument for price stability, while the RR ratio policy deals mainly with financial stability. We explore the role and effectiveness of the tightening in the RR ratio as a macro-prudential tool. Contrary to Gumata and Ndou (2017), this chapter links the RR with the liquidity channel of banks as defined by Koray et al. (2016). Furthermore, given that the RR ratio has been a dormant policy tool in South Africa, this chapter tests the presence of the 'cost channel' of the RR.

17.2 Features of South African Banking System: Unchanged Required Reserves Ratio

From a historical perspective, unlike the forex reserve accumulation strategy, the RR ratio has largely been a dormant policy tool in South Africa at a fixed rate (as a ratio to liabilities to the public) despite the amount of the reserves fluctuation at low levels, as shown in Fig. 17.1. The minimum required cash reserve balances of banks were set at 2.5 per cent of the banks' liabilities since April 1998. This ratio has never been adjusted,[1] as shown by the grey line in Fig. 17.1.

In addition, the minimum required (LAH of banks were set at 5 per cent of the banks' total liabilities in April 1993 and this percentage has not been adjusted since then. However, it is evident in Fig. 17.1b and c that there was a persistent divergence between the minimum required LAH and the actual LAH by banks since January 2009. The excess LAH by banks as a percentage of total liabilities to the public are currently above 5 per cent.

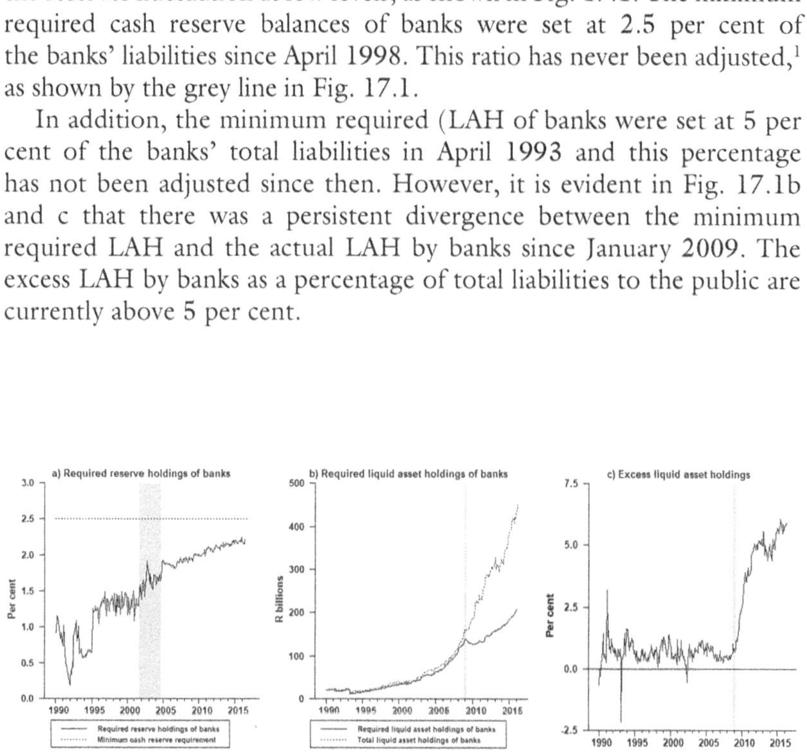

Fig. 17.1 The evolution of banks' required reserves and liquid asset holdings. (Note: In (c) Excess liquid asset holdings of banks are expressed as a percentage of liabilities. Source: South African Reserve Bank and authors' calculations)

[1] But the ratio of banks' vault cash holdings that qualifies as part of cash reserves was reduced and phased out over four years from 100 per cent to 0 per cent between September 2001 and 2004.

17.3 The Liquidity Channel of the Transmission of Changes in the Required Reserves

In the case of South Africa, the accommodation system operates on the basis of a shortage system of accommodating banks' funding needs to effect changes in the repo rate. This means that the central bank drains surplus liquidity from the money market via open market operations (OMO) to make sure that banks make use of the funding from the central bank. In addition, the RR is not remunerated, and banks can access the RR during the maintenance period[2], if during the maintenance period banks hold the minimum required percentage of the RR. This is quite different from what is done in other countries. Hence, we ask: In such a case as South Africa, how does the cost channel of the RR arise or occur?

Like Koray et al. (2016), we construct a liquidity ratio[3] to test the existence of the liquidity channel. However, we differ from these authors in how we define the liquidity ratio. Koray et al. (2016) define and calculate the liquidity ratio as total securities held by banks as a fraction of total liabilities. We differ from them and define the liquidity ratio as shown in Eq. 17.1.

$$\text{Liquidity ratio} = \left(\frac{\text{excess liquid asset holdings}}{\text{total liabilities to the public}} \right) * 100 \qquad (17.2)$$

Where,

$$\text{excess liquid asset holdings} = \text{total liquid asset holdings} \\ -\text{required liquid asset holdings} \qquad (17.3)$$

This is because the RR and the LAH ratios have been unchanged in South Africa. We show the constructed liquidity ratio and its relationship to the RR ratio in Fig. 17.2. Koray et al. (2016) postulate that a negative relationship exists between the increase in the RR ratio and the excess LAH.

This is because the tightening in the RR ratio acts as a liquidity shock on the banking system and increases the amount of liquid assets that banks must pledge as collateral when borrowing from the central bank. Indeed,

[2] The maintenance period lapses on the 15th day of each month. This arrangement or approach to the RR policy compensates for the fact that banks do not earn interest on the RR.

[3] Koray et al. (2016) also refer to the liquidity ratio as the banks' liquidity buffers.

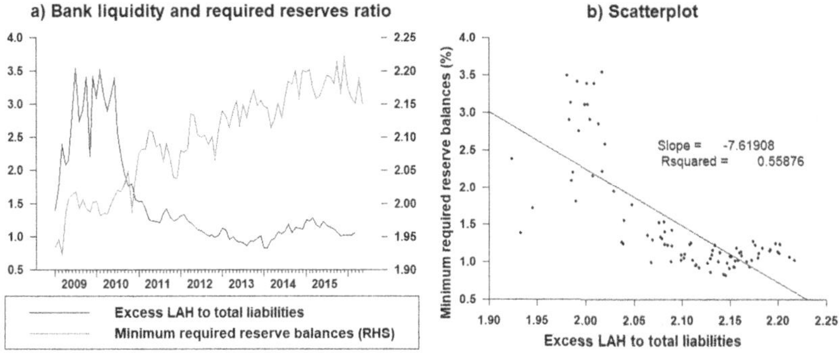

Fig. 17.2 Bank liquidity and required reserves ratio changes. (Source: South African Reserve Bank and authors' calculations)

we find a negative relationship between changes in the excess LAH of banks in Fig. 17.2. This means that the RR ratio can play a meaningful role in transmitting changes to bank liquidity.

17.4 How Significant Is the Cost Channel via the Consumer Deposit and Lending Rates due to the Tightening RR ratio Shock?

We start by estimating Eq. (17.4) to identify the cost channel of the transmission of changes in the RR. The cost channel is defined as a tax imposed by the increase in the RR ratio on bank intermediation. Alternately, we test the direct impact of RR changes on the money market interest rates of various maturities:

$$Y_t = \{\text{RRR}_{\text{rat}}, \text{ELAH}_{\text{Tliab}}, \text{LR}, \text{DR}, \text{Spread}, R/US\$\} \tag{17.4}$$

where RRR_{rat} is the required reserves as a ratio of total liabilities to the public, $\text{ELAH}_{\text{Tliab}}$ is excess LAH as a ratio of total liabilities to the public, LR is the consumer weighted average lending rate, *DR* is the consumer weighted average deposit rate, the spread is the difference between the lending and the deposit rate, and *R/US$* is the log changes in the rand-US dollar exchange rate. Due to the nature of the bank funding sources and the possibility that they will react differently, we estimate different models as we replace the lending rate, deposit rate and the deposit rate-lending rate spread. However, the *R/US$* exchange rate is kept in all models.

The ***first model*** uses the Johannesburg inter-bank agreed rate (Jibar), repo rate and their spread. The ***second model*** uses the three-month negotiable certificate of deposits (NCDs), repo rate and their spread. The ***third model*** uses the three-month Treasury bill rate (TB), repo rate and their spread. The NCD rate captures the impact of the RR ratio shock on wholesale funding given the fact that Glocker and Towbin (2015) suggest that the RR ratio policy becomes ineffective if banks can compensate the higher deposit rate due to a tight RR ratio by financing themselves via alternative markets such as the wholesale market.

The models use two lags as chosen by AIC and the impulse responses are generated from 10,000 Monte Carlo draws. The shock is one positive (increase or tightening) standard deviation shock to the RR ratio. The sample period spans 1999Q1 to 2016Q3 due to the availability of data for the lending and deposit rates. Fig. 17.3 shows that a positive shock to the RR ratio has no significant effect on excess LAH of banks.[4] The repo rate and the average deposit and lending rates rise significantly but in a transitory manner. Their increase is in line with theoretical predictions.

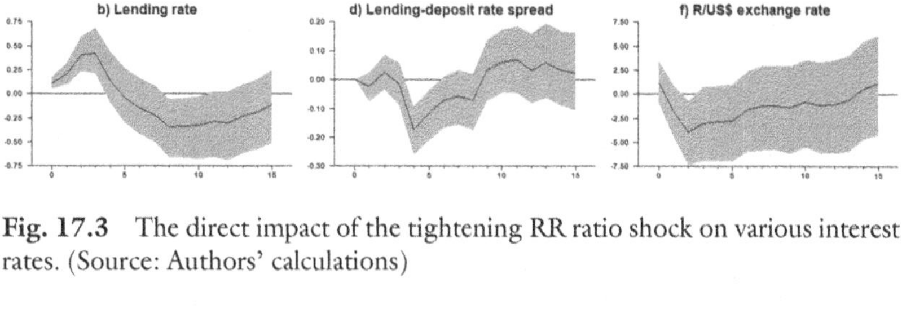

Fig. 17.3 The direct impact of the tightening RR ratio shock on various interest rates. (Source: Authors' calculations)

[4]We explored the role of large-scale asset purchases in reducing excess LAH in earlier chapters.

This means that the cost channel of tightening by increasing the RR ratio affects the banks' funding needs and the liquidity position, resulting in a significant impact on the bank deposit and lending and the interest rate spread. This implies that the central bank's provision of liquidity is not a perfect substitute for bank deposits. Thus, we conclude that the increase in the RR ratio acts as a cost or an implicit tax on the banking system induced by the increase in the RR ratio, which also affects financial banks' intermediated funds via the increase in the lending rate.

These results imply that the central bank credit (funding from the central bank via the accommodation system) and bank deposits from the public are not close substitutes when compared to the alternative sources of bank funding.[5] A tightening shock in the RR ratio results in changes in the deposit and lending rates. The eventual impact of the adjustments in the RR ratio on money and credit markets and economic activity will not be neutral. These results occur even though RR bank deposits are not remunerated and banks can access RR deposits during the maintenance period. It is possible that limiting the access to RR deposits by banks during the maintenance period to smooth out the costs associated with the tightening in the RR might increase the potency of the RR ratio policy to achieve maximum desired effects.

Furthermore, a tightening shock in the RR ratio results in the increase in interest rates and the appreciation in the R/US$ exchange rate in Fig. 17.3. This channel of transmission is in line with the interest rate differential view or the risk-taking channel articulated by, for instance, Bruno and Shin (2013), who show that low interest rates in advanced economies (AEs) act as a driver of cross-border capital flows and affect exchange rates, and macroeconomic and financial stability.

In addition, Fig. 17.4 shows that the magnitudes and the timing of the peak impact of the RR ratio tightening on the repo, deposit and lending rates differ. The repo rate peaks at 0.472 percentage points in the third quarter, the deposit rate peaks at 0.438 percentage points in the fourth quarter and the lending rate peaks at 0.424 percentage points, in Fig. 17.4b. As a result, the adjustment of the deposit and lending rate spreads or margins relative to the repo rate differ as shown in Fig. 17.4c.

[5] In earlier chapters, we explored the policy implications of lengthening the maturities of repurchase agreements for the pricing of lending by banks, for funding constraints experienced by banks with respect to the housing sector and small, micro and medium enterprises (SMMEs).

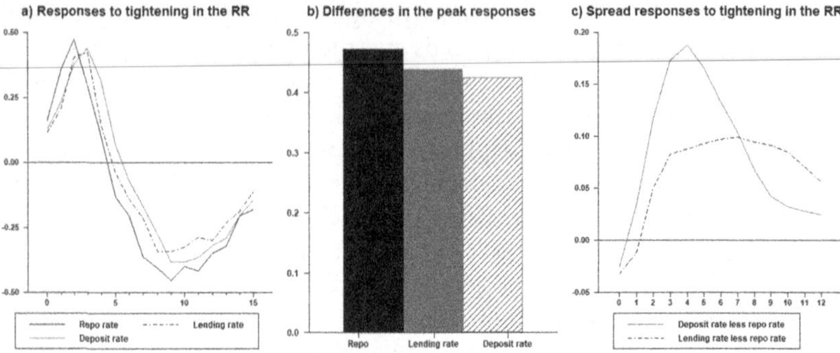

Fig. 17.4 The impact of a tightening shock in the RR ratio on deposit and lending interest rates. (Source: Authors' calculations)

The deposit rate-repo rate spread increases sharply and peaks at around 0.20 percentage points in the fifth quarter and the lending rate-repo rate spread increases gradually and peaks around 0.10 percentage points in the third quarter.

17.5 What Do Rates from Varied Funding Market Segments Reveal About Other Funding Rate Responses?

We show the existence of the cost channel of the RR ratio via the liquidity channel using the consumer deposit and lending rates as these may differ from the rates used by banks in sourcing other funds. Consequently, we focus on the dynamics of the inter-bank, wholesale and government funding markets. Hence, this section estimates the same VAR model as in the previous section but without the repo rate as shown in Eq. 17.5.

$$Y_t = \{\text{RRR}_{\text{rat}}, \text{ELAH}_{\text{Tliab}}, \text{Jibar}, \text{Spread}, R/US\$\} \qquad (17.5)$$

Where, RRR_{rat} is the required reserves as a ratio of total liabilities to the public, $\text{ELAH}_{\text{Tliab}}$ is excess LAH as a ratio of total liabilities to the public, Jibar is the Johannesburg inter-bank agreed rate and the spread is the Jibar less repo rate. The other two models will replace the Jibar and its repo rate margin with the (i) NCD, which is the three-month Negotiable Certificate of Deposits and its spread to the repo rate, and (ii) TB, which is the three-month Treasury Bill rate and its spread to the repo rate. The results in

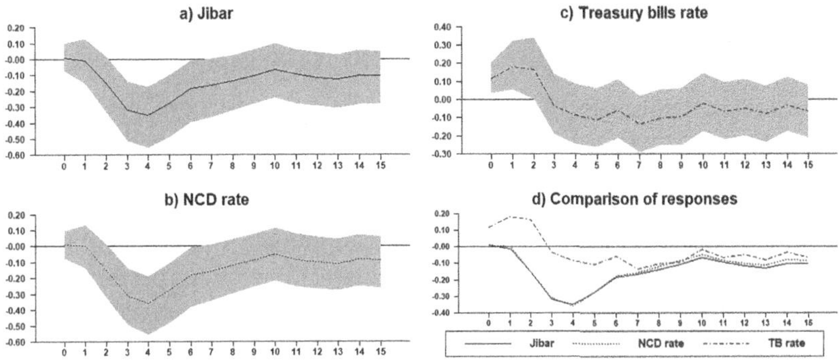

Fig. 17.5 The direct impact of the tightening RR ratio shock on funding interest rates. (Source: Authors' calculations)

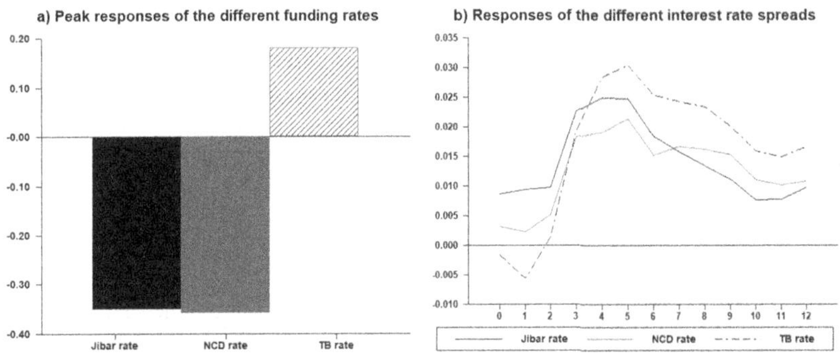

Fig. 17.6 The direct impact of a tightening RR ratio on various interest rates. (Source: Authors' calculations)

Fig. 17.5 indicate that the tightening in the RR ratio exerts different effects on the funding rates. It is evident that the three-month Jibar and NCD rates decline on impact as opposed to an increase observed on the three-month TB rate in Fig. 17.5c.

Furthermore, Fig. 17.6 shows that the peak magnitudes for the Jibar and the NCD rates are marginally different but the NCD rate declines more. On the other hand, the three-month TB rate increases and peaks at 0.2 percentage points. Similarly, the margins relative to the repo rate adjust differently to the tightening in the RR ratio in Fig. 17.6b. The Treasury Bill rate margin increases more than that on the Jibar and the NCD rates.

17.6 Policy Implications from Inter-bank and Wholesale Funding Markets

The policy implication of the results of the RR ratio tightening on the funding rates suggests that bank deposits are easily substituted by wholesale funding. For instance, the fact that the increase in the RR ratio exerts downward pressure on the Jibar and NCD rates suggest that banks access wholesale funding to supplement banks' deposits in the event of a tight RR ratio. This means that alternative funding sources are perfect substitutes for bank deposits. This has implications for the effectiveness of the RR ratio policy and the desired macro-economic effects.

However, the fact that the spreads of the Jibar and the NCD rates relative to the repo rate increase in response to the RR ratio tightening implies that the cost of borrowing from the public adjusts more compared to the rate of borrowing from the central bank. The adjustments in the cost channel are more visible particularly in the inter-bank market as shown by the adjustment of the Jibar rate-repo rate spread compared to the wholesale funding market as shown by the adjustment of the NCD rate-repo rate spread in Fig. 17.6b. The increase in the spread is consistent with the implicit tax on deposits or the cost channel of the RR ratio. There is more interest rate risk priced into funding in the inter-bank market as opposed to that attached to funding in the wholesale market.

17.7 Policy Implications of the Treasury Bill Rate Response

The responses of the three-month TB rate are characteristic of the regulatory impact of changes in the banking regulations as was the case with the Basel III. In this case, the responses of the TB rate speak to the impact of the adherence to the Liquidity Coverage Ratio (LCR), which compelled banks to hold a high level of government securities. Hence, the responses of the TB rate are not only characterised by the expected response of lending rates in the traditional sense but also reflect the distortionary effects of financial regulation. This is because despite the increase in the TB rate, which is associated with an increase in the excess LAH, this invariably means that the increase in the borrowing rate did not result in lower credit to government. The regulatory changes resulted in the increase in credit to government at the expense of credit to the private sector.[6] Hence, there was a sectorial redistribution of credit induced by the regulatory changes. The policy implication is that regulatory changes have a bearing on the effectiveness of macro-prudential tools and their macro-economic effects are not neutral. We test for the macro-economic effects of the tightening in the RR ratio and the excess LAH as a propagating channel.

17.8 The Role of the Excess LAH as a Propagator of the RR Ratio Tightening Policy Shock

This section concludes the analysis by exploring the role of excess LAH as the propagator of RR ratio tightening shocks. We estimate the VAR models in Eqs. (17.4) and (17.5) and assess the role excess LAH plays in propagating the RR ratio tightening shocks on various interest rates. We use the counterfactual scenarios to show the role of the bank liquidity channel in transmitting the RR ratio tightening shocks.

The results in Fig. 17.7 show that in the absence of the RR ratio tightening shocks, the lending and deposit rates increase more. This means that the RR ratio tightening shocks exert the desired effects of imposing costs on bank intermediation.

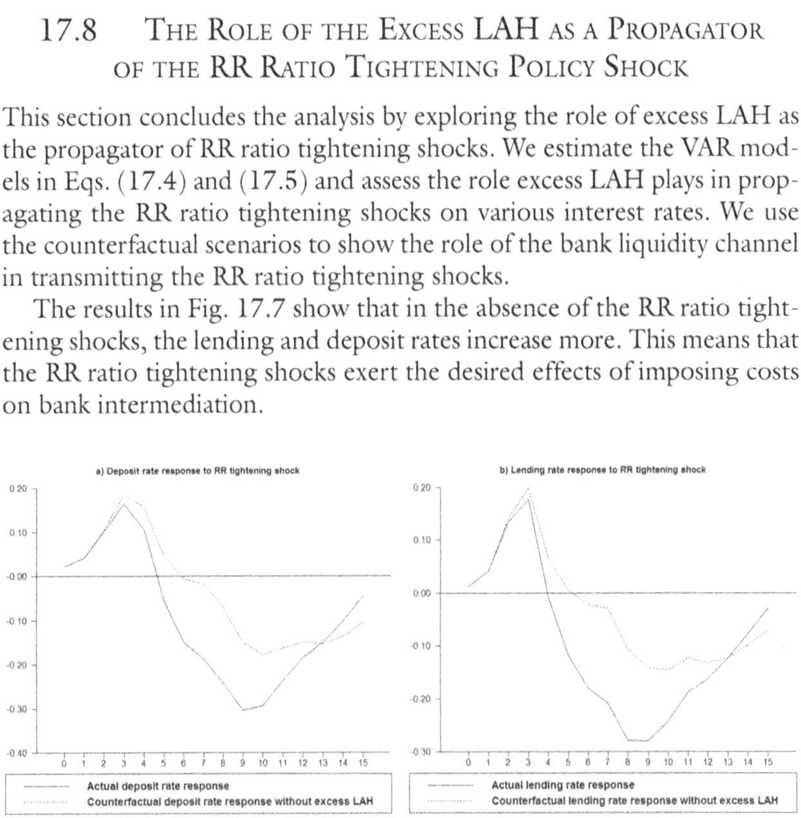

Fig. 17.7 Deposit and lending rates responses to an RR ratio tightening shock

[6] Earlier chapters showed that there is a negative association between credit to government and the private sector. Credit to the private sector declines in response to positive shocks to credit to government. An increase in bank credit to government tends to depress credit to the private sector.

17.9 Conclusion and Policy Implications

This chapter set out to explore the effects of RR ratio tightening shock and excess LAH on the funding and consumer interest rates. We establish the existence of an RR ratio cost channel. This means that the tightening in the RR ratio imposes a cost on bank intermediation. However, the effects of the RR ratio tightening shock on consumer and funding interest rates differ. The implications of the results is that policy makers must be cognizant of the varying effects of different policy tools on consumer and funding rates, and the role of financial regulatory changes in propagating the negative effects.

Furthermore, the regulatory impact on the deposit funding base of banks indirectly assisted the central bank in raising the money market liquidity, but this was at the expense of a sustained increase in the spread of funding rates in the inter-bank, wholesale and government markets. Nonetheless, the policy implication is that to make the RR ratio policy effective, the SARB will have to exploit the effects that regulatory changes and the structure of the banks' balance sheet induce on the rand deposit funding base. This means that there is a role for coordinating the financial regulation and monetary policy tools to achieve the desired effects.

In addition, the results imply that to make the RR ratio policy effective and the transmission of policy changes, the SARB has to re-look at the current approach of allowing banks to access their reserve deposits intra-month. Accessing the reserves intra-month is meant to smooth the liquidity constraints faced by banks due the binding nature of the RR ratio over and above the fact that they are not remunerated. Theoretically, if the RR deposits are remunerated at the going market rate, the RR ratio effects are rendered macro-economically neutral. Hence, if the SARB introduces (or phases in) the approach of restricting access to the RR deposits intra-month, this may make the RR ratio a binding constraint, thus making the RR ratio policy more effective. However, the gradual phasing in of such a policy change has to be coordinated with that of gradually phasing in the autonomous use of the deposit rate facility to manage bank liquidity or excess reserves at the central bank as recommended in earlier chapters.

References

Basci E and Kara H. 2011. Financial Stability and Monetary Policy. Working Papers 1108, Research and Monetary Policy Department, Central Bank of the Republic of Turkey.

Bruno V and Shin H S. 2013. Capital Flows, Cross-Border Banking and Global Liquidity. NBER Working Paper No. 19038.

Glocker C and Towbin P. 2015. Reserve requirements as a macroprudential instrument – Empirical evidence from Brazil. Journal of Macroeconomics, Elsevier, vol. 44(C), pages 158–176.

Gumata N and Ndou E. 2017. Bank Credit Extension and Real Economic Activity in South Africa: The Impact of Capital Flow Dynamics, Bank Regulation and Selected Macroprudential Tools. Palgrave Macmillan. ISBN 978-3-319-43550-3.

Koray A, Mahir B, Selva D, Hakan K, and Pınar O. 2016. "Reserve Requirements, Liquidity Risk, and Bank Lending Behavior," Koç University-TUSIAD Economic Research Forum Working Papers 1612, Koc University-TUSIAD Economic Research Forum.

CHAPTER 18

The Impact of Large-Scale Asset Purchases on Non-residents' Purchases of South African Assets

Research Questions Explored

- Assess the impact of positive shocks to the South African Reserve Bank (SARB) balance sheet on non-residents' activity in the South African financial markets, especially the bond market.
- Whether positive shocks to SARB assets growth amplify or dampen the impact of non-residents' purchases of South African bonds on the R/US$ exchange rate volatility and its components.
- Explore the impact of different sizes of positive shocks to the SARB balance sheet on the R/US$ exchange rate volatility and its components.

18.1 Introduction

Ndou et al. (2017) showed that capital flows are volatile and transitory in nature, and in particular, the bond flows. Furthermore, evidence showed that there is a significant bilateral volatility of spillovers from net equity flows to exchange rate changes. This means that not only is it difficult to predict longer-term net asset purchases based on the information conveyed by current flows, but there is a significant positive feedback loop and that reinforces the effects. The authors concluded that from a policy

N. Gumata, E. Ndou, *Achieving Price, Financial and Macro-Economic Stability in South Africa*,
https://doi.org/10.1007/978-3-030-66340-7_18

perspective, there are serious implications for the design of policies aimed at controlling capital flows, reducing financial market distortions and the associated exchange rate movements. Leaning on this evidence, this chapter assesses the impact of large-scale asset purchases (LSAPs) by the SARB on non-residents' purchases of South African assets. Do positive shocks to SARB assets growth, alternatively LSAPs by the SARB, impact non-residents' purchases of South African assets, in particular government bonds? Furthermore, do positive shocks to LSAPs amplify or dampen the impact of non-residents' purchases of South African bonds on the R/US$ exchange rate volatility and its components?

Figure 18.1 shows non-residents' activity in the South African equity and debt (bond) markets. The trends shown by the cumulative net purchases of bonds and equities indicate that the participation of non-residents in the South African financial markets increased and almost doubled post the financial crisis in 2007 and recession in 2009. The period post-2009 was characterised by LSAPs (quantitative easing or QE) by central banks in advanced economies (AEs). The injection of liquidity by the central banks and low interest rates in AEs via the search for yield and global investor risk appetite was channelled to emerging market economies, including South African markets.[1]

Bauer and Neely (2014) and Neely (2015) find evidence that the effects of the Federal Reserve's asset purchase program spilled over to

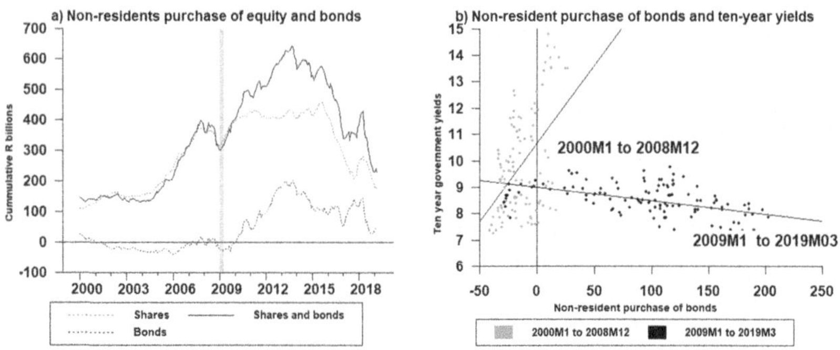

Fig. 18.1 Non-residents' activity in the South African equity and debt (bond) markets. (Source: South African Reserve Bank)

[1] See Cœuré (2017).

international bond yields. This international spillover depends on two factors: (i) the size of asset purchases relative to the size of the pool of substitutable assets, and (ii) the degree of substitutability of domestic and foreign bonds. Put differently, international investors in the bonds issued by small open economies are highly price sensitive because of the existence of a large set of similar (i.e. highly substitutable) assets. In contrast, if US Treasury bonds are special in certain ways and cannot be substituted easily (i.e. because of the reserve currency status of the dollar), the price-taking element is to a large extent eliminated. Furthermore, Fig. 18.1 shows that the association between cumulative net non-resident purchases of bonds and the ten-year government yield changed post-2009. Whereas the relationship was positive between 2000M1 and 2018M12, it became negative post-2009. Thus, an increase in non-resident participation in the domestic bond market influenced the ten-year government bond yields.

In addition, the trends in Fig. 18.1 show that on a net cumulative basis, non-residents have bought more South African bonds post-2009 compared to shares. These trends can be partly explained by the increase in the budget deficit considering the conduct of counter-cyclical fiscal policy and the inclusion of South African government bonds in the World Global Bond Index (WGBI) in October 2012. South African government bonds constitute 0.32 per cent of the WGBI. Non-residents hold around 40 per cent of government bonds, as shown in Fig. 18.2.[2]

This chapter contributes to literature by examining the impact of the positive shocks to the SARB balance sheet on non-residents' activity in the South African financial markets, in particular the government bond market. In addition, this study contributes to literature on the policy interventions and instruments that can be used to deal with the exchange rate volatility. The study uses several quantitative techniques to establish the robustness of the findings and thus policy recommendations.

[2] See also the Global Financial Stability Report (2019): the role of global and EM index benchmarks as drivers of an unusually large share of their local currency government debt, which is held by foreign investors in countries such as South Africa, Hungary, Malaysia, Poland and Colombia.

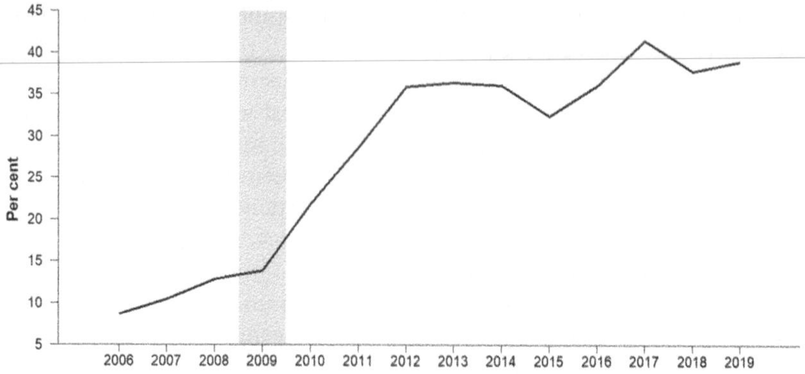

Fig. 18.2 Non-residents' holdings of South African government bonds. (Source: National Treasury)

18.2 The Impact of Positive Shocks to the SARB Balance Sheet on Non-residents' Cumulative Net Purchases of South African Shares and Bonds

We start by estimating a VAR model which includes growth in SARB assets and non-residents' cumulative net purchases of South African shares and bonds. Thereafter, we estimate a VAR model that disaggregates non-residents' cumulative net purchases of South African shares and bonds to assess which of the components is more responsive to the positive SARB assets growth shock. The VAR models are estimated for the sample 2000M1 to 2018M12. The growth rates are annual rates. The VAR models are estimated using two lags and 10,000 Monte Carlo simulations. The shock is a one standard deviation to the SARB balance sheet.

The results in Fig. 18.3 indicate that a positive shock to SARB assets growth depresses non-residents' cumulative net purchases of South African shares and bonds, especially the purchase of bonds. This means that as the SARB increases its purchases of South African government bonds, the effects will reduce or depress the purchase of domestic assets by non-residents. The results also imply that positive shocks to SARB assets growth will also spill over to non-residents' purchases of shares or equities. These results concur with international evidence showing that LSAPs by central banks due to the fact that they constrain the supply of government assets (supply effects) available to private investors result in the rebalancing of assets held by investors largely due to the portfolio rebalancing channel.

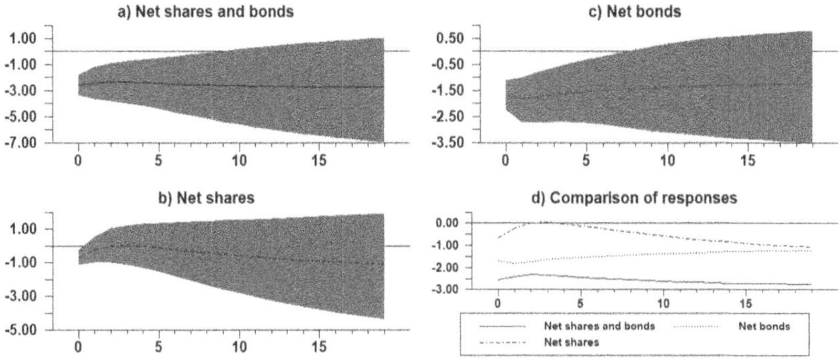

Fig. 18.3 Responses of disaggregated non-resident cumulative net purchases of South African shares and bonds to positive SARB assets growth shocks. (Source: Authors' calculations)

The portfolio rebalancing channel works via changes in the composition of private-sector portfolios. When assets (and liabilities) are imperfect substitutes, changes in the relative supplies of financial securities brought about by central bank operations can significantly affect the composition of portfolios, alter investor behaviour and induce an adjustment in relative yields and asset prices.

18.3 Do Large-Scale Asset Purchases Propagate the Effects of Non-residents' Purchases of Bonds on the Exchange Rate Volatility and Its Components?

The previous section showed that positive shocks to LSAPs dampen the purchase of non-residents' purchases of South African bonds. This section assesses whether the effects of LSAPs presented in Fig. 18.4 spill over to the exchange rate volatility and its components?[3] We estimate a counterfactual VAR model which includes growth in SARB assets, cumulative net

[3] Ndou et al. (2017) find that capital flows are volatile and transitory, in particular bond flows. Net asset purchases by non-residents are very transitory or short term. Furthermore, there is significant bilateral volatility of spillovers from net equity flows to the exchange rate changes and the rand exchange rate depreciation shock has a bigger impact on the slowdown in net equity purchases by non-residents. There is a significant positive feedback loop that reinforces these effects.

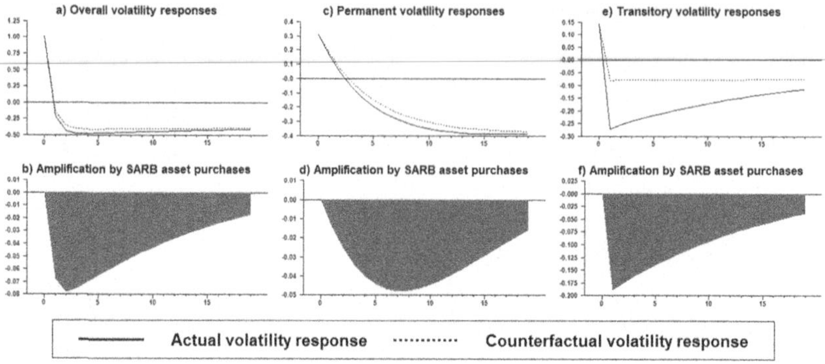

Fig. 18.4 Responses to non-residents' purchases of bonds and propagation by the SARB asset purchases channel. (Source: Authors' calculations)

purchases of South African bonds by non-residents and the various components of the R/US$ exchange rate volatility. The R/US$ exchange rate volatilities are, overall, permanent and transitory volatility.[4] The R/US$ exchange rate volatility components enter the VAR model separately. In the counterfactual VAR models, we are interested in knowing whether positive shocks to SARB assets growth dampen or propagate the impact of non-residents' purchases on South African bonds. The model is estimated using one lag and 10,000 Monte Carlo simulations. The sample spans 2000M1 to 2018M12 and all growth rates are annual rates.

The results in Fig. 18.4 indicate that the SARB asset purchase channel dampens the positive shock effects due to non-resident purchases of domestic bonds on all the components of the R/US$ exchange rate volatility. A comparison of the dampening effects in Fig. 18.5 shows that the most impact is on the transitory R/US$ exchange rate volatility component compared to other exchange rate volatility components. The implication of the results is that because positive shocks to SARB assets growth dampen the net purchases of South African bonds largely due to the supply effects, these effects are also transmitted to all measures of the R/US$ exchange rate volatility as well. Thus, LSAPs by the SARB will

[4] See Ndou et al. (2017) for the details of the methodology to estimate the various exchange-rate volatility components.

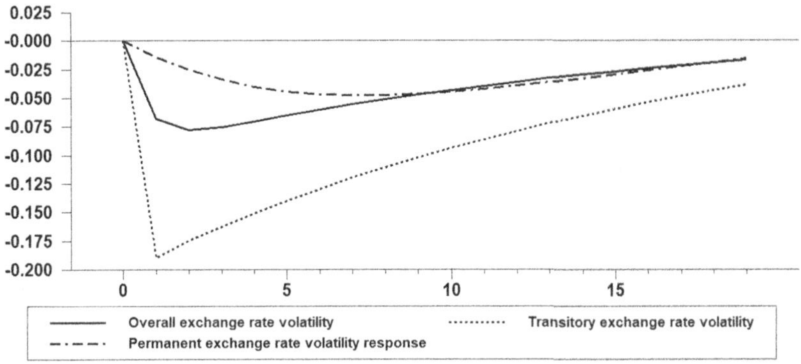

Fig. 18.5 Comparison of the propagation effects of SARB asset purchases on the R/US$ exchange volatility. (Source: Authors' calculations)

complement other policy initiatives and tools aimed at curbing the R/US$ exchange rate volatility.

18.4 Are There Asymmetric Effects Induced by Positive Shocks to SARB Assets on the R/US$ Exchange Rate Volatility?

This section assesses the robustness of the results in the previous section by exploring whether different positive shock sizes to SARB assets asymmetrically impact the components of the R/US$ exchange rate volatility. We use the modified Kilian and Vigfusson (2011) approach to assess the effects of one, two, four or ten positive standard deviation shocks to SARB assets growth on the three components of the R/US$ exchange rate volatility. The results in Fig. 18.6 indicate that large shocks to purchases of government bonds by the SARB exert more downward pressure on all components of the R/US$ exchange rate volatility. Thus, there is robust evidence that large-scale asset purchases by the SARB will contribute to policies aimed at dampening the R/US$ exchange rate volatility.

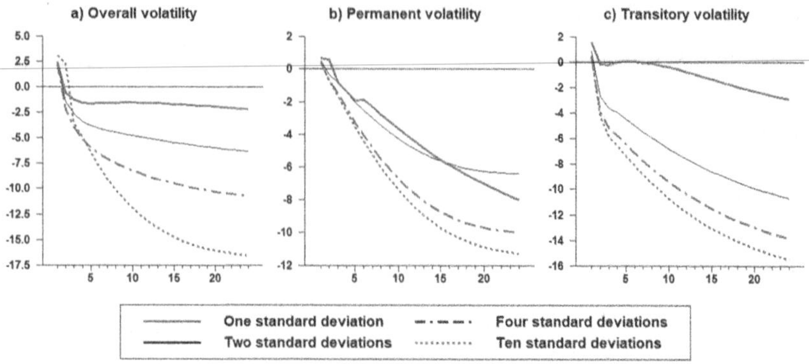

Fig. 18.6 Cumulative effects of SARB asset purchase shocks on the R/US$ exchange volatility. (Source: Authors' calculations)

18.5 Conclusion and Policy Implications

Do positive shocks to the SARB balance sheet impact non-residents' activity in the South African financial markets, especially the bond market? We find that a positive shock to SARB assets growth depresses non-residents' cumulative net purchases of South African shares and bonds, especially the purchase of bonds. This means that as the SARB increases its purchase of South African government bonds, this will reduce and even depress the purchase of domestic assets, especially government bonds by non-residents. The results also imply that positive shocks to SARB assets will also spill over to non-residents' purchases of shares or equities. These results concur with international evidence showing that LSAPs by central banks due to the fact that they constrain the supply of government assets (supply effects or supply-induced portfolio rebalancing) available to private investors result in the rebalancing of assets held by investors largely due to the portfolio rebalancing channel.

Furthermore, evidence shows that LSAPs by the SARB exert the most impact on the transitory R/US$ exchange rate volatility component compared to the other exchange rate volatility components. The implication of the results is that because positive shocks to SARB assets dampen the net purchases of South African bonds largely due to the supply effects, these effects are also transmitted to all measures of the R/US$ exchange rate volatility as well. Thus, LSAPs by the SARB will complement other policy initiatives and tools aimed at curbing the R/US$ exchange rate volatility. In addition, large shocks to purchases of government bonds by the SARB exert more downward pressure on all components of the R/US$ exchange rate volatility. In policy terms, LSAPs by the SARB are part of the policy tools that will contribute to policy interventions aimed at dampening the R/US$ exchange rate volatility. In addition, such a balance sheet strategy addresses the main financial stability risks associated with changes in global investor risk appetite emanating from a large share of local currency government debt held by foreign investors.

References

Bauer M D and Neely C J. 2014. International channels of the Fed's unconventional monetary policy. Journal of International Money and Finance, Elsevier, vol. 44(C), pages 24–46.

Cœuré B. 2017. The international dimension of the ECB's asset purchase programme. Speech at the Foreign Exchange Contact Group meeting. https://www.ecb.europa.eu/press/key/date/2017/html/ecb.sp170711.en.html.

Global Stability Report. 2019. Vulnerabilities in a Maturing Credit Cycle. https://www.imf.org/en/Publications/GFSR/Issues/2019/03/27/Global-Financial-Stability-Report-April-2019.

Kilian L and Vigfusson R J. 2011. Are the Responses of the U.S. Economy Asymmetric in Energy Price Increases and Decreases? Quantitative Economics, 2(4): 419–453.

Ndou E, Gumata N, and Ncube M. 2017. Global Economic Uncertainties and Exchange Rate Shocks: Transmission Channels to the South African Economy. ISBN 978-3-319-62280-4.

Neely C J. 2015. Unconventional monetary policy had large international effects. Journal of Banking & FinanceVolume 52, March 2015, Pages 101–111.

Opricǎ S and Weistroffer C. 2019. Institutional presence in secondary bank bond markets: how does it affect liquidity and volatility? ECB Working Paper Series No 2276 / May 2019. https://www.ecb.europa.eu/pub/pdf/scpwps/ecb.wp2276~09300538fd.en.pdf.

Yeşin P. 2016. Capital Flows and the Swiss Franc. SNB Working Papers 8/2016. https://www.snb.ch/n/mmr/reference/working_paper_2016_08/source/working_paper_2016_08.n.pdf.

CHAPTER 19

Large-Scale Asset Purchases and Activity in the Primary and Secondary Share and Bond Markets

Research Questions Explored

- Assess the impact of positive South African Reserve Bank (SARB) asset growth shocks on activity in the primary and secondary share (equity) and bond markets.
- Explore whether positive SARB asset growth shocks propagate the effects of real economic activity indicators such as manufacturing output growth on activity in the primary and secondary share (equity) markets.
- Understand the impact of positive SARB asset growth shocks on the financing conditions of corporations as proxied by the Corporate Default Swap (CDS) spreads, the Eskom bond yield and the credit conditions index (CCI).

19.1 Introduction

This chapter extends the analysis on the impact of large-scale asset purchases (LSAPs) by the SARB on activity in the primary and secondary share (equity) markets. Do large-scale asset purchases affect activity in the primary and secondary share and bond markets? In the previous chapters, we assessed the impact of LSAPs on government bond yields, non-resident purchases of domestic assets and the banks' holdings of excess liquid assets. This chapter extends the analysis to the impact of LSAPs on activity

N. Gumata, E. Ndou, *Achieving Price, Financial and Macro-Economic Stability in South Africa*,
https://doi.org/10.1007/978-3-030-66340-7_19

in the primary and secondary share (equity) markets. After the collapse of Bear Stearns, the United States Federal Reserve Bank (US Fed) (i) announced purchases of housing agency debt and agency mortgage-backed securities (MBS), (ii) decided to substantially expand its purchase of agency-related securities (iii) and to purchase longer-term Treasury securities as well. The intention was to provide greater support to mortgage lending and housing markets, and to improve financial conditions in the private credit market.

Similarly, the Bank of England (BoE) introduced a Special Liquidity Scheme (SLS) that allowed banks and building societies to swap high-quality but temporarily illiquid mortgage-backed and other securities for UK Treasury bills. A Discount Window Facility was also launched in October 2008 as a permanent liquidity insurance facility. The BoE also set up the Asset Purchase Facility Fund (APF) as its subsidiary whose remit was subsequently expanded to be used as a monetary policy tool. The BoE Monetary Policy Committee (MPC) was given the option to finance purchases under the APF by issuing central bank reserves, and the range of eligible assets was expanded to include gilts. The BoE Quantitative Easing and the Funding for Lending Scheme (FLS) were used as complementary monetary policy tools. Quantitative Easing (QE) reduces yields and has a wider effect on asset prices, whereas FLS operates directly through the banking sector by reducing their funding costs and increasing incentives to lend. At the BoE, the MPC decided that it would purchase both private and public sector assets using central bank reserves, though most securities purchased would be United Kingdom government securities (gilts). The purchase of corporate bonds and commercial paper was aimed at improving the functioning of those markets and therefore improving access to credit for firms.

In 2016, the European Central Bank (ECB) started the outright purchases of investment-grade euro-denominated bonds issued by non-bank corporations on the primary and secondary markets under the programme named Corporate Sector Purchase Programme (CSPP). As such, because the CSPP specifically targeted corporate securities, it provides an opportunity for the analysis of the effects of LSAP on the financing conditions of corporations. Zaghini (2019) finds that the CSPP programme by the ECB's QE had a significant impact on yield spreads. The results are evident on both directly purchased and targeted bonds and indirectly on all other bonds consistent with the portfolio rebalancing channel. Similarly, Joyce et al. (2010) find that QE may have depressed gilt yields and that the largest part of the impact of QE came through the portfolio rebalancing channel. The authors find that the effects of QE also spilled over to other asset prices, as the corporate yields also declined, liquidity in the corporate bond markets improved, and net equity and corporate bond issuance increased after the implementation of QE.

Gagnon et al. (2010) establish evidence that LSAPs by the Fed led to economically meaningful and long-lasting reductions in longer-term interest rates on a range of securities, including securities that were not included in the asset purchase programmes. The reductions in interest rates primarily reflect lower risk premiums, including term premiums, rather than lower expectations of future short-term interest rates. They find an even more powerful effect of LSAPs on agency debt and agency mortgage-backed securities. Evidence also shows that liquidity injections via longer-term refinancing operations (LTROs) by the ECB played a key role in averting a major credit crunch. Lengthening the maturity of LTROs helped to relax the banks' financial constraints. Altavilla et al. (2015) find that euro area asset purchases had a sizeable effect on asset prices and reinforced other channels due to the interaction between LSAPs and the asset composition of the asset purchase programme. Targeting assets at long maturity supported the duration and the credit channels. At the same time, the low degree of financial stress prevailing at time of the announcement of the programme weakened the local supply channel and facilitated spill-over to non-targeted assets. Furthermore, Andrade et al. (2016) find that the ECB's LSAPs programme significantly and persistently reduced sovereign yields on long-term bonds and raised the share prices of banks that held more sovereign bonds in their portfolios. This evidence is consistent with the potency of the portfolio rebalancing channel (alternatively, the asset valuation channel) acting through the removal of duration risk and the relaxation of leverage constraints for financial intermediaries (alternatively, the bank capital relief channel).

We fill policy and academic research gaps by analysing the impact of positive SARB asset growth shocks on activity in the primary and secondary bond and share (equity) markets.[1] We use the Eskom bond yield and the South African CDS spread as proxies for the corporate sector bond market and financing conditions. For the robustness test of the results, we use the credit conditions index (CCI), which is a broader indicator of the corporate sector financing conditions that includes financial indicators such as the spread between the South African and the US government bond

[1] Largely due to limited data availability on the South African balance sheets, we limit the analysis on activity in the primary and secondary bond and share (equity) markets.

yields, banks' non-performing loans, banks' return-on-equity and tier-one capital adequacy ratio. Furthermore, we assess whether positive SARB asset growth shocks propagate or dampen the effects of primary and secondary bond and share (equity) market activity on manufacturing production growth.

19.2 How Have Activity and Prices in the Bond and Share Markets Evolved over Time?

We start by showing the evolution of activity in the primary and secondary bonds and equity (share) markets in Fig. 19.1. The data used in this section is monthly (M) spanning the sample period 2000M1 to 2019M6. The trends in Fig. 19.1a show that activity in the primary bond and share markets has been just below R20 billion post-2009.

Nonetheless, it is evident that activity in the primary share market has been especially subdued below R10 billion post-2017. This contrasts with the secondary share market capitalisation, which increased from just below R5 trillion in 2008 to above R15 trillion in 2019. Similarly, the bond market capitalisation increased from just below R1 trillion in 2008 to above R3 trillion in 2019. This trend in market activity was reflected in the share price indices and government bond yields, as shown in Fig. 19.2. The trends show that all the share prices increased from below 100 index points in 2009 and reached varying peaks thereafter. A further disaggregation of the share price indices shows that industrials and financials were the

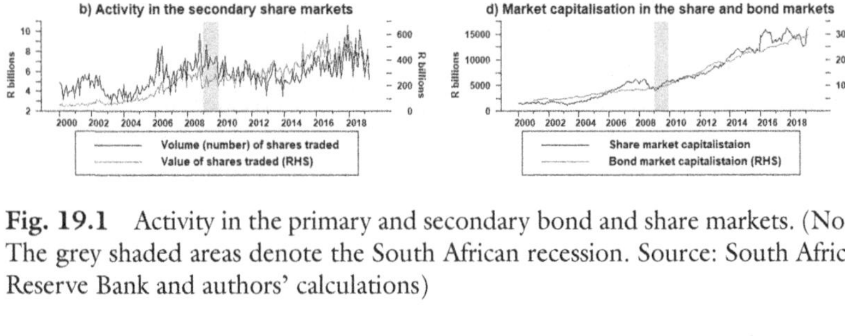

Fig. 19.1 Activity in the primary and secondary bond and share markets. (Note: The grey shaded areas denote the South African recession. Source: South African Reserve Bank and authors' calculations)

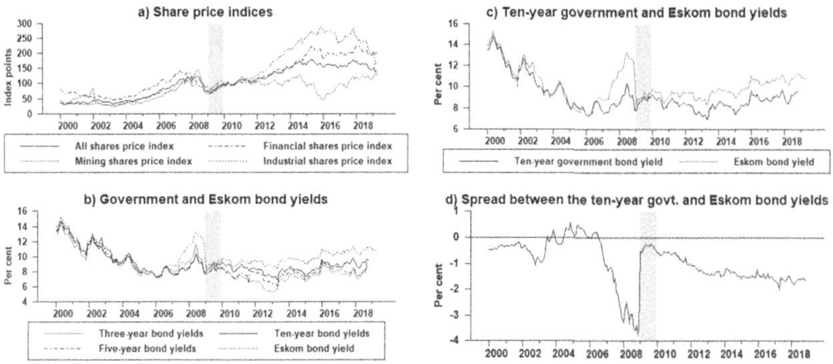

Fig. 19.2 Share prices, government bond yields and Eskom bond yields. (Note: The grey shaded areas denote the South African recession. Govt. = government. Source: South African Reserve Bank and authors' calculations)

main drivers of the performance of the All-shares price index. It is also evident that government bond yields also declined to multiyear low levels post-2009, although this trend has reversed in recent years.

The trends in Fig. 19.2 also show that the Eskom bond yield followed a similar trend to that of government bond yields and the spread was very narrow until the end of 2005. Since then, the spread between the ten-year government bond yield and the Eskom bond yield has widened and is currently around 200 basis points. It is also evident that at the peak of the electricity crisis, the spread between the ten-year government bond yield and the Eskom bond yield peaked at around 400 basis points.

19.3 Large-Scale Asset Purchases, Liquidity and Issuance in the Corporate Share Markets

This section estimates the effects of LSAPs on activity in the corporate bond and share (equity) markets. Joyce et al. (2010) find that corporate yields also declined, liquidity in the corporate bond markets improved, and net equity and corporate bond issuance increased after the implementation of QE. To measure activity in the corporate bond and equity market, we use the market capitalisation in the bond and equity (share) markets, and the number (volume) and value of shares and bonds traded in the secondary market. For the primary market indicators, we use the share capital raised by companies on the Johannesburg Stock Exchange (JSE). The data is monthly (M) for the sample period 2000M1 to 2019M6.

The growth rates are annual rates. For the primary share market indicators, Fig. 19.3a shows that the share capital raised on the JSE is positively associated with SARB assets growth.

We establish that there is also a positive relationship between the secondary share market indicators and SARB assets growth in Fig. 19.3b–d. These stylised facts mean that an increase in SARB assets growth can lead to an increase in the primary and secondary share market activity on the JSE. The bilateral relationships presented in Fig. 19.4 indicate that there

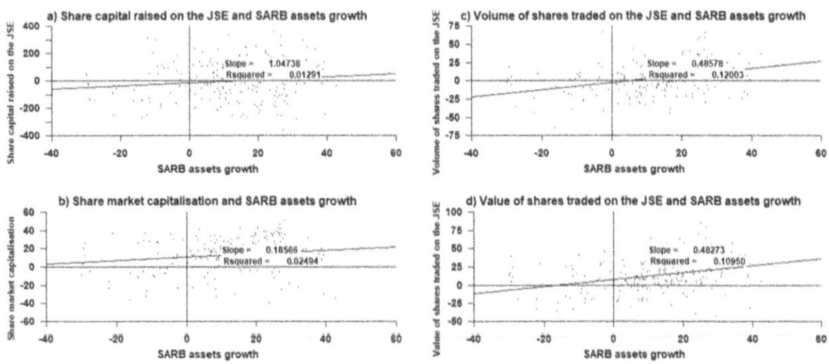

Fig. 19.3 Share (equity) market activity and SARB assets growth. (Note: JSE = Johannesburg Stock Exchange. Source: South African Reserve Bank and authors' calculations)

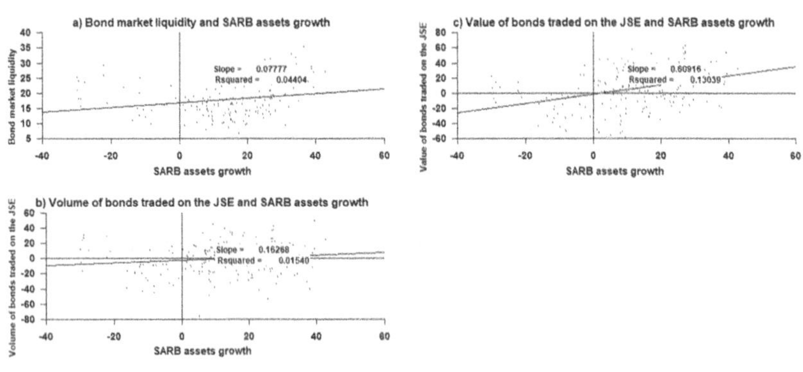

Fig. 19.4 Bond market activity and SARB assets growth. (Note: JSE = Johannesburg Stock Exchange. Source: South African Reserve Bank and authors' calculations)

is also a positive relationship between selected bond market activity indicators and SARB assets growth. Thus, the bilateral relationships presented in this section indicate that an increase in SARB assets growth can stimulate activity in the primary and secondary share (equity) and bond markets.

19.4 The Impact of Large-Scale Asset Purchases, Liquidity and Issuance in the Corporate Share Markets: Evidence from VAR Model

This section estimates VAR models to assess the impact of positive SARB assets growth on primary and secondary activity in the corporate share market. We estimate a VAR model that includes SARB assets growth, growth in share capital raised by companies on the JSE, market capitalisation in the bond and equity (share) markets, and the number (volume) and value of shares and bonds traded in the secondary market. The data is monthly (M) for the sample period 2000M1 to 2019M6. The growth rates are annual rates. The shock is a one-unit shock to SARB asset growth. The model is estimated using 10,000 Monte Carlo draws and two lags. The shock is a unit shock to SARB asset growth.

The results in Fig. 19.5 show that the primary and secondary share market activity indicators increase in response to positive SARB asset growth shocks. These results concur with the findings in Joyce et al.

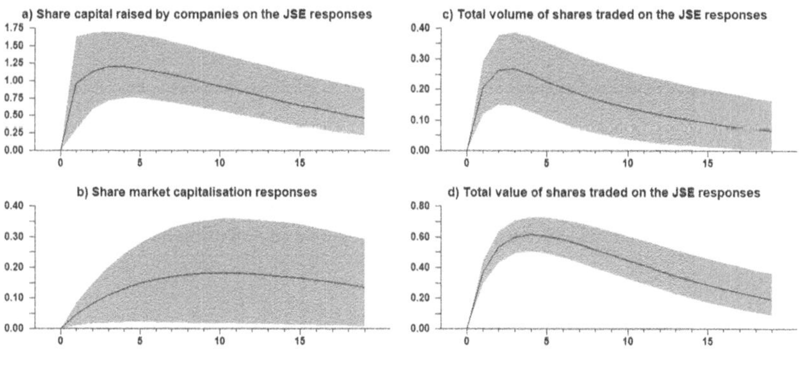

Fig. 19.5 Responses to positive SARB asset growth shocks. (Note: The grey-shaded area bands denote the 16th and 84th percentile confidence bands. Source: Authors' calculations)

(2010), which show that liquidity in the corporate bond markets improved and corporate bond issuance increased after the implementation of QE in the euro area.

19.5 The Impact of Large-Scale Asset Purchases, Liquidity and Issuance in the Corporate Share and Bond Markets: Evidence from the Modified Kilian and Vigfusson (2011) Approach

Does SARB asset growth exert asymmetric shocks to primary and secondary share market indicators? To answer this question, we estimate various bivariate asymmetric VAR models using the modified Kilian and Vigfusson (2011) methodology to compute non-linear impulse responses to a positive SARB growth asset shock. We estimate several VAR models that include SARB assets growth and growth in the JSE market indicator. The growth in the JSE market indicators include the share capital raised by companies on the JSE, market capitalisation in the bond and equity (share) markets, and the number (volume) and value of shares and bonds traded in the secondary market. These are include separately in the model. The data is monthly (M) for the sample period 2000M1 to 2019M6. The growth rates are annual rates.

The results in Figs. 19.6 and 19.7 indicate that incremental positive shocks to SARB asset growth exert asymmetric effects on selected primary and secondary market share and bond market indicators.

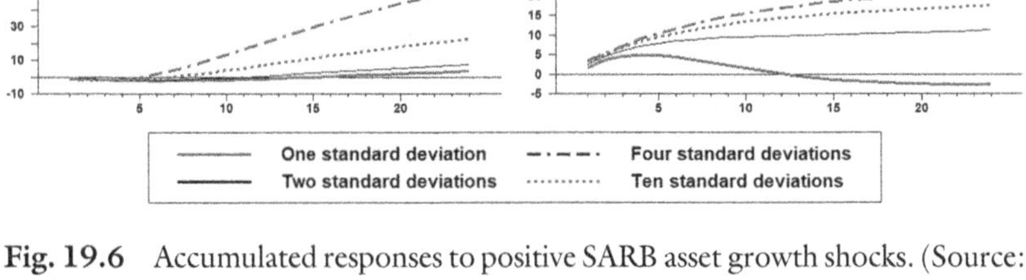

Fig. 19.6 Accumulated responses to positive SARB asset growth shocks. (Source: Authors' calculations)

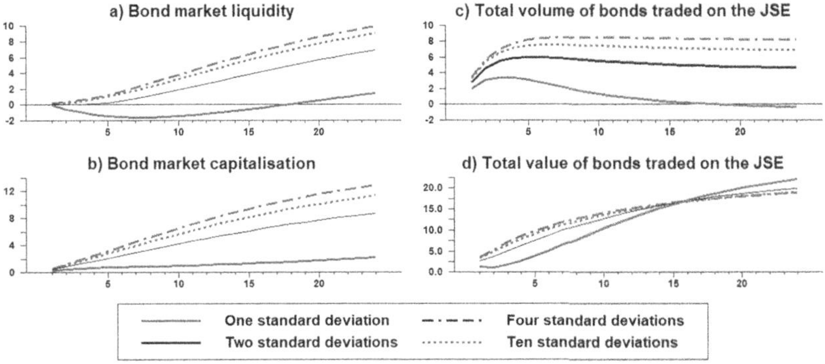

Fig. 19.7 Accumulated responses of the primary and secondary bond market activity to positive SARB asset growth shocks. (Source: Authors' calculations)

19.6 Do Large-Scale Asset Purchases Propagate the Impact of Manufacturing Production Growth on Liquidity and Issuance in the Corporate Share and Bond Markets?

This section assesses whether SARB asset growth amplifies or dampens the effects of positive manufacturing production growth shocks on primary and secondary share market activity. We estimate a number of counterfactual VAR models, which include manufacturing production growth, share capital raised by companies on the JSE growth, market capitalisation in the bond and equity (share) markets growth, the number (volume) and value of shares and bonds traded in the secondary market growth, and SARB asset growth. The counterfactual models estimated are (i) manufacturing production growth, share capital raised by companies on the JSE growth, market capitalisation and SARB asset growth; (ii) manufacturing production growth, the number (volume) and value of shares traded growth, and SARB asset growth; (iii) manufacturing production growth, bond market liquidity and bond market capitalisation growth, and SARB asset growth; and (iv) manufacturing production growth, total volume and value of bonds traded growth, and SARB asset growth. We use manufacturing production growth as a proxy for real economic activity. The data is monthly (M) for the sample period 2000M1 to 2019M6. The growth rates are annual rates. The models are estimated using 10,000 Monte Carlo draws and two lags. The counterfactual responses are derived from estimations

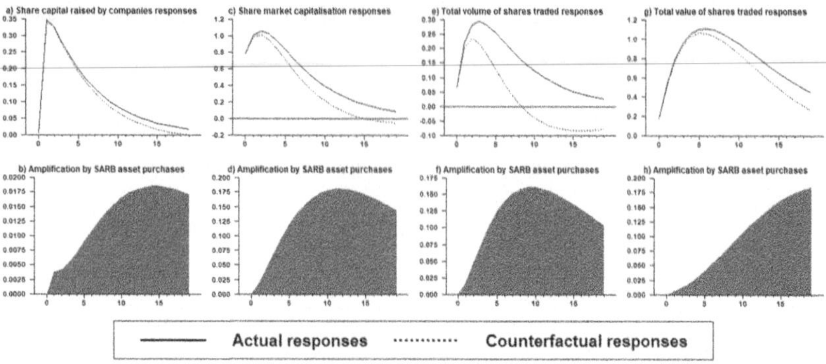

Fig. 19.8 Share market activity responses to positive manufacturing production growth shocks and amplification by the SARB asset growth channel. (Source: Authors' calculations)

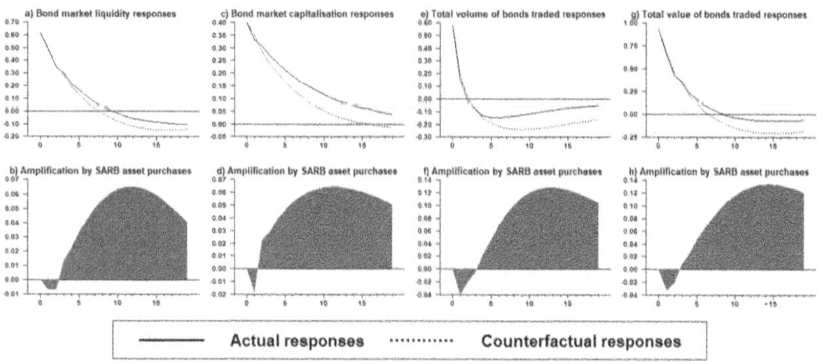

Fig. 19.9 Bond market activity responses to positive manufacturing production growth shocks and amplification by the SARB asset growth channel. (Source: Authors' calculations)

where the role of SARB assets (SARB asset growth channel) is closed (not active) in the model. The propagation or dampening effects are the difference between the actual and the counterfactual responses.

The results in Fig. 19.8 show that SARB asset growth propagates the effects of positive manufacturing production growth shocks to primary and secondary share market activity. Similarly, we find that SARB asset growth propagates the responses of bond market primary and secondary market activity to manufacturing output growth in Fig. 19.9.

19.7 The Effects of LSAPs on the Financing Conditions of Corporations

This section concludes the analysis by assessing the impact of positive SARB asset growth shocks on selected indicators of the corporate bond market and financing conditions of the corporate sector. We use the two-year CDS spreads and the Eskom bond yield as indicators of the financing conditions of the corporate sector. To measure activity in the bond market, we use the bond market capitalisation and liquidity. The estimated VAR model includes SARB asset growth, two-year CDS spreads and the Eskom bond yield, bond market capitalisation and liquidity. The data is monthly (M) for the sample period 2000M1 to 2019M6. The growth rates annual rates. The models are estimated using 10,000 Monte Carlo draws and two lags. The shock is a unit shock to SARB asset growth. For robustness analysis, we reverse the ordering of the variables in the model.

The results in Fig. 19.10 show that the two-year CDS spreads and the yield on the Eskom bond decline in response to positive SARB asset growth shocks, whilst the bond market capitalisation and liquidity increase. The results are robust to changes in the model specification when we replace the two-year CDS spreads with the five-year CDS spreads, as shown in Fig. 19.13 in the appendix.

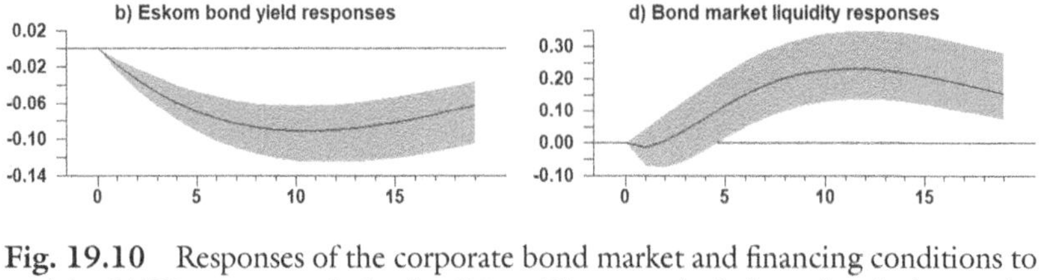

Fig. 19.10 Responses of the corporate bond market and financing conditions to positive SARB asset growth shocks. (Note: The grey-shaded area bands denote the 16th and 84th percentile confidence bands. Source: Authors' calculations)

For robustness analysis of the impact of positive SARB asset growth on the financing conditions of corporations, we use the credit conditions index (CCI) constructed in Gumata and Ndou (2017). The CCI is constructed using the variables shown in Table 19.1.[2]

We estimate a VAR model which includes SARB asset growth, manufacturing production growth and the credit conditions index. The growth rates are annual rates. The model is estimated using two lags and 10,000 Monte Carlo draws. The shock is a unit shock to SARB asset growth. The results in Fig. 19.11 show that a positive shock to SARB asset growth

Table 19.1 Components of the credit conditions index

Debt market indicators	*Banking indicators*
5-year spread between SA and US government bond	Non-performing loans
Spread between 10-year government bond and 28-day SARB debentures	Return on equity
Spread between corporate and government bonds	Tier 1 capital adequacy ratio
Bond market liquidity ratio	Spread between banks and government bonds
5-year SA banks credit default swap	Spread between bank lending and deposit rate

Source: Gumata and Ndou (2017)

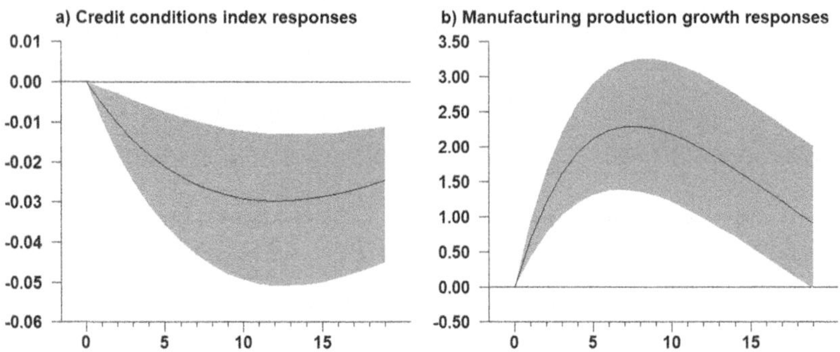

Fig. 19.11 Responses of the credit conditions and manufacturing output growth to positive SARB asset growth shocks. (Note: The grey shaded area bands denote the 16th and 84th percentile confidence bands. Source: Authors' calculations)

[2] For further details on the construction of the credit conditions index, see Gumata and Ndou (2017).

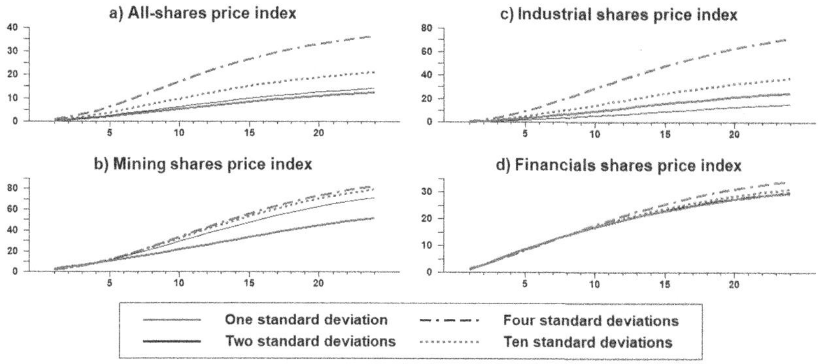

Fig. 19.12 Accumulated responses of share price indices growth to positive SARB asset growth shocks. (Source: Authors' calculations)

loosens the credit conditions as the credit conditions index declines. On the other hand, manufacturing output growth increases.

In addition, we consider the impact of asymmetric effects of positive SARB asset growth shocks on the share price indices by estimating a bivariate VAR model using the modified Kilian and Vigfusson (2011) methodology. We establish that the different sizes of positive SARB asset growth shocks lead to incrementally large increases on the different components of the All-shares price indices, as shown in Fig. 19.12.

19.8 Conclusion and Policy Implications

Do large-scale asset purchases affect activity in the primary and secondary share and bond markets? Evidence in this chapter shows that the primary and secondary bond and share market activity indicators increase in response to positive SARB asset growth shocks. Furthermore, the results indicate that incremental positive shocks to SARB asset growth exert asymmetric effects on selected primary and secondary market share and bond market indicators. In addition, we establish that SARB asset growth propagates the effects of positive manufacturing production growth shocks to primary and secondary share market activity. The two-year CDS spreads and the yield on the Eskom bond decline in response to positive SARB asset growth shocks, whilst the bond market capitalisation and liquidity increase. On the other hand, positive shock to SARB asset growth loosens the credit conditions and this is transmitted to an increase in the manufacturing output growth.

Appendix

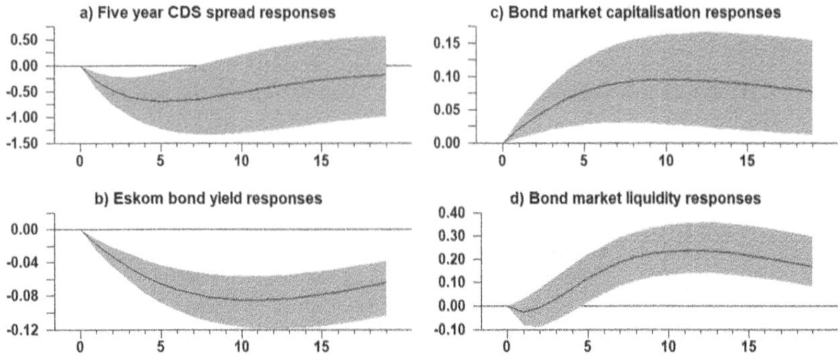

Fig. 19.13 Responses of the corporate bond market and financing conditions to positive SARB asset growth shocks. (Note: The grey shaded area bands denote the 16th and 84th percentile confidence bands. Source: Authors' calculations)

References

Altavilla C, Motto R and Carboni G. 2015. Asset purchase programmes and financial markets: lessons from the euro area. ECB Working Paper Series No. 1864.

Andrade, P., Breckenfelder, J., De Fiore, F., Karadi, P., and Tristani, O. 2016. "The ECB's asset purchase programme: an early assessment". ECB Working Paper 1956.

Gagnon, J, Raskin, M, Remache, J and Sack, B. 2010. Large-scale asset purchases by the Federal Reserve: did they work? Federal Reserve Bank of New York, Staff Report No, 441.

Gumata N and Ndou E. 2017. Bank Credit Extension and Real Economic Activity in South Africa: The Impact of Capital Flow Dynamics, Bank Regulation and Selected Macroprudential Tools. Palgrave Macmillan. ISB 978-3-319-43550-3.

Joyce M, Lasaosa A, Stevens I and Tong M. 2010. The financial market impact of quantitative easing. Bank of England Working Paper No. 393.

Kilian L and Vigfusson R J. 2011. Are the Responses of the U.S. Economy Asymmetric in Energy Price Increases and Decreases? Quantitative Economics, 2(4): 419–453.

McCauley N R. 2019. Safe assets: made, not just born. BIS Working Papers No 769. https://www.bis.org/publ/work769.pdf.

Zaghini A. 2019. The CSPP at work: yield heterogeneity and the portfolio rebalancing channel. ECB Working Paper No 2264. https://www.ecb.europa.eu/pub/pdf/scpwps/ecb.wp2264~c4382400c5.en.pdf.

CHAPTER 20

The Stock and Flow Effects of Large-Scale Asset Purchases: Evidence from Persistent Versus Transitory Shocks

Research Questions Explored

- Assess the stock and flow effects of large-scale asset purchases on various financial and macro-economic variables.
- Explore whether the stock effects of large-scale asset purchases are more potent and persistent compared to flow effects.

20.1 Introduction

What are the stock and flow effects of large-scale asset purchases? How persistent are the stock and flow effects of large-scale asset purchases (LSAPs)? This chapter extends the analysis of the effects of LSAPs by exploring the different effects of stock and flow effects of LSAPs. Literature shows that there are stock and flow effects involved in the conduct of LSAPs and the persistence of these effects matters. D'Amico and King (2013) define the stock effects of LSAPs as persistent or lasting changes in prices that result from movements along the government securities' demand curves. On the other hand, the flow effects are defined as the response of prices to the ongoing or continuing purchase operations.[1] Various studies establish that there are sizeable and significant

[1] The flow effects can reflect the portfolio rebalancing activity due to the outcome of the purchases, impairments in liquidity and functioning that lead to sluggish price discovery.

N. Gumata, E. Ndou, *Achieving Price, Financial and Macro-Economic Stability in South Africa*,
https://doi.org/10.1007/978-3-030-66340-7_20

announcement effects related to the stock or outstanding LSAPs and these effects are active whenever investors receive new information about the parameters or boundaries of the LSAPs programme, such as its size, duration and composition. For instance, Altavilla et al. (2015) find that the major impact of the asset purchase programmes arises at the announcement of the key programme parameters, that is, the stock effects. However, the flow effects generated by the actual implementation of the purchases are limited.[2]

Furthermore, Altavilla et al. (2015) show that the stock effects of asset purchases on bond yields are transmitted through the financial markets' response to current and expected future withdrawals of bond supply, in anticipation to the actual purchases taking place. These effects to bond yields are largely transmitted through the local supply or asset scarcity and the duration channels. In addition, they establish that in contrast to existing literature findings of a large impact of asset purchases only in periods of high financial distress, the impact of the asset purchase programme on asset prices in the euro area was sizeable and significant even though the programme was announced at a time of low financial distress. This is because targeting assets at long maturity and spanning the investment-grade space supported the duration and the credit channels. Furthermore, the low level of financial stress existing at the announcement of the asset purchase programme, while diminishing the local supply channel, facilitated the spillovers to non-targeted assets. Kettemann and Krogstrup (2013) also find evidence of a significant fall in the term premium on covered bonds following the announcement and implementation of the Swiss National Bank bond purchase programme. Their results suggest the presence of stock and flow effects largely via the expected or actual portfolio balance channel.

Similarly, De Santis and Holm-Hadulla (2017) establish that most of the downward pressure of the Public Sector Purchase Programme (PSPP) on sovereign bond yields was due to the stock effects. These effects arose in anticipation of and upon the announcement of the programme parameters. However, the flow effect of the PSPP operations led to a temporary decline in sovereign bond yields on the day of purchase. As such, the flow

The percentage change in the price of the securities issued on each day is used to estimate the flow effects (D'Amico and King 2013).

[2] See also D'Amico and King (2013), Joyce and Tong (2012), Breedon et al. (2012), and De Santis and Holm-Hadulla (2017).

effects accounted for a limited share of the downward pressure of PSPP on sovereign yields. Figure 20.1 presents the stylised supply and demand effects of the LSAPs. It is a graphical representation of the interaction between the central bank acting as a buyer of securities and potential sellers in the secondary market.

In Fig. 20.1a the demand curves of the central band denoted by D_{CB} are vertical to signify that the central bank demand is expected to be largely price inelastic. This is because the main objective of the central is not to minimise costs or to maximise profits but rather to create the financial conditions required to achieve price stability and financial stability. In contrast, the supply curves in Fig. 20.1b are a convex function because, as the demand for securities increases, the supply is likely to become increasingly constrained. The demand curves for private investors in Fig. 20.1b are linear and downward sloping indicating that they are price elastic (sensitive). Central bank asset purchase programmes effectively constrain the supply of bonds available to private price-sensitive market participants. These bond supply effects result in an inward shift of the supply curve in Fig. 20.1b, leading to an increase in bond prices and a decline in bond yields. According to Altavilla et al. (2015), the bond supply effects shown in Fig. 20.1b are transmitted via the local supply channel or the scarcity channel and the duration channel or the long maturities channel. As a result, the central bank purchases tend to have large and significant effects on targeted assets over which preferred-habitat financial market

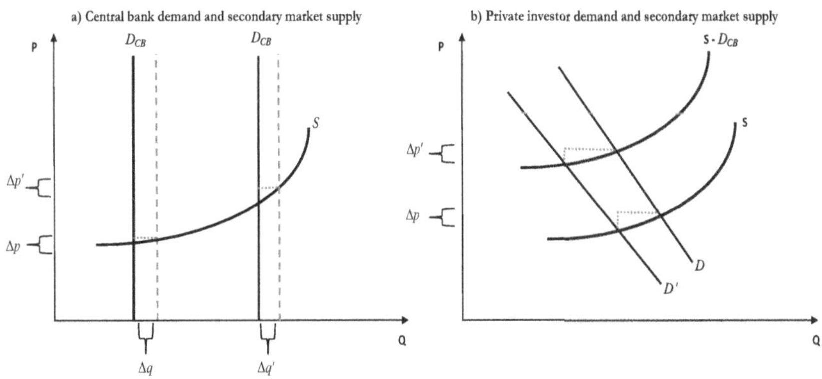

Fig. 20.1 Stylised representation of large-scale asset purchases stock effects. (Source: Authors' drawing and adapted from Cœuré (2018))

participants have a specific demand. In such cases, preferred-habitat financial market participants are willing to engage in transactions with central banks only if the expected returns of these bonds decrease, thus signifying the local supply channel or scarcity channel. To this effect, D'Amico and King (2013) show that the LSAP programme changes the stock of government securities and affects yields on these securities in specific sectors where purchases occurred. This phenomenon is referred to as the local supply effect. On the other hand, the changes in the government securities' supply also affect the term structure by changing the total quantity of the duration risk that arbitrageurs must hold. This is referred to as the duration effect and is distinct from the local-supply effect.

In addition, the effectiveness of the central bank asset purchases shown by the shift of the demand curves in Fig. 20.1a is expected to increase over time indicating the ***persistence*** of the stock effects. The stock effects shift the private sector supply curve upwards (inwards) in Fig. 20.1b, which becomes steeper as bonds become scarcer. According to Coeure (2018), the outward shift in the central bank demand curve can be operationalised through an extension of the asset purchase programme until it achieves the desired effects. The aspect of the extension and changes in the parameters of the central bank LSAPs also relates to the persistence of the effects of asset purchases.

We contribute to literature by assessing the impact of the level (stock) and flow (changes), and persistent and transitory shocks to the SARB balance sheet on various financial and macro-economic indicators using several econometric techniques. It is well documented in literature that event studies used in a large body of research have little to say about the persistence of asset purchase programmes long after they are announced (announcement effects). As a result, other studies that use time-series analysis suggest that the expected persistence of the supply shock is important (Coeure 2018). First, we use the historical counterfactual VAR analysis to assess the impact of the forex reserves accumulation programme the SARB embarked on between 2004M1 and 2008M12. As discussed in detail in earlier chapters, the SARB balance more than doubled between 2004M1 and 2018M12 largely on account of the forex reserves accumulation programme. Foreign currency reserves constitute almost 90 per cent of the SARB's balance sheet. Second, we use VAR modelling techniques to assess the impact of persistent versus transitory SARB balance sheet shocks on several macro-economic variables. Like De Santi (2016), we net the effects of transitory and persistent effects to estimate the potential incremental impact of LSAPs and how their impact is likely to accumulate over time.

20.2 The Effects of Stocks and Flow Effects on Ten-Year Yields: Evidence from the Historical Decompositions

To assess the different impact of stock and flow effects, we start by estimating counterfactual VAR models which include the yield on the ten-year government bond, R/US$ exchange rate and SARB assets to capture the effects of LSAPs. The first counterfactual VAR model is estimated using data for SARB assets and the R/US$ exchange rate in log levels to signify the stock effects. The second counterfactual VAR model uses the variables but as changes or growth rates over twelve-months to signify the effects of flows. However, we are more interested in the historical decompositions to assess the contributions of the LSAPs shock to the ten-year yields, especially for the period 2004M1 to 2008M12 when the SARB started accumulating forex reserves, thus growing the size of its balance sheet.

The intention is to assess the impact of the increase in the level (stock) and the flows (changes) in the SARB balance sheet on long-term bond yields over this period. In the estimation of the counterfactual historical decompositions, the role of the SARB assets channel in levels and changes is closed to derive an estimate of what the ten-year yields would have been in the absence of this channel.[3] The VAR models are estimated using two lags and 10,000 Monte Carlo draws. The shocks refer to a one standard deviation shock.

The results in Fig. 20.2 show that positive shocks to SARB assets had stock and flow effects and exerted downward pressure on ten-year yields. For instance, in levels (stocks), the LSAPs positive shock induced a prolonged decline in ten-year yields between 2003M1 and 2007M12 compared to when considering changes (flows). The downward pressure of LSAPs changes (flows) on ten-year yields was much larger during 2003, after which these effects turned positive. The comparison of these different

[3] This approach is like that adopted by D'Amico and King (2013).

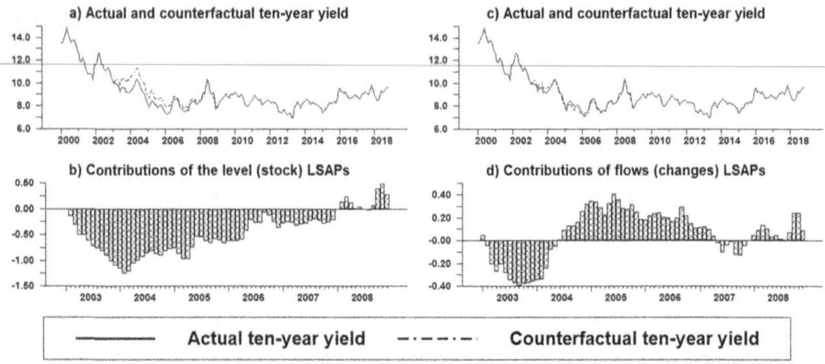

Fig. 20.2 The contributions of the stock and flows of LSAPs shocks to ten-year yields between 2003M1 and 2008M12. (Source: Authors' calculations)

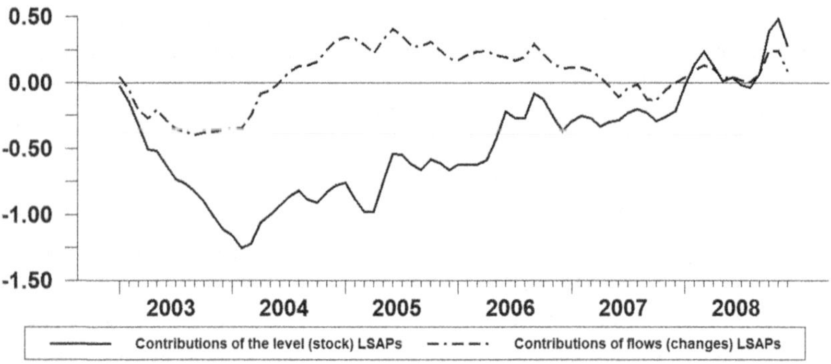

Fig. 20.3 Comparison of the contributions of stock and flows of LSAPs shocks to ten-year yields between 2003M1 and 2008M12. (Source: Authors' calculations)

effects is clear in Fig. 20.3, which shows that the ten-year yields declined more and for a prolonged period due to the positive stock effects of LSAPs shocks compared to when we use flows (changes) in the model. This implies that the stock effects on account of the forex reserves accumulation had persistent effects on ten-year bond yields compared to the flow effects. These results concur with those in D'Amico and King (2013), Joyce and Tong (2012), Breedon et al. (2012), and De Santis and

Holm-Hadulla (2017) who establish that the bulk of the impact of the central bank asset purchase programmes arises at announcement of the key programme parameters.

Similarly, Joyce et al. (2010) show that the imperfect substitutability of assets involved in the central bank asset purchase programmes provides a channel through which they affect asset prices by inducing financial market participants to rebalance their asset portfolios. The impact through the portfolio rebalancing channel may occur on announcement of the asset purchase programme and over time as investors adjust their portfolios. Since the portfolio rebalancing channel depends on the perceptions of the path of the outstanding stock of bonds and whether it is likely to be persistent.

20.3 Persistent Versus Non-persistent Effects of Stock and Flow Effects of SARB Asset Purchases on Various Financial and Macro-economic Indicators

This section assesses the effects of persistent and non-persistent positive shocks to SARB assets on various macro-economic variables to get an indication of what a persistent rise (increase) over time of the stock of asset purchases by the SARB is compared to flow shock effects. We estimate two seperate VAR models which include the variables in log levels and growth rates. The one model uses variables in growth rates while the other model uses variables in logs.

The variables included in the VAR models are SARB assets growth, output growth, employment growth, unemployment rate, Gini coefficient growth, household consumption growth, household financial assets growth and the all-share price index (equity price index) growth. The variables enter the VAR models separately and all growth rates are at annual rate. The sample starts in 2000Q1 to 2018Q4. The VAR models are estimated using two lags and 10,000 Monte Carlo draws. All the shocks are a one standard deviation shock. We calculate the net shock effects as the difference between persistent and non-persistent shock effects to demonstrate the cumulative effects of these shocks over time.

The results in Figs. 20.4 and 20.5 show that persistent shocks to the level and growth rates of SARB assets have persistently and cumulatively larger effects compared to transitory shocks. In addition, the stock effects of positive shocks to SARB assets in Fig. 20.4 have cumulatively larger effects on GDP and employment overtime compared to the flow effects in Fig. 20.5.

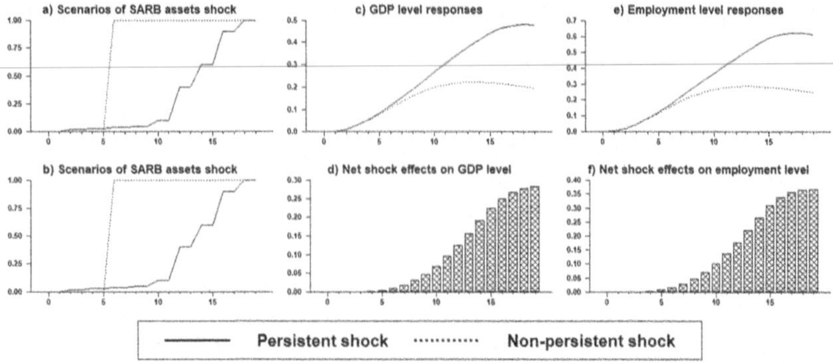

Fig. 20.4 The impact of persistent and non-persistent positive SARB asset shocks on GDP and employment levels. (Source: Authors' calculations)

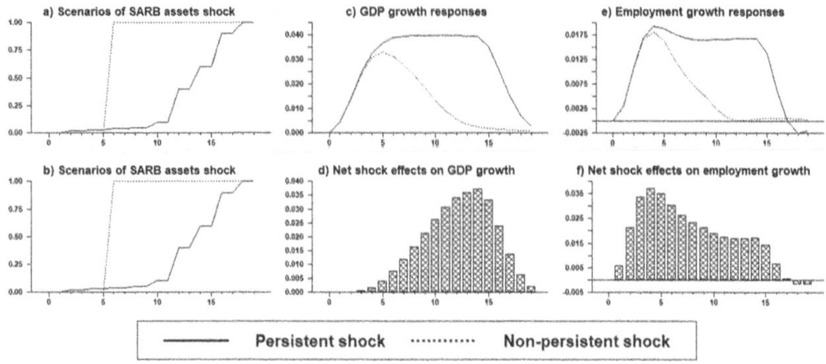

Fig. 20.5 The impact of persistent and non-persistent positive SARB asset growth shocks on GDP growth and employment growth. (Source: Authors' calculations)

We establish the same results for stock effects versus flow effects on household consumption expenditure growth and unemployment in Figs. 20.6 and 20.7. The positive shocks to the stock of SARB assets exert persistent and larger net effects on the level of household consumption expenditure and unemployment.

The results of the shock effects on household consumption and unemployment are consistent with findings in Lenza and Slacalek (2019), who establish that quantitative easing in the euro area through the European Central Bank (ECB) Asset Purchase Programme (APP) stimulated economic activity and asset prices and these in turn positively affected household employment, income and wealth.

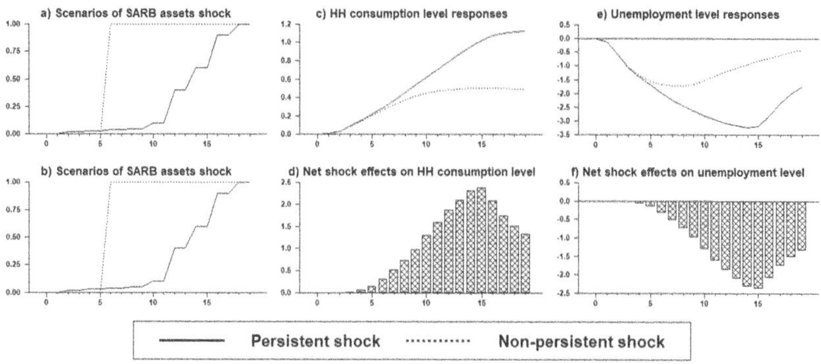

Fig. 20.6 The impact of persistent and non-persistent positive SARB asset shocks on the level of household consumption and unemployment. (Note: HH = households. Source: Authors' calculations)

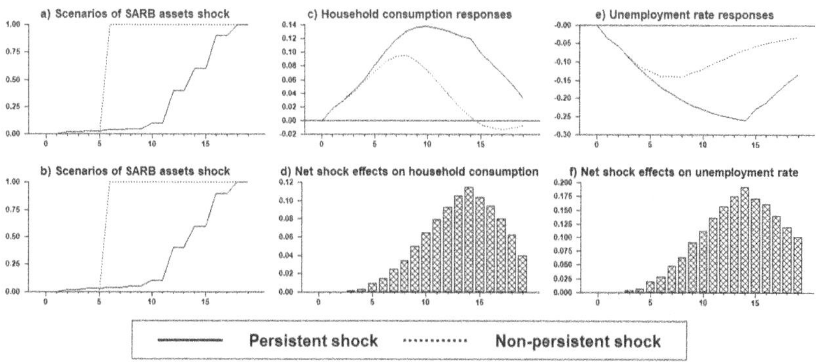

Fig. 20.7 The impact of persistent and non-persistent positive SARB asset growth shocks on household consumption growth and the unemployment rate. (Source: Authors' calculations)

The authors show that the ECB APP decreased income inequality mostly by reducing the unemployment rate for poorer households and increasing the wages of the employed. They also establish that quantitative easing helped to reduce net wealth inequality slightly through its positive impact on house price growth. Furthermore, Ampudia et al. (2019) show that distributional effects of monetary policy, especially QE on households' income, wealth and consumption in the euro area, led to a reduction of income inequality.

The ECB APP resulted is a disproportionately large drop in the unemployment rate of low-income households. They establish that these heterogeneous effects of monetary policy on households occurred largely through the indirect effect of the responses of prices and wages, labour income and employment. The heterogeneous indirect effects on households further occurred through the degree to which the ECB APP exerted different effects in the elasticities of low- versus high-skilled employment and expenditure.

We establish the results for the effects of stock and flow effects on the level of the all-share price index, house prices and household total assets and financial assets in Figs. 20.8, 20.9, 20.10, and 20.11. These results are consistent with recent evidence showing that central bank asset purchases positively affected household wealth because of the changes in the value of real estate, stocks and bonds.

Furthermore, Ampudia et al. (2019) show that the direct and indirect channels of asset purchases by the ECB propagated and reinforced the effects of household income and wealth on household consumption. Such propagation effects are very significant and important especially when the marginal propensity to consume out-of-transitory-income shocks varies across households.

To conclude this section, the results in Figs. 20.12 and 20.13 show that positive shocks to the level of SARB assets lower the level of the Gini coefficient and the ratio of government interest cost to its expenditure. The channels of transmission to a lower Gini coefficient and interest costs are

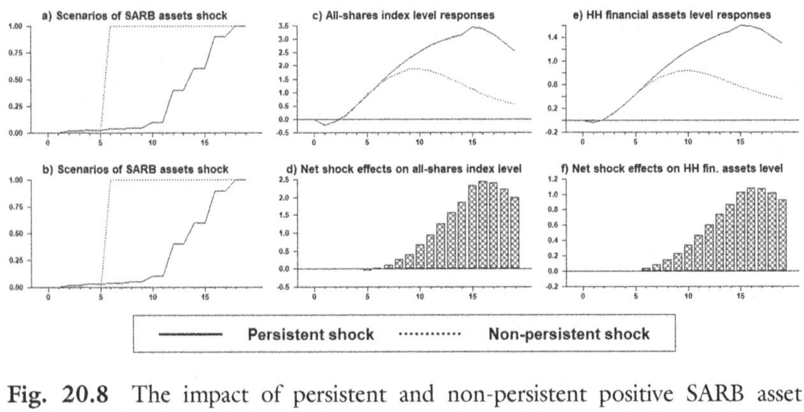

Fig. 20.8 The impact of persistent and non-persistent positive SARB asset shocks on the level of the all-share price index and household financial assets. (Note: HH = households. Source: Authors' calculations)

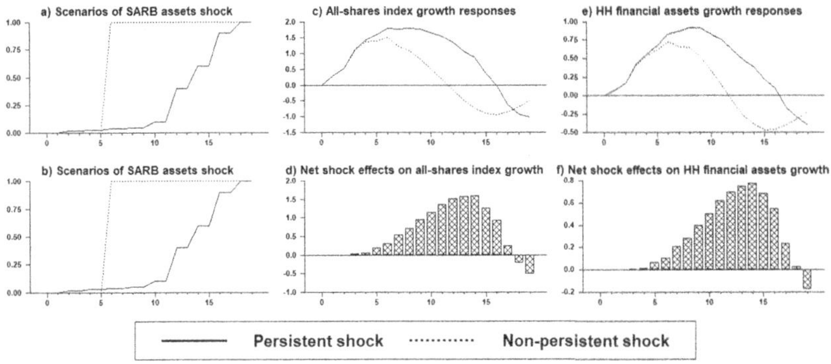

Fig. 20.9 The impact of persistent and non-persistent positive SARB asset growth shocks on all-share index and household financial assets growth rates. (Note: HH = households. Source: Authors' calculations)

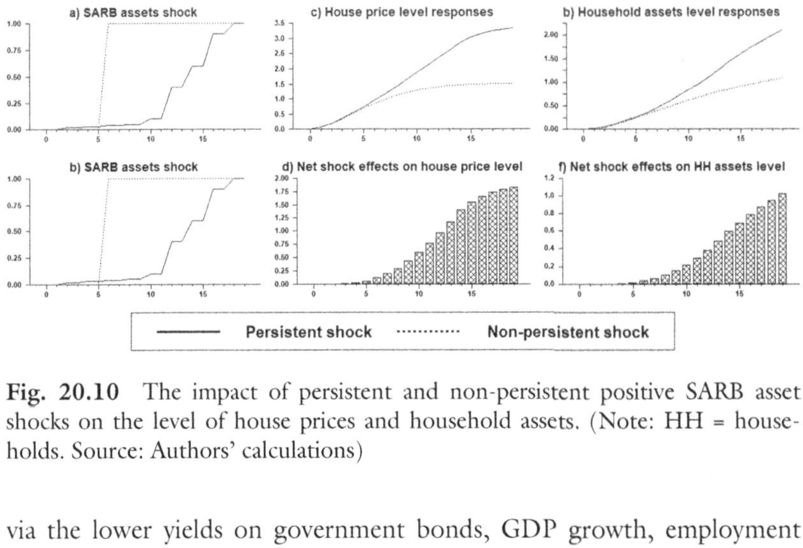

Fig. 20.10 The impact of persistent and non-persistent positive SARB asset shocks on the level of house prices and household assets. (Note: HH = households. Source: Authors' calculations)

via the lower yields on government bonds, GDP growth, employment growth and asset price growth.

Thus, we conclude that the stock effects of LSAPs are more persistent and potent compared to the flow effects. This means that the size, duration and composition of LSAPs matter. It also matters how a given stock of asset purchases is accumulated and composed because such parameters of the asset purchase programme interact with the monetary policy stance to influence financial and macro-economic variables.

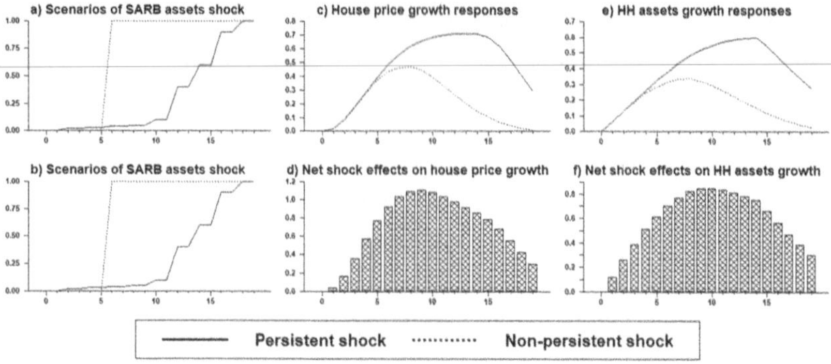

Fig. 20.11 The impact of persistent and non-persistent positive SARB asset growth shocks on house prices growth and household assets growth. (Note: HH = households. Source: Authors' calculations)

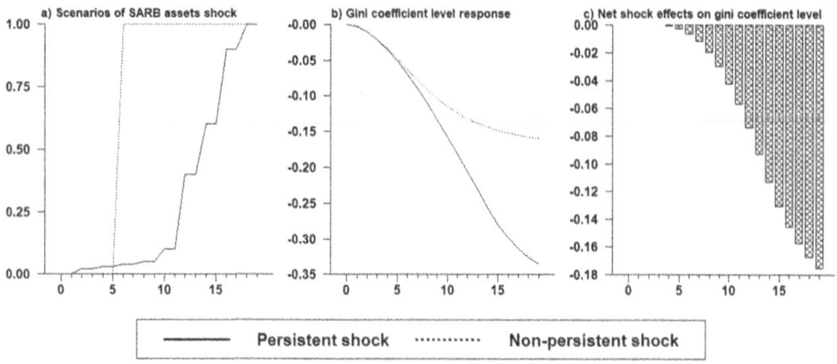

Fig. 20.12 The impact of persistent and non-persistent positive SARB asset shocks on the level of the Gini coefficient. (Source: Authors' calculations)

20.4 Conclusion and Policy Implications

Are the stock effects of large-scale asset purchases more potent and persistent relative to the flow effects? We find that positive shocks to the level of SARB assets lowers yields on long-term government, the unemployment rate, Gini coefficient and the ratio of government interest cost to its expenditure. The channels of transmission are via the lower yields on government bonds an increase in GDP growth, employment growth and asset price growth. The historical decompositions of the LSAPs shocks to

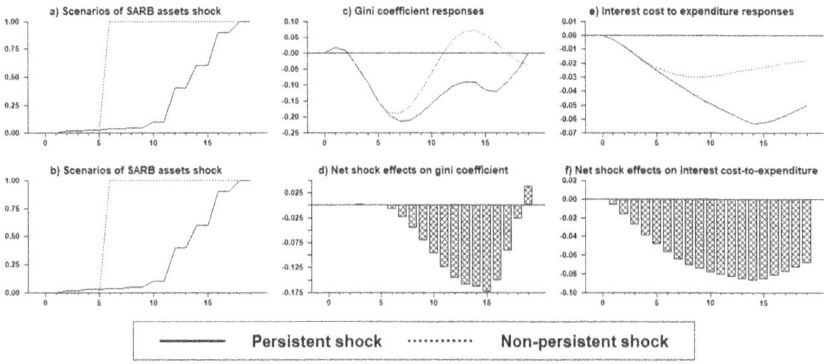

Fig. 20.13 The impact of persistent and non-persistent positive SARB asset shocks on the Gini coefficient. (Source: Authors' calculations)

ten-year yields for the period 2004M1 to 2008M12 when the SARB started accumulating forex reserves thus growing the size of its balance sheet, show that shows that ten-year yields declined more and for a prolonged period due to positive shocks to the level (stock effects) of the SARB sheet compared to flows effects (changes). Thus, stock effects of LSAPs are more persistent and potent compared to flow effects. This means that the size, duration and composition of LSAPs matter. We conclude that it matters how a given stock of asset purchases is accumulated and composed because such parameters of the asset purchase programme interact with the monetary policy stance to influence financial and macroeconomic variables.

References

Altavilla C, Carboni G, and Motto R. 2015. Asset purchase programmes and financial markets: lessons from the euro area. ECB Working Paper Series No 1864. https://www.ecb.europa.eu/pub/pdf/scpwps/ecbwp1864.en.pdf.

Ampudia M, Georgarakos D, Slacalek J, Tristani O, Vermeulen P, Violant G L. 2019. Monetary policy and household inequality. ECB Working Paper No 2170 / July 2018. https://www.ecb.europa.eu/pub/pdf/scpwps/ecb.wp2170.en.pdf?utm_source=ecb_twitter&utm_medium=social&utm_campaign=20181227_end_of_year_thread&utm_term=July_inequality.

Bernanke B S. 2014. Some reflections on Japanese monetary policy. https://www.brookings.edu/wp-content/uploads/2017/05/es_20170523_bernanke_boj_remarks.pdf.

Blattner T S and Joyce M. 2017. "Net debt supply shocks in the euro area and the implications for QE", ECB Working Paper No 1957. https://www.ecb.europa.eu/pub/pdf/scpwps/ecbwp1957.en.pdf?b4968a7e8c1fdce45065c6b694a39c70.

Breedon, F., Chadha, J.S., and Waters A. 2012. "The financial market impact of UK quantitative easing" Oxford Review of Economic Policy, Oxford University Press, Vol. 28(4), 702–728.

Cahill M E, Canlin L, and Sears J S. (2013) "Duration Risk versus Local Supply Channel in Treasury Yields: Evidence from the Federal Reserve's Asset Purchase Announcements", Federal Reserve Board, Finance and Economics Discussion Series 201335.

Cœuré B. 2018. The persistence and signalling power of central bank asset purchase programmes. Speech at the 2018 US Monetary Policy Forum, New York City, 23 February 2018.

Constâncio V. 2017a. Inequality and macroeconomic policies. Speech at the Annual Congress of the European Economic Association Lisbon, 22 August 2017. https://www.ecb.europa.eu/press/key/date/2017/html/ecb.sp170822.en.html.

Constâncio V. 2017b. Inequality and macroeconomic policies. Speech at the Annual Congress of the European Economic Association Lisbon, 22 August 2017. https://www.ecb.europa.eu/press/key/date/2017/html/ecb.sp170822.en.html.

D'Amico S and King T B. 2013. "Flow and stock effects of large-scale Treasury purchases: Evidence on the importance of local supply", *Journal of Financial Economics* 108(2): 425–448. https://www.federalreserve.gov/Pubs/feds/2012/201244/201244pap.pdf.

De Fiore F, Hoerova M, Uhlig H. 2019. Money markets, collateral and monetary policy. ECB working paper No 2239. https://www.ecb.europa.eu/pub/pdf/scpwps/ecb.wp2239~eb47cf93c2.en.pdf.

De Santi R A. 2016. Impact of the asset purchase programme on euro area government bond yields using market news. Working Paper Series, No 1939. https://www.ecb.europa.eu/pub/pdf/scpwps/ecbwp1939.en.pdf.

De Santis R A and Holm-Hadulla F. 2017. Flow effects of central bank asset purchases on euro area sovereign bond yields: evidence from a natural experiment. Working Paper series, No 2052. https://www.ecb.europa.eu/pub/pdf/scpwps/ecb.wp2052.en.pdf.

Gagnon J, Raskin M, Remache J, and Sack B. 2011. The Financial Market Effects of the Federal Reserve's Large-Scale Asset Purchases. International Journal of Central Banking March 2011. https://www.ijcb.org/journal/ijcb11q1a1.pdf.

Greenwood R, Hanson S, and Vayanos D. 2015. "Forward Guidance in the Yield Curve: Short Rates versus Bond Supply", NBER Working Paper No 21750. https://www.nber.org/papers/w21750.pdf.

Harrison R. 2017. Optimal quantitative easing. Bank of England Staff Working Paper No. 678. https://www.bankofengland.co.uk/working-paper/2017/optimal-quantitative-easing.

Joyce M A S and Tong M. 2012. "QE and the Gilt Market: A Disaggregated Analysis", The Economic Journal, Vol. 122 (564), F348—F384.

Joyce M, Lasaosa A, Stevens I and Tong M. 2010. The financial market impact of quantitative easing. Bank of England Working Paper No. 393.

Kettemann A and Krogstrup S. 2013. Portfolio balance effects of the SNB's bond purchase program. Swiss National Bank Working Paper 2013–1. https://www.snb.ch/n/mmr/reference/working_paper_2013_01/source/working_paper_2013_01.n.pdf.

Krishnamurthy and Vissing-Jorgensen. 2013. "The Ins and Outs of LSAPs", mimeo, Federal Reserve Bank of Kansas City.

Krishnamurthy A. and Vissing-Jorgensen A. 2011. "The Effects of Quantitative Easing on Long-term Interest Rates", Brookings Papers on Economic Activity, Fall 2011, 215–265.

Krogstrup S, Reynard S, and Sutter B. 2012. Liquidity Effects of Quantitative Easing on Long-Term Interest Rates. Swiss National Bank Working Paper 2012–2. https://www.snb.ch/n/mmr/reference/working_paper_2012_02/source/working_paper_2012_02.n.pdf.

Lenza M and Slacalek J. 2019. Quantitative easing did not increase inequality in the euro area. ECB Research Bulletin No. 54. https://www.ecb.europa.eu/pub/economic-research/resbull/2019/html/ecb.rb190129.en.html.

See Li C and Wei M. 2013. "Term Structure Modeling with Supply Factors and the Federal Reserve's Large-Scale Asset Purchase Programs", *International Journal of Central Banking*, 9(1), 3–39. https://www.federalreserve.gov/pubs/feds/2014/201407/201407pap.pdf.

Weidmann J. 2019. The role of the central bank in a modern economy: a European perspective speech at the University of South Africa. https://www.bundesbank.de/en/press/speeches/the-role-of-the-central-bank-in-a-modern-economy%2D%2D-a-european-perspective-776448.

CHAPTER 21

Is There a Case for the Public Investment Corporation to Increase Its Holdings of Government Debt Securities?

Research Questions Explored

- Assess whether there is a case for the public investment corporation (PIC) to increase its holdings of government debt securities.
- Explore the effects of incremental positive shocks to the share and growth rate of government bonds in the PIC balance sheet on the yield on the ten-year government bond.
- Test whether positive shocks to the share and growth rate of government bonds in the PIC balance sheet propagate the effects of large-scale asset purchases (LSAPs) of government bonds by the South African Reserve Bank (SARB).
- Evaluate the persistent versus non-persistent effects of government bond purchases by the PIC on ten-year government bond yields.

21.1 Introduction

Is there a case for the Public Investment Corporation (PIC) to increase its holdings of government debt securities? We ask this question as is it is related to the impact of the increased participation of the PIC in the primary and secondary government bond markets and its effects on government bond yields. The trends in Fig. 21.1 show that the share of government fixed income securities (bonds) and bills (Treasury Bills) has declined over the years.

N. Gumata, E. Ndou, *Achieving Price, Financial and Macro-Economic Stability in South Africa*,
https://doi.org/10.1007/978-3-030-66340-7_21

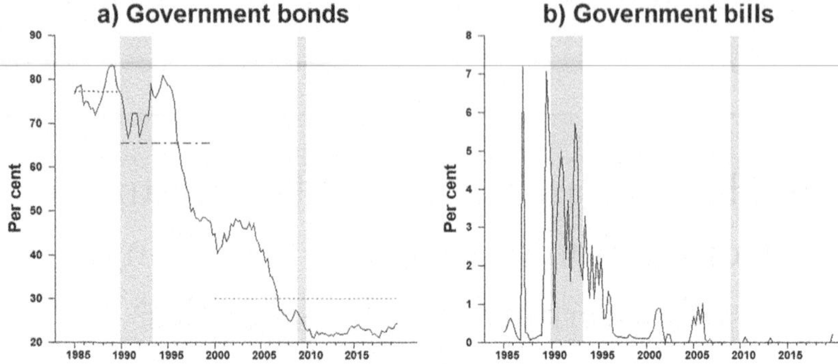

Fig. 21.1 Government bonds and bills as a share of PIC assets. (Source: South African Reserve Bank and authors' calculations. Note: The grey shaded areas denote the periods of domestic recessions. The horizontal dotted lines in (a) indicate the averages referred to in the text)

In the case of government bonds, Fig. 21.1a shows that the share of government bonds declined from an average of 77.26 per cent between 1985Q1 and 1989Q4 to an average of 65.51 per cent between 1990Q1 and 1999Q4 and an average of 30.13 per cent between 2000Q1 and 2019Q4. At the same time the holdings of government bills declined from an average of 1.28 per cent between 1985Q1 and 1989Q4 to an average of 1.72 per cent between 1990Q1 and 1999Q4 and an average of 0.11 per cent between 2000Q1 and 2019Q4. Thus, the PIC has almost reduced its share of government debt securities to a bare minimum post-2000.

It is against this background that we assess the impact of increasing the share of government bonds and Treasury Bills in the PIC balance sheet on government bond yields. We use three approaches to assess the impact of positive shocks to the share and growth rate of government bonds and Treasury Bills in the PIC balance sheet. First, we use the modified Kilian and Vigfusson (2011) approach to assess for the effects of one, four, six or ten positive standard deviation shocks to the share and growth rate of government bonds in the PIC balance sheet. Second, we use the counterfactual VAR models to assess whether positive shocks to the share and growth rate of government bonds in the PIC balance sheet propagate the effects of LSAPs of government bonds by the SARB. We explore this aspect considering the recent announcement by the SARB that it has started to purchase government bonds across the maturity spectrum to ensure the proper function in the markets and assist with the transmission mechanism of monetary policy decisions. Third, we use persistent versus non-persistent shock scenarios in a VAR model to assess the impact of stock and flow shocks of bond purchases by the PIC.

We contribute to academic literature and policy discussions by exploring the role the asset reallocation by the PIC can play in achieving the set objectives of price stability, financial stability and macro-economic stability. The role the PIC balance sheet can play in assisting policymakers to achieve these objectives has not been explored. We argue that the PIC balance sheet is another tool that can be used to achieve these set objectives in a prudent manner. The PIC balance sheet can be used alongside the SARB balance sheet to achieve these national objectives. Hence, we assess whether bond purchases by the PIC reinforce the positive shock effects of LSAPs by the SARB. It is also worth noting that this analysis does not differentiate between the effects of the bond purchases by the PIC in the primary and secondary market, as it can participate in both segments of the market.

21.2 What Is the Impact of the Incremental Effect of Positive Shocks to the Share and Growth Rate of Government Bonds in the PIC Balance Sheet on the Ten-Year Yield?

To answer this question, we use the modified Kilian and Vigfusson (2011) approach to assess for the effects of one, four, six and ten positive standard deviation shocks to the share and growth rate of government bonds in the PIC balance sheet on the ten-year yield. We use the share and growth rates of the government bonds in the PIC balance sheet to assess for the robustness of the impact of the shock. The model uses quarterly (Q) data from 2000Q1 to 2019Q4. The growth rates are at an annual rate.

The results in Fig. 21.2a and b show that they are robust to using the share and growth rates of government bonds in the PIC balance sheet. Incremental positive shocks to the share and growth rate of government bonds in the PIC balance sheet result in a decline in the ten-year government bond yield. It is also evident that the larger the positive shock to the share and growth rates of government bonds in the PIC balance sheet, the

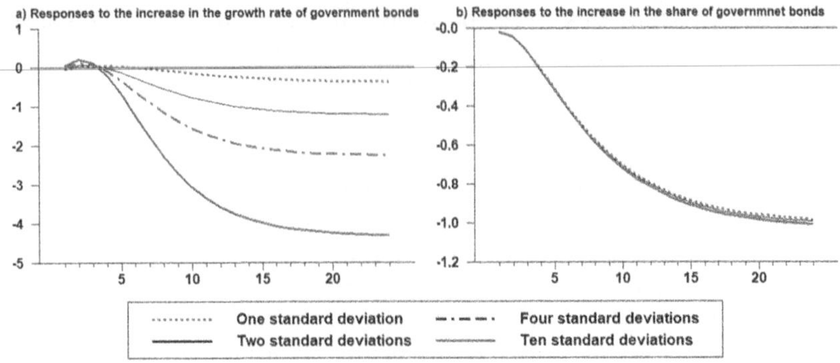

Fig. 21.2 Responses to positive shocks to the share and growth rate of government bonds on the PIC balance sheet. (Source: Authors' calculations)

larger the decline in the ten-year government bond yield. The asymmetries induced by the different positive shock sizes to the share and growth rate of government bonds in the PIC balance sheet on the ten-year yield are mostly evident when using growth rates in Fig. 21.2a. This is because growth rate represents the flow effects (changes) of the size of government bonds in the balance sheet as opposed to the share which largely represents the size or stock effects. Both effects are important in the effectiveness of LSAPs.

Literature shows that there are stock and flow effects involved in the conduct of LSAPs and the persistence of these effects matters. D'Amico and King (2013) define the stock effects of LSAPs as persistent changes in prices that result from movements along Treasury demand curves. On the other hand, the flow effects are defined as the response of prices to the ongoing purchase operations.[1] Various studies establish that there are sizeable announcement effects related to the stock of LSAPs and these effects are active whenever investors receive new information about the parameters of the LSAPs programme, such as its size, duration and composition. For instance, Altavilla et al. (2015) find that the bulk of the impact of the asset purchase programmes arises at the announcement of the key

[1] The flow effects can reflect the portfolio rebalancing activity due to the outcome of the purchases, impairments in liquidity and functioning that lead to sluggish price discovery. The percentage change in the price of the securities issued on each day is used to estimate the flow effects (D'Amico and King 2013).

programme parameters, that is, the stock effects, whereas the flow effects generated by the actual implementation of the purchases are limited.[2]

21.3 Do Bond Purchases by the PIC Reinforce the Positive Shock Effects of LSAPs by the SARB?

We use the counterfactual VAR approach to answer this section. The estimated counterfactual VAR model includes the SARB assets growth rate, ten-year government yield and the PIC government bonds purchases growth rate. We use this small-scale counterfactual VAR model because we are mostly interested in the shock effects on bond yields. The growth rates are at an annual rate. The actual response is derived when the PIC government bonds purchases growth rate channel is active in the model. However, the counterfactual response is derived when this channel is not active in the model. The intention is to assess the amplification effects of the PIC government bonds purchases growth rate channel. The amplification effects are the difference between the actual and counterfactual responses.

The results in Fig. 21.3 show that the ten-year government bond yield declines in response to positive shocks to the SARB assets and the PIC government bonds purchases growth rate channel amplifies these shock effects. The actual ten-year government bond yields decline more than the counterfactual response when the PIC bonds purchases growth rate channel is closed or inactive in the model. Therefore, the PIC bonds purchases growth rate channel leads to a larger decline in the ten-year government bond yields and amplifies the decline. We conclude that it is a worthwhile strategy to use the PIC balance sheet alongside the SARB balance sheet to achieve these national objectives of price stability, financial stability and macro-economic stability in a prudent manner.

[2] See also D'Amico and King (2013), Joyce and Tong (2012), Breedon et al. (2012), and De Santis and Holm-Hadulla (2017).

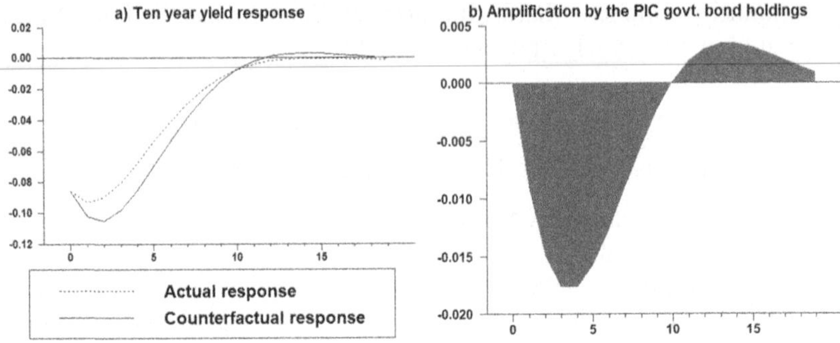

Fig. 21.3 Responses to a positive SARB assets growth shock and amplification by the increase in the PIC government bonds growth rate. (Source: Authors' calculations)

21.4 Persistent Versus Non- persistent Effects of Government Bond Purchases by the PIC on Ten-Year Government Bond Yields

To conclude the analysis, we assess the impact of persistent versus non-persistent effects of government bond purchases by the PIC on ten-year government bond yields. For robustness analysis, we assess the impact of stock (the share) and flow (changes or growth rates) effects of government bond purchases by the PIC on ten-year government bond yields.

The results in Figs. 21.4 and 21.5 show that the persistent positive government bond purchases by the PIC on ten-year government bond yields whether measured as a growth rate (flow) or as a share (stock) have a much larger downward effect compared to transitory (non-persistent) shocks. The cumulative effects of persistent versus non-persistent shock effects as measured by their difference in Figs. 21.4c and 21.5c show the downward effects of persistent shocks increase of the forecast horizon.

These results concur with those in D'Amico and King (2013), Joyce and Tong (2012), Breedon et al. (2012), and De Santis and Holm-Hadulla (2017) who establish that the bulk of the impact of the central bank asset purchase programmes arises at the announcement of the key programme parameters. Similarly, Joyce et al. (2010) show that the imperfect substitutability of assets involved in the asset purchase programmes provides a channel through which LSAPs affect asset prices by inducing investors to rebalance their asset portfolios. The impact through the portfolio

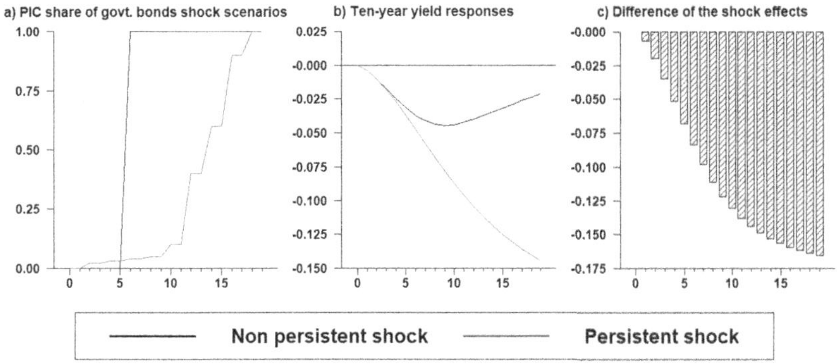

Fig. 21.4 Responses to positive persistent and non-persistent PIC share of purchases of government bonds shocks. (Source: Authors' calculations)

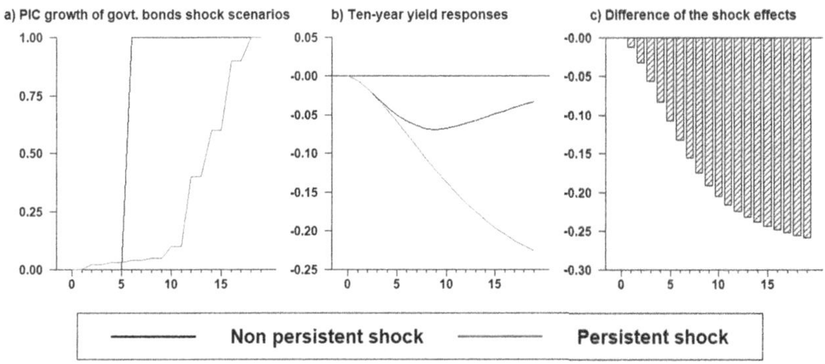

Fig. 21.5 Responses to positive persistent and non-persistent PIC growth rate of purchases of government bonds shocks. (Source: Authors' calculations)

rebalancing channel may occur on announcement and over time as investors are able to adjust their portfolios. Since the portfolio rebalancing channel depends on perceptions of the path of the outstanding stock of bonds, it is likely to be persistent. Thus, we conclude that there is a case for the PIC to increase its holdings of government debt securities. The PIC balance sheet can be used alongside the SARB balance sheet to achieve the earlier stated national objectives. This is especially the case given that the effects of the bond purchases by the PIC can reinforce LSAPs by the SARB in the primary and secondary market, as the PIC can participate in both segments of the market. However, the effects will depend on the design of the PIC bond purchase programme by policymakers involved. Based on the trends shown in Fig. 21.1, there is room to do some portfolio rebalancing on the PIC balance sheet.

21.5 Conclusion and Policy Implications

Is there a case for the PIC to increase its holdings of government debt securities? Yes, there is. There is room to do portfolio rebalancing on the PIC balance sheet. We find that incremental positive shocks to the share (stock effects) and growth rate (flow effects) of government bonds in the PIC balance sheet result in a decline in the ten-year government bond yield. Large positive shocks to the share and growth rates of government bonds in the PIC balance sheet result in a larger decline in the ten-year government bond yield. The asymmetries induced by the different positive shock sizes to the share and growth rate of government bonds in the PIC balance sheet on the ten-year yield are mostly evident when using growth rates.

Furthermore, the ten-year government bond yield declines in response to positive shocks to the SARB assets growth rate and the PIC government bonds purchases growth rate channel amplifies these shock effects. The PIC bond purchases growth rate channel leads to a larger decline in the ten-year government bond yields and amplifies their decline. In addition, persistent positive government bond purchases by the PIC shocks on the ten-year government bond yields whether measured as a growth rate (flow) or as a share (stock), have a much larger downward effect compared to transitory (non-persistent) shocks. The cumulative effects of persistent versus non-persistent shock effects as measured by their difference show that the downward effects of persistent shocks increase the forecast horizon. Thus, it is a worthwhile strategy to use the PIC balance sheet alongside the SARB balance sheet to achieve the national objectives of price stability, financial stability and macro-economic stability in a prudent manner. This is especially the case given that the effects of the bond purchases by the PIC can reinforce LSAPs by the SARB in the primary and secondary market, as the PIC can participate in both segments of the market. However, the effects will depend on the design of the PIC bond purchase programme by the policymakers involved, because it matters how a given stock of asset purchases is accumulated and composed.

References

Altavilla C, Carboni G, and Motto R. 2015. Asset purchase programmes and financial markets: lessons from the euro area. ECB Working Paper Series No 1864. https://www.ecb.europa.eu/pub/pdf/scpwps/ecbwp1864.en.pdf.

Blattner T S and Joyce M. 2017. "Net debt supply shocks in the euro area and the implications for QE", ECB Working Paper No 1957. https://www.ecb.europa.eu/pub/pdf/scpwps/ecbwp1957.en.pdf?b4968a7e8c1fdce45065c6b694a39c70.

Breedon F, Chadha J S and Waters A. 2012. The financial market impact of UK quantitative easing. BIS Papers chapters in: Bank for International Settlements (ed.), Threat of fiscal dominance?, volume 65, pages 277–304, Bank for International Settlements.

D'Amico S and King T B. 2013. "Flow and stock effects of large-scale Treasury purchases: Evidence on the importance of local supply", *Journal of Financial Economics* 108(2): 425–448. https://www.federalreserve.gov/Pubs/feds/2012/201244/201244pap.pdf.

De Santis R A and Holm-Hadulla F. 2017. Flow effects of central bank asset purchases on euro area sovereign bond yields: evidence from a natural experiment. Working Paper series, No 2052. https://www.ecb.europa.eu/pub/pdf/scpwps/ecb.wp2052.en.pdf.

Gagnon J, Raskin M, Remache J, and Sack B. 2011. The Financial Market Effects of the Federal Reserve's Large-Scale Asset Purchases. International Journal of Central Banking March 2011. https://www.ijcb.org/journal/ijcb11q1a1.pdf.

Greenwood R., Hanson S, and Vayanos D. 2015. "Forward Guidance in the Yield Curve: Short Rates versus Bond Supply", NBER Working Paper No 21750. https://www.nber.org/papers/w21750.pdf.

Haldane A G, Roberts-Sklar M, Wieladek T, and Young C. 2016. QE: the story so far. Bank of England Staff Working Paper No. 624. https://www.bankofengland.co.uk/working-paper/2016/qe-the-story-so-far.

Joyce M A S and Tong M. 2012. QE and the Gilt Market: a Disaggregated Analysis. The Economic Journal, Volume 122, Issue 564, November 2012, Pages F348–F384.

Joyce M, Lasaosa A, Stevens I and Tong M. 2010. The financial market impact of quantitative easing. Bank of England Working Paper No. 393.

Kilian L and Vigfusson R J. 2011. Are the Responses of the U.S. Economy Asymmetric in Energy Price Increases and Decreases?. Quantitative Economics, 2(4): 419–453.

Krogstrup S, Reynard S, and Sutter B. 2012. Liquidity Effects of Quantitative Easing on Long-Term Interest Rates. Swiss National Bank Working Paper 2012–2. https://www.snb.ch/n/mmr/reference/working_paper_2012_02/source/working_paper_2012_02.n.pdf.

See Li C and Wei M. 2013. "Term Structure Modeling with Supply Factors and the Federal Reserve's Large-Scale Asset Purchase Programs", *International Journal of Central Banking*, 9(1), 3–39. https://www.federalreserve.gov/pubs/feds/2014/201407/201407pap.pdf.

South African Reserve Bank. 2020a. Amendments to the Money Market Liquidity Strategy of the South African Reserve Bank. https://www.resbank.co.za/Lists/News%20and%20Publications/Attachments/9810/QA%20on%20Amendments%20to%20Money%20Market%20Liquidity%20Strategy%20of%20the%20SARB.pdf.

South African Reserve Bank. 2020b. Further amendments to the money market liquidity management strategy of the South African Reserve Bank and additions to the Monetary Policy Portfolio. https://www.resbank.co.za/Lists/News%20and%20Publications/Attachments/9805/Further%20amendments%20to%20the%20money%20market%20liquidity%20management%20strategy%20of%20the%20SARB.pdf.

CHAPTER 22

Has the Inflation Target Band Impacted the Natural Rate of Unemployment in South Africa? Evidence from the Accelerationist Philips Curve

Research Questions Explored

- Determine the influence of the different inflation bands on the non-accelerating inflation rate of unemployment (NAIRU).
- Explore whether expansionary monetary policy impacts the NAIRU using the 4.5 per cent inflation threshold.
- Show the role of monetary policy on the unemployment rate in South Africa.
- Establish the role of the GDP growth channel, investment growth channel, credit growth channel, unit labour costs channel and the exchange rate channel in amplifying or dampening the effects of accommodative monetary policy shocks in lowering the unemployment rate above the NAIRU.

22.1 Introduction

Has the inflation target band impacted the natural rate of unemployment in South Africa based on the accelerationist Philips curve? Furthermore, to what extent can the expansionary monetary policy impact the unemployment rate above the non-accelerating inflation rate of unemployment (NAIRU) when using the 4.5 per cent inflation threshold? Figure 22.1 shows the distribution of the official unemployment rate for the period 2000Q1 to 2019Q2. This chapter examines the role of monetary policy

N. Gumata, E. Ndou, *Achieving Price, Financial and Macro-Economic Stability in South Africa*,
https://doi.org/10.1007/978-3-030-66340-7_22

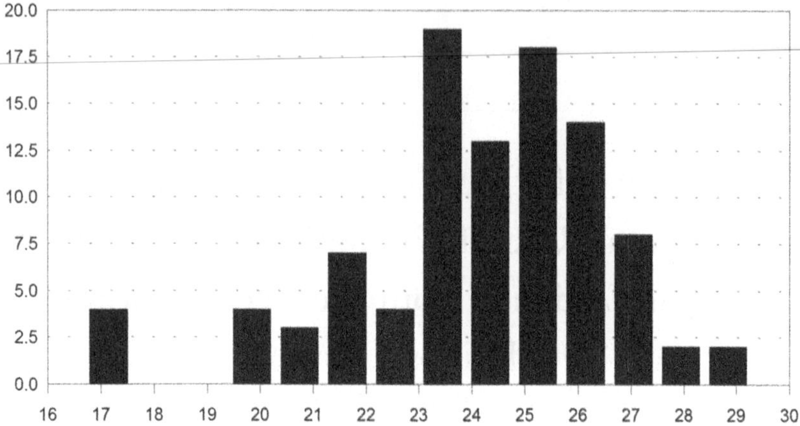

Fig. 22.1 The distribution of the official unemployment rate: 2000Q1 to 2019Q2. (Source: Authors' calculations)

on the unemployment dynamics via two ways. First, the chapter determines the influence of the different inflation bands on the NAIRU. Second, it explores whether expansionary monetary policy impacts the NAIRU using the 4.5 per cent inflation threshold. We explore the effects of this threshold because monetary policymakers have repeatedly stated their preference to keep inflation below 4.5 per cent which is the midpoint of the 3–6 per cent inflation target band. The purpose of this chapter is to show the role of monetary policy on the unemployment rate in South Africa and that there are channels that should operate very well to help monetary policy to deal with the unemployment rate above the NAIRU.

This chapter fills existing policy and academic research gaps by showing that price stability measured by inflation bands leads to a lower NAIRU compared to when the inflation bands are not considered. Second, we show that expansionary monetary policy lowers the unemployment rate above the NAIRU. This suggests that monetary policy has a role to play in dealing with the unemployment issues. This chapter shows the channels through which expansionary monetary policy is transmitted to lower the unemployment rate. In addition, we show instances during which the effects of expansionary monetary policy in reducing the unemployment rate can be frustrated or hampered.

The evidence in this chapter suggests that monetary policy has a role to play in dealing with the unemployment problem above the NAIRU and this is contrary to the evidence put forward that there is little or nothing that monetary policymakers can do. Evidence shows that expansionary monetary policy lowers the unemployment rate and these effects are amplified by high economic growth, investment growth, credit growth, the exchange rate appreciation and unit labour costs below trend growth. However, the impact of expansionary monetary policy on the unemployment rate above the NAIRU is hampered by the exchange rate depreciation and high unit labour costs above trend growth. This evidence shows that studies which do not control for the influence of inflation bands miss an important aspect in the determination of the NAIRU in South Africa. Such findings can lead to policymakers dismissing certain important policy tools which are also potent in dealing with the unemployment rate.

22.2 Model Approach

The analysis in this section uses a basic version of the expectations augmented Phillips curve or accelerationist Phillips curve given by Eq. (22.1). Where, π_t denotes the consumer price inflation rate at time t, U_t denotes the official unemployment rate at time t and U^n denotes the steady state unemployment rate or the natural unemployment rate:

$$\pi_t - \pi_{t-1} = \beta_2 \left(U_t - U^n\right) + u_t \tag{22.1}$$

Expanding Eq. (22.1) leads to Eq. (22.2):

$$\pi_t - \pi_{t-1} = -\beta_2 * U^n + \beta_2 * U_t + u_t \tag{22.2}$$

This can be written as Eq. (22.3):

$$\pi_t - \pi_{t-1} = \beta_1 + \beta_2 * U_t + u_t, \tag{22.3}$$

where, $\beta_1 = -\beta_2 * U^n$

The natural unemployment rate is calculated using Eq. (22.4) below:

$$U^n = {}^{-\beta_1}\!/_{\beta_2} \tag{22.4}$$

The main purpose of this chapter is to determine the influence of price stability on the NAIRU by testing for the effects of different inflation bands. Hence, we modify Eq. (22.1) and (22.2) to include the inflation bands. The modified equations are given in Eqs. (22.5) and (22.6) below:

$$\pi_t - \pi_{t-1} = \beta_1 + \beta_2 U_t + \beta_3 * U_t * D_{\text{band}} + \varepsilon_t \tag{22.5}$$

where, D_{band} is a dummy variable which refers to inflation in the following inflation bands: (i) inflation below 6 per cent, (ii) inflation above 6 per cent, (iii) inflation between 3 and 6 per cent, (iv) inflation below 4.5 per cent, (v) inflation above 4.5 per cent and (vi) estimations without inflation bands. The D_{band} dummy equals to the value of inflation in the indicated band and zero otherwise. The natural rate of unemployment or non-accelerating inflation rate of unemployment is given by

$$U^n = -\beta_1 / (\beta_2 + \beta_3) \tag{22.6}$$

22.3 Does the Inflation Target Band Impact the NAIRU?

This chapter uses quarterly (Q) data spanning 2000Q1 to 2019Q2. Table 22.1 shows the different NAIRU estimates based on the role of inflation bands according to the inflation bands included in the model and the significance level of the calculated NAIRU and F-Value of the estimated model. The results for the different inflation bands are based on Eq. (22.6). The results of the model without inflation bands in the equation are based on Eq. (22.2). The p values shown in Table 22.1 were used to determine whether the calculated NAIRU is significant or not.

A graphical comparison of various estimated NAIRU according to inflation bands is shown in Fig. 22.2. The results show that the NAIRU varies according to the role of the inflation band. In all instances, the NAIRU is the highest when inflation exceeds 6 per cent (above 6 per cent) compared to when inflation is below 6 per cent. On the other hand, the NAIRU is the lowest when inflation is below 4.5 per cent relative to when it exceeds this threshold value. The results also show that the NAIRU is lower when inflation is within the 3–6 per cent inflation target band compared to when there are no inflation regimes considered in the estimations. Of importance is the robustness of the results indicating that the

Table 22.1 NAIRU estimates based on the inflation bands

Inflation band used	*Estimated NAIRU coefficient in per cent*	*Standard errors*	*T statistics*	*p value*
No inflation bands	25.3	0.8	31.1	0.00
3–6 per cent band	24.8	1.1	23.1	0.00
Above 6 per cent band	26.9	1.9	14.1	0.00
Below 6 per cent band	24.5	1.0	23.5	0.00
Above 4.5 per cent band	25.8	1.2	21.9	0.00
Below 4.5 per cent band	24.1	1.5	15.9	0.00
Above 3 per cent band	25.6	1.0	26.7	0.00
Below 3 per cent band	23.0	2.7	8.5	0.00

Source: Authors calculations

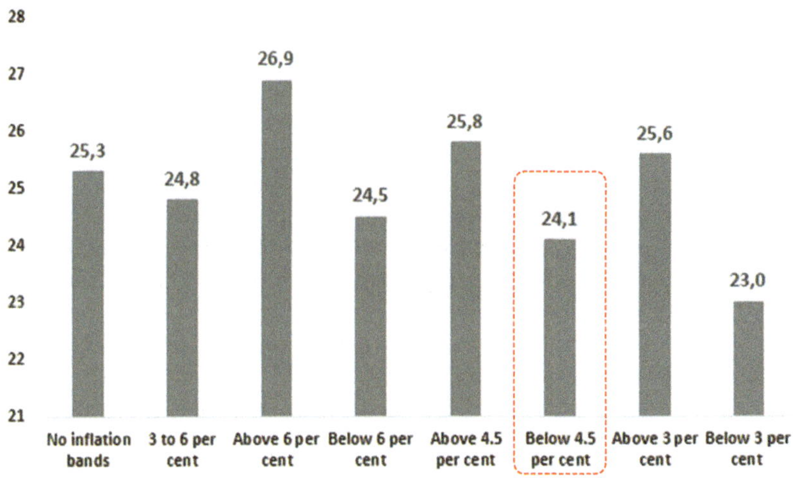

Fig. 22.2 Comparison of NAIRU estimates based on different inflation bands. (Source: Author's calculations)

NAIRU is the lowest when inflation is below 4.5 per cent as shown by the fact that the NAIRU is the lowest when inflation is below 3 per cent compared to when inflation exceeds this threshold. These results show that minimising inflation matters for lowering the NAIRU.

This analysis reveals that inflation bands matter for the influence of price stability on the NAIRU. Hence, studies which estimate the NAIRU without controlling for the influence of price stability measured by the inflation bands omit a very important component in the policy discussions.

22.4 Does the Expansionary Monetary Policy Shock Impact the Unemployment Rate When It Is Above the NAIRU Calculated Using the 4.5 Per Cent Target?

This section examines the extent to which expansionary monetary policy shocks impact the unemployment rate when it exceeds 24.1 per cent. We use the NAIRU of 24.1 per cent which is calculated using the inflation band below 4.5 per cent because the Monetary Policy Committee has communicated their preference for inflation to be below 4.5 per cent. We use various VAR models under different model assumptions which are estimated using 10,000 Monte Carlo draws and two lags. The estimation of various VAR models is to determine the robustness of the results to different model assumptions and specifications. The models use a dummy variable that assume all values of the negative repo rate changes (repo rate cuts) to capture the accommodative monetary policy stance. The dummy variable for accommodative monetary policy takes on all the values of the negative repo rate changes (repo rate cuts) and zero otherwise. The unemployment rate dummy variable is equal to the values of the unemployment rate which exceed the NAIRU value of 24.1 per cent which is calculated using the 4.5 per cent inflation target band and zero otherwise. All growth rates are at annual rate.

22.4.1 *The Models Are Specified as Follows*

(1) Model 1 is a VAR model which includes the unemployment rate dummy, the accommodative monetary policy dummy and govern-

ment consumption growth as endogenuos variables. The exogenous variables in this model include a constant and consumer price inflation.

(2) Model 2 is a VAR model which includes the accommodative monetary policy dummy, the unemployment rate dummy and government consumption growth as endogenous variables.
(3) Model 3 is a VAR model which includes the unemployment rate dummy, GDP growth and the accommodative monetary policy dummy as endogenous variables.
(4) Model 4 is a VAR model which includes the unemployment rate dummy and the accommodative monetary policy dummy as endogenous variables.
(5) Model 5 is a linear regression model and regresses the unemployment rate dummy on its own four lags, the accommodative monetary policy dummy first two lags and the consumer price inflation first two lags.

The VAR models are estimated using two lags and 10,000 Monte Carlo draws. The results in Fig. 22.3 show that the unemployment rate declines significantly due to an expansionary monetary policy shock. The decline in the unemployment rate is robust to different model specifications.

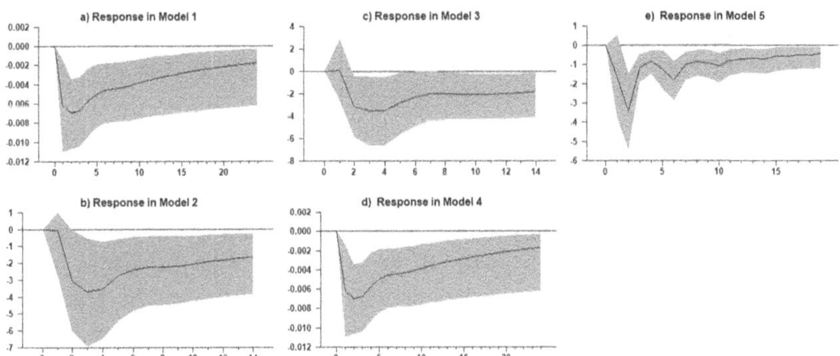

Fig. 22.3 Responses to an unexpected 1 per cent repo rate reduction. (Note: The grey shaded areas denote the 16th and 84th percentile confidence bands. Source: Authors' calculations)

22.5 Which Channel Transmits Accommodative Monetary Policy Shocks to the Unemployment Rate Above the NAIRU?

This section estimates the counterfactual VAR models to determine the channels which transmit expansionary monetary policy shocks to the unemployment rate above the NAIRU. We estimate three-variable counterfactual VAR models. The models include the accommodative monetary policy dummy, the unemployment rate dummy and either the GDP growth channel, or investment growth channel, or credit growth channel, or unit labour costs growth channel or the exchange rate change channel. The dummy variables are as defined earlier. The models are estimated using two lags and 10,000 Monte Carlo draws. The influence of a channel is determined by the gap between the actual and counterfactual inflation rate. When the actual response is more than the counterfactual response, this suggests that the channel included in the model amplifies the response of the unemployment rate due to expansionary monetary policy shocks. When the counterfactual response is more than the actual response, this suggests the channel included in the model dampens the response of the unemployment rate due to expansionary monetary policy shocks.

22.5.1 What Are the Roles of GDP Growth, Investment Growth and Credit Growth Channels?

This section examines the role of the GDP growth (GDP_G), gross fixed capital formation (CAP_FORMG) and credit growth (CREDIT) channels in transmitting expansionary monetary policy shocks to the unemployment rate when it exceeds the NAIRU of 24.1 per cent. The cumulative responses shown in Fig. 22.4 indicate that the actual unemployment rate declines more than the counterfactual suggests. This happens when GDP growth, investment growth and credit growth are included in the model compared to when they are shut off in the model. This shows the potency of the high GDP growth, investment growth and credit growth in transmitting expansionary monetary policy shocks. In addition, the results in Fig. 22.4 show that the biggest amplification of accommodative monetary policy shocks is due to credit growth. This suggests that credit growth and the availability of finance magnify the transmission of expansionary monetary policy shocks in reducing the unemployment rate above the NAIRU.

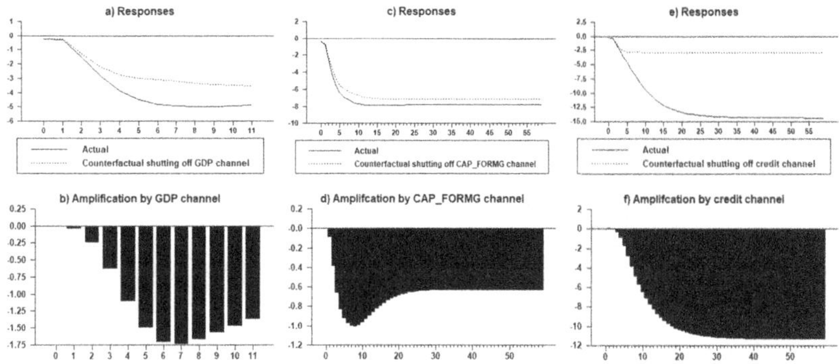

Fig. 22.4 Unemployment rate responses to expansionary monetary policy shocks and the transmission channels. (Source: Authors' calculations)

22.5.2 *The Role of the Economic Growth Channel*

This section separates the role of GDP growth into positive (GDP_POS) and negative (GDP_NEG) growth to establish whether there are differential effects in the transmission of expansionary monetary policy shocks to the unemployment rate above the NAIRU of 24.1 per cent. Figure 22.5 shows the cumulative unemployment rate responses to a one standard deviation expansionary monetary policy shock and roles of the positive and negative GDP growth channels. The results indicate that expansionary monetary policy shocks have a bigger impact in decreasing the unemployment rate when GDP growth is negative compared to during expansionary phases.

22.5.3 *The Role of the Unit Labour Costs Channel*

This section examines whether the role of the unit labour costs channel depends on whether it is above or below the Hodrick-Prescott filtered trend level. We calculate the unit labour cost gap as a difference between the Hodrick-Prescott filter trend of the log of unit labour costs and actual unit labour costs. Thereafter, we decompose the unit labour costs gap into positive unit labour costs gap (ULC_POS) and negative unit labour cost (ULC_NEG). The ULC_POS dummy equals to the values of the positive unit labour cost gap and zero otherwise. The ULC_NEG dummy equals to the values of the negative unit labour costs gap and zero otherwise.

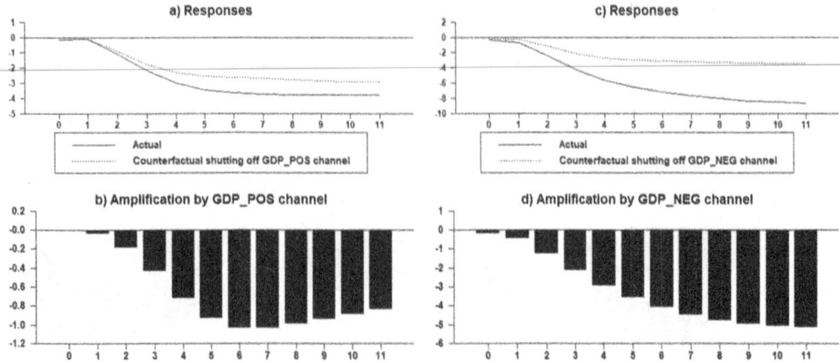

Fig. 22.5 Unemployment rate responses to expansionary monetary policy shocks and the role of the GDP growth channel. (Source: Authors' calculations)

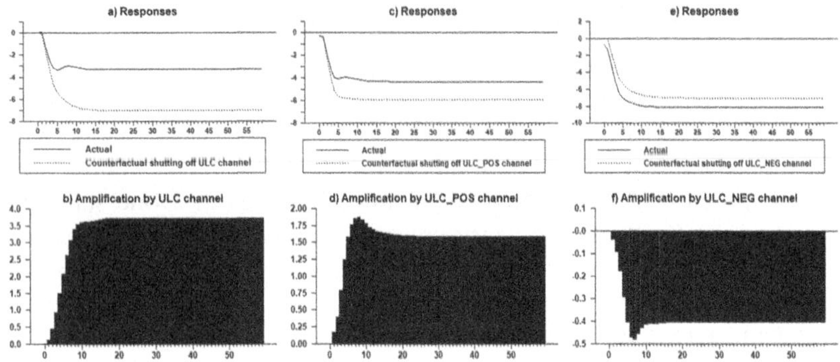

Fig. 22.6 Unemployment rate responses to expansionary monetary policy shocks and the role of the unit labour costs channel. (Source: Authors' calculations)

These dummy variables replace the unit labour growth (ULC) in the model and are included separately in the model.

In Fig. 22.6 the counterfactual response (which shuts off the role of the unit labour costs channel) declines more than the actual response. This suggests that high unit labour costs (above the trend) mitigate the decline in the unemployment rate above the NAIRU. The negative unit labour costs amplify the decline in the unemployment rate above the

NAIRU. In contrast, rising unit labour costs growth reduces the decline in the unemployment rate above the NAIRU. This suggests that expansionary monetary policy will be effective in lowering the unemployment rate above the NAIRU especially when unit labour costs are below the trend. In addition, a comparison of the responses based on the absolute values indicates the presence of the asymmetric amplification of positive and negative unit labour costs gap. The results show that positive unit labour costs are more potent in compared to negative unit labour costs in transmitting expansionary monetary policy shocks. This suggests that there is a need to lower unit labour costs (increase labour productivity) if expansionary monetary policy shocks are to reduce the unemployment rate above the NAIRU.

22.5.4 *The Role of the Exchange Rate Channel*

This section determines the role the exchange rate channel in transmitting expansionary monetary policy shocks to the unemployment rate above the NAIRU. We decompose the annual exchange rate changes into the exchange rate appreciations and depreciations. We use the real effective exchange rate (REER) annual changes. The REER_APP dummy variable equals to the positive REER changes and zero otherwise. The REER_DEPP dummy variable equals to the negative REER changes and zero otherwise. These dummy variables are included separately in the model.

The results in Fig. 22.7 indicate that the unemployment rate above the NAIRU declines more than the counterfactual response suggests when the REER changes and REER_APP are included in the model compared to when these are shut off in the model. This suggests that the exchange rate appreciation amplifies the decline in the unemployment rate above the NAIRU. In contrast, the counterfactual unemployment rate declines more than the actual response suggests. This suggests that the exchange rate depreciation prevents the reduction in the unemployment towards the NAIRU. In addition, there are asymmetry responses due to the REER appreciation and depreciations. The REER appreciations have are more potent compared to REER depreciations in transmitting expansionary monetary policy shocks to the unemployment rate above the NAIRU.

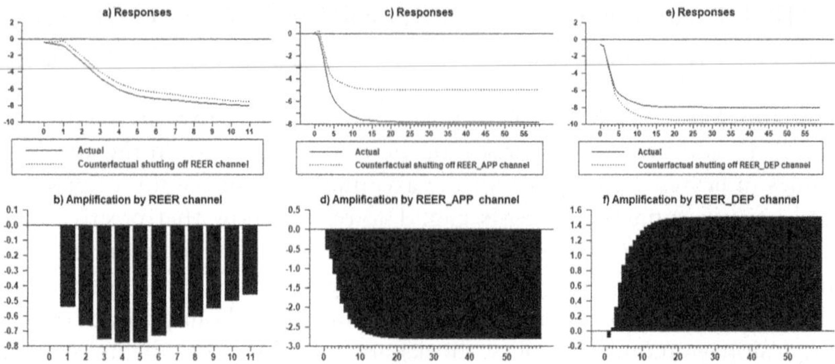

Fig. 22.7 Unemployment rate responses to expansionary monetary policy shocks and the role of the exchange rate channel. (Source: Authors' calculations)

22.6 Conclusion and Policy Implications

Has the inflation target band impacted the natural rate of unemployment in South Africa based on the accelerationist Philips curve? Furthermore, to what extent can expansionary monetary policy impact the unemployment rate above the NAIRU when using the 4.5 per cent inflation threshold? Evidence in this chapter suggests that monetary policy has a role to play in dealing with the unemployment problem above the NAIRU and this is contrary to the evidence put forward that there is little or nothing that monetary policymakers can do. We find that price stability measured by all the inflation bands below 4.5 per cent lead to a lower NAIRU compared to when the inflation bands are not considered. Expansionary monetary policy lowers the unemployment rate above the NAIRU. We find that expansionary monetary policy lowers the unemployment rate and these effects are amplified by high economic growth, investment growth, credit growth, the exchange rate appreciation and unit labour costs below the trend growth (alternatively, positive labour productivity shocks). The results show that positive unit labour costs gap are more potent compared to negative unit labour costs in transmitting expansionary monetary policy shocks. This suggests that there is a need to lower unit labour costs (increase labour productivity) if expansionary monetary policy shocks are to reduce the unemployment rate above the NAIRU. However, the impact of expansionary monetary policy on the unemployment rate above the NAIRU is hampered by the exchange rate depreciation and high unit labour costs above the trend growth. This evidence shows that studies which do not control for the influence of inflation bands miss an important aspect in the determination of NAIRU in South Africa. Such findings can lead to policymakers dismissing certain important policy tools which are also potent in dealing with the unemployment rate.

References

Ball L and Mankiw G. 2002. The NAIRU in Theory and Practice. Journal of Economic Perspectives, 16(4), pp 115–136.

Cusbert T. 2017. Estimating the NAIRU and the Unemployment Gap. Reserve Bank of Australia Quarterly Bulletin Article. June Quarter 2017.

PART III

Financial Regulations, Selected Macroprudential Tools, the Quality of the Banks' Loan Books and the Transmission of Capital Flow and Monetary Policy Shocks

CHAPTER 23

Do Financial Regulatory Tools Impact the Transmission of Capital Inflow Shocks into Credit Extension and Induce a Reallocation of Sectoral Credit Shares?

Research Questions Explored

- Investigate the role of excess capital adequacy ratio (CAR) and liquid asset holding (LAH) in the transmission of capital flow shocks to the domestic economy.
- Determine the role excess CAR and excess LAH play in the transmission of gross capital inflow and outflow shocks on credit growth.
- Determine the conduits and amplification channels in the transmission of capital inflow and outflow shocks on sectorial credit shares.

23.1 Introduction

Earlier chapters established that capital inflow shocks affect credit growth directly and indirectly via the credit conditions and credit risk channels. Furthermore, we established that aggregate credit growth and sector credit thresholds contribute to the design of the macro-prudential tools aimed at dealing with sectorial capital requirements under the countercyclical capital buffer (CCyB) insofar as they complement policies aimed at increasing the household's financial resilience during economic slumps. Evidence indicates that periods of excessively high credit growth tend to be associated with boom and bust episodes. The busts tend to be followed by persistent real economic costs. Hence, the evidence concurs with the

N. Gumata, E. Ndou, *Achieving Price, Financial and Macro-Economic Stability in South Africa*,
https://doi.org/10.1007/978-3-030-66340-7_23

rationale put forward for the use of the CCyB to moderate the impact of credit cycles on the business cycles. Nonetheless, earlier chapters and those in Gumata and Ndou (2019)[1] did not assess the role and impact of the financial regulatory tools on the transmission of capital flow shocks into credit growth and whether they induce a reallocation of sectoral credit shares. Hence, this chapter explores the role that excess CAR and the excess LAH of banks play in the transmission of gross capital inflow and outflow shocks on credit growth and the reallocation of sectoral credit shares.

Igan and Tan (2015) provide evidence that capital inflows loosen the credit and financial constraints in countries with weak banking sectors. Thus, what is the role of excess CAR and excess LAH in the transmission of capital inflow shocks into the domestic economy? Are excess CAR and excess LAH conduits in the transmission of capital inflow and outflow shocks on credit growth and the reallocation of sectorial credit shares? Furthermore, is it plausible that regulatory tools are responsible for the muted response of credit growth to positive capital inflow shocks? What can empirical evidence reveal about the policy relevance of excess CAR and excess LAH post-2007?

Figure 23.1 shows a plausible inverse relationship between credit growth and excess CAR and excess LAH, suggesting that an increase (decrease) in excess CAR and excess LAH results in a decrease (increase) in credit growth. We focus on excesses CAR and excess LAH as opposed to the minimum required holdings because the excesses act as buffers or shock absorbers as discussed in earlier chapters.

In addition, Fig. 23.2 shows that high levels of excess CAR and excess LAH post-2008 coincided with the decline in the share of credit to companies and an increase in the share of credit to households. Thus, what is the role of excess CAR and excess LAH in the transmission of capital inflow shocks to sectorial credit shares? What policy lessons and recommendations can an empirical analysis contained in this chapter offer in terms of the design of policy tools to deal with capital inflow shocks?

[1] See Gumata and Ndou (2019) on how an increase in capital inflows leads to a reduction in the share of credit to household. The authors show that there is significant reallocation of credit to households due to FDI bank and non-bank flow shock as well as to portfolio bank flow shock. Furthermore, increased capital inflows whether in the form of bank and non-bank flow lead to an increase in the share of credit to companies. The share of credit to companies is more sensitive to the bank portfolio inflows compared to the non-bank category.

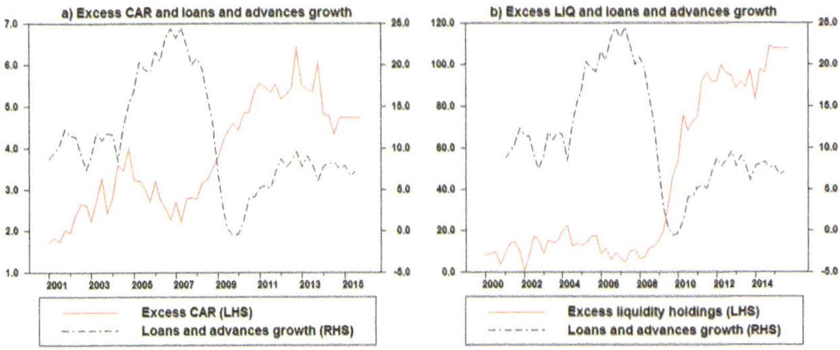

Fig. 23.1 Excess capital adequacy ratio, excess liquid asset holdings and credit growth. (Source: South African Reserve Bank and authors' calculations)

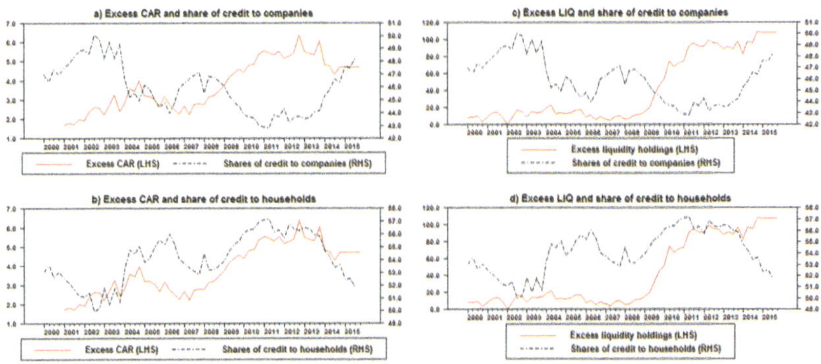

Fig. 23.2 Excess CAR and excess LAH and the shares of credit to companies and households. (Source: South African Reserve Bank and authors' calculations)

23.2 What Is the Impact of Capital Inflows and Outflows on Credit Growth?

This section uses a VAR approach and two versions of counterfactual analysis in the form of (i) an endogenous–exogenous and (ii) the counterfactual approach that shuts off the variable or channel of interest to determine the amplification effects of excess CAR and excess LAH as financial regulatory tools. The quarterly (Q) data used in this chapter spans the period 2001Q1 to 2015Q4. The model uses capital flows (gross inflows, gross outflows, portfolio banking inflows and non-banking inflows) variables as

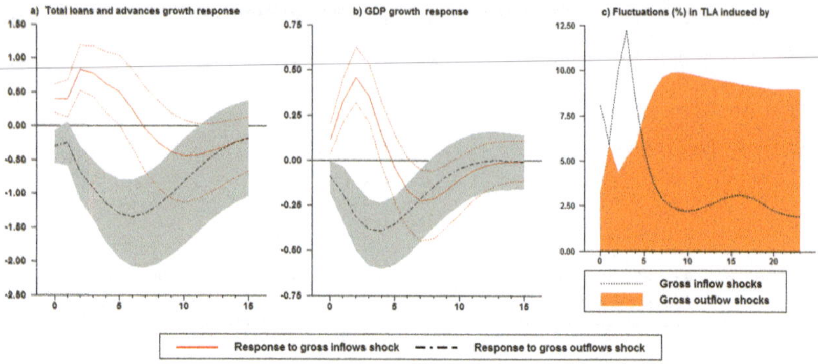

Fig. 23.3 Responses to positive gross capital outflow and inflow shocks. (Note: TLA refers to total loans and advances growth. Source: Authors' calculations)

per cent of GDP, GDP growth, aggregate credit growth, shares of credit to households and companies, inflation, excess CAR, excess LAH and loan loss provisions. The sectoral shares of credit are expressed as per cent of aggregate credit. The data is sourced from the South African Reserve Bank database. All growth rates are an annual rate. The model is estimated using two lags as selected by AIC and uses 10,000 Monte Carlo draws. The shocks refer to one positive standard deviation shocks.

Figure 23.3 shows that a positive gross capital outflow shock has a bigger effect on credit growth and GDP growth as these variables decline significantly compared to their reaction due to a positive gross capital inflow shock. In addition, in Fig. 23.3c gross capital outflow shocks induce more fluctuations in credit growth than the gross capital inflow shocks.

Evidence shows that a positive gross capital outflow shock depresses total credit growth. So, what are the effects on sectorial credit shares? Figure 23.4 shows that positive gross capital inflow and outflow shocks move the shares of credit to companies and households in different directions. This implies that gross capital inflow and outflow shocks have an impact on sectoral credit allocations. Capital flow shocks impact total credit directly and indirectly via sectorial reallocations.[2]

[2] See Gumata and Ndou (2019) for further corroborating evidence on the interaction of capital flows and the sectoral credit reallocation.

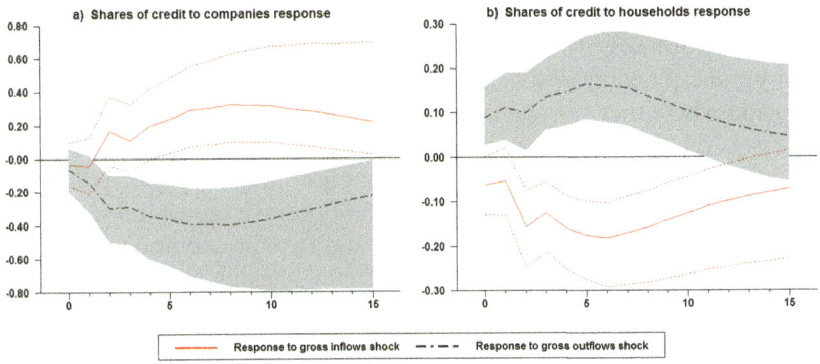

Fig. 23.4 Responses of sectorial credit shares to gross capital inflow and outflow shocks. (Source: Authors' calculations)

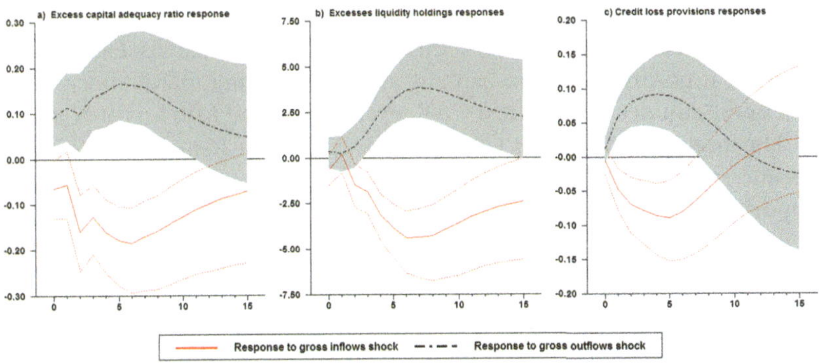

Fig. 23.5 Responses of regulatory tools to positive gross capital inflow and outflow shocks. (Source: Authors' calculations)

23.2.1 What Is the Impact of Gross Capital Inflow and Outflow Shocks on Excesses of CAR and LAH?

The financial regulatory standards set the minimum requirements, but banks also maintain excess holdings. Can excess CAR and excess LAH in part be attributed to shocks to capital flows? Are the credit provisions also impacted by gross capital inflow and outflow shocks? Evidence in Fig. 23.5 shows that positive (negative) gross capital inflow shocks lead to a significant reduction (increase) in excess CAR, excess LAH and loan loss provisions. The periods of significant impact for both gross capital outflow and capital inflow shocks on excess CAR, excess LAH and loan loss provisions last for about nearly 13, 15 and 8 quarters, respectively. The results imply that gross capital inflow shocks loosen the credit and financial constraints of banks where they operate in, since they have an impact on excess CAR, excess LAH and loan loss provisions. These results concur with those established in earlier chapters showing that non-performing loans and the credit conditions impact the transmission of positive capital inflow shocks to credit growth. Evidence showed that tight credit conditions lead to a lower transmission of positive portfolio capital banking inflow shocks into credit growth. During periods of severe global and domestic financial constraints, the direct and indirect ability of positive capital inflow shocks to stimulate credit growth are highly neutralised by the prevailing tight credit conditions. Thus, prevailing credit conditions are conduits through which capital inflow shocks are transmitted to credit growth.

Does the composition of capital inflows matter? We extend the analysis to show the effects of positive portfolio banking and non-banking flow shocks on excess CAR and excess LAH, and loan loss provisions. Figure 23.6 shows that positive portfolio banking and non-banking inflow shocks lead to a significant decline in excess CAR, excess LAH and loan loss provisions.

The finding that excess CAR, excess LAH and loan loss provisions decline (increase) in response to gross capital inflow (outflow) shocks is important but it tells us very little about the impact of the adjustments in regulatory tools on total credit growth and the sectorial credit allocation. This is explored in the next section.

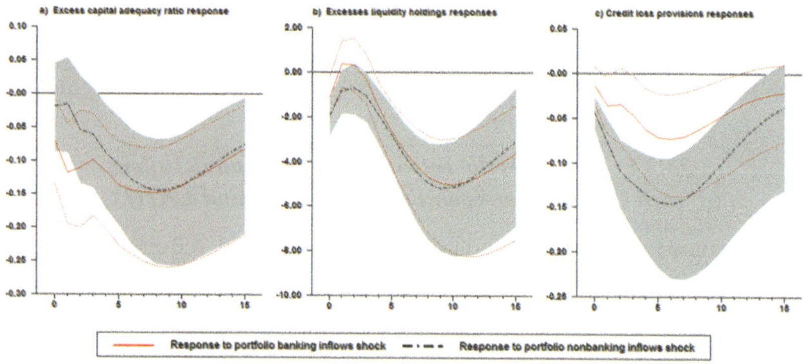

Fig. 23.6 Responses of excess CAR, excess LAH and loan loss provisions to positive portfolio banking and non-banking inflow shocks. (Source: Authors' calculations)

23.2.2 *The Role of Excess CAR and Excess LAH on Credit Growth Dynamics*

Earlier sections showed that positive gross capital inflow and outflow shocks have different effects on the excess CAR, excess LAH and loan loss provisions responses. Furthermore, the data trends presented earlier showed different relationships pre-2008 and post-2008Q1. We therefore use two dummy variables to capture these structural shifts in excess CAR during the sample period. The first dummy variable for excess CAR pre-2008 equals to the value of excess CAR from the beginning of sample to 2007Q4 and zero otherwise. The second dummy variable equals to the value of excess CAR from 2008Q1 to the end of the sample and zero otherwise. These dummy variables are included separately in the VAR estimations.

Figure 23.7 shows the role of excess CAR pre- and post-2008Q1 and evidence indicates that the responses of total credit growth tend to decline more than the counterfactual responses due to positive gross capital outflow shocks. This indicates that excess CAR depresses aggregate credit growth following positive gross capital outflow shocks. The peak amplification in Fig. 23.7c and 23.8c is large in the period post-2008Q1 compared to pre-2008.

In addition, the gross capital inflow shocks increase credit growth but the increases are below what the counterfactual suggests. This indicates that excess CAR dampens the actual increase in total credit growth following a positive gross capital inflow shock. Thus, indeed excess CAR acts as a buffer or a shock absorber.

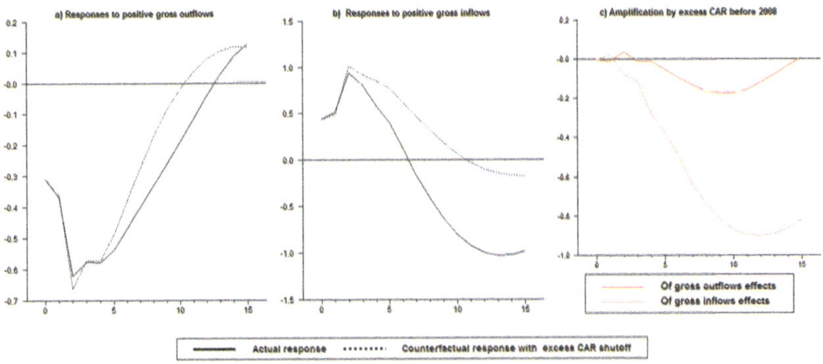

Fig. 23.7 Responses of credit growth and the role excess CAR pre-2008 to positive gross capital flow shocks. (Source: Authors' calculations)

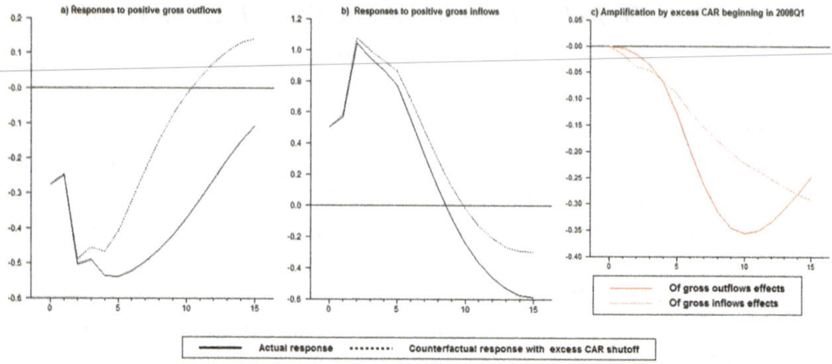

Fig. 23.8 Responses of credit growth and the role excess CAR post-2008 to positive gross capital flow shocks. (Source: Authors' calculations)

These results show that positive gross capital outflow shocks lead to a pronounced amplification on aggregate credit growth. This can indicate asymmetric effects between capital inflows and outflows on total credit. Positive gross capital outflow shocks may have adverse effects on aggregate credit growth which may linger for a prolonged period.

23.2.3 *Evidence from the Endogenous–Exogenous VAR Approach*

This section assesses the robustness of the preceding findings by using the endogenous–exogenous VAR approach. Figure 23.9 shows that indeed excess CAR leads to a pronounced contraction due to positive gross capital outflow shocks when excess CAR is endogenous in the model compared to when it is exogenous in the model. This suggests that excess CAR dampens aggregate credit growth following a positive gross capital outflow shock. The evidence is robust to the role of excess CAR pre- and post-2008Q1.

23.2.4 *The Transmission of Shocks via Sectorial Credit Reallocations Based on the Endogenous–Exogenous Approach*

This section explores the transmission of capital outflow and inflow shocks via sectoral credit growth. We estimate the endogenous–exogenous VAR model and replace aggregate credit growth with the household and company credit shares. The results in Fig. 23.10 show that a positive gross capital outflow shock increases the share of credit to households at the

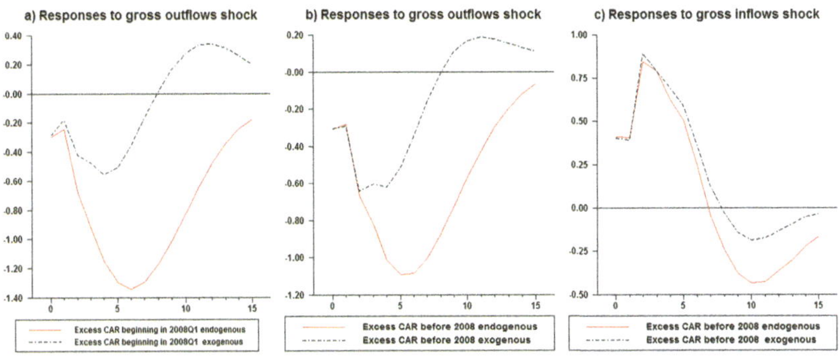

Fig. 23.9 Credit growth responses to positive gross capital flow shocks. (Source: Authors' calculations)

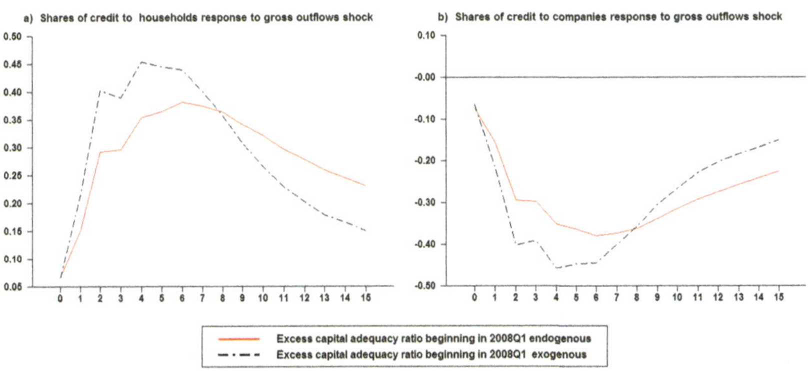

Fig. 23.10 Responses to positive gross capital outflow shocks. (Source: Authors' calculations)

expense of a decline in the share of credit to companies. This means that positive gross capital outflow shocks operate via sectorial reallocation of credit. The share of credit to households increases more when excess CAR is exogenous in the model than when it is endogenous. This evidence concurs with Gumata and Ndou (2019) who show that foreign direct investment (FDI) bank inflow, FDI non-bank inflow and portfolio bank inflow shocks result in a significant reallocation of credit to households.

In addition, the results indicate a pronounced decline in the share of credit to companies when excess CAR is exogenous in the model compared to when it is endogenous in the model. This implies that excess CAR cushioned the contraction in the share of credit to companies. Overall, this means that excess CAR as a financial regulatory tool also works via its impact on the reallocation of sectoral credit shares following gross capital inflow shocks.

23.2.5 *How Robust Are the Channels of Transmission via Sectorial Credit Reallocation?*

This section examines the robustness of the sectorial reallocation effects induced by positive gross capital outflow shocks via the counterfactual VAR approach. We shut off the excess CAR channel to assess its role. The impulse response when the excess CAR channel is shut off measures the amplifying effect of this financial regulatory tool. Figure 23.11 shows that the counterfactual share of credit to household increases more than the actual increase. This means that excess CAR dampens the increase in the share of credit to households. At the same time, excess CAR cushions against a severe decline in the share of credit to companies.

This means that excess CAR dampens the increase in the share of credit to households. At the same time, excess CAR cushions against a severe decline in the share of credit to companies.

23.2.6 *How Different Is the Role of Excess LAH?*

This section explores the role of excess LAH as a conduit and amplification channel of positive shocks to gross capital flows. We replace excess CAR with excess LAH in the counterfactual VAR estimations. Figure 23.12

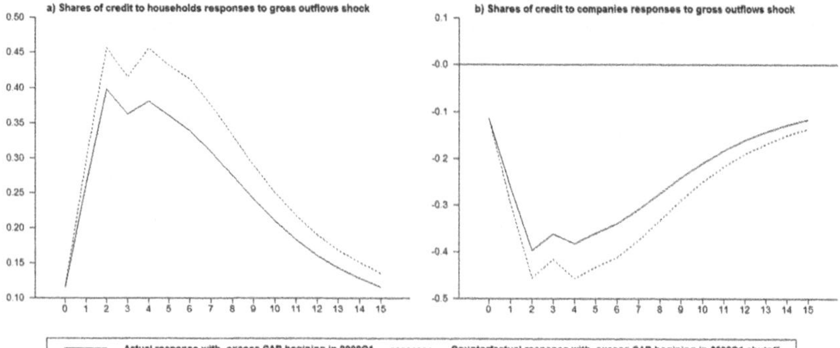

Fig. 23.11 Responses of sectorial credit shares to a positive gross capital outflow shock. (Source: Authors' calculations)

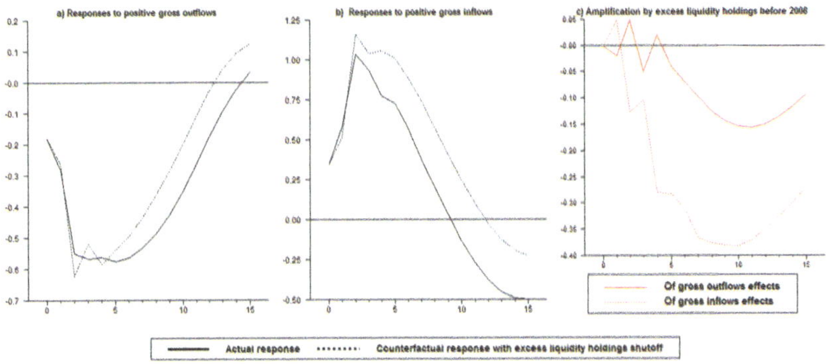

Fig. 23.12 Responses of credit growth to positive gross capital outflow and inflow shocks and the role of excess LAH. (Source: Authors' calculations)

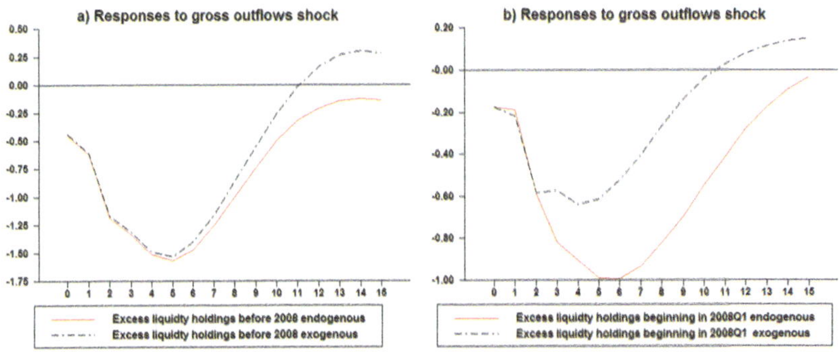

Fig. 23.13 Total credit growth responses to positive gross capital outflow shocks and the role of excess LAH. (Source: Authors' calculations)

shows that aggregate credit growth declines (increases) more than the counterfactual due to positive gross capital outflows (inflows) shocks. This indicates that excess LAH cushions (dampens) the decline (increase) in aggregate credit growth.

23.2.7 Does the Evidence of the Role of Excess LAH Differ When the Endogenous–Exogenous Approach Is Used?

The results in Fig. 23.13 indicate that total credit growth declines more when excess LAH is endogenous in the model than when it is exogenous. This means that excess LAH also has a worsening effect on aggregate credit growth contraction following a positive gross capital outflow shock. Like the results established for excess CAR, the depressing effects on credit growth may be prolonged.

23.2.8 *How Potent Is the Sectorial Credit Reallocation via the Excess LAH Channel?*

We conclude the analysis by looking at the role of excess LAH on the sectoral reallocation of the shares of credit to companies and households using the endogenous–exogenous VAR approach. We use excess LAH as an endogenous in one model and as an exogenous variable in another model. Figure 23.14 shows the responses of the sectoral credit shares of credit to companies. The share of credit to companies increases (declines) due to positive gross capital inflow (outflow) shocks. This evidence suggests that the share of credit to companies would have increased more when excess LAH is exogenous in the model than when it is endogenous in the model. This means that excess LAH dampens the increases in the share of credit to companies following a positive gross capital inflow shock. In addition, excess LAH mitigates a big contraction in the share of credit to companies due to a positive gross capital outflow shock.

Figure 23.15 shows that a positive gross capital inflow shock lowers the share of credit to households and the gross capital outflows increase the share. When excess LAH is exogenous in the model, the share of credit to households declines more indicating that excess LAH neutralises the contraction in the share of credit to households. In addition, Fig. 23.15(b)

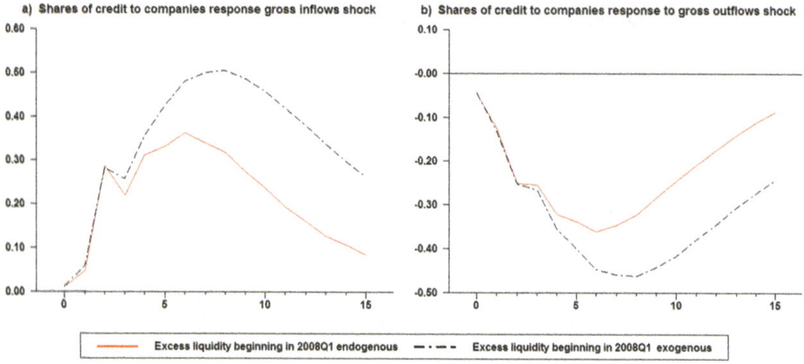

Fig. 23.14 Responses to positive gross capital outflow and inflow shocks. (Source: Authors' calculations)

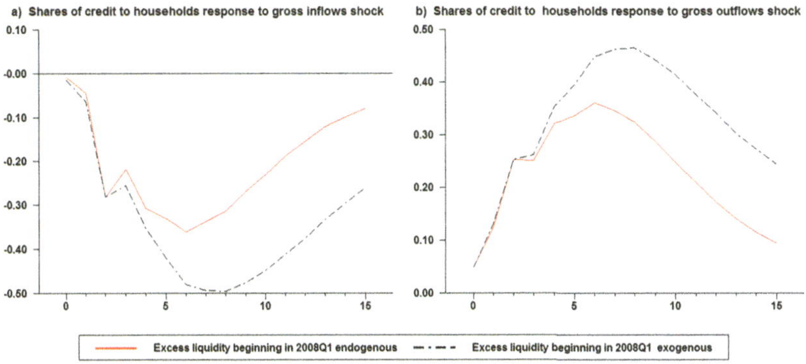

Fig. 23.15 Responses to positive gross capital outflow and inflow shocks. (Source: Authors' calculations)

shows that the household credit share increases less when excess LAH is exogenous in the model.

23.2.9 Are the Amplification Effects Exerted by Excess LAH and Excess CAR Like Those of Monetary Policy Shocks?

To facilitate a comparison of two tools, this section shows which one between excess CAR and excess LAH has severe depressing effects on aggregate credit growth due to positive gross capital outflow shocks. We create dummy variables for excess LAH and excess CAR which take on the values for these variables post-2007 and zero pre-2007. The results in Fig. 23.16 show that although excess CAR and excess LAH move aggregate credit growth in the same direction, excess CAR amplifies the depressing effects of gross capital outflow shocks compared to excess LAH.

In addition, we show the role of contractionary repo rate shocks and compare their amplification effects to those due to excess CAR using the endogenous and exogenous VAR model. Figure 23.17 shows that excess CAR and excess LAH move aggregate credit growth in the same direction as that due to a contractionary monetary policy shock. Thus, tight monetary policy during periods of positive gross capital outflow shocks leads to a pronounced decline in aggregate credit growth.

The results in this chapter concur with those established in Gumata and Ndou (2017) showing that the National Credit Act (NCA), loan-to-value (LTV) ratio and repayment-to-income (RTI) ratio as macro-prudential tools complement monetary policy in lowering inflation expectations and

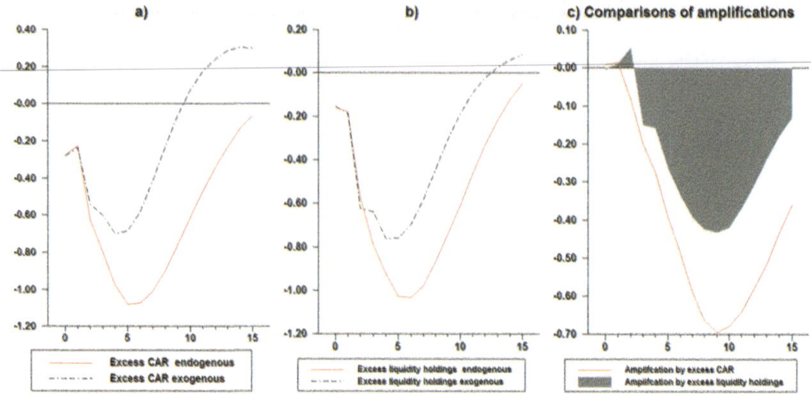

Fig. 23.16 Credit growth responses to gross capital outflow shocks and the amplification by excess LAH and excess CAR. (Source: Authors' calculations)

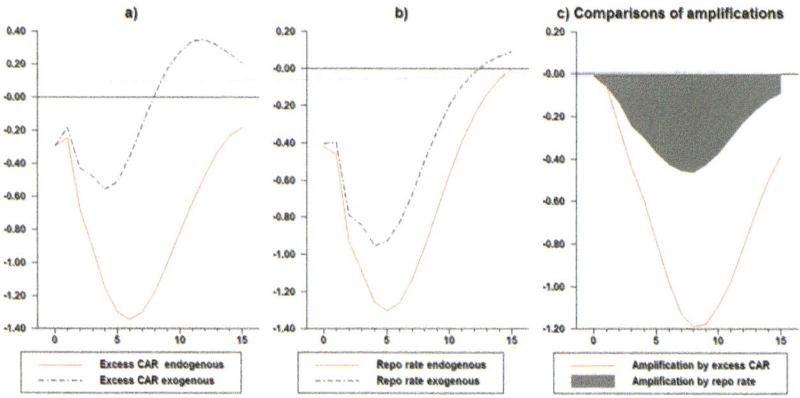

Fig. 23.17 Credit growth responses to gross capital outflow shocks and the amplification by excess LAH and tight repo rate. (Source: Authors' calculations)

dampening credit demand-driven inflationary pressures. The financial regulatory tools in the form of excess CAR and excess LAH play a part in moderating aggregate and sectoral credit cycles due to gross capital flow shocks. Thus, excess CAR and excess LAH complement monetary policy in mitigating against capital flow episodes, credit booms and severe busts.

Evidence indicates that they are suitably placed to guard or cushion against the capital flow effects on credit growth, credit booms and busts.

However, excess CAR and exces LAH impose quantity as well as price effects or costs on banks. Hence, they possibly act as supply and demand shocks via increasing the availability of credit but at the same time increasing the cost of credit via the lending rate spreads. This means that they also neutralise monetary policy accommodation. At the same time, they reinforce monetary policy tightening on the macro-economy. This is particularly important given that capital flow shocks tend to act in the same fashion as large financial and supply shocks such as the exchange rate which shift the policy trade-off.

23.3 Conclusion and Policy Implications

This chapter assessed whether excess CAR and excess LAH are conduits or channels in the transmission of gross capital inflow and outflow shocks on credit growth and the reallocation of sectorial credit shares. First, evidence establishes a plausible inverse relationship between credit growth and excess CAR and excess LAH, suggesting that an increase (decrease) in excess CAR and excess LAH results in a decrease (increase) in credit growth. Furthermore, high excess CAR and excess LAH post-2008 coincided with the decline in the share of credit to households and an increase in the share of credit to companies Second, positive gross capital outflow (inflow) shocks depress (increase) credit growth and GDP growth but move the shares of credit to companies and households in different directions. In addition, gross capital outflow shocks induce more fluctuations in credit growth than gross capital inflow shocks.

Do shocks to gross capital flows impact excess CAR and excess LAH and loan loss provisions? Evidence shows that positive (negative) gross capital inflow shocks lead to a significant reduction (increase) in excess CAR, excess LAH and loan loss provisions. Similarly, positive (negative) portfolio banking inflow and non-banking inflow shocks lead to a significant decline (increase) in excess CAR, excess LAH and loan loss provisions. Thus, capital flow shocks loosen the credit and financial constraints banks operate in since they have an impact on excess CAR, excess LAH and loan loss provisions. Furthermore, evidence shows that excess CAR exerted asymmetric effects on aggregate credit growth due to positive gross capital inflow and outflow shocks pre- and post-2008Q1. Excess CAR cushioned (dampened) aggregate credit growth following a positive gross capital outflow (inflow) shock. The peak amplification effects were large post-2008Q1 compared to pre-2008. Thus, indeed excess CAR acts a buffer as or a shock absorber.

Does excess CAR and excess LAH play a role in the transmission of gross capital inflow and outflow shocks via sectorial credit shares? Evidence shows that a positive gross capital outflow shock increases the share of credit to households at the expense of a decline in the share of credit to companies. In addition, the results indicate that excess CAR and excess LAH cushioned the contraction in the share of credit to companies. Excess CAR and excess LAH play different amplification effects on sectoral credit. On the one hand, excess CAR and excess LAH dampen the increase in the share of credit to households. At the same time, excess CAR and excess LAH cushion against a severe decline in the share of credit to companies. Furthermore, contractionary monetary policy, excess CAR and excess LAH shocks exert the same downward effects on aggregate credit growth.

Overall, this means that excess CAR and excess LAH as financial regulatory tool also works via their impact on the reallocation sectoral credit shares following gross capital inflow shocks. Excess CAR and excess LAH exert the same effects on aggregate credit growth and sectoral credit shares in response to gross capital inflow and outflow shocks. But excess CAR exerts pronounced adverse effects on aggregate credit growth compared to excess LAH. At the same, contractionary monetary policy, excess CAR and excess LAH propagate each other's effects and move aggregate credit growth in the same direction. Thus, as financial regulatory tools, excess CAR and excess LAH complement each other and the effects of contractionary monetary policy on aggregate credit growth.

However, excess CAR and excess LAH impose quantity as well as price effects or costs on banks. They act as supply and demand shocks via increasing the availability of credit but at the same time increasing the cost of credit via the lending rate spreads. This means that they also neutralise monetary policy accommodation. They reinforce monetary policy tightening on the macro-economy. This is particularly important given that capital flow shocks tend to act in the same fashion, as large financial and supply shocks such as the exchange rate which shift the policy trade-off. Macro-prudential tools such as the NCA, LTV ratio and RTI ratio also exert additional effects on credit growth and the macro-economy. Hence, we recommend the coordination of the financial regulation, macro-prudential and monetary policy tools.

References

Gumata N and Ndou E. 2017. Bank Credit Extension and Real Economic Activity in South Africa: The Impact of Capital Flow Dynamics, Bank Regulation and Selected Macroprudential Tools. Palgrave Macmillan. ISB 978-3-319-43550-3.

Gumata N and Ndou E. 2019. Capital Flows, Credit Markets and Growth in South Africa: The Role of Global Economic Growth, Policy Shifts and Uncertainties. Palgrave Macmillan ISBN 978-3-030-30882-2.

Igan D and Tan Z. 2015. Capital Inflows, Credit Growth, and Financial Systems. IMF Working paper WP/15/193.

CHAPTER 24

What Role Do Non-performing Loans Play in Propagating the Excess Liquid Asset Holdings Shock Effects on Sectoral Credit Re-allocation?

Research Questions Explored

- Establish whether non-performing loans play a role in propagating the excess LAH shock effects on sectoral credit reallocation.
- Determine whether the effects of excess LAH differ during 2000Q1 to 2015Q4 and 2008Q1 to 2015Q4.

24.1 Introduction

Earlier chapters showed that capital inflow shocks loosen the credit and financial constraints and impact how banks operate since they have an impact on the excess capital adequacy ratio (CAR), excess liquid asset holdings (LAH) of banks and loan loss provisions. Furthermore, excess CAR and LAH as financial regulatory tools exert the same effects on aggregate credit growth and sectoral credit shares in response to capital inflow and outflow shocks. At the same time, contractionary monetary policy, excess CAR and LAH propagate each other's effects and move aggregate credit growth in the same direction. However, earlier chapters did not assess the role of bank credit risk as captured by non-performing loans (NPLs). It is against this background that this chapter extends the analysis and explores the role of NPLs in propagating the excess LAH shock effects on sectoral credit re-allocation.

N. Gumata, E. Ndou, *Achieving Price, Financial and Macro-Economic Stability in South Africa*,
https://doi.org/10.1007/978-3-030-66340-7_24

Figure 24.1 shows that LAH of banks exceeded the minimum required. Excess LAH increased from 20 per cent in 2008 to more than 100 per cent in 2015Q4. During this period, credit to government in Fig. 24.2 increased given that purchases of government securities by banks represent credit to government.

Thus, excess LAH of banks almost matched credit to government one-to-one. While the purpose of holding excess liquid assets may be for

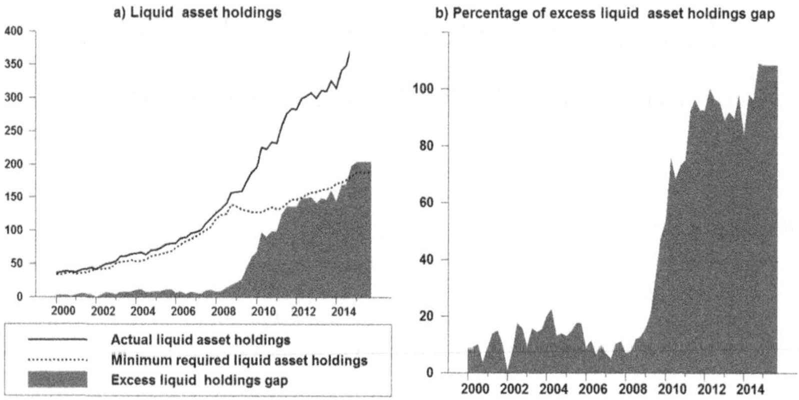

Fig. 24.1 Actual and minimum required liquid asset holdings. (Source: South African Reserve Bank and authors' calculations)

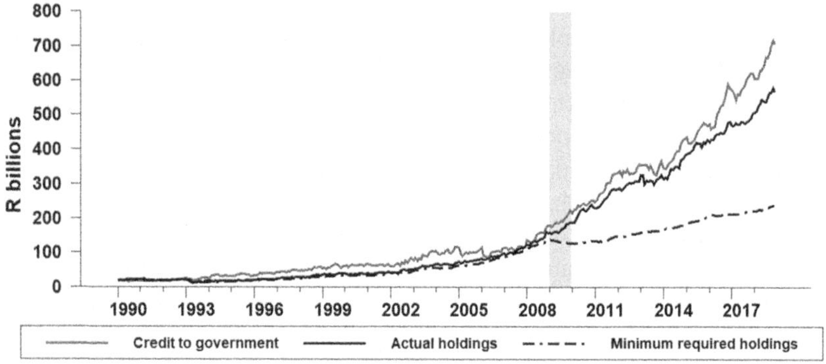

Fig. 24.2 Actual and minimum required liquid holdings and credit to government. (Source: South African Reserve Bank and authors' calculations)

financial regulatory concerns, it is also important for policy analysis to assess its effects on the sectoral allocation of credit. Excess LAH by banks could also mean that there are distortions in the allocation of credit that could be used to support productive economic activities.

This chapter fills academic and policy research gaps by establishing whether NPLs as a credit risk measure play a role in propagating the excess LAH shock effects on sectoral credit reallocation. In addition, we determine whether the effects of excess LAH differ during 2000Q1 to 2015Q4 and 2008Q1 to 2015Q4.

24.2 Evidence of the Amplification Role of the Excess LAH on Aggregate Credit Growth

To assess the role of NPLs in propagating the excess LAH shock effects on aggregate credit growth, this section uses the counterfactual and endogenous–exogenous VAR approaches. We modify the Pentecôte and Rondeau (2015) and Cerra and Saxena (2008) approaches and apply them to the credit Eq. (24.1):

$$Credit_t = constant + \sum_{i=1}^{4} \beta_i credit_{t-i} + \sum_{i=0}^{4} c_i EXC\_LIQH_{t-i} + \sum_{i=0}^{2} d_i Dummy_{t-i} + \varepsilon_t \tag{24.1}$$

where, ε_t denotes the error term, EXC_LIQH denotes the excess LAH. Dummy refers to an adverse financial shock starting in 2007Q3. The adverse financial shock is defined using a dummy variable which equals one for the period 2007Q3 to the end of the sample and zero otherwise. This dummy variable encompasses the beginning of the global financial crisis, domestic and global recession, various rounds of quantitative easing in advanced economies and periods of global economic instability associated with the euro area sovereign debt crisis. We determine the actual and counterfactual aggregate credit growth responses. The actual (counterfactual) aggregate credit growth responses refer to aggregate credit growth responses when a specific transmission channel is included (excluded) in the model. The propagating (magnifying) or restraining (stifling) ability of the specific variable and channel is determined by the gap between the actual and counterfactual responses. The analysis uses quarterly (Q) data spanning 2000Q1 to 2015Q4. We use aggregate credit growth, GDP growth, excess LAH and NPLs expressed as a ratio of aggregate credit. The data is sourced from the South African Reserve Bank. All growth rates are at an annual rate.

24.2.1 Does the Excess Liquidity Holdings Matter for the Transmission of Adverse Financial Shocks Effects to GDP Growth?

This section assesses the response of aggregate credit growth and GDP growth using Eq. (24.1). In the VAR estimations, when assessing the role of GDP growth, we replace credit growth with GDP growth in Eq. (24.1). We test for the effects of the increase in excess LAH and credit to government by subdividing the sample into (i) 2000Q1 to 2015Q4 and (ii) 2008Q1 to 2015Q4. Figure 24.3 shows the cumulative responses of credit growth to an adverse financial shock. The gap between the actual and counterfactual responses indicates the degree of propagation induced by excess LAH. Evidence in Fig. 24.3a shows that an adverse financial shock lowers credit growth. But the decline is more pronounced in the presence of excess LAH for the sample period 2008Q1 to 2015Q4. Figure 24.3c shows that excess LAH was much more of a drag on credit growth during 2008Q1 to 2015Q4 compared to the 2000Q1 to 2015Q4.

A similar pattern emerges in Fig. 24.4 showing that excess LAH acts as a conduit in the transmission of adverse financial shocks into GDP growth.

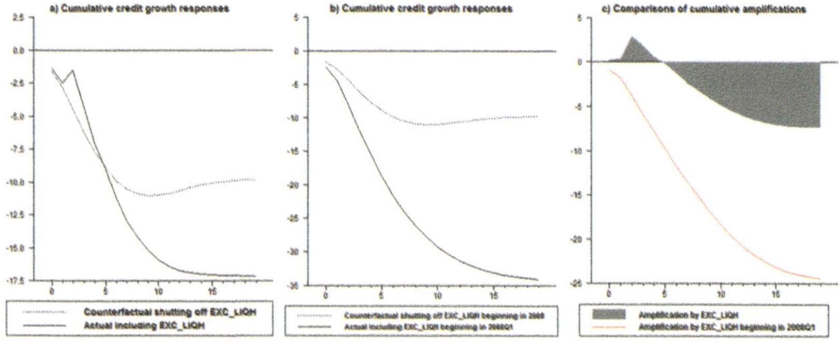

Fig. 24.3 Cumulative credit growth responses to an adverse financial shock and the role of excess LAH. (Source: Authors' calculations)

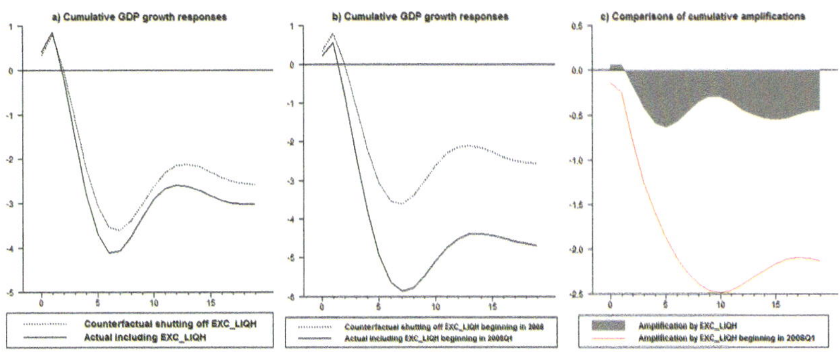

Fig. 24.4 Cumulative GDP growth responses to an adverse financial shock and the role of excess LAH. (Source: Authors' calculations)

GDP growth declines due to an adverse financial shock and the contraction is larger in the presence of excess LAH. Figure 24.4c shows that excess LAH had pronounced negative effects during 2008Q1 to 2015Q4. This evidence shows that excess LAH during economic turbulence and uncertainty may exacerbate the economic growth contraction.

24.2.2 *The Different Role of Excess LAH Shocks and Non-performing Loans on Sectorial Credit Shares*

How did excess LAH impact the sectorial credit shares? Were excess LAH shocks transmitted via NPLs? This section uses a VAR model with the excess LAH dummy indicator, GDP growth, inflation, sectoral credit shares and NPLs. We use NPLs as an exogenous and endogenous variable in different models. The models are estimated using two lags and 10,000 Monte Carlo draws. The sectorial credit shares refer to the shares of credit to households and companies and are included separately in the model. The excess liquid asset holdings dummy indicator refers to two separate dummies. The first dummy liquidty_2007Q4 equals the value of excess LAH for the period 2000Q1 to 2007Q4 and zero otherwise. The second dummy liquidty_2008Q1 equals the value of excess LAH during 2008Q1 to 2015Q4 and zero otherwise.

Figure 24.5 shows that a positive excess LAH shock has different effects pre- and post-2007Q4. Pre-2007Q4, a positive excess LAH shock, increased credit to the households ($\text{Credit}_{\text{hh}}$) but results in a decline post-2008.

Furthermore, the NPLs dampen the increase in the share of credit to households due to a positive shock to excess LAH in Fig. 24.5a. This means that NPLs accentuated the contraction in the share of credit to households. What about the effects of excess LAH shock on credit to companies ($\text{Credit}_{\text{comp}}$). Evidence in Fig. 24.6 shows that credit to companies contracted due to excess LAH shock pre-2007Q4. The excess liquidity shock impacted the credit to companies differently before and after 2007Q4.

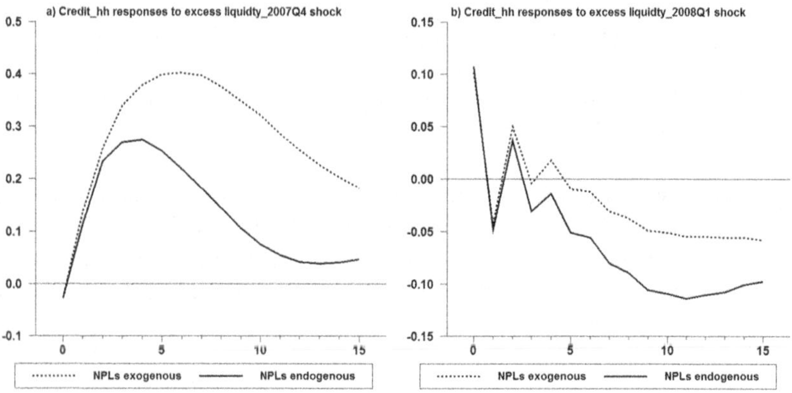

Fig. 24.5 Responses of credit to households to positive excess LAH shocks and the role of non-performing loans. (Source: Authors' calculations)

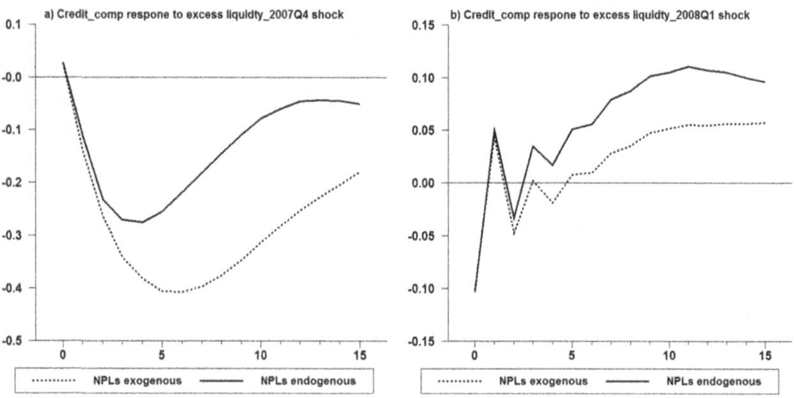

Fig. 24.6 Responses of credit to companies to positive excess liquidity shocks and the role of non-performing loans. (Source: Authors' calculations)

24.3 Conclusion and Policy Implications

Do the excess LAH of banks matter for the transmission of adverse financial shock effects to credit growth and GDP growth? First, we establish that LAH of banks exceeded the minimum required and increased from 20 per cent in 2008 to more than 100 per cent in 2015Q4. The increase in excess LAH moved one-to-one with credit to government. Second, evidence shows that an adverse financial shock lowers credit growth and GDP growth and excess LAH resulted in a more pronounced decline for the sample period 2008Q1 to 2015Q4. Excess LAH was a drag on credit growth more during 2008Q1 to 2015Q4 compared to 2000Q1 to 2015Q4.

How did excess LAH impact the sectorial credit shares? Were excess LAH shocks transmitted via NPLs? Evidence shows that positive shocks to excess LAH did impact the share of credit to households and companies, and the effects differed between 2000Q1 to 2015Q4 and 2008Q1 to 2015Q4. During 2000Q1 to 2015Q4, a positive excess LAH shock increased credit to the households and companies compared to a decline during 2008Q1 to 2015Q4. Furthermore, the NPLs dampened the increases in the share of credit to households due to a positive shock to excess LAH. This means that NPLs accentuated the contraction in the share of credit to households. Thus, excess LAH during 2008Q1 to 2015Q4 resulted in the sectoral credit reallocation from the households and corporate sector to government. The adverse shock effects of excess LAH on sector credit allocation were exacerbated by the increase in credit risk as captured by the NPLs. Excess LAH by banks in compliance with the financial regulatory standards dampened credit growth and GDP growth, and amplified the adverse effects of heightened credit risk. Hence, the evidence contained in this chapter further reinforces the policy recommendation of the coordination of financial regulation, macro-prudential and monetary policy tools.

References

Cerra V and Saxena C S. 2008. Growth Dynamics: The Myth of Economic Recovery. American Economic Review. VOL. 98, NO. 1, March 2008 (pp. 439–57).

Gumata N and Ndou E. 2017. Bank Credit Extension and Real Economic Activity in South Africa: The Impact of Capital Flow Dynamics, Bank Regulation and Selected Macroprudential Tools. Palgrave Macmillan. ISB 978-3-319-43550-3.

Gumata N and Ndou E. 2019. Capital Flows, Credit Markets and Growth in South Africa: The Role of Global Economic Growth, Policy Shifts and Uncertainties. Palgrave Macmillan ISBN 978-3-030-30882-2.

Igan D and Tan Z. 2015. Capital Inflows, Credit Growth, and Financial Systems. IMF Working paper WP/15/193.

Pentecôte J-S and Rondeau F. 2015. Trade spillovers on output growth during the 2008 financial crisis. International Economics, CEPII research center, issue 143, pages 36–47.

CHAPTER 25

Is the Excess Capital Adequacy Ratio Beneficial in Neutralising Excessive Credit Growth and Inflationary Pressures? What Are the Implications for Monetary and Financial Policy?

Research Questions Explored

- Examine the role of excess capital adequacy ratio (CAR) in amplifying the effects of positive shocks such as aggregate demand and supply shocks on credit growth.
- Assess the impact of excess CAR in propagating or dampening positive cost pull or push shocks to inflation.
- Show periods during which the impact of excess CAR was beneficial in neutralising inflationary pressures and excessive credit growth and the impact on GDP growth.
- Compare the persistence of excess CAR shocks on inflation, credit growth and GDP growth.

25.1 Introduction

Earlier chapters showed that excess capital adequacy ratio (CAR) and excess liquid asset holdings (LAH) of banks reinforce tight monetary policy shocks. Furthermore, excess CAR exerts pronounced adverse effects on aggregate credit growth compared to excess LAH. At the same time,

N. Gumata, E. Ndou, *Achieving Price, Financial and Macro-Economic Stability in South Africa*,
https://doi.org/10.1007/978-3-030-66340-7_25

contractionary monetary policy, excess CAR and LAH propagate each other's effects and move aggregate credit growth in the same direction. Evidence also showed that excess LAH by banks in compliance with the financial regulatory standards dampened credit growth and GDP growth, and amplified the adverse effects of heightened credit risk as captured by the non-performing loans. However, these chapters did not assess whether excess CAR and LAH by banks were beneficial in neutralising inflationary pressures, excessive credit growth and therefore the impact on the pace, magnitude and duration of the repo rate changes. Thus, this chapter asks: What is the impact of excess CAR on excessive credit growth and inflationary pressures? Did excess CAR neutralise the repo rate adjustments to inflationary pressures?

As a precursor to the analysis, Fig. 25.1 shows the evolution of excess CAR and how it is related to GDP growth. It is evident that excess CAR increased more post-2008, at a time when GDP growth was subdued compared to what it was when GDP growth was buoyant pre-2008. This indicates that excess CAR is another channel through which a tightening in the financial regulatory stance is transmitted through the banking sector to affect real economic activity.

This chapter fills academic and policy research gaps by examining the role of excess CAR in amplifying the effects of positive aggregate demand and supply shocks on credit growth. In addition, we assess the impact of excess CAR in propagating or dampening positive cost pull or push shocks to inflation. We show periods during which the impact of excess CAR was beneficial in neutralising inflationary pressures, excessive credit growth and the impact on GDP growth. The analysis in the chapter also compares the persistence of excess CAR shocks on inflation, credit growth and GDP growth.

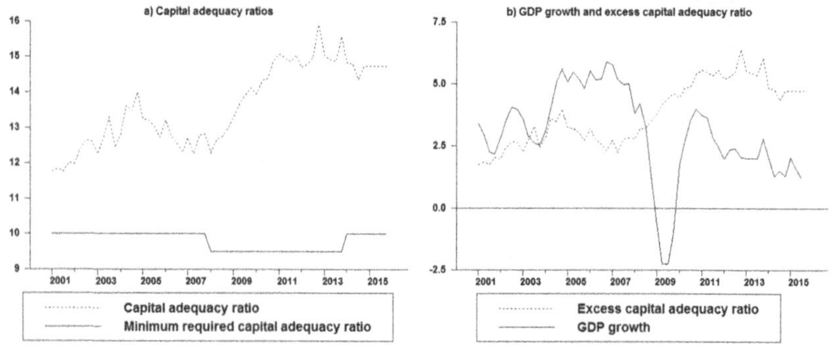

Fig. 25.1 The evolution of the capital adequacy ratio and GDP growth. (Source: South African Reserve Bank and authors' calculations)

25.2 Evidence of the Amplification Role of Excess CAR

This section uses the modified Pentecôte and Rondeau (2015) and Cerra and Saxena (2008) counterfactual VAR approaches to Eq. (25.1).

$$Credit_t = Constant + \sum_{i=1}^{4} \beta_i credit_{t-i} + \sum_{i=0}^{4} c_i CAR_{t-i} + \sum_{i=0}^{4} d_i Dummy_{t-i} + \varepsilon_t \quad (25.1)$$

where ε_t denotes the error term, *CAR* denotes the capital adequacy ratio and *Dummy* refers to the dummy variable used to determine the different effects of various shocks. The first dummy is equal to the value of excess CAR from 2000Q1 to 2007Q4 and zero otherwise. The second dummy is equal to the value of excess CAR from 2008Q1 to 2015Q4 and zero otherwise. These dummies are used separately in the estimations. We determine the actual and counterfactual credit growth responses. The actual (counterfactual) credit growth responses refer to credit growth responses when a specific transmission channel from that variable is included (excluded) in the model. The propagating (magnifying) or restraining (stifling) ability of the specific variable and channel is determined by the gap between the actual and counterfactual responses. The analysis uses quarterly (Q) data spanning 2000Q1 to 2015Q4. The VAR models include credit growth, GDP growth, inflation, minimum required CAR, excess CAR and the repo rate. All growth rates are at annual rate. The data is sourced from the South African Reserve Bank database.

25.2.1 *The Role of Excess CAR in Amplifying Selected Economic Responses Pre- and Post-2007*

The analysis in this section starts by examining the role of excess CAR in amplifying the effects of positive shocks such as aggregate demand and supply shocks on credit growth. Figure 25.2 shows that the actual response of credit growth to a positive shock to excess CAR exceeds the counterfactual responses. This means that excess CAR (EX_CAR) dampened the increase in credit growth due to positive demand shocks, especially post-2008 in Fig. 25.2(c).

We replaced credit growth in Eq. (25.1) with GDP growth to assess the role of excess CAR in transmitting positive demand shocks to real

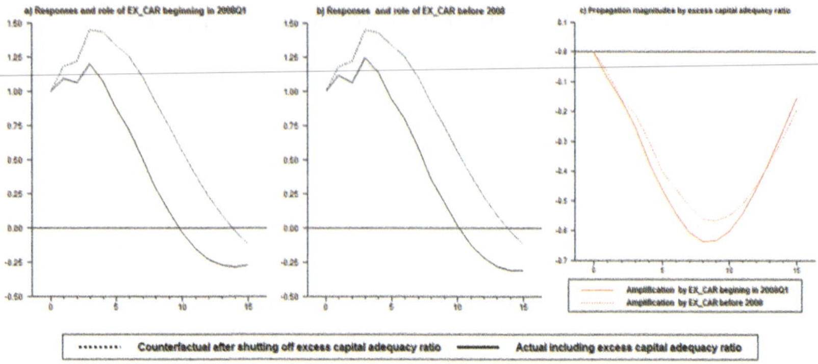

Fig. 25.2 Responses of credit growth to positive demand shocks and the role of excess CAR. (Source: Authors' calculations)

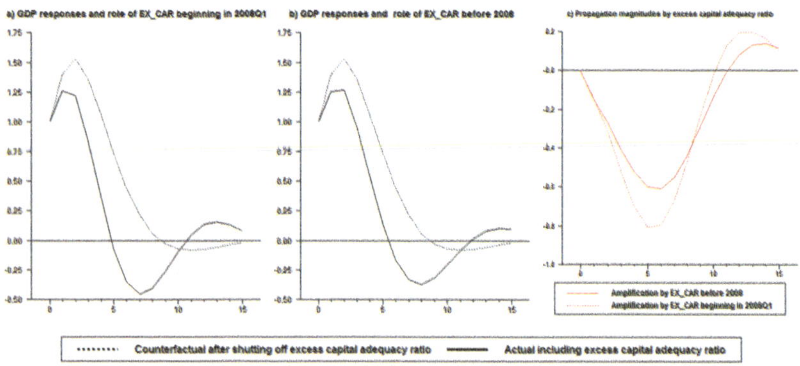

Fig. 25.3 GDP growth responses to positive demand shocks and the role of excess CAR. (Source: Authors' calculations)

economic activity. Figure 25.3 shows that the increase in GDP growth due to positive demand shocks is dampened by excess CAR (EX_CAR). The amplification effects in Fig. 25.3(c) show that excess CAR depressed GDP growth especially post-2008Q1. Thus, excess CAR dampens the impact of demand shocks on credit growth and GDP growth in line with the intended primary purpose of countering the financial cycle. But it is also true that excess CAR propagates and amplifies adverse demand shocks on credit growth and GDP growth as was the case post-2007. Hence, in part credit growth and GDP growth remained subdued post-2008.

What is the impact of excess CAR on inflation? To answer this question, we replaced credit growth with inflation in Eq. (25.1) to examine the role of excess CAR in transmitting positive cost pull or push shocks to inflation. Evidence shows that actual inflation increases less than the counterfactual response in Fig. 25.4 suggesting that excess CAR dampened inflationary pressures post-2008Q1.

25.2.2 *Did Excess CAR Cushion or Propagate the Response of Credit Growth and GDP Growth to the Adverse Financial Shock in 2007Q3?*

To determine the role of excess CAR during periods of adverse financial shocks we create a dummy variable and define an adverse financial shock as a dummy equal to one for the period 2007Q3 to the end of the sample and zero otherwise. The period 2007Q3 to 2015Q4 includes the domestic recession, global financial crisis and the euro area sovereign crisis. Figure 25.5 shows that GDP growth declines more due to adverse financial shocks.

However, the decline depicted by the counterfactual GDP growth response is less severe than the actual impulse responses. This shows that excess CAR worsened the decline in GDP growth due to an adverse financial shock. In addition, Fig. 25.5(c) shows that excess CAR post-2008Q1 had larger cumulative depressing effect on GDP growth. This means that the increase in excess CAR worsened the response of

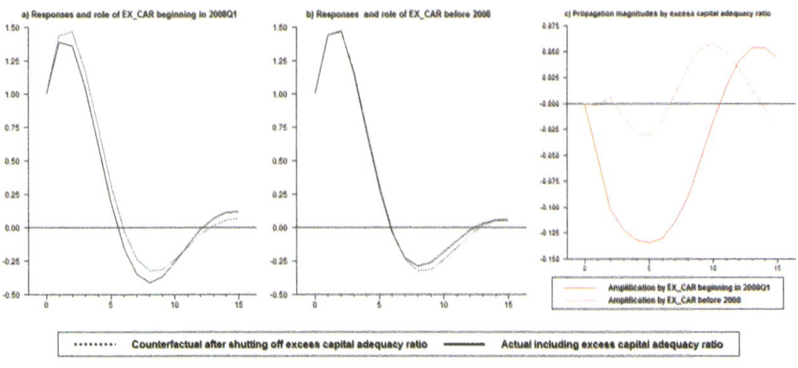

Fig. 25.4 Inflation responses to positive shocks and the role of excess CAR. (Source: Authors' calculations)

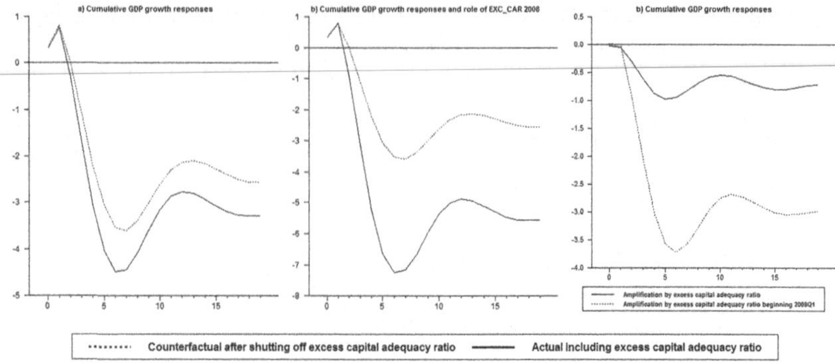

Fig. 25.5 Cumulative GDP growth responses to adverse financial shocks and the role of excess CAR. (Source: Authors' calculations)

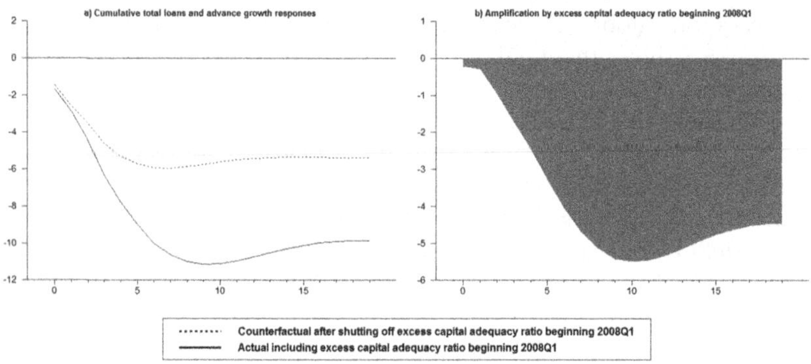

Fig. 25.6 Credit growth responses to adverse financial shocks and the role of excess CAR post-2008Q1. (Source: Authors' calculations)

GDP growth to adverse financial shocks. This indicates that excess CAR propagates financial shocks via the financial accelerator mechanism. Excess CAR plays its intended role as a cushion for banks and prevents balance sheet damage due to severe financial shocks and adverse shocks to the business cycle. But at the same time excess CAR is detrimental to growth because it restricts the supply of credit during severe financial shocks.

Did the excess CAR transmit the effects of adverse financial shocks to credit growth and inflation? Fig. 25.6(b) shows that excess CAR post-2008Q1 exacerbated the decline in credit growth as the decline in the actual credit growth responses is more than what the counterfactual suggests.

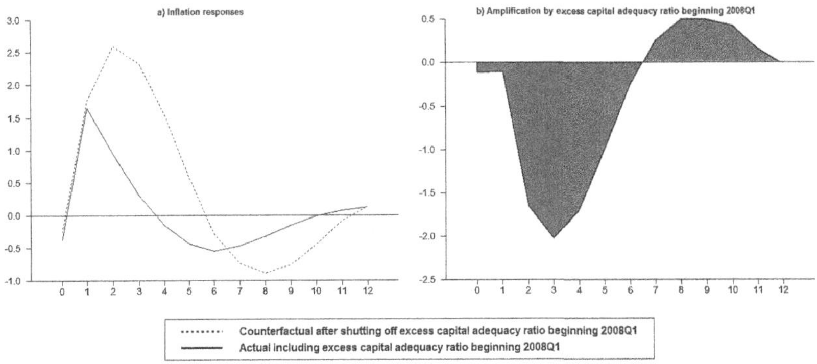

Fig. 25.7 Inflation responses to adverse financial shocks and the role excess CAR. (Source: Authors' calculations)

Figure 25.7(b) shows that excess CAR dampened the actual increase in inflation during the adverse financial shocks post-2008Q1. Hence, the increase in actual inflation is lower compared to the counterfactual. However, the impact on inflation has not been as persistent as that on credit growth as it dies out after seven quarters.

25.2.3 If Excess CAR Dampened Inflationary Pressures, Did It Neutralise Repo Rate Adjustments?

For the analysis of excess CAR on the repo rate adjustments to inflationary pressures, this section starts by showing the effects of monetary policy tightening shocks and positive excess CAR shocks in Fig. 25.8. The impulse responses show that monetary policy tightening and excess CAR shocks lower GDP growth significantly in Fig. 25.8 (a) and (d). In Fig. 25.8(b) and (e) credit growth declines for nearly 11 quarters and the peak decline is between 1 and 2 percentage points.

How do tight monetary policy and excess CAR interact? Do their responses depend on which shocks precede the other? Fig. 25.8(c) shows that excess CAR increases with a delay following a monetary policy tightening shock. This occurs in mitigating potential credit defaults in line with prudential practices. In addition, Fig. 25.8(f) shows that a positive excess CAR shock leads to monetary policy loosening. This channel of transmission could be triggered by the contraction in credit growth which slows GDP growth. Hence, monetary policy in the absence of inflationary pressures loosens policy settings to stimulate economic activity.

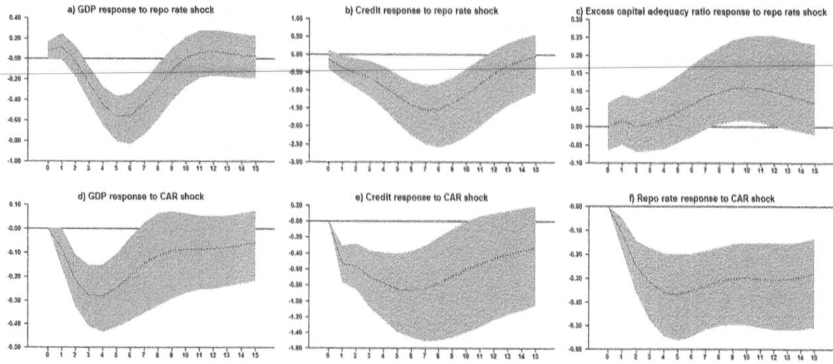

Fig. 25.8 Responses to tight monetary policy and excess CAR shocks. (Source: Authors' calculations)

25.2.4 *The Counterfactual Scenarios*

The evidence in the preceding section shows interdependencies between the tight monetary policy and positive excess CAR shocks. This section uses the counterfactual VAR approach to assess how these two policy tools interact. Figure 25.9 (a) and (b) show that excess CAR accentuates the responses of credit growth and GDP growth to tight monetary policy shocks. This means that excess CAR is a potent propagator of tight monetary policy to credit growth and GDP growth.

25.2.5 *Evidence from the Exogenous–Endogenous Model*

This section estimates the exogenous–endogenous VAR approach. We estimate two models: (i) one which includes excess CAR as an endogenous variable and (ii) the other model includes excess CAR as an exogenous variable with its first and second lags. The exogenous model shuts off the contemporaneous effects of excess CAR and feedback effects. The importance of the amplification due to excess CAR is captured by the gap between the two impulse responses. Figure 25.10 shows that credit growth and GDP growth responses decline more when excess CAR is endogenous in the model. The effects are severe for credit growth and this means that the presence of excess CAR worsens credit growth and GDP growth responses due to tight monetary policy shocks. This evidence suggests that excess CAR exacerbates the adverse effects of tight monetary policy shocks on credit growth and GDP growth.

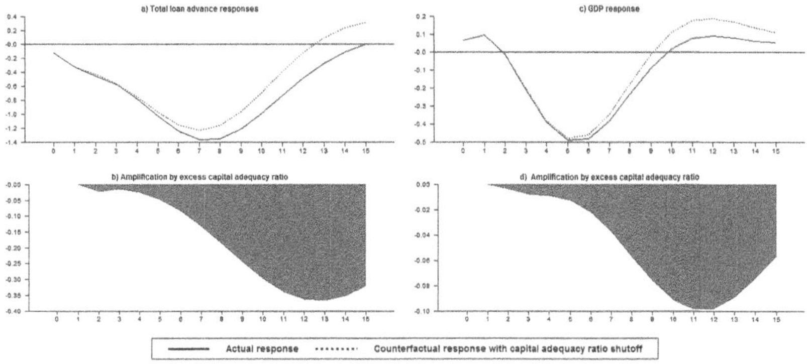

Fig. 25.9 Actual and counterfactual GDP growth and credit growth responses to tight monetary policy. (Source: Authors' calculations)

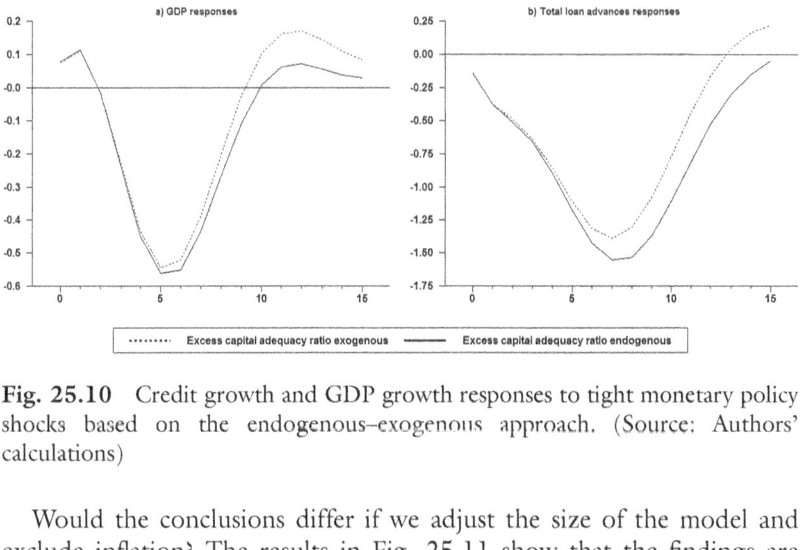

Fig. 25.10 Credit growth and GDP growth responses to tight monetary policy shocks based on the endogenous–exogenous approach. (Source: Authors' calculations)

Would the conclusions differ if we adjust the size of the model and exclude inflation? The results in Fig. 25.11 show that the findings are robust to changes in the model size and specification. Tight monetary policy shocks lower credit growth and GDP growth more when excess CAR is endogenous in the model than when it is exogenous. This shows that excess CAR worsens the decline of these macro-economic variables.

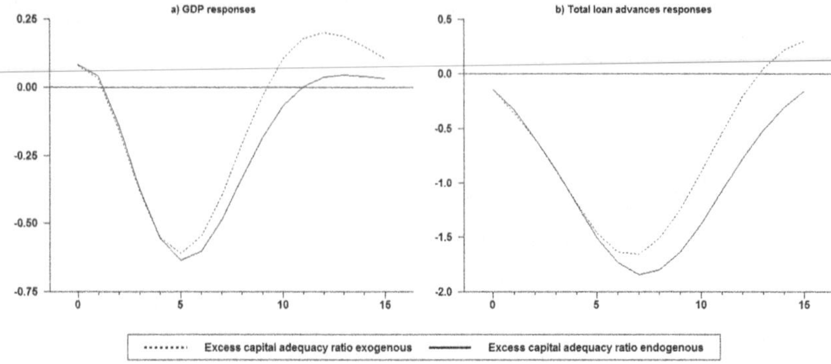

Fig. 25.11 GDP growth and credit growth responses based on the endogenous–exogenous approach in a small model. (Source: Authors' calculations)

25.2.6 Implications for Monetary Policy Responses to Positive Inflation Shocks

Figure 25.12 shows that there is a small difference in the repo rate responses to positive inflation shocks. The actual repo rate is tightened by smaller magnitudes relative to the counterfactual repo rate in Fig. 25.12(a). This suggests that in the absence of credit demand shocks, the role of excess CAR results in muted repo rate adjustments.

In addition, this may be motivated by the indirect effects working via GDP growth when excess CAR is not shut off in the model in Fig. 25.12(b). This is additional evidence showing that the repo rate responses to positive inflation shocks are dampened by excess CAR. The amplification magnitudes are shown in Fig. 25.12(b) and (d).

25.2.7 What Does the Historical Decomposition Reveal?

This section concludes the analysis by looking at the role of excess CAR via a historical decomposition approach. We construct the counterfactuals by shutting off the role of excess CAR and compare the generated series without contributions from this regulatory tool to counterfactual inflation. Figure 25.13(a) and (b) show that the counterfactual credit growth and GDP growth rates exceed the actual values between 2009 and 2014. This suggests that excess CAR dampened the GDP growth and credit growth.

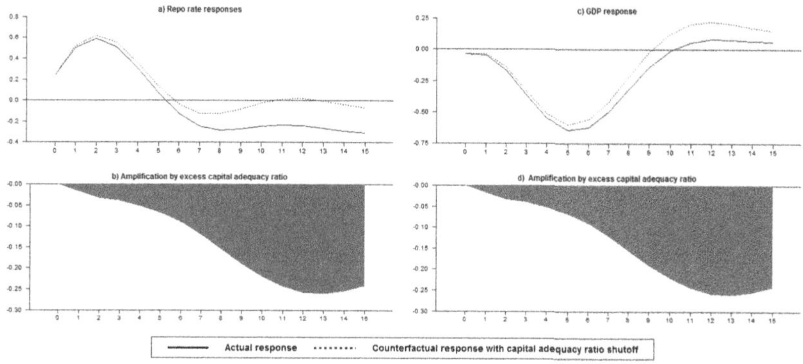

Fig. 25.12 Repo rate and GDP growth responses to positive inflation shocks and role of excess CAR. (Source: Authors' calculations)

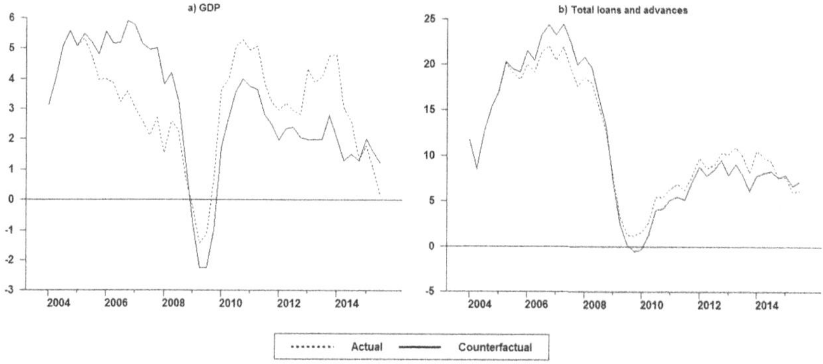

Fig. 25.13 Actual and counterfactual GDP growth and credit growth and the role of excess CAR. (Source: Authors' calculations)

What is the role of excess CAR in the evolution of inflationary pressures and the repo rate? Fig. 25.14 shows that the actual repo rate was lower than the counterfactual between 2009 and 2014. This suggests that excess CAR leads to a lower repo rate than that would have prevailed. This is further evidence that excess CAR interacts with monetary policy. However, the effects on inflation are marginal because actual inflation was slightly lower than the counterfactual between 2009 and 2014.

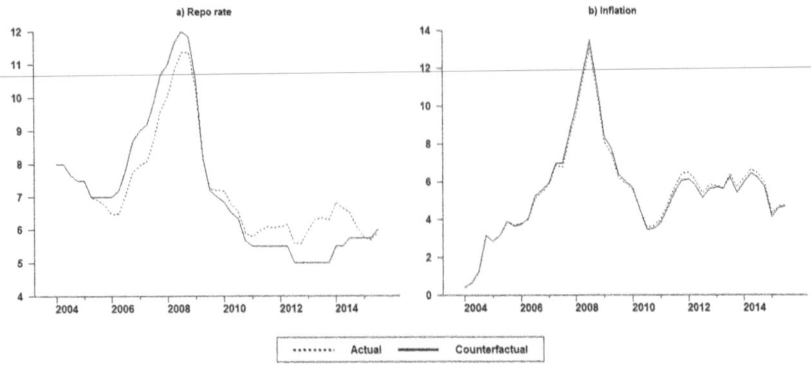

Fig. 25.14 Actual and counterfactual inflation and repo rate and the role of excess CAR. (Source: Authors' calculations)

This means that although excess CAR assisted in lowering inflationary pressures via muted credit demand, other macro-economic factors placed upward pressure on inflation. Excess CAR is not that potent in neutralising other inflationary processes such as the exchange rate passthrough.

25.3 Conclusion and Policy Implications

What is the impact of excess CAR on excessive credit growth and inflationary pressures? Did excess CAR neutralise the repo rate adjustments? Evidence shows that excess CAR dampens the impact of demand shocks on credit growth and GDP growth in line with the intended primary purpose of countering the amplitude and duration of the financial and business cycles. But it is also true that excess CAR propagates and amplifies adverse demand shocks on credit growth and GDP growth as was the case post-2007. Excess CAR is detrimental to credit growth and GDP growth because it restricts the supply of credit during severe financial shocks and demand shocks. Furthermore, excess CAR becomes pro-cyclical during severe financial and business cycles downturns. Hence, in part credit growth and GDP growth remained subdued post-2008. In addition, excess CAR dampened the transmission of positive cost pull or push shocks to inflation especially post-2008Q1, thus sustaining muted inflationary pressure. Excess CAR propagates financial shocks via the financial accelerator mechanism and plays its intended role as a cushion for banks and prevents balance sheet damage due to severe financial shocks and adverse shocks to the business cycle.

How do tight monetary policy and excess CAR interact? Evidence shows that monetary policy tightening and excess CAR shocks lower credit growth and GDP growth. But excess CAR increases with a delay following a monetary policy tightening shock, in line with prudential practices aimed at mitigating potential credit defaults. Evidence based on the counterfactual scenarios shows that excess CAR accentuates the responses of credit growth and GDP growth to tight monetary policy shocks. This means that excess CAR is a potent propagator of tight monetary policy shocks to credit growth and GDP growth. These two policy tools interact and reinforce each other's effects in the same direction.

But, evidence based on the excess CAR channel shows that a positive shock to excess CAR leads to monetary policy loosening. This channel of transmission could be triggered by the contraction in credit growth which slows GDP growth and inflation. Evidence shows that positive shocks to excess CAR affect the pace and magnitude at which the repo rate is tightened in response to inflationary shocks. In the absence of credit demand shocks, the positive shocks to excess CAR result in muted repo rate adjustments. The repo rate responses to positive inflation shocks are dampened by excess CAR. Thus, excess CAR as a financial regulation and prudential tool interacts with tight monetary policy and dampens credit demand driven inflationary pressures. In the process, excess CAR lowers the pace and magnitudes of the repo rate responses to inflationary pressures. However, evidence shows that excess CAR is not potent in neutralising other inflationary processes driven by factors such as the exchange rate passthrough to inflation. In that sense, other policy tools possess superior properties and are well positioned to complement monetary policy.

References

De-Ramon S, Francis W, and Harris Q. 2016. Bank Capital Requirements and Balance Sheet Management Practices: Has the Relationship Changed after the Crisis? Bank of England Working Paper No. 635

Pentecôte J S, and Rondeau F. 2015. Trade spill overs on output growth during the 2008 financial crisis, *Journal of International Economics* 143, 36–47

Cerra V, and Saxena S W. 2008. Growth Dynamics: The Myth of Economic Recovery, *American Economic Review* 98 (1), 439–457

CHAPTER 26

Do Non-Performing Loans Propagate the Transmission of Monetary Policy Tightening Shocks to Sectorial Credit?

Research Questions Explored

- Investigate the role of credit risk as proxied by non-performing loans (NPLs) in affecting the responses of aggregate credit growth and sectorial shares of credit to monetary policy tightening shocks.
- Determine the extent to which NPLs propagate the effect of tight monetary policy on credit growth and induce sectoral credit shifts.
- Assess whether the amplification capabilities of NPLs changed pre- and post-2008.

26.1 Introduction

Recent developments shown in Fig. 26.1 indicate that the share of credit to households is trending downwards while that to companies is rising. This trend coincided with the monetary policy tightening as shown in Fig. 26.2. Earlier chapters showed that adverse shock effects of excess LAH on the sector credit allocation were exacerbated by the increase in credit risk as captured the NPLs. Excess LAH by banks in compliance with the financial regulatory standards dampened credit growth and GDP growth, and amplified the adverse effects of heightened credit risk. Hence, this chapter extends the investigation of the factors that drive sectorial credit shifts by

N. Gumata, E. Ndou, *Achieving Price, Financial and Macro-Economic Stability in South Africa*,
https://doi.org/10.1007/978-3-030-66340-7_26

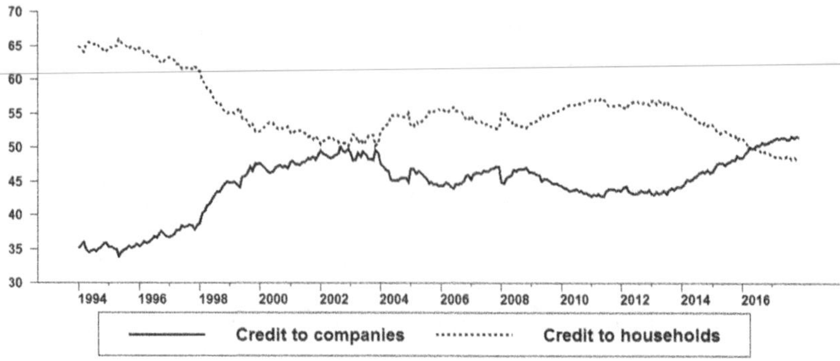

Fig. 26.1 Shares of credit to household and companies. (Source: South African Reserve Bank)

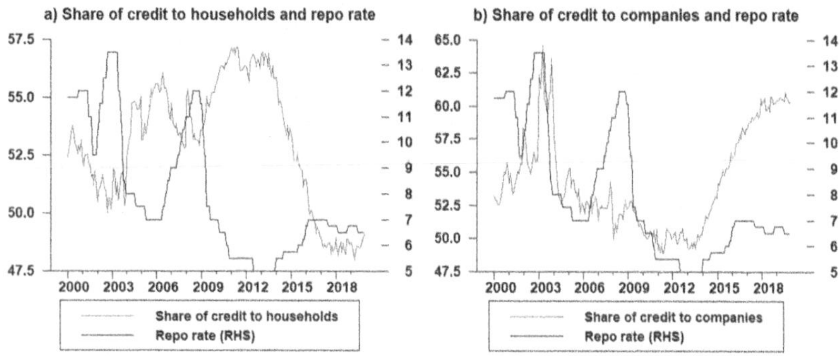

Fig. 26.2 Shares of credit to households and companies and repo rate. (Source: South African Reserve Bank)

exploring the role of credit risk as proxied by NPLs in the responses of aggregate credit growth and sectoral credit shares to monetary policy tightening shocks. Do NPLs propagate the effect of tight monetary policy on credit growth and induce sectorial shifts? Have the amplification capabilities of NPLs changed pre- and post-2008?

Fig. 26.2 shows the evolution of the shares of credit to households and companies and the repo rate over time. The trends show a negative relationship between the repo rate and the share of credit to households. At the same time, the share of credit to companies commoves with changes

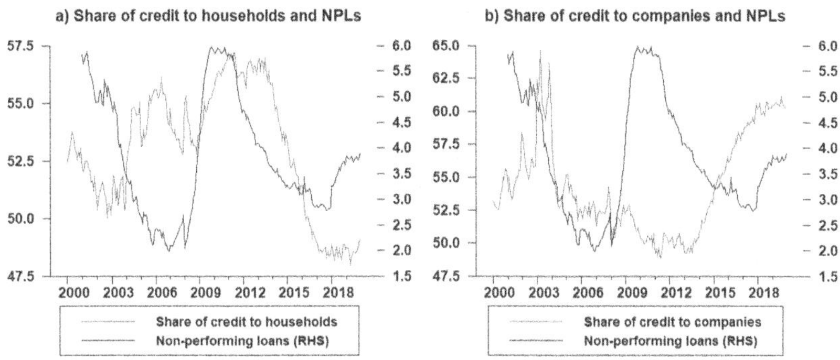

Fig. 26.3 Shares of credit to households and companies and non-performing loans. (Source: South African Reserve Bank)

in the repo rate. Does this mean that monetary policy tightening has differential effects on sectorial credit shares?

Figure 26.3 shows the trends between NPLs and the shares of credit to households and companies.

The shares of credit to households increased more between 2004 and 2007 when NPLs were exceptionally low and the negative relationship indicates a countercyclical relationship. But post-2008 there is a positive correlation (pro-cyclical relationship) between the share of credit to households and NPLs. In contrast, Fig. 26.3(b) shows that pre-2008 the share of credit to companies moved in the same direction with NPLs (pro-cyclical), but post-2008 they are moving in the different directions (countercyclical).

This chapter fills academic and policy research gaps by investigating the role of credit risk as proxied by NPLs in affecting the responses of aggregate credit growth and sectorial shares of credit to monetary policy tightening shocks. In addition, we determine the extent to which NPLs propagate the effect of tight monetary policy on credit growth and induce sectoral credit shifts. We also assess whether the amplification capabilities of NPLs changed pre- and post-2008.

26.2 Evidence of the Amplification Role of Non-Performing Loans on Credit Growth Dynamics

To assess the amplification role of the NPLs, this section modifies the Pentecôte and Rondeau (2015) and Cerra and Saxena (2008) approaches and applies them to the credit Eq. (26.1):[1]

$$Credit_t = Constant + \sum_{i=1}^{4} \beta_i credit_{t-i} + \sum_{i=0}^{4} c_i NPL_{t-i} + \sum_{i=0}^{4} d_i Dummy_{t-i} + \varepsilon_t \qquad (26.1)$$

where ε_t denotes a error term, *NPL* is Non-performing loans and *Dummy* refers to the dummy variable that is used to determine the different effects of various shocks explored in the study. We use Eq. (26.1) to determine the actual and counterfactual credit growth responses. The actual (counterfactual) credit growth responses refer to credit growth responses when a specific transmission channel from that variable is included (excluded) in the model. The propagating (magnifying) or restraining (stifling) ability of the specific variable and channel is determined by the gap between actual and counterfactual responses. We apply the counterfactual approach to test for the influence of NPLs on aggregate credit growth and sectorial credit shifts. We use the endogenous–exogenous approach to test for the robustness of the results.

The analysis uses quarterly (Q) data for the period 2000Q1 to 2015Q4. The variables included in the model include GDP growth, aggregate credit growth, credit to households and companies as a share of aggregate credit, and non-performing loans as a share of aggregate credit, inflation and the repo rate. The data is sourced from the South African Reserve Bank database. All growth rates are at an annual rate.

[1] Figure 26.12 shows the responses of aggregate and sectoral credit to repo rate shocks in VAR model with the same variables. Positive shocks to the repo rate exert differential effects on sectoral credit growth. Credit growth to households declines and remains depressed for a prolonged period, whereas credit growth to the corporate sector remains positive throughout the forecast horizon. The results are comparable to Den Haan et al. (2007), who find that real estate and consumer loans decline sharply following a monetary policy tightening shock compared to an increase in industrial and commercial loans.

26.2.1 Does the Quality of Loans Matter for the Transmission of Adverse Financial Shocks Effects to GDP Growth?

This section starts by assessing the response of GDP growth to an adverse financial shock pre-2007Q3. The financial dummy equals one pre-2007Q3 to end of sample and zero otherwise and encompasses the global financial crisis, domestic and global recession, euro area sovereign crisis and various rounds of quantitative easing in advanced economies. To estimate the role of the financial shock on GDP growth, we replace credit growth with GDP growth in Eq. (26.1). The models are estimated using two lags and 10 000 Monte Carlo draws. Figure 26.4 shows that an adverse financial shock leads to a decline in GDP growth irrespective of whether NPLs are included or not in the model.

However, the magnitudes differ and GDP growth declines more when NPLs are included in the model compared to when they are shut off in Fig. 26.4(a). This means that the deterioration in the banks' credit books and the increase in credit risk exacerbate the effects of an adverse financial shock on GDP growth as shown by the cumulative amplifications in Fig. 26.4(b).

26.2.2 Is There a Changing Role of NPLs Post-2008 in Transmitting Positive Shocks to Credit Growth?

For this analysis, we replace GDP growth with aggregate credit growth in Eq. (26.1) and split the sample for NPLs into two by constructing two

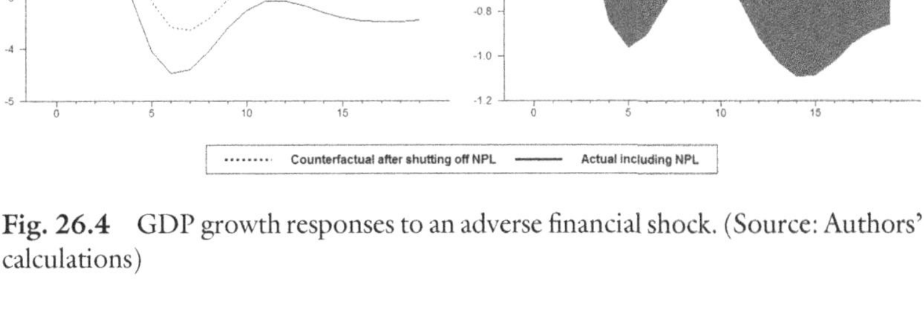

Fig. 26.4 GDP growth responses to an adverse financial shock. (Source: Authors' calculations)

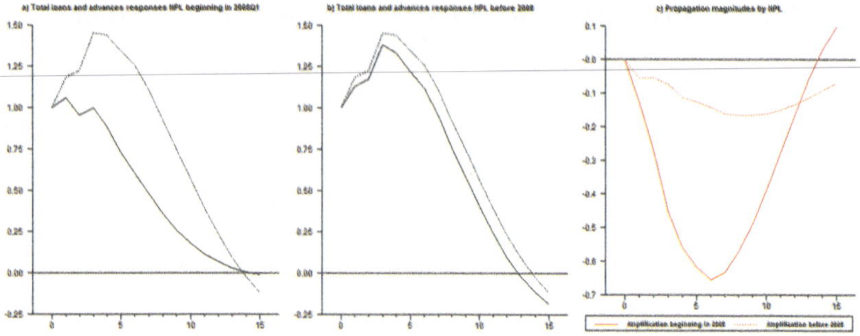

Fig. 26.5 Credit growth responses to positive shocks and the role of non-performing loans. (Source: Authors' calculations)

separate dummies. The first dummy captures NPLs pre-2008 and zero otherwise. The second dummy captures NPLs post-2008Q1 to the end of the sample and zero otherwise. Figures 26.5(a) and (b) show that in the absence of NPLs, aggregate credit growth would increase at a robust pace, meaning that NPLs had a severe dampening effect on aggregate credit growth post-2008Q1.

What is the impact of NPLs on sectorial credit? For insight into this effect, we replace aggregate credit in Eq. (26.1) with the shares of credit to households and companies. The variables enter the model one at a time in separate estimations. Figures 26.6 and 26.7 show that positive shocks to the shares of credit to households and companies do increase but the effects are muted when NPLs are active in the model.

This means that NPLs dampen the rate of increase of credit to the households and corporate sectors. But there are noticeable differences in the magnitudes involved. The share of credit to households and companies declines more pre-2008Q1. This evidence concurs with observations in Restoy (2018) and Lane (2018) who show that the abundance of non-performing assets[2] adversely affects the profitability of the banking sector in Europe. They contend that the increased level of non-performing assets may partly explain the slack in the credit supply in the most affected economies in Europe.

[2] Non-performing assets can either be non-performing loans or foreclosed properties.

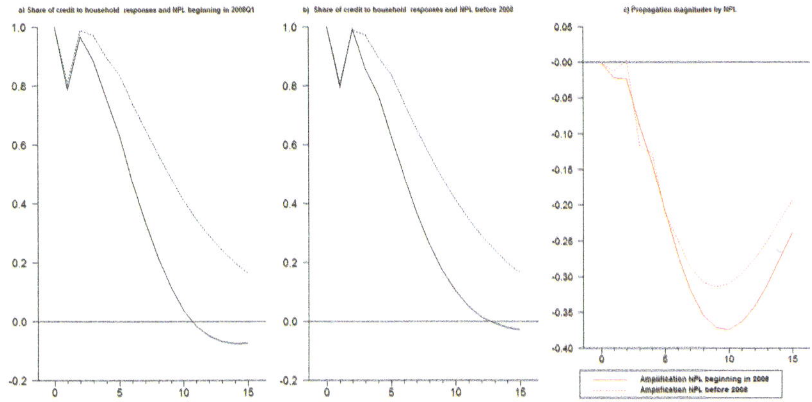

Fig. 26.6 Share of credit to households' responses to positive shocks and the role of non-performing loans. (Source: Authors' calculations)

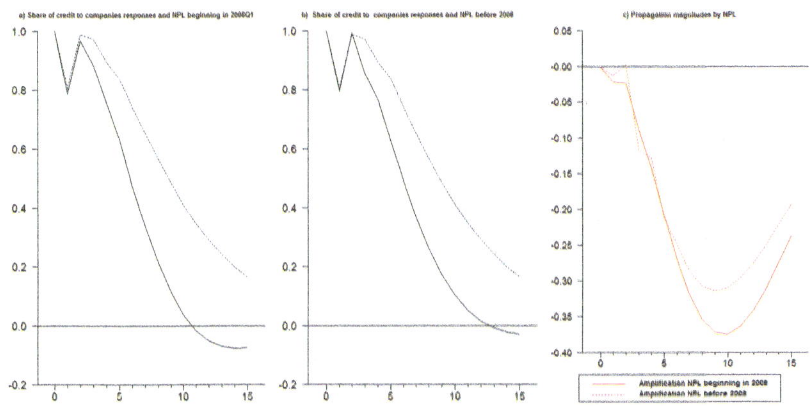

Fig. 26.7 Share of credit to companies responses to positive shocks and the role of non-performing loans. (Source: Authors' calculations)

26.3 What Are the Amplification Effects of Monetary Policy Tightening by NPLs on Aggregate Credit Growth?

This section does not use Eq. (26.1) as used in the preceding analysis but introduces the endogenous–exogenous VAR model approach to test for the robustness of the earlier results. We estimate two endogenous–exogenous

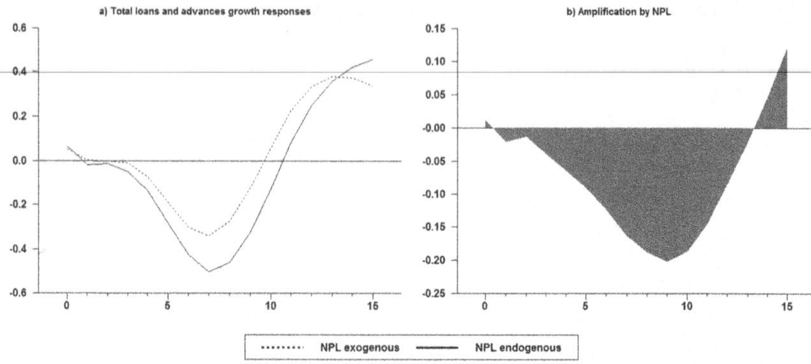

Fig. 26.8 Credit growth responses to monetary policy tightening shocks based on the endogenous–exogenous model. (Source: Authors' calculations)

VAR models which include (i) NPLs as an endogenous variable in one model and (ii) NPLs as an exogenous variable in another model and use the first and second lags of NPLs. The exogenous model shuts off the contemporaneous effects of NPLs. The importance of the amplification due to NPLs is captured by the gap between the two impulse responses. Figure 26.8(a) shows that credit growth declines more when NPLs are endogenous in the model. This means that the presence of NPLs worsens the response of credit growth to a monetary policy tightening shock. Thus, NPLs exacerbate the adverse effects of tight monetary policy shock on credit growth.

What about sectorial credit? Fig. 26.9(a) shows that monetary policy tightening shocks increase the share of credit to companies but lead to a decline in the share of credit to households. However, NPLs dampen the increases in the share of credit to companies in Fig. 26.9(b).

Figure 26.10(b) shows that the monetary policy tightening shocks increase the share of credit to companies. But the actual responses lie below the counterfactual suggesting that NPLs dampen the increase in the share of credit to companies.

The historical decompositions in Figs. 26.10 and 26.11 indicate that since 2013 the actual share of credit to households was lower than the counterfactual. On the other hand, in Fig. 26.11 the actual share of credit to companies is higher than the counterfactual, which means that NPLs did not affect credit to companies.

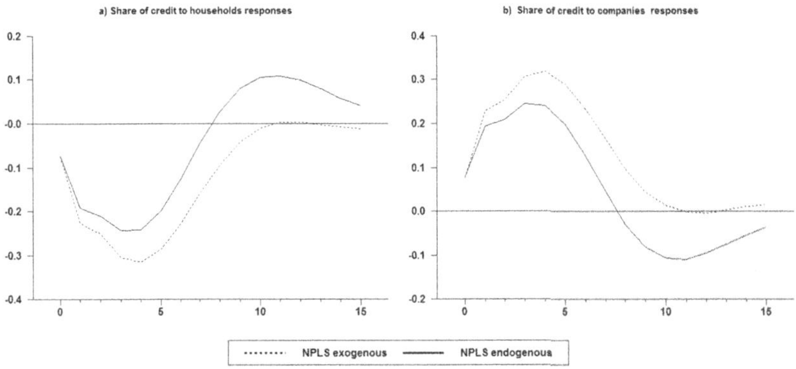

Fig. 26.9 Responses of credit to companies and households to monetary policy tightening shocks and the role of non-performing loans. (Source: Authors' calculations)

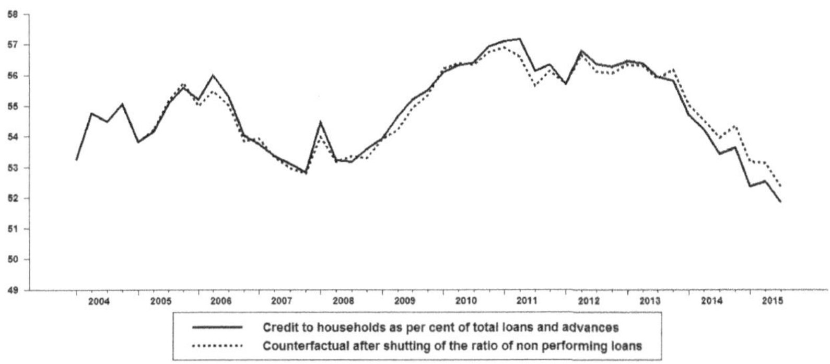

Fig. 26.10 Actual and counterfactual share of credit to households and the role of non-performing loans. (Source: Authors' calculations)

The increase in credit risk was mainly associated with the decline in the households' sector credit share. Thus, heightened credit risk exerts disproportionate monetary policy tightening effects on credit to the households' sector.

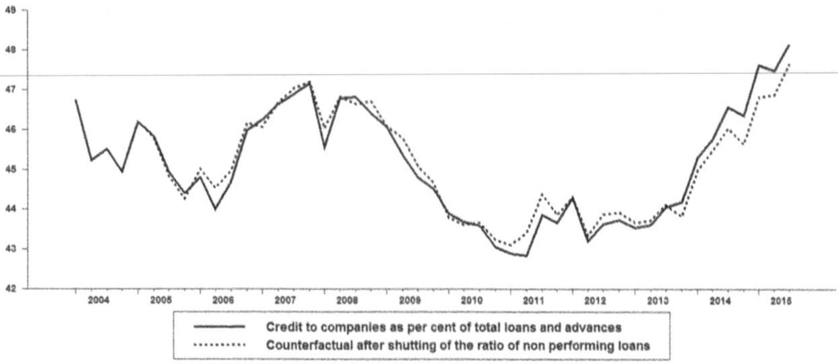

Fig. 26.11 Actual and counterfactual share of credit to companies and the role of non-performing loans. (Source: Authors' calculations)

26.4 Conclusion and Policy Implications

Do NPLs propagate the effect of tight monetary policy on credit growth and induce sectorial shifts? Have the amplification capabilities of NPLs changed pre- and post-2008? First, evidence shows that the deterioration in the banks' credit books and the increase in credit risk exacerbate the effects of an adverse financial shock on aggregate credit growth and GDP growth. In the absence of NPLs aggregate credit growth would increase at a robust pace. This means that NPLs had a severe dampening effect on aggregate credit growth post-2008Q1. Second, NPLs dampen the rate of increase of credit to the households and corporate sectors. But there are noticeable differences in the magnitudes involved. The share of credit to households and companies declines more pre-2008Q1. Third, the presence of NPLs worsens the response of credit growth to a monetary policy tightening shock. Thus, NPLs exacerbate the adverse effects of tight monetary policy shocks on credit growth.

Does this mean that monetary policy tightening has differential effects on sectorial credit shares? Evidence shows that monetary policy tightening shocks increase the share of credit to companies but lead to a decline in the share of credit to households. However, NPLs dampen the increases in the share of credit to companies. The historical decompositions indicate that since 2013 the actual share of credit to households was lower than its counterfactual compared to the share of credit to companies. This suggests that the increase in credit risk was mainly associated with the decline in the households' sector share of credit as opposed to that of companies. The propagation of tight monetary policy shocks effects by credit risk was disproportionate and resulted in a decline in the share of credit to the households' sector. Therefore, heightened credit risk exerts disproportionate monetary policy tightening effects on credit to the households' sector.

Appendix

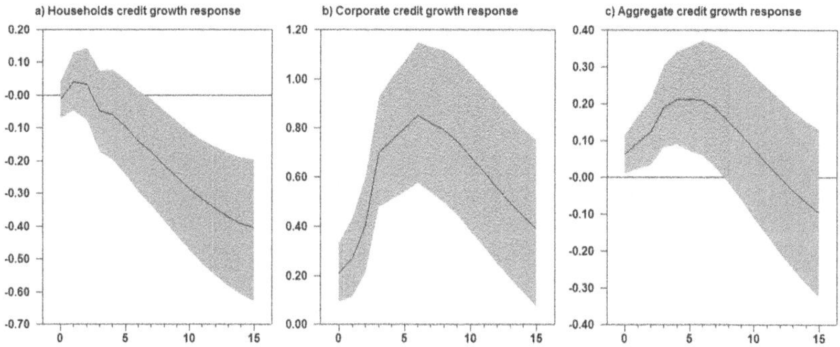

Fig. 26.12 Responses of aggregate credit growth and sectoral credit shares to repo rate shocks. (Source: Authors' calculations)

References

Cerra V and Saxena C S. 2008. Growth Dynamics: The Myth of Economic Recovery. American Economic Review. VOL. 98, NO. 1, March 2008 (pp. 439–57).

Den Haan W J, Sumner S W, and Yamashiro G M. 2007. Bank loan portfolios and the monetary policy transmission mechanism. Journal of Monetary Economics 54 904–924.

Gumata N, and Ndou E. 2019. Capital Flows, Credit Markets and Growth in South Africa: The Role of Global Economic Growth, Policy Shifts and Uncertainties. Palgrave Macmillan. ISBN 978-3-030-30882-2

Gumata N, and Ndou E. 2017. Bank Credit Extension and Real Economic Activity in South Africa: The Impact of Capital Flow Dynamics, Bank Regulation and Selected Macroprudential Tools. Palgrave Macmillan. ISB 978-3-319-43550-3

Igan D, and Tan Z. 2015. Capital Inflows, Credit Growth, and Financial Systems. IMF Working paper WP/15/193

Lane P R. 2018. The macro-financial environment in Ireland in spring 2018. Speech to the Institute for International and European Affairs (IIEA), Dublin, 9 March 2018.

Pentecôte J-S and Rondeau F. 2015. Trade spillovers on output growth during the 2008 financial crisis. International Economics, CEPII research center, issue 143, (pp. 36–47).

Restoy F. 2018. The post-crisis regulatory agenda: What is missing? Speech to Círculo Financiero La Caixa Barcelona, Spain, 19 February 2018.

CHAPTER 27

How Effective Is the Relaxation of the Countercyclical Capital Buffer at a Time When Other Residential Macro-prudential Tools Are Tight?

Research Questions Explored

- Construct various mortgage market credit conditions indices (MMCIs) and assess what they say about the state of the housing market.
- Assess the impact of changes to the countercyclical capital buffer (CCyB) and the MMCI on GDP growth, inflation, repo rate and lending rate spreads.
- Establish the role of MMCIs and lending rate spreads as conduits and channels for the transmission of shocks to the CCyB.

27.1 Introduction

Kganyago (2016) indicated that given the weak state of bank lending, the Financial Stability Committee (FSC) decided to set the countercyclical buffer (CCyB) for banks at zero. Furthermore, the speech states that the macro-prudential tool-kit is still being refined.[1] Cognisant of the fact that it is not only the state of credit conditions and GDP growth that are subdued but also that labour markets and the fiscal policy stance are tight, this

[1] See https://www.resbank.co.za/Lists/Speeches/Attachments/484/Address%20by%20Governor%20Kganyago%20at%20the%20SACCI%20Annual%20Convention.pdf.

N. Gumata, E. Ndou, *Achieving Price, Financial and Macro-Economic Stability in South Africa*,
https://doi.org/10.1007/978-3-030-66340-7_27

chapter assesses the interaction of the CCyB,[2] mortgage market credit conditions index (MMCI) and the labour market conditions index (LMCI). How effective is the relaxation of the countercyclical capital buffer at a time when other residential macro-prudential tools are tight?

The results in earlier chapters indicate that although the CCyB was relaxed in 2016Q4, the benefits mainly accrued to the corporate sector and had a very limited impact on household and mortgage advances credit growth.[3] Furthermore, evidence in earlier chapters showed that heightened credit risk as proxied by non-performing loans was mainly associated with the decline in the household sector share of credit as opposed to that of companies. The propagation of tight monetary policy shock effects by credit risk was disproportionate on sector credit, resulting in a decline in the share of credit to the household sector. Thus, heightened credit risk exerts disproportionate monetary policy tightening effects on credit to the household sector. At the same time, earlier chapters showed that excess CAR and liquid asset holding (LAH) of banks as financial regulatory tools also work via their impact on the re-allocation of sectoral credit shares following capital inflow shocks. Contractionary monetary policy, excess CAR and LAH propagate each other's effects and move aggregate credit growth in the same direction. As financial regulatory tools, excess CAR and LAH complement each other and the effects of contractionary monetary policy on aggregate credit growth.

Furthermore, excess CAR and LAH impose quantity as well as price effects or costs to banks. They act as supply shocks via decreasing (increasing) the availability of credit but simultaneously increasing (decreasing) the cost of credit via the lending rate spreads. This means that depending on the monetary policy cycle, they also neutralise accommodative monetary policy and reinforce the monetary policy tightening effects on the macro-economy. This is particularly important given that credit risk and capital inflow shocks tend to act in the same fashion as financial shocks.[4]

[2] The CCyB referred to in this chapter is the excess capital adequacy (CAR). The labour market conditions index (LMCI) is sourced from Gumata and Ndou (2017b).

[3] See the evolution of aggregate credit, mortgage credit and sectoral credit growth relative to their estimated credit threshold in earlier chapters. The corporate sector credit recovered post-2009 and has been briefly above the upper threshold. On the other hand, mortgage credit has been a drag on aggregate and household credit growth post-2009 despite the significant recovery in corporate credit growth.

[4] Ndou et al. (2017) show that capital inflow shocks also act as large financial and supply shocks, such as the exchange rate, which shift the monetary policy trade-off.

Adverse shocks to macro-prudential tools such as the National Credit Act (NCA) and loan-to-value (LTVs) and repayment-to-income ratios (RTIs) also exert additional negative effects on credit and financial conditions, credit growth and the macro-economy. Hence, this chapter extends the analysis of the impact of the CCyB by asking how effective is the relaxation of the countercyclical capital buffer at a time when other residential macro-prudential tools are tight?

First, this chapter constructs several mortgage market credit conditions indices (MMCIs) from several housing market indicators to assess for consistency in the message they convey about the mortgage market conditions. Second, we estimate several VAR models to compare the shock effects of a lowering (loosening) of the CCyB and the MMCI on GDP growth, inflation and lending rate spreads. We are assessing the role of the MMCI and lending rate spreads as conduits and channels for the transmission of shocks to the CCyB.

In earlier chapters we stated that changes in the CCyB are part of the macro-prudential tools aimed at influencing the supply of credit and these are mainly targeted at influencing the risk-taking behaviour of banks. On the other hand, changes to the residential macro-prudential tools such as the loan-to-value (LTVs) and the repayment-to-income ratios (RTIs) are mainly aimed at influencing the demand for credit and are supposed to alter the borrowing constraints faced by firms and households via channels such as the balance sheet and asset prices. Hence, these macro-prudential tools target the supply side of the credit markets in the case of adjustments in the CCyB and the demand side of credit markets in the case of the LTVs and RTIs. So, they are supposed to complement each other.[5] Benetton et al. (2018) show that lenders use the down payment size to price unobservable borrower risk. They find that a 20-percentage point smaller down payment is associated with a 22 basis-point higher interest rate at origination, and a higher ex-post default rate. Lenders see a down payment as a signal for unobservable risk, but the relative importance of this

[5] Furthermore, earlier chapters showed that changes in the CCyB are indeed a powerful and effective macro-prudential tool mainly targeted at influencing the risk-taking behaviour of banks. But literature also shows that changes to the CCyB do not specifically target household's resilience or indebtedness. The CCyB falls short of directly addressing household demand for credit or the household sector's financial resilience and indebtedness. Hence, changes in the complementary tools such as the NCA, LTVs and RTIs are necessary to propagate the effectiveness of changes in the CCyB in boosting the household sector credit growth.

signal is limited, as it accounts for only 10 per cent of the difference in mortgage rates between loans with 75 per cent and 95 per cent LTV ratio.

If the loosening of the CCyB implies a positive credit supply shock, how do we assess that such a policy intervention has had the desired effects? This is particularly important when the National Credit Act (NCA), alternatively the lending criteria, labour market conditions, fiscal and monetary policy are tight. Earlier chapters showed that credit to the corporate sector recovered post-2009 while credit to the household sector and mortgage advances remained subdued. Hence it becomes important to also assess how lending rate margins (spreads)[6] respond to changes in the CCyB and MMCI as the channels of transmission of credit supply shocks. Do lending rate margins (spreads) narrow in response to shocks to the CCyB? Does their narrowing suggest that banks take on more risk on their balance sheets to channel the surge in the supply of credit or transmit the loosening in the credit supply conditions? Furthermore, how does the repo rate respond to changes in the CCyB? Do shocks to the CCyB effectively mean that monetary policy has been loosened? Does it effectively give the Monetary Policy Committee room for manoeuvre for a persistently longer period?

27.2 What Can We Infer from the Evolution of Excess CAR, Sectoral Credit and Risk Weighted Assets?

If the intention of adjusting the CCyB is as stated above, what can we infer from the data about the actual behaviour of excess CAR and risk-weighted assets (RWAs)? Figure 27.1 shows that effectively the lowering of the CCyB means that banks are instructed to reduce or hold no excess CAR.[7] This means that due to the lag effects of applying this regulatory change on the part of the banks, we expect to see the level of excess CAR in Fig. 27.1a eventually moving persistently towards the minimum requirement of 9.75 per cent over a prolonged period of time. In addition, Fig. 27.1 shows that RWAs are negatively associated with excess CAR.

[6] The lending rate margins used in the empirical section specifically apply to the household sector.

[7] Given that there is no indication of what a positive and neutral (non-binding) level of the CCyB is, an assumption can be made that banks are instructed to hold minimum CAR as required by the regulations. Literature shows that there exists a neutral or non-binding setting for CCyB. The neutral or non-binding level of the CCyB is defined as that level at which there are no current heightened risks and no policy constraints are intended.

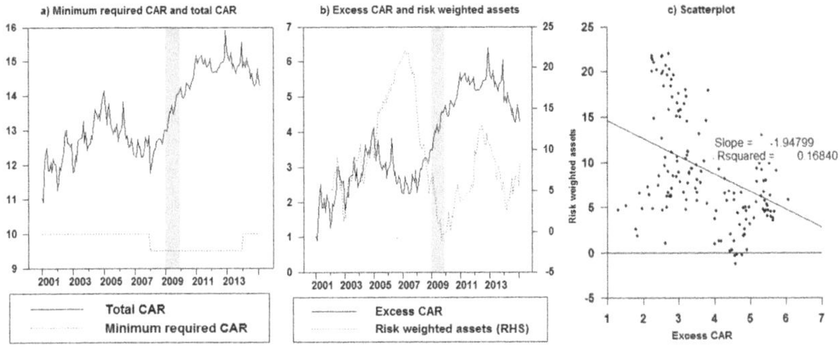

Fig. 27.1 Risk-weighted assets and total and excess capital adequacy ratio. (Source: South African Reserve Bank and authors' calculations)

Furthermore, if we use the change in the RWAs as a proxy for banks' risk appetite and the transmission of changes in the CCyB to credit supply, this means that the inverse relationship that holds between excess CAR and RWAs will be triggered. Meaning that, we expect to see an increase in RWAs as banks channel excess funds to the real economy to fund various investment projects and consumption expenditure. Effectively, the loosening of CCyB implies that the credit supply constraint has been partially addressed and banks can lend depending on their risk appetite.

Figure 27.2 shows excess CAR, and credit to households, companies and mortgage advances. The trends show that high excess CAR post-2008 coincided with the decline in mortgage and sectoral credit growth. There is a negative association of excess CAR with mortgage and sectorial credit growth. For instance, changes in excess CAR explain around 52 per cent and more than 25 per cent of mortgage credit growth and sectoral credit growth, respectively. The results imply that heightened excess CAR is associated with a decline in mortgage credit growth and sectoral credit growth. These associations are far higher compared to those established for RWAs in Fig. 27.1, indicating that aggregation can mask a lot of information regarding the disaggregated credit data as shown in Fig. 27.2.[8]

What do the above estimated relationships mean for the pricing of credit? We show the evolution and relationship between the weighted average deposit and lending rate margins relative to the repo rate and

[8] Figure 27.12 in the appendix shows that aggregate credit and RWAs are positively related. Changes in RWAs explain 78 per cent of the variation in aggregate credit growth.

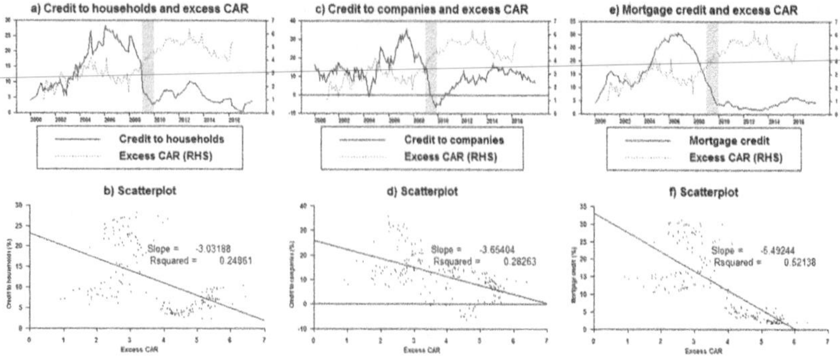

Fig. 27.2 Excess CAR, mortgage credit growth and sectoral credit growth. (Source: South African Reserve Bank)

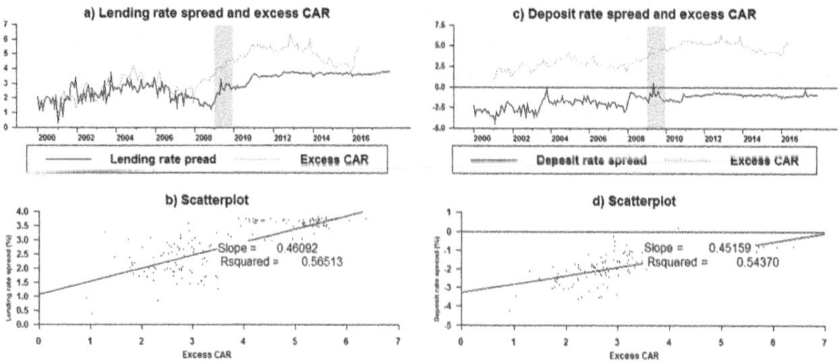

Fig. 27.3 Deposit and lending rate spreads and excess CAR. (Source: South African Reserve Bank and authors' calculations)

excess CAR in Fig. 27.3. We establish a positive relationship between excess CAR, deposit and lending rate margins. The results imply that as excess CAR increases, and bank credit extension declines, banks adjust the price of deposits and credit to compensate for the sources of funds and profitability. As the volume of credit declines, banks rely more on the pricing of credit to compensate and boost profitability as shown by the positive association of the deposit and lending rate margins with excess CAR in Fig. 27.3.[9] Changes in excess CAR explain 57 per cent and 53 per cent of the variation in the lending and deposit rate spreads, respectively. Pre-2008, the lending rate margins were highly correlated with excess CAR.[10] This evidence is in line with findings in Basten and Koch (2015), which show that the CCyB changes the composition of mortgage supply, as relatively capital-constrained and mortgage-specialised banks raise prices (interest rates) more than their competitors do.

We stated earlier that to be effective, the adjustment of the CCyB is also expected to be transmitted via lending conditions and standards such as the loosening (tightening) of the LTV and RTI ratios. The loosening of the lending criteria signifies changes in the banks' risk appetite. Figure 27.4 shows that there is an inverse relationship between LTVs, RTIs and excess CAR.

This means that the adjustments in the CCyB as a policy tool does get transmitted via other macro-prudential tools in the residential property market. In this case, heightened excess CAR also coincided with tighter LTVs and RTIs. Thus, it is possible that the spill-overs of the adjustments

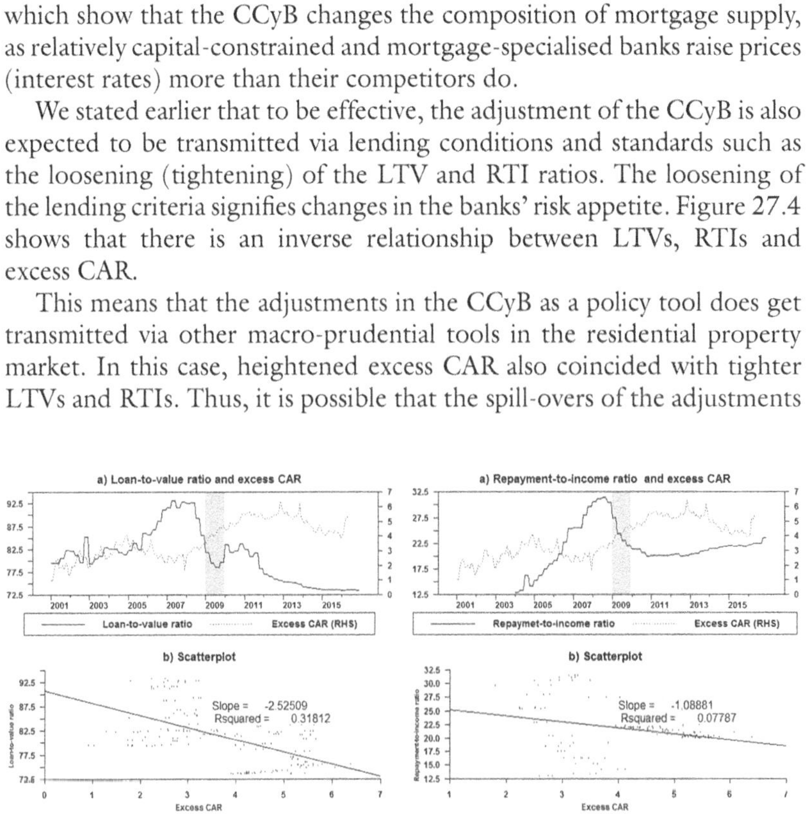

Fig. 27.4 Excess CAR and average weighted LTV and RTI. (Source: South African Reserve Bank and authors' calculations. Note: A higher (lower) LTV and RTI = loose (tight) lending criteria)

[9] The positive relationship holds even during periods when banks lower excess CAR, as was the case between 2000M1 and 2008M12 in Fig. 27.13 in the appendix.

[10] Furthermore, lending rate spreads remained elevated despite the successive (persistent) decline in the repo rate post-2009. Figure 27.3 also shows that the lending rate spreads remained elevated post-2016 despite the relaxation of the CCyB.

to the CCyB will be reinforced by the tightening (easing) of the lending criteria in the residential property market. Figure 27.4 also shows that at the height of lower excess CAR during 2005M1 to 2007M12, the LTVs and RTIs were highly accommodative (loose). This evidence corroborates that in Gumata and Ndou (2017a), who showed that LTVs and RTIs are complementary tools and that the repo rate and LTV and RTI tightening shock effects reinforce each other. In addition, the transmission of the LTV and RTI shocks occurs through the same channels as those that are impacted by tight monetary policy shock. Similarly, Spencer (2018) shows that LTVs have assisted the Reserve Bank of New Zealand in achieving their economic and financial stability objectives. The LTVs have reduced housing related risk in the banking system and also helped to ease housing market pressures.[11]

27.3 The Construction of Mortgage Market Credit Condition Indices

This section discusses the estimation of the MMCIs. Because the housing market is characterised by a variety of elements that hinder or propagate the supply of credit and are too diverse to consider individually, we construct several MMCIs using different variables specific to the mortgage market. We use the principal component analysis (PCA) approach to extract the common factors in the data and derive the MMCIs. The data is in log changes and demeaned prior to the construction of the factors. Due to issues related to data availability and limitations, the sample sizes for the estimated MMCIs span the period 1990Q1 to 2016Q2. The sample size is adjusted in cases where the data start in 1994Q1 and 2004Q1. The data and variables used for the different factors are presented in Table 27.1.

The variables included in the construction of the various MMCIs capture the different segments of the housing market that are key to the asset, wealth and collateral channels of the monetary policy transmission mechanism. In addition, we include variables that represent the demand side of credit for housing that are mostly related to the affordability of the households. The residential activity indicators such as residential fixed

[11] The Bank of Ireland uses LTVs and serviceability or the loan-to-income ratio (LTI) dimensions of borrower risk with separate limits on each dimension for different categories of borrowers. On the other hand, the Bank of England places a limit on high LTI lending as an insurance policy aimed at preventing a deterioration in lending standards.

Table 27.1 Variables included in the various mortgage market credit condition indices

Variable	*MMCI1*	*MMCI2*	*MMCI3*	*MMCI4*
Asset prices/collateral values/valuation				
Aggregate house price	Y	Y		
Small			Y	Y
Medium			Y	Y
Large			Y	Y
Price-to-rent ratio	Y	Y	Y	Y
Household financial position/affordability				
Household debt to income	Y	Y	Y	
Mortgage repayment to income	Y	Y	Y	
Prime rate	Y	Y	Y	Y
Residential investment/activity/strength				
Residential gross fixed capital formation	Y	Y	Y	
Estate duty collected	Y	Y	Y	Y
Labour market				
Employment rate: official	Y	Y	Y	Y
Quality of the mortgage book				
NPL number				Y
NPL value				Y
Lending criteria/sentiment/confidence				
LTV ratio				Y
RTI ratio				Y
CCI	Y	Y	Y	Y
BCI	Y	Y	Y	Y

Source: South African Reserve Bank and authors' calculations

Abbreviations: *BCI* business confidence index, *CCI* consumer confidence index, *LTV* loan-to-value, *MMCI* mortgage market credit conditions index, *NPL* non-performing loan, *RTI* repayment-to-income

investment and the duty collected are included to capture the strength of the residential property market.

Labour market conditions are important for equilibrating demand and supply in the housing market. Hence, we include changes in the official employment rate. Furthermore, the quality of the banks' mortgage books is an important determinant of the profitability of the banking sector and the ability to lend more (supply of credit).[12] In this regard, the inclusion

[12] See Restoy (2018) and Lane (2018) on the impact of NPLs on the supply of credit.

of the number and value of non-performing loans captures the profitability and non-profitability lending in the mortgage market space.

Last, we include a collection of variables that capture the state of the business and consumer confidence in the economy, as well as the key variables that are used as indicators of the lending criteria in the residential property market. We estimate several MMCIs to present the robustness of the estimated mortgage market conditions. This is also aimed at quelling off unnecessary criticism that can suggest that the exclusion of some indicators that are available for a short sample period (and cannot be used in the estimations due to the degrees of freedom issues) may lead to biased estimations. However, in the empirical estimations we use the MMCIs that start in 1990.

Figure 27.5 shows all the estimated MMCIs. The trends show that by and large credit conditions in the residential property market are not as tight as they were at the height of the financial crisis. Having been neutral for the most part of 2013 and 2014, mortgage credit conditions tightened since the beginning of 2015.

27.4 How Does GDP and Inflation Respond to a Positive Shock to MMCIs?

We estimate a few VAR models for the sample period 2001Q1 to 2016Q2, which include the MMCI, GDP growth, inflation, repo rate and the lending rate spread. The sample size is adjusted to start in 2001Q1 due to the

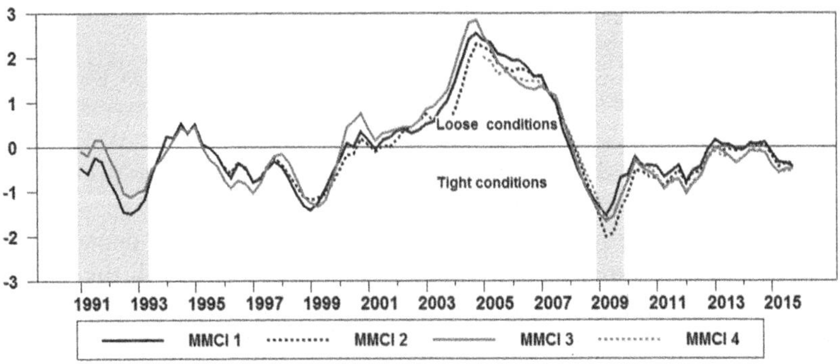

Fig. 27.5 Mortgage Market Credit Condition Indices. (Source: Authors' calculations. Note: Positive means loose mortgage credit conditions and negative means tight conditions)

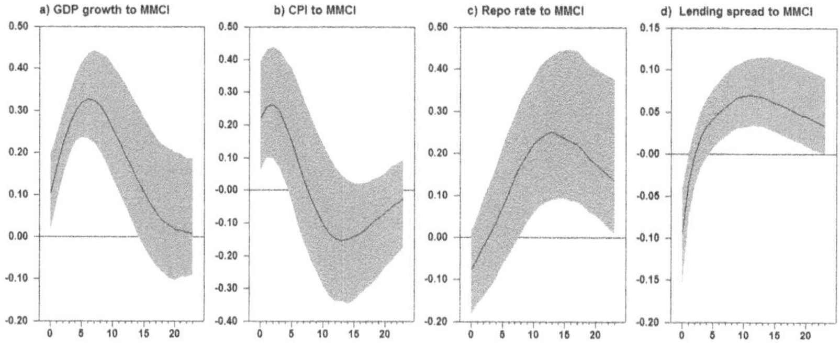

Fig. 27.6 Responses to loose MMCI shock. (Source: Authors' calculations)

availability of the data for excess CAR. In later models we replace MMCI with excess CAR to assess whether they exert different effects. The models were estimated with 2 lags as chosen by the Akaike information criterion (AIC) and 10,000 Monte Carlo draws. The growth rates for GDP and inflation are at annual rates. The data are sourced from the South African Reserve Bank database. We assess the positive (loose or increase) shocks to the MMCI and an unexpected reduction in excess CAR. To capture the positive (loose or increase) MMCI values only, we create a dummy variable that takes only the positive values of the MMCI and zero otherwise. A shock that captures an unexpected reduction in excess CAR is a negative (decline) shock.

Figure 27.6 shows that GDP growth increases in response to loosening in the MMCI and lending spreads decline, albeit transitorily. This means that the loosening in the MMCI is transmitted via a decline in the lending spreads to have a positive impact on GDP growth. But inflation increases in response to loose MMCI, which may indicate the spill-over of accommodative monetary policy to macro-prudential policies largely via the short-lived contraction in the lending spreads. Lending spreads are influenced by changes in the repo rate,[13] which increases in response to heightened inflationary pressures in Fig. 27.6b.

What about an unexpected negative shock (reduction) in excess CAR? Figure 27.7 shows that GDP growth and inflation do increase in response

[13] Figure 27.14 shows that the repo rate explains roughly around 95 per cent and 92 per cent of the variation in the lending and deposit rate levels.

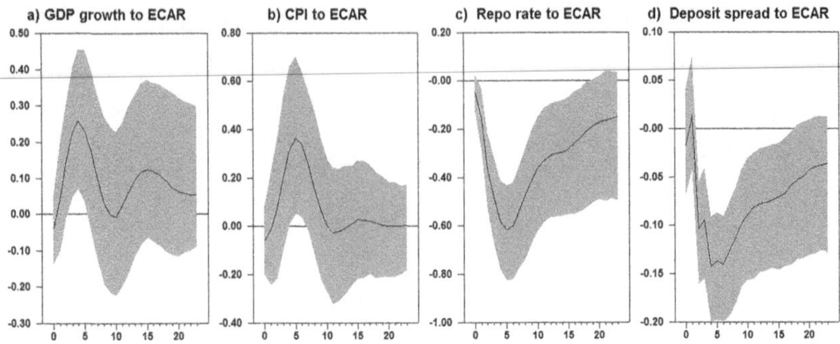

Fig. 27.7 Responses to unexpected negative (reduction) in excess CAR. (Source: Authors' calculations)

to unexpected reduction in excess CAR. True to the nature of credit supply shocks, an unexpected negative shock (reduction) in excess CAR depresses the lending spread in Fig. 27.7c.

On a comparison basis, GDP growth and inflation increases more due to loose MMCI than to an unexpected reduction in excess CAR. This means that indeed lowering the CCyB is transmitted into bank lending partly via the residential property market lending. But the lending spreads decline more in response to the lowering of excess CAR compared to the loosening of the MMCI. Thus, the reduction in excess CAR and the loosening of the MMCI do exert the desired effects of compressing the lending rate spread and result in an increase in GDP growth.

How does the repo rate respond to the reduction in the CCyB? Figures 27.6 and 27.7 show that the repo rate decline. Thus, negative shocks to the CCyB effectively mean that monetary policy has been loosened. But the responses of the lending rate spread indicate that there is more to the transmission of excess CAR shocks. The benefits of the increased credit supply possibly induced by the reduction in excess CAR are neutralised by the banking sector specific factors such as the pricing of risk due to a number of factors such as increased non-performing loans.[14] Thus, other banking sector specific factors neutralise the accommodative effects of monetary policy, financial regulation and macro-prudential tools.

[14] Earlier chapters showed that credit risk as measured NPLs propagates the effects of tight monetary policy shocks and exerts disproportionate effects on the share of credit to the household sector.

27.5 GDP Growth Responses and the Propagation Role of MMCI and Excess CAR

The earlier section showed that a reduction in excess CAR and loosened MMCIs result in a decline in the lending rate spreads, which is transmitted into the real economy. But the estimations did not show how loose MMCIs and the reduction in excess CAR propagate each other's effects on the selected macro-economic variables. Hence, this section looks at the propagation role of excess CAR and the MMCI. We estimate VAR models with GDP growth, inflation, the lending rate spread, excess CAR and the MMCI. The MMCI and the excess CAR enter the estimations in separate VAR models. The models are estimated for the sample period 2001Q1 to 2016Q2 with two lags chosen by AIC criterion and 10,000 Monte Carlo draws. Comparisons of the propagation effects by loose MMCIs and the effects of the reduction in excess CAR on GDP growth are shown in Figs. 27.8 and 27.9. The results suggest that loose MMCI and the reduction in excess CAR play different roles and exert different magnifying roles in the responses of GDP growth.

The peak effects show that loose MMCI play a smaller role compared to an unexpected reduction in excess CAR in propagating GDP growth responses. This means that indeed the lowering of excess CAR is necessary over and above the loosening of MMCI to exert significantly large magnifying effects on GDP growth.

Similarly, Figs. 27.10 and 27.11 show that loose MMCI and the reduction in the CCyB reinforce each other's effects and lower the lending rate

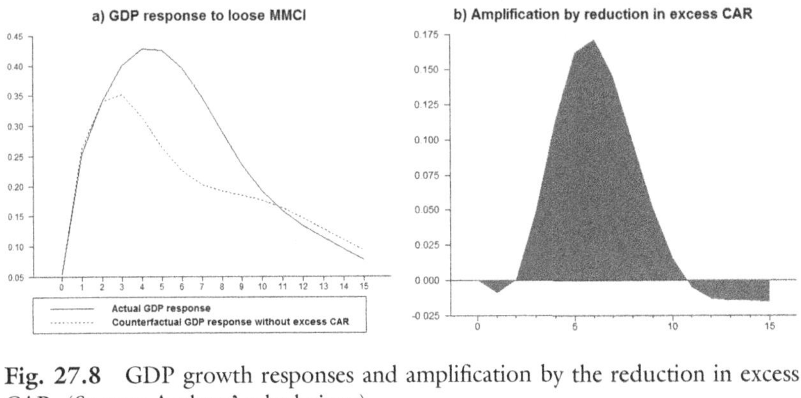

Fig. 27.8 GDP growth responses and amplification by the reduction in excess CAR. (Source: Authors' calculations)

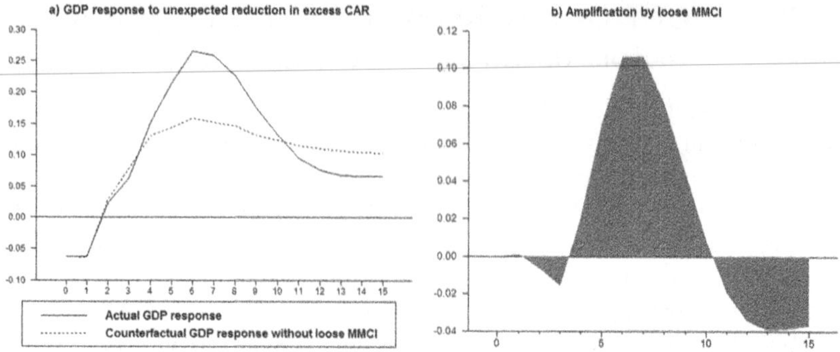

Fig. 27.9 GDP growth responses and amplification by loose MMCI. (Source: Authors' calculations)

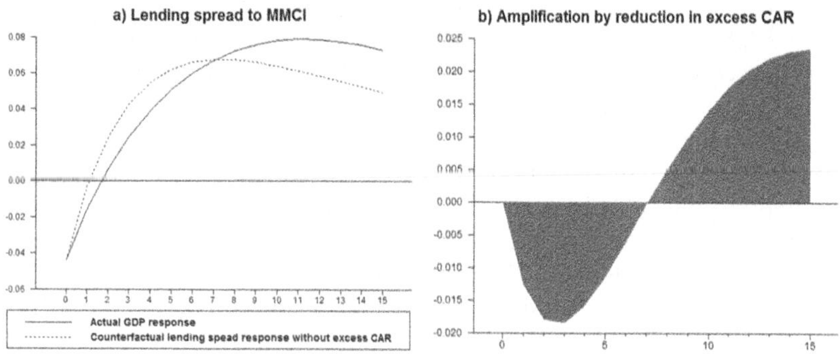

Fig. 27.10 Lending rate spread responses and amplification by the reduction in excess CAR. (Source: Authors' calculations)

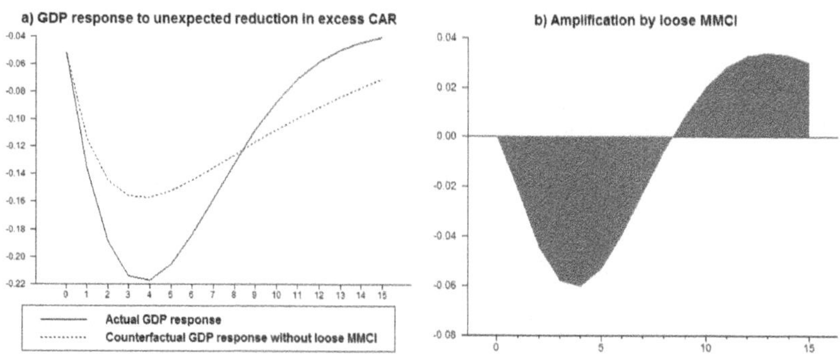

Fig. 27.11 Lending rate spread responses and amplification by loose MMCI. (Source: Authors' calculations)

spread. But the reduction in the CCyB depresses the lending rate spread more compared to loose MMCIs alone.

At peak decline, the reduction in excess CAR lowers the lending spread by 22 basis-points compared to a mere 5 basis points due to loose MMCIs. The results are consistent with those in Figs. 27.6 and 27.7, which showed that loose MMCIs result in a transitory decline in lending rate spreads compared to a larger and persistent compression due the reduction in excess CAR.

27.6 Conclusion and Policy Implications

How effective is the relaxation of the countercyclical capital buffer at a time when other residential macro-prudential tools are tight? First, evidence shows that excess CAR is negatively associated with RWAs, mortgage credit growth, credit to companies and households, LTVs and RTIs but positively associated with the lending rate margins. This implies that excess CAR leads to a decline in risk taking by banks, which manifests in tighter lending criteria, a decline in credit growth and an increase in the lending rate margins. Second, all the estimated MMCI trends show that by and large credit conditions in the residential property market are not as tight as they were at the height of the financial crisis. Having been neutral for the most part of 2013 and 2014, mortgage credit conditions tightened since the beginning of 2015.

Third, evidence shows that GDP growth increases in response to loosening in MMCI and a decline in excess CAR as the repo rate and lending spreads decline. This means that the loosening in the MMCI is transmitted via a decline in the repo rate and lending spreads to have a positive impact on GDP growth. At the same time, the decline in excess CAR is largely transmitted via the loosening of the MMCI and the lending rate spreads. Thus, we conclude that the decline in the CCyB and loose lending conditions imply an accommodative monetary policy stance. But inflation increases in response to loose MMCI, which may indicate the spill-over of accommodative monetary policy to macro-prudential policies largely via the short-lived contraction in the lending spreads. On a comparison basis, GDP growth and inflation increase more due to loose MMCI compared to an unexpected reduction in excess CAR. But a negative shock (reduction) to the CCyB true to its characteristic of a credit supply shock depresses the lending rate spread more than the loosening in the MMCI. This means that indeed the lowering of the CCyB and the loosening of the MMCI are transmitted into bank lending via the same channels and they exert different effects.

Fourth, loose MMCI and the reduction in the CCyB reinforce each other's effects and accommodative monetary policy on GDP growth and the compression in the lending rate spreads. The policy implication is that the reduction in CCyB as a positive credit supply shock requires the loosening of credit lending standards to reinforce its positive effects on lending rate spreads and GDP growth. Thus, the relaxation of the CCyB is more potent when other residential macro-prudential tools are loosened. The relaxation of the CCyB and loose lending conditions complement accommodative monetary policy and move the lending rate spread and GDP growth in the same direction. Hence, these tools need to be systematically co-ordinated to have the desired effects on real economic activity.

Appendix

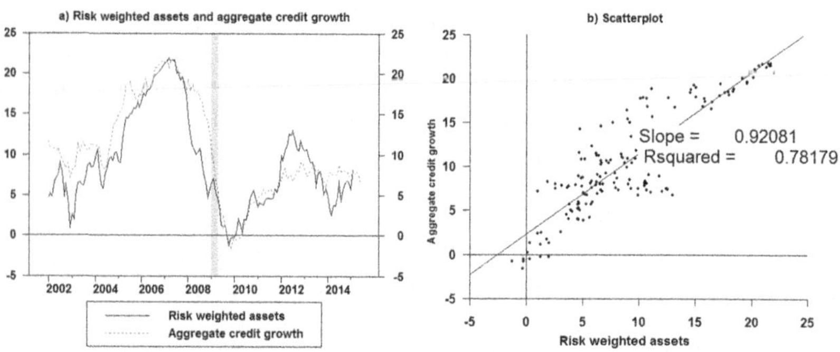

Fig. 27.12 Risk-weighted assets and aggregate credit growth. (Source: Authors' calculations)

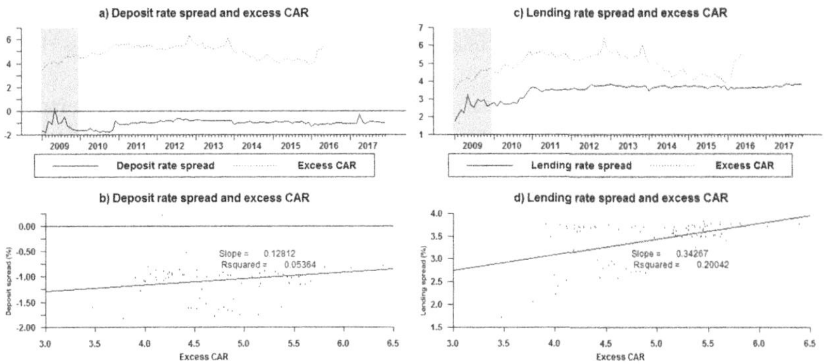

Fig. 27.13 Deposit and lending rate spreads and excess CAR. (Source: South African Reserve Bank and authors' calculations)

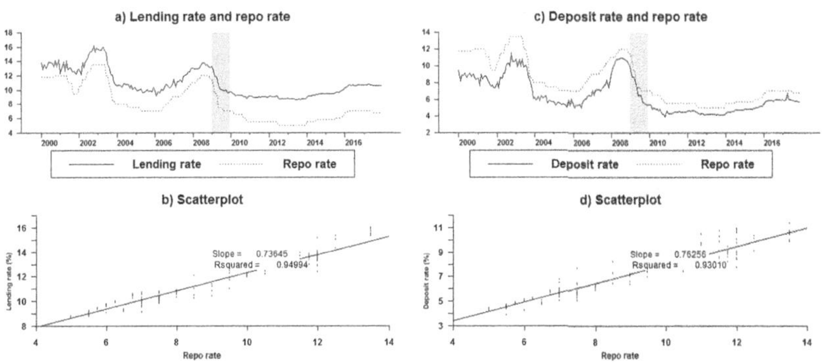

Fig. 27.14 Repo, lending and deposit rates. (Source: South African Reserve Bank and authors' calculations)

References

Aikman D, Andrew G, Haldane A G, Hinterschweiger M, and Kapadia S. 2018. Rethinking Financial Stability. Bank of England. Staff Working Paper No. 712.

Basten C, and Koch C. 2015. Higher Bank Capital Requirements and Mortgage Pricing: Evidence from the Countercyclical Capital Buffer (CCB). BIS Working Papers No. 511.

Benes J, Laxton D, and Mongardini J. 2016. Mitigating the Deadly Embrace in Financial Cycles: Countercyclical Buffers and Loan-to-Value Limits. IMF Working Paper WP/16/87.

Benetton M, Bracke P, and Garbarino N. 2018. Down Payment and Mortgage Rates: Evidence from Equity Loans. Bank of England Staff Working Paper No. 713.

De-Ramon S, Francis W, and Harris Q. 2016. Bank Capital Requirements and Balance Sheet Management Practices: Has the Relationship Changed after the Crisis? Bank of England Working Paper No. 635.

Gerdrup K R, Hansen F, Krogh T, and Maihy J. 2016. Leaning Against the Wind When Credit Bites Back. Norges Bank Working Paper No. 9 (2016).

Gumata N and Ndou E. 2017a. Bank Credit Extension and Real Economic Activity in South Africa: The Impact of Capital Flow Dynamics, Bank Regulation and Selected Macroprudential Tools. Palgrave Macmillan. ISB 978-3-319-43550-3.

Gumata N and Ndou E. 2017b. Labour Market and Fiscal Policy Adjustments to Shocks: The Role and Implications for Price and Financial Stability in South Africa. Palgrave Macmillan. ISBN ISBN 978-3-319-66520-7.

Kganyago L. 2016. Speech Given at the Annual Convention of the South African Chamber of Commerce and Industry (SACCI) Emperors Palace, Johannesburg 20 October 2016.

Lane P R. 2018. The Macro-financial Environment in Ireland in Spring 2018. Speech to the Institute for International and European Affairs (IIEA), Dublin, 9 March 2018.

Ndou E, Gumata N, and Ncube M. 2017. Global Economic Uncertainties and Exchange Rate Shocks: Transmission Channels to the South African Economy. Palgrave Macmillan. ISBN ISBN 978-3-319-62280-4.

Restoy F. 2018. The Post-crisis Regulatory Agenda: What is Missing? Speech to Círculo Financiero La Caixa Barcelona, Spain, 19 February 2018.

Serija T S. 2015. Application of the Countercyclical Capital Buffer in Lithuania. Bank of Lithuania.

Spencer G. 2018. Getting the Best Out of Macro-prudential Policy Speech to INFINZ, Auckland, 13 March 2018.

Tunc C, and Yavas A. 2015. Not All Credit is Created Equal: Mortgage vs Non-Mortgage Debt and Private Saving Rate in Turkey. Working Papers 1526. Research and Monetary Policy Department, Central Bank of the Republic of Turkey.

PART IV

Money Demand, Exchange Rate Depreciation Shocks, Household Wealth and Credit Conditions

CHAPTER 28

Revisiting the Role of the Money Demand Function: Does the Shortfall in Money Demand Impact the Inflation Responses to the Exchange Rate Depreciation Shocks?

Research Questions Explored

- The importance of the correct specification of the money demand function for the policy makers.
- The information content of the money demand overhang (excess) and shortfall for policy makers.
- Assess whether redefining and improving the money demand function via *the portfolio balance approach* to money demand renders it relevant for the price and financial stability policy objectives.
- Whether the excess or shortfall in money demand affects the transmission of the rand depreciation shocks to inflation.

28.1 Introduction

The money demand function can be used to link money growth and inflation. In addition, the real money demand states that $M/P = L(Y,R)$, where M/P is real money balances and Y denotes income and R is interest rate. Two measures of imbalances arise: (i) excess money demand occurs when

N. Gumata, E. Ndou, *Achieving Price, Financial and Macro-Economic Stability in South Africa*,
https://doi.org/10.1007/978-3-030-66340-7_28

$M/P > L(Y,R)$ and (ii) shortfall occurs when $M/P < L(Y,R)$. It is these indicators of disequilibrium states that matter for the analysis in this chapter. This chapter puts forward an argument that it is appropriate to revisit the role of monetary aggregates. The aim is to assess whether there is a case to redefine and improve the money demand function to be relevant for the price and financial stability policy objectives. Does the excess or shortfall in money demand affect the transmission of the rand exchange rate depreciation shocks to inflation? If so, does this depend on whether the money demand function includes or excludes wealth variables?

It is a well-established fact that the information content of the money supply aggregates and the income velocity of money weakened in the 1990s in part due to financial liberalisation and globalisation. Figure 28.1 shows that the income velocity was stable between 1980Q1 and 1993Q4 but was on a long-term decline from 1994Q1 to 2009Q2. The downward trend changed post-2010Q1.[1]

Indeed, a number of South African empirical studies have investigated the stability of the money demand function and the information content

Fig. 28.1 Income velocity of money: M3 (log scale). (Source: Authors' calculations)

[1] The income velocity of money is derived using Eq. (28.1) based on the quantity equation $MV = Py$, where M is the total stock of money, V is the per-period turnovers of the money stock which must be equal to the nominal value of income and Py is real GDP. The income velocity of M3 can be estimated via a linear equation *Income velocity of M3* $= -(m - p - y)$, W where m is the log of real M3 balances and y is the log of real GDP.

Table 28.1 Key findings of selected money demand studies in South Africa

	Technique	*Sample*	*Coefficient*				
			GDP	*CPI*	*SR*	*LR*	*Wealth*
Jonsson (2000)	SVEC	1970Q1 to 1998Q2	1.14		0.02	-0.04	
Ricci (2006)	VECM	1970Q1 to 2002Q4	1.03	1.07	0.01	-0.04	
Nell (1999)	VECM	1965Q1 to 1997Q4	1.28			-0.1	
Wesso (2002)	VECM	1971Q1 to 2000Q4	1.84		-5.11	-2.76	
Todani (2007)	VECM	1980Q1 to 2003Q4	3.20		6.30	-6.30	
Hall et al. (2007)	VECM and TVC	1970Q1 to 2006Q4	1.46		-0.02		0.31

Source: Authors' calculations

Note: SR is the short-term interest rate and LR is the long-term interest rate

of M3 money supply for inflation as shown in Table 28.1.[2] But their focus was on the magnitudes of the income elasticities, the stability of the money demand function and largely driven by establishing the validity of the quantity theory of money presupposed one-for-one relationship between money growth and inflation. Contrary to these studies, this chapter (i) extends the definition of the money demand function by including the role of real aggregate and financial household wealth; (ii) derives the measures of money demand disequilibria from the estimated money demand functions; and (iii) uses the money demand disequilibria to derive policy implications of the excess (shortfall) money demand in the transmission of the exchange rate deprecation shock to inflation. The rationale is that this is another approach to examine the role of the extended money demand

[2] Wesso (2002) established a time-varying income coefficient in the money demand function consistent with an increasing degree of financial intermediation. Ricci (2006) established a stable money demand function and the income elasticity close to one. On the other hand, Todani (2007) estimated high-income elasticity and attributed this to omitted variable bias. Hall et al. (2007) used the stock-market valuation as a proxy for the level of wealth and conclude that the exclusion of wealth in the money demand function leads to biased estimates and that M3 growth does provide useful information about medium- to long-term inflation.

function in capturing the interaction between financial stability and monetary policy, a channel that has not been explored in South Africa.

Furthermore, this chapter differs from Koivu et al. (2005), Hall et al. (2007) and De Bondt (2009) who use either equity prices or excess returns on equities or equity prices as a ratio of income as proxies for wealth. This chapter uses two estimates of real household wealth, namely real aggregate and real financial wealth. For policy and robustness analysis, the estimated periods of excess (shortfall) M3 growth are used to assess the rate at which they propagate inflationary pressures of the rand exchange rate depreciation shocks.

The chapter fills various academic and policy research gaps by determining the importance of the correct specification of the money demand function for the policymakers. We show the information content and importance of the money demand overhang (excess) and shortfall for policymakers. In addition, we assess whether redefining and improving the money demand function via *the portfolio balance approach* to money demand renders it relevant for the price and financial stability policy objectives. We also determine whether the excess or shortfall in the money demand affects the transmission of the rand exchange rate depreciation shocks to inflation.

28.2 Does the Conventional Money Demand Function Differ from the Augmented Specification with Financial Wealth Variables?

The study is conducted for the sample period 1990Q1 to 2015Q4. The data is sourced from the South African Reserve Bank database. All growth rates are at an annual rate. This section starts by estimating the conventional money demand function (referred to as the benchmark model) or the long-run money–inflation relationship as specified in Eq. (28.1) and the augmented version is given by Eq. (28.2):[3]

$$(m-p)=\beta_0+\beta_1 GDP+\beta_2(IRspread) \tag{28.1}$$

$$(m-p)=\beta_0+\beta_1 GDP+\beta_2(Wealth)+\beta_3(IRspread) \tag{28.2}$$

[3] See Calza, Gerdesmeier and Levy (2001) for further details.

where $(m - p)$ is the log of the stock of real money balances (M3 money supply deflated by the GDP deflator P_t) and y is the real GDP. The *IR spread* is the difference between the ten-year yield on the government bond and the 12-month Negotiable Certificate of Deposit (NCD) rate and captures the opportunity cost of holding money. Two household wealth variables, real aggregate wealth (RAW) and real financial wealth (RFW), are used in Eq. (28.2) in different estimations. All the measures of wealth are deflated with the GDP deflator. Equations (28.1) and (28.2) are estimated by the Johansen (1998) vector error correction model (VECM).

Table 28.2 shows that all the variables are I(1) and Table 28.3 shows that the maximum eigenvalues and the trace test establish the existence of one cointegration equation. Table 28.4 shows the VECM results from models which include real aggregate and financial household wealth (RAW and RFW).[4] The real money balances are positively linked to real income and negatively associated with interest rates. The VECM results in Table 28.4 indicate that the point elasticity for GDP ranges between 1.89 and 1.65. The income elasticity of GDP is more than one and the coefficient for the interest rate spread implies that interest rates are relevant for the money demand function. The interest rate spread coefficient is -0.05 and -0.002. The magnitudes of the coefficients for GDP and the interest rate spread are comparable to those in Hall et al. (2007), Beyer (2009), De Santis et al. (2008) and Brand and Cassola (2004), amongst other studies.

Table 28.2 Order of integration and unit root tests

Variable	*PP*	*ADF*
NCD rate	I(1)	I(1)
SA ten-year yield	I(1)	I(1)
GDP	I(1)	I(1)
GDP deflator	I(1)	I(1)
Inflation	I(1)	I(1)
M3	I(1)	I(1)
Total wealth	I(1)	I(1)
Financial wealth	I(1)	I(1)

Source: Authors' calculations

Note: Significance at 5 per cent**, at 10 per cent*

[4]We estimated a VECM for real household net wealth and the results are comparable to those derived using real aggregate wealth.

Table 28.3 Johansen test for cointegration rank test

$H_0: Rank \leq p$	*Trace*	*Max-eigenvalues*
	Equation 13.1	
$p = 0$	31.82	21.95
	(0.03)**	(0.04)**
$p \leq 1$	9.86	9.25
	(0.29)	(0.27)
Equation 13.2 including real aggregate wealth (RAW)		
$p = 0$	67.23	36.16
	(0.00)**	(0.00)**
$p \leq 1$	31.08	25.80
	(0.04)**	(0.01)**
$p \leq 2$	5.28	5.25
	(0.78)	(0.71)
Equation 13.2 including real financial wealth (RFW)		
$p = 0$	70.22	41.05
	(0.00)**	(0.00)**
$p \leq 1$	29.17	23.64
	(0.06)**	(0.03)**

Source: Authors' calculations

Note: Significance at 5 per cent**, at 10 per cent*

Table 28.4 Cointegration equation for the conventional money demand function

	Conventional money demand	*Augmented with real aggregate wealth*	*Augmented with real financial wealth*
LGDP	1.878 (31.461)**	1.866 (16.384)**	1.645 (11.043)**
RAW		0.0339 (5.329)**	
RFW			0.031 (6.197)**
Spread	-0.049 (6.475)**	-0.064 (4.058)**	-0.002 (0.198)***
ECT	-0.09 (2.313)**	-0.0299 (2.405)**	-0.033 (3.708)**

Source: Authors' calculations

Note: ** indicates significance at 5 per cent significance level

Does the inclusion of wealth variables matter? Yes, that seems to the case. First, the results mean that the extension of the money demand functions via the wealth channel and portfolio–balance approaches is supported by the data. Second, the estimated income elasticities are lower in models with the financial wealth variables in comparison to those estimated under the conventional money demand function.

This implies that the inclusion of the financial wealth variables lowers the sensitivities of income in the money demand function, with respect to the specification that includes real financial wealth. This may be due to the role of financial wealth in price and financial stability. The slow speed of adjustment means that the disequilibrium takes longer when considering the role of wealth than is the case under the conventional money demand function. This is consistent with the recent empirical evidence showing that financial cycles take longer to adjust. Last, from the interaction of monetary policy and financial stability perspective this means that the extension of the money demand function can capture aspects related to asset price inflation and wealth channels in the transmission mechanism.

28.2.1 *Are the Elasticities in the Money Demand Functions Time Varying?*

Figure 28.2 shows the time-varying properties of the estimated coefficients in the various money demand functions.

The rolling long-run coefficients for GDP and the interest rate spread vary overtime but are stable and bounded within the error bands. The coefficient for income declined significantly between 2008Q1 and 2012Q4 but has recovered as reflected in the income velocity of M3 in Fig. 28.1. Hence, the results can be interpreted to mean that the sharp decline in the

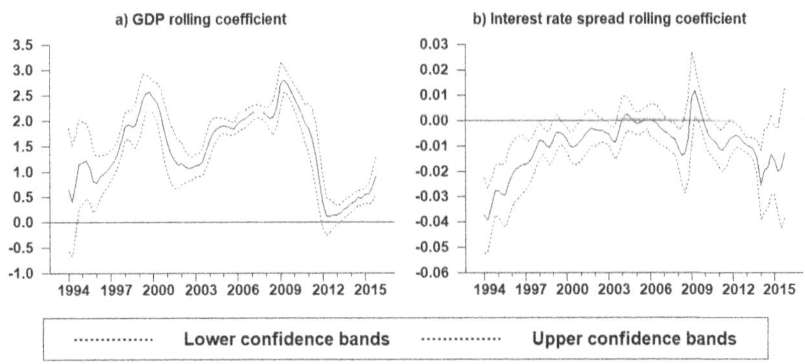

Fig. 28.2 Rolling long-run coefficients. (Source: Authors' calculations)

income coefficient and the income velocity of M3 do not necessarily imply the instability of the money demand function per se, but rather that there was a structural break in the relationship. Indeed, this may mean that the money demand function as traditionally specified can be improved.

28.3 Does the Excess Money Supply and Shortfall Impact the Transmission of Rand Exchange Rate Depreciation Shocks into Inflation?

The excesses and shortfalls estimated by the conventional money demand relationship derived from Eq. (28.1) are shown in Fig. 28.3 and indicate that since 2014 the real money balances are below the long-term trend. This means that there is a shortfall in the money demand by almost 5 per cent compared to the recent overhang during 2009Q1 and 2013Q4.

Furthermore, the money demand disequilibria estimated via the extended money demand functions in Fig. 28.4 show that the extended money demand functions including real financial wealth suggest that there was excess money demand which peaked at 2 per cent during 2014 but has since corrected. On the other hand, the demand function derived from the real aggregate wealth equation suggests that the shortfall since 2013 has corrected.

First, the implication is that both measures of the error correction are picking up the role of financial and non-financial asset price inflation post the global financial crisis which is absent in the conventional money

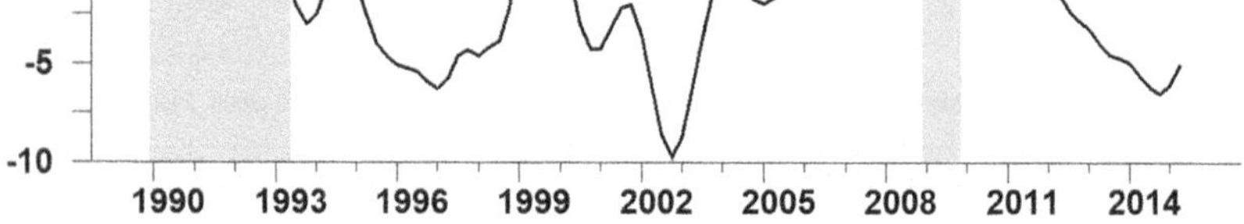

Fig. 28.3 Estimates of excess and shortfall in the conventional money demand function. (Source: Authors' calculations)

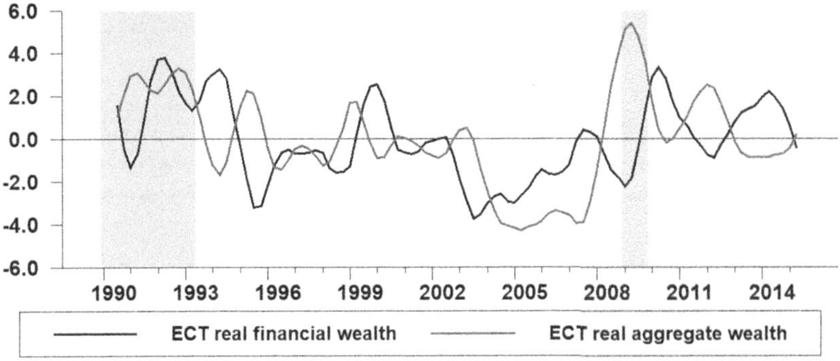

Fig. 28.4 Estimates of excess and shortfall in the augmented money demand function. (Source: Authors' calculations)

demand function as it still indicates a substantial and persistent money demand shortfall. Second, there might be substitution effects since real financial wealth will mostly reflect the valuation of non-monetary financial and non-financial assets. The performance of financial assets post-2009 possibly indicates the role of various rounds of quantitative easing (QE) from key central banks of financial assets. It is common knowledge that equity prices performed better than other asset classes such as housing which would be included in aggregate wealth.

28.4 The Role of the Shortfall and Excess Money Demand from the Model with Real Household Aggregate Wealth Shortfall

So, how do the estimated money demand overhang and shortfall impact the transmission of the rand exchange rate depreciation shocks to inflation? We answer this question by creating two dummy variables: (i) the excess money demand dummy variable which equals to the value of excess money demand and zero otherwise; (ii) the money demand shortfall dummy variable equals to the value of the shortfall and zero otherwise. We estimate a counterfactual VAR model using quarterly data from 2000Q1 to 2015Q4 which includes annual rand per US dollar changes (R/US$), inflation and the dummy variables for either excess or money demand shortfall indicator. The models are estimated with two lags and 10,000 Monte Carlo draws. The role of the dummy variables is shut off to determine the amplification effects of the excess or shortfall in money demand.

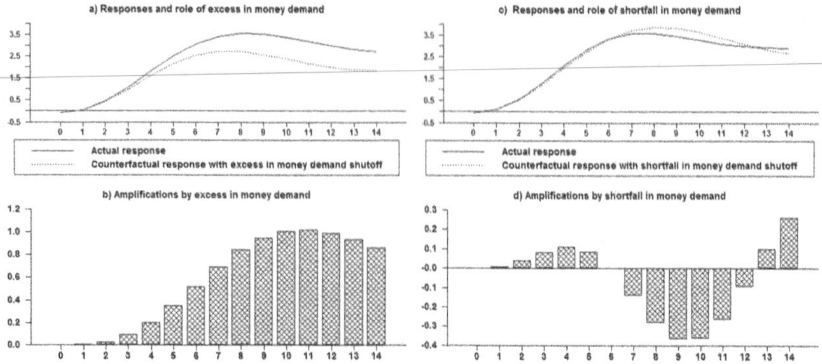

Fig. 28.5 Inflation responses to rand depreciation shock and the role of the excess and shortfall money demand channels. (Source: Authors' calculations)

Figure 28.5c and d shows that excess (shortfall) money demand amplifies (neutralises) the inflation responses to the rand exchange rate depreciation shocks. But it is evident that the shortfall in the money demand in Fig. 28.5d neutralises the exchange rate depreciation effects after a considerable lag of about six quarters.

28.4.1 How Does the Money Demand Shortfall Impact The Rand Exchange Rate Depreciation Shocks Transmission into Inflation?

For the robustness analysis of the effects of the rand exchange rate depreciation episodes on inflation and the role of the money demand disequilibria, we use Eq. (28.3):

$$Inflation_t = constant + \sum_{i=1}^{4} \beta_i Inflation_{t-i} + \sum_{i=1}^{4} \beta_i Shortfall_{t-i} + \sum_{i=0}^{4} q_i Rand\ depreciation_{t-i} + \varepsilon_t \quad (28.3)$$

where ε_t denotes an error term and ***Rand depreciations*** refers to dummy variables which equals to one for the rand exchange rate depreciations only and zero otherwise. The money demand *Shortfall* dummy equals to the value of the shortfall and zero otherwise. The counterfactual responses are determined by setting all coefficients of the money demand shortfall equal to zero. The actual responses refer to inflation responses when the money demand shortfall is included in the model, whereas the counterfactual responses refer to when the money demand shortfall is shut off in the model.

28.4.2 *Evidence from the Money Demand Shortfall in Equations Augmented with Real Aggregate and Financial Wealth*

Figure 28.6 shows the role of the money demand shortfall based on the augmented money demand function with real household aggregate wealth. The counterfactual impulse responses exceed the actual inflation responses, which mean that the money demand shortfall dampens the pass-through of the rand exchange rate deprecations shock to inflation. In the absence of the money demand shortfall inflation would be higher.

Does the shortfall from real financial wealth make a difference? We find in Fig. 28.7 that the money demand shortfall from the model augmented with real financial wealth indicates a delay in the dampening effects on the pass-through of rand exchange rate depreciations shocks to inflation. In cumulative terms, real aggregate wealth exerts a more depressing effect on inflation compared to real financial wealth. This implies that the wealth channel of the monetary policy transmission plays a significant role in inflation developments.

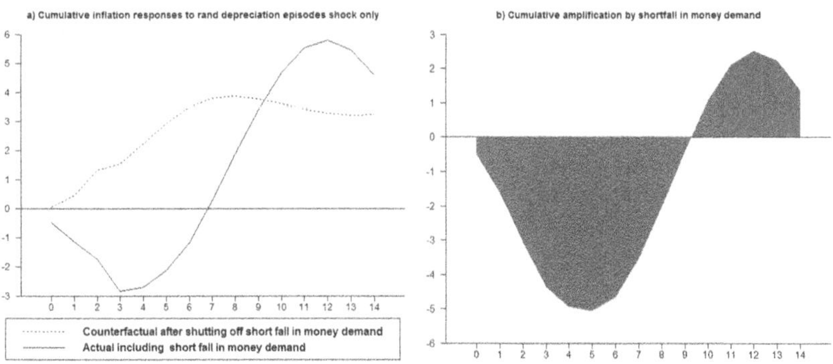

Fig. 28.6 Accumulated responses and the role of the money demand shortfall from a model with real aggregate wealth. (Source: Authors' calculations)

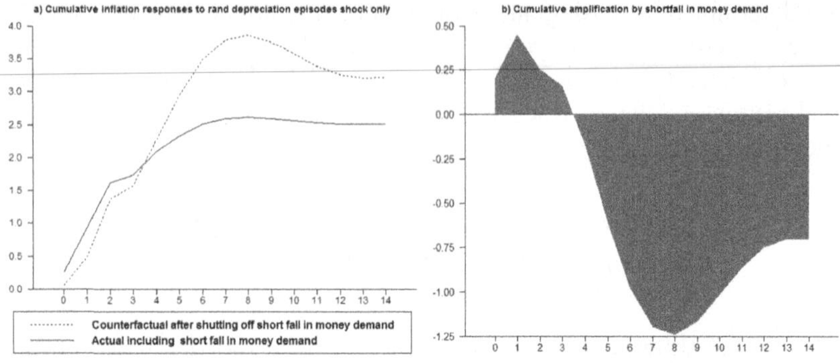

Fig. 28.7 Accumulated responses and the role of the money demand shortfall from a model with real financial wealth. (Source: Authors' calculations)

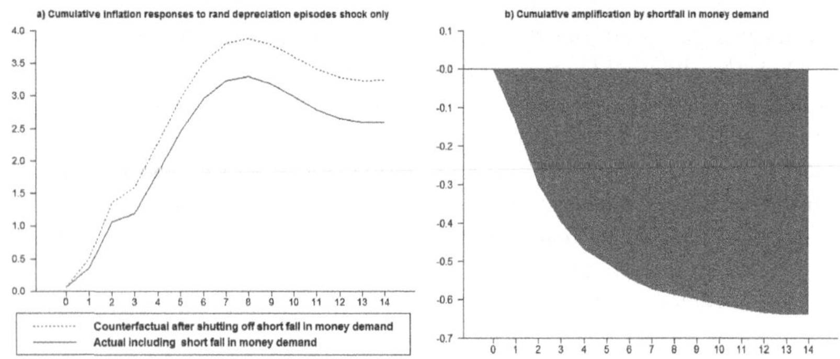

Fig. 28.8 Accumulated responses and the role of the money demand shortfall from the conventional money demand model. (Source: Authors' calculations)

How do the money demand disequilibria impact the pass-through effects from the extended money demand function compared to the conventional money demand function? Figure 28.8 shows that the money demand shortfall derived from the conventional money demand function also dampens inflationary pressures, but in cumulative terms it exerts less downward pressure compared to those due to the extended money demand functions.

This means that the extended money demand functions do indeed contain more relevant information about inflationary pressures compared to the conventional money demand function. The inclusion of real wealth variables adds valuable information in relation to the price stability mandate.

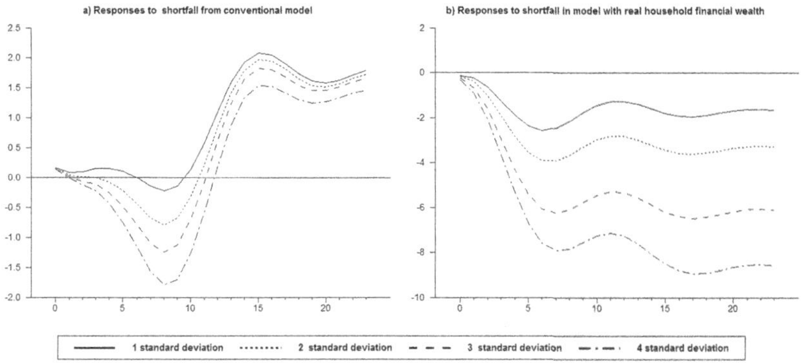

Fig. 28.9 Inflation responses to money demand shortfall shocks of different magnitudes. (Source: Authors' calculations)

28.4.3 *The Asymmetric Effects of Conventional, Real Aggregate and Financial Wealth Shortfalls*

This section concludes the analysis by showing the inflation responses to the estimated money demand shortfall shocks using a bivariate VAR model. The model enables us to test for the asymmetric effects due to the money demand disequilibria based on the size of the shortfall. Figure 28.9 shows that inflation declines more due to large money demand shortfall shocks. This means that the money demand shortfall has a direct and indirect impact on inflation via the transmission of the rand exchange rate depreciations shocks. In addition, the nature of the money demand disequilibria matters given that the responses of the conventional money demand function seem to suggest that the effects it exerts are sharp but very transitory. This contrasts with those exerted by the shortfall derived from the extended money demand functions which suggests that the dampening effects on inflationary pressures seem to be more persistent. The results imply that the nature of the money demand disequilibrium from models augmented with financial variables conveys valuable information for price and financial stability objectives.

28.5 Conclusion and Policy Implications

This chapter put forward the argument that it is appropriate to revisit the role of monetary aggregates to assess whether there is a case to redefine and improve the money demand function to be relevant for price and financial stability policy objectives. Contrary to earlier papers that have explored the money demand in South Africa, this chapter focused on what the indicators of the money demand disequilibrium states mean for policymakers. Does the excess or shortfall in the money demand affect the transmission of the rand exchange rate depreciation shocks to inflation? If so, does this depend on whether the money demand function includes or excludes wealth variables?

Evidence shows that the extension of the money demand functions via the wealth channel and portfolio-balance approaches is supported by the data. The estimated income elasticities are lower in models with financial variables in comparison to those estimated under the conventional money demand function. This means that the inclusion of the wealth variables lowers the sensitivities of income in the money demand function. This is particularly the case with the respect to the inclusion of real financial wealth. This may be due to the role of financial wealth in the price and financial stability.

Furthermore, the inclusion of wealth variables results in the slow speed of adjustment. This means that the correction from the point of disequilibrium takes longer when considering the role of wealth than is the case under the conventional money demand function. This is consistent with the recent empirical evidence showing that financial cycles take longer to adjust. From the interaction of monetary policy and financial stability perspective this means that the extension of the money demand function can capture aspects related to asset price inflation and wealth channels of the transmission mechanism.

Evidence from the indirect role of the money demand based on the counterfactual analysis concludes that excess money demand and shortfall do impact the transmission of the R/US$ exchange rate depreciation shocks to inflation. The money demand shortfall shock dampens the pass-through of rand exchange rate deprecation shocks to inflation. The decline in inflation is pronounced due to large money demand shortfall shocks than small shocks. Hence, we conclude that the money demand shortfall directly and indirectly affects inflation via the transmission of the rand exchange rate depreciations shocks.

In addition, the results show that the nature of the money demand disequilibria matters. This is because the responses of the conventional money demand function seem to suggest that it exerts sharp but very transitory effects on the exchange rate pass-through. These contrast with those exerted by the shortfall derived from the extended money demand functions which suggest that the dampening effects on inflationary pressures seem to be more persistent and consistent with the effects of financial cycles. The results imply that the nature of the disequilibrium in the money demand function from models augmented with financial variable conveys valuable information for price and financial stability objectives.

References

Beyer A. 2009. A stable model for euro area money demand revisiting the role of wealth. ECB Working Paper Series No 111.

Boone L, Mikol F, and Van den Noord P. 2004. Wealth Effects on Money Demand in EMU. OECD Working Paper No. 411.

Brand C and Cassola N. 2004. A money demand system for euro area M3, Applied Economics, Vol. 36, 817–838.

Bruggeman A, Donati P, and Warne A. 2003. Is the Demand for Euro Area M3 Stable? ECB Working Paper No. 255.

Calza A, Gerdesmeier D, and Levy J. 2001. Euro area money demand:measuring the opportunity costs appropriately. IMF Working Paper WP/01/179.

De Bondt G. 2009. Euro Area Money Demand: Empirical Evidence on the Role of Equity and Labour Markets. ECB Working Paper Series No. 1086.

De Santis R A, Favero C A, and Roffia B. 2008. Euro area money demand and international portfolio allocation: A contribution to assessing risks to price stability, A flow-of-funds perspective on the financial crisis, 46–93.

Dreger C, and Wolters J. 2009. Money Velocity and Asset Prices in the Euro Area. Empirica, 36, 51–63.

Gerdesmeier D. 1996. The Role of Wealth in Money Demand. Deutsche Bundesbank Discussion Paper 5/96. Frankfurt am Main.

Goodhart C and Hofmann B. 2007. House Prices and the Macroeconomy: Implications for Banking and Price Stability. Oxford University Press.

Hall S G, Hondroyiannis G, Swamy P A V B, and Tavlas G. 2007. A portfolio balance approach to euro area money demand in a time varying environment. Bank of Greece.

Johansen S. 1988. Statistical Analysis of Cointegration Vectors. Journal of Economic Dynamics and Control, Vol. 12, No. 2–3, pp. 231–254.

Jonsson G. 2000. Inflation, money demand, and purchasing power parity in South Africa. IMF Staff Papers, 48, 243–265.

Ricci L A. 2006. Bringing Inflation Under Control. IMF.

Koivu M, Pennanen T, and Ziemba W T. 2005. Cointegration analysis of the FED model. Finance Research Letters, 2: 248–259.

Nell K S. 1999. The Stability of Money Demand in South Africa, 1965–1997. Studies in Economics, 99(5).

Todani K R. 2007. A cointegrated VAR model of M3 demand in South Africa, South African Reserve Bank, Discussion Paper No.04.

Wesso G R. 2002. Broad Money Demand and Financial Liberalisation in South Africa, South African Reserve Bank, Occasional Paper No. 18, November, (2002), Pretoria.

CHAPTER 29

Do the Shortfalls and Overhangs Derived from Money Demand in South Africa Augmented with Portfolio Balances Impact Inflation Dynamics?

Research Questions Explored

- Show the relevance of asset price such as the price/earnings (P/E) ratios based on *international portfolio balance approach* to the conventional money demand in South Africa.
- Show the effects of the *international portfolio balance approach* to the money demand shortfall and overhang on inflation when inflation is above and below the 6 per cent threshold.
- Establish the nature of the relationship between international portfolio flows and M3 money growth.

29.1 Introduction

The earlier chapter considered the role of the wealth channel and the portfolio balance approach to the money demand function. The analysis in the chapter only considered South African variables in the *portfolio balance approach* to money demand. This chapter extends the analysis of the potential explanatory variables of the determinants of the money demand function in South Africa by exploring the role of external variables and applying

N. Gumata, E. Ndou, *Achieving Price, Financial and Macro-Economic Stability in South Africa*,
https://doi.org/10.1007/978-3-030-66340-7_29

the *international portfolio balance approach* to money demand. In contrast to the earlier chapter, the analysis in this chapter asks: Does the inclusion of foreign assets and capital flows in the conventional money demand functions influence the effects of the derived shortfall and overhang (excess) on inflation dynamics above and below the 6 per cent threshold?

The *international portfolio balance approach* to money demand suggests that the relative portfolio allocation among risky assets depends on domestic and non-resident agent asset expected returns on domestic and foreign assets, relative to their own rate of return on money. Why does an analysis from the perspective of the international portfolio balance approach to money demand matter? First, this matters because the period post the global financial crisis was characterised by (i) the decline to zero and even negative policy rates; and (ii) in some instances negative long-term yields in some advanced economies. This widened the interest rate differentials with most emerging market economies (EMEs). Second, we show the relevance of asset price such as price/earnings (P/E) ratios. The *international portfolio-balance approach* (FED model) associates the decline in excess returns on equities with the deviation of the P/E ratio from the long-term government bond yield. The implication is that when investors expect returns to decline, they reallocate assets, thus resulting in shifts in equity and bond prices that restore equilibrium in the asset markets.

This chapter fills policy and academic research gaps by including the international portfolio choice of assets in the modelling of the money demand function. From the monetary policy perspective, the period post the global financial crisis has been characterised by the role of excess global liquidity, capital flow surges and external financial imbalances had become a topical policy issue for the mandates of price and financial stability. Hence, this chapter assesses the relevance of the international portfolio balance approach to the money demand function and the information content of the derived shortfall and excess of money demand. The approach adopted in this chapter differs from Hall at al. (2007), De Santis et al. (2008) and Carstensen (2003, 2006), who included a measure of equity market price returns and volatility, and confined their analysis to the United States (US) and the euro area.

This chapter explores the role of (i) the international portfolio inflows on the South African (SA or domestic) money demand function, (ii) the interest rate differential between domestic and G4[1] foreign interest rates,

[1] The G4 includes the U.S., the euro area, the United Kingdom (UK) and Japan.

and (iii) asset price returns on the SA money demand function. This means that the analysis in this chapter estimates the money demand functions largely based on the evolution of several asset price returns. We then test whether the derived money demand overhang and shortfall have an impact on domestic inflation. The chapter further fills the existing policy research gaps regarding (i) the sectorial re-distribution effects of money holding induced by the international portfolio allocation shifts between the risky and safe haven motives for holding money and (ii) the money stock or holding effects induced by transactions between money-creating counterparties.

29.2 What Happened to Price/Earnings Ratios and Other Asset Prices?

To put context into the investigation in the study, Fig. 29.1 shows that the relationship between SA P/E ratios and the ten-year government bond yield diverged since 2003. On the other hand, the US and SA P/E ratios diverged during the mid-1990s but have since moved in the same direction with SA P/E ratios higher than those in the US.

Similarly, the long-term bond yields in the two countries have tended to trend in the same direction and have persistently declined since the 1990s. The trends observed may have implications for the *international portfolio balance approach* to money demand. The divergence of the asset prices may lead to substitution effects amongst assets and wealth effects within the domestic and international asset portfolios.

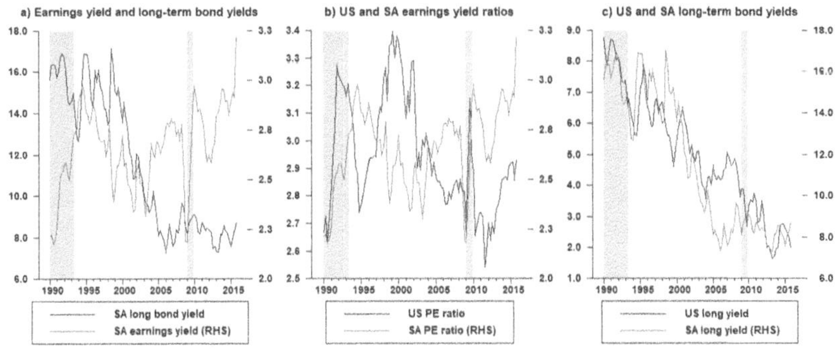

Fig. 29.1 SA and US bond yields and price/earnings ratios. (Source: South African Reserve Bank)

29.2.1 *Do International Portfolio Inflows Impact the Demand for Money?*

This section is motivated by De Santis et al. (2008), who establish a breakdown in the relationship between M3 growth and inflation in the euro area due to the strong positive link between net cross-border capital (portfolio) inflows and M3 growth. The study finds that the link occurs via the *substitution portfolio balance effect.* The substitution effect arises largely due to heightened financial market and geopolitical uncertainty triggering portfolio shifts and thus impacting developments in the monetary aggregates.

Does capital inflow activity impact money demand in South African? Yes, evidence in Fig. 29.2 shows that M3 growth increases with a delay of about one quarter due to positive shocks to portfolio inflows.[2] The peak effects of positive capital inflow shocks occur between five and six quarters. The responses imply that indeed cross-border portfolio inflow transactions do affect M3 money supply growth.

When did capital inflows uplift and drag M3 growth? To answer this question, we perform a historical decomposition analysis based on a counterfactual VAR model shown in Fig. 29.3 to determine what would

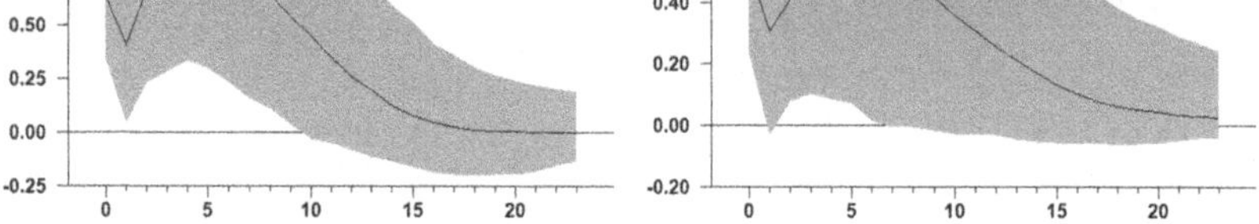

Fig. 29.2 M3 growth responses to gross and net portfolio inflows. (Source: Authors' calculations)

[2] The results are based on a VAR model for the period 1990Q1 to 2015Q4, which includes GDP growth, the interest rate spread, and gross or net portfolio flows, which are included separately in the estimations. The model is estimated with two lags chosen by AIC and 10,000 Monte Carlo draws. All growth rates are at an annual rate and the data is sourced from the South African Reserve Bank database.

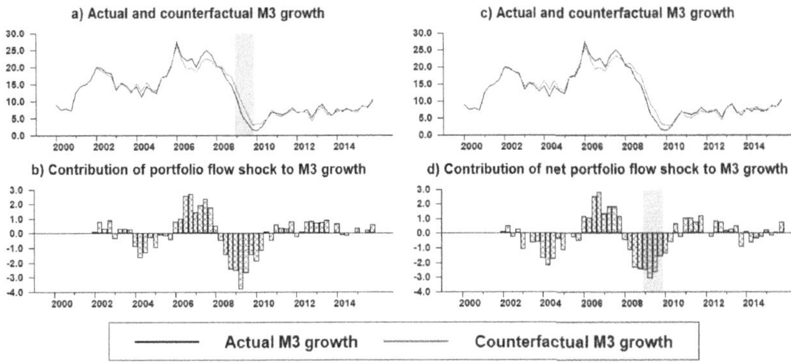

Fig. 29.3 Actual and counterfactual broad M3 money growth and the role portfolio inflow shocks. (Source: Authors' calculations)

have happened to M3 growth in the absence of gross and net portfolio inflows. The counterfactual responses are based on estimations where the gross and net capital inflow channel is shut off in the model.

Evidence indicates that between 2006Q1 and 2008Q1, gross and net portfolio inflows contributed as much as 3 per cent to the increase in M3 growth. This trend was reversed during the recession in 2009 as capital inflows contributed to a decline in M3 growth.

Furthermore, since 2010Q1, portfolio inflows contributed less than 1 per cent to the increase in M3 growth. This implies that despite quantitative easing (QE) interventions by central banks in advanced economies and the subsequent capital flow surge, monetary assets offered very limited returns compared to other asset classes, hence the muted contribution of portfolio inflow shocks to M3 growth. Based on the impulse responses and historical decomposition, we conclude that M3 growth is impacted by international portfolio inflows. In addition, these results corroborate earlier findings in Gumata and Ndou (2017), who find that international capital inflow shocks play an exceedingly small and limited role in credit extension. The authors conclude that the most significant drivers of credit may be primarily domestically generated and oriented rather than highly dependent on foreign capital inflow shocks. In addition, the implication is that bank-based funding in the economy can remain stable in the case of their withdrawal or volatility.

29.2.2 Money Demand Function Specifications

Three money demand functions are estimated, which include the conventional money demand function and two augmented versions. Equation (29.1) is the conventional money demand function, while Eqs. (29.2) and (29.3) are the augmented versions. Equation (29.2) suggests that the relative portfolio allocation among risky assets depends on asset returns expected by domestic and non-resident agents on domestic and foreign assets, relative to their own rate of return on money. The specification in Eq. (29.2) suggests that domestic residents as holders of money balances maximise their returns by holding both domestic and foreign-currency assets. In addition, the domestic and foreign interest rates and asset price return variables capture the role of international capital mobility. An increase in foreign interest rates and returns subsequently leads to a decline in the demand for domestic assets. Equation (29.3) suggests that the demand for domestic monetary assets cannot be realistically estimated without considering the impact of foreign factors.

$$(m-p)=\beta_0+\beta_1 GDP+\beta_2 (IR spread) \tag{29.1}$$

$$\begin{aligned}(m-p)=\beta_0+\beta_1 GDP+\beta_2\left(PE^{SA}\right)+\beta_3\left(IR spread^{SA}\right)\\ +\beta_4\left(PE^{US}\right)+\beta_5\left(spread^{SAUS}\right)\end{aligned} \tag{29.2}$$

$$\begin{aligned}(m-p)=\beta_0+\beta_1 GDP+\beta_2\left(PE^{SA}\right)+\beta_3\left(IR spread^{SA}\right)\\ +\beta_4\left(PE^{UKEAJap}\right)+\beta_5\left(spread^{SAUKEAJap}\right)\end{aligned} \tag{29.3}$$

(m - p) is the log of the stock of real money balances (money supply M3 deflated by the GDP deflator P_t), y is the real GDP. The *IR spread* is the difference between the ten-year yield on the government bond and the 12-month Negotiable Certificate of Deposit (NCD) rate, and captures the opportunity cost of holding money. PE^{SA} and PE^{US} are the SA and US P/E ratios. The $spread^{SA\ US}$ is the difference between the SA and US ten-year government bond yields. $PE^{UK\ EA\ Jap}$ is the common factor for the P/E ratios for the UK, the euro area and Japan; and $spread^{UK\ EA\ Jap}$ is the difference between the SA and the factor for the UK, euro area and Japan ten-year government bond yields. Equation (29.3) is an extended version of Eq. (29.2) and includes the UK, euro area and Japan P/E ratios and ten-year government bond yields to assess for robustness of the estimated money demand function to model parameter changes and sample size.

29.3 Data

The empirical estimation of the money demand functions uses data from SA, the US, the UK, the euro area and Japan for the sample period 1995Q1 to 2015Q4. We use SA M3 money supply, GDP, the GDP deflator, the 12-month NCD and the SA ten-year government bond yields to calculate the deposit rate spread. The domestic M3 money supply is deflated with the GDP deflator. All variables enter the estimations in log form except for the interest rates. The three-month rates and long-term government bond yields are used to calculate the deposit rate spread or the opportunity cost of holding and the interest rate differential between SA and the G4 countries. The P/E ratios are the proxies for the Sharpe ratios.

Theoretically, the portfolio shares and allocation of all assets depends on the Sharpe ratios which capture the risk associated with asset prices. Due to the availability of data for the P/E ratios for some of the G4 countries, we adjust the sample size to start in 2001Q1 to 2015Q4. In addition, to avoid biased estimations, we extract the common component of the UK, euro area and Japan P/E ratios and ten-year government bond yields by using the principal component analysis. Thereafter, we use the derived factors in the estimations of the money demand function.

29.3.1 Johansen Cointegration Results

The Johansen cointegration test indicates that one long-run relationship exists between the variables included in the model for the sample period.[3] Table 29.1 shows that the variables are I (1).

The cointegration rank tests for Eqs. (29.1) to (29.3) in Table 29.2 indicate that the maximum eigenvalues and the trace tests show that there is one cointegration equation.

[3] De Santis et al. (2008) argue that returns on asset prices rule out the presence of a deterministic trend in the long-run equilibrium for bond and stock prices. This means that the tests for the cointegration rank will exclude a deterministic trend. The maximum eigenvalues and the trace tests show that there is one cointegration equation.

Table 29.1 Unit root tests

Variable	PP	ADF
SA NCD rate	I(1)	I(1)
US three-month rate	I(1)	I(1)
UK three-month rate	I(1)	I(1)
Euro area three-month rate	I(1)	I(1)
Japan three-month rate	I(1)	I(1)
SA ten-year yield	I(1)	I(1)
US ten-year yield	I(1)	I(1)
UK ten-year yield	I(1)	I(1)
Euro area ten-year yield	I(1)	I(1)
Japan ten-year yield	I(1)	I(1)
SA GDP growth	I(1)	I(1)
SA GDP deflator	I(1)	I(1)
SA M3 growth	I(1)	I(1)
SA PE ratio	I(1)	I(1)
US PE ratio	I(1)	I(1)
UK PE ratio	I(1)	I(1)
Euro area PE ratio	I(1)	I(1)
Japan PE ratio	I(1)	I(1)
SA portfolio inflows	I(1)	I(1)

Source: Authors' calculations

Note: Significance at 5 per cent **, at 10 per cent*

The cointegration rank and equations suggest that only one long-run relationship exists between the variables included in the model for the sample period. The long-run relationship is interpreted as the money demand equation and that there is at least some form of arbitrage that exists between the bond yields, returns on equities and money (monetary assets) across countries. In addition, the equity returns and bond yields are the key drivers of the money supply developments. As a result, the positions of the dis-equilibria can be interpreted within the asset price and monetary developments nexus.

Table 29.3 shows the vector error correction model (VECM) results from three estimated models. The real money balances are positively linked to real income and negatively to the interest rate spreads, as predicted by theory. The point elasticity for GDP is high (1.88) in the conventional model and low (1.096) in model augmented with asset prices. This low value in the augmented models implies that the inclusion of asset price returns and the interest rate differentials impacts the money demand aspects that are not captured by the income velocity of money.

Table 29.2 Johansen test for cointegration rank tests

$H_o : Rank \leq p$	*Trace*	*Max-eigenvalues*
	Equation 14.1	
$p = 0$	31.82	21.95
	(0.03)**	(0.04)**
$p \leq 1$	9.86	9.25
	(0.29)	(0.27)
	Equation 14.2 SA and US variables only	
$p = 0$	95.75	40.07
	(0.00)**	(0.00)**
$p \leq 1$	69.81	33.87
	(0.06)**	(0.13)**
	Equation 14.3. SA, US, UK, euro area and Japan variables included	
$p = 0$	95.75	40.078
	(0.00)**	(0.00)**
$p \leq 1$	69.82	33.88
	(0.18)**	(0.35)**

Source: Authors' calculations

Note: ** indicates significance at 5 per cent significance level

Table 29.3 Cointegration equation for the conventional money demand function

	Conventional money demand	*Augmented with SA US variables*	*Augmented with SA, UK, EA and Japan variables*
LGDP	1.878 (31.461)**	1.300 (11.92)**	1.096 (9.226)**
IR Spread^{SA}	-0.049 (-6.475)**	-0.031 (-5.626)**	-0.015 (-3.861)**
Spread$^{SA\ U.S.}$		-0.054 (-5.115)**	
Spread$^{SA\ UK\ EA\ Jap}$			-0.110 (-10.373)**
PE^{SA}		-0.014 (-2.661)**	-0.153 (-2.214)**
PE^{US}		-0.013 (-2.185)**	
PE$^{U.K.\ EA\ Jap}$			-0.014 (-1.918)**
Error correcting term	-0.09 (-2.313)**	-0.179 (-5.34)**	-0.255 (-6.468)**

Source: Authors' calculations

Note: ** indicates significance at 5 per cent significance level

The impact of the SA interest rate spread ranges between -0.05 and -0.02 and those of the foreign spreads are between -0.05 and -0.11. The magnitudes of the coefficients for GDP and the interest rate spread are comparable to those of Hall et al. (2007), Beyer (2009), De Santis et al. (2008) and Brand and Cassola (2004), amongst other studies. The impact of the estimated coefficients indicates that the income effect is larger than the interest rate differential effect in absolute terms.

Is there a *substitution effect*? Furthermore, asset price returns are negatively related to money demand and their coefficients range between -0.013 and -0.153. The coefficients in absolute terms are slightly higher than those of the interest rate differentials but lower than those of income. This means that the *substitution effect* due to the asset returns is significant but slightly smaller in comparison to the portfolio balance effect induced by income effects. However, both the *substitution effects* and *international portfolio balance* effects play a role in determining the demand for money.

The error correction terms of the augmented model are bigger in absolute terms than those implied by the conventional money demand function. In the conventional money demand, the dis-equilibria corrects at a rate of 9 per cent per quarter. This is smaller compared to 18 per cent and 26 per cent in the models that include international asset price returns and the interest rate differential. This means that the inclusion of international asset price returns and the interest rate differentials in

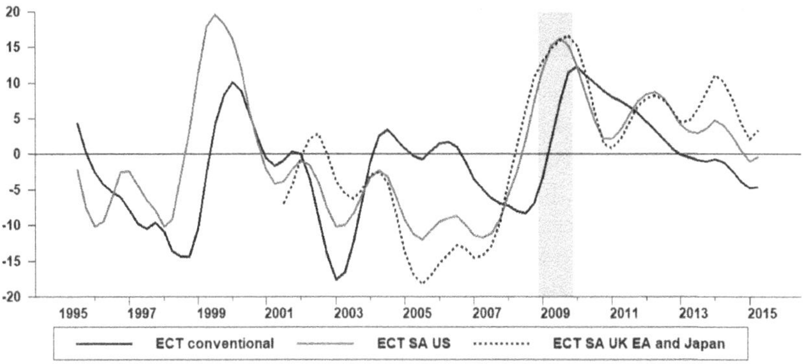

Fig. 29.4 Estimates of excess and shortfall from all money demand equations. (Source: Authors' calculations)

the money demand results in a slightly higher rate of correction of the dis-equilibrium positions.

Figure 29.4 indicates that money balances derived from the conventional money demand function are below the long-term trend. This means that there is a shortfall in the money demand by almost 5 per cent compared to the recent overhang of 10 per cent during 2009Q1 and 2013Q4.

On the other hand, the cointegration relations derived from the money demand function, augmented with international asset price returns and the interest rate differential, suggest that there has been a persistent money demand overhang since 2008Q1, which has varied between 15 and 10 per cent. This implies that both measures from the augmented model are picking up the role of asset price returns and the interest rate differentials post the global financial crisis. This is absent in the conventional money demand function as it still indicates a substantial and persistent money demand shortfall.[4] The performance of financial assets post-2009 possibly indicates the role of various rounds of QE from central banks on financial assets. It is common knowledge that bond yields and equity price performed better than other asset classes.

[4] Since the models including international asset-price returns explain monetary developments in a system that includes the evolution of a broad set of asset returns, this means that models are picking up the developments in money demand conditional on the behaviour of asset prices. The dis-equilibria positions possibly indicate the asset-market disequilibria, which is incompatible with the long-term asset-price behaviour. Growth in money supply must be analysed in a system that includes a broader set of asset-price developments for it to be policy relevant.

29.3.2 Do Excess Shortfall and Overhang from the Augmented Money Demand Functions Impact Inflation Dynamics?

We conclude the analysis of the relevance of the international portfolio balance approach to money demand by assessing the responses of inflation to positive shocks to the estimated dis-equilibria positions from the augmented money demand functions. We estimate a bivariate VAR model which includes either a measure of the money demand shortfall or overhang from the two augmented money demand functions and inflation. The models are estimated using two lags and 10,000 Monte-Carlo draws.

Figure 29.5a and b show that positive shocks to the money demand dis-equilibria in the augmented money demand functions raise inflation for two to six quarters. In addition, Fig. 29.6 shows that inflation increases (declines) due to positive shocks to the money demand overhang (shortfall). Thus, the money demand disequilibria have implications for inflationary pressures and the augmented money demand functions contain more information about inflation developments.

Furthermore, Fig. 29.7 shows that there are asymmetries induced by different sizes of the money demand dis-equilibria. Figure 29.7 shows that larger sizes of the money demand short-fall result in a decline in inflation relative to the 6 per cent threshold. Large money demand shortfall shocks lead to a pronounced deceleration in inflation.

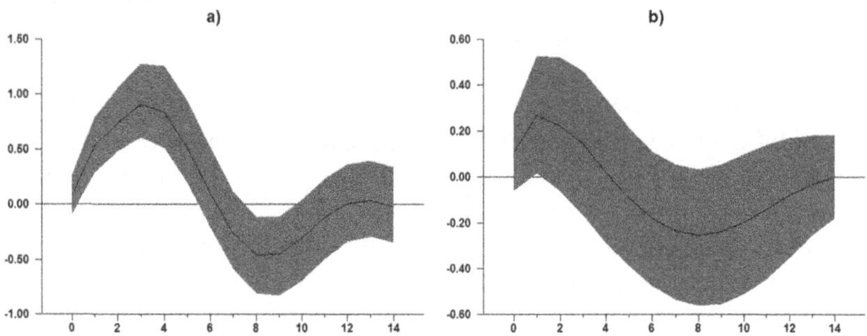

Fig. 29.5 Inflation responses to positive shocks to the augmented money demand dis-equilibria. (Source: Authors' calculations. Note: (a) shows responses due to money demand dis-equilibria in SA-US variables and (b) is based on SA, UK, euro area and Japan variables)

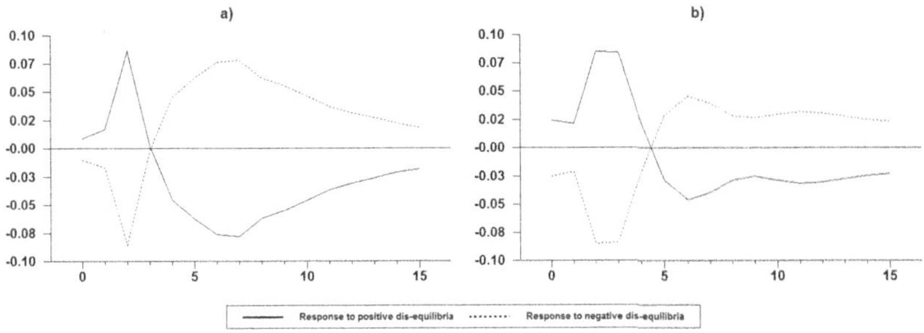

Fig. 29.6 Inflation responses to positive shocks to the augmented money demand dis-equilibria. (Source: Authors' calculations. Note: (a) shows responses due to dis-equilibria in SA-US variables and (b) is based on SA, UK, euro area and Japan variables)

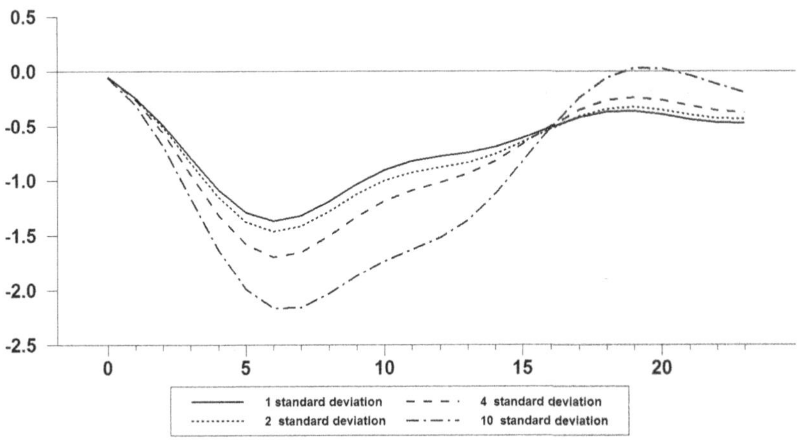

Fig. 29.7 Inflation responses to different shocks in the augmented money demand shortfall. (Source: Authors' calculations)

29.4 Conclusion and Policy Implications

This chapter tested the applicability of the *international portfolio balance approach* to the South African money demand function. Three VECM models representing the (i) conventional money demand function (ii) money demand function augmented with the South African and US asset price returns and the interest rate differential, and (iii) money demand function augmented with the South African, UK, euro area and Japan asset price returns and the interest rate differentials, are estimated.

We find that M3 growth is impacted by international portfolio inflows. The implication is that international capital inflow shocks play a very small and limited role in credit extension. The most significant drivers of credit growth may be primarily domestically generated and oriented rather than highly dependent on foreign capital inflow shock. This implies that bank-based funding in the economy can remain stable in the case of their withdrawal or volatility. The VECM results also indicate that real money balances are positively linked to real income and negatively to the interest rate spreads as predicted by theory.

Furthermore, augmenting the money demand function with asset price returns lowers the point elasticity for GDP. This means that the augmented the money demand functions can explain developments in monetary aggregates via the ***substitution and international portfolio balance effects.*** The cointegration relations derived from the money demand function augmented with asset price returns and the interest rate differential suggest that there has been a persistent money demand over-hang since 2008Q1 which has varied between 15 and 10 percent. The implication is that both measures are picking up the role of asset price returns and the interest rate differentials post the global financial crisis which is absent in the conventional money demand function as it still indicates a substantial and persistent money demand shortfall.

The responses of inflation relative to the 6 per cent inflation threshold to measures of the augmented money demand dis-equilibria indicate that the asset market dis-equilibria are incompatible with long-term inflation behaviour. Alternatively, inflation is not neutral to asset price developments. This means that the inclusion of international asset returns in the behaviour of money demand explains the effects of perpetual structural changes and financial innovation. Furthermore, developments in asset price dis-equilibria can undermine price, financial and macro-economic stability.

References

Beyer A. 2009. A stable model for euro area money demand revisiting the role of wealth. ECB Working Paper Series No 111.

Boone L, Mikol F, and Van den Noord P. 2004. Wealth Effects on Money Demand in EMU. OECD Working Paper No. 411.

Brand C and Cassola N. 2004. A money demand system for euro area M3, Applied Economics, Volume 36, 817–838.
Bruggeman A, Donati P, and Warne A. 2003. Is the Demand for Euro Area M3 Stable? ECB Working Paper No. 255.
Carstensen, K. 2003. "Is European money demand still stable?", Kiel Working Paper Series, No 1179, Kiel Institute for the World Economy.
Carstensen, K. 2006. "Stock market downswing and the stability of European Monetary Union money demand", Journal of Business and Economic Statistics, Vol. 25, pp. 395–402.
De Bondt G. 2009. Euro Area Money Demand: Empirical Evidence On the Role of Equity and Labour Markets. ECB Working Paper Series No. 1086.
De Santis R A, Favero C A and Roffia B. 2008. Euro area money demand and international portfolio allocation: A contribution to assessing risks to price stability, A flow-of-funds perspective on the financial crisis, 46–93.
Dreger C, and Wolters J. 2009. Money Velocity and Asset Prices in the Euro Area. Empirica, 36, 51–63.
Gerdesmeier D. 1996. The Role of Wealth in Money Demand. Deutsche Bundesbank Discussion Paper 5/96. Frankfurt am Main.
Gumata N and Ndou E. 2017. Bank Credit Extension and Real Economic Activity in South Africa: The Impact of Capital Flow Dynamics, Bank Regulation and Selected Macroprudential Tools. Palgrave Macmillan. ISB 978-3-319-43550-3.
Hall S G, Hondroyiannis G, Swamy P A V B, and Tavlas G. 2007. A portfolio balance approach to euro area money demand in a time varying environment. Bank of Greece.

CHAPTER 30

Do the Exchange Rate Depreciation and Volatility Shocks Impact Money Demand in South Africa?

Research Questions Explored

- Explore whether the exchange rate depreciation shocks impact money demand in South Africa.
- Establish whether there is the prevalence of the currency substitution effect following the exchange rate-depreciation shock.
- Whether the exchange rate volatility channel transmits the exchange rate depreciation shocks to money demand.

30.1 Introduction

This chapter investigates the link between the exchange rate depreciation shocks and money demand in South Africa. Literature argues that external factors such as changes in exchange rates can affect the composition of optimal money holdings. According to Robert Mundell, the demand for money, while determined by the income level and interest rates, may also depend on the exchange rate. However, theory indicates that the direction of the effect of the exchange rate on money demand can be either negative or positive. Hence, this chapter explores whether the exchange rate depreciation shocks impact money demand in South Africa. Trends in Fig. 30.1

N. Gumata, E. Ndou, *Achieving Price, Financial and Macro-Economic Stability in South Africa*,
https://doi.org/10.1007/978-3-030-66340-7_30

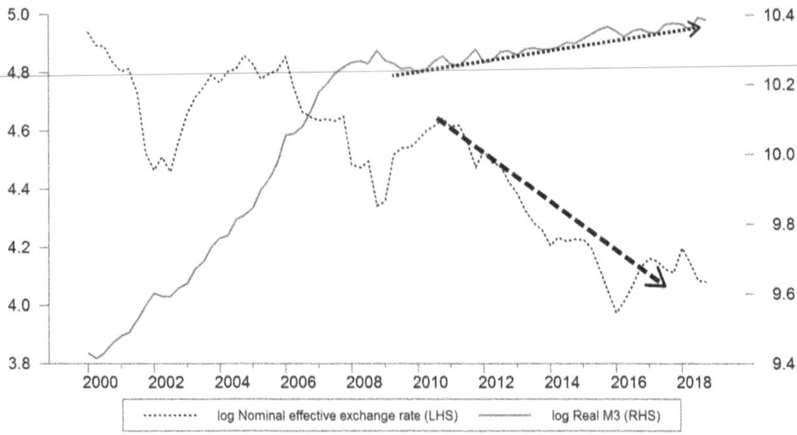

Fig. 30.1 M3 money demand and the nominal effective exchange rate dynamics. (Source: Authors' calculations)

show that real money supply flattened post-2007 and this coincides with trend nominal effective exchange rate (NEER) depreciation.

There are two theories which link the exchange rate depreciation and money demand. The first theory suggests that wealth holders evaluate their asset portfolios in terms of their domestic currency following the currency depreciation.[1] This theory suggests that the exchange rate depreciation would increase the demand for domestic currency. The second theory postulates that exchange rate movements may generate a currency substitution effect. This happens when there is an expectation that the exchange rate will depreciate further following the initial depreciation, which makes wealth holders to raise their share of foreign assets in their portfolios.[2] In this theory, the exchange rate depreciation lowers the money demand. Thus, the slowdown in money demand may delay the recovery of economic growth during periods of large exchange rate depreciation. This chapter fills policy and academic research gaps by showing the extent to which the exchange rate depreciation and volatility shocks affect money demand. In addition, we use the counterfactual analysis to explore whether

[1] Theory suggests that when investors maintain a fixed share of their wealth invested in domestic assets, they will repatriate part of their foreign assets to domestic assets, including domestic currency.

[2] This theory argues that currency depreciation implies a higher opportunity cost of holding domestic money following currency depreciation.

exchange rate volatility shocks are conduits that link exchange rate depreciation shocks and money demand.

30.2 Empirical Results

This section estimates various VAR models to determine the link between money demand and the exchange rate. The various VAR models are estimated with variables expressed in levels format to avoid discarding the existence of any cointegration relationship amongst the variables. The unit root tests establish that CPI inflation is intergrated oder 1. The estimated model specifications are as stated below:

- The baseline VAR model (Model 1) includes log real money, log GDP, log NEER, CPI inflation and the repo rate as endogenous variables.
- Model 2 is a linear regression model which regresses log real money on a constant, four lags of log real money, two lags of log NEER, four lags of log GDP and four lags of the repo rate.
- Model 3 is a VAR model which includes log real money, log GDP, CPI inflation, repo rate and log NEER as endogenous variables.
- Model 4 is a VAR model which includes log real money, log GDP and log NEER as endogenous variables. The exogenous variables include a constant, log CPI and repo rate.
- Model 5 is a VAR model which includes log real money, log GDP, repo rate and log NEER as endogenous variables. The exogenous variables include a constant and log CPI.
- Model 6 is a linear regression model which regresses log real money on a constant, four lags of log real money, two lags of log NEER, four lags of log GDP and four lags of the repo rate.

Real money demand is M3 deflated by the consumer price level. GDP captures the income effects, while the repo rate and inflation rates capture the opportunity costs of holding money. We assume that money supply equals money demanded in equilibrium, ceteris paribus. The exogenous variables in the model include the recession dummy. The dummy equals to one for the domestic recessions in 2009Q1–2009Q3 and 2018Q1–2018Q2 and zero otherwise. We use quarterly data from 2000Q1 to 2018Q4. The models are estimated using two lags and 10,000 Monte Carlo draws. All shocks refer to a 1 per cent NEER shock.

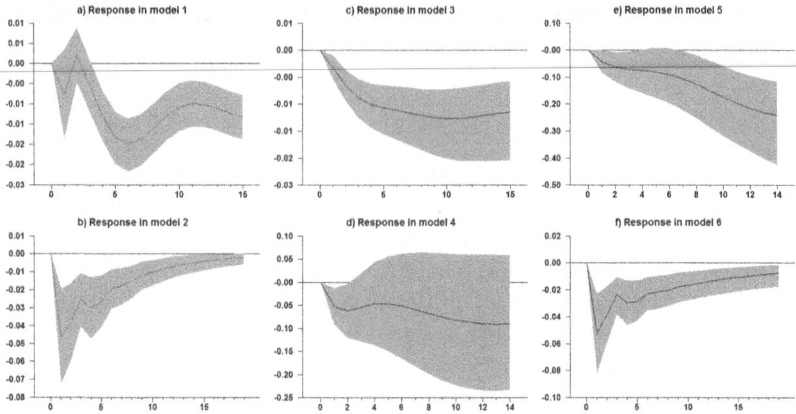

Fig. 30.2 Responses to NEER depreciation shocks. (Note: The grey-shaded area bands denote the 16th and 84th percentile confidence bands. Source: Authors' calculations)

The results in Fig. 30.2 show that the NEER shock reduces real money demand, irrespective of how the model is specified. This finding supports the prevalence of the currency substitution effect following the exchange rate depreciation shock. The VAR results are robust to different ordering in the models.

30.3 Does the Exchange Rate Volatility Channel Transmit the Exchange Rate Depreciation Shocks to Money Demand?

We conclude the analysis by determining the role of exchange rate volatility in transmitting the exchange rate depreciation shocks to real money demand. This is motivated by Ndou et al. (2018), who showed that the exchange rate volatility exerts adverse macroeconomic effects. We estimate two counterfactual VAR models to determine the role of the exchange rate volatility in transmitting the exchange rate depreciation shocks to money demanded. These two models determine the robustness of the role of the exchange rate volatility channel in different model specifications. In both models, the exchange rate volatility channel is shut off to calculate

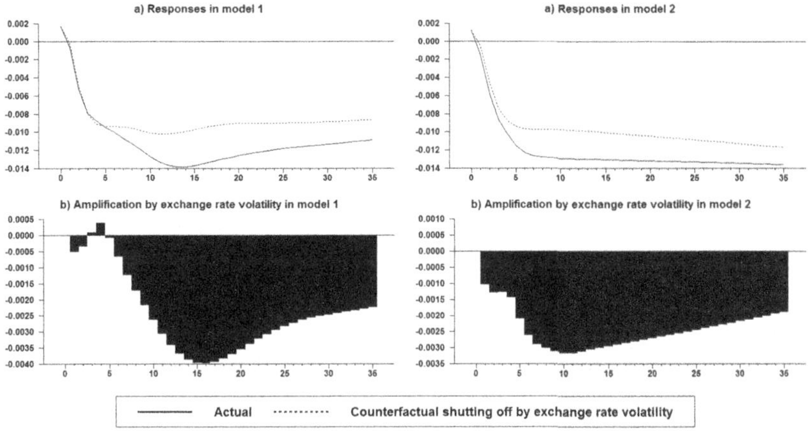

Fig. 30.3 Actual and counterfactual responses to exchange rate depreciation shocks. (Source: Authors' calculations)

the counterfactual responses of money demand to the exchange rate depreciation shock.

The results in Fig. 30.3 show that the exchange rate depreciation shock lowers the real money demand. In both models, the decline in money demand is accentuated by elevated exchange rate volatility. This evidence suggests that the exchange rate depreciation shocks and the accompanying elevated exchange rate volatility shocks matter for real money demand. Thus, policymakers should consider the adverse effects of the exchange rate depreciation and volatility shocks on money demand. The information on money supply growth has implications for economic growth prospects and inflation dynamics.

30.4 Conclusion and Policy Implications

This chapter investigated the extent to which the exchange rate deprecation and volatility shocks drive money demand in South Africa. Evidence indicates that the exchange rate depreciation reduces money demand, and this supports the prevalence of the currency substitution effect. Furthermore, the decline in money demand is accentuated by elevated exchange rate volatility. This evidence suggests that the exchange rate depreciation shocks and the accompanying elevated exchange rate volatility shocks matter for real money demand. Thus, both the exchange rate depreciation shocks and the elevated exchange rate volatility shocks matter for real money demand. Hence, policymakers should consider the adverse effects of the exchange rate depreciation and volatility shocks on money demand. The information on money supply growth has implications for economic growth prospects and inflation dynamics.

References

Hlatshwayo S and Saxegaard M. 2016. The Consequence of Policy Uncertainty: Disconnects and Dilutions in the South African Real Effective Exchange Rate-Export Relationship, IMF Working Paper WP/16/113.

Ndou E, Gumata N, and Ncube M. 2018. Global Economic Uncertainties and Exchange Rate Shocks, Transmission Channels to the South African Economy. Palgrave Macmillan. ISBN 978-3-319-62280-4.

CHAPTER 31

Does Economic Policy Uncertainty Impact Real Money Demand in South Africa?

Research Questions Explored

- Assess whether economic policy uncertainty affects money demand.
- Explore whether the responses of money demand to heightened economic uncertainty shocks are consistent with the hypothesis which suggests that increased economic uncertainty generates a substitution effect away from cash in favour of less volatile assets.
- Establish whether inflation regimes impact the effects of economic policy uncertainty shocks on inflation and GDP growth.
- Assess the role of the credit conditions channel in transmitting economic uncertainty shocks to real money demand.

31.1 Introduction

Theory suggests that increased uncertainty about the economy affects the demand for money.[1] As a precautionary measure, the public will increase their cash holdings when faced with heightened economic uncertainty. This kind of behaviour suggests that elevated uncertainty has a positive

[1] The demand for money can increase when the public becomes pessimistic about the future course of the economy.

N. Gumata, E. Ndou, *Achieving Price, Financial and Macro-Economic Stability in South Africa*,
https://doi.org/10.1007/978-3-030-66340-7_31

effect on the money demanded. In contrast, Choi and Oh (2003) postulate that increased economic uncertainty can adversely affect the demand for money and this depends on the degree of substitutability between money and other less volatile assets.[2] Why is it important to examine the link between economic policy uncertainty and money demand? First, theory suggests that there is important information regarding future economic developments that is contained in money demand or growth. Second, there is a high likelihood that a sequence of negative shocks that hit the economy since the 2007 financial crisis, domestic recessions in 2009Q1–2009Q3 and 2018Q1–2018Q2, the prolonged currency trend depreciations and increased economic policy uncertainty have impacted money demand. Literature indicates that during recessions, there maybe problems in the banking sector and this eventually affects money demand. Evidence indicates the demand for money decreases due to any unexpected elevation in economic policy uncertainty. The decline is worsened by the tightening of credit conditions. Given these diverging views about the role of economic uncertainty on money demand, this chapter examines the extent to which increased economic policy uncertainty impacts real money demand in South Africa.[3]

This chapter fills academic and policy research gaps by exploring whether the responses of money demand to heightened economic uncertainty shocks are consistent with the hypothesis which suggests that increased economic uncertainty generates a substitution effect away from cash in favour of less volatile assets. In addition, we determine whether inflation regimes impact the effects of economic policy uncertainty shocks on inflation and GDP growth. We also assess for the role of the credit conditions channel in transmitting economic uncertainty shocks to real money demand.

[2] There are also conditions which may raise the demand for money. For instance, investors tend to withdraw their monies from banks during uncertain economic conditions. In addition, the uncertain economic conditions may increase precautionary saving by households. Thus, uncertainty does impact money demand, but the direction of the impact is an empirical issue.

[3] See Ndou et al. (2018) for the depiction of the detailed transmission channels of economic uncertainty shocks.

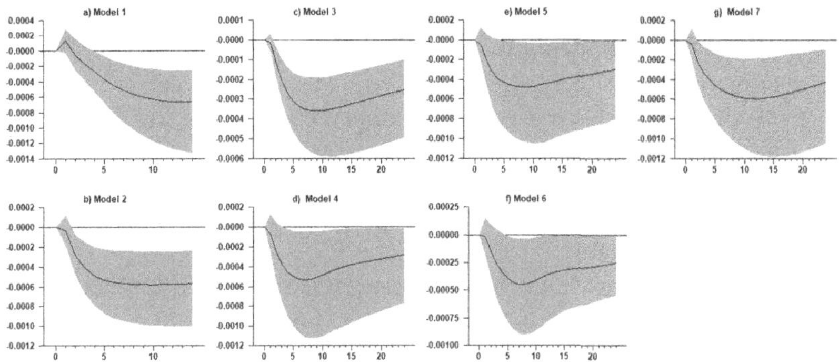

Fig. 31.1 Real money responses to positive economic policy uncertainty shocks. (Note: The grey shaded area bands denote the 16th and 84th percentile confidence bands. Source: Authors' calculations)

31.2 Empirical Results

We estimate various VAR models to determine the effect of positive economic policy uncertainty shocks on real money demand, as shown in Fig. 31.1. The economic policy uncertainty index is sourced from Hlatshwayo and Saxegaard (2016) and the other data is obtained from the South African Reserve Bank database. We use data from 2000Q1 to 2015Q4. Real money is measured by M3 money supply divided by the consumer price level. We assume that M3 money supply equals to the money demand at equilibrium, ceteris paribus. The unit root tests inficate that CPI inflation is integerated of order one. We estimate models that include various variables that are the determinants of the money demand as estimated in literature. The shocks denote a unit increase in economic policy uncertainty. The various estimated VAR models are specified as shown below:

- Model 1 includes log economic policy uncertainty, log real money, CPI inflation, log GDP and log nominal effective exchange rate (NEER) as endogenous variables. The exogenous variables are a constant and the recession dummy.
- Model 2 includes log economic policy uncertainty and log real money as endogenous variables. The exogenous variables are a constant and the recession dummy.

- Model 3 includes log economic policy uncertainty, log GDP, log real money as endogenous variables and a constant as an exogenous variable.
- Model 4 includes log economic policy uncertainty, log GDP, CPI inflation, repo rate and log real money as endogenous variables.
- Model 5 includes log economic policy uncertainty, log GDP, repo rate and log real money as endogenous variables and a constant as an exogenous variable.
- Model 6 includes log economic policy uncertainty, CPI inflation and log real money as endogenous variables and a constant as an exogenous variable.
- Model 7 includes log economic policy uncertainty, log NEER and log real money as endogenous variables and a constant as an exogenous variable.

In Fig. 31.1, the real money demand declines due to positive economic policy uncertainty shock. The decline is robust to different model specifications. These findings are also robust to the different ordering of the variables in the model, using one lag and to different specifications of the model. The decline in money demand is consistent with the hypothesis which suggests that increased uncertainty generates a substitution away from cash in favour of less volatile assets.

31.3 Do Inflation Regimes Impact the Effects of Economic Policy Uncertainty Shocks on Inflation and GDP Growth?

We determine the impact of positive economic policy uncertainty shocks on consumer price inflation by estimating different VAR models which include the log economic policy uncertainty, log real money, log GDP, repo rate and CPI inflation or the inflation dummy. The exogenous variables include a constant and the dummy for domestic recessions in 2009Q1–2009Q3 and 2018Q1–2018Q2 and zero otherwise. The variables used in the estimations are the determinants of the money demand functions in empirical literature. The models are estimated using two lags and 10,000 Monte Carlo draws. To determine the role of price stability, we show the responses of GDP growth and inflation to positive economic policy uncertainty shocks. This is motivated by the link between inflation and the output gap. A negative output gap should imply subsiding demand related to inflationary pressures. Hence, it is important to show the effects below and above the 6 per cent inflation threshold. In addition, inflation bands capture the existence of nonlinear responses of inflation to positive economic policy uncertainty shocks.

We show the response of inflation according to inflation bands separated into (1) less than 4.5 per cent, (2) between 4.5 and 6 per cent, (3) between 3 and 6 per cent, (4) below 6 per cent and (5) above 6 per cent. To determine the influence of these inflation bands, we create dummy variables for each inflation band. Each dummy variable equals to the value of inflation in the indicated band and zero otherwise.

Figure 31.2 shows that the responses of inflation to positive economic policy uncertainty shocks depends on the inflation band. Inflation rises significantly when inflation regimes are not considered in the model and when inflation is above 6 per cent. Inflation declines (although insignificant) due to positive economic policy uncertainty shocks when inflation is (1) between 4.5 and 6 per cent (2) betweeen 3 and 6 per cent and (3) below 6 per cent. Overall, the results show that inflation declines significantly when it is below 4.5 per cent. The results imply that it matters where the inflation is relative to the target band. The decline in inflation occurs when we include the NEER depreciation in the model. This suggests that the exchange-rate pass-through to inflation is weaker when

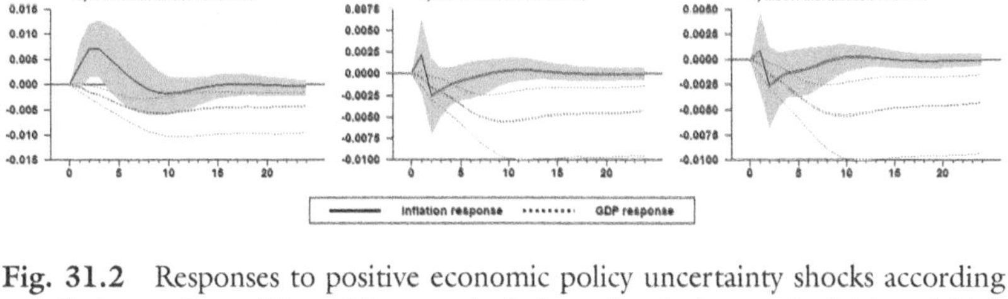

Fig. 31.2 Responses to positive economic policy uncertainty shocks according to inflation regimes. (Note: The grey shaded area bands denote the 16th and 84th percentile confidence bands. The red dotted lines are the confidence bands for the black dotted impulse responses. Source: Authors' calculations)

inflation is below 6 per cent, especially when it is below 4.5 per cent, compared to when it is above these inflation thresholds. These results imply that an unexpected increase in policy uncertainty should not threaten price stability when inflation is below the 6 per cent threshold. Thus, inflation regimes matter for the transmission of heightened economic uncertainty shocks to the money demand. The results are robust to different ordering of variables in the model and the inclusion of the NEER.

31.4 What Is the Role of the Credit Conditions Channel in Transmitting Economic Uncertainty Shocks to Real Money Demand?

This section examines the role of the credit conditions channel in transmitting positive economic policy uncertainty shocks to real money demand.[4] We estimate a counterfactual VAR model to assess the role of the credit conditions index as an amplifier or neutralising channel of heightened economic policy uncertainty shocks on money demand. The counterfactual impulse response is calculated by shutting off the credit conditions index channel in transmitting positive economic policy uncertainty shocks to real money demand in the model.

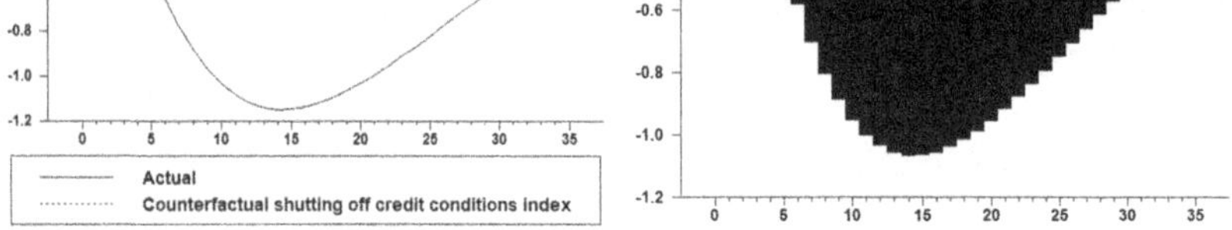

Fig. 31.3 Responses to positive economic policy uncertainty shocks and the role of the credit conditions channel. (Source: Authors' calculations)

[4] The credit conditions index is sourced from earlier chapters in this book. See Gumata and Ndou (2017) for the discussion of the methodology of constructing the credit conditions index.

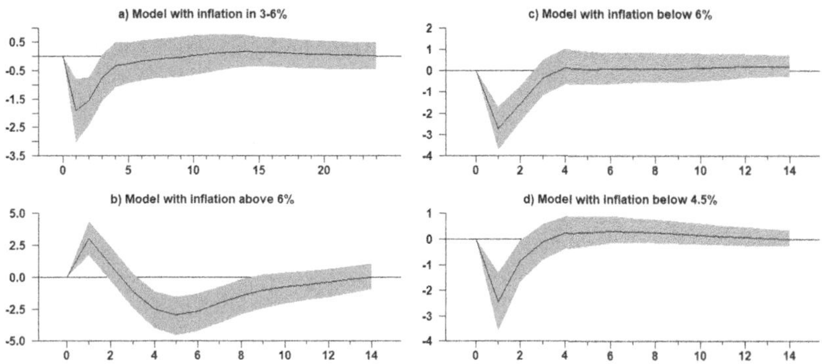

Fig. 31.4 Inflation responses to tight credit conditions shocks according to inflation regimes. (Note: The bands denote the 16th and 84th percentile confidence bands)

The results in Fig. 31.3 show that real money demand declines more when the credit conditions channel is operating in the model compared to when it is shut off. This arises because the positive economic policy uncertainty shocks lead to a tightening of the credit conditions, which accentuates the decline in real money demand.

Furthermore, the results in Fig. 31.4 show that an unexpected tightening in credit conditions lowers inflation when inflation is (1) below 6 per cent, (2) between 3 and 6 per cent and (3) between 4.5 and 6 per cent. However, inflation declines with a delay when inflation is above 6 per cent.

31.5 Conclusion and Policy Implications

Does economic policy uncertainty impact real money demand in South Africa? Evidence reveals that the elevated economic policy uncertainty lowers the real money demand and that the credit conditions channel and inflation regimes matter for the transmission of such shocks. The results show that inflation declines due to positive economic policy uncertainty shocks when inflation is below 6 per cent and especially when it is below 4.5 per cent. Inflation also declines when considering the effects of the NEER depreciation shocks, suggesting that the exchange rate pass-through to inflation is weaker in low-inflation regimes. In addition, positive policy uncertainty shocks tighten credit conditions and lower GDP growth, and these effects assist in attaining price stability especially when inflation is below 6 per cent. Hence, inflation regimes matter for the transmission of economic policy uncertainty shocks to money demand.

References

Choi W G, and Oh S. 2003. A Money Demand Function with Output Uncertainty, Monetary Uncertainty, and Financial Innovations. Journal of Money, Credit and Banking 35: 685–709.

Gumata N, and Ndou E. 2017. Bank Credit Extension and Real Economic Activity in South Africa: The Impact of Capital Flow Dynamics, Bank Regulation and Selected Macroprudential Tools. Palgrave Macmillan. ISB 978-3-319-43550-3.

Hlatshwayo S, and Saxegaard M. 2016. The Consequence of Policy Uncertainty: Disconnects and Dilutions in the South African Real Effective Exchange Rate-Export Relationship, IMF Working Paper WP/16/113.

Ndou E, Gumata N, and Ncube M. 2018. Global Economic Uncertainties and Exchange Rate Shocks, Transmission Channels to the South African Economy.

CHAPTER 32

Is a Single Sectorial Credit Growth Threshold Too Restrictive? Evidence from the Output and Inflation

Research Questions Explored

- Determine the lower and upper thresholds for aggregate and sectorial credit growth.
- Show how the double thresholds lead to non-linearities on GDP growth and inflation.

32.1 Introduction

The 2007 global financial crisis demonstrated the importance of credit and financial conditions. Adverse credit and financial shocks can cause large and persistent recessions. In addition, the existence of frictions due to information asymmetries and contractual rigidities in credit markets can act as non-linear propagators of aggregate demand and supply shocks on economic activity. Financial markets and institutions can be sources of shocks and conduits that transmit shocks domestically and across borders. Furthermore, Balke (2000) establishes evidence that credit conditions exert threshold and asymmetric effects on macro-economic responses over the lending cycle.[1] However, Avdjiev and Zeng (2014) argue that single-

[1] Calza and Sousa (2005), Avdjiev and Zeng (2014).

N. Gumata, E. Ndou, *Achieving Price, Financial and Macro-Economic Stability in South Africa*,
https://doi.org/10.1007/978-3-030-66340-7_32

threshold models tend to be too restrictive and cannot capture all the non-linearities in the data. It is against this background that this chapter asks: Does the role of double thresholds for sectorial credit lead to non-linearities on GDP growth and inflation? How do the results above the upper credit threshold compare to those below the lower credit threshold?

Why is the analysis of double thresholds important? Avdjiev and Zeng (2014) assert that a single threshold may not fully capture all the non-linearities in the data. Therefore, this chapter establishes the levels at which the lower and upper thresholds for sectorial credit occur. We apply the Tsay (1998) approach to establish the double thresholds which allow us to delineate between three credit growth regimes. Similar to Avdjiev and Zeng (2014), we identify the regimes as (1) subpar when credit growth is below the lower threshold; (2) moderate when credit growth is between the lower and upper thresholds; and (3) high when credit growth is above the upper credit threshold. We estimate the regime-dependent impulse responses to assess whether there are different GDP growth and inflation responses based on lower and upper threshold effects. Alternatively, are the responses of GDP growth and inflation to shocks different in the sub-par and high credit growth regimes? This evidence will reveal the extent of the non-linear propagation of shocks across credit growth regimes. Furthermore, establishing the sectorial credit growth rates contributes to the design of the macro-prudential tools aimed at dealing with sectorial capital requirements as envisaged by the countercyclical capital buffer (CCyB). For instance, the Bank of Ireland (2014) shows that while the CCyB increases the banks' capacity to absorb losses in a downturn, it does not specifically target the household's resilience or indebtedness. The CCyB falls short of directly addressing the household demand for credit or the household sector financial resilience and indebtedness. The establishment of sectorial credit thresholds can fill this existing policy research gap and assist in setting the guidelines on targeted tools such as the loan-to-value ratios and the repayment-to-income ratios over the credit cycle.

This chapter fills academic and policy research gaps by establishing the lower and upper thresholds for aggregate credit growth and sectorial credit growth. In addition, we show how the double thresholds lead to non-linear responses in GDP growth and inflation.

32.2 Does Sectorial Credit Follow a Non-linear Process and What Are the Lower and Upper Thresholds?

This section conducts tests for non-linearity and thresholds for sectorial credit growth. The sample spans the period 1995Q1 to 2015Q4 and the data is sourced from the South African Reserve Bank database. All growth rates are at annual rates. On average, credit to the household sector accounts for 56 per cent of the total credit to the private sector for the sample period. On the other hand, credit to the corporate sector accounts for 44 per cent of the total credit to the private sector for the same period.[2]

The results in Table 32.1 shows that all the series follow a non-linear process. The credit variables have breakpoints (thresholds) and follow a non-linear process. In all instances in Table 32.1, the null hypothesis that there is no threshold is rejected.

We estimate the best point and upper threshold levels, and use them to identify the non-linear credit shock effects in three different phases: (1) below the best point threshold; (2) in between the best point and upper threshold; and (3) above the upper threshold. The estimated thresholds are based on a VAR model with GDP growth, household credit or credit to companies, lending rate, inflation and nominal house prices. We include nominal house price growth in the estimation of the credit thresholds in different VAR models to assess for the robustness of the estimated thresholds. Table 32.2 shows the estimated best and upper threshold values for aggregate, household and corporate credit growth.

Table 32.1 Tests for non-linearity

Test	*Null Hypothesis*	*Decision*	
		Credit to household	*Credit to companies*
Arranged Autoregression Test	No break	Break	Break
Hansen Threshold test	No break	Threshold	Threshold
STAR test	Linearity	Non-linearity	Non-linearity

Source: Authors' calculations

Note: STAR means smooth transition autoregressive

[2] Mortgage advances account for 47 per cent of total credit to the private sector and 84 per cent of credit to the household sector for the sample period.

Table 32.2 Estimated threshold points

Balke (2000)	*Best point threshold*	*Upper threshold*
Aggregate credit	9.50	12.70
Household credit	9.60	12.45
Credit to companies	9.20	12.60

Source: Authors' calculations

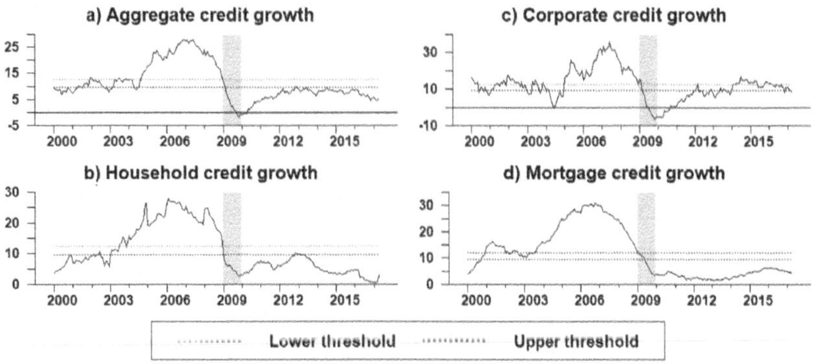

Fig. 32.1 Household and corporate credit growth and estimated threshold values. (Source: Authors' calculations)

The best threshold values for aggregate credit and sectorial are all below 10 per cent and the upper thresholds are below 13 per cent, which indicates that there is convergence in terms of points at which the non-linear threshold values occur. Figure 32.1 shows aggregate, household and corporate, together with their estimated thresholds over the business cycles.

In the empirical section, we use the estimated threshold values to delineate two credit growth regimes, which correspond to (1) subpar credit growth versus (2) high credit growth. We estimate different models with varied specifications and the threshold levels to assess the distinct responses in the specific credit regimes.

32.3 Empirical Analysis

We estimate regime-dependent impulse responses based on the identified thresholds using a recursive Cholesky ordering identification scheme in which GDP growth is ordered first, followed by inflation, house prices growth, credit growth and the lending rate. Similar, to Balke (2000) and Calza et al. (2005), the ordering scheme followed in the study implies that shocks to real GDP affect all the other variables in the system contemporaneously. The positioning of the real sector variables before those related to credit and housing markets is standard in the empirical literature. In addition, the ordering scheme is informed by the assumption that financial markets adjust simultaneously to macro-economic shocks. On the other hand, the real sector reacts sluggishly to shocks to financial variables. The shocks refer to a one standard deviation shock in the sectorial credit growth. The model is estimated with two lags chosen by the AIC and HIC information criteria and 10,000 bootstrap draws. The error bands around the impulse responses denote the 16th and 84th percentile confidence bands.

32.3.1 Evidence from Household Credit

This section shows the GDP growth and inflation responses to positive shocks in household credit growth and the role of thresholds. Figure 32.2 shows the responses to household credit growth shocks. GDP growth rises significantly when credit is below 9.6 per cent and the response is nonsignificant above 12.5 per cent. In addition, inflation increases significantly above 12.5 per cent compared to the insignificant response below 9.6 per cent.

The results show that in cases where household credit growth is below 9.6 per cent, GDP growth peaks at a higher rate compared to when household credit growth is above 12.5 per cent. The difference is due to inflation responses. Inflation increases by more than double at peak response when household credit growth exceeds 12.5 per cent compared to when household credit growth is below 9.6 per cent.

In cumulative terms, Fig. 32.3 shows that GDP growth accelerates more when credit growth is below 9.6 per cent compared to when credit growth is above 12.5 per cent. In addition, inflation increases more when credit growth exceeds 12.5 per cent than when credit is below 9.6 per cent. The results imply the presence of an inverse relationship between inflation and GDP growth, and this depends on the credit growth threshold levels.

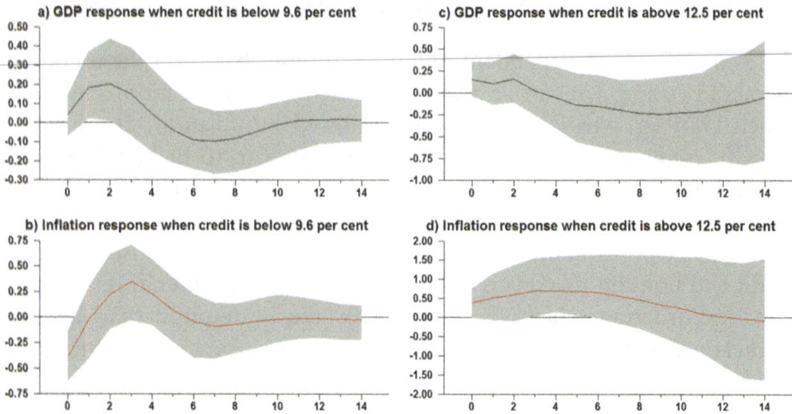

Fig. 32.2 GDP growth and inflation responses to positive credit shocks to the household sector according to the thresholds. (Source: Authors' calculations)

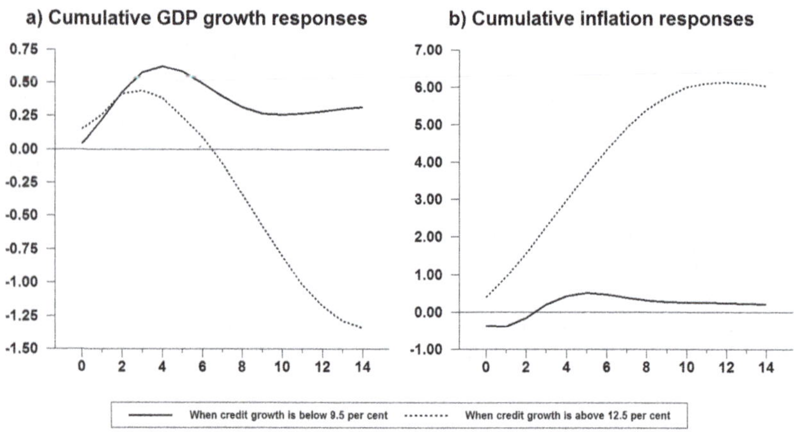

Fig. 32.3 Responses to positive credit shocks to the household sector according to the thresholds. (Source: Authors' calculations)

32.3.2 Evidence from Corporate Credit

Are there discernible differences in responses below lower and above the upper thresholds of growth in corporate credit? Figure 32.4 shows that GDP growth responds to positive corporate credit shocks more when

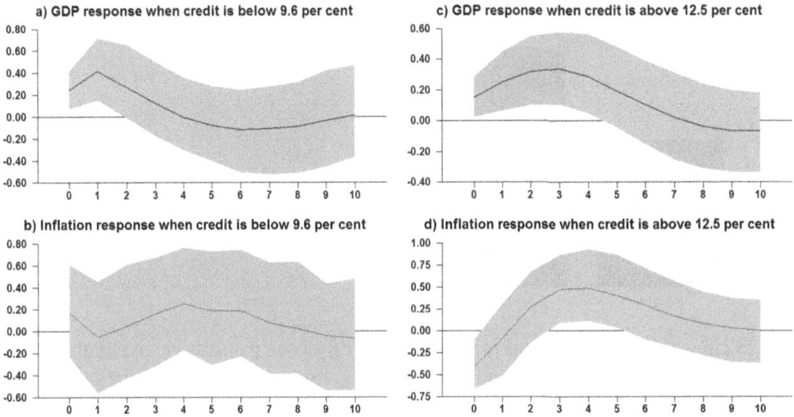

Fig. 32.4 GDP growth and inflation responses to positive credit shocks to the corporate sector according to the thresholds. (Source: Authors' calculations)

corporate credit growth is below 9.2 per cent than when it exceeds 12.6 per cent. The difference is related to the inflation responses being lower and insignificant when corporate credit growth is below 9.2 per cent compared to when credit growth exceeds 12.6 per cent as shown in Fig. 32.4.

The peak responses for GDP growth and inflation when credit is below 9.2 per cent and above 12.6 per cent in Fig. 32.5 suggest an inverse relationship. For instance, GDP growth peaks at a higher level when credit growth is below 9.2 per cent compared to when credit growth is above 12.6 per cent.

The results imply that sectorial credit thresholds and regimes exert non-linear GDP growth and inflation responses. Periods of high credit growth are characterised by high inflationary pressures and do not necessarily result in higher GDP growth. The implication is that additional aggregate and sectorial credit does not necessarily result in incrementally higher GDP growth but result in higher inflation responses.

What proportion of the movements in GDP and inflation is induced by positive credit shocks when household credit growth is below 9.6 per cent and above 12.5 per cent? Evidence indicates that positive credit shocks explain a larger variation in inflation and GDP growth above the 12.5 per cent threshold. In addition, inflation fluctuates more than GDP growth, further corroborating the evidence of decreasing returns. This means that

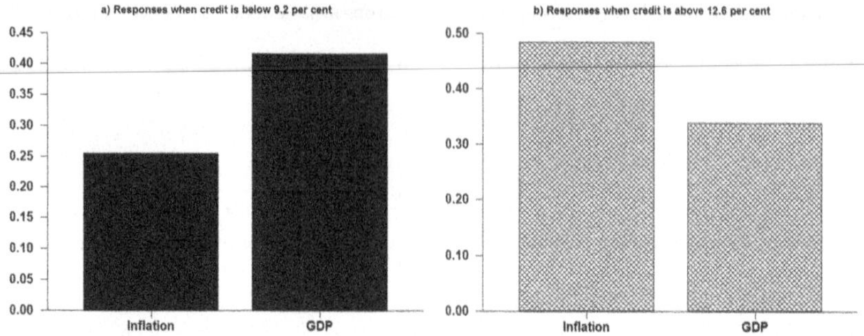

Fig. 32.5 GDP growth and inflation peak responses to positive credit shocks to the corporate sector and the role of thresholds. (Source: Authors' calculations)

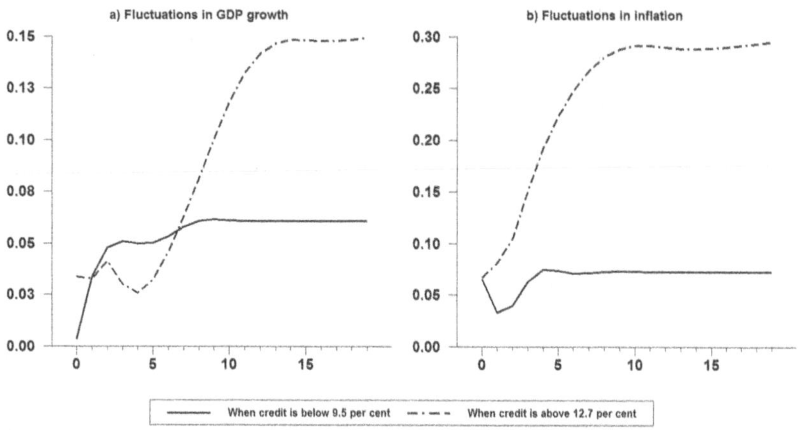

Fig. 32.6 Proportion of movements in GDP growth and inflation induced by positive shocks in credit to households and the role of thresholds. (Source: Authors' calculations)

incremental increases in credit growth generate credit-driven inflationary pressures. The peak fluctuations induced by household credit in Fig. 32.6 exceed those from corporate credit growth. Thus, shocks to corporate credit growth lead to less variation in GDP growth and inflation in Fig. 32.7.

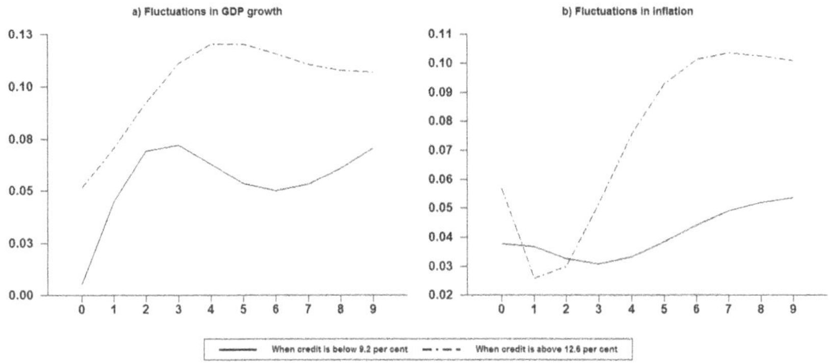

Fig. 32.7 Proportion of movements in GDP growth and inflation induced by positive shocks in credit to corporate and the role of thresholds. (Source: Authors' calculations)

32.4 Conclusion and Policy Implications

The chapter tested for double thresholds and the non-linear process in aggregate and sectorial credit growth. The estimated thresholds were later used to assess for the asymmetric effects of the aggregate and sectorial credit growth regimes on GDP growth and inflation. The results show that the lower and upper threshold levels for aggregate and sectorial credit occur around 9.20 per cent and 12.70 per cent, respectively. We use these thresholds to classify credit regimes: (1) subpar credit growth, (2) moderate credit growth and (3) high credit growth.

First, evidence shows that in cases where household credit growth is below 9.5 per cent, GDP growth tends to peak at a higher rate compared to when household credit growth is above 12.6 per cent. The difference is due to inflation responses. Inflation increases by more than double at peak response when household credit growth exceeds 12.6 per cent compared to when household credit growth is below 9.6 per cent.

Second, evidence shows that GDP growth responds to credit shocks more when corporate credit growth is below 9.2 per cent than when it exceeds 12.6 per cent. The difference is related to the inflation responses being lower and insignificant when corporate credit growth is below 9.2 per cent compared to when credit growth exceeds 12.6 per cent.

The policy implication is that additional credit growth above the normal and high credit growth regimes does not necessarily result in accelerated and incremental GDP growth, but rather induces higher inflation responses. Furthermore, credit growth below the normal credit growth helps to contain inflationary pressures and is consistent with price and financial stability to the degree that excessive debt-driven household consumption is contained. Thus, the established credit thresholds contribute to the design of the macro-prudential tools aimed at dealing sectorial capital requirements under the countercyclical capital buffer in as far as they complement policies aimed at increasing households' resilience in an economic downturn.

References

Avdjiev F and Zeng Z. 2014. Credit Growth, Monetary Policy, and Economic Activity in a Three-Regime TVAR Model. BIS Working Papers No 449.

Balke N S. 2000. Credit and Economic Activity: Credit Regimes and Nonlinear Propagation of Shocks. The Review of Economics and Statistics, MIT Press, 82(2), 344–349.

Calza A and Sousa J. 2005. Output and Inflation Responses to Credit Shocks: Are There Threshold Effects in the Euro Area? Studies in Nonlinear Dynamics & Econometrics 10 (Issue 2, Article 3).

Central Bank of Ireland. 2014. Financial Stability Review.

Gumata N and Ndou E. 2017. Bank Credit Extension and Real Economic Activity in South Africa: The Impact of Capital Flow Dynamics, Bank Regulation and Selected Macroprudential Tools. Palgrave Macmillan. ISB 978-3-319-43550-3.

Gumata N and Ndou E. 2019. Capital Flows, Credit Markets and Growth in South Africa: The Role of Global Economic Growth, Policy Shifts and Uncertainties. Palgrave Macmillan ISBN 978-3-030-30882-2.

Tsay R S. 1998. Testing and modelling multivariate threshold models, Journal of the American Statistical Association 93, 1188–1202, 1998.

CHAPTER 33

Does the Threshold for Household Debt Growth Matter for GDP Growth and the Response of Monetary Policy to Inflation Shocks?

Research Questions Explored

- Determine the level at which the household debt threshold exerts non-linear effects on output growth.
- Show that the household debt threshold matters for GDP growth and monetary policy responses to inflation shocks.
- Show the propagation effects of loose labour market conditions in the low and high household debt regimes.
- Show the link between the price and financial stability objectives of the central bank via the household debt channel and regimes.

33.1 Introduction

Mian et al. (2015) show that an increase in the household debt-to-GDP ratio predicts subsequent lower output growth and higher unemployment. The authors conclude that household debt is a source of instability and lowers economic growth. Is this the case for South Africa? This chapter argues that this is an empirical question which depends on the threshold analysis and putting non-linearities at the centre of the policy discussions and recommendations. For instance, Fig. 33.1 shows that there exists a positive relationship between household debt growth and GDP growth.

N. Gumata, E. Ndou, *Achieving Price, Financial and Macro-Economic Stability in South Africa*,
https://doi.org/10.1007/978-3-030-66340-7_33

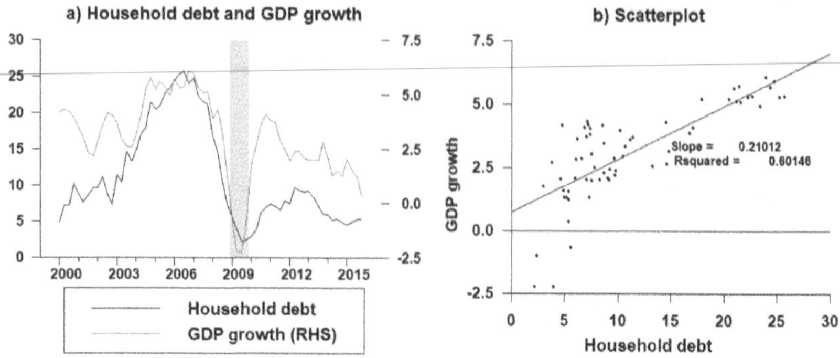

Fig. 33.1 Household debt growth and GDP growth. (Source: South African Reserve Bank and authors' calculations)

The scatterplots indicate that on a bilateral basis, household debt explains 60 per cent of changes in GDP growth. In addition, there may be persistent lag effects in the dynamics of the relationship. At what level does the household debt threshold that exerts non-linear shock effects on output growth occur? Does the threshold for household debt growth matter for GDP growth and the responses of monetary policy to inflation shocks?

This chapter fills academic and policy research gaps by examining the differential effects at which the household debt threshold exerts non-linear effects on GDP growth and the monetary policy reaction to inflationary pressures. What role does household debt play in the evolution of output growth? To show policymakers the extent to which current low levels of debt possibly explain sluggish GDP growth, we examine the evidence of the asymmetric effects of positive and negative household debt growth as deviations from the household debt threshold on GDP growth. In addition, we show that negative deviations from trend household debt growth have more potent effects on GDP growth compared to positive deviations. To enrich the analysis further, we explore the extent to which the labour markets transmit positive inflation shocks to the policy rate depending on the household debt regimes. In this way, the analysis links the price and financial stability objectives of the central bank via the household debt channel.

33.2 Does Growth in Household Debt Follow a Linear or Non-linear Process?

This section establishes whether household debt growth has a breakpoint by using several tests that allow for structural breaks in the data. The objective of testing for the presence of the breakpoint is not to establish the dates during which the breaks in the series occurred but to show that the tests converge to the existence of the break points in the data. The results of the break point test in Table 33.1 indicate that the household debt series does indeed have a break. This means that the household debt series follows a non-linear process, and we can use non-linear approaches in the estimations.

We stated earlier that the intention of the chapter is to establish the threshold at which growth in household debt exerts different effects on GDP growth. We show the robustness tests of the existence of the threshold evidence by using several approaches to establish the thresholds, as indicated in Table 33.2. The results indicate that there is convergence and the estimated thresholds for household debt are robust to changes in the specification and techniques used.

To simplify the analysis and the estimation of the threshold effects, we use the average of the best threshold points estimated in Table 33.2, which amounts to 9.62 per cent to delineate the high and low household debt growth regimes. Figure 33.2 shows household debt growth over time in relation to the estimated threshold. It is notable that household debt is currently below the estimated threshold.

Table 33.1 Tests for non-linearity in household debt growth

Test	*Null hypothesis*	*F-value*	*P value*	*Decision*
Tsay arranged test	No break point	2.37973	(0.00)**	Break
Hansen Threshold test	No break point	-19.2465	(0.00)**	Break
STAR test	Linearity	4.6294	(0.00)**	Non-linearity
Zivot and Andrews (1992)	No break point	23.3183	(0.00)**	Break
Lumsdaine and Papell (1997)	No break point	6.74	(0.00)**	Break

Note: The numbers in (.) denote the *p*-value. * denote significance at 1 per cent. ** denotes significance at 10 per cent

Source: Authors' calculations

Table 33.2 Tests for the household debt growth threshold

Test	*Best point threshold*
Tsay (1998)	9.00
Hansen Threshold test	9.89
Balke (2000)	9.98

Source: Authors' calculations

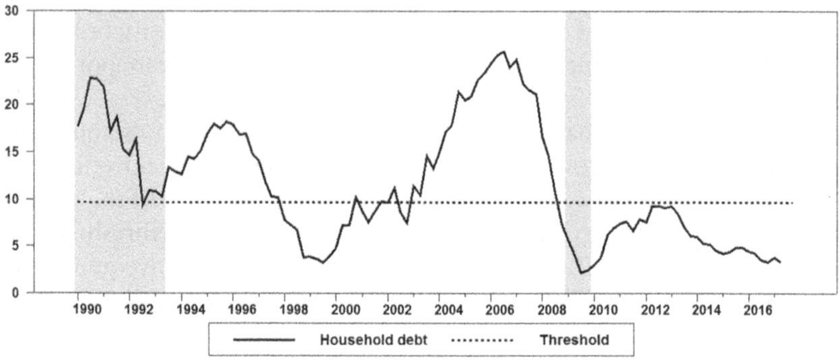

Fig. 33.2 Household debt growth and the estimated threshold. (Source: South African Reserve Bank and authors' calculations)

33.3 What Does the Threshold VAR Model Suggest About the Asymmetric Effects Introduced by the Household Debt Threshold?

We apply different techniques to establish the asymmetric effects induced by the household debt threshold. We decompose household debt into cycles and trends so that we can focus on the effects of household debt cycles on GDP growth. We use bivariate and multivariate TVAR models to assess for the household debt asymmetric effects. The estimated VAR models include GDP growth, household debt growth, household disposable income, the lending rate, inflation employment growth, the labour market conditions index, non-performing loans, labour productivity growth and the repo rate. The baseline TVAR model includes the household debt growth, GDP growth, employment growth, lending rate and inflation. The sample spans the period 1990Q1 to 2015Q4 and the data is sourced from the South African Reserve Bank database. The labour market conditions index is sourced from Gumata and Ndou (2017). All the variables enter the model at annual growth rates except for the interest rates.

Household debt growth is placed first, followed by GDP growth, employment growth, the lending rate and inflation.[1] In other estimations, we replace employment growth with either disposable income or labour productivity or non-performing loans. The ordering of output before the non-performing loans is in line with much of the monetary VAR literature. Furthermore, the broad credit view suggests that decisions on issuing bank loans are directly affected by the size of the external finance premium, which depends on the creditworthiness of borrowers. Hence, we order non-performing loans before the lending rate, which also quantitatively measures the credit risk premium and the quality of banks' loan books. We order the repo rate last and this implicitly assumes that monetary policy responds contemporaneously to output, labour and credit market conditions. The models are estimated using two lags and 10,000 Monte Carlo draws. The grey-shaded areas around the impulse responses denote the 16th and 84th percentiles error bands. All shocks refer to a positive one standard deviation shock.

We start the discussion by presenting a comparison of the GDP growth responses to positive household debt shocks in models where (i) there is no household debt threshold; (ii) household debt is below the threshold of 9.62 per cent; and (iii) household debt is above the threshold of 9.62 per cent.

Figures 33.3 and 33.4 indicate that the household debt thresholds induce asymmetric responses in GDP growth and employment growth due to a positive household debt growth shock. The responses in the models with no thresholds and during high household debt regimes lead to high and persistent responses. The responses in the models with no thresholds and during high debt regimes lead to high and persistent responses.

[1] We exclude bank credit in the specification because it constitutes almost 95 per cent of household debt and can thus bias the estimations.

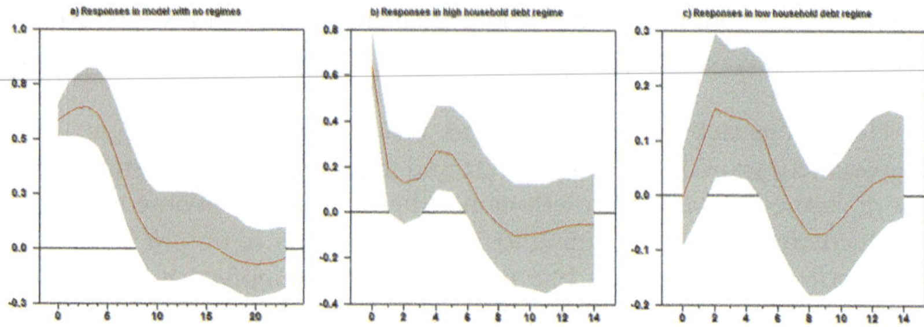

Fig. 33.3 GDP growth responses to positive household debt shocks below and above the household debt thresholds. (Source: Authors' calculations)

33.3.1 Are Symmetric Effects Based on Cyclical Deviation Impacts?

What are the asymmetric effects of negative and positive household debt cycles on GDP growth? The cycles in Fig. 33.5 are derived via the Hodrick-Prescott and extended Kalman filters for the period 1980Q1 to 2015Q4. Figure 33.5(a) shows the positive (negative) cycles, which are the periods during which household debt was above (below) the long trend level.

It is evident that there are four cycles during which household debt was persistently above trends (debt overhang) during the sample period. The recent trend during 2004 to 2010 was the highest positive deviation on record. The HP and the extended Kalman filters estimate that the deviation was nearly 10 per cent above trend at peak. The sensitivity of GDP growth to positive and negative household debt deviations shown in Fig. 33.5(b) is based on the linear regression coefficients of positive (negative) household debt gaps[2] on GDP growth. The sizes of the effects indicate that there are potential asymmetries. Positive (negative) household debt gaps result in an increase (decline) in GDP growth, but it is also evident that the sensitivity of GDP growth is different. Figure 33.5(b) indicates that GDP growth is more sensitive to negative household debt gaps compared to positive gaps. The same trends are evident in subsamples 2000Q1 to 2015Q4 and 2010Q1 to 2015Q4, although not shown here.[3]

[2] We generated dummy variables for periods of positive and negative household debt gaps for the HP and extended Kalman filter cycles and regressed them on GDP growth.

[3] Results are not shown here and can be availed upon request.

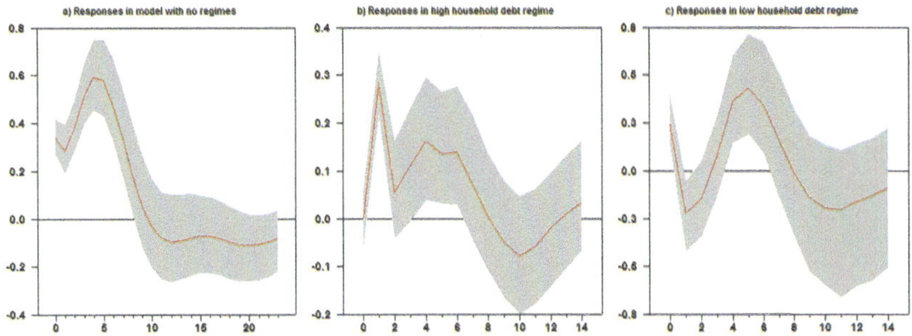

Fig. 33.4 Employment growth responses to positive household debt shocks below and above the household debt thresholds. (Source: Authors' calculations)

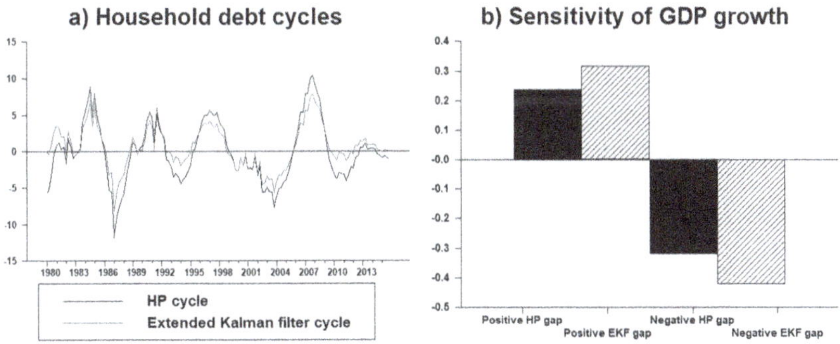

Fig. 33.5 Household debt cycles and GDP growth. (Source: Authors' calculations)

33.3.2 Evidence Based on Bivariate Asymmetric Model

This section uses a bivariate VAR model following Kilian and Vigfusson (2011) to assess the evidence of the asymmetric GDP growth responses to positive and negative household debt shocks. The analysis focuses on different sizes and signs of the deviations of household debt growth from the estimated threshold. We inverted the responses to positive household debt shocks to enable a comparison with negative shocks given that the current growth in household debt is below the threshold.

Figure 33.6 shows that a large negative one standard deviation shocks to household debt has a larger adverse impact on GDP growth compared to small negative shocks. This indicates the asymmetric effects of adverse

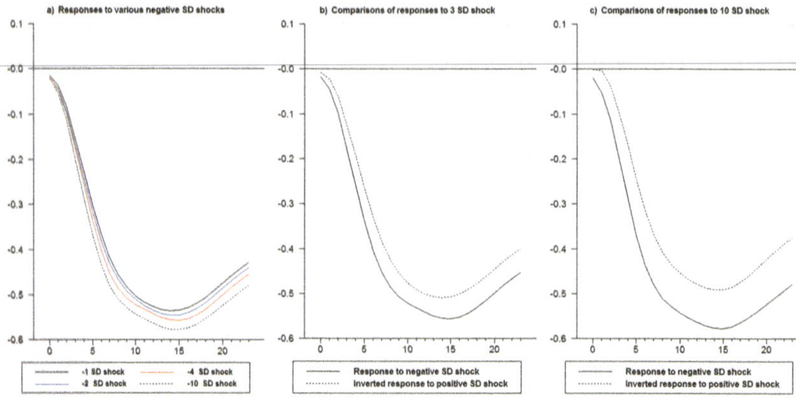

Fig. 33.6 GDP growth responses to positive and negative household debt shocks. (Source: Authors' calculations)

developments in growth in household debt below the threshold and suggests that household debt dynamics contribute to sluggish GDP growth. In addition, Figs. 33.6(b) and (c) show that large negative shocks have more impact on GDP growth than positive shocks of the same size.

33.4 What Are the Implications of the Household Debt Threshold for Price Stability in the Inflation-Targeting Era?

This section examines the effects of positive inflation shocks on the repo rate by estimating a counterfactual VAR model. In the counterfactual VAR model, the role of household debt in transmitting positive inflation shocks to the repo rate is shut off. The VAR model includes inflation, repo rate and household debt. The model is estimated using two lags and 10,000 Monte Carlo draws. Figure 33.7 shows the actual and counterfactual impulse responses, the size of the policy response and the amplification by household debt.

The results show that the policy rate is tightened due to positive inflationary pressures, but the actual policy rate increases more than the counterfactual, meaning that household debt transmits positive inflation shocks to the policy rate. How does the repo rate respond to positive inflation shocks when inflation exceeds 6 per cent? Further analysis of the role of

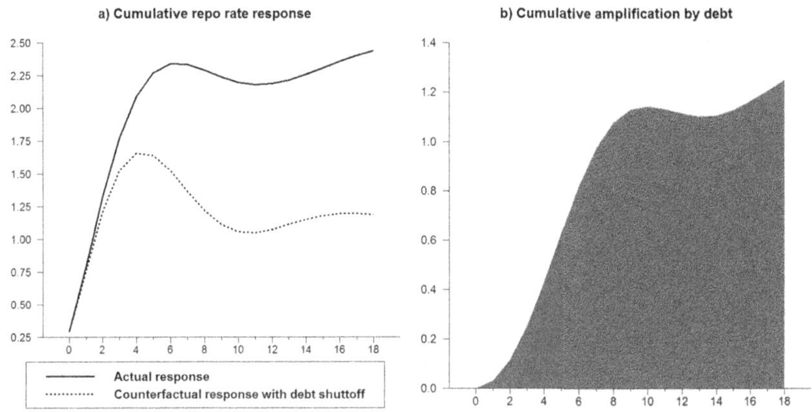

Fig. 33.7 Repo rate responses to positive inflation shocks and the role of household debt. (Source: Authors' calculations)

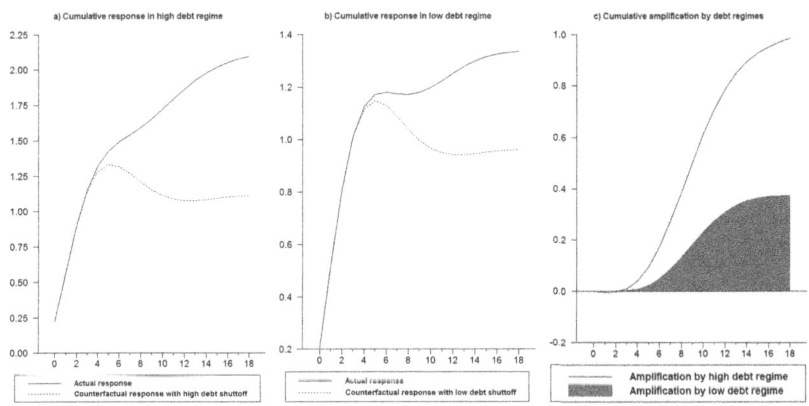

Fig. 33.8 Repo rate responses to positive inflation shocks above 6 per cent and the role of debt regimes. (Source: Authors' calculations)

the inflation threshold relative to the 6 per cent inflation upper band in Fig. 33.8 shows that the repo rate is tightened more in the high debt regime as household debt amplifies the inflationary pressures more in Fig. 33.8(c). The amplification size by household debt in the high debt regime is nearly double that in the low debt regime. The implication of these results is that the level of household debt (household debt regimes) as one of the indictors of financial stability plays a meaningful role in the price stability mandate and the responses of the policy rate.

33.5 Do Labour Market Conditions Act as a Conduit of Positive Inflation Shocks Depending on the Household Debt Regime?

This section examines the role of labour market conditions in transmitting positive inflation shocks to the repo rate and the role of household debt regimes. The counterfactual VAR model estimated in this section includes inflation, the labour market conditions index and the repo rate. Figure 33.9 shows that the actual repo rate is tightened in the high and low debt regimes but is tightened more in the high household debt regimes.

In cumulative terms, the repo rate increases by 175 basis points at peak in the high household debt regime compared to 50 basis points in the low household debt regime. This shows that loose labour market conditions amplify the repo rate tightening in response to inflationary pressures in the high household debt regime. In addition, Fig. 33.10 shows that the repo rate increases more when labour market conditions are loose. Furthermore, tight labour market conditions play a limited amplifying or dampening role in the low household debt regime in the first five months.

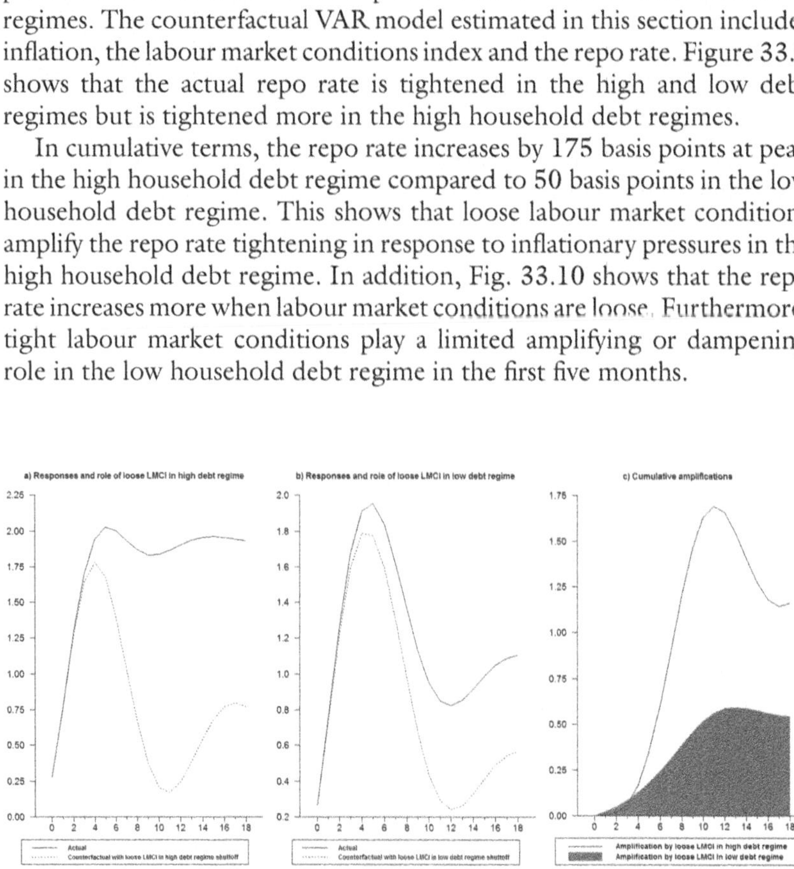

Fig. 33.9 Repo rate responses to positive inflation shocks and the role of loose labour market conditions. (Source: Authors' calculations)

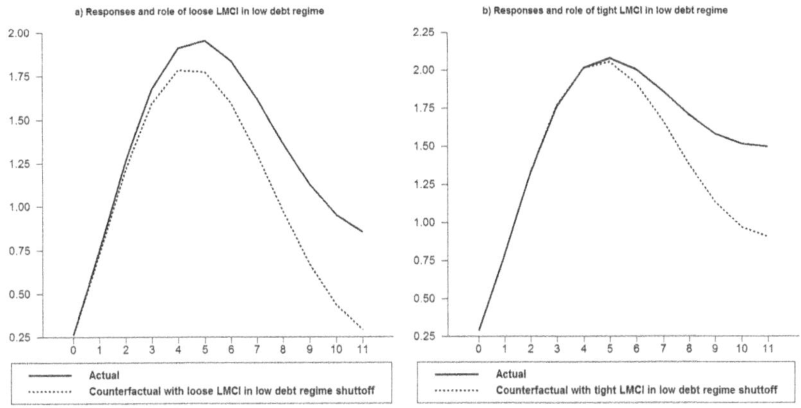

Fig. 33.10 Repo rate responses to positive inflation shocks and the role of labour market conditions. (Source: Authors' calculations)

This evidence corroborates earlier findings that loose labour market conditions, household debt regimes and inflationary pressures interact and have an influence on the monetary policy settings.

33.6 Conclusion and Policy Implications

This chapter assessed whether household debt regimes lead to subsequent lower output growth and higher unemployment. Mian et al. (2015) establish that household debt is a source of instability and lower economic growth. First, we establish that on a bilateral basis, household debt explains 60 per cent of changes in GDP growth. Second, the household debt threshold that exerts non-linear shock effects on output growth occurs around 9.62 per cent. Third, the household debt threshold matters for output growth, inflation and the monetary policy response. The results show that the policy rate is tightened in the high household debt regime due to positive inflationary pressures. In cumulative terms, the repo rate increases by 175 basis points at peak in the high household debt regime compared to 50 basis points in the low household debt regime. This shows that loose labour market conditions amplify the repo rate tightening in response to inflationary pressures in the high household debt regime. Furthermore, loose labour market conditions amplify the repo rate tightening in response to inflationary pressures in the high household debt regime. This means that household debt regimes transmit positive inflation shocks to the policy rate.

Loose labour market conditions, household debt regimes and inflationary pressures interact and have an influence on the monetary policy settings. The amplification size by household debt in the high debt regime is nearly double that in the low debt regime. The policy implication is that the level of household debt (household debt regimes) as one of the indictors of household financial standing and financial stability plays a meaningful role in the price stability mandate and the responses of the policy rate. There is a strong link between the price and financial stability objectives of the central bank via the household debt channel.

References

Avdjiev F, and Zeng Z. 2014. Credit Growth, Monetary Policy, and Economic Activity in a Three-Regime TVAR Model. BIS Working Papers No 449.

Balke, N S. 2000. Credit and Economic Activity: Credit Regimes and Nonlinear Propagation of Shocks. The Review of Economics and Statistics, MIT Press, 82(2), 344–349.

Calza A, and Sousa J. 2005. Output and Inflation Responses to Credit Shocks: Are There Threshold Effects in the Euro Area? Studies in Nonlinear Dynamics & Econometrics 10(2), 1253–1253.

Gumata N, and Ndou E. 2017a. Bank Credit Extension and Real Economic Activity in South Africa: The Impact of Capital Flow Dynamics, Bank Regulation and Selected Macro-prudential Tools. Palgrave Macmillan. ISBN 978-3-319-43551-0.

Gumata N, and Ndou E. 2017b. Labour Market and Fiscal Policy Adjustments to Shocks: The Role and Implications for Price and Financial Stability in South Africa. Palgrave Macmillan. ISBN 978-3-319-66520-7.

Gumata N, and Ndou E. 2019. Capital Flows, Credit Markets and Growth in South Africa: The Role of Global Economic Growth, Policy Shifts and Uncertainties. Palgrave Macmillan. ISBN 978-3-030-30888-9.

Kilian L, and Vigfusson R J. 2011. Are the responses of the U.S. economy asymmetric in energy price increases and decreases? Quantitative Economics, ISSN 1759-7331, Wiley, Hoboken, NJ, Vol. 2, Iss. 3, pp. 419–453.

Lumsdaine R, and Papell D. 1997. Multiple trend breaks and the unit root hypothesis. Review of Economics and Statistics, 79, 212–218.

Mian A R, Sufi A, and Verner E. 2015. Household Debt and Business Cycles Worldwide NBER Working Paper No. 21581.

Tsay R S. 1998. Testing and modelling multivariate threshold models, Journal of the American Statistical Association 93, 1188–1202, 1998.

Zivot E, and Andrews D. 1992. Further evidence of great crash, the oil price shock and unit root hypothesis. Journal of Business and Economic Statistics, 10, 251–270.

PART V

The Role of the Flow-of-Funds Approach in Monetary and Financial Policy Analysis

CHAPTER 34

How Does a Tight Monetary Policy Shock Affect the Household Sector Intermediation? Evidence from Households' Flow-of-Funds Data

Research Questions Explored

- Show the effects of an unexpected tight monetary policy shock on the households' incurrence of liabilities and acquisition of financial assets.
- Establish whether net financial asset flows fluctuate more due to positive GDP growth and inflation shocks compared to monetary policy tightening shocks.
- Examine the role of GDP growth shocks in magnifying the response of household liability flows due to a tight monetary policy shock.
- Establish the role of household gross assets and net financial asset flows in the response of GDP growth to inflation shocks and the role of the household liability flows in the response of GDP growth to a tight monetary policy shock.
- Offer insight into the interaction between monetary and macroprudential policy in relation to household debt levels and the deleveraging process.

N. Gumata, E. Ndou, *Achieving Price, Financial and Macro-Economic Stability in South Africa*,
https://doi.org/10.1007/978-3-030-66340-7_34

34.1 Introduction

The effects of monetary policy shocks on flows of borrowing and lending by households have not been investigated in South Africa.[1] This is the case despite the findings by Bernanke and Gertler (1989) and the lingering adverse effects of the recent global financial crisis indicating that shocks to the borrowers' balance sheets and net worth may induce undesirable fluctuations in economic activity. Bonci (2011) suggests that policy lessons from the recent global financial crisis indicate that the information content provided by the flow-of-funds provides a comprehensive framework for the analysis of the household sector borrowing, lending activities and their financial instruments with the rest of the economy. It is against this background that this chapter uses the flow-of-funds data for the household sector to assess the impact of a tight monetary policy shock on the household sector intermediation. Does an unexpected tight monetary policy shock induce households to cut the incurrence of liabilities and the acquisition of financial assets?

To properly bring into the policy discourse the role of flow-of-funds, it is appropriate to highlight the location of flow-of-funds in economic theory. The flow-of-funds can be traced back to theory of exchange equation. The equation of exchange shown in Eq. (34.1) shows the relationship between the money supply (M), the income velocity of money (V), the price level (P) and transaction[2] (T). Thus, the equation of exchange directly links the price and financial stability aspects of the central bank mandate. Papademos and Stark (2010) indicate that the transactions in Eqs. (34.1) and (34.2) comprise both the real and financial transactions and those due to the intermediary transactions along the production line. Similar to the quantity theory of money, which replaces (T) with income (Y) in Eq. (34.2), this equation relates increases in the money supply (M) to increases in the overall level of prices (P).[3]

$$MV = PT \tag{34.1}$$

$$M = \frac{PT}{V} \tag{34.2}$$

[1] Flows based on the flow-of-funds approach and not stocks.

[2] Or an index of expenditures.

[3] The quantity theory of money is given by $M = kPY$ where $k = (1/v)$.

In addition, we can get an indicator for the demand for money from the theory of exchange in Eq. (34.2). This linkage reaffirms through the equation of exchange that the flows-of-funds via transactions are complementary to the monetary analysis. Given the diverse transactional activities, these flow-of-fund accounts report the transactions of the economy according to (i) sectors and (ii) financial instruments. In addition, the flow-of-fund accounts place explicit emphasis on financial transactions whilst giving a comprehensive coverage of the financial system.

The preview of the theory of equation of exchange enhances the view that policymakers should consider the role of the flow-of-funds in policy-making decisions. The presence of prices, transactions and money in the theory of exchange assures the policymakers of the direct link between price and financial stability. Papademos and Stark (2010) indicate that in a policy perspective, the flow-of-funds accounting identity requires that total sources of funds must equal total uses of funds for each instrument in each sector and economy. Furthermore, the flow accounts track funds as they move from sectors such as households to other sectors.[4] So, the imbalances are indicative of certain financial instabilities or blockages that the monetary and financial stability policymaker should pay attention to. Second, the balance sheet shocks to some sectors may lead to a chain reaction which leads to adverse financial positions in other sectors.

If evidence matters and is indispensable in policy discussions, the recent empirical work on the origins and evolution of the recent financial crisis encourages policymakers to pay attention to the flow-of-funds data to identify signs of imbalances in sectors.[5] Papademos and Stark (2010) indicate that the accounting identities remind policymakers that things have to add up from the flow-of-funds viewpoint. This requires financial asset flows to be matched by financial liability flows. At the same time, expanding debt should lead to rising payment flows.

This chapter fills academic and policy research gaps by showing the effects of a tight monetary policy shock on the households' incurrence of liabilities and acquisition of financial assets. We establish whether net financial asset flows fluctuate due to positive GDP growth and inflation

[4] Households are sources of funds, through intermediaries to sectors that use the funds to acquire physical and financial assets.

[5] This happens despite the flow-of-funds being less informative about the underlying drivers of the financial processes and cannot include financial asset flows to forecast the implication of developments in these flows for economic dynamics.

shocks compared to monetary policy tightening shocks. We examine the role of GDP growth shocks in magnifying the response of household liability flows due to a tight monetary policy shock. We establish the role of household gross assets and net financial asset flows in the response of GDP growth to inflation shocks, as well as the role of household liability flows in the response of GDP growth to the a tight monetary policy shock. The study offers insight into the interaction between monetary and macroprudential policy in relation to household debt levels and the deleveraging process.

34.2 What Can Policymakers Learn from the Crosschecking Based on the Sectoral Perspective?

Financial asset flows can be used for crosschecking economic realities and theoretical predictions. The crosschecking requires actively reconciling varied pieces of information from varied perspectives in the same coherent framework. Hence, we argue that crosschecking is useful for identifying inconsistencies, and developing a coherent and consistent picture in the sector. Based on developments during the financial crisis in 2007Q3, not all sectors sold risky assets simultaneously in flight to safety. Hence, in a broader sense, changes in the assets and liabilities which indicate saving and investment imbalances require these to match across sectors.

34.2.1 Are Households Net Borrowers or Lenders Based on the Flow-of-Funds and Are There Signs of Households Deleveraging?

The flow-of-funds in the household sector allows for the reconciliation of the identity of saving and real capital formation in any period in this sector. According to Bonci and Columba (2008), the households have the option to invest in real assets more or less than they have saved. The difference between fixed investment and gross saving leads to a change in the net financial position as shown in identity Eq. (34.3):

$$Investment - Saving = Net\ financial\ assets\ of\ household\ sector \quad (34.3)$$

To be consistent with the definition used in the flow-of-funds in the South African Reserve Bank, we define net financial asset flows by using the identity in Eq. (34.4). The households' financial asset (liability) flows refer to the net acquisition (incurrence) of financial assets (liability).

$$\begin{aligned} &\textit{Net financial assets of household sector} \\ &= \textit{Households' financial asset flows} \\ &- \textit{Households' financial liability flows} \end{aligned} \tag{34.4}$$

These identities require the financial asset flows and liabilities to balance. If not so, the negative (positive) sign on the second identity implies net borrowing (net lending) by households. We use data sourced from the South African Reserve Bank database. The sample spans the period 2000Q1 to 2014Q3.

The density and box whisker plots in Fig. 34.1(a) show that the net financial asset flows are negatively skewed, which indicates net borrowing by households in period 2000Q1 to 2014Q3. *First*, the flow-of-funds as a tool for crosschecking signs of imbalances in the economy using net financial asset flows from the density plots concludes that households are net borrowers. In addition, in Fig. 34.1(b) we reject the hypothesis that household financial asset and liability flows are distributed similarly, which indicates imbalances exist. Household financial asset flows are mostly distributed around R20 billion while liability flows are more evenly spread

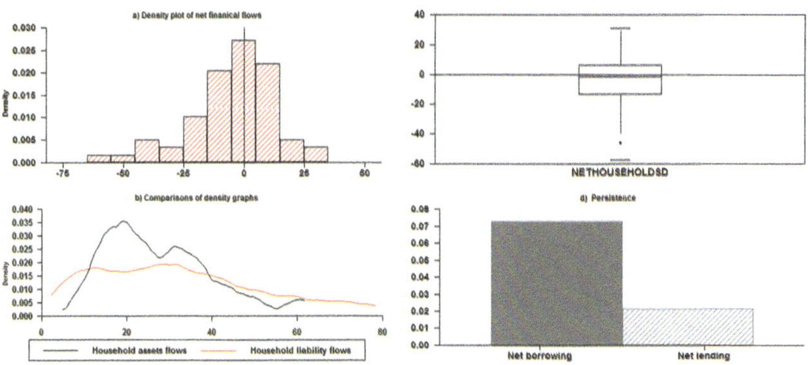

Fig. 34.1 Various aspects of net financial asset flows. (Source: South African Reserve Bank and authors' calculations)

between R15 billion and R40 billion. However, above R66 billion we find only liability flows reach a peak of nearly R80 billion.

If signs of deleveraging require the flows to show persistence in one direction for some time, then, what do the measures of persistence conclude? Figure 34.1(d) shows the persistence magnitudes based on first-order correlation. Both net borrowing and net lending display less persistence despite slight differences in magnitudes. The less persistent magnitudes indicate high volatility of net financial asset flows and that it cannot remain in one state for long periods. *Second*, crosschecking using flow-of-funds based on persistent magnitudes, it is difficult to conclude clearly regarding extent of households' deleveraging process.

34.2.2 Did the Periods of the Low Repo Rate Lead to an Improvement in the Households' Financial Asset Flows After 2007Q2?

To answer this question, this section uses the largest net borrowing value reached pre-2007 as a benchmark of whether periods of low interest rates help reduce borrowing. Figure 34.2 shows the pre-crisis borrowing cut-off and the evolution in the trends of the household sector financial assets, liabilities and the net value for the period 2000Q1 to 2014Q3.

When net borrowing by households is viewed relative to the highest value recorded (R26.979 billion) before the financial crisis, the results

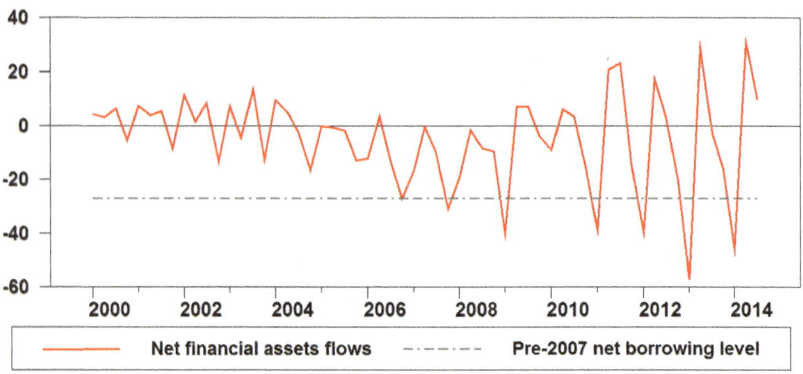

Fig. 34.2 Household sector financial asset flows (R billion). (Source: South African Reserve Bank and authors' calculations)

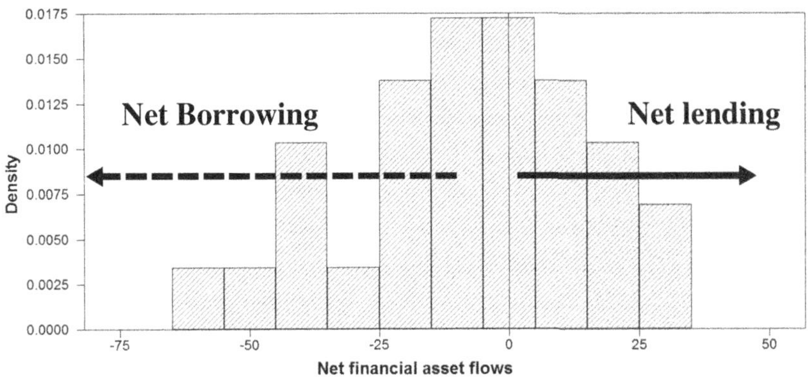

Fig. 34.3 Density plots of net financial asset flow distribution after 2007Q2. (Source: Authors' calculations)

show that the net household borrowing increased by bigger amounts after 2010 relative to the pre-2007 borrowing level. The negative skewness exhibited by the density plot in Fig. 34.3 indicates that net borrowing was more prevalent than net lending since 2007Q3. *Third*, the crosschecking based on financial asset flows of the household sector puts doubt on assertions that households were reducing borrowing consistent with the deleveraging process in period of low interest rates.

34.3 What Does VAR Evidence Suggest?

This section estimates various VAR models using different techniques to complement the descriptive statistical approaches used in the previous section. The VAR models determine: (i) whether the impact of a tight monetary policy shock is large on impact or not, (ii) the rate at which the impact dissipates, (iii) the substitution effects, (iv) the propagation effects, and (v) the magnitudes of fluctuations in net financial asset flows induced by different shocks. The baseline VAR model has three variables, which comprises of the GDP level, the consumer price index and the repo rate. The GDP level and consumer price index are log transformed and then multiplied by 100. This enables the interpretation of the impulse responses as deviations from the trend. In addition, using variables in level form allows for implicit cointegration like justifications cited in literature. The

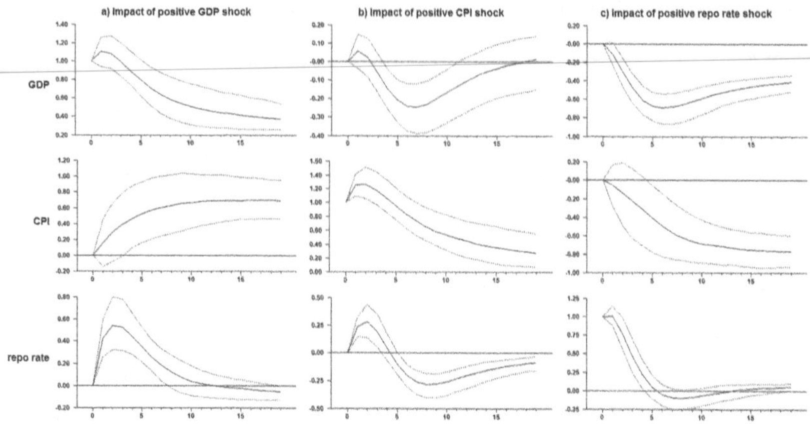

Fig. 34.4 Responses in the baseline model. (Source: Authors' calculations)

baseline model is the initial step, which we augment with the flow-of-fund variables. The augmenting involves adding the flow-of-fund variables individually according to the marginal strategy to determine their response to a tight monetary policy shock.

The VAR model is estimated using two lags selected by the Akaike information criterion (AIC). The variables are ordered such that GDP is the most exogenous variable. The repo rate is placed last in the sequence, suggesting that monetary policy has lagged effects on consumer prices and GDP. The results for the baseline model are shown in Fig. 34.4.

Figure 34.4, column (a), shows that a positive GDP shock leads to an increase in the consumer price level and repo rate. The repo rate increases to curb inflation.[6] Column (b) shows that a positive consumer price shock has adverse effects on real economic activity, as it reduces GDP growth significantly for nearly 11 quarters. Consistent with a forward-looking monetary policy conduct that mitigates inflationary pressures, the repo rate is tightened for nearly a year. The peak increase in the repo rate coincides with the maximum increase in the consumer price level. However, as the inflationary pressures begin to diminish towards the pre-shock level,

[6] For instance, based on the Philips curve, increased demand pressures lead to heightened inflationary pressures when actual output exceeds potential output.

the repo rate falls significantly after six quarters. Figure 34.4, column (c), shows the effects of a tight monetary policy shock on GDP and CPI. A tight monetary policy shock does not lead to a price puzzle. The consumer price level and GDP responses affirm the expected monetary policy effects on aggregate demand consistent with economic theory. Furthermore, this evidence shows that the model can be used to assess the impact of tight monetary policy shocks on the flow-of-fund dynamics in the household sector. Thus, the baseline evidence shows that a monetary policy tightening shock leads to a higher repo rate, weaker economic activity and a decline in the consumer price level.

34.3.1 *The Impact of a Tight Monetary Policy Shock on Household Sector Net Financial Assets Flows*

This section applies the marginal method in which we add the last variable in the VAR model to be net financial asset flows or a component of asset or liability flows. The economic intuition from the marginal method suggests that the repo rate does not react in the short term to changes in these flow variables. But these variables react within the same quarter to the repo rate shock. The marginal strategy will enable us to test several economic hypotheses to ascertain the usefulness of the flow-of-funds as a crosschecking tool. We begin by testing Hypothesis 1 to determine whether households participate in capital markets.

Hypothesis 1: No evidence of limited household participation in capital markets This Hypothesis 1 arises from Christiano et al. (1996) who find evidence indicating limited participation of US households in capital markets. Limited participation prevented US households from adjusting their financial assets and liabilities following a tightening monetary policy shock. According to Bonci (2011), evidence of limited participation could be linked to limited data in the past, because recent data reveal that households' participation has risen over time. The tight monetary policy shock refers to a 1 per cent positive repo rate shock.

Figure 34.5 shows that the household sector net financial asset flows decline due to a tight monetary policy shock. This indicates that households become net borrowers for nearly two quarters. This occurs through the revaluation of outstanding debt following a new high interest rate. In

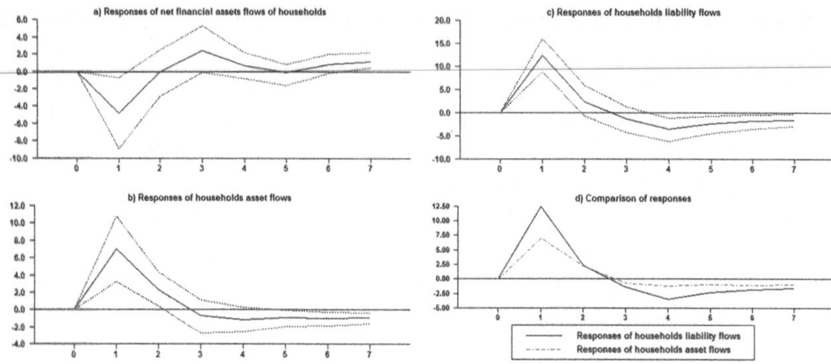

Fig. 34.5 Responses of the household sector net financial asset flows, assets, and liabilities (in billion Rands) to a tight monetary policy shock. (Source: Authors' calculations)

addition, households may borrow more to smooth consumption since the decline in GDP may coincide with decline in household disposable income.

Which component of the household balance sheet is highly responsive to a tight monetary policy shock? To answer this question, we determine which of the components of the household balance sheet flows is highly responsive to a tight monetary policy shock. Figure 34.5(c and d) shows that both the liability and asset flow components are transitorily impacted by a tight monetary policy shock. The worsening of the household net lending position is due to increased liability flows, which indicate more borrowing, possibly to smooth out their obligations and consumptions.

How do these conclusions compare to evidence reported in other studies? As shown in Table 34.1, these findings differ from the Christiano et al. (1996) conclusion that US households do not adjust their net financial position following a monetary policy tightening shock. This reflects the predictions of limited participation model, which indicates the existence of certain degree of rigidities in the households' decisions of financial choices. Furthermore, the findings in this study are contrary to those in Bonci and Columba (2008) who conclude that Italian households become net lenders following a tight monetary policy shock. However, our findings concur with those studies focusing on the euro area and Portugal, indicating that the household sector becomes a net borrower. In addition, Gameiro and Sousa (2010) conclude that the maximum net funds borrowed by the household sector occurs in the first quarter in Portugal, which is like the South African household sector response.

Table 34.1 Evidence of household sector responses to a tight monetary policy shock

Country	*Net funds raised/ financial asset flows*	*Financial liability flows*	*Financial asset flows*	*Authors of the study*
US	Unchanged	Decreased	Not significant	Christiano et al. (1996)
euro area	Net borrower	Decreased	Decreased	Bonci (2010)
Italy	Net lender	Decreased	Increased	Bonci and Columba (2008)
Portugal	Net borrower	Decreased	Decreased	Gameiro and Sousa (2010)
South Africa	Net borrower	Increased	Increased	Gumata and Ndou (2019)

Note: These studies (excluding South African one) used net funds raised, defined as financial liability less financial asset flows, and the negative sign implies net lender and the positive sign implies net borrower

Source: Authors' calculations

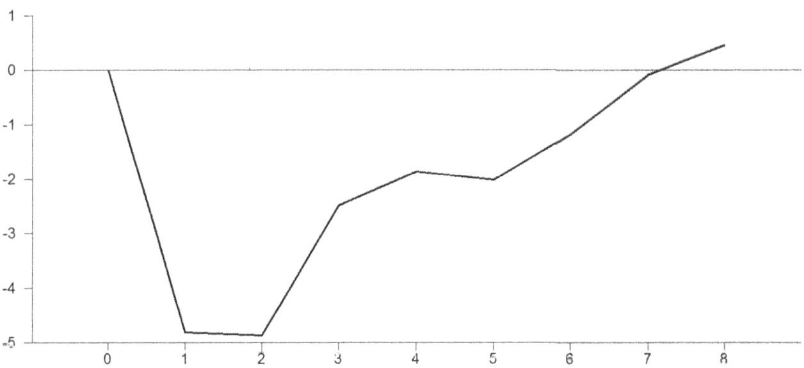

Fig. 34.6 Cumulative net financial asset flow responses to a tight monetary policy shock. (Source: Authors' calculations)

We find evidence that South African households do participate in capital markets. The household sector adjusts financial liabilities more than assets following a tight monetary policy shock. In cumulative terms, the household sector becomes a net borrower for a prolonged period as shown in Fig. 34.6. *Fourth*, using the flow-of-funds as a crosschecking tool we conclude that households do not deleverage following policy tightening shock.

34.3.2 *Are There Any Differences in the Responses of the Households' Asset Flow Components to an Unexpected Tight monetary Policy Shock?*

To identify the channels involved in the adjustments of the household sector net financial asset flows, this section investigates the role of specific assets. To determine the degree of asset substitutability, we separate the households' asset flows into bank and non-bank deposits as well as various instruments. Figure 34.7 shows the responses of various maturities of deposits into banks following a monetary policy tightening shock. The monetary policy tightening shock significantly increases short- and medium-term monetary deposits in Fig. 34.7(a). The short-term and medium-term deposits include M1 and M2, which are deposits held for transactional and precautionary purposes. Long-term deposits in Fig. 34.7(b) decline albeit insignificantly; the decline may indicate switching from these assets into short- and medium-term deposits and deposits with other financial institutions shown in Fig. 34.7(c). This switching may suggest that financial intermediaries adjust interest rates paid on liquid instruments to take advantage of higher interest rates in Fig. 34.7(c).

Hypothesis 2: No substitution effect amongst deposits

We compare the response of short- and medium-term deposits, long-term monetary deposits, and currency and deposits in Fig. 34.8(a) to test

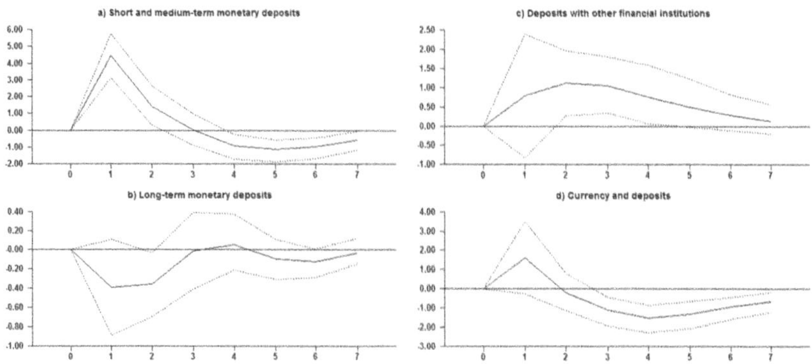

Fig. 34.7 Responses of deposit components to a tight monetary policy shock. (Source: Authors' calculations)

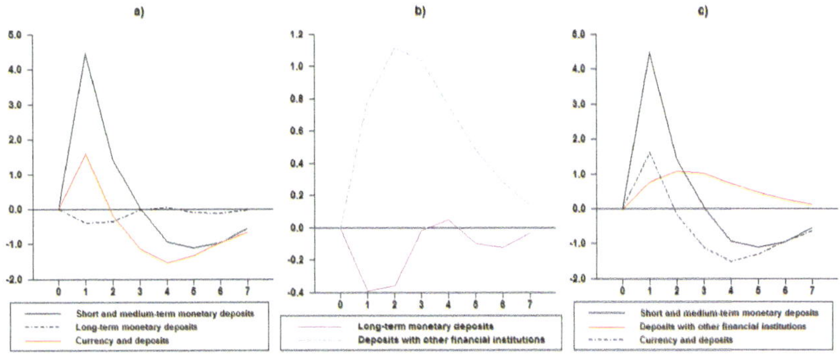

Fig. 34.8 Comparisons of various deposits' responses to a tight monetary policy response. (Source: Authors' calculations)

Hypothesis 2. Yes, we find evidence indicating partly switching of deposits by households from long-term deposits to short-term and medium-term deposits, because households may want to recall their deposits when interest rates rise to meet their obligations. This suggests that households switch for transactional and precautionary savings following a tighter monetary policy shock. Thus, evidence rejects Hypothesis 2.

Hypothesis 3: No substitution effects between bank and non-bank deposits

To test Hypothesis 3, we compare the response of deposits with other financial institutions and long-term monetary deposits. Figure 34.8(b) shows that deposits with other institutions increase while long-term monetary deposits tend to decline. This suggests that households switch their portfolios from long-term monetary deposits to deposits with other institutions. Thus, we conclude that evidence rejects Hypothesis 3.

Hypothesis 4: No substitution between bank deposits of short- and medium-term maturity and non-bank deposits

To test Hypothesis 4, evidence in Fig. 34.8(c) shows that there is a switch from bank short-term and medium-term deposits towards other deposits with other financial institutions. The switching occurs after three quarters and may be due to high relative returns offered and the safety of deposits from other institutions, which include mutual funds. Thus, evidence rejects Hypothesis 4.

Based on evidence presented in this section we conclude that the decline in long-term deposit flows is probably linked to the households reallocating their funds for precautionary purposes as they seek to smooth consumption and meet their debt servicing obligations following an interest rate increase. In addition, as shown in the baseline model, GDP growth declines following the tightening in the repo rate. Thus, the switch to short-term deposits may reflect expected effects of reduced GDP growth which may be felt via the reduction in income and employment opportunities. Bonci (2011) suggests that this means that households have an incentive to draw on their long-term bank deposits to finance expenditure or consumption as disposable income slows down. Furthermore, using the flow-of-funds for crosschecking the prevalence of the substitutability of assets, we find evidence of re-composition and re-allocation of households' portfolios from long-term maturity assets to short-term liquid assets.

34.3.3 Evidence from Non-Deposit Financial Assets Flows

The results in Fig. 34.9(a) show that the interest rate in the retirements and life funds increases significantly and peaks at nearly R3 billion in the first quarter. In addition, securities other than shares rise significantly in the second quarter.

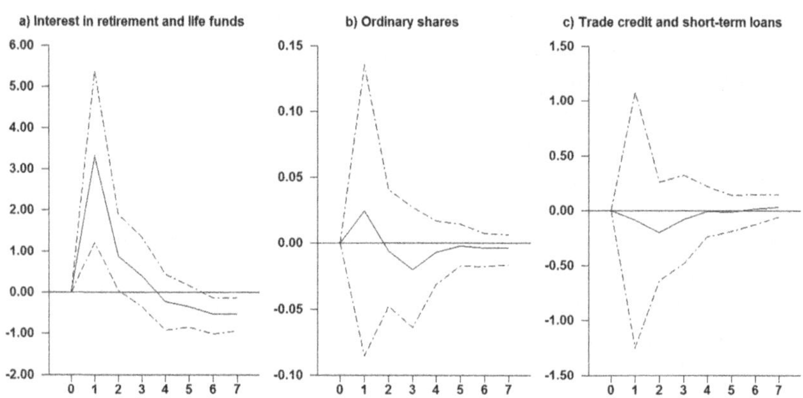

Fig. 34.9 Responses of other financial asset flows to a tight monetary policy shock. (Source: Authors' calculations)

Studies in other countries examine the role of ordinary shares. Despite this asset class not being prominent in this country, we include it in this analysis for comparative purposes. The results show that ordinary shares do not respond significantly in Fig. 34.9(b) to a tight monetary policy shock, indicating this is not a prominent channel for the household financial asset flows. This does not mean that this asset class channel is completely ineffective. Rather, it might be effective via flows in other sectors. The trade credit and short-term loans in Fig. 34.9(c) are not responsive possibly because their lending rates are guided by National Credit Regulation Act, which historically were not directly linked to the prevailing policy rates.

34.3.4 *Evidence from the Liability Flows*

Do households cut back on the demand for loans after a tight monetary policy shock? Evidence in this section indicates that bank loans and advances in Fig. 34.10(a) rise transitorily reaching a peak in the first quarter and decline after two quarters. The bank loans and advances consist of short-term loans, mostly of small magnitudes. Based on this composition, the transitory increase is consistent with households bridging finance in which households may draw from their pre-committed credit lines at lending rates observed before the shock. The delayed decline in bank loans and advances may reflect the adverse effects of economic activity slowdown, which prompts banks to apply tighter credit lending criteria.

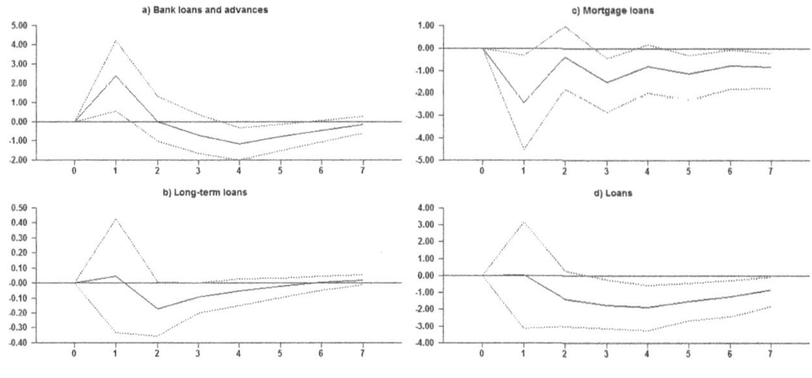

Fig. 34.10 Responses of household liability sector components to a tight monetary policy shock. (Source: Authors' calculations)

The long-term loans in Fig. 34.10(b) increase (although insignificantly) in the first quarter followed by a contraction. The long-term loans refer to loans offered by non-banks such as borrowing from a life insurance or retirements funds, the once-off increase may be indicative that households tend to borrow slightly more from these institutions, possibly based on their life policies.

Mortgage loans tend to decline following a tight monetary policy shock. The decline may reflect these are long-term maturity loans of big magnitudes. So, lending institutions will tighten their credit lending standards as interest rates on these loans rise due to the screening of customers leading to a significant decline in loans granted. In addition, Bonci (2011) suggests that the decline relative to the baseline is probably caused by demand and supply factors, when credit institutions adjust credit lending standards due to the deteriorating GDP outlook.

34.3.5 Variance Decompositions

This section applies a variance decomposition approach, which shows the proportions of movements in a variable due to a specific shock. These proportions should add up to 100 per cent. However, we focus on those fluctuations induced by positive shocks to GDP, CPI and repo rate for comparative purposes. Figure 34.11 shows that a shock to GDP explains less than 13 per cent of the variation in the household sector net financial asset flows in the long run. This is followed by a positive shock to the consumer price level, which explains about 12 per cent of the variation in the long run. Over the entire forecast horizon, a tight monetary policy shock contributes less than 2 per cent to variations in net household financial asset flows.

The results suggest that apart from net household financial asset flows explaining their own fluctuations for most periods (not shown here), GDP and consumer price level dynamics matter more than tight monetary policy shocks.

34.3.6 To What Extent Do Financial Asset Flows Amplify and Dampen the Response of Macro-economic Variables to a Positive Economic Shock?

To derive policy implications regarding the role of flow-of-funds, this section applies a counterfactual approach. The counterfactual effect is measured by the gap of certain responses when specific channels are

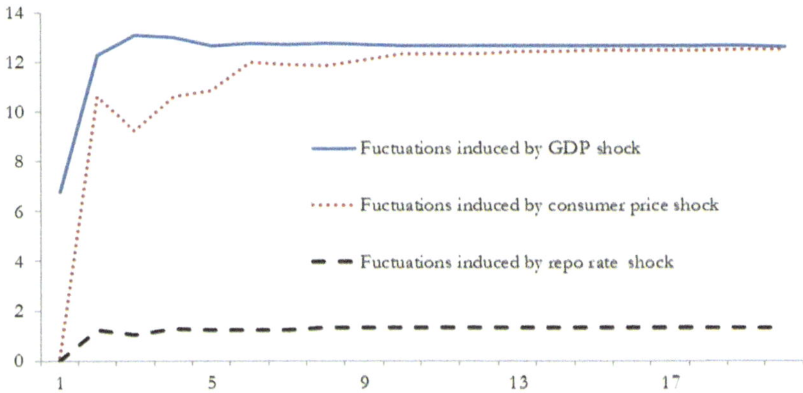

Fig. 34.11 Fluctuations in net household sector financial asset flow induced by various shocks. (Source: Authors' calculations)

shut-off compared to when they are not shut-off in the model. We argue that the counterfactual analysis matters for several reasons. The flow-of-funds links monetary and financial stability via the financial sector as a propagator of macro-financial shocks. Papademos and Stark (2010) and various other studies indicate that the recent financial crisis shows that non-bank financial intermediaries propagate financial shocks in the securitised finance. This practice blurred the distinction between bank and market-based financial systems on account of financial globalisation.

Due to economic developments post-2009, we assess the roles of GDP, net financial asset flows as well as their liability and asset flows. In addition, this is motivated by evidence that liability flows increase more leading to the deterioration in the net financial asset flows of households. Second, we established in the earlier section that GDP leads to more fluctuations in the net financial asset flows of households. Third, high inflation regimes during periods characterised by low economic growth may exacerbate households' net financial asset flows.

34.3.7 Does GDP Amplify or Dampen the Response of Households' Liability Flows to a Tighter Monetary Policy Shock?

Does GDP amplify or dampen the reaction of household liability flows due to tightening monetary policy shocks? Papademos and Stark (2010) suggest that a propagation channel will arise in the presence of contagion when shocks spread from the real sector to financial sector via the net lending positions of different sectors. This section adopts a similar approach to the earlier sections examining the responses of the households' liability flows to a positive 1 per cent tightening in monetary policy shock. We compare the responses of liability flows when GDP is shut-off and allowed to be active in the model. The gap between the two responses measures the magnifying or dampening effect of GDP.

Figure 34.12 shows that the households' liability flows increase for a year following a tight monetary policy shock, but the magnitudes are different. The households' liability flows increase more when GDP is shut-off in the model, indicating the dampening ability of GDP. At peak magnitude, GDP induces an increase of nearly R1 billion in liability flows, which is lower than the R2.5 billion reached when GDP is shut-off in the model. This suggests that robust GDP dampens the households' liability flows possibly by providing employment opportunities that generate income hence discouraging the household incurrences of liability flows. The magnitudes of the GDP dampening effects are shown in Fig. 34.12(b). Thus, robust GDP growth is needed to mitigate the high incurrence of liability flows after a monetary policy tightening shock.

We further argue that a propagation channel arises via the excessive incurrence of liability flows, which increases risk exposures and induces more volatility in key balance sheet items with spill-over effects to economic activity. Hence, in Fig. 34.13 we find that increased household

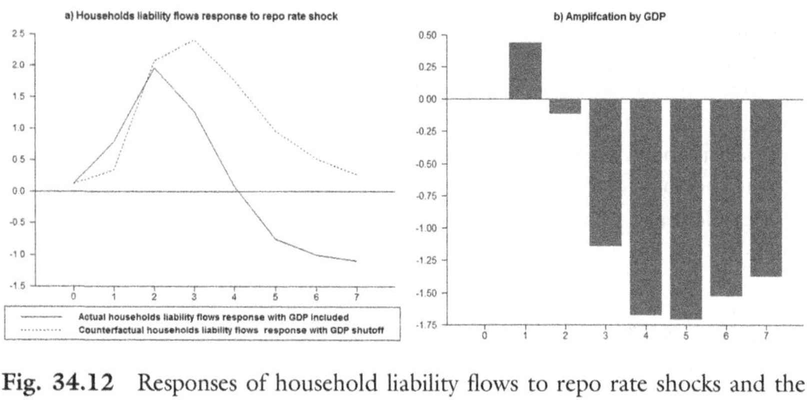

Fig. 34.12 Responses of household liability flows to repo rate shocks and the role of GDP. (Source: Authors' calculations)

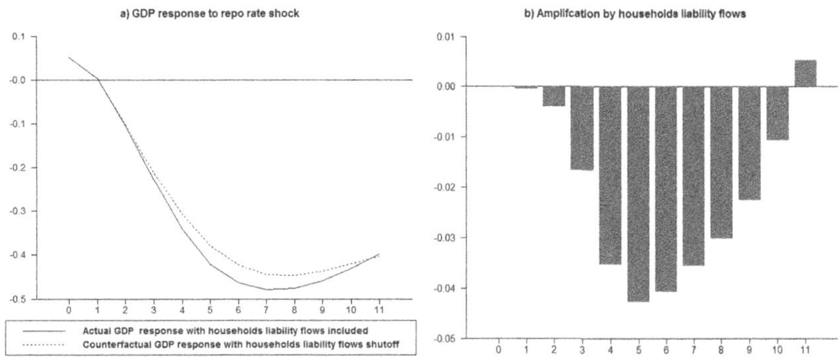

Fig. 34.13 Responses of GDP to repo rate shocks and the role of household liability flows. (Source: Authors' calculations)

liability flows worsen the GDP response to a tight monetary policy shock. This suggests that increased households' liability flows will worsen the GDP contraction probably through increased risk exposure and high household indebtedness, thereby slowing down consumption. The amplification by the household liabilities suggests that the GDP contraction can worsen by nearly 0.05 per cent as shown in Fig. 34.13(b). Furthermore, the increased incurrences of households' liability flows worsen the GDP contraction probably through increased risk exposure and high household indebtedness, thereby slowing down consumption.

34.3.8 Do Household Financial Asset Flows Dampen the Response of GDP to Positive Inflation Shocks?

This section extends the analysis by looking at the role of the households' financial asset flows to determine whether they amplify or dampen the GDP responses to positive inflation shocks. This asset accumulation channel is important from the financial stability perspective. It is a channel through which shocks may spread through the system with possible spillover effects into those areas initially not vulnerable to the shock but that become affected though interconnections with the sector. So, does increased asset accumulation amplify or dampen the GDP response to positive inflation shocks? We measure the amplification or dampening effects exerted by the households' flow-of-funds by the gap between the counterfactual and actual GDP responses a positive inflation shock.

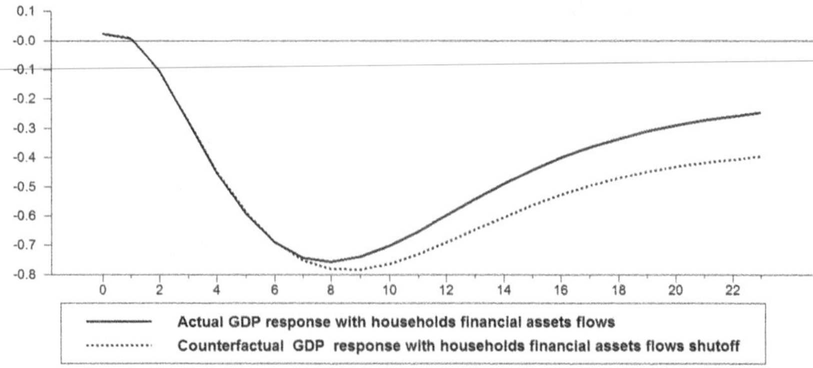

Fig. 34.14 GDP growth responses to positive inflation shocks and the role of the households' financial asset flows. (Source: Authors' calculations)

Figure 34.14 shows that GDP declines due to positive inflation shocks irrespective of whether the household sector asset flows are shut-off or not in the model. The decline in GDP is pronounced when the households' financial asset flows are shut-off in the model. This suggests that the improvement in the households' financial asset flows would to some extent mitigate the effects of the GDP decline due to a positive inflationary shock. Thus, we conclude that increased accumulation of households' assets dampens the GDP decline, pointing to the importance of healthy households' financial asset flows.

34.3.9 Do Household Financial Asset Flows Dampen the Response of the Monetary Policy Rate to Positive Inflation Shocks?

This section concludes the analysis by looking at whether the improved household financial assets may impede the policy rate response to positive inflation shocks, thus impacting the price stability mandate. This may arise when households switch their financial assets as part of hedging strategies, thereby possibly impacting the transmission of policy shocks. We find in Fig. 34.15 that the repo rate increases to curb inflationary pressures. However, the gap between whether the household financial assets are included or shut-off in the model is exceedingly small suggesting the minimal effect exerted by these financial asset flows on the repo rate response to inflationary shocks as shown in Fig. 34.15.

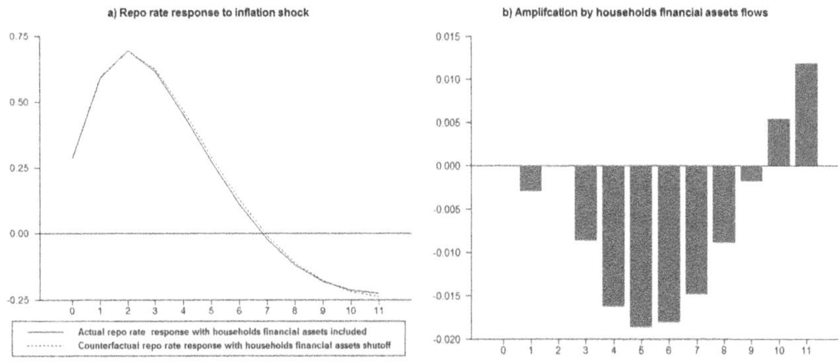

Fig. 34.15 Repo rate responses to positive inflation shocks and the role of the households' financial asset flows. (Source: Authors' calculations)

34.4 Conclusion and Policy Implications

This chapter explored whether a tight monetary policy shock induces households to cut the incurrence of liabilities and the acquisition of financial assets? First, evidence shows that there are signs of imbalances in the economy. The household financial asset and liability flows are not distributed similarly, indicating that imbalances exist. Second, the results show that the net household borrowing increased by bigger amounts after 2010 relative to the pre-2007 borrowing level. Net borrowing was more prevalent than net lending since 2007Q3. Third, evidence based on the financial asset flows of the household sector puts doubt on assertions that households were reducing borrowing consistent with the deleveraging process in periods of low interest rates. Furthermore, a positive GDP shock leads to an increase in the consumer price level and repo rate. The repo rate increases to curb inflation. This is consistent with a forward-looking monetary policy conduct that mitigates inflationary pressures. On the other hand, a contractionary monetary policy shock leads to a higher repo rate, weaker economic activity and a decline in the consumer price level.

Which component of the household balance sheet is highly responsive to a tight monetary policy shock? Evidence shows that the household sector net financial asset flow declines due to a tight monetary policy shock. This indicates that households become net borrowers, and this occurs through the revaluation of outstanding debt following a new high interest rate. In addition, households may borrow more to smooth consumption since the decline in GDP may coincide with a decline in household disposable income. The worsening of the household net lending position is due to increased liability flows, which indicates more borrowing, possibly to smooth out their obligations and consumptions.

From the policymaking perspective, the financial assets flow evidence indicates that households participate in capital markets. For instance, households switch deposits amongst asset classes of different maturities following a positive interest rate shock. The monetary policy tightening shock significantly increases short- and medium-term monetary deposits, which are held for transactional and precautionary purposes. Long-term deposits decline indicating the switching from these assets into short- and medium-term deposits and deposits with other financial institutions. This switching may suggest that financial intermediaries adjust interest rates paid on liquid instruments to take advantage of higher interest rates. Thus, households switch and reallocate assets for transactional and precautionary savings following a tight monetary policy shock. This means that households have an incentive to draw on their long-term bank deposits to finance expenditure or consumption as disposable income slows down. Hence, we conclude that there is a substitution effect between bank and non-bank deposits.

Furthermore, the net financial asset flows fluctuate more due to positive shocks to GDP and the consumer price level shocks compared to a positive monetary policy tightening shock. The households' liability flows increase more when GDP is shut-off in the model, indicating the dampening ability of GDP. The results suggest that robust GDP dampens the households' liability flows possibly by providing employment opportunities that generate income hence discouraging the household incurrences of liability flows. Thus, robust GDP growth is needed to mitigate high incurrence of liability flows after a policy tightening shock. In addition, a propagation channel arises via the excessive incurrence of liability flows, which increases risk exposures and induces more volatility in key balance sheet items with spill-over effects to economic activity. Increased households' liability flows worsen the GDP contraction through increased risk exposure and high household indebtedness, thereby slowing down consumption.

In addition, from a financial stability perspective, the channels through which shocks may spread through the system with possible spill-over effects into those areas initially not vulnerable to the shock but that become affected though interconnection, evidence shows that the improvement in households' financial asset flows would to some extent mitigate the effects of the GDP decline due to a positive inflationary shock. Thus, increased accumulation of households' assets dampens the GDP decline, pointing to the importance of healthy households' financial asset flows.

References

Bernanke B, and Gertler M. 1989. Agency Costs, Net Worth, and Business Fluctuations. The American Economic Review, Vol. 79, No. 1 (Mar., 1989), pp. 14–31.

Bonci R. 2011. Monetary policy and the flow of funds in the euro area. ECB Working Paper No. 1402.

Bonci R, and Columba F. 2008. Monetary Policy Effects: New Evidence from the Italian Flow of Funds. Bank of Italy Economic Working Papers No. 678.

De Bondt G. 2009. Euro Area Money Demand: Empirical evidence on the role of equity and labour markets. ECB Working Paper Series No 1086.

Boone L, Mikol F, and Van den Noord P. 2004. Wealth Effects on Money Demand in EMU. OECD Working Paper No. 411.

Bruggeman A, Donati P, and Warne A. 2003. Is the demand for euro area M3 stable? ECB Working Paper no. 255.

Christiano L, Eichenbaum M, and Evans C. 1996. The Effects of Monetary Policy Shocks: Evidence from the Flow of Funds. The Review of Economics and Statistics, MIT Press, vol. 78(1), pages 16–34, February.

Dreger C, and Wolters J. 2009. Money velocity and asset prices in the euro area. Empirica, 36, 51–63.

Gameiro I, and Sousa J. 2010. Monetary Policy Effects: Evidence from the Portuguese Flow of Funds. Banco de Portugal Working Papers No. 201014.

Gerdesmeier D. 1996. The role of wealth in money demand. Deutsche Bundesbank Discussion Paper 5/96. Frankfurt am Main.

Gumata N, and Ndou E. 2019. Capital Flows, Credit Markets and Growth in South Africa: The Role of Global Economic Growth, Policy Shifts and Uncertainties. Palgrave Macmillan ISBN 978-3-030-30888-9.

Papademos L D, and Stark J. 2010. Enhancing monetary analysis. 2010. European Central Bank.

CHAPTER 35

To What Extent Are the Public and Private Sector Financial Asset Flows Impacted by a Monetary Policy Tightening Shock?

Research Questions Explored

- Determine the extent to which the net private and public sector financial asset flows are impacted by a tight monetary policy shock.
- Determine whether the effects of a monetary policy tightening shock on the public and private sector net financial asset flows differ from those of a negative shock to GDP shocks.

35.1 Introduction

Earlier chapters showed that households participate in capital markets and switch deposits amongst asset classes of different maturities following a tight monetary policy shock. The monetary policy tightening shock significantly increases short- and medium-term monetary deposits which are held for transactional and precautionary purposes. Long-term deposits decline indicating the switching from these assets into short- and medium-term deposits and deposits with other financial institutions. This switching may suggest that financial intermediaries adjust interest rates paid on liquid instruments to take advantage of higher interest rates. Thus, households switch and re-allocate assets for transactional and precautionary savings following a tighter monetary policy shock. This means that

N. Gumata, E. Ndou, *Achieving Price, Financial and Macro-Economic Stability in South Africa*,
https://doi.org/10.1007/978-3-030-66340-7_35

households have an incentive to draw on their long-term bank deposits to finance expenditure or consumption as disposable income slows down. Hence, there is a substitution effect between bank and non-bank deposits. This evidence indicates that the monetary policy tightening cycle has implication for the sectorial intermediation of funds measured by transactions. It is against this background that this chapter asks: To what extent are the net private and public sector financial asset flows impacted by a tight monetary policy shock? Which between a monetary policy tightening shock and a negative shock to GDP has a bigger impact on the private and public sector financial asset flows? Do these shocks reinforce each or move the sectoral financial asset flows in different directions?

Therefore, this chapter extends the analysis of the sectoral financial asset flow impact of a tight monetary policy shock using the flow-of-funds approach. As a precursor to the empirical analysis, Fig. 35.1 shows that there is a negative relationship between public and private sector financial asset flows as they tend to move in different directions. This implies that the net public sector deficit (surplus) should be offset by net private sector surplus (deficit). This is primarily consistent with the role of flows-of-funds in restoring the balance between the two sectors. Hence, this chapter completes the analysis by including the private sector.

At the same time, Fig. 35.1 reveals a persistent decline in the net public sector financial asset flows since 2007. The widening public sector deficit has been persistent during the onset of the global financial crisis,

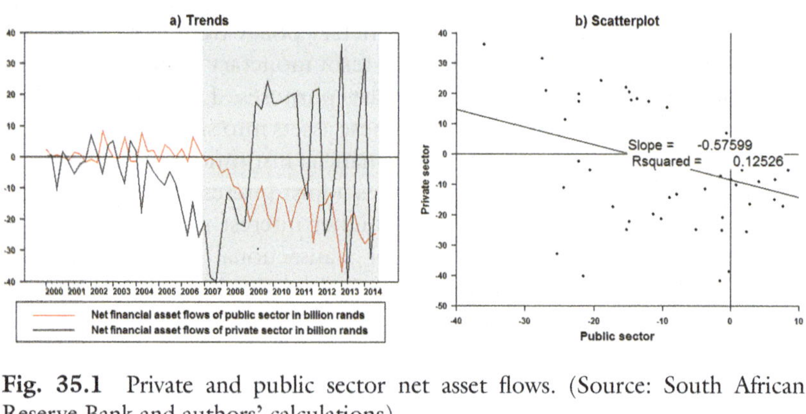

Fig. 35.1 Private and public sector net asset flows. (Source: South African Reserve Bank and authors' calculations)

subsequent global recession and the South African recession in 2009Q1–Q3.[1] In contrast, the private sector in most periods experienced intermittent surplus funds suggesting that it is a net lender. This private sector behaviour is consistent with a procyclical investment strategy.

This chapter fills academic and policy research gaps by determining the extent to which the net private and public sector financial asset flows are impacted by a tight monetary policy shock. We determine whether the effects of a monetary policy tightening shock on the public and private sector net financial asset flows differ from those due to a negative shock to GDP.

35.2 What Do the Descriptive Statistics Suggest?

This chapter examines various aspects of the relationship between the net public and private sector financial asset flows. We begin by assessing the lead effects and the role of changes in the sensitivity of the bilateral relationships. We find a negative cross-correlation between the public and private sector net financial asset flows in Fig. 35.2. This suggests that the net private (public) sector financial asset flows decline when preceded by increases in net public (private) sector financial asset flows.

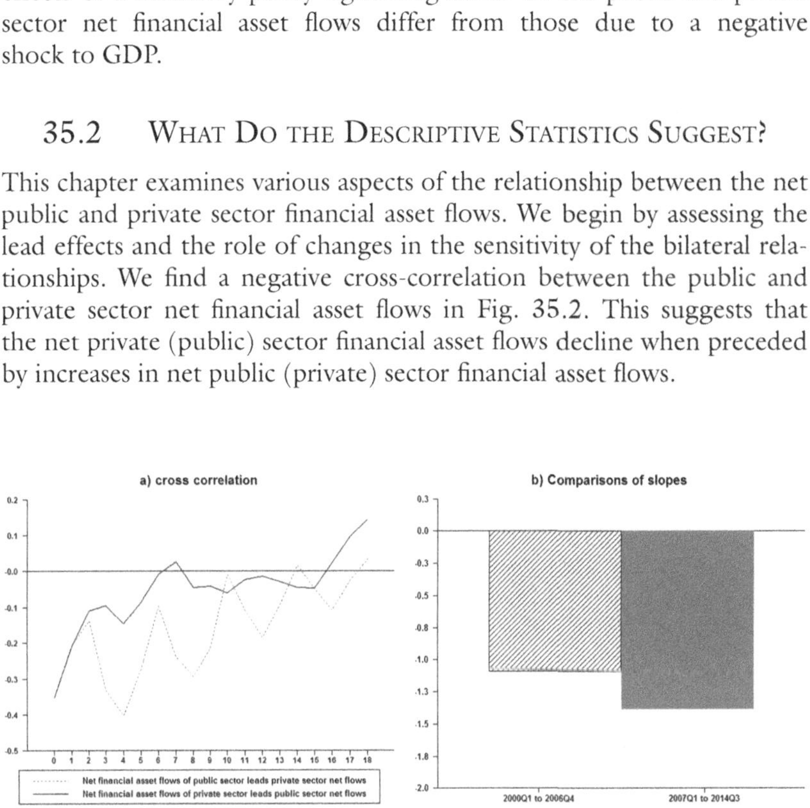

Fig. 35.2 Cross-correlation and the magnitudes of regression slopes. (Source: Authors' calculations)

[1] This trend in part indicates the countercyclical public sector investment spending via large public corporations (such as Transnet, Sanral).

Has the bilateral relationship changed between the two sectors? Fig. 35.2(b) shows that the magnitudes of the slopes based on the regression of the net public sector on net private sector financial asset flows are bigger during 2007Q1–2014Q3 compared to 2000Q1–2006Q4.

We use the density plots to determine the skewness of the net financial flow asset values of the private and public sector financial asset flows. Negative (positive) skewness indicates the net borrowing (lending) or deficit.

Figure 35.3 shows that the net financial assets of the public sector are negatively skewed indicating a public sector deficit. In a contrast, the negative skewness of the net private sector financial asset flows is not as large as that exhibited by the net public sector financial asset flows. Furthermore, Fig. 35.4 shows the persistence of the public and private sector net financial asset flows based on the cross-correlation and first-order autoregressions.

We find that the net public sector financial asset flows exhibit more persistence compared to the private sector. In addition, the net public sector financial asset flows exhibit high persistence in 2000Q1–2014Q3 and 2007Q1–2014Q3 in Fig. 35.4(b and c).

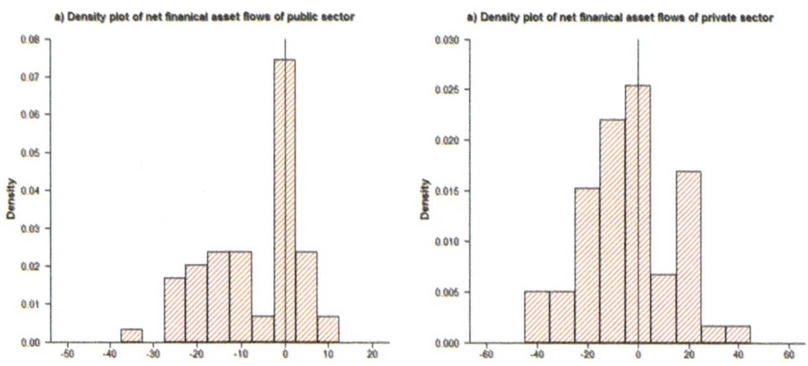

Fig. 35.3 Distributions of the net funds of non-financial sector in billion Rands. (Source: Authors' calculations)

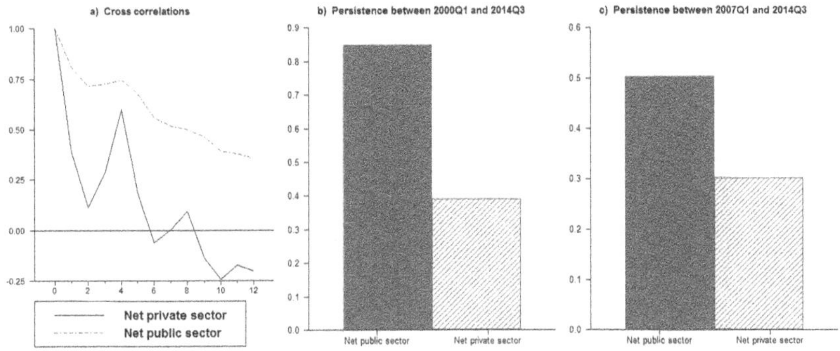

Fig. 35.4 Cross-correlation and the magnitudes of persistence. (Note: 'Net private sector' means net private sector financial asset flows. 'Net public sector' means net public sector financial asset flows. Source: Authors' calculations)

35.3 To What Extent Does the Net Public and Private Sector Financial Asset Flows Respond to Monetary Policy Tightening Shocks?

To answer this question, this section estimates a four-variable VAR model using quarterly (Q) data from 2000Q1 to 2014Q3. We estimate a baseline VAR which uses GDP, CPI and the repo rate. In later sections, we augment the baseline VAR model with the net public sector or private sector financial asset flows and their asset and liability components. These variables are added individually in the VAR models. The models are estimated using 2 lags selected by the Schwartz Bayesian criterion (SBC) and use 10,000 Monte Carlo replications. The monetary policy shock refers to a positive 1 per cent increase in the repo rate shock. The data is sourced from the South African Reserve Bank database.

We start the analysis by testing Hypotheses 1 and 2 as stated below:

Hypothesis 1: A tight monetary policy shock induces public sector deficits and private sector surplus

Hypothesis 2: A negative GDP shock induces public sector deficits and private sector surplus

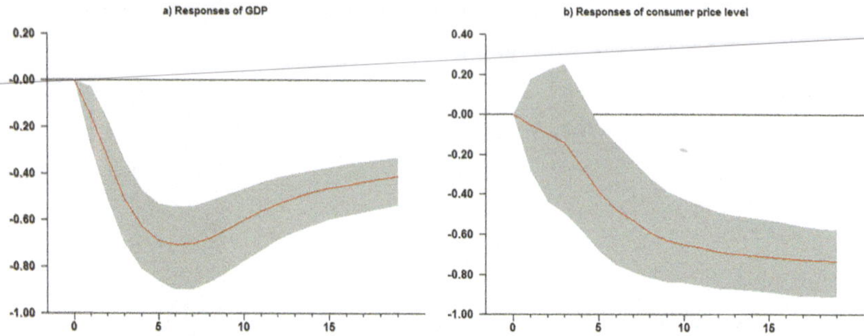

Fig. 35.5 GDP and consumer price level responses to tight monetary policy shocks. (Source: Authors' calculations)

Figure 35.5 shows that GDP and the consumer price level decline due to a monetary policy tightening shock. The consumer price level does not display a price puzzle. As a result, we proceed to examine the two hypotheses stated above.

35.3.1 The Impact of the Monetary Policy Tightening Shock on the Public and Private Sector Financial Asset Flows

Figure 35.6 shows the responses of the public and private sectors to a tight monetary policy shock and a negative shock to GDP. We assess the sensitivity of the responses to changes in the sample size for the periods 1995Q1 to 2014Q3 and 2000Q1 to 2014Q3. Figure 35.6(a) shows that the sign of the responses of the public sector deficit to a tight monetary policy shock is robust to changes in the sample size. But a tight monetary policy shock leads to a wider public sector deficit during 1995Q1 to 2014Q3 compared to 2000Q1 to 2014Q3. This evidence is contrary to expectations that the public sector financial asset flows do not respond to a tight monetary policy shock. At peak effects, the public sector deficit widens by a bigger magnitude due to a negative shock to GDP compared to a positive repo rate shock. The widening of the public sector deficit due to a tight monetary policy shock lasts for nearly eight quarters, which is twice longer than the responses of the deficits induced by a negative shock to GDP. Thus, the negative shocks to GDP and tight monetary policy shocks lead to the widening of the public sector financial asset flow deficits.

We find that the net private sector financial asset flows increase for a prolonged period due to a monetary policy tightening shock and a negative shock to GDP. However, there is lack of a statistically significant difference during the two sample periods in the impulses of the net private sector financial asset flows due to a tight monetary policy shock. This behaviour is consistent with cash hoarding by the private sector following adverse shocks to the repo rate and GDP.

So, which shock between a tight monetary policy shock and a negative GDP shock leads to a widening of the net public sector deficits? Figure 35.6 shows that the public sector deficits decline by more than R2.5 billion due to a negative GDP shock and this exceeds the R1.5 billion due to a tight monetary policy shock.[2] In addition, the net private sector financial asset flows reach a high peak due to a negative GDP shock compared to those induced by a monetary policy tightening shock. The findings of the widening of the public sector deficits compared to the net private sector surpluses are robust to changes in the sample size. Thus, evidence confirms Hypotheses 1 and 2. A tight monetary policy shock induces public sector deficits and private sector surplus, while a negative GDP shock induces public sector deficits and private sector surplus.

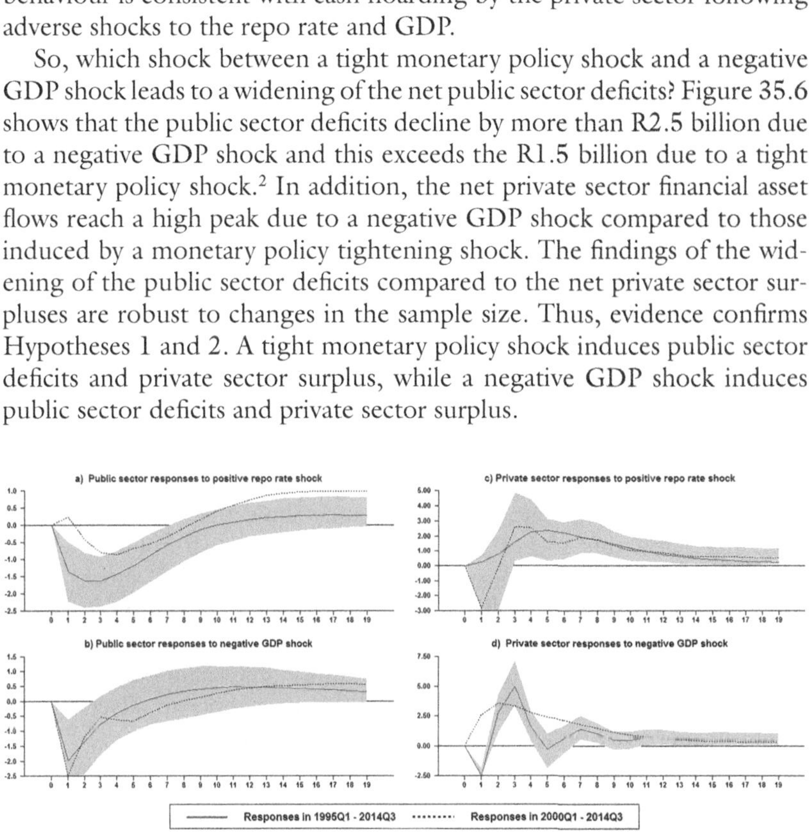

Fig. 35.6 Responses of the net financial asset flows of the public and private sectors to a tight monetary policy and negative GDP shocks. (Note: ‘Net private sector’ means net private sector financial asset flows. ‘Net public sector’ means net public sector financial asset flows. Source: Authors’ calculations)

[2] Studies showed that the net funds raised by the public sector increased in the United States of America and Italy and were not significant in the euro area and Portugal.

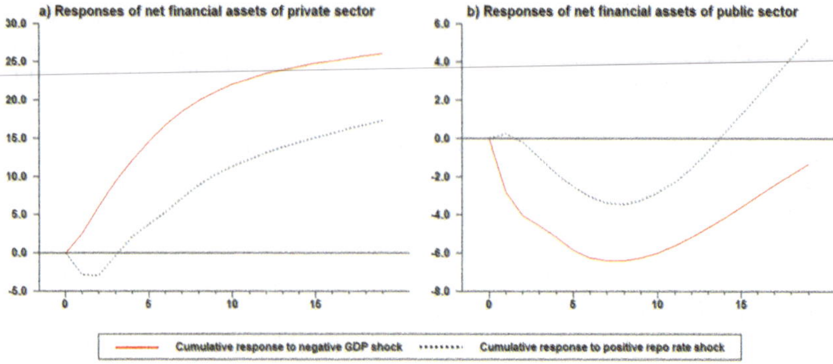

Fig. 35.7 Cumulative impulse responses to a tight monetary policy shock. (Source: Authors' calculations)

35.3.2 *What Are the Accumulated Effects?*

This section shows the accumulated responses so that we can compare which shock has a bigger effect over the entire horizon under review. Figure 35.7(b) shows that the cumulative net public sector deficits are more pronounced in response to a negative GDP shock compared to a tight monetary policy shock.

In contrast, the private sector responses show the net surpluses or a lending status due to both shocks. The elevated cash holdings of the private sector are more pronounced due to negative GDP shocks compared to a tight monetary policy shock. These results are robust to changes in the sample size. The results indicate that GDP plays a significant role compared to the repo rate dynamics. In addition, the results show that the private and public sectors respond in a different manner to adverse GDP and tight monetary policy shocks.

35.3.3 *Would the Results Change If the Net Public and Private Sector Financial Asset Flows Are Simultaneously Included in the Model?*

The results in the preceding sections are based on the estimations which include the public and private sector variables individually in the models. Thus, the assumption is that the public and private sectors make decisions independently. However, this may not be the case, hence this section includes the private and public sector variables simultaneously in the VAR

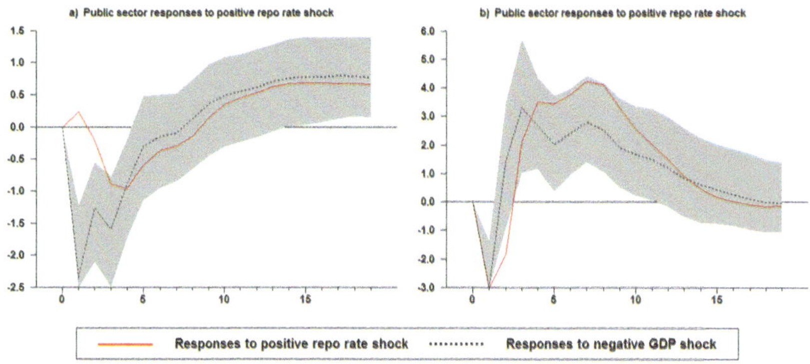

Fig. 35.8 Comparison of the sector responses to shocks during the inflation targeting period. (Source: Authors' calculations)

model to examine whether there are significant differences. The main conclusions do not change as evidence in Fig. 35.8 indicates that a negative GDP shock has the opposite effects on the private and public sectors as found in the preceding sections. The net public sector deficit worsens more due to a negative GDP shock compared to a tight monetary policy shock. However, after four quarters the effects are not significantly different.

In addition, the results in Fig. 35.8 show that the negative GDP shock and a tight monetary policy shock lead to the net private sector financial asset flow surpluses. The effects are not significantly different from each of the shocks after two quarters. Thus, we conclude that the main conclusions are robust to the simultaneous inclusion of the net public and private sector financial asset flows in the VAR model.

35.3.4 What Proportion of Fluctuations in The Net Sector Flows Is Explained by Macro-economic Variables in the Model?

This section compares the fluctuations in the net private and oublic sector flows induced by adverse shocks to GDP, consumer price level and monetary policy. The monetary policy tightening shocks explain extraordinarily little movement in the net public sector financial asset flows in Fig. 35.9. We find that a negative GDP shock explains about 30 per cent of fluctuations in the public sector financial asset flows and this is nearly five times larger than the fluctuations due to the adverse consumer price level and monetary policy tightening shocks in Fig. 35.9.

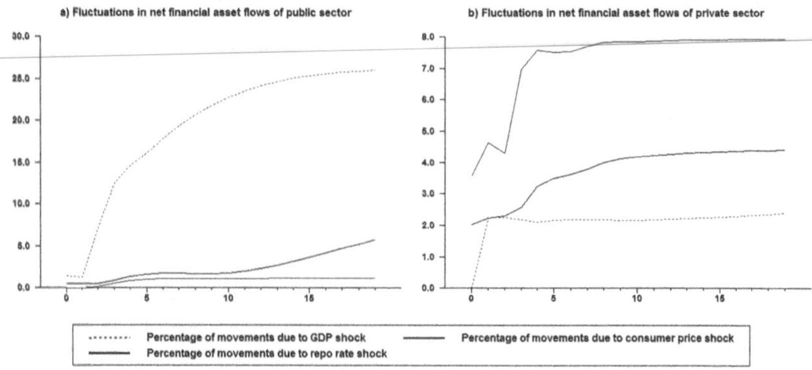

Fig. 35.9 Fluctuations in the net funds of the public sector due to negative GDP and tight monetary policy shocks. (Source: Authors' calculations)

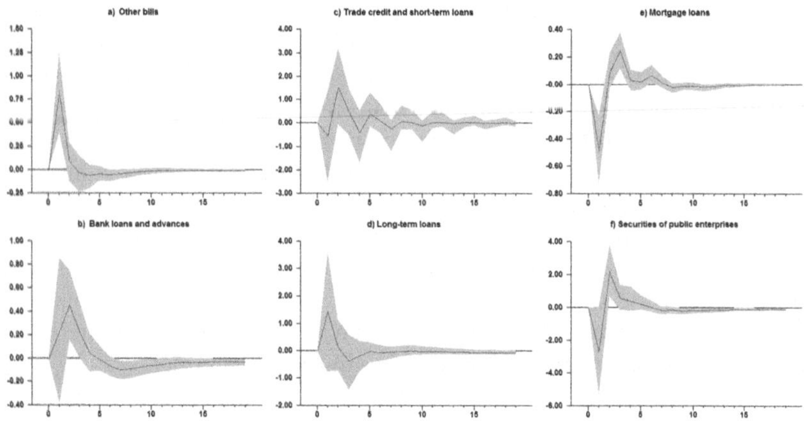

Fig. 35.10 Responses of the public sector financial *liability* flows to a tight monetary policy shock. (Source: Authors' calculations)

Thus, in a comparative sense amongst the macro-economic shocks, monetary policy shocks play a small role compared to the adverse consumer price level and GDP shocks. The adverse consumer price shock induces more fluctuations in the net private sector financial asset flows compared to the GDP shock.

35.3.5 *How Do Different Components of the Private and Public Sector Financial Liability and Asset Flows React to A Monetary Policy Tightening Shock?*

This section examines the responses of selected financial assets and liability components of the private and public sectors to a monetary policy tightening shock. Figure 35.10 and Figs. 35.14 and 35.15 in the Appendix show selected responses from the private and public sector financial asset flows, which include cash and demand money deposit, short- and medium-term monetary deposits, long-term deposits and deposits with other financial institutions. Amongst the financial asset flows, only cash and demand monetary deposits as well as short- and medium-term monetary deposits in the private sector financial asset flows react transitorily to monetary policy shocks. The public sector other bills increase significantly over two quarters, with a peak effect occurring in the first quarter. The trade credit and short-term loans do not respond significantly to the monetary policy tightening shock.

The difference exists regarding the private and public sector long-term loan and mortgage loan responses as shown in Fig. 35.11. The long-term loans in the public sector financial liability flow responses are not significant to the monetary policy tightening shocks in contrast to a significant decline in the private sector financial liability flows. In addition, mortgage loans in the private sector financial liability flows remain depressed after three quarters. This behaviour contrasts with the mortgage loan response in the public sector financial liability flows, which show a significant transitory decline in first quarter which is followed by a significant recovery after three quarters. There are similarities in the public and private sector bank loans and advances liability responses. Bank loans and advances increase significantly in first four quarters but decline significantly between four and ten quarters as shown in Fig. 35.11.

The initial increase might reflect the use of credit lines that were previously agreed and still available and due to credit commitments these cannot be changed immediately. Gameiro and Sousa (2010) suggests that corporations with pre-committed loan facilities will continue to obtain funds on cheaper terms and under less quantitative restrictions on credit than other firms. Examining the private sector flow liabilities reveals that ordinary shares and other loan stock and preference shares decline although insignificantly due to a tight monetary policy shock.

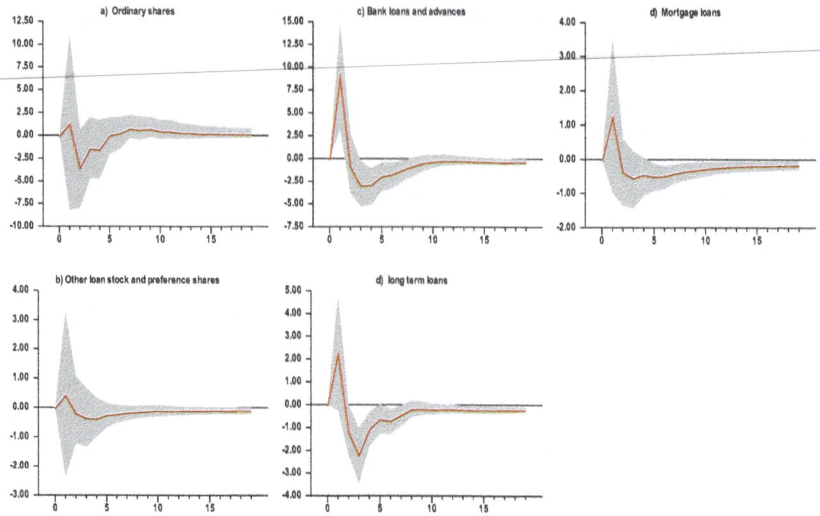

Fig. 35.11 Responses of the private sector financial *liability* flows to a tight monetary policy shock. (Source: Authors' calculations)

35.3.6 Do Public Sector and Private Sector Net Financial Asset Flows Affect the Response of the Monetary Policy Rate to Positive Inflation Shocks?

To answer this question, this section uses the counterfactual VAR approach. The counterfactual analysis shuts off the role of the private and public sector net financial flows individually in the model. The results in Fig. 35.12 show that the repo rate is tightened due to a positive inflation shock. There is a significantly different increase in the repo rate when the private and public sector net financial asset flows are included in the model, suggesting that the monetary policy adjustment to positive inflation shocks is not impacted by the private and public sector net financial asset flows.

35.4 Conclusion and Policy Implications

This chapter examined the extent to which the intermediations of net funds of non-financial corporations as well as the net funds of the public sector are impacted by a tight monetary policy shock and a negative GDP

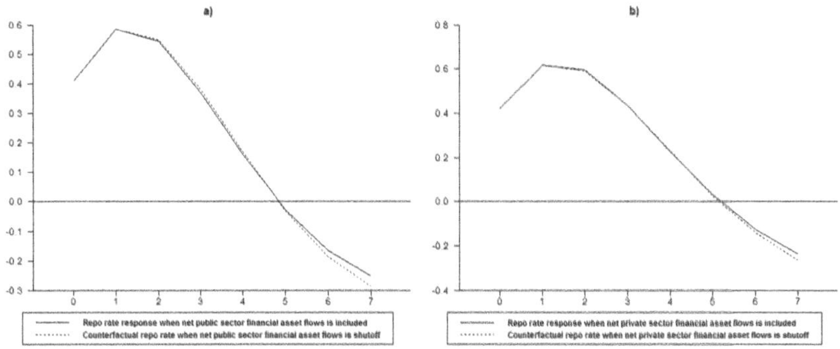

Fig. 35.12 Repo rate responses to positive inflation shocks and the role of net public and private financial asset flows. (Source: Authors' calculations)

shock. First, we establish that there is a negative relationship between public and private sector financial asset flows as they tend to move in different directions. This implies that the net public sector deficit (surplus) should be offset by the net private sector surplus (deficit). The widening of the public sector deficit was persistent post-2009Q1–Q3. In contrast, the private sector experienced intermittent surplus funds suggesting that it is a net lender. This private sector behaviour is consistent with a procyclical investment strategy whereas the public sector exhibits a countercyclical investment strategy.

Which between a monetary policy tightening shock and a negative shock to GDP has a bigger impact on the private and public sector financial asset flows? Evidence shows that a negative shock to GDP and a tight monetary policy shock induce wider public sector deficits. This evidence is contrary to expectations that public sector financial asset flows do not respond to a monetary policy shock. But at peak effects, the public sector deficit widens by a bigger magnitude that is more persistent due to a negative shock to GDP compared to a tight monetary policy shock. Thus, the negative shocks to GDP and tight monetary policy shocks lead to the widening of the public sector financial asset flow deficits. In addition, GDP shocks explain a high proportion of net public sector financial asset flow fluctuations compared to those induced by the monetary policy shocks.

On the other hand, we find that net private sector financial asset flows increase for a prolonged period due to a monetary policy tightening shock and a negative shock to GDP. This behaviour is consistent with cash hoarding by the private sector following adverse shocks to the repo rate and GDP. Furthermore, the net private sector financial asset flows reach a high peak due to a negative GDP shock compared to those induced by a monetary policy tightening shock. The private sector responses exude net surpluses or a lending status, indicating that elevated cash holdings of the private sector are more pronounced due to negative GDP shocks compared to a positive repo rate shock. Thus, monetary policy tightening shocks and adverse GDP shocks induce diverging responses (movements in opposite directions) on public and private sector financial asset flows. But GDP plays a significant role compared to repo rate dynamics. The private and public sectors respond in a different manner to adverse GDP and repo rate shocks. Public sector financial asset flows tend to be countercyclical whereas the private sector financial asset flows tend to be procyclical. But adverse shocks to GDP matter more for the public and private sector financial asset flows.

Appendix

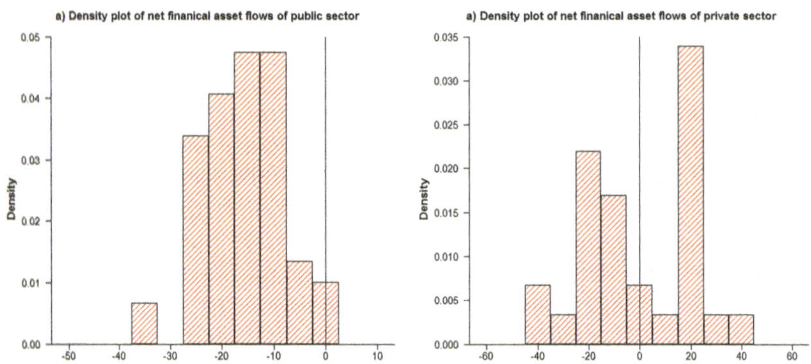

Fig. 35.13 Density plots post-2007. (Source: Authors' calculations)

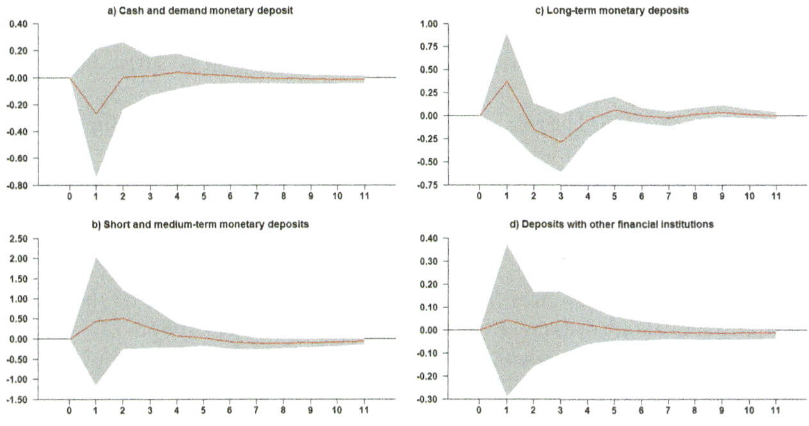

Fig. 35.14 Responses of public sector financial *asset* flows to a repo rate shock. (Source: Authors' calculations)

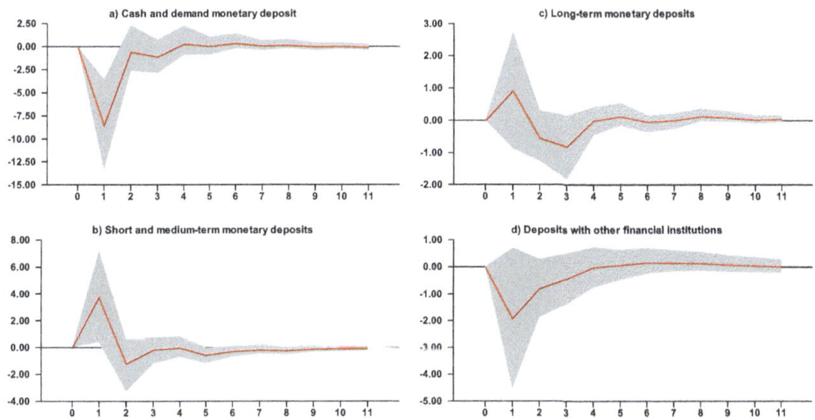

Fig. 35.15 Responses of private sector financial *asset* flows to a repo rate shock. (Source: Authors' calculations)

References

Papademos L D and Stark J. 2010. Enhancing monetary analysis. 2010. European Central Bank.

Gerdesmeier D. 1996. The role of wealth in money demand. Deutsche Bundesbank Discussion Paper 5/96. Frankfurt am Main.

Gameiro I and Sousa J. 2010. Monetary Policy Effects: Evidence from the Portuguese Flow of Funds. Banco de Portugal Working Papers No. 201014.

Dreger C, and Wolters J. 2009. Money velocity and asset prices in the euro area. Empirica, 36, 51–63.

De Bondt G. 2009. Euro Area Money Demand: Empirical evidence on the role of equity and labour markets. ECB Working Paper Series No 1086.

Boone L, Mikol F, and Van den Noord P. 2004. Wealth Effects on Money Demand in EMU. OECD Working Paper No. 411.

Bruggeman A, Donati P, and Warne A. 2003. Is the demand for euro area M3 stable? ECB Working Paper no. 255.

CHAPTER 36

Conclusion

This chapter offers a summary of the findings in the book. The book explored the policy mix that can be pursued for operationalising and achieving the set objectives in the National Development Plan (NDP) and expanding the central bank mandate to include maximum employment as an objective. The book argued that there is a need for policy co-ordination, especially between monetary and fiscal policy, to reinforce the effectiveness of nominal demand management policies. Furthermore, that the repo rate (monetary policy rate) alone is an insufficient instrument to simultaneously achieve an expanded mandate and a lower inflation target. This book offered empirical analysis that answers this question and many other important questions relating to the co-ordination of policies in pursuit of fiscal sustainability and price, financial and macro-economic stability. The book strengthened the arguments in academic and policy discussions regarding the use of the central bank balance sheet in its entirety by presenting the theoretical perspectives and empirical analysis. Below, we present the summary of the main findings and policy implications formulated under the five main themes. Evidence presented in the book shows the following.

N. Gumata, E. Ndou, *Achieving Price, Financial and Macro-Economic Stability in South Africa*,
https://doi.org/10.1007/978-3-030-66340-7_36

36.1 Theme One: Capital Flow Episodes, Fiscal Shocks, Commodity Price and House Price Boom Effects on Credit Growth Dynamics

1. We establish that there are asymmetric effects in the transmission of portfolio banking inflow shocks due to prevailing credit conditions. Tighter credit conditions had a larger dampening effect on credit growth post-2008Q1 compared to the period pre-2008. During periods of severe global and domestic financial constraints, the direct and indirect ability of positive capital inflow shock to stimulate credit growth is highly neutralised by the prevailing tight credit conditions. Prevailing credit conditions are conduits through which capital inflow shocks are transmitted to credit growth. Policy initiatives that loosen (tighten) credit conditions tend to lead to the amplification (dampening) of capital flow shock on credit growth.
2. We find that the tightening in credit conditions, credit lending standards, house prices and the monetary policy stance have a disproportionate effect on the household sector compared to the corporate sector. Tight credit conditions neutralise the effects of the R/US$ exchange rate depreciation shock on inflationary pressures. As a result, tight credit conditions and muted GDP growth lead to less aggressive monetary policy responses to inflationary pressures. In the absence of credit driven demand pressures on inflation, tight credit conditions and muted GDP growth have a significant impact on the pace and magnitude of monetary policy responses to inflation.
3. Evidence in the book shows that household credit contributed to the prolonged duration of aggregate credit growth during the recent credit boom whereas credit to companies contributed more to the amplitude of the boom. At the same time, the duration and amplitude of nominal house prices also played a significant role in the recent credit boom. Credit growth and house price downward (busts) cycles tend to be severe and last longer compared to upturns (booms). Furthermore, mortgage credit plays a significant role in propagating the house price boom episodes. Mortgage credit growth is an important conduit through which house price boom episode shocks are transmitted to credit growth and GDP growth.
4. Synchronised boom episodes propagate inflationary pressures and result in pronounced increases in the repo rate. The occurrence of

house price and credit boom periods amplifies the monetary policy responses to positive inflation shocks. The amplification due to house price and credit boom is enormously higher compared to that induced by non-boom periods. As such, synchronised house price and credit growth boom episodes result in aggressive monetary policy tightening to inflationary pressures especially when inflation exceeds the 6 per cent threshold.

5. Contractionary fiscal policy shocks interact with various macroeconomic variables to affect credit demand. We find that a positive tax shock has an adverse effect on credit growth. However, spending cut shocks induce more fluctuations in credit growth compared to a positive tax shock. This is because GDP growth declines more due to spending cut shocks compared to positive tax shocks and this is transmitted into credit growth. Hence, the GDP growth channel is a potent channel through which the contractionary fiscal shocks are transmitted to credit growth.

36.2 Theme Two: Interaction of the South African Reserve Bank, Public Investment Corporation and Banks' Balance Sheets: Effects on Fiscal and Monetary Policy Tools

1. Large-scale asset purchases (LSAPs) play an important role in lowering government bond yields across the maturity spectrum, the risk premium and the cost of government debt. LSAPs loosen the domestic financial conditions and the fiscal constraints. However, government debt growth regimes matter for the impact of LSAPs and foreign currency reserves accumulation policy on government debt yields and interest costs. Evidence in the book shows that a policy strategy that contains growth in government debt below 10 per cent coupled with a foreign currency reserves accumulation policy and LSAPs will have a positive effect on long-term government bond yields, the risk premium and interest costs.
2. The fiscal policy stance as measured by the government debt regimes interacts with monetary policy through its effects on inflation (price stability). Monetary policy balance sheet tools amplify

the effects of the fiscal policy stance as measured by the government debt regimes.

3. LSAPs assist the SARB in achieving its price stability mandate and have stabilisation effects on the macro-economy. For instance, evidence shows that largely due to the supply effects, LSAPs result in the appreciation of the R/US$ exchange rate thus lowering inflation outcomes and expectations. Furthermore, LSAPs assist in achieving macro-economic stability as they result in an increase in GDP growth, investment growth and employment growth and a decline in the unemployment rate and the Gini coefficient (income inequality).
4. Evidence in the book shows that GDP growth and employment growth increase in response to positive shocks to forex reserves accumulation, whereas the unemployment declines. Furthermore, larger-sized shocks to forex reserves accumulation exert larger positive effects on GDP growth and employment growth resulting in larger declines in the unemployment rate. Thus, large and persistent foreign currency reserves accumulation shocks will complement other policies aimed at enforcing a stable exchange rate, moderate increases in government funding costs and macro-economic stability in the form of a lower unemployment rate, robust GDP growth and employment growth.
5. These outcomes are consistent with the SARB mandates of price, financial and macro-economic stability. Furthermore, the book argued for a broad approach to the foreign currency reserves accumulation policy that complements sound macro-economic and prudential policy frameworks that limit the country's vulnerability to multiple shocks. This speaks for much-needed policy co-ordination within the flexible inflation targeting framework, which includes the exchange rate stabilisation policy. This means that the forex reserves accumulation policy can be pursued for non-precautionary savings objectives such as to provide a stream of investment income to help finance part of the annual government budget, alternatively, for intergenerational savings or an endowment fund.
6. LSAPs affect the banks' balance sheets and curb excess liquid asset holdings (LAH) by banks. Evidence in the book shows that LSAPs by the SARB result in a decline in the excess LAH by banks. The decline in the excess LAH by banks leads to a decrease in bank credit to government, credit conditions become looser, the inter-

est rate pass-through increases and the bank loan intermediation mark-up declines.

7. Furthermore, evidence shows that lengthening of the maturities of funding options available to banks at the accommodation window at the SARB can result in the substitution of funding sources by banks on their liabilities side of the balance sheets and the cost of funding. Most importantly, long-term repurchase agreements will also affect the way banks price lending on their asset side. As such, lengthening of the maturities of funding options available at the accommodation window can loosen the funding constraints experienced by banks and this will spill-over to funding conditions of important markets such as the housing sector and small, SMMEs.
8. From a policy and regulatory perspective, the lengthening of the maturity of the funding options for banks is especially important given the long-standing regulatory concern of the maturity mismatch risks induced by funding long-term assets such as housing using deposits which are of a short duration. At the same time, such a strategy will neutralise the impact of sterilisation and other costs associated with the forex reserves accumulation programme.
9. When conducting LSAPs and accumulating foreign currency reserves, the central bank creates reserves. The book explored approaches that can be adopted by the SARB to manage excess reserves and liquidity created by LSAPs and the accumulation of foreign currency reserves. Evidence in the book shows that the interbank rate volatility is dependent on the banks' excess reserves regimes. The overnight forex rate volatility increases more compared to the South African benchmark overnight rate (Sabor) in response to positive shocks to excess banks' reserves. Positive shocks to banks' excess reserves explain a larger variance in the overnight forex rate volatility compared to the Sabor rate volatility.
10. The results based on the transition function imply that the estimated threshold within the interest rate corridor can be used to tier excess reserves in the management of banking liquidity. The interest rate corridor allows the central bank to separate the monetary policy stance from the liquidity management policy. This means that policymakers can gradually phase in the autonomous use of the deposit rate to manage bank liquidity or excess reserves. This gradual phasing in of the autonomous use of the deposit rate to manage bank liquidity or excess reserves can take the approach

of tiering excess reserves and use the estimated threshold as a guideline—remunerating reserves in excess of some threshold, in this instance the estimated R100 billion, at the corridor between the repo rate (mid-point) and the deposit rate. This is especially important because the forex reserves accumulation and LSAP policies will result in the creation of excess reserves.

11. The book also looks at the impact of LSAPs on non-resident purchases of South African assets. The Global Financial Stability Report (GFSR 2019), refers to the unusually large share of the local currency government debt that is held by foreign investors as one of the main financial stability risks that can be brought about by changes in global investor risk appetite. Evidence in the book shows that LSAPs depress the non-resident's cumulative net purchases of South African shares and bonds, especially the purchase of bonds, largely due to the supply effects; and these effects are also transmitted to all measures of the R/US$ exchange rate volatility, especially the transitory R/US$ exchange rate volatility. These results imply that LSAPs are part of the policy tools that will contribute to policy interventions aimed at dampening the R/US$ exchange rate volatility and financial stability risks.
12. We also find that LSAPs improve activity in the primary and secondary bond and share market. Incremental positive SARB asset growth shocks exert asymmetric effects on selected indicators of primary and secondary market share and bond market. The two-year credit default swap (CDS) spreads and the yield on the Eskom bond declines in response to positive SARB asset growth shocks, whilst the bond market capitalisation and liquidity increase. On the other hand, positive SARB asset growth shock loosens the credit conditions as the credit conditions decline and manufacturing output increases.
13. Price stability measured by inflation below the 4.5 per cent inflation threshold leads to a lower non-accelerating inflation rate of unemployment (NAIRU) compared to when the inflation bands are not considered. Expansionary monetary policy lowers the unemployment rate above the NAIRU. Evidence shows that expansionary monetary policy lowers the unemployment rate and these effects are amplified by high economic growth, investment growth, credit growth, the exchange rate appreciation and unit labour costs below the growth trend (alternatively, positive labour productivity shocks).

36.3 Theme Three: Financial Regulations, Selected Macro-prudential Tools, the Quality of Banks' Loan Books and the Transmission of Monetary Policy Shocks

1. A positive capital inflow shock leads to the loosening of credit conditions. The capital inflow shocks affect credit growth via their impact on the credit risk as captured by non-performing loans (NPLs). Capital inflow shocks loosen the credit and financial constraints banks operate in since they have an impact on excess capital adequacy ratio (CAR), excess LAH and loan loss provisions. Furthermore, evidence shows that excess CAR exerted asymmetric effects on aggregate credit growth due to positive capital inflow and outflow shocks pre- and post-2008Q1. Evidence indicates that excess CAR cushioned (dampened) aggregate credit growth following a positive capital outflow (inflow) shock. The peak amplification effects were large post-2008Q1 compared to pre-2008. Thus, indeed excess CAR acts as a buffer or a shock absorber.
2. Furthermore, evidence shows that a positive gross capital outflow shock increases the share of credit to households at the expense of a decline in the share of credit to companies. Contractionary monetary policy, excess CAR and excess LAH shocks exert the same downward effects on aggregate credit growth.
3. The quality of the banks' balance sheets as proxied by NPLs interacts with financial regulation and macro-prudential tools to impact credit growth. For instance, NPLs dampened the increases in the share of credit to households due to a positive shock to excess LAH during 2008Q1 to 2015Q4. This means that NPLs accentuated the contraction in the share of credit to households. In addition, excess LAH during 2008Q1 to 2015Q4 resulted in the sectoral credit reallocation from the households and corporate sector to the government. The adverse shock effects of excess LAH on the sector credit allocation were exacerbated by the increase in credit risk as captured by the NPLs. The deterioration in the banks' credit books and the increase in credit risk exacerbate the effects of an adverse financial shock on aggregate credit growth and GDP growth.

4. Excess CAR dampens the impact of demand shocks on credit and GDP growth in line with the intended primary purpose of countering the amplitude and duration of the financial and business cycles. Furthermore, monetary policy tightening and excess CAR shocks lower credit and GDP growth. Evidence based on the counterfactual scenarios shows that excess CAR accentuates the responses of credit and GDP growth to tight monetary policy shocks. This means that excess CAR is a potent propagator of tight monetary policy to credit and GDP growth. These two policy tools interact and reinforce each other's effects in the same direction.
5. Evidence shows that excess CAR as a financial regulation and prudential tool interacts with tight monetary policy and dampens credit demand driven inflationary pressures. In the process, excess CAR lowers the pace and magnitude of the repo rate responses to inflationary pressures. However, excess CAR is not potent in neutralising other inflationary processes driven by factors such as the exchange rate pass-through to inflation. In that sense, other SARB balance sheet policy tools such as the accumulation of foreign currency reserves possess superior properties and are well positioned to complement the repo rate as the monetary policy tool.

36.4 Theme Four: Money Demand, Exchange Rate Depreciation Shocks, Household Wealth and Credit Conditions

1. The money demand function from models augmented with financial variables conveys valuable information for price and financial stability objectives. In addition, augmenting the money demand function with asset price returns yields the desired results of lowering the point elasticity for GDP. The augmented money demand functions can explain developments in monetary aggregates via the ***substitution and international portfolio balance effects***. Furthermore, evidence from the indirect role of the money demand based on the counterfactual analysis shows that the money demand shortfall shock dampens the pass-through of rand depreciation shocks to inflation. The exchange rate depreciation and elevated economic

policy uncertainty shocks reduce the money demand indicating the prevalence of the currency substitution effect. The decline in the money demand is further accentuated by elevated exchange rate volatility.

2. From a flow-of-funds analytical framework, evidence shows that the household sector net financial asset flow declines due to a tight monetary policy shock. This is because households become net borrowers, and this occurs through the revaluation of outstanding debt following a new high interest rate. In addition, households may borrow more to smooth consumption since the decline in GDP may coincide with decline in household disposable income.

36.5 Theme Five: The Role of the Flow-of-Funds Approach in Monetary and Financial Policy Analysis

1. Furthermore, using the flow-of-funds analytical framework, we find that a negative shock to GDP growth and a tight monetary policy shock induce wider public sector deficits. This evidence is contrary to the expectations that public sector financial asset flows do not respond to a monetary policy shock. Negative shocks to GDP growth and tight monetary policy shocks lead to the widening of the public sector financial asset flow deficits.
2. On the other hand, we find that net private sector financial asset flows increase for a prolonged period due to a monetary policy tightening shock and a negative shock to GDP growth. This behaviour is consistent with cash hoarding by the private sector following adverse shocks to the repo rate and GDP growth. Monetary policy tightening shocks and adverse GDP growth shocks induce diverging responses (movements in opposite directions) on public and private sector financial asset flows. But GDP growth plays a more significant role compared to repo rate adjustments. Adverse shocks to GDP growth matter more for the public and private sector financial asset flows. Public sector financial asset flows tend to be countercyclical whereas the private sector financial asset flows tend to be procyclical.

The findings in the book indicate that there is a need for the co-ordination of financial regulation, macro-prudential tools and the SARB balance sheet tools to assist in the achievement price, financial and macro-economic stability mandates. Evidence presented in the book shows that there needs to be a structural change in the composition of the SARB, PIC and private banks' balance sheets to facilitate, and in some instances to catalyse, the achievement of the set objectives in the NDP. The structural changes proposed in the book can take the form of: (i) the SARB balance sheet to conduct LSAPs and using the PIC balance sheet to reinforce these effects; (ii) embarking on another long-term programme of foreign currency reserves accumulation policy to support the exchange rate policy and as a form of non-precautionary savings buffer to provide a stream of investment income to help finance part of the annual government budget, for intergenerational savings, or an endowment fund; (iii) lengthening the maturity of funding options for banks offered by the SARB to facilitate and loosen funding of important markets such as the housing sector and SMMEs, and neutralise the impact of sterilisation and other costs associated with the forex reserves accumulation programme; (iv) curbing excess liquid asset holdings by banks to release funding that has been disproportionately skewed towards funding the government as opposed to the private sector; and (v) dealing with the build-up of banks' excess reserves created by the SARB policies so at to adopt the excess reserves tiering approach and an interest rate corridor floor that allows the central bank to separate the monetary policy stance from the liquidity management policy.

Index[1]

[1] Note: Page numbers followed by 'n' refer to notes.

N. Gumata, E. Ndou, *Achieving Price, Financial and Macro-Economic Stability in South Africa*,
https://doi.org/10.1007/978-3-030-66340-7

The manufacturer's authorised representative in the EU is Springer Nature Customer Service Centre GmbH, Europaplatz 3, 69115 Heidelberg, Germany. If you have any concerns regarding our products, please contact ProductSafety@springernature.com

Printed and bound by CPI Group (UK) Ltd, Croydon, CR0 4YY

30/09/2026

02225321-0016